Time Out

London
for Children

www.timeout.com

Time Out Guides Limited
Universal House
251 Tottenham Court Road
London W1T 7AB
Tel + 44 (0)20 7813 3000
Fax + 44 (0)20 7813 6001
Email guides@timeout.com
www.timeout.com

Editorial
Editor Ronnie Haydon
Deputy Editor Phil Harriss
Copy Editors Jan Fuscoe, Hugh Graham
Listings Editor Cathy Limb
Researchers Ravneet Ahluwalia, James Cartwright, Francis Gooding, Laura Macaulay
Indexer Anna Norman

Managing Director Peter Fiennes
Financial Director Gareth Garner
Editorial Director Sarah Guy
Series Editor Cath Phillips
Editorial Manager Holly Pick
Accountant Ija Krasnikova

Design
Art Director Scott Moore
Art Editor Pinelope Kourmouzoglou
Senior Designer Henry Elphick
Junior Graphic Designer Kei Ishimaru
Digital Imaging Simon Foster
Ad Make-up Jodi Sher

Picture Desk
Picture Editor Jael Marschner
Deputy Picture Editor Tracey Kerrigan
Picture Researcher Helen McFarland

Advertising
Sales Director & Sponsorship Mark Phillips
Sales Manager Alison Wallen
Advertising Sales Ben Holt, Alex Matthews, Jason Trotman
Advertising Assistant Kate Staddon
Copy Controller Declan Symington

Marketing
Group Marketing Director John Luck
Marketing Manager Yvonne Poon
Sales & Marketing Director, North America Lisa Levinson

Production
Group Production Director Mark Lamond
Production Manager Brendan McKeown
Production Coordinator Caroline Bradford

Time Out Group
Chairman Tony Elliott
Financial Director Richard Waterlow
TO Magazine Ltd MD David Pepper
Group General Manager/Director Nichola Coulthard
Managing Director, Time Out International Cathy Runciman
TO Communications Ltd MD David Pepper
Group Art Director John Oakey
Group IT Director Simon Chappell

Sections in this guide were written by
Introduction Ronnie Haydon. **The Story of London** *Education: Dr Thomas Barnardo; Robert Baden-Powell; Edward Alleyn* Paul Edwards. **Festivals & Events** Hugh Graham, Cathy Limb. **Around Town Introduction** Ronnie Haydon; **South Bank & Bankside** Ronnie Haydon *The fun don't stop* Maeve Hosea; **The City** *Know your boundary* Rick Jones; **Holborn & Clerkenwell** *Ghouls, greens and ghastly goings-on* Cathy Limb; **Bloomsbury & Fitzrovia** *Stuff to consider* Sue Webster; **Covent Garden & the Strand** Ronnie Haydon; **West End** *Hit the shops* Kelley Knox; **Marylebone** Ronnie Haydon; **Westminster** *Dig for Victory* Rick Jones; **Paddington & Notting Hill** Andrew Humphreys; **South Kensington & Chelsea** Holly Pick *Monumental sacrifice* Sue Webster; **North London** *Round Camden way* Joseph Bindloss; **East London** *Thinking outside the pod* Simon Coppock, *The river east* Joseph Bindloss; **South-east London** Ronnie Haydon, *Walk the line* Rick Jones; **South-west London** *Royal haunts* Deborah Nash; **West London** *The river west* Deborah Nash; **Eating** Phil Harriss, *Eat your way around the world, Eating posh* Sue Webster; **Shopping** Ronnie Haydon *To market, to market* Maeve Hosea; **Arts & Entertainment** *Cinematic city, In the Club* Chloë Lola Riess, *Creative spirit* Maeve Hosea, *Drawing on the experience* Sue Webster; **Parties** Ronnie Haydon, Chloë Lola Riess, *Shooting party* Sara O'Reilly; **Sport & Leisure** *Jump to it*, Blades of glory Cyrus Shahrad; **Days out** Ronnie Haydon; **Directory** Ronnie Haydon.

The Editor would like to thank Bevin Anandarajah, Jane, Bruce and John Jones, Finn Jordan, Julien Sauvalle, Teresa Trafford and all contributors to previous editions of *Time Out London for Children*, whose work forms the basis for parts of this book.

Maps john@jsgraphics.co.uk

Cover photography Rob Greig

Photography pages 3, 5, 7, 8, 9, 11, 28, 29, 79, 85, 94, 96, 97, 102, 105, 106, 163, 165, 176, 178, 179, 180, 187, 188, 201, 206, 212, 213, 216, 230, 253, 276, 277 Heloise Bergman; page 13 Roger-Viollet/Topfoto; page 14 Austrian Archives/Corbis; page 16 Getty Images; pages 16, 17 City of Westminster Archive Centre, London/Bridgeman Art Library; page 19 (top) TopFoto; page 19 (bottom) Mary Evans Picture Library; page 24 Gabriele Stabile; pages 31, 57, 63, 69, 71, 74, 92, 114, 198, 203, 221, 227, 228, 229, 257, 265, 266, 284, 285 Andrew Brackenbury; pages 37, 89 Olivia Rutherford; pages 40, 215, 289 Tricia de Courcy Ling; pages 44, 48, 50, 53, 59, 117, 118, 119, 125, 131, 134, 171 Tove Breitstein; pages 67, 73, 82, 101, 120, 121, 132, 208 Britta Jaschinski; pages 76, 159 Jonathan Perugia; page 77 Zoological Society of London; page 81 Abigail Lelliott; pages 90, 172 Alys Tomlinson; page 137 Maritime Museum; pages 141, 147, 149, 156, 182, 202, 210, 262, 263 Tricia de Courcy Ling; pages 273, 281 Cathy Limb.

The following images were provided by the featured establishments/artists: pages 9, 10, 26, 27, 33, 54, 111, 220, 234, 235, 240, 244, 245, 249.

Printer Cooper Clegg, Shannon Way, Tewkesbury Industrial Centre, Tewkesbury, Gloucestershire GL20 8HB.

ISBN 978-1-905042-16-6
      1-905042-16-7
ISSN 1753-7916
Distribution by Seymour Ltd (020 7429 4000)
For details of distribution in the Americas, see www.timeout.com

Contents

Introduction

London? Child friendly? The very idea, say those detractors wrung out by the city's demands on their sanity. True, this cacophonous capital may instil more shock than awe. The trick is to approach its complicated layers in a spirit of adventure, an impulse that comes easily to the young, but is more of a challenge for their parents. That's where this guide comes in – it tells you all about the picture postcard pin-ups as well as Londoners' own favourite places, both in central London and outside the Orbital.

Sometimes it's the simplest attractions that make London special for children. They may love their ride in an Eye pod, but their trip on the front seat of a driverless DLR train through Docklands will also stick in the memory. The West End musical they've read about may have a certain glamour, but the free performances outside the National Theatre during the summer festival has them jumping for joy. The royal palaces, dripping with history and priceless treasures, are worth gawking at, but it's the remnants of the Roman Wall and crumbling old city churches that summon up the ghosts of the past. Both London's tourist honeypots and her less obvious charms are celebrated in these pages, which prove beyond doubt, that London, for children, is as friendly as you want it to be.

TIME OUT LONDON FOR CHILDREN GUIDE

This is the seventh edition of the *Time Out London for Children Guide*, produced by the people behind the successful listings magazines and travel guide series. It is written by resident experts to provide you with all the information you'll need to explore the city, whether you're a local or a first-time visitor.

THE LOWDOWN ON THE LISTINGS

Addresses, phone numbers, websites, transport information, opening times, admission prices and credit card details are included in the listings.

Details of facilities, services and events were all checked and correct as we went to press. Before you go out of your way, however, we'd advise you to phone and check opening times, ticket prices and other particulars. While every effort has been made to ensure the accuracy of the information contained in this guide, the publishers cannot accept any responsibility for any errors it may contain.

FAMILY-FRIENDLY INFORMATION

Having visited all the places with our children, we've added essential information for families. Where we think it's important, we've stated whether a building can accommodate pushchairs ('buggy access'), or if there's a place to change a nappy ('nappy-changing facilities'). We've also listed the nearest picnic place.

Attractions are required to provide reasonable facilities for disabled visitors, although it's always best to check accessibility before setting out.

Disabled visitors requiring information about getting around the city contact GLAD (Greater London Action on Disability) through their website, www.glad.org.uk.

PRICES AND PAYMENT

We have noted where venues accept the following credit cards: American Express (AmEx), Diners Club (DC), MasterCard (MC) and Visa (V).

THE LIE OF THE LAND

Map references are included for each venue that falls on our street maps (starting on p310), but we recommend that you follow the example of the locals and invest in a standard A-Z map of the city.

PHONE NUMBERS

The area code for London is 020. All phone numbers given in this guide take this code unless otherwise stated, so add 020 if calling from outside London; otherwise, simply dial the number as written. The international dialling code for the UK is 44.

Sponsors & advertisers

We would like to thank our sponsor Cartoon Network for its involvement in this guide. However, we would like to stress that no establishment has been included because it has advertised in any of our publications and no payment of any kind has influenced any review. The opinions given in this book are those of Time Out writers and editors and are entirely independent.

In Context

Features

We love London

London life gave **Dr Michele Elliott** a new perspective on childcare.

More than two million children across the UK have reason to be glad that a certain American fell in love with London. Dr Michele Elliott, founder of Kidscape, the campaign for children's safety, started a new life here in the 1970s, and looks back on those early days, bringing up her sons in the city with great fondness.

'We've lived in the same west London flat practically since we came to London. We brought our children proudly home from Queen Charlotte's hospital, and now the kids come to visit us.'

'Kensington Gardens was just across the road from our flat. These days they have all this really child-friendly play equipment, but in my day all they had was a slide that seemed to be 100 feet high, with concrete on the bottom. Oh, and I remember the sandpit, because my son peed in it. All the other kids went 'yeuch!' and I pretended he wasn't mine!'

Happy days?

'Of course. It's all much more sanitised now but in those days you knew they were going to come home with all sorts of scrapes and bumps. They didn't mind.'

Michele Elliott was brought up in the States. Her mum was a British woman who married an American after the war. Michele came over in 1970, initially curious to meet the grandfather she'd believed was dead. While visiting him, and discovering other relatives she didn't know she had, she developed a strong attachment to England.

'We (my husband and I) loved it so much we decided to quit our jobs and move to this country. My relatives in the States wonder when we're going to stop 'playing' over here and come home, but I think I will spend the rest of my life here.'

During those early days as a young mum in West London, going to parks, theatres, museums and ensuring her sons enjoyed a happy stable childhood, Michele's work as a child psychologist in Westminster was casting a darker shadow.

'My work involved going into schools and dealing with children who had been abused and bullied. It seemed I was picking up the pieces all the time, dealing with hurt children, yet nothing was being done to prevent children suffering at the hands of bullies. It frustrated me.

'I felt I wanted make the world a safer place. I know that sounds mushy but you look at your own kids and you want to protect them.'

'I started Kidscape in 1984. I decided to write a little book about protecting children from bullying after I'd carried out a lot of research, talking to many school children in my area, Paddington. I printed the book in the local Prontoprint and it received a lot of publicity. High-profile writers such as Claire Rayner, Miram Stoppard and Anna Raeburn all mentioned it in their newspaper columns, then the wider media got hold of it.

The *Today Programme* on Radio 4, television news programmes, it seemed that everyone wanted to talk to me. There I was, a working mother of two little boys, who had done some research in Paddington, totally unprepared for all the fuss. It was like holding on to the tail of a tiger!'

The reason her research caused such as stir was that it suggested that, although 'stranger danger' was widely taught to children by police school liaison officers, the threat to their safety was in fact more likely to come from people known to them, such as bullies, friends, or even family members.

It was clear that a child protection programme – one that worked to keep children safe before harm occurs – needed to be established.

Michele took out a second mortgage on her flat and started Kidscape, registered as a charity in 1985.

Kidscape is based on the premise that: 'All children have the right as individuals to the knowledge and skills that will help them be safe, independent and to be able to express their feelings and concerns' and 'All adults have the responsibility to keep children safe, to listen to the feelings and concerns of children and take them seriously.'

Today, Michele employs a staff of 12. Kidscape advises over 12,000 children and parents through its anti-bullying helpline, and distributes over 250 child safety packs each week.

'The most marvellous thing we do is our ZAP courses' (these are assertiveness courses for children and young people aged nine to 15 who have been bullied). Kids come on them all demoralised, and they learn through the course that the reason they're being bullied is that the bully has a problem. These are beautful intelligent, creative children, who may have been victimised because they moved school, or simply that they were in the wrong place at the wrong time.'

'Of course, the bullies need help too, but the bullies don't come on the courses. We teach the victims that if they allow the words of the bully to get into their soul it gives them a hand hold. If you don't react they have no hold over you. I love to work with these kids and their parents. I'm still

My London Dr Michele Elliott, founder and director of Kidscape.

What is your favourite part of London?
Hyde Park and Kensington Gardens. My kids learned to ride their bikes there and were, ahem, very fond of the sandpit.

Favourite view?
From the top of London Eye I love it. I'm a big fan every time we have visitors, I take them on it. When you look across at the Houses of Parliament from a pod you're on a level with the clock face on St Stephen's Tower.

Where would you recommend people take their children?
Regent's Park (we spent many a Saturday morning watching the kids play football there) and the zoo; Hampstead; for a walk along the South Bank, past Shakespeare's Globe.

How do you get around London?
On the bus. I love the buses. I take the 148 into work every day. I know all the bus routes.

What is the best thing about bringing up children in London?
The choice, all the museums and parks you can visit free. We love the Imperial War Museum, for example. This is a wonderful, vibrant city for kids to explore.

What were your feelings when you heard we were staging the Olympics?
At first there was euphoria; everyone in the office was jumping up and down. Then, I have to admit, my heart sank when I heard about the enormous cost of staging such an event. I work for a charity. If someone gave us half a million pounds I could run Kidscape forever.

very hands-on, very involved with children and young people in my working life even though my own kids have grown up.'

Her line of work means that Michele Elliott is often consulted about aspects of modern childcare, especially the dangers inherent in bringing up children in a city like London. Did she have worries about letting her young sons loose in the city? At what stage does she think children should be allowed to travel on buses alone, for example?

'Age 40!' she quips. 'Seriously, though, I met a woman once who insisted on accompanying her son everywhere – and he was 21.'

'It's understandable: everyone worries. The first time my son Charles went out alone I ran down the stairs from our flat to watch him from the front door. I reckon children can go on buses alone when they're about 11. When my sons were that age I knew all the things that could happen but I had to let them go. I'd met too many parents whose children had had bad things happen to them so I had to try not to be over protective. I gave them practical advice: 'Don't be macho, always run into a shop if you feel in danger.'

'You have to teach the techniques they need to protect themselves, then turn them loose. Worry comes with the placenta: you have the baby, then you have the worry. And it never goes away.'

Dr Michele Elliott is the author of 23 books, including *501 Ways to be a Good Parent* available in bookshops and from www.kidscape.org.uk.

What is your favourite part of London?
The River Thames is London's most precious and visible natural asset. The river has played a vital part in London's history, and remains central to the capital's success today. From the wonderful Thames Festival (*see p26*) to the internationally acclaimed New Year's Eve fireworks display, the Thames has become an unrivalled backdrop for social and cultural activities that bring Londoners and visitors together.

Favourite view?
I have an amazing view from my office at City Hall. From my desk I am able to look out at Tower Bridge, the City, the Thames and across to the east of the Capital where the Olympics will be. I often look at the cranes in the distance to the east of the city and the regeneration. It reminds me of the benefits that will come with the Olympics and also how beautiful and diverse the city is.

Where would you recommend people take their children?
I love Kew Gardens and London Zoo. I think everybody, whether they are young or old, should go to these at some point. I have been going to the zoo since I was a child and recently went to the new gorilla enclosure.

How do you get around London?
I get the tube and bus to and from work every day. I prefer the tube to cars because (when I can get a seat) I can catch up on some paperwork.

What is the best thing about bringing up children in London?
London is one of the most exciting and creative cities in the world. Where else can you find the world in one city? Over 300 languages are spoken in London, many of them in our schools. There is an opportunity to celebrate everyone's culture and there is great acceptance among Londoners of people's traditions and beliefs as long as what you do doesn't harm others.

What were your feelings when you heard that we were staging the Olympics?
I was in Singapore with the London 2012 team for the announcement. As we waited for the result, all of the world's media had positioned themselves in front of the Paris team so I began to brace myself for what seemed to be a win for Paris and didn't want to visibly show my disappointment. When Jacque Rogge said those words 'The winner is the city of London', for a brief moment I was stunned, but then as I heard the cheers around me, I realised that in fact we had won. I felt tremendously proud of London and the team for winning not only the greatest prize in sport, but also the opportunity to regenerate one of the most polluted and poorest areas in the country.

In Context

Street theatre on the **South Bank**. *See p36.*

The Story of London

Once upon a Thames…

Prior to the arrival of the Romans, the area that was to become London was almost certainly open countryside. The site was probably chosen because it was the first place up river where the River Thames could easily be bridged.

It was once thought that Londinium started as a fort to defend the crossing, and later developed into a civilian settlement. Archaeologists from the Museum of London, however, who have been working on London's Roman beginnings for decades, have never unearthed much to convince them that a military occupation took place, so it's probable that Londinium grew up on private enterprise – as a busy river crossing it was a perfect place for traders from across the Empire to set up business.

The Latin name Londinium could have any number of ancient origins. 'Llyn-don', for example, means town ('don') by the stream ('llyn'); 'lunnd' means marsh; 'Laindon', long hill; while the adjective 'londos' translates as fierce. The first bridge across the Thames, which crossed at roughly the point of the present-day London Bridge, was also a Roman achievement. It was built after the British outpost of the Empire was sacked by Boudicca, who led her armies against the soldiers who had seized her lands and raped her daughters. The settlement was almost destroyed, but the Romans rebuilt and surrounded their town with a defensive wall in an attempt to keep out rebellions. Another 200 years passed with the Romans in charge, but with the eventual decline of the Empire, the last troops were withdrawn in 410 and London was left to Angles and Saxons.

CITY FARMS

Much of what happened in London after the Romans left is stuff of legend, rather than history. Saxon settlers crossed the North Sea to set up homes and farms in eastern and southern England during the fifth and sixth centuries. Lundenwic, 'wic' meaning marketplace, stood about where Covent Garden is today. What is now Trafalgar Square was the site of farm buildings. The Strand is so called because it used to be just that, a strand, or beach for grounding ships. London's first bishop, Mellitus, was a missionary sent by the Pope. He converted the East Saxon King

Sebert to Christianity and, in 604, founded a wooden cathedral, dedicated to St Paul, inside the old city walls. Although his people turned back to paganism after Sebert's death, later generations of Christians rebuilt St Paul's. In the ninth century another wave of invaders arrived: the Vikings. They crossed the North Sea to ransack London, forcing the king of the time, Alfred of Wessex, to reoccupy the old Roman town. In 1013, London Bridge was burned down by King Ethelred in an attempt to divide the invading forces. This episode reputedly inspired the well-known nursery rhyme.

As the Saxon city prospered, harassment from the Vikings continued until the 11th century when a Danish king – Cnut (Canute) took power. During this time London replaced Winchester as the capital. Edward the Confessor, an English king, gained the throne in 1042 and set to building Westminster Abbey. He died a week after his abbey was consecrated in December 1065.

Edward's death was a pivotal moment in history. His cousin William, Duke of Normandy, swore that his kinsman had promised him the crown. But Edward's brother-in-law Harold was a solid favourite with the English people. Their armies tried to settle the matter at Hastings. On 14 October 1066 William defeated Harold and marched to London. He was crowned in Westminster Abbey on Christmas Day.

TALKING SHOP

William knew he had to keep things sweet with the wealthy merchants in the City of London, so he gave them independent trading rights in return for taxes. The charter stating these terms is kept at the Guildhall. But the king was still bothered by the possibly rebellious population, so he ordered strongholds to be built along the city wall. One of these is the White Tower, the tallest building in the Tower of London.

The city became a hotbed of political struggle. Fighting for supremacy were three powerful bodies: the king and aristocracy; the Church; and the lord mayor and city guilds. In the early Middle Ages, the king made all the laws in the country, aided by lords and bishops. During the 14th and 15th centuries, the Palace of Westminster became the seat of law and government, and the king's meetings with the noblemen and clergy – called Parliaments – became increasingly important. As the number of advisors to the king grew, Parliament divided into two groups, the House of Lords (populated by nobles and members of the clergy chosen by the king) and the House of Commons (powerful people elected by rich merchants and landowners). Trade with Europe grew. Imports of spices, cloth, furs, precious metals and wine filled the wharves by London Bridge. The City's markets, already established, drew produce from miles around. The street markets, or 'cheaps', around Westcheap (now Cheapside) were crammed with goods. Foreign traders and craftsmen settled around the port of London. The population rocketed from about 18,000 in 1100 to more than 50,000 in the 1340s.

PLAGUED BY RATS

Overcrowding brought hygiene problems. The water supply, which came more or less directly from the Thames, was limited and polluted. In the east, Houndsditch gained its name because people threw dead dogs into the boundary ditch. At Smithfield meat market, meanwhile, butchers dumped animal guts willy-nilly. Such conditions led to the greatest catastrophe of the Middle Ages: the Black Death of 1348 and 1349. The plague came to London from Europe, carried by rats on ships. In this period about 30 per cent of the population died of disease. The epidemic recurred

in London on several occasions over the next three centuries, each time devastating the population.

With the plague killing so many, London was left with a labour shortage, resulting in unrest among the overworked peasants. A poll tax – a charge of a shilling a head – was introduced, which prompted the poor to revolt. In 1381 thousands of them, led by Wat Tyler from Kent and Jack Straw from Essex, marched on London. In the rioting and looting that followed, the Savoy Palace on the Strand was destroyed, the Archbishop of Canterbury was murdered and hundreds of prisoners were set free. Eventually a 14-year-old King Richard II rode out to face the angry mob at Smithfield, but the Lord Mayor William Walworth, angered by Tyler's belligerence, stabbed the rebel leader to death. This stopped the rioting, and the ringleaders were hanged.

HEADS ROLL

The city blossomed under the Tudors and Stuarts. Buoyed up by trade from newly discovered lands, London became one of the largest cities in Europe. Henry VII left his mark on London by commissioning the building of the Henry VII Chapel in Westminster Abbey, where he and his queen are buried. His successor was, of course, the notorious wife collector (and dispatcher) Henry VIII. His first marriage to Catherine of Aragon failed to produce an heir, so the king, in

In Context

Charles I is executed. See p17.

Robert Baden-Powell – Education outdoors

The founder of the Scout movement was born in Paddington, London, 150 years ago. The first experimental camp was held in 1907: that's a whole century of knobbly-kneed scoutmasters and ging-gang-gooly round the campfire. The whole bizarre cult is still going strong, though perhaps ever so slightly out of sync with our modern times. Scouting, after all, rests on the twin pillars of obedience to authority and gung-ho patriotism; not exactly modern yoof's cup of tea.

Baden-Powell himself, though, remains a larger-than-life, fascinating figure. Impeccably middle-class, he was educated at Charterhouse School, the son of an Oxford professor. His father died when Baden-Powell was only three, and the future Chief Scout of the World was driven forward throughout his life by a formidable mother. A distinguished military career followed. During his service as an officer in India, South Africa and the Mediterranean, he became an expert in the skills of military scouting and helped train new recruits. He also worked as an intelligence officer. His advanced reconnaissance skills came to the fore during the siege of Mafeking in the second Boer War, when a vastly outnumbered British force withstood a Zulu siege for 217 days. He was promoted to Major-General and became a national hero.

Returning to England, he found that a military training manual he had written called *Aids to Scouting* had become a national bestseller. He rewrote the book – in Wimbledon, as it happens (*see p148*) – for a youth audience and in 1907 tried out his ideas at a camp on Brownsea Island

(Dorset) for 22 boys of mixed social background. *Scouting for Boys* was published in 1908; it was such a success that spontaneously girls and boys began to form scout troops. It became a national, then an international, obsession; a worldwide movement had been born, almost by accident. Baden-Powell left the army in 1910 and became, for the remainder of his life, Chief Scout of the World, aka Bronze Wolf.

The rest of his career is a roll-call of honours that includes the Order of Merit (the most exclusive British club), the Nobel Peace Prize (or nearly, in the end not awarded because World War II had broken out) and the title of Baron. But through this fog of distinction there are shafts of humour allowing you to see another side of Baden-Powell; his Rolls-Royce for attending jamborees was known as the Jam-Roll, the Eccles caravan it towed became of course the Eccles Cake.

At the age of 55 he married. His wife was only 23. Every scout paid a penny towards his wedding present. Subsequently even girls were allowed to join the campfire-and-badges club; his wife became Guide-in-Chief. BP was a prolific artist as well as writer, in love with the African Outdoors more than any other. He died in 1941 and was buried near Mount Kenya. His gravestone bears a scouting symbol, a circle around a dot, meaning: I have gone home. Yes, he has indeed gone home, a long time ago now, but what he has left us with is unclear.

Wanting to spend many hours in the company of young boys in shorts, at night, in the woods, could never seem entirely innocent, especially in these distrustful days but, in spite of suggestions of an ulterior motive for all this mucking about with boys, nothing was ever proved – and Robert Baden-Powell's honourable legacy continues to this day. The London connection is kept strong by the Baden Powell House Hostel (Scout Activity Centre) in South Kensington (*see p88*). As for the centenary, what are the scouts doing to celebrate? They are bringing out a special badge/patch, of course, and LIVE 07 at the O_2 arena (*see p134*) is billed as a Festival of Scouting (24 November 2007). Visit www.scouts.org.uk for more information.

You're 'avin' a bubblebarf with

CARTOON NETWORK.

Cockney to English translation: You are having a laugh with Cartoon Network.

Dr Thomas Barnardo – Education for the poor

Thomas Barnardo was a well-intentioned young Dubliner who arrived in London in the 1860s to study medicine in order to become a missionary in China. Instead he devoted his life to running the orphaned and destitute children running wild in the streets of the capital, becoming one of the most famous men in Victorian Britain and revolutionising the field of philanthropy. Within seven years, fired by evangelical zeal, he had single-handedly founded a ragged school, a mission church, an employment agency, a children's magazine and no fewer than twelve Barnardo's homes in the East End of London.

Victorian London (as we know from our Dickens) was a place of exploding population where orphaned or abandoned children slept in gutters and on rooftops and died from exposure, hunger or disease. Some had been maimed from factory work and had no resort but begging. In 1866, for example, the year Barnardo arrived, a cholera epidemic killed more than 3,000 people in the East End. Barnardo was at first sufficiently moved by the plight of poor children in London to open his first 'ragged school'(*pictured*) in 1867. But while working there he was taken one night by one of his pupils, Jim Jarvis, on a tour of the places in the East End where children were sleeping rough. This convinced him to spend a lifetime working for the destitute. In 1870 the first of his homes for boys was opened in Stepney. Later, in another incident emotionally recounted by Barnardo himself an unfortunate eleven-year-old boy called John Somers, nicknamed 'Carrots', was found dead of cold and hunger days after being turned away from one of his shelters. From then on a sign hung outside the door of every Barnardo home which read: No Destitute Child Ever Refused Admission.

One of Barnardo's original Ragged Schools in east London has been re-opened as a museum (*see p115*). It's a popular place for school trips; today's pampered darlings are for some strange reason quite thrilled by the recreation of a Victorian classroom experience, complete with cane-swishing teacher in a period whaleboned frock.

When Barnardo died in 1905, his charity ran 96 homes caring for more than 8,000 children. He had also founded a kind of village of homes for girls in Barkingside, where 1,500 girls were housed in cottages around a village green. In the homes boys learnt a trade and girls were educated in domestic skills.

As the twentieth century progressed, the essentially Victorian idea behind the children's homes began to fall out of favour. Barnardo, like many a bewhiskered philanthropist of the age, had set up a well-meaning dictatorship. Poverty was seen as shameful and therefore the lives of the

1527, decided (in defiance of the Catholic Church) that the union should be annulled. Demanding to be recognised as Supreme Head of the Church of England, Henry ordered the execution of anyone who refused to comply (including his chancellor Sir Thomas More). So England began its transition to Protestantism. The subsequent dissolution of Catholic monasteries changed the face of London: the land sold off was given over to streets. Henry also founded the Royal Dockyards at Woolwich. The land he kept for hunting became the Royal Parks (Hyde, Regent's, Greenwich and Richmond). Henry's daughter Queen Mary's five-year reign saw a brief Catholic revival. She was dubbed 'Bloody Mary' following her order to burn at the stake nearly 300 Protestants.

Mary's half-sister Elizabeth I oversaw a huge upsurge in commerce: the Royal Exchange was poor could be ruled by their superiors without consultation. The homes were also seen by many children as cold and cruel institutions, and some were rife with bullying and abuse.

Finally, in 1946, a national report (the Curtis Report) concluded that children's emotional needs were best met by a family and not by an institution. This revolutionised childcare and tolled the death knell for residential homes. Today Barnardo's is simply one more charity in a crowded landscape, working with families and involved in fostering. History has forced it to adapt. But without Dr Thomas Barnardo, who never did make it out to China and died in his fifties from overwork, how much more suffering would children have had to endure? An old-fashioned Victorian, he can never become a present-day hero since his ideas seem so Martian to us with our touchy-feely child-centredness, but he is yet another of that era's great and saintly figures. For more information visit www.barnardos.org.uk.

founded by Sir Thomas Gresham in 1566, and London became Europe's leading commercial centre. With Drake, Raleigh and Hawkins sailing to America and beyond, new trading enterprises were developed. By 1600 there were 200,000 people living in London; 12,000 of whom were beggars. Conditions were overcrowded, insanitary and infested with rats and fleas, so plague was a constant threat.

CITY OF CULTURE?

London was a cultural centre, however, as well as a death trap. Two theatres, the Rose (1587) and the Globe (1599), were built on the south bank of the Thames, and the plays of William Shakespeare and Christopher Marlowe first performed. Earthier dramas took place on the street. At Bankside, people visited taverns and brothels, and engaged in bear-baiting and cockfighting.

London was a violent place. Elizabeth's successor, the Stuart James I, narrowly escaped being blown up. The Gunpowder Plot was instigated by a group of Catholics led by Guy Fawkes, who planned to protest at their persecution by dynamiting the Palace of Westminster from the cellar. Unfortunately for Fawkes, one of his co-conspirators warned his brother-in-law not to attend Parliament on 5 November – prompting a thorough search and the foiling of the scheme. Four plotters were killed while resisting arrest, while the remainder of the gang were dragged through the streets and executed, their heads displayed on spikes.

James I had escaped death, but his son Charles I wasn't so lucky. He stirred up trouble by throwing his weight around in the House of Commons, threatening the City of London's tax-free status and sparking a civil war: Charles and his Royalists were the losers. The king was tried for treason and beheaded outside the Banqueting House in Whitehall in 1649. Oliver Cromwell's Puritans declared Britain a Commonwealth, and theatres and gambling dens were closed down.

LONDON'S BURNING

The exiled Charles II was restored to the throne in 1660, and Londoners were relieved. But there was trouble ahead: the 1664-65 bubonic plague killed nearly 100,000 Londoners. At the height of the epidemic, 10,000 people were dying each week. When plague was diagnosed in a house, the occupants were locked inside for 40 days, while watchmen outside ensured no one escaped. London reeked of death. The following year, an oven in Farriner's bakery in Pudding Lane started a fire that lasted three days and destroyed four-fifths of the City. Rumours of a Popish plot were everywhere, and Frenchman Robert Hubert was forced to confess to starting the fire and hanged. Today Christopher Wren's Monument marks a spot near where the fire broke out. London was rebuilt in brick and stone. As well as completing his greatest work, the new St Paul's Cathedral, Wren oversaw the rebuilding of 51 city churches.

London was a veritable hotbed of dissent between 1680 and the early 19th century; there was a riot almost every weekend, as Professor

In Context

Clive Bloom, author of *Violent London: 2000 years of Riots, Rebels and Revolts* writes. The worst example of such disorganised violence in London was the 1780 Gordon Riots, an outpouring of anti-Catholic rage that lasted a week and left hundreds dead.

Around this time George III was on the throne and the Whig Party, led by Sir Robert Walpole, was in power. Walpole was the first prime minister and was given 10 Downing Street as an official home. This address has been occupied by the serving prime minister ever since. More crossings over the river were built: Westminster Bridge (1750) and Blackfriars Bridge (1763) joined London Bridge, which until then had been the only bridge to span the river. While the well-to-do enjoyed their Georgian homes, life for the poor was squalid. Living in slums, ruined by plentiful gin, people turned to street crime. Gangs emerged, who enjoyed near immunity from arrest. The Gregory Gang, one of many that preyed on travellers, included highwayman Dick Turpin.

In 1751 the writer Henry Fielding and his brother John established a volunteer force of 'thief takers' to help the parish constables catch these criminals. This force, originally known as the Bow Street Runners, eventually became the Metropolitan Police (established 1829).

The rich had never had it so good when Victoria was crowned in 1837. Progress was impressive: five more bridges spanned the Thames and the city's first railway line (London Bridge to Greenwich) had been laid. Yet this city, the administrative and financial capital of the British Empire, had a dark underbelly. Crammed into slums, the urban masses led a miserable – and malodorous – life. The summer of 1858 smelled particularly bad: the 'Great Stink' meant that politicians in the Houses of Parliament could not work with their windows open. The stink so got up the noses of MPs that Benjamin Disraeli, the Chancellor of the Exchequer was able to rush through a bill allocating some £3 million to construct a new sewerage system in London.

DEVASTATED BY WAR

The new century started merrily enough, with Edward VII taking the throne in 1901, but the gaiety and glamour that had been so lacking in the last years of Queen Victoria's reign wouldn't last. World War I saw the first bomb to be dropped on London. It came from a Zeppelin and landed near the Guildhall. Terrifying nightly raids continued throughout the Great War, killing 650 people.

When it was finally over, those soldiers who had survived were promised 'homes for heroes' on their return. Yet few homes materialised and the nation's mood was bleak. Political change was set in motion. In 1924 David Lloyd George's Liberal Party was deposed in favour of a promised fresh start with the Labour Party, under Ramsay MacDonald. While the upper classes partied their way through the Roaring Twenties, the working classes were in the grip of mass unemployment. Dissatisfaction was expressed when all the workers downed tools to support the striking miners. The General Strike of 1926 lasted for nine days: the army distributed food, and students drove buses. After nine days of chaos the strike was called off by the Trades Union Congress. Unemployment continued to rise. The New York Stock Exchange crash of 1929 had a knock-on effect; the British economic situation was grim.

The London County Council worked to improve conditions for its people. As the city's population grew (8.7 million in 1939), so did its sprawl. Suburbia expanded, and with it the Tube lines. The main entertainment for people was the radio, until 1936, when the first television broadcast went out live from the British Broadcasting Corporation (BBC) at Alexandra Palace studios.

On 3 September 1939 Britain declared war on Germany. Londoners dug air-raid shelters and sent children and pregnant women to the countryside. In fact, the air raids did not begin until almost a year later. In September 1940, 600 German bombers devastated east London and the docks. The raids continued for 57 nights in a row. Nearly 30,000 bombs were dropped on the city; around 15,000 people were killed and 3.5 million houses destroyed or damaged. People sheltered in the Tube stations. They were safe unless the stations were hit. This happened at Marble Arch, Bank and Balham.

In 1944 a new type of bomb began flattening Londoners' homes – the fearsome V1 flying bomb, or doodlebug. These caused widespread destruction, as did their successor, the more powerful V2 rocket. By the end of the war, about a third of the city was in ruins.

PREFAB SPROUT

In the General Election that took place soon after VE Day, Churchill was defeated by the Labour Party under Clement Attlee. The National Health Service was founded in 1948; public transport and communications were overhauled. But life in the city still seemed drab and austere. For Londoners facing a housing shortage there were ambitious initiatives. Some of the buildings whisked up – prefabricated bungalows – were supposed to be temporary, but many are still inhabited more than 60 years later. Many new high-rise estates were shoddy and many have since been pulled down.

Edward Alleyn – Education for the rich

Edward Alleyn was not only one of the two most famous actors of his day (alongside Richard Burbage) and a mate of Shakespeare's, but also a theatre-entrepreneur and landowner who became seriously rich and well-connected – a sort of Elizabethan Larry Olivier, Andrew Lloyd-Webber and Lord Melvyn Bragg of Cumbria all rolled into one. His name lives on today mainly as the founder of Dulwich College, the distinguished public school in south London.

Born into a working-class family, Alleyn played leading roles at the Rose theatre (near the Globe) from 1587. He then made a smart career move: he married the stepdaughter of his friend and employer, Philip Henslowe, owner of the Rose. Together they built the Fortune theatre to compete with Shakespeare's Globe. He finally retired from acting in 1604, when he and Henslowe jointly held the patent as Master of the Royal Game of Bears, Bulls and Mastiff Dogs. In other words, the popular business of bear-baiting and the like made them very rich men. Forget Melvyn Bragg now, he

had become the Simon Cowell of popular live entertainment. With all this money Alleyn bought the Manor of Dulwich in 1605 for an absolute snip at £35,000. He began building the College of God's Gift on his newly-acquired land in 1613 and Dulwich College (*pictured*) was founded in 1619. Is this the origin of the expression: 'They think they're God's gift, that lot?'

Alleyn's original foundation stipulated that twelve poor scholars aged six to 18 years old were to be educated by resident Fellows. He also stipulated the detail of the uniform ('good cloth of sad colour') and diet for the pupils (on three days of the week the poor boys were to have 'beere without stint'). Some of the arrangements laid down by Alleyn are now disregarded; the college no longer needs to hire a ploughboy (and the boys probably drink less beer these days too). The basic principle of providing an education for the well-off majority and also, charitably, a free education for a less well-off minority still exists, technically, but it has been watered down. Scholarships are available for the brightest. This is a relic of the 'poor scholars' idea. But scholarships now pay only one tenth of the eye-wateringly high tuition fees. In Elizabethan times it was simply accepted that only those 'of good family' could afford an education; hence the need for foundations like this to even up the playing-field. But even Alleyn's vast wealth doesn't seem to have reached into the present.

Alleyn built the Hope theatre on Bankside in 1614 on the site of the Bear Garden. In 1616 he inherited, on Henslowe's death, most of his friend's assets. He re-married, in 1623, one of the daughters of poet John Donne and died a rich man three years later, a vivid demonstration of the upward mobility an actor could achieve in Elizabethan England. Henslowe's papers, left to his friend Alleyn, have ended up in the library of Dulwich College and provide invaluable research material for anyone studying Elizabethan theatre.

In Context

Key events

c66 BC Ludgate built by King Lud (legendary).
AD 43 The Roman invasion. Londinium is founded.
61 Boudicca sacks the city.
122 Emperor Hadrian visits Londinium.
200 Rebuilt Londinium is protected by a city wall.
410 The last Roman troops finally leave Britain.
c600 Saxon London is built to the west of the city.
604 The first St Paul's Cathedral is built.
841 First Viking raid.
c871 The Danes occupy London.
886 King Alfred retakes London.
1013 The Danes take London.
1042 King Edward builds Westminster Abbey.
1066 William, Duke of Normandy, defeats Harold.
1067 Work begins on the Tower of London.
1099 First recorded flood in London.
1123 St Bartholomew's Hospital founded.
1197 Henry Fitzailwyn becomes the first mayor.
1240 First Parliament sits at Westminster.
1294 First recorded mention of Hammersmith.
1348-9 The Black Death ravages London.
1357 The first Sanitary Act passed in London.
1381 Wat Tyler leads the Peasants' Revolt.
1388 Tyburn, near Marble Arch, becomes a place of execution.

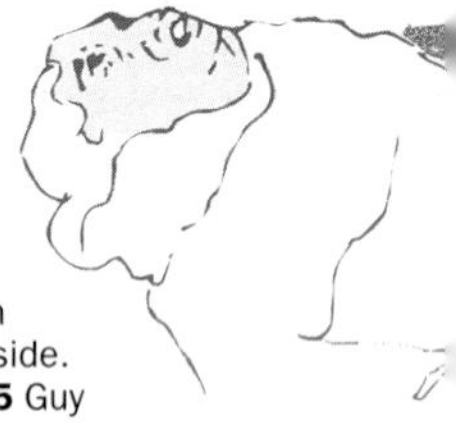

1397 Richard (Dick) Whittington becomes Lord Mayor.
1497 The first image of London published in a 'Chronycle of Englonde'.
1513 Henry VIII founds Woolwich Royal Dockyard.
1534 Henry VIII breaks from the Catholic Church.
1554 300 Protestant martyrs burned at Smithfield.
1599 The Globe Theatre is built on Bankside.
1605 Guy Fawkes's fiendish Gunpowder Plot is discovered.
1635 London's first public postal service established.
1642 The Puritans defeat the Royalists at Turnham Green.
1649 Charles I is tried for treason and beheaded.
1664-5 The Great Plague kills thousands.
1666 The Great Fire destroys London.
1675 Building starts on a new St Paul's.
1680 Downing Street built.
1686 The first May Fair celebration takes place at Mayfair.
1694 The Bank of England opens at Cheapside.
1711 St Paul's is completed.
1742 Thomas Coram founds his orphanage.
1750 Westminster Bridge is built.
1769 Blackfriars Bridge opens.
1803 The first railway opens.
1820 Regent's Canal opens.
1824 National Gallery founded.
1827 Regent's Park Zoological Gardens open.
1829 The first horse-drawn bus runs. The Metropolitan Police Act is passed.
1833 The London Fire Brigade is established.

Takako Okuma

In Context

1835 The Madame Tussaud's collection opens.
1843 Trafalgar Square is laid out in Nelson's honour.
1851 The Great Exhibition.
1858 The Great Stink permeates London.
1863 World's first underground railway opens.
1866 Sanitation Act is passed.
1868 The last public execution takes place in Newgate Prison.
1869 The first J Sainsbury grocery opens in Drury Lane.
1884 Greenwich Mean Time is established.
1888 Jack the Ripper haunts East End women.
1890 First electric underground railway opens.
1897 Motorised buses introduced.
1898 The first escalator installed in London.
1915-18 Zeppelins bomb London.
1916 Horse-drawn buses disappear.
1940-4 The Blitz destroys much of the city.
1948 The Olympic are Games held in London.
1951 The Festival of Britain takes place on the south bank of the Thames.
1952 The last of the city's infamous 'pea-souper' fogs
1953 Queen Elizabeth II is crowned.
1966 England win the World Cup at Wembley.
1975 Work begins on the Thames flood Barrier.
1982 The last of London's docks close.
1986 The Greater London Council is abolished.
1990 Poll Tax protestors riot.
1992 Canary Wharf opens.
1997 A Labour government is elected; Britain mourns Princess Diana.
2000 Ken Livingstone elected Mayor.
2001 The Labour Government is re-elected for a second term.

2002 Queen Mother dies aged 101.
2003 A massive public demonstration – against the war on Iraq – is the biggest ever seen in London.
2004 Mayor Ken Livingstone is re-elected.
2005 A euphoric London wins bid to host the 2012 Olympics. One day later four suicide bombers kill 52 people.
2006 The Queen celebrates her 80th birthday with a children's party at Buckingham Palace.
2007 London marks the bicentennial of the Slave Trade Act. Blair resigns.

In Context

It was not all doom for Londoners, though. The city hosted the Olympic Games in 1948 and, in 1951, the Festival of Britain, which celebrated all that was great about British technology and design. The festival took place on derelict land on the south bank of the river, which eventually became the site of the South Bank Centre arts complex. During the 1950s Britain enjoyed a gradual return to relative prosperity. Families were inspired to move to new towns away from the city, where air pollution was a problem. The Clean Air Acts, the first introduced in 1956 as a result of the Great Smog four years earlier, finally ensured the reduction of noxious gas emissions. Inner London was also facing a labour shortage. Workers from the country's former colonies, particularly the West Indies, were recruited for London Transport and in the hospitals. Many immigrants faced an unfriendly reception from indigenous Londoners: matters came to a head in the Notting Hill race riots of 1958. Some parts of London were more tolerant; Soho, with its jazz joints and clubs, for one. The 1960s saw London – fashion capital of the world – swing.

To find out where the gigs were, people bought a weekly guide to London called *Time Out*; the first issue came out in August 1968. People flocked to Abbey Road, NW8, because of the Beatles album of the same name. Hyde Park was the place to be in the summer of '69 when the Rolling Stones played for half a million fans.

In the 1970s the lights went out, often literally, on London's glamour. Inflation, unemployment, strikes, IRA bombs and an increasingly fractured Labour government all contributed to an air of gloom. The rebellious punk explosion made a few sparks fly, but that was shortlived. Margaret Thatcher came to power in 1979, and the 1980s are regarded as her decade. Her Conservative government made sweeping changes, and stood up for 'market forces'. This was the era of the yuppie (Young Urban Professional), who cashed in on the Conservatives' monetarist policies and the arrival of the global economy. It did not take long for the city's underdogs to snarl and riot, first in Brixton, in 1981, and four years later in Tottenham, north London.

One lasting legacy of the Thatcher era in London is the Docklands redevelopment. Set up in 1981 to create a business centre in the docks to the east of the City, the scheme was slow to take shape, but to this day businesses and residents continue to move into buildings around the Isle of Dogs, and the area exudes prosperity. But this is a prominent area of London with a split personality, because little of the wealth from the banks and businesses is filtering through to the community. In 1986 the Greater London Council, with its anti-Thatcher outlook, was abolished, and County Hall was sold to a Japanese corporation. But hisory has a way of turning on you – the GLC's former leader, 'Red' Ken Livingstone, bided his time and, in 2000, was voted mayor with authority over all the city.

LABOUR'S DAYS

London in the early 1990s hit the buffers. A slump in house prices saw the reign of the yuppies come to an end. The last straw for beleaguered Londoners was the poll tax. Demonstrations led to riots in Trafalgar Square. It marked the loosening of Thatcher's grip, leading to her replacement by John Major in 1990. The recession continued. The numbers of rough sleepers rose in London as people lost their homes through unemployment and mortgage-rate rises. The IRA stepped up its campaign against the mainland, bombing the City in 1992 (destroying the medieval church of St Ethelburga the Virgin) and Docklands in 1996. Many cheered up when Tony Blair's New Labour ousted the Tories in May 1997, but went into shock when, later that year, Princess Diana was killed. The gates of Kensington Palace were the focus for the nation's tears and bouquets.

Fireworks for the new millennium weren't confined to the celebratory kind. Labour continued with the Conservative-conceived Millennium Dome project. But the spectacular tent on the once-derelict Greenwich Peninsula failed to capture the zeitgeist, and angry voices were raised about the massive sums of money swallowed up by the enterprise. After many false starts, the Dome has been renamed the O_2 and is finally being transformed into a 20,000-seat sports and entertainment complex. And London still has problems. Housing is both expensive and in short supply, leading some to campaign for a reintroduction of tower blocks. Transport is taking a long time to improve, but much new work is now under way in preparation for the 2012 Olympics. When London was named as the venue, mass euphoria broke out in Trafalgar Square. The happiness was shortlived, however; terrorist bombs killed 52 people and injured 700 not 24 hours later.

Very quickly after the tragedy the first 'Not Afraid' T-shirts began to appear and London emerged with a revitalised sense of itself. The city in 2007 promises much to keep the mood buoyant. As Tony leaves, Gordon remains hopeful and Ken oversees a number of inner-city regeneration schemes. There's an Olympian urgency behind a will to make our sporting facilities the best in the world. Meanwhile the tourists keep coming, and Londoners still take pride in their chaotic capital.

Festivals & Events

Whatever the season, London finds good reason to celebrate.

It seems there's always some sort of shindig going on in this city. Recent years have seen an increase in outdoor festivals, usually during the summer, as well as some imaginative sponsored seasons and one-off events. Check *Time Out* magazine every week for the news, and for details of fairs and circuses coming to a park near you. Zippo's, London's largest traditional touring circus, has a new show every year. See www.zipposcircus.co.uk for details of new acts, plus venues and dates for 2008.

Summer

Coin Street Festival

Bernie Spain Gardens (next to Oxo Tower Wharf), SE1 9PH (7401 2255/www.coinstreetfestival.org). Southwark tube/Waterloo tube/rail. **Date** June-Sept 2007. **Map** p318 N7.
A series of culturally themed weekday and weekend events celebrating different communities in the capital. Festivities take place on the South Bank and include music, dance and performance events for all ages, with craft and refreshment stalls and workshops for families at each one. This year's events include *Turkish Fest* (14-15 July), with a bazaar and live music. Check the website for details near the time.

Beating Retreat

Horse Guards Parade, Whitehall, Westminster, SW1A 2AX (booking 7414 2271). Westminster tube/Charing Cross tube/rail. **Date** 6-7 June 2007. **Map** p317 K8.
This patriotic ceremony begins at 7pm, with the 'Retreat' beaten on drums by the Mounted Bands of the Household Cavalry and the Massed Bands of the Guards Division.

Trooping the Colour

Horse Guards Parade, Whitehall, Westminster, SW1A 2AX (7414 2271). Westminster tube/Charing Cross tube/rail. **Date** 16 June 2007. **Map** p317 K8.
Though the Queen was born on 21 April, this is her official birthday celebration. At 10.45am she makes the journey from Buckingham Palace to Horse Guards Parade, then scurries back home to watch a noon Royal Air Force flypast and receive a formal gun salute from Green Park.

London Garden Squares Weekend

Various venues across London (www.opensquares.org). **Date** 9-10 June 2007; check website for 2008 dates.
For one weekend only, the London Parks & Gardens Trust opens many of them to the public. Tickets allow entry to all participating gardens, from Japanese-style retreats to secret 'children-only' play areas, and cost £6 in advance or £7.50 during the weekend. Under-12s go free.

City of London Festival

Venues across the City, EC2-EC4 (7796 4949/www.colf.org). St Paul's tube/Bank tube/DLR/Blackfriars, Cannon Street, Farringdon or Moorgate tube/rail. **Date** 22 June-12 July 2007.
Now in its 45th year, the City of London Festival takes place in some of the finest buildings in the Square Mile, among them the Guildhall and St Paul's. The programme is wide-ranging, with music, visual art, drama and film screenings, alongside architecture walks, talks and other outdoor events. This year takes a colourful Japanese theme; in addition to a number of concerts, there will be a family fun day at Hampstead Heath (24 June) with kite-making and origami workshops and demonstrations.

London Youth Games

Various venues in London (8778 0131/www.youthgames.org.uk). **Dates** 30 June-1 July 2007.
This mini-Olympics, now in its 30th year, attracts 12,000 sporting hopefuls, all of them under 17, representing the 33 London boroughs in 28 different sports. The teams are selected locally, and activities include archery, fencing, canoeing, football, tennis, athletics and show jumping. Check the website for a programme. The finals are held at Crystal Palace Sports Ground, where various entertainments including DJs, street sports, graffiti art and dance demonstrations complement the main event.

Wimbledon Lawn Tennis Championships

All England Lawn Tennis Club, PO Box 98, Church Road, Wimbledon, SW19 5AE (8944 1066/info 8946 2244/www.wimbledon.org). Southfields tube/Wimbledon tube/rail. **Date** 25 June-8 July 2007.
Plan ahead for this prestigious tennis tournament. For Centre Court and Court Number One seats, you'd have had to request an application form from the All England Lawn Tennis Club between August and the end of November the year before; this form gives you access to the public ticket ballot. If you queue on the day, you should gain entry to the outside courts. In the afternoon, returned show-court tickets are available from the booth opposite Court One, so it may be worth hanging about to see stars in action on one of the most famous courts ion the world.

Greenwich & Docklands International Festival (GDIF)

Various venues in Greenwich & Docklands (8305 1818/www.festival.org). **Date** 21-24 June 2007.
An annual mix of free theatrical, musical and site-specific outdoor events, this always family-friendly festival will be celebrating its tenth anniversary this year. Look out for human mobiles spectacularly suspended from cranes, stilt artists, plenty of pyrotechnics and the grand 'birthday party' finale on the last day. See the website for details of the 2008 event nearer the time.

In Context

Henley Royal Regatta

Henley Reach, Henley-on-Thames, Oxon RG9 2LY (01491 572153/www.hrr.co.uk). Henley-on-Thames rail. **Date** 4-8 July 2007; 2-6 July 2008.

First held in 1839, and under royal patronage since 1851, Henley is still going strong; it's now a five-day affair. Boat races range from open events for men and women through club and student crews to juniors. There are two events for junior boys under the age of 19.

Royal National Theatre Summer Festival

South Bank, SE1 9PX (7452 3400/www.national theatre.org.uk). Waterloo tube/rail. **Date** 6 July-16 September 2007. **Map** p318 M7.

One of our favourite annual arts events, Watch This Space, is a free outdoor festival of entertainment in Theatre Square. It showcases the best street theatre, circus, cinema, music, art and dance from all over the world.

Royal National Theatre Summer Festival: circus tricks, silly costumes and much more.

Special events include A Day to Play (family day) on 4 August (1-7pm). Look out for last year's hit, the Insect Circus Museum, which is making a triumphant return (26-28 July). Other events too good to miss include Belgium's Circo Ripopolo miniature circus (21 July) and Compost Mentis, an hilariously organic show about a living compost heap by the Whalley Range All Stars on 11 August.

Tour de France Grand Depart
Trafalgar Square, SW1 (www.tourdefrancelondon.com). **Date** 6-8 July 2007.
The opening ceremony will light up Trafalgar Square on the Friday with a spectacular celebration of Tour de France arrivals in London. On Saturday the Tour opens with an individual race around the streets of central London, from 2pm. On the Sunday, riders leave the Mall at 10.25am, there's a ceremony at Tower Bridge at 10.40am and the riders bowl south-eastward to Greenwich, thence to Canterbury, after that. It's being seen as a dress rehearsal for the 2012 Olympics.

BBC Sir Henry Wood Promenade Concerts
Royal Albert Hall, Kensington Gore, South Kensington, SW7 2AP (box office 7589 8212/www.bbc.co.uk/ proms). Knightsbridge or South Kensington tube/9, 10, 52 bus. **Date** 13 July-8 September 2007. **Map** p313 D9.
This annual event brings together an eclectic range of mainly classical concerts over the course of two months. Most are televised, but there's nothing like seeing them in person. If you choose carefully, you should able to find something in the grown-up Proms programme that the children will enjoy. The '5 BBC Music Intro' concerts can be seen for £5 per family member; all under- 16s can get half-price tickets to every Prom across the season (apart from the Last Night). Otherwise, check the website for details of the Blue Peter Proms (22 & 23 July).

Lambeth Country Show
Brockwell Park, SE24 0NG (7926 9000/www.ubique leisure.co.uk). Brixton tube/rail then 2, 3, 68, 196 bus/Herne Hill rail. **Date** 21-22 July 2007.
This free annual urban country show fills the rolling hills of Brockwell Park with a mix of farmyard and domestic animal attractions (horse show, dog show, farm animals and birds of prey). Aside from meeting and greeting the beasts, children can have fun on numerous bouncy castles and fairground rides, and there are also international food and craft stalls, and a whole lot of music and dancing.

Sundae on the Common
Clapham Common, SW4 (www.benjerry.co.uk/sundae). Clapham Common tube. **Date** last weekend of July 2007.
As we went to press the dates and line-up were yet to be announced (check the website for updates), but expect a huge chunk of the Common to be fenced off for this fun family festival. With a farmyard corner with livestock from a local city farm, a children's area with bouncy castle (and quieter tent for the tinies), the festival is a true crowd pleaser. Parents can watch live bands while their offspring hurtle down the Helter Skelter and queue for free ice-cream all day long. The proceeds go towards regenerating the Clapham Common bandstand. In 2006, Ben himself (or was it Jerry?) was wandering around the site; see if you can spot those famous beards again this year.

Summer in the Square
Trafalgar Square, Westminster, WC2 (7983 4100/www.london.gov.uk/trafalgarsquare). Embankment tube/Charing Cross tube/rail. **Date** 2-19 August 2007. **Map** p317 K7.
An annual programme of free (and usually fun) live cultural performances for all ages, Summer in the Square is keenly supported by the Mayor of London. As we went to press programme details had not been confirmed; check the website nearer the time.

Free Time Festival
Somerset House, Strand, WC2R ORN (7845 4600/ www.somerset-house.org.uk). Covent Garden or Temple tube (closed Sun)/Charing Cross tube/rail. **Date** 26-29 July 2007. **Map** p317 M7.
The courtyard here provides a handsome stage for events during the summer holidays, and the Family Free Time Festival promises fun, song, laughter and games.

Peter Pan in Kensington Gardens
Kensington Gardens, W8 2UH (www.gosh.org/tickets 7239 3111). High Street Kensington, Lancaster Gate or Queensway tube/9, 12, 28, 49, 148 bus. **Date** 28-29 July 2007. **Tickets** £7.50; free under-2s. **Map** p310 C7.
Bring a picnic and a sense of fun to this open-air performance in Kensington Gardens by Chalkfoot Theatre Arts, who promise to bring Neverland to the park. Wear fancy dress; there are prizes for the best costumes.

Innocent Village Fete
Gloucester Green, north-east corner of Regent's Park, NW1 (8600 3939/www.innocentdrinks.co.uk). Baker Street or Regent's Park tube. **Date** 4-5 August 2007. **Map** p314 G3.
No Fruitstock this year as the 2006 one became too frantic. There will be no massive music stage, and no dance tent. The fete instead will focus on gentler pastimes – picnics, own-made buns, the tombola, lying around in the grass. And there will be music, comedy, arts and crafts and fancy dress games for children, lessons in massage and yoga lessons and, possibly, snail racing. Tickets go on sale a few weeks before the event; check the website for details.

Carnaval del Pueblo
www.noticias.co.uk. **Date** 5 August 2007 free entry.
The UK's largest Latin American celebration. It begins with a parade from Tower Bridge to Burgess Park with every country of South America represented. The parade then leads into Burgess Park to be greeted by five stages, hundreds of stalls, funfair and activities.

Underage
Victoria Park, Old Ford Road, E3 5DS (8985 1957/www.myspace.com/underage_club). Mile End tube/Cambridge Heath or Hackney Wick rail/8, 26, 30, 55, 253, 277, S2 bus. **Date** 10 August 2007. **Tickets** £20.
Underage, the World's first strictly under-17s music festival, promises some of the best indie/rock/electronic music of the day for young music fans. With a capacity of 5,000, it will be a smaller more intimate affair than the big festivals. The bars will serve soft drinks only. Confirmed bands at time of going to press included Crystal Castles, Cajun Dance Party, Foals, The Teenagers and Xerox Teens.

Notting Hill Carnival

*Notting Hill, W10, W11 (0870 059 1111/www.
lnhc.org.uk). Ladbroke Grove, Notting Hill Gate
& Westbourne Park tube.* **Date** 26-27 Aug bank
holiday 2007.

Sunday is traditionally children's day at this annual
shindig, second in the world only to Rio in terms of sheer
scale. It livens up this posh neighbourhood with mas-
querades, steel bands, decorative floats and more sound
systems than you could shake a paper plate of curried goat
at. Its reputation for bringing short, sharp spikes to the
annual crime charts continues to court controversy, but
increasing commercialism and a strong police presence
have made the carnival safer than ever.

Autumn

Young Pavement Artists Competition

Venue tbc/www.muscular-dystrophy.org/pavementart.
Date *Exhibition* Autumn 2007.

The Young Pavement Artists Competition (YPAC) is a
national competition to raise awareness of muscular dys-
trophy. Schools, community and youth groups can take
part by holding their own creative pavement event to help
raise funds for the charity. Participants who find it difficult to get down to the pavement can use chalks on paper
to create their own visions. Each year has a different theme
and winners of the local events can enter the national competition. Children aged four to 19 can compete, with pitches costing around £1 per entrant. Photographs of the day's
winners are then entered into the national competition,
judged by members of the Tate Britain and Royal
Academy of Arts. Winners are displayed at an exhibition
this autumn (venue to be announced). Guidelines for organ-
ising your own event are detailed on the website.

Regent Street Festival

*Regent Street, W1 (7287 9601/www.regentstreet
online.com). Oxford Circus or Piccadilly Circus tube.*
Date 2 September 2007. **Map** p316 J7.

An annual celebration in one of the capital's smartest
streets, which closes to traffic for the day to make room
for fairground rides, theatre, street entertainers,
storytelling, a variety of live music and, of course,
shopping. There's usually plenty of input from the busy
toy emporium, Hamley's, *see p208.*

Trafalgar Great River Race

*Thames, from Ham House, Richmond, Surrey,
to Island Gardens, Greenwich, E14 (8398 9057/
www.greatriverrace.co.uk).* **Date** 8 September 2007.

More than 260 'traditional' boats – from Chinese dragon
boats to Viking longboats – vie for the title in the UK traditional boat championships over a 35-kilometre (22-mile)
course. The race begins at 12.55am and reaches the finish
at around 4.30pm. The best viewing point is riverside at
Richmond Bridge, or along the South Bank, on the
Millennium and Hungerford bridges. Or, for a special treat,
take a trip on the boat and watch the action up close (£25;
£10 concessions, free under-6s).

Mayor's Thames Festival

*Between Westminster & Blackfriars Bridges (7983
4100/www.thamesfestival.org). Blackfriars or Waterloo
tube/rail.* **Date** 15-16 September 2007.

Always fun and occasionally spectacular, this waterfest
celebrating the sweet Thames runs from noon to 10pm all
weekend and is highlighted by an atmospheric lantern
procession and a noisy and spectacular firework finale on
Sunday evening. Before the pyrotechnics kick off, there are
riverside market stalls, various environmental activities
and creative workshops, and a lively assortment of dance
and music performances.

Summer in the Square. *See p25.*

Horseman's Sunday

Church of St John's Hyde Park, Hyde Park Crescent, W2 2QD (7262 1732/www.stjohns-hydepark.com/ horsemans). Edgware Road or Lancaster Gate tube/ Paddington tube/rail. **Date** 23 September 2007. **Map** p313 E6.

This ceremony dates back to 1967, when local stables, threatened with closure, held an outdoor service to protest. At noon, after morning service, the vicar of St John's rides out to bless and present rosettes to a procession of horses and riders, and delivers a short service with hymns and occasional guest speakers. To mark its 40th anniversary this year there will also be games, face painting and other fun laid on for kids in a special area next to the church.

City Farms Festival

Capel Manor Gardens, Bullsmoor Lane, Enfield, Middx BN1 4RQ (8366 4442/www.capel.ac.uk). Turkey Street rail (Closed Sun)/217, 310 bus. **Date** 22 September 2007.

The urban farms we all love have a pleasant day oufor this agricultural extravaganza. Events include a farm-animal show and arena events, such as milking and shearing demonstrations, vegetable and plant sales, displays by craftspeople and food stalls.

Children's Book Week

Booktrust, 45 East Hill, SW18 2QZ (8516 2977/ www.booktrust.org.uk). **Date** 1-7 October 2007.

This annual event is dedicated to children's literacy. It is run by Booktrust, the independent national charity that encourages people of all ages and cultures to enjoy reading. It also administers the Children's Laureate award, sponsored by Waterstones's. The countrywide schedule of activities includes hands-on events and author visits. Libraries and schools will have details of local events, otherwise visit the Booktrust website.

Pearly Kings & Queens Harvest Festival

St Martin-in-the-Fields, Trafalgar Square, Westminster, WC2N 4JJ (7766 1100/www.pearlysociety.co.uk). Leicester Square tube/Charing Cross tube/rail. **Date** 7 October 2007. **Map** p317 L7.

Pearly kings and queens – so called because of the shiny white buttons sewn in elaborate designs on their dark suits – have their origins in the 'aristocracy' of London's early Victorian costermongers, who elected their own royalty to safeguard their interests. Now charity representatives, today's pearly monarchs gather for this 3pm thanksgiving service in their traditional 'flash boy' outfits.

Punch & Judy Festival

Covent Garden Piazza, Covent Garden, WC2 (0870 780 5001/www.coventgardenmarket.co.uk). Covent Garden tube. **Date** 1st Sun October 2007. **Map** p315 L6.

More domestic incidents involving the crocodile, a policeman and Mr Punch giving Judy a few slaps (and vice versa). Performances take place around the market building. Puppetry means prizes, and there's also puppet-related merchandise for sale. Call to confirm this year's date as it hadn't been finalised as we went to press.

The Baby Show

Earl's Court Exhibition Centre, SW5 9TA (booking line 0870 122 1313/www.thebabyshow.co.uk). Earl's Court tube. **Date** 19-21 October 2007; 29 February-2 March 2008.

Anything you need to know about how to have a healthy pregnancy, and how to bring up splendid, cherubic babies and toddlers, you can find out here – and check out an obscene amount of nursery equipment, stimulating toys another paraphernalia into the bargain. To try to list what's there would be an exercise in futility; for best results, consult the website and search for yourself.

In Context

Tutankhamun & the Golden Age of the Pharaohs

O2 Centre, Drawdock Road, SE10 0BB (01753 565656/www.kingtut.org). North Greenwich tube. **Date** November 2007.
Older parents may remember the thrill (and the queues) of a visit to the British Museum's Tutankhamun exhibition in 1972. Now, 35 years later, the staggering treasures from the boy king's tomb (including his magnificent gold coffin and mask) will be on display in London again, this time in the centre formerly known as the Dome. Treasures from other royal graves in the Valley of the Kings – such as the tomb of Tutankhamun's great-grandparents Yuya and Tuyu – will also be displayed. Fill out an online registration form to guarantee your ticket when they go on sale.

Trafalgar Day Parade

Trafalgar Square, Westminster, WC2 (7928 8978/ www.ms-sc.org). Charing Cross tube/rail. **Date** 21 October 2007. **Map** p401 K7.
More than 500 sea cadets parade with marching bands and musical performances. Events culminate in the laying of a wreath at the foot of Nelson's Column.

Bonfire Night

Date 5 November 2007.
Most public displays of pyrotechnics to commemorate the Gunpowder Plot are held on the weekend nearest 5 November; among the best in London are those at Battersea Park, Alexandra Palace and Crystal Palace. Alternatively, try to book a late ride on the relevant nights on the British Airways London Eye (*see p33*).

London to Brighton Veteran Car Run

From Serpentine Road, Hyde Park, W2 (01327 856 024/www.lbvcr.com). Hyde Park Corner tube. **Date** 4 November 2007. **Map** p311 F8.
Get up at the crack of dawn to catch this parade of 500 vintage motors. The shiny fleet sets off from Hyde Park between 7.30am and 9am, aiming to reach Brighton before 4pm – their maximum speed capacity is 32 kmh (20mph). Otherwise, join the crowds lining the rest of the route. The handsome, buffed-up vehicles are on display in Regent Street (10am-4pm) on Saturday 3 November.

Lord Mayor's Show

Various streets in the City (7332 3456/www.lord mayorsshow.org). **Date** 10 November 2007.
This is the day when, under the conditions of the Magna Carta, the newly elected Lord Mayor is presented to the monarch, or his or her justices. Amid a procession of around 140 floats, the Lord Mayor leaves the Mansion House at 11am and travels through the City to the Royal Courts of Justice on the Strand, where he makes some vows before returning to Mansion House. The procession takes around an hour and a quarter to pass. The event is rounded off by a fireworks display from a barge moored on the Thames between Waterloo and Battersea bridges.

Discover Dogs

Earl's Court 2 (entrance on Lillie Road), SW5 9TA (7518 1012/www.the-kennel-club.org.uk). West Brompton tube/rail. **Date** 10-11 November 2007. **Map** p312 A11.

This canine extravaganza continues to go from strength to strength. It's far less formal than Crufts: you can meet more than 180 dogs, discuss pedigrees with breeders, and gather info on all matters of the mutt. There are competitions in categories as wide-ranging as 'dog that looks most like a celebrity' to OAP (over seven years old). The Good Citizen Dog Scheme offers discipline and agility courses, and you can also meet husky teams and watch police-dog agility demonstrations and Heelwork to Music displays.

State Opening of Parliament

House of Lords, Palace of Westminster, Westminster, SW1A 0PW (7219 4272/www.parliament.uk). Westminster tube. **Date** November 2007 (phone for details & changes). **Map** p317 L9.
In a ceremony that has changed little since the 16th century, the Queen officially reopens Parliament after its summer recess. You can see what goes on inside only on telly, but if you join the throngs on the streets, you can watch Her Maj arrive and depart in her Irish or Australian State Coach, attended by the Household Cavalry.

Children's Film Festival

Main venue: Barbican Centre, Silk Street EC2Y 8DS (Barbican box office 7638 8891/www.londonchildren film.org.uk). Barbican tube. **Date** 17-25 November 2007. **Map** p318 P5.
Following the resounding success of the first and second festival in 2005 and 2006, the third is planned with the same principles in mind: to attract children from all backgrounds with films from all corners of the globe. Few of the films screened would find a multiplex slot, but if the encouraging outcome of last year's festival is anything to go by, children appreciate more than just blockbusters: the First Light Young Juries scheme, in which children (aged between 7 and 16) are invited to be film critics and vote for their favourites, once again came up with two winners,

Chinese New Year Festival. *See p30.*

both from the world-cinema category with subtitles. Last year's costume and make-up workshops – many of which were free – were so popular that a range of activities to complement the screenings is again planned for this year. Organisers aim to keep ticket prices low (last year they were just £2 if you booked in advance).

LIVE 07

O2 Centre/0845 300 1818/www.scouts.org.uk. **Date** 24 November 2007.
As the Scouting movement celebrates its centenary, be prepared for lots of fun. Two epic shows are planned in the huge O₂ arena, which, we're promised will be transformed into a Scouting theme park. More than 3,000 Scouts from around the country will descend on the venue, watching circus antics, bands and all sorts of other performers. There will be performances items from all Sections across the country, with elements from the World Scout Jamboree, Brownsea Island in Dorset where the first Scout held his first camp (*see p16* **Robert Baden-Powell: Eucation outdoors**), local Scouting events, Scout bands and award presentations from famous ex-Scouts.

Christmas Lights & Tree

Covent Garden (0870 780 5001/www.coventgarden market.co.uk); Oxford Street (7976 1123/www. oxfordstreet.co.uk); Regent Street (7152 5853/ www.regent-street.co.uk); Bond Street (www.bond streetassociation.com); Trafalgar Square (7983 4234/www.london.gov.uk). **Date** November-December 2007.
Much of the childhood wonder still remains in the glittering lights on St Christopher's Place, Marylebone High Street, Bond Street and Kensington High Street. The giant fir tree in Trafalgar Square each year is a gift from the Norwegian people, in gratitude for Britain's role in liberating their country from the Nazis.

Winter

The London International Horse Show

Olympia, Hammersmith Road, Kensington, W14 8UX (01753 847900/www.olympiahorseshow.com). Kensington (Olympia) tube/rail. **Date** 17-22 December 2007.
This annual extravaganza for equestrian enthusiasts has dressage, show-jumping and more frivolous events, such as the Shetland Pony Grand National, mounted police displays and dog agility contests. There are more than 100 trade stands, so you can do some Christmas shopping.

Bankside Frost Fair

Bankside Riverwalk, by Shakespeare's Globe, SE1 9DT (details from Tourism Unit, Southwark Council, 7525 1139/www.visitsouthwark.com). London Bridge tube/rail. **Date** 14-16 December 2007.
This tradition started in the winter of 1564, when the Thames froze over and Londoners set up stalls of mulled wine and roast meats on the ice. Sadly, no ice can be expected these days (although the ice slide outside Tate Modern was a blast last year). But the fifth annual frost fair will go ahead nonetheless, opening with a lantern parade on Friday evening. It has a wonderful community feel, with crafts, food and wine stalls, huskies to hug, ice sculptors, children's shows and festive singalongs on Bankside. It all makes for terrific entertainment in the run-up to Christmas.

Peter Pan Swimming Race

The Serpentine, Hyde Park, W2 2UH (7298 2100/ www.royalparks.gov.uk). Hyde Park Corner tube. **Date** 25 Dec.
Established in 1864 by *Peter Pan* author JM Barrie, this chilly swimming race draws competitors and fans to the

In Context

Serpentine every Christmas. It's a 100-yard race with a ceremony afterwards. However mild the weather is, the Serpentine always looks less than inviting.

London International Mime Festival

Various venues across London (7637 5661/www. mimefest.co.uk). **Date** January 2008.
Surely the quietest festival the city has to offer, LIMF will invite 20 companies from the UK and abroad to perform a variety of shows for all ages. This year's highlight is the French outfit Compagnie 111, which will perform a slapstick show at the South Bank's Queen Elizabeth Hall. Free brochures are available via phone or website.

Chinese New Year Festival

Around Gerrard Street, Chinatown, W1, Leicester Square, WC2, & Trafalgar Square, WC2 (7851 6686/ www.chinatownchinese.co.uk). Leicester Square or Piccadilly Circus tube. **Date** 7 February 2008 (phone to confirm date). **Map** p317 K7.
Kung hei fat choi! ('congratulations and be prosperous') is the traditional greeting for the new year celebrations. This is the most important of the Chinese festivals, so expect quite a bunfight around London's Chinatown. Celebrations for the Chinese Year of the Rat begin at 11am with a children's parade from Leicester Square gardens to Trafalgar Square, where the lion and dragon dance teams perform traditional dances. And there are, of course, firework displays (at lunchtime and at 5pm).

National Storytelling Week

Various theatres, bookshops, libraries, schools & pubs around London (contact Del Reid 8866 4232/ www.sfs.org.uk). **Date** 26 January-2 February 2008.
This annual storytelling week, now in its 8th year, sees venues across the country hosting events for tellers and listeners. It is held by the Society for Storytelling, an organisation that aims to increase public awareness of the art, practice and value of oral storytelling and the narrative traditions of the peoples and cultures of the world. In 2007 over a thousand storytelling events and performances were organised, in theatres, bookshops, libraries, schools, museums and arts centres all over the UK. Expect more of the same in 2008. Note: stories cater to all ages.

Spring

Great Spitalfields Pancake Day Race

Dray Walk, Old Truman Brewery, 91 Brick Lane, E1 6QL (7375 0441/www.alternativearts.co.uk). Liverpool Street tube/rail. **Date** 5 February 2008. **Map** p319 S5.
The action starts at 12.30pm, with teams of four tossing pancakes as they run (it's all done for the charity Save The Children). Phone in advance if you want to take part (kids have their own race so they aren't trampled underfoot), or just show up if all you're after is seeing silly costumes and pancakes hit the pavement.

St Patrick's Day Parade & Festival

Trafalgar Square, Leicester Square & Covent Garden (7983 4100/www.london.gov.uk). **Date** March 2008 (check website for date). **Map** p317 K7.
This fun, colourful and noisy parade departs from Hyde Park Corner at noon and continues to romp through the streets until 6pm. Expect lots of Irish music, food, dancing, crafts and various other activities for all ages.

London Marathon

Greenwich Park to the Mall via the Isle of Dogs, Victoria Embankment & St James's Park (7902 0200/ www.london-marathon.co.uk). **Date** 13 April 2008.
One of the world's biggest metropolitan marathons, the London Marathon started in 1981 and nowadays attracts 35,700 starters, many in outrageous costumes. Spectators are advised to arrive early; the front runners reach the 13-mile mark near the Tower of London at around 10am. If you think you're fit enough, you must apply by the October before the race. The 2008 entry system, opening on 1 August 2007, is via an entry form in a free magazine called *Marathon News*, available from major sports stores.

London Harness Horse Parade

Phone for venue details (01737 646 132/www. lhhp.co.uk). **Date** 24 March 2008. **Map** p313 F13.
A must for pony-mad children, this equine parade takes place on Easter Monday. More than 300 working horses, donkeys and mules with various commercial and private carriages assemble for the main parade (noon-1pm). At the time of press, the venue for 2008 was yet to be decided.

Shakespeare's Birthday

Various venues around South Bank & Bankside. **Date** 23 April 2008.
The days leading up to and after the Bard's birth date are busy ones at Shakespeare's Globe and Southwark cathedral (*see p46*), when performances, readings and walks mark the great man's contribution to literature.

Canalway Cavalcade

Little Venice, W9 (01923 711114/www.waterways. org.uk). Warwick Avenue tube. **Date** 1st May bank hol weekend 2008.
This three-day bank-holiday boat transforms the pool of Little Venice with an assembly of more than 100 colourful narrowboats, all decked out in bunting and flowers. Events include craft, trade and food stalls; kids' activities; music and boat trips. The beautiful lantern-lit boat procession is a must-see – pray for fine weather.

May Fayre & Puppet Festival

St Paul's Church Garden, Bedford Street, Covent Garden, WC2E 9ED (7375 0441/www.alternativearts. co.uk). Covent Garden tube. **Date** 11 May 2008. **Map** p317 L7.
Celebrating the first recorded sighting of Mr Punch in England (by Pepys, in 1662), this free event offers puppetry galore from 10.30am to 5.30pm. A grand brass-band procession around Covent Garden is followed by a service held in St Paul's (*see p67*), with Mr Punch in the pulpit. Then there are puppet shows, booths and stalls, as well as workshops for puppet-making and dressing up.
At 10.30am there's a procession with a brass band around the neighbourhood of Covent Garden starting at the church garden gate; at 11.30am, there's a special service in St Paul's Church. The puppet shows and workshops run from noon to 5.30pm. Folk music and maypole dancing, clowns and jugglers are added bonuses.

Around Town

Features

Introduction

London up close.

This being the best city break destination in the world, you're spoilt for choice in the sightseeing stakes. These Around Town pages list all the best, from the star-turn museums, galleries and royal parks and palaces, to the more obscure local treasures, such as city farms and libraries.

Orientation

The chapters are organised into eight central London areas and five outer London areas. In central London, we start with the **South Bank** the centre of the nation's arts scene, *(pp36-48)*, **Bankside**, to the east, home of Tate Modern *(p45)*. In the historic **City** *(pp49-56)* reminders of London's past jostle with today's citadels of high finance. West of here **Holborn & Clerkenwell** *(pp57-60)* is where the City meets the West End, Holborn is the legal quarter and Clerkenwell the arty one. **Bloomsbury & Fitzrovia** is dominated by the British Museum *(p60)*. **Covent Garden & the Strand** *(pp67-70)* is entertainment, shopping and theatres. In the **West End** chapter *(pp71-75)* Soho, Leicester Square and Chinatown bustle in their own sweet ways. **Marylebone** has shopping, the Regent's Park and the Zoo *(pp76-79)*. The **Westminster** chapter *(p80-85)* takes in the official centre of London, Trafalgar Square, as well as its political centre, the Houses of Parliament. The west-central region incorporates **Notting Hill & Paddington** *(pp86-87)* and **Kensingon & Chelsea**, the repository of the city's top museums for families *(pp88-95)*. Out of Zone 1, the further reaches of town are organised as North *(p96-107)*, East *(pp108-124)*, South-east *(pp125-140)*, South-west *(pp141-153)* and West London *(pp154-162)*. We've given opening times and admission prices, but always ring to check.

The Tube is the quickest way to get around (*see p290*), but the bus is more scenic. Good routes for sightseeing are the 7, 8, 11 and 12 (all double deckers) and, for the river, the RV1.

A couple of old-style Routemaster buses – numbers 9 and 15 – run as Heritage Routes, operating between Trafalgar Square and Tower Hill (15) and the Royal Albert Hall and Aldwych. Normal fares apply; see www.routemaster.org.uk.

Useful Information

If your sightseeing programme includes expensive places, a London Pass (01664 485020/www.london pass.com), which gives you pre-paid access to more than 50 attractions, may be of interest. Phone or check the website for prices.

The initials 'LP' before the admission price in our listings means your London Pass grants free admission. 'EH' means English Heritage members, and their kids, get in free. 'NT' means National Trust family members get free admission.

Trips and tours

On the buses

Big Bus Company *48 Buckingham Palace Road, Victoria, SW1W 0RN (0800 169 1365/7233 9533/www.bigbustours.com)*. **Departures** every 10-15 mins. *Summer* 8.30am-6pm daily. *Winter* 8.30am-4.30pm daily. **Pick-up** Green Park (near the Ritz); Marble Arch (Speakers' Corner); Victoria (outside Thistle Victoria Hotel, 48 Buckingham Palace Road, SW1W 0RN). **Fares** £22 (£20 if booked online); £10 5-15s; free under-5s. Tickets valid for 24hrs, interchangeable between routes. **Credit** AmEx, DC, MC, V.
Open-top buses, with commentary, stop at the major tourist sights, where customers can hop on and hop off at will (tickets are valid for 24 hours). Big Bus also runs cruises and walking tours.
Original London Sightseeing Tour *8877 1722/ www.theoriginaltour.com*. **Departures** *Summer* 9am-6pm daily. *Winter* 9am-5pm daily. **Pick-up** Grosvenor Gardens; Marble Arch (Speakers' Corner); Baker Street tube (forecourt); Haymarket (Piccadilly Circus); Embankment tube; Trafalgar Square. **Fares** £19; £12 5-15s; free under-5s. £1.50 discount if booked online. **Credit** AmEx (not internet), MC, V.
Kids' Club tours include a special activity pack.

Pedal power

London Bicycle Tour Company *7928 6838/ www.londonbicycle.com*. **Fares** £3/hr; £18 1st 24hrs, £8 thereafter; £48/wk.
In addition to bicycles, kids' trailers are also available.
London Pedicabs *7093 3155/www.london pedicabs.com*. **Fares** from £3 per person (per mile). Rickshaws based around Covent Garden and Soho.

Take a walk

Original London Walks *7624 3978/www. walks.com*. **Tours** £6; £5 concessions; 1 free under-15 per adult.

Waterways

For visitors to London, travel on the Thames is not only more pleasurable than squeezing on to overcrowded buses and trains, but it also offers access to dozens of London's key attractions – and traffic-free connections between them. Although the Thames has always been central to London's development, it's been a long time since it was used properly as a transport link. In the 18th century, the Pool of London was so crammed with vessels it was said you could cross the river just by stepping from one boat to the next. Of course it's unlikely the river will ever be so busy again, but there are moves to win back the Thames for ordinary travellers. **Thames Clippers**, whose fast, reliable boat service between the Embankment and Tower Bridge is a top commute for City workers, transports a million passengers every year and plans to double its fleet to 13 boats in 2007, so that boats will run every 15 minutes, making river travel a viable option again.

Tourists already get a pretty good deal out of the Thames. You can feel the wind in your hair courtesy of **London RIB Voyages**. The rigid inflatable boat ambles from Waterloo to Tower Bridge before cranking things up to zoom downriver to the Thames Barrier at an exhilarating 30 knots. More sedately, and infinitely more eccentrically, **London Duck Tours** trundles a decommissioned DUKW amphibious truck (*pictured*), built for use in World War II, around the major sights of the West End before ducking into the river. Then there's Thames Clippers' tourist boats, notably the Tate to Tate Damien Hirst dotty number (*see p84*). The Clippers Rover Roamer hop-on hop-off ticket (£7.30) is a tip top way to see the sights. **City Cruises** also organise sightseeing tours and sells Rail & River Rover tickets (*see also p292*). For free river travel float on down to Woolwich, where the ferries ply their course between the distant river banks way out east. Inland, tourists can enjoy boat trips with the **London Waterbus Company** on the Regents' Canal, from Camden to Regent's Park. This is the best way to get to the zoo, as the boats tie up right inside their premises (*see p76*).

City Cruises
7740 0400/www.citycruises.com.

London Duck Tours
55 York Road, SE1 7NJ (7928 3132/ www.londonducktours.co.uk). **Tours** Check website for departure details. **Fares** £17.50; £14 concessions, 13-15s; £12 under-12s; £53 family (2+2). **Credit** MC, V,

London RIB Voyages
Kiosk, British Airways London Eye, Millennium Pier, SE1 7PB (7401 8834/www.londonrib voyages.com). **Tours** Check website for departure details. **Fares** £25; £15 under-12s. 10% discount for families (2+2). **Credit** MC, V.

London Waterbus Company
7482 2660/www.londonwaterbus.com. **Tours** *Check website for departure details.* **Fares** Single £6.00; £4.30 3-15s. Return £8.40, £5.40 children. **No credit cards**.

Thames Clippers
0870 781 5049, www.thamesclippers.com.

Around Town

Staying over?

There's a hotel boom in London at the moment, expected to continue till the 2012 Olympics, by which time at least 20,000 rooms will have been added. In the long term, this should provide more options for the beleaguered family looking for an affordable berth in central London. In the short term, however, London is one of the most expensive cities in the world, especially where decent hotels are concerned. The Youth Hostels Association can help here, which is why we've listed the best London branches below. Sadly, the most handsome youth hostel – in a wing of Holland House, a stately Kensington mansion built in 1607 (0870 770 5866) – doesn't have family rooms (dorms are for eight to 20 people, so not great for youngsters).

While scouting for cut-price rooms, don't dismiss the chains. The formula might be a bit corporate, but when you can bag a double room with two extra child beds and a cot on the South Bank for £92 (Premier Travel Inn Metro London County Hall, www.travelinn.co.uk) or a family room with access to a swimming pool and free meals for kids for £99 (a recent half-term special from Holiday Inn, www.holiday-inn.com) or a family room in the heart of touristy Covent Garden (Travelodge; www.travelodge.co.uk) for £26, who gives a monkey's about institutional decor?

If you prefer self-catering, consider a Citadines apartment (www.citadines.com). Studios, which sleep up to six people, have a kitchenette and baby facilities. You can even bring the family pet. The Citadines complex at Trafalgar Square cannot be beaten for location, and the apartments, if snug, are clean and well equipped.

Amsterdam Hotel

7 Trebovir Road, Earl's Court, SW5 9LS (0800 279 9132/fax 7244 7608/www.amsterdam-hotel.com). Earl's Court tube. **Rates** *£90-£100 double; £132-£148 family.* **Credit** *AmEx, DC, MC, V.*
Located near the tube, the Amsterdam is popular with tourists; the bright, clean cut of its jib is similarly appealing. There are 28 en suite rooms with televisions. The suites, with a small sitting area and kitchenette, are in demand. Downstairs there's an internet room and a sheltered garden open April to October in clement weather. The staff can provide high chairs, cots and push-chairs for babies and toddlers.

Arran House Hotel

77-79 Gower Street, Bloomsbury, WC1E 6HJ (7636 2186/fax 7436 5328/www.london-hotel.co.uk). Goodge Street or Tottenham Court Road tube. **Rates** *£77-£100 double; £95-£118 triple; £101-£122 quad; £110-£135 quint.* **Credit** *MC, V.*

The place to come for huge en suite family rooms, (with space to add a couple of bunks or cots), interconnecting pairs of rooms, or double rooms with a twin bed and bathroom across the corridor. The clean, simply furnished rooms have a television and some have DVD players (there's also a DVD player in the sitting room). The communal rooms are pleasant places to linger. When the kitchen is free, after 3pm, guests are welcome to use the facilities to cook up family suppers to eat around the big kitchen table in the breakfast room (provided they clear up after themselves). It's unusual to find such easy-going homeliness in a central London guesthouse.

City of London Youth Hostel

36 Carter Lane, EC4V 5AB (0870 770 5764/ www.yha.org.uk). St Paul's tube. **Open** *24 hours daily.* **Rates** *£34; £20.50 children; family rooms from £47.* **Credit** *MC, V.*
Fancy a room only 100 metres away from St Paul's Cathedral? That's what you get at this three-star hostel, set in the rather gothic looking building that used to be the choir boys' school. The hostel has 190 beds, including several small rooms for singles and couples, but the majority are four-to-eight bed spaces, which are ideal for families. There is a restaurant for breakfast (included in the price of the stay and quite a continental spread – cereals, yoghurts, pastries, toast, hard boiled eggs, cheese, cold meats and fruit), as well as snacks included in the price.

Draycott Hotel

26 Cadogan Gardens, SW3 (7730 6466/ www.draycotthotel.com) Sloane Square tube. **Rates** *£230 double; £290 triple; £750 family.* **Credit** *AmEx, MC, V.*
A lovely hotel with a country manor feel, the Draycott is a luxury option. Guests are plied with little treats – tea and biscuits at 4pm, champagne at 6pm, cocoa at 10pm. And although there is no dedicated restaurant (there are too many good ones in the area), there is a chef on duty to prepare light lunches and room-service suppers. The 35 rooms, which include several delightful family suites, are huge and gracious. All the mod cons and comforts – free Wi-Fi, CD/DVD and satellite television, air-conditioning, bath tubs and power showers, massive double beds – are much appreciated by family groups. Ask about the Family Package, which gives two adults and two children a garden-view double room with adjacent single room, Playstation availability, babysitting, Big Bus Tour tickets, teddy bears, children's bathrobes and gift pack and a breakfast of boiled egg and soldiers (£280 per family).

Earl's Court Hostel

38 Bolton Gardens, SW5 OAQ (0870 770 5804/www.yha.org). Gloucester Road or South Kensington tube. **Open** 24 hours daily. **Rates** from £20.50; £18.95 under-18s; family rooms £57-£79.50. **Credit** MC, V.

The YHA's young and trendy outpost has 180 four-to-six-bed rooms. Its proximity to the Kensington museums, shopping centres and Earl's Court and Olympia, and easy access to Heathrow Airport, make it a big draw, particularly with foreign students, although families in the know recommend it too. Breakfast is not included in the price of an overnight stay. There is a self-catering kitchen and any number of cafés, restaurants and supermarkets just nearby.

Garden Court Hotel

30-31 Kensington Gardens Square, Bayswater, W2 4BG (7229 2553/fax 7727 2749/www. gardencourthotel.co.uk). Bayswater or Queensway tube. **Rates** £75-£110 double; £90-£145 triple; £100-£165 quad. **Credit** MC, V.

This tastefully appointed, but unfussy family hotel is moderately priced. It's close to Portobello Road Market and Hyde Park, which gives it a real London buzz, emphasised by the Beefeater statue standing to attention in reception. The communal area is pleasant, with its polished wood floors and squashy leather sofas, and the 34 cheery rooms are even better. They have bright, modern sprigged wallpaper, desks and chairs and space to move around. The family room, with its three windows, is a particularly comfortable place to set up camp for the weekend. As the name suggests, the hotel has a small walled garden of impressive lushness; guests have access to the private square too (a rare privilege in London).

Hampstead Village Guesthouse

2 Kemplay Road, Hampstead, NW3 1SY (7435 8679/www.hampsteadguesthouse. com). Hampstead tube/Hampstead Heath rail. **Rates** £50-£95 single; £75-£95 double; £95-£170 studio. **Credit** AmEx, MC, V.

Annemarie van der Meer's handsome Hampstead homestead has been one of London's favourite guesthouses for 25 years. It has a gloriously bohemian air, which puts families at their ease. There are lots of toys around, as Annemarie's grandchildren are frequent visitors, and every one of the nine guest rooms is quirky and characterful. Each room has a fridge, a basin, telephone and Wi-Fi. Downstairs, there's a dining room, a music room and a picturesque kitchen, where a jumble of pots, pans and chinaware create a scene of arty domestic bliss. Outside, in the pretty paved garden, there are places to play and tables and chairs for family meals.

Hart House Hotel

51 Gloucester Place, W1U 8JF (7935 2288/ www.harthouse.co.uk). Marble Arch tube. **Rates** £110 double; £135 triple; £165 quad. **Credit** AmEx, MC, V.

Handy for London Zoo and Regent's Park, Hart House occupies a Tardis-like Georgian townhouse. A gloomy corridor leads to the reception area, liberally festooned with tourist brochures. Upstairs the rooms are gratifyingly bright. Triple rooms are spacious for a family of four, and cots and Z-beds are easily moved in. All the rooms have televisions and are en suite. Family suites, with connecting rooms, can be arranged. Full English breakfast included.

London Thameside Youth Hostel

20 Salter Road, Rotherhithe SE16 5PR (7232 2114/www.yha.org.uk). **Rates** £26.50; £22.50 under-18s; family rooms from £48-£65. **Credit** MC, V.

Thameside is a purpose-built hostel. All of its rooms, whether they are cosy two-person arrangements, rooms for families of up to six, or eight- and ten- bedded dorms, have bunks to sleep in and basic en suite bathroom facilities (shower and toilet) and a little kettle. They're pretty functional, but bright and modern. In the basement there's a television lounge with games, books and toys for children.

St Pancras YHA Hostel

79-81 Euston Road, King's Cross, NW1 2QE (0870 770 6044/www.yha.org.uk). King's Cross tube/rail. **Open** 24 hours daily. **Rates** from £26.50; £22.50 under-18s; family rooms £48-£65. **Credit** MC, V.

Right opposite St Pancras Station, and a minute away from King's Cross station (Euston is about five minutes), the YHA's Euston Road hostel is conveniently located for transport links in and out of the city centre. The King's Cross hostel is a four-star one, which means there are rooms with en suite bathrooms and double bed (hard to find in YHA land) as well as family rooms that sleep four, five and six.

Vicarage Hotel

10 Vicarage Gate, W8 4AG (7229 4030/www. londonvicaragehotel.com). High Street Kensington or Notting Hill Gate tube. **Rates** £85-£110 double; £105-£140 triple; £112-£155 quad. **Credit** AmEx, MC, V.

A handsome, 19-room Kensington terrace hotel with spacious family rooms. Families can take a double with a smaller twin-bedded across the way and a bathroom on the same landing, or the larger, en-suite triple.

Around Town

South Bank & Bankside

Tales of the riverbank: a big wheel, a big fish, big art and a big ship.

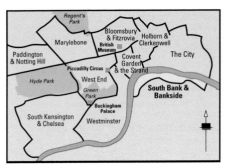

London's most popular Sunday walk destination for families continues to scrub up well. For centuries it was notable for all the wrong reasons – bear baiting, brothels and hard drinking being just a few examples – but the transformation from rough to buff has been continuing since 1951, when the Festival of Britain opened the way for the building of the blockish South Bank Centre. Yet it took the run-up to the Millennium festivities in the late 1990s to effect the metamorphosis of this district. The **British Airways London Eye**, designed by architects Marks Barfield, and the magnificent **Tate Modern** are symbols of the success of the South Bank's regeneration. The elegant Millennium and Hungerford footbridges continue the theme. Add to these the **IMAX** cinema (*see p218* for screenings), **Shakespeare's Globe**, the **Design Museum**, and the regenerated patch, called More London Riverside, incorporating the **Unicorn Theatre** (*see p231*) and you can see why the South Bank and Bankside are now the arts and entertainment showpiece of the capital.

A useful starting point for the first-time visitor is the Tourist Information Centre, in Vinopolis wine museum (1 Bank End, SE1 9BU, 7357 9168/www.visitsouthwark.com).

The South Bank

Walk east from Lambeth Bridge for a spectacular view of the Houses of Parliament. These sit opposite St Thomas's Hospital, where you'll find the **Florence Nightingale Museum** and the new £60 million Evelina Children's Hospital, a glass, seven-storey building.

Jubilee Gardens (*see p43* **The fun don't stop**), adjacent to the London Eye, is being landscaped. County Hall – once the home of the Greater London Council – houses the **Dalí Gallery**, noisy **Namco Station** and the **London Aquarium**.

The **Southbank Centre** (the arts centre formerly known as the South Bank Centre; *see p217*) has recently undergone a massive renovation and rebranding programme. The £91 million redevelopment to restore and improve the Royal Festival Hall was nearly ready to be unveiled as we went to press (*see p236*). Under Waterloo Bridge the Riverside Walk Market displays second-hand books on trestle tables. The kids might prefer to see the source of the rumblings and thuds of the skateboarders and rollerbladers practising ollies and grinds in the graffitied concrete space under Queen Elizabeth Hall, also part of the Southbank Centre. Nearby, the gorgeous new **BFI Southbank National Film Theatre** (www.bfi.org.uk) now has a good-looking café and numerous screens and galleries (*see p218*).

Strolling on east, the handsome Oxo Tower Wharf, with its deco tower advertising the stock-cube company, was saved from demolition in the 1970s by the Coin Street Community Builders, who are also responsible for the high-spirited **Coin Street Festival** every summer (*see p23*). Gabriel's Wharf – all pastel-coloured crafty shops and friendly cafés – is another Coin Street enterprise. For more information about what to see when you're walking in this area, check the website (www.southbanklondon.com).

British Airways London Eye

Riverside Building (next to County Hall), Westminster Bridge Road, SE1 7PB (bookings and customer services 0870 990 8883/www.ba-londoneye.com). Westminster tube/Waterloo tube/rail. **Open** Oct-May 10am-8pm daily. *June-Sept* 10am-9pm daily. **Admission** £14.50; £11 concessions (not applicable weekends or in July or Aug); £7.25 5-15s; free under-5s. Fastrack tickets £25. **Credit** AmEx, MC, V. **Map** p317 M8.

The world's largest big wheel keeps on turning, its 32 capsules carrying an average of 10,000 people each day, more than 20 million visitors since it opened in 2000. The Eye was designed by architects David Marks and Julia Barfield, whose dream took seven years to become reality. They suffered several setbacks, not least the ignominy of learning

Around Town

South Bank

Top 5 Feasts for the senses

A **sight** for sore eyes: the view from the **British Airways London Eye**. See p36.

The **sound** of music: pop goes the gamelan at the **Festival Hall**. See p236.

Wake up and **smell** the coffee (plus the chocolate and organic burgers) in **Borough Market**. See p208.

Taste the heaven that is **Konditor & Cook**'s chocolate brownie. See p166.

Feel a damp squid – or at least the briefest brush of a passing ray – at the **London Aquarium**. See p38.

that this, their entry in a big competition for the ultimate Millennium structure, had come second. The first prize-winner has been conveniently forgotten. Pre-book online to get a 10% discount, taking a gamble with the weather. The Eye gets festive with fairy lights at Christmas and there are other holiday specials (Hallowe'en, Easter). A guide to the landmarks, and photos of your trip, are sold (£7.50). Check the website for details of packages that combine a turn in the Eye with a trip down the river.
Buggy access. Café. Disabled access: toilets. Nappy-changing facilities. Nearest picnic place: Jubilee Gardens. Shop.

Dalí Universe

County Hall (riverfront entrance), Riverside Building, SE1 7PB (7620 2720/www.daliuniverse.com). Westminster tube/Waterloo tube/rail. **Open** 10am-5.30pm daily. **Admission** £12; £10 concessions; £8 8-16s; £5 4-7s; free under-4s. £30 family (2+2) **Credit** AmEx, DC, MC, V. **Map** p317 M8.
The main exhibition, curated by long-term Dalí friend Benjamin Levi, includes wall-mounted quotes by, and (silent) videos and photographs of, this eccentric artist. There are sculptures, watercolours, rare etchings and lithographs. Many of the works seem like artistic comedy: melting clocks, long-legged elephants, crutches, lobsters, ants and stretched buttocks casting shadows over dreamy sunny plains. The gallery also shows work by new artists.
Buggy access. Disabled access: lift, ramp, toilets. Nearest picnic place: Jubilee Gardens. Shop.

Florence Nightingale Museum

St Thomas's Hospital, 2 Lambeth Palace Road, SE1 7EW (7620 0374/www.florence-nightingale.co.uk). Westminster tube/Waterloo tube/rail. **Open** 10am-5pm Mon-Fri; 10am-4.30pm Sat, Sun (last entry 1hr before closing). **Admission** (LP) £5.80; £4.80 5-18s, concessions; free under-5s; £16 family (2+2). **Credit** AmEx, MC, V. **Map** p317 M9.
Florence's celebrity status on Key Stage One and Two of the National Curriculum means that school holidays are busy here at the museum dedicated to her life (1820-1910). Mementoes and tableaux depict the harshness of the field hospitals of Scutari, where Nurse Nightingale first came to public attention, but details of her privileged life before

this, and the studious time thereafter, are just as interesting. A 20-minute film tells Florence's story. Other displays include clothing, furniture, books, letters and portraits. Florence's pet owl, Athena (now stuffed), is also on show.
A temporary exhibition: 'Hospital Voices: Stories From Nightingale To Now' runs until 23 December 2007, drawing on personal stories of patients and nurses and displaying previously unseen objects to build a picture of daily life at the hospitals from the 1930s to the present. Among the contributors recalling their encounters with hospital life are politician Tony Benn; Gill Hicks, survivor of the 7/7 London bombings, and one of the nurses who cared for her, Louise Danks, deputy ward sister at St Thomas's Hospital.
Free trails for children aged from five are available at all times. Family activities are held on the second weekend of every month and during half-term and the Easter holidays. Events may include craft work (such as making your own lamp), poetry and performance sessions with actors playing the parts of nurses Nightingale and Seacole, or object handling and dressing-up. Check the website for details.
Buggy access. Disabled access: toilets. Nearest picnic place: benches by hospital entrance/Archbishop's Park. Shop. (In hospital: Café. Nappy-changing facilities. Restaurant.)

Hayward Gallery

Belvedere Road, SE1 8XX (7960 5226/box office 0870 169 1000/www.hayward.org.uk). Embankment tube/Waterloo tube/rail. **Open** subject to change; check website for details. **Admission** £8; £7; £5 concessions; £4 12-16s; free under-12s. Prices vary, phone to check. **Credit** AmEx, MC, V. **Map** p318 M8.
Inside the light, bright pavilion, designed by Daniel Graham, casual visitors can watch cartoons on touch screens or just wander around the visually confusing space created by curved, two-way mirrors. The neon tower on the gallery roof was commissioned by the Arts Council in 1970. Its yellow, red, green and blue tubes are controlled by changes in the direction and strength of the wind. Until August 2007 the big exhibition is by Anthony Gormley. Family activities linked to the current exhibitions might include poetry workshops or puppet making sessions; consult the gallery's website for details.
Buggy access. Café. Disabled access: lift. Nappy-changing facilities. Nearest picnic place: Jubilee Gardens/riverside benches. Shop.

London Aquarium

County Hall (riverfront entrance), Riverside Building, SE1 7PB (7967 8000/tours 7967 8007/www. londonaquarium.co.uk). Westminster tube/Waterloo tube/rail. **Open** Oct-June 10am-6pm daily (last entry 5pm) July-Sept 10am-7pm (last entry 6pm) Phone for late opening during holidays. Closed 25 Dec. **Tours** (groups of 10 or more) phone for details. **Admission** (LP) £13.25; £11.25 concessions, disabled; £9.75 3-14; £8.25 disabled children; free under-3s; £44 family (2+2). **Credit** MC, V. **Map** p317 M9.
The impressive million-litre (220,000-gallon) Pacific tank is the big draw for children. Here they watch the Brown, Sandtiger, Nurse and Zebra sharks with gleeful fascination. The aquarium's 14 aquatic zones cover habitats from freshwater streams to coral reefs to rainforest. They contain some 350 species of marine life that occupy 50 tanks on two floors beneath County Hall. Steer your shoal to the tropical tanks, which are aglow with seahorses, angelfish,

Burning curiosity at the **London Fire Brigade Museum**.

pufferfish and that celebrity species, the clownfish. Other exotic environments are recreated in the Atlantic, Mangrove, Rainforest and Coral tanks. The touch pool attracts large crowds of children keen to stroke the long-suffering rays as they skim along the surface. Feeding times are fun for children: every day you can watch the rays being fed (11.30am) and listen to a talk about coral (3.30pm); on Monday, Wednesday and Friday divers feed the Atlantic tank inhabitants (rays, dogfish) at noon; on Tuesday, Thursday and Saturday the sharks are fed at 2.30pm, and there are daily shark talks at 2pm and 4pm. Conservation and breeding programmes are part of the Aquarium's brief; it has links to campaigning organisations such as the Shark Trust, London Wildlife Trust, Seawatch Foundation and Marine Conservation Society. Children pick up an activity sheet as they go in, and the education department runs regular activities for children during school holidays. Queues are long school holidays and at weekends; book online for fast-track advance tickets.
Buggy access. Café. Disabled access: lift, ramp, toilets. Nappy-changing facilities. Nearest picnic place: Jubilee Gardens. Shop.

London Fire Brigade Museum

Winchester House, 94A Southwark Bridge Road, SE1 0EG (7587 2894/www.london-fire.gov.uk). Borough tube/Southwark tube/rail/344 bus. **Tours** by appointment 10.30am, 2pm Mon-Fri. Closed bank hols. **Admission** £3; £2 7-14s, concessions; £1 under-7s; £20 school groups. **Credit** MC, V. **Map** p318 O9.
Any child who wants to be a firefighter when grown up should be taken on one of the daily tours of this friendly museum, housed in eight small rooms within the London Fire Brigade Training Centre. Packed with firefighting memorabilia, photographs, paintings and equipment, the museum presents an entertaining potted history of fire-fighting since the Great Fire of 1666. Exhibits include uniforms dating from the early 20th century, a 17th-century manual firefighting pump, and paintings by firemen and firewomen. Tours take in the appliance bay, where pumps dating back to 1708 stand in tribute to blazes past. Small children are encouraged to draw any of the 20 fire engines, ranging from a horse-drawn, hand-pumped 1830s model to shiny red and brass vehicles from the early 20th century, and today's more streamlined heavyweights. Sadly, climbing on the vehicles is not allowed, but children can try on the uniforms. *See p40.*
Buggy access. Disabled access: toilets. Nappy-changing facilities. Nearest picnic place: Mint Street Park. Shop.

Museum of Garden History

Church of St Mary-at-Lambeth, Lambeth Palace Road, SE1 7LB (7401 8865/www.museumgardenhistory.org). Waterloo tube/rail then 507 bus/Lambeth North tube/C10, 3, 77 bus. **Open** 10.30am-5pm Tue-Sun. **Admission** free; suggested donation £3 (£2.50 concessions). **Credit** *Shop* (over £10) AmEx, MC, V. **Map** p317 L10.
The world's first museum dedicated to gardening is contained within the deconsecrated and refurbished church of St Mary's. The Tradescants (a pioneering family of gardeners and botanists), Captain William Bligh (of *Bounty* fame), along with half a dozen Archbishops of Canterbury, are entombed in the graveyard. A replica of a 17th-century knot garden is a living memorial to the Tradescants. Look out for the Pedlar's Window, a stained-glass window illustrating a man and his dog. History has it that an early 16th-century pedlar came into an acre of land (now the site of County Hall) and donated it to the church on condition that an image of him be preserved in glass. The current window is the fourth, made in 1956 after its predecessor was destroyed in 1941.

Permanent exhibitions include a multimedia local history display about the borough of Lambeth over the past 1,000 years, horticultural practices through the ages, plant hunting, and garden-designer Gertrude Jekyll. They are joined by occasional temporary displays (check the website for details). It's quite a child-friendly place (especially if yours are green-fingered sprogs). Free activities for children take place during the school holidays. Past events have included making seasonal mini gardens and paper models.
Buggy access. Café. Disabled access: ramps, toilets. Nappy-changing facilities. Nearest picnic place: Archbishop's Park. Shop.

Namco Station

County Hall (riverfront entrance), Westminster Bridge Road, SE1 7PB (7967 1066/www.namcoexperience. com). Westminster tube/Waterloo tube/rail. **Open** 10am-midnight daily. **Admission** free; games prices vary. **Map** p317 M9.
A noisy hideaway harbouring more than 200 types of video games, with dodgem cars, techno bowling and pool tables lurking downstairs. This pleasure dome shares its entrance with McDonald's: talk about teen paradise.
Bar. Buggy access. Disabled access: lift, toilets. Nappy-changing facilities. Nearest picnic place: Jubilee Gardens.

Royal National Theatre

South Bank, SE1 9PX (info 7452 3400/box office 7452 3000/www.nationaltheatre.org.uk). Waterloo tube/rail. **Open** 9.30am-11pm Mon-Sat. *Box office* 9.30am-8pm Mon-Sat. Closed 24, 25 Dec, Good Friday. **Tickets** *Olivier & Lyttelton* £10-£39.50. *Cottesloe* £10-£29. *Standby* £10, £18.50. *Backstage tours* £5; £4 concessions, under-18s. **Credit** AmEx, DC, MC, V. **Map** p318 M8.
The outdoor space – Theatre Square – has done much to draw families' attention toward Sir Denys Lasdun's landmark concrete theatre complex. It's the home of the terrific Watch This Space season every summer (July to Sept 2007), which includes street theatre and comic performance suitable for a family audience at lunchtimes and in the early evening every day. Look out for the Whalley Range All Stars and the Insect Circus Museum in summer 2007. Indoors, the National is full of bright ideas to secure tomorrow's audiences. Around the ground-floor refreshment area, free exhibitions and music events take place throughout the year. You can catch free music concerts Mon-Fri in the early evenings before the plays begin; the bands perform both at lunchtime and in the evening on Saturdays. The NT runs educational activity programmes, from half-term shows by visiting theatre companies to school-based initiatives (visit the website for details). For more on the work of the National and selected regional partners in England, log on to Stagework (www.stagework.org), commissioned and funded by Culture Online, part of the Department for Culture, Media and Sport and managed by the National Theatre. Stagework aims to increase the understanding of theatre. More tangible demystifying of the art-form is offered by the National's backstage tours (not suitable for under-sevens), which may be booked at the information desk (£5, £4 under-18s). Tours take in the rehearsal rooms, workshops where costumes and props are made, dressing rooms and the stages.
Café. Disabled access: lift, toilets. Nappy-changing facilities. Nearest picnic place: Bernie Spain Gardens. Restaurants. Shop.

Bankside

The riverside stretch between London Bridge and Blackfriars Bridge was once the epicentre of bawdy Southwark, presided over by various money-grabbing Bishops of Winchester. All that remains of the Palace of Winchester, home of successive bishops, is the rose window of the Great Hall on Clink Street, just around the corner from the fun-filled **Golden Hinde**.

The parish church during Shakespeare's time was St Saviour's, known since 1905 as **Southwark Cathedral**, which sits modestly away from the river. The **Millennium Bridge** in front of Tate Modern provides a pedestrian carriageway to the puffed-up other cathedral across the water, namely **St Paul's** (*see p54*). The wonkily ancient terrace of houses between Tate Modern and the Globe is owned by Southwark Cathedral; Sir Christopher Wren is reputed to have stayed in one of them during the building of St Paul's in 1680.

Borough Market, (www.boroughmarket. org.uk) hard by Southwark Cathedral, is the best food market in town – fitting for an area known in the 17th century as the 'larder of London'. Borough Market Trustees have plans to deliver the good food news to the twizzler generation. The market, they say, is 'a wonderful open-air classroom' in which children can learn about good food and its provenance. They plan to open the Borough Market Food School, at No.1 Cathedral Street, where students from as young as four will be taught how to choose, prepare and enjoy good food. All involved in the cooking workshops will sit down together to eat what they have cooked;

Top 5 | Living history

Rest easy as a Tudor sailor during a sleep-over on board the the **Golden Hinde**. *See p43.*

Be a groundling, but don't chuck anything at the actors, at **Shakespeare's Globe**. *See p45.*

Don a bloody apron and learn the grisly details of operations before anaesthetics at **St Thomas's Old Operating Theatre & Herb Garret**. *See p45.*

Tune in and hear officers and crew chat, work, reminisce and sink the *Scharnhorst* on mess-deck, galley and bridge on board **HMS *Belfast***. *See p48.*

Visit an air raid shelter and explore a bombed-out street in Blitz-ravaged London at **Winston Churchill's Britain at War Experience**. *See p47.*

Around Town

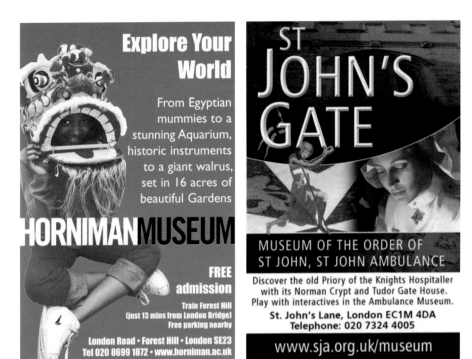
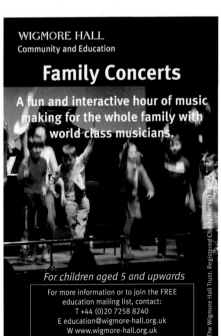

children will be able to invite their families to attend special events there.

Fundraising for the Food School is proceeding apace; for more information contact juliet@boroughmarket.org.uk.

Bramah Museum of Tea & Coffee

40 Southwark Street, SE1 1UN (7403 5650/www. teaandcoffeemuseum.co.uk). London Bridge tube/ rail. **Open** 10am-6pm daily. **Admission** £3; £2.50 concessions; £10 family (2+4). **Credit** AmEx, MC, V. **Map** p317 P8.
Edward Bramah founded this refreshing little museum. He's the master of the perfect brew (one of his coffee machines is displayed in the Science Museum). The displays and exhibitions constitute an informative tribute to the history of top hot beverages, and set out to explain the tea trade's power to influence the course of history. You don't have to visit the museum to enjoy a pot (plus scones, muffins and cakes) in the old-fashioned tea rooms; here a

pianist often tinkles away and the walls are adorned with vintage posters advertising the two great brews. *Buggy access. Café. Disabled access: toilets. Nearest picnic place: Southwark Cathedral Gardens. Shop.*

Clink Prison Museum

1 Clink Street, SE1 9DG (7403 0900/www.clink.co.uk). London Bridge tube/rail. **Open** June-Sept 10am-9pm daily. *Oct-May* 10am-6pm daily. **Tours** pre-booking essential; minimum 10 people. **Admission** £5; £3.50 5-15s, concessions; free under-5s; £12 family (2+2). *Tours* phone for prices. **Credit** MC, V. **Map** p318 P8.
Like its close neighbour the London Dungeon, the Clink Prison Museum informs visitors of the hideous practices that were meted out to wrongdoers of London past, but there the similarity ends. The Clink might not employ live actors or use gimmicky special effects to act out the dastardly deeds of yore, but it is nonetheless fascinating. Much of the material is shown on wall panels that are generally well-presented if unsettling. A few waxwork models and props, like old beds with straw mattresses, are used to

The fun don't stop

It's a wonder the Thames isn't bubbling with anticipation. As an increasing number of day trippers and tourists converge on the riverside area from Waterloo to Tower Bridge, there are ever-more impressive developments on the cards to keep the strollers entertained. South Bank & Bankside is now the focus of an innovative regeneration project producing new open spaces and cultural activities every year. The aim is to broaden access to the arts and make cultural experience a priority.

Plans for landscaping work already in progress make full use of the riverside location and add welcome colour to the urban landscape. These include: new green spaces where you can play frisbee or eat lunchtime sandwiches; the addition of twinkling low-energy tree-lighting arrangements along the river; and upgrades to walkways, including the notoriously grotty IMAX underpass at Waterloo. A new signage system is to be piloted here too, as part of a bigger city-wide project, 'legible London', to make way-finding more straightforward. There are also plans to introduce more public toilets to the area.

Jubilee Gardens, just by the London Eye, is set to undergo a major transformation over the next few years. The plan is to create a lush park with 'softly undulating hills' and trees and flowering plants chosen to provide colour all year round. The project aims to mix peaceful spaces, excellent views of the river and top facilities for public events and performances, with a dedicated play area for children.

Farther east, the Coin Street neighbourhood centre, on the corner of Coin Street and Stamford Street, is currently under construction and will be ready by September 2007. This is yet another masterstroke from the Coin Street Community Builders, who have, since 1977, been directing

their energies into turning 13 acres (53,000m2) of what was derelict warehouses, into an exemplary social enterprise. The not-for-profit organisation has already created a South Bank riverside walkway, the lovely Bernie Spain Gardens and Gabriel's Wharf market. It refurbished the Oxo Tower Wharf for mixed uses (including shops, restaurants, retail design studios and flats) and built 220 affordable homes for four fully-mutual housing cooperatives. The Coin Street community makes the most of the great outdoors throughout the summer, with an annual festival (www.coin streetfestival.org; *see p23*) that brings music, dance, children's workshops, food and craft stalls to the area from June and throughout the summer.

Keep walking to City Hall to see more regeneration in action. Buildings, in the form of mini glass towers resembling daleks, are on the drawing board. When built they should rise up around the recently regenerated Potter's Fields. A £3 million investment has greatly improved this park, allowing the visiting hordes to picnic alongside the herbaceous borders, practise ball skills on the greensward overlooking the river, or benefit from the free Wi-Fi by using their laptops. Potter's Fields has an educational remit, so workshops for children on such matters as recycling and conservation are planned.
To keep up to date with all the developments in this restless stretch of London, log on to www.southbanklondon.com, where you can search for family-friendly events at all the venues in the area. The website also has a 'plan' option for users to create an itinerary and email it to friends.

Old Operating Theatre, Museum & Herb Garret

bring scenes to life. The prison was in operation from 1247 until 1780, the year it burned down. This museum is on the site of the original Clink (so called, it's said, because the inmates clanked their chains) and was where thieves, prostitutes, debtors and priests served their sentences; some had hideously long incarcerations and suffered unimaginable tortures. The museum is a useful resource for students at Key Stage Three who are learning Tudor and medieval history, particularly as it deals with issues such as the power of the church and the role of the monarchy. There isn't much gore inside, apart from a number of unsavoury devices, such as a 'scolds bridle' (used by husbands to keep their wives in check) and a few 'hands on' execution blocks, fetters and foot crushers, thumb screws and chains, 70% of which are original.
Buggy access. Disabled access. Nearest picnic place: Southwark Cathedral Gardens. Shop.

Golden Hinde

St Mary Overie Dock, Cathedral Street, SE1 9DE (0870 011 8700/www.goldenhinde.org). Monument tube/London Bridge tube/rail. **Open** daily, times vary; phone for details. *Tours* phone for times. **Admission** £6; £4.50 concessions; £4.50 4-13s; free under-4s; £18 family (2+3). **Credit** MC, V. **Map** p319 P8.
Children love this replica of Sir Francis Drake's 16th-century flagship, which was the first ship to circumnavigate the globe (1577 and 1580). It was built in 1973 to commemorate the admiral-pirate's 400th birthday, after which it sailed to San Francisco. The main gun deck can't be more than 3ft (0.9m) high. The five levels, recreated in minute detail, are fascinating. 'Living History' overnighters are popular with families and school groups, all of whom have to dress ahead to live the Tudor life at sea. These take place on Saturdays and cost £39.95 per person (minimum age is six), costumes and entertainment provided – bring a sleeping bag. During the school holidays there arestorytelling sessions, craft activities and special workshops every weekend; details are on the website. You can also have a party here; ring or check online.
Nearest picnic place: Southwark Cathedral Gardens/riverside benches. Shop.

London Dungeon

28-34 Tooley Street, SE1 2SZ (7403 7221/www. thedungeons.com). London Bridge tube/rail. **Open** times vary, phone or check website for details. **Admission** £17.95; £14.95 concessions; £13.95 5-14s; £2 reduction for registered disabled; free carers, under-5s. **Credit** AmEx, MC, V. **Map** p319 Q8.
A horrific attraction, on a mission to scare the general public witless, the London Dungeon is clearly on to a winner, judging from the length of the weekend queues outside the Victorian railway arches that form its home (you can purchase fast-track tickets online to avoid queueing). There are always plenty of young children waiting to get in, but we would advise against taking anyone under ten. The Dungeon offers the chance to revisit various gruesome eras of London history, including the Great Plague exhibition (with skulls, rats and scabs), the Great Fire (from which you escape through a rotating drum filled with dry ice), and the 'Traitor Boat Ride to Hell' (visitors play the part of condemned prisoners – death sentence guaranteed). Costumed actors are on the prowl, emerging through wreaths of dry-ice fog and letting out blood-curdling screeches. Guaranteed to generate a scream or two is 'Labyrinth of the Lost', a horror mirror maze, the largest

scary mirror labyrinth in the world. Then there's a gruesome section devoted to Jack the Ripper, and another to Sweeney Todd, the demonic 18th-century barber. If that's not enough depravity, new for 2007 is Extremis: Drop Ride to Doom!, which recreates the experience of being hanged in a slightly more fairground way: 'Taste the fear and feel the adrenaline pump as the trap-door opens and your heart shoots into your throat as you drop, screaming into the darkness below…' Delightful: kids'll love it.
Buggy access. Café. Disabled access; toilets. Nappy-changing facilities. Picnic place: Hay's Galleria. Shop.

Old Operating Theatre, Museum & Herb Garret

9A St Thomas's Street, SE1 9RY (7188 2679/www. thegarret.org.uk). London Bridge tube/rail. **Open** 10.30am-5pm daily (last entry 4.45pm). Closed 15 Dec-5 Jan. **Admission** (LP) £5.25; £4.25 concessions; £3 6-16s; free under-6s; £12.95 family (2+4). **No credit cards. Map** p319 Q8.
Why is there an operating theatre in the roof space of a baroque church? Because the south wing of St Thomas's Hospital was built around St Thomas's Church. Britain's only surviving 19th-century operating theatre was used from 1822 largely for amputations and the treatment of superficial wounds, before being boarded up and forgotten until 1956. The rest of the museum displays hideous-looking surgical instruments and images of early surgical procedures – the museum is not for the squeamish or those who are terrified of surgery – alongside bunches and jars of dried herbs in the atmospheric 300-year-old herb garret. Check the website for weekend and school-holiday events, which include surgery 'demonstrations', hands-on pill and poultice-making, and object-handling sessions. Free trails and worksheets are available for children.
Nearest picnic place: Southwark Cathedral Gardens. Shop.

Shakespeare's Globe

21 New Globe Walk, Bankside, SE1 9DT (7401 9919/tours 7902 1500/www.shakespeares-globe. org). Mansion House tube/London Bridge tube/rail. **Open** Box office theatre bookings, April-Oct 2007 10am-6pm daily. **Tours** 9am-5pm daily. From May-Sept, afternoon tours only visit the Rose Theatre, not the Globe. **Tickets** £5-£32. *Tours* £9; £7.50 concessions; £6.50 5-15s; free under-5s; £20 family (2+3). **Credit** AmEx, MC, V. **Map** p318 P7.
This reconstruction of the Bard's own theatre, built less than 100 metres from where the original stood, was the brainchild of actor Sam Wanamaker, who died before it was finished. Tours of the theatre take place all year, but the historically authentic performances in the 'wooden O' (*Othello, The Merchant of Venice* and *Love's Labour's Lost* will play in rep during the 2007 season) run from May to October. Workshops and events for students of all ages include a range of half-term activities for children, with costume dressings and sword-fighting displays. Expect lots of fun around the time of Shakespeare's birthday (23 April) too. In the summer, drama sessions for eight to 11 year-olds accompany the theatre season; consult the website or ring 7902 1433 for details. The remains of the Rose theatre, where many of Shakespeare's works were originally staged, lie around the corner in the basement of an office block (log on to www.rosetheatre.org.uk).
Café. Disabled access: lift, toilet. Nappy-changing facilities. Restaurant. Shop.

Southwark Cathedral

London Bridge, SE1 9DA (7367 6700/tours 7367 6734/www.dswark.org/cathedral). London Bridge tube/rail. **Open** from 8am daily (closing times vary). *Restaurant* 10am-5pm daily. Closed 25 Dec, Good Friday, Easter Sunday. *Services* 8am, 8.15am, 12.30pm, 12.45pm, 5.30pm Mon-Fri; 9am, 9.15am, 4pm Sat; 8.45am, 9am, 11am, 3pm, 6.30pm Sun. **Admission** (LP) *Audio tour* £2.50; £2 OAPs; £1.25 under-16s, students. Donations appreciated. **Credit** MC, V. **Map** p319 P8.
The oldest Gothic building in London, this small but handsome cathedral was known as St Saviour's Church back in the 13th century. The part dating from these medieval days is the retro-choir and lady chapel and the north transept. The nave was rebuilt for the fourth time in the 1890s. The church fell into disrepair after the Reformation, but in 1905 was reclaimed as a cathedral. It now has an Education Centre, a shop and a refectory. Memorials include one to the 51 victims of the 1989 *Marchioness* riverboat tragedy, as well as others to Shakespeare (whose roustabout brother Edmund is buried here), John Gower and John Harvard. The windows contain images of Chaucer (who set off on pilgrimage to Canterbury from a pub in Borough High Street) and John Bunyan (who preached locally). In the much-improved churchyard there is a flattish, ribbed stone monument to Mahomet Weyomon, a Mohegan chief buried in the churchyard in 1735. This unfortunate native American was ill-used by the English during the Mohegan Land Dispute and died of disease after travelling here to state his case. The Queen unveiled the monument in November 2006, and representatives of the Mohegan tribe flew to the UK to be honoured in the ceremony.

The cathedral choir is one of the UK's best. Hear them sing evensong on Mondays and Thursdays (girls) and Tuesdays, Fridays and Sundays (boys). An all-male choir usually sings morning Eucharist, except on high days and holidays. Joining the choir gives children a fantastic musical education and the lads have a useful footie team too. Ring the above number for details of audition dates. *Buggy access. Disabled access: lifts, ramps, toilets. Nappy-changing facilities. Nearest picnic place: gardens. Restaurant. Shop.*

Tate Modern

Bankside, SE1 9TG (7887 8000/www.tate.org.uk). St Paul's tube/Blackfriars tube/rail. **Open** *Galleries* 10am-6pm Mon-Thur, Sun; 10am-10pm Fri, Sat. Last admission 45mins before closing. **Admission** free (charge for special exhibitions). **Credit** AmEx, DC, MC, V. **Map** p318 O7.
Just trotting around this awesome space is an event in itself. The architects who converted the structure from power station to gallery in 2000 left relics of the building's industrial days – the original gantries and lifting gear in the vast Turbine Hall, where the Unilever Series of large-scale commissions are displayed, changing in the autumn every year. Last year's Carsten Holler slides are sadly missed; we can only hope that the next artist, Doris Salcedo, comes up with something entertaining for her show (9 October 2007 to 24 March 2008). Other temporary exhibitions for 2007/8 include a big Dali and Film show, as well as Louise Bourgeois for autumn. The permanent collections (many of which will excite the children) are

 Lunch box

For recommended restaurants and cafés in the area, *see reviews p164.*

Amano *Victor Wharf, Clink Street, SE1 9DG (7234 0000).*
Auberge *35 Tooley Street, SE1 2PJ (7407 5267).*
Arancia *52 Southwark Park Road, SE16 3RS (7394 1751).*
Azzuro *1 Sutton Walk, SE1 7ND (7620 1300).*
Café Rouge *Hay's Galleria, SE1 2HD (7378 0097).*
Doggett's *(pub) 1 Blackfriars Bridge, SE1 9UD (7633 9081).*
EAT *Oxo Tower Wharf, Bargehouse Street, SE1 9PH (7928 8179); Royal Festival Hall riverside level, SE1 8XX (7401 2989).*
Film Café *Charlie Chaplin Walk, South Bank, SE1 8XR (7960 3118).*
Founders' Arms *(pub) 52 Hopton Street, SE1 9JH (7928 1899).*
Giraffe *Riverside, Royal Festival Hall, Belvedere Road, SE1 8XX (7928 2004).*
House of Crêpes *56 Upper Ground, SE1 9PP (7401 9816).*
Laughing Gravy *154 Blackfriars Road, SE1 8EN (7721 7055).*
Masters Superfish *191 Waterloo Road, SE1 8UX (7928 6924).*
Nando's *225-227 Clink Street, SE1 9DG (7357 8662).*

Ned's Noodle Bar *3e Belvedere Road, SE1 7GQ (7593 0077/www.nedsnoodlebar.com)*
Ping Pong *Festival Terrace, Southbank Centre, Belvedere Road, SE1 8XX (7960 4160).*
Pizza Express *4 Borough High Street, SE1 9QQ (7407 2995); 24 New Globe Walk, SE1 9DS (7401 3977); The Cardamom Building, 31 Shad Thames, SE1 2YR (7403 8484); The White House, 9 Belvedere Road, SE1 8YP (7928 4091).*
Real Greek Souvlaki & Bar *Units 1 & 2, Riverside House, 2A Southwark Bridge Road, SE1 9HA (7620 0162).*
Southwark Cathedral Refectory *Southwark Cathedral, Montague Close, SE1 9DA (7407 5740).*
Starbucks *Winchester Wharf, Clink Street, SE1 9DG (7403 0951).*
Strada *Royal Festival Hall riverside level, SE1 8XX (7401 9126).*
Studio Six *56 Upper Ground, SE1 9PP (7928 6243).*
Tate Modern Café: Level 2 *2nd Floor, Tate Modern, Bankside, SE1 9TG (7401 5014).*
Table *83 Southwark Street, SE1 0HX (7401 2760).*
Wagamama *Royal Festival Hall riverside level, SE1 8XX (7021 0877).*
Yo Sushi! *Unit 3B, County Hall, Belvedere Road, SE1 7GP (7928 8871).*

organised into four wings on Levels 3 and 5. Themes include: Cubism, Futurism and Vorticism; Surrealism and Surrealist tendencies; Abstract Expressionism and European Informal Art; and Minimalism.

There are plenty of resources to help children negotiate the art collection. Family activities are mostly available from Level 3. A pack called Start, which contains puzzles, art materials and an architectural trail, is available every Sunday (11am-5pm) and in school holidays. There's a children's audio tour too. Also on Level 3 you'll find the Family Zone and can pick up a Tate Teaser paper trail and play art-related games. On Level 5, Bloomberg Learning Zone holds a collection of interactive activities. The café has a decent children's menu if you can get near it (there are often queues). Signing up for the email bulletin via the website is a good way of keeping tabs on the Tate. Plans for a colossal expansion programme are underway; the current proposal of an extension resembling a stack of glass boxes looks bold and not a little crackers.

Buggy access. Café. Disabled access: lifts, toilets. Nappy-changing facilities. Nearest picnic place: grounds. Restaurant. Shops.

Winston Churchill's Britain at War Experience

64-66 Tooley Street, SE1 2TF (7403 3171/www. britainatwar.co.uk). London Bridge tube/rail. **Open** *Apr-Sept* 10am-5.30pm daily. *Oct-Mar* 10am-5pm daily. Last entry 30mins before closing. Closed 24-26 Dec. **Admission** £9.95; £5.75 concessions; £4.85 5-16s; free under-5s; £25 family (2+2). **Credit** AmEx, MC, V. **Map** p319 Q8.
Enter via an original London Underground lift into a reconstructed Blitz-era Underground air raid shelter, where the set – which gives the impression the place is still in use – includes bunks, a temporary kitchen and library, original posters and newsreel clips from the time. Other displays show the roles of women at war, the life of evacuated children and rationing. There's a BBC broadcasting room and a pub, and visitors can experience Morrison and Andersen bomb shelters. The visit culminates in a full-size street scene where a bomb has just exploded, chillingly staged to make you feel the action happened moments before. Children can try on a variety of wartime regalia in the dressing-up corner.

Buggy access. Disabled access: toilets. Nearest picnic place: Southwark Cathedral Gardens. Shop.

Tower Bridge & Bermondsey

This stretch of the Thames Path from London Bridge towards Tower Bridge is known as the Pool of London. Before visiting the area with children check www.poolonlondon.co.uk/familyfriendly, from which you can download free self-guiding family trails and find out about events in the area. Walking along the riverside from London Bridge will take you through Hay's Galleria: an echoey, touristy enclave where there's a sparkly Christmas shop, a few high-street favourites, stalls selling crafts and London souvenirs, and a Café Rouge. Back on the river looms **HMS** *Belfast*, the floating wing

of the Imperial War Museum. Continue along the Thames Path towards Tower Bridge and you come to the 13-acre (53,000m2) riverside development known as More London. You can cool your feet in the fountains inset in the piazza on a hot summer's day and enjoy the newly landscaped parkland (*see p43* **The fun don't stop**). The area's main landmark is City Hall, the bulbous glass-sided headquarters of Mayor Ken Livingstone, the London Assembly and the Greater London Authority. The ground floors (with exhibitions and café) are open to the public. Outside, The Scoop is a sunken amphitheatre that stages free events throughout the year; check www.morelondon.com for details. The £13 million **Unicorn Theatre** (www.unicorntheatre.com), opened in 2005, is the first specially designed theatre for kids in central London; *see also p231*.

Nearby is Tower Bridge; a noticeboard announces when the bridge will next open for tall ships to pass through (it does so about 500 times a year). This is what a wealthy American developer allegedly thought he was buying when he invested in London Bridge, back in 1968, and had it shipped, stone by stone, to Arizona. Cross Tower Bridge to reach the **Tower of London** (*see p54*).

Further east, on Shad Thames (the main thoroughfare behind the wharves) is the **Design Museum**. Years ago dockworkers unloaded tea, coffee and spices to be stored in the warehouses around here. Now listed buildings, the warehouses have been converted into upmarket apartments, offices and the restaurants of Butlers Wharf.

Up past the Design Museum, across Jamaica Road and down Tanner Street, is historic Bermondsey Street. Nearby, St Saviour's Dock was a place of execution for pirates. Once this part of Bermondsey was all slimy tidal ditches surrounding a nasty neighbourhood called Jacob's Island. Charles Dickens, appalled by conditions here, chose it as the place for Bill Sikes to meet his end in *Oliver Twist*. Bermondsey antiques market, on the corner of Bermondsey Street and Long Lane (Fridays 4am-2pm), has been around for some 60 years. Nearby Bermondsey Square is undergoing redevelopment; works to provide a hotel, apartments, shops and an outdoor cinema are due to be completed in spring 2008. For decades Bermondsey was know as Biscuit Town, because of the preponderance of confectionery factories in this part of Southwark. Sadly for Jammy Dodger fans, the last biscuit factory, Peek Freans, closed down in 1989. Note that the flamboyant **Fashion & Textile Museum** (83 Bermondsey Street, SE1 3XF (7407 8664, www. ftmlondon.org) is closed until November 2007,

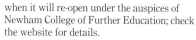

Design Museum

when it will re-open under the auspices of Newham College of Further Education; check the website for details.

Design Museum

Shad Thames, SE1 2YD (7403 6933/www.design museum.org). Tower Hill tube/London Bridge tube/ rail/47, 100, 188 bus. **Open** *10am-5.45pm 7 days.* **Admission** £7; £4 concessions; free under-12s. **Credit** AmEx, MC, V. **Map** p319 S9.

Design in all its forms is celebrated within this stylish, white building. Outside, in the riverside Design Museum Tank, a little outdoor gallery features installations by contemporary designers and a taster of exhibitions in the museum. Forthcoming events include Zaha Hadid: Architecture & Design (29 June-31 October 2007).

The museum's acclaimed programme of children's creativity workshops – design-and-make sessions for those aged six to 12 – cost £4. They take place on Sunday afternoons 2-5pm; all children must be accompanied by a paying adult. Recent highlights have included hat workshops with Philip Treacy and a special Architecture Week series. Booking is essential, either by phone or email at education@designmuseum.org. Keep an eye on the website for news of a proposed move upriver.

Buggy access. Café. Disabled access: lift, toilets. Nappy-changing facilities. Nearest picnic place: Butler's Wharf riverside benches. Shop.

HMS Belfast

Morgan's Lane, Tooley Street, SE1 2JH (7940 6300/ www.iwm.org.uk). Tower Hill tube/London Bridge tube/rail. **Open** *Mar-Oct 10am-6pm daily. Nov-Feb 10am-5pm daily. Last entry 45mins before closing.*

Admission (LP) £9.95; £6.15 concessions; £3.50 disabled and carers; free under-16s (must come with an adult). **Credit** MC, V. **Map** p319 R8.

A favourite place to visit in school holidays, when wacky trails have you climbing all over the ship, HMS *Belfast* is also a challenging workout. In Hunt the Rat, for instance, children go in search of rodents, then make one out of clay. This 11,500-ton World War II battlecruiser, enjoying a peaceful retirement on the Thames, is a vast playground of narrow ladders, stairs and walkways connecting the nine decks. There are guided tours, but it's fun to scramble around the ship, bridge to boiler room, visiting the galley, sick bay, dentist's, NAAFI canteen and mess deck. There's even an operating theatre on board. Models of sailors chatting, eating, cooking, and having their teeth drilled add to the entertainment. The permanent exhibition 'HMS *Belfast* in War and Peace' tells the story of the ship's inception in 1938, through her wartime service to her retirement in 1971, when the decision was made to turn her into a museum. The guns that destroyed the German battleship *Scharnhorst* on Boxing Day in 1943 and supported the D-Day landing a year later are, literally, a big attraction. There's usually a queue to climb into the port-deck Bofors gun, which enthusiasts can swivel, elevate and aim. The audio tour – available in adult, children or family versions and in English, French, German and Spanish – has testimonies from HMS *Belfast* veterans, as well as historical and technical information about the ship.

On the last weekend of every month there are free drop-in family activities (11am-1pm and 2-4pm), which might involve art, craft, music or dance activities, or sessions about life on board ship. Although buggies can be left on the quarterdeck, you'll be exhausted hoicking a baby around the ship; this attraction is most suited to over-fives.

Café. Disabled access; lift, toilets (check website for limitations). Nearest picnic place: Potters Field. Shop.

The City

A wealth of possibilities.

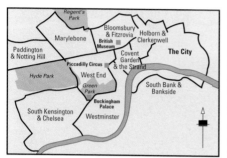

The famous Square Mile, first enclosed by the Romans, who built their wall to protect it (*see p53* **Know your boundary**) was the sum total of the city for more than a millennium. London spread beyond this boundary after the medieval period, when the City and Westminster (money and politics) joined forces. The City walls protected a fiercely independent population of merchants, who planted the seeds of economic growth. Today the City remains the economic heart of the capital, with billions of pounds changing hands every day on the trading floor of the stock exchange. But don't let that put you off. This square mile's fascinating history and culture is etched in its many treasures. Established by the Romans, ransacked by Boudicca, occupied by royalty, and the tomb of national heroes – there are stories to enthrall children here. Conveniently, one of the best places to hear them, the **Museum of London**, is right at its centre.

As shipping on the Thames decreased, and London turned its attention from trade goods to the money markets, this area on the north Bank of the Thames exchanged housing for the offices of huge corporations. The middle classes moved to new suburbs like Brixton, the well-off moved to the West End and the poor to the East.

From a peak population of around 200,000 in the 17th century, the City is now home to only about 7,500. It would be much less if it were not for the **Barbican Centre** complex, built in 1981. Over 300,000 commuters invade the square mile from Monday to Friday but leave the streets gloriously crowd-free for the rest of the time, which makes the City perfect for weekend family visits.

The City's history has shaped its governance. It is the only local authority in London that isn't run on a party political basis and has its own police force. The Corporation of London dates from the ninth century, making it older than Parliament, and its administration still retains elements of the feudal system it developed from. Centuries ago residents essentially paid off the monarchs in return for a measure of independence and self-governance. The Corporation is also unique in that it benefits from the wealth generated from the rental of the many company buildings erected on its common land. This enormous private income is known as City's Cash.

Some of London's most imposing monuments, old and new, are here. Modern landmarks like the Lloyd's Building (1 Lime Street) and the The Gherkin (30 St Mary Axe) are now as recognisable a part of the skyline as **St Paul's Cathedral**. The recently redeveloped Paternoster Square to the north of St Paul's is a gift for families, a smartly pedestrianised refreshment spot full of cafés with outside tables. Less imposing historic churches swell the numbers of ancient buildings. Tiny St Ethelburga's was flattened by an IRA bomb but rose from the ruins as a centre for peace and reconciliation. It stands bravely on Bishopsgate, the mighty Gherkin looming over it. Many peaceful pockets among the concrete and glass exist because of tragedies that scarred the City – Bunhill Fields, once set aside for victims of the Great Plague, remained unconsecrated and became a dissenters' graveyard. It's like a secret garden, with its mossy graves tilted at odd angles and its memorials to nonconformists such as William Blake, Daniel Defoe and members of Oliver Cromwell's family. Other, smaller public gardens were created from spaces left by the Blitz.

The City is a fascinating place to walk round after dark; indeed, it is the venue for one of the most popular peregrinations organised by London Walks (7624 3978, www.walks.com). Even a child with no appetite for history and a positive distaste for walking can be lured on to a tour with talk of ghosts, ghouls and the shadowy possibility of seeing something spooky after dark, which is why Ghosts of the Old City (choose the Saturday evening one, when the storyteller dresses up) is a hit with the younger generation.

Around Town

Happy Birthday. The **Barbican Centre** celebrates 25 years in 2007.

Bank of England Museum

Entrance on Bartholomew Lane, off Threadneedle Street EC2R 8AH (7601 5491/cinema bookings 7601 3985/www.bankofengland.co.uk/museum). Bank tube/ DLR. **Open** 10am-5pm Mon-Fri. Closed bank hols. **Admission** free; £1 audio guide. **Credit** *Shop* MC, V. **Map** p319 Q6.

The history of the institution is set out through a re-creation of an 18th-century banking hall (with bewigged and bestockinged mannequins) and displays of notes, coins and early handwritten cheques. An introductory film describes the Bank's origins, and there's an interactive foreign exchange-dealing desk. Special events take place throughout the year. There are calligraphy lessons, chances to design your own bank notes and fridge-magnet making in the school summer holidays of 2007 and equally creative events for the October half term 2007. On 10 Nov 2007 (Lord Mayor's Show), face painters will turn children into characters from the *Wind in the Willows*. The connection? That'll be Kenneth Grahame, who was Secretary of the Bank (1898-1908). Consistently popular, though, is the gold bar – insert a hand into a perspex case and try to lift the bar encased within. Its weight 12.7kg (28lb) – is shocking to anyone who has ever fantasised about running off with a load of gold bullion. *Buggy access. Disabled: ramp, toilet. Nappy-changing facilities. Nearest picnic place: St Paul's Cathedral Garden. Shop.*

Barbican Centre

Silk Street, EC2Y 8DS (7638 4141/box office 7638 8891/www.barbican.org.uk). Barbican tube/Moorgate tube/rail. **Open** *Box office* 9am-8pm. **Admission** free; phone for details of ticket prices for events. **Credit** AmEx, MC, V. **Map** p318 P5.

Study the maps and follow the notices on the walkways carefully and you need not get lost in this rather complex arts complex. The centre also contains 6,500 handsome flats and is a very desirable pace to live. There are also some pockets of pleasant calm for everyone to enjoy: the fountains in the inner courtyard; the Waterside Café, with its children's menu; the exotic plants and lazy koi carp in the conservatory (open to the public on Sunday afternoons); and the library, with its extensive children's section. You see remains of the Roman walls on which the Barbican was built. A £12.5-million refurbishment has resulted in a bright new look for the public spaces.

The Barbican's range of cultural offerings is certainly big (*see p216*) and 2007 offers even more dates for the diary, as the centre lays on activities to mark its 25th year. The annual two-week London Children's Film Festival in November is also a must. To join the Family News mailing list and find out more about the festival, as well as LSO and Barbican projects for children, call the Education Department on 7382 2333.

Bars. Buggy access. Cafés. Disabled access: lift, toilet. Nappy-changing facilities. Nearest picnic place: Barbican Lakeside Terrace. Restaurants. Shops.

Broadgate Arena

Broadgate Circle, EC2A 2BQ (7505 4068/www. broadgateice.co.uk). Liverpool Street tube/rail. **Open** *Mid Oct-early Apr* noon-2.30pm, 3.30-5.30pm Mon-Thur; noon-2.30pm, 3.30-6pm, 7-9pm Fri; 11am-1pm, 2-4pm, 5-7pm Sat, Sun. *Early Apr-mid Oct* phone for details. **Admission** £8; £5 under-16s (incl skate hire). **No credit cards. Map** p319 Q5.

The rink has a circular form, enclosed by a sort of amphitheatre of offices and shops in Broadgate Circle. The tiny rink is a good place to support the clinging kids in their first, hair-raising experience of the ice; skates avail-

able here range from child's size six. From April to October the arena is used for corporate events, outdoor drama and music – phone for details. *See also p265.*
Buggy access. Cafés. Nappy-changing facilities. Nearest picnic place: Finsbury Circus. Shops.

College of Arms

Queen Victoria Street, EC4V 4BT (7248 2762/ www.college-of-arms.gov.uk). Mansion House tube/ Blackfriars tube/rail. **Open** 10am-4pm Mon-Fri. Closed bank hols. **Tours** by arrangement 6.30pm Mon-Fri; prices vary. **Admission** free. **Map** p318 O7.
This beautiful 17th-century house is the official repository of the coats of arms and pedigrees of English, Welsh, Northern Irish and Commonwealth families and their descendants. Note that Scottish folk aren't included – clans are not their bag. The college was responsible for creating a new coat of arms for Camilla, Duchess of Cornwall, to signify her new position as wife to Prince Charles. Unfortunately not all of us are eligible – you must either have a coat of arms formally granted to you or be descended in the legitimate male line from someone to whom arms were granted in the past. However, you can get help with your family tree by making an appointment, to which you should bring along as much genealogical information as possible; a fee is charged for the work according to how long it is expected to take.
Buggy access. Nearest picnic place: St Paul's Cathedral garden. Shop.

Dr Johnson's House

17 Gough Square, off Fleet Street, EC4A 3DE (7353 3745/www.drjohnsonshouse.org). Chancery Lane or Temple tube/Blackfriars tube/rail. **Open** May-Sept 11am-5.30pm Mon-Sat. *Oct-Apr* 11am-5pm Mon-Sat. Closed 1 Jan, 24-26 Dec, bank hols. **Tours** by arrangement (groups of 10 or more). **Admission** £4.50; £1.50 under-18s; £3.50 concessions; free under-10s; £10 family (2+unlimited children). *Tours* free. *Evening tours* by appointment only. **No credit cards.** **Map** p318 N6.
A faithfully restored Georgian house, where the witty lexicographer (Dr Johnson was the author of the *Dictionary of the English Language*, the first ever English dictionary), lived with his very fine cat, Hodge. Hodge is remembered with a statue outside the house, and is one of the few items that will really interest children about the collection here. There are pictures of Dr Johnson and his eclectic social circle; a 20-minute film gives you a decent introduction to the man's life. Another child-friendly element is trying on replica Georgian costumes in the garret on the top floor. There are occasional family workshops at the house. The current exhibition, Behind the Scenes: The Hidden Life of Georgian Theatre 1737-1784, runs until 18 September 2007.
Nearest picnic place: Lincoln's Inn Fields. Shop.

Guildhall

Gresham Street, EC2P 2UJ (7606 3030/tours 7606 3030 ext 1463/www.corpoflondon.gov.uk). St Paul's tube/Bank tube/DLR/Moorgate tube/rail. **Open** May-Sept 9.30am-5pm daily. *Oct-Apr* 9.30am-5pm Mon-Sat. Last entry 4.30pm. Closes for functions; phone ahead to check. **Tours** by arrangement; groups of 10 or more only. **Admission** free. **Map** p318 P6.
The Guildhall survived both the Great Fire of London and the Blitz, making it one of the few structures in the City that dates before 1666. Now it's the seat of local govern-

ment; the Court of Common Council meets at 1pm on various Thursdays each month, in the cathedral-like 15th-century Great Hall (visitors are welcome; phone for dates). You can also visit the Hall when it is not being used for official business. The impressive space has a vaulted ceiling, marble monuments, and banners and shields of 100 livery companies on the walls. Every Lord Mayor since 1189 gets a namecheck on the windows. Two large wooden statues of Gog and Magog stand in the West Gallery. These giants, carved in 1953 to replace those destroyed by the Blitz, represent the mythical conflict between Britons and Trojan invaders; the result of this struggle was the founding of Albion's capital city, New Troy, on whose site London is said to stand. On the north wall hangs a fascinating list of notable trials and chilly executions. Visits to the Guildhall's enormous medieval crypt are allowed only in the context of group tours.
Of more immediate appeal is a room beyond the library devoted to a collection of watches, clocks and marine chronometers belonging to the Worshipful Company of Clockmakers. This small museum contains 700 historic timepieces dating back to the 14th century, including a silver skull watch said to have belonged to Mary Queen of Scots (though more likely to be of 19th-century vintage), important pieces by John Harrison and the watch Edmund Hillary wore to the top of Everest. The museum does a good job of explaining historical developments in the watchmaker's art.
Buggy access. Disabled access: lift, ramp, toilet. Nappy-changing facilities. Nearest picnic place: grassy area by London Wall. Shop.

Guildhall Art Gallery

Guildhall Yard, off Gresham Street, EC2P 2EJ (7332 3700/www.guildhall-art-gallery.org.uk). Mansion House or St Paul's tube/Bank tube/DLR/Moorgate tube/rail/8, 25, 242 bus. **Open** 10am-5pm Mon-Sat (last entry 4.30pm); noon-4pm Sun (last entry 3.45pm). **Admission** £2.50; £1 concessions; free under-16s. Free to all after 3.30pm daily, all day Fri. **Credit** (over £5) MC, V. **Map** p318 P6.
This gallery was opened in 1999 after a break of over 50 years; its predecessor was destroyed by World War II bombing. Upstairs, the Main Gallery is decorated chiefly with stuffy portraits of dead politicians, paintings and marble busts of kings and queens and various dignitaries connected to London. Mrs Thatcher's statue (repaired after having its head lopped off by a visitor in 2002) is on loan here. The centrepiece is the vast *Siege of Gibraltar* by John Copley – the largest painting in Britain.
The Victorian Galleries hold more dramatic and recognisable art to interest the kids. There's a full-sized marble Hamlet, Topham's vivid painting of a child's escape from a locked plague house and Millais's *My First Sermon* and *My Second Sermon* (by which time the young sitter, his daughter, has nodded off). Dotted around are art materials and tables and chairs for children's use. In October the gallery takes part in the annual nationwide Big Draw, and there are family workshops during half-terms.
Down in the basement lie the scant remains of London's only amphitheatre. It was known from written accounts that there was one somewhere in the city, but its location was a mystery until Roman masonry was unearthed during the rebuilding of the gallery. Despite only the foundations of the walls and entrance surviving, the slick presentation of the site does an excellent job of suggesting how the amphitheatre would have looked, with the

staggered seats printed on a screen along with dynamic illustrations of gladiators and sound effects to boot.

In the absence of a café, packed lunches can be scoffed in the cloakroom area, which has a water cooler. *Buggy access. Disabled access: lift, toilet. Nappy-changing facilities. Nearest picnic place: grassy area by London Wall. Shop.*

The Monument

Monument Street, EC3R 8AH (7626 2717/www.city oflondon.gov.uk). Monument tube. **Open** 9.30am-5pm **Admission** £2; £1 5-15s; free under-5s. **No credit cards. Map** p319 Q7.

A glass pavilion and a new square now surround this monument to the Great Fire of London, all refurbished in 2006. The 61-metre (202ft) column is 61 metres (202ft) from the exact spot of the bakery in Pudding Lane where the fire broke out in 1666. It was built by Sir Christopher Wren and, despite the many skyscrapers being built nearby, it still stands out thanks to the golden urn of flames on top. Children who make it up the 311 stairs can expect two treats: the view from the top and a certificate, given out at the bottom, to commemorate their climbing feat. If you choose to stay below, admire the hundreds of pieces of mirrored glass on the new pavilion's roof – these reflect a golden orb at the top of the Monument. *Nearest picnic place: riverside by London Bridge.*

Museum of London

150 London Wall, EC2Y 5HN (0870 444 3852/ www.museumoflondon.org.uk). Barbican or St Paul's tube/Moorgate tube/rail. **Open** 10am-5.50pm Mon-Sat; noon-5.50pm Sun (last admission 5.30pm). **Admission** free. *Exhibitions* £5; £3 concessions. **Credit** *Shop* MC, V. **Map** p318 P5.

Navigating the Museum of London is easy – laid out chronologically, it traces a logical trail from prehistoric London to the 21st-century capital. But be warned: its lower galleries (those housing displays from 1666 onwards) will remain closed until 2009. There's still lots to see, though, such as foyer exhibitions on topical subjects; the

Know your boundary

Ironically, the Romans who built London put a wall round their city to keep the British out. What a cheek. They built a fort where the Barbican is (a barbican is a watch-tower over the gate of a castle or fortified town); bits of both wall and fort still remain. You can walk a square mile route around what would have been the Roman sentry's beat. The wall ran for 1.75 miles (2.8km) from Tower Bridge round to Blackfriars Bridge, incorporating the great gates – Aldgate, Bishopsgate, Cripplegate, Aldersgate and Newgate – and following Cooper's Row, Jewry Street, Bevis Marks, London Wall, Newgate Street and Blackfriars Lane. It enclosed an area of about one square mile, still known as The City. Indeed, the City of London has been built on top of Londinium. And remnants are still there, buried underneath the hard core of two millennia.

There is a huge piece of wall left near Tower Gate tube, as well as a bench to gaze at it from. The top part is medieval: after the Romans left, the lazy Saxons just built on to what was already there. The Roman half has much better brickwork. Alongside it are a bronze statue said to be of Emperor Trajan and some Latin, the oldest piece of writing in the country, carved into a stone. This is a replica. The original is in the British Museum.

An even larger section of wall looms over the café tables outside Grange Hotel. You can see the double staircase up which the sentry marched. Holes which secured wooden beams now house pigeons. At Aldgate the position of the wall is marked out in the underpass.

Some of the wall was blown up by an IRA bomb in Bishopsgate in 1993. Other parts, especially those along London Wall and at the Barbican, were only revealed by German bombs in 1943. The Barbican lake is there now, as well as a herb garden and a peaceful expanse of lawn among the uncovered Roman ruins, walls and watchtowers, around St Giles Cripplegate.

A large amount of wall runs through a sunken garden alongside Noble Street towards Aldersgate. There are benches from which to contemplate them and their brutal past outside the church of St Anne and St Agnes. The city gates were also prisons and therefore places of execution. Pepys saw the severed limbs of men hung, drawn and quartered here in 1660. They stuck them on the wall near the gate as a deterrent against bad behaviour. Such are the uses of a wall.

Roman city walls

Museum of London. *See p53*.

London Before London, Roman and Medieval London galleries also remain open throughout the building work.

To get the kids absorbed, pick up an activity sheet or family activity bag on your way in. Not that they'll need much help: every effort has been made to bring history to life here. Displays of archaeological artefacts alternate with vivid reconstructions and quizzes; there are opportunities to touch objects along the way and kids can try on an old-fashioned fireman's hat or medieval costumes.

A recent addition to the museum is the London's Burning exhibition (free, open until September 2009), which dramatically recreates the Great Fire using the stories of survivors. Aimed at under-sevens, it features a video installation and quizzes to get the kids engaged.

Every Sunday there's a kids' event (usually free). Half-term and holidays feature extra events: you might listen to the tales of a Saxon storyteller, meet an iron-age woman or paint a medieval street scene. Sessions are led by actors, who hold the attention of the most fidgety kids.

Buggy access. Café. Disabled access: lift, toilet. Nappy-changing facilities. Nearest picnic place: Barber Surgeon's Garden. Shop.

Museum of Methodism & John Wesley's House
Wesley's Chapel, 49 City Road, EC1Y 1AU (7253 2262/www.wesleyschapel.org.uk). Moorgate or Old Street (exit 4) tube/rail. **Open** 10am-4pm Mon-Sat. Closed bank hols. **Tours** ad hoc arrangements on arrival; groups of 10 or more must phone ahead. **Admission** free; £4 donation requested. *Tours* free. **Credit** *Shop* MC, V. **Map** p319 Q4.
This lovely chapel, with its gated courtyard ringed by Georgian buildings, is a haven from the thunderous traffic of City Road. Known as the cathedral of world Methodism, it was built by John Wesley in 1778. Museum displays in the crypt allude to Methodism's beginnings. Hogarthian prints portray the effects of poverty, alcoholism and moral degradation in 18th-century England. John Wesley devoted his life to serving God and helping the poor, and his rigorous and methodical programme of prayer, fasting and lifestyle led to him being dubbed a Methodist. The house has been restored and shows a kitchen with a range and no running water. Much of the furniture in the house is of the period, although the tiny four-poster in the bedroom is reproduction, as is the chamber horse in the study. The latter is a curious article – a bouncing chair that simulated a good gallop – useful if Wesley felt he wasn't getting enough equestrian exercise.
Buggy access. Disabled access: lift, toilet. Nappy-changing facilities. Nearest picnic places: enclosed courtyard at entrance; Barber Surgeon's Garden; Bunhill Field Cemetery. Shop.

Postman's Park
Between King Edward Street & Aldersgate Street, EC1R 4JR (www.cityoflondon.gov.uk). St Paul's tube. **Open** 8am-dusk daily. **Admission** free. **Map** p318 O6.
Named after its proximity to a large sorting office (long ago demolished), this green space is most famous for its Heroes' Wall, a canopy-covered expanse of ceramic plaques, inscribed in florid Victorian style, that pay tribute to ordinary people who died trying to save others. Frederick Alfred Croft, Inspector, aged 31, begins one typical thumbnail drama. Saved a Lunatic Woman from Suicide at Woolwich Arsenal Station, But was Himself Run Over by the Train, Jan 11, 1878. Many of the dead heroes were children who tried to rescue drowning companions; their fates offer gruesome morals for their modern peers. *Buggy access.*

St Bartholomew's Hospital Museum
West Smithfield, EC1A 7BE (7601 8152/www.hidden london.com). Barbican or St Paul's tube. **Open** 10am-4pm Tue-Fri. Closed for Easter, Christmas, bank hols. **Tours** 2pm Fri. **Admission** free. *Tours* Church & Great Hall £4; £3 concessions; accompanied children free. **No credit cards. Map** p318 O6.
One of London's medieval hospitals, St Bart's was built in 1123 by Rahere, a courtier of Henry I, after a near-death brush with malaria. The museum recalls the hospital's origins as a refuge for the chronically sick hoping for a miraculous cure. Leather lunatic restraints, a wooden head used by medical students to practise their head-drilling techniques (but also, apparently, as a football) and photographs documenting the slow progress of nurses from drudges to career women make mildly edifying exhibits. Don't miss the huge painting by William Hogarth on the stairs. Hogarth was born in Bartholomew's Close and offered his services free when he heard the hospital governors were about to commission a Venetian artist.
Buggy access (ramp by arrangement). Café (in hospital). Nearest picnic place: hospital grounds. Shop.

St Paul's Cathedral
Ludgate Hill, EC4M 8AD (7236 4128/www.stpauls. co.uk). St Paul's tube. **Open** 8.30am-4pm Mon-Sat. *Galleries, crypt & ambulatory* 9.30am-4pm Mon-Sat. Closed for special services, sometimes at short notice. *Tours* 11am, 11.30am, 1.30pm, 2pm Mon-Sat. **Admission** (LP) *Cathedral, crypt & gallery* £9.50; £3.50 6-16s; £8.50 concessions; free under-6s; £22.50 family (2+2). *Tours* £3; £1 6-16s; £2.50 concessions; free under-6s. *Audio guide* £3.50; £3 concessions. **Credit** MC, V. **Map** p318 O6.
Approaching its 300th anniversary, St Paul's – the capital's most famous cathedral – looks radiant. A decade of restoration has stripped it of Victorian grime and the main façade looks as spectacular as must have done in 1708, when it was built. We have Sir Christopher Wren's dogged persistence to thank for this monument – the authorities nearly vetoed his project as too ambitious and expensive.

The audio guide does a grand job in bringing the place to life for children. Quirky facts about everything from the organ pipes (some big enough to crawl through) to Nelson's corpse (they had a hell of a time getting it back to England for the funeral) enliven the tour. During Christmas and Easter holidays there are trails with a small prize at the end, and parents who need help for a self-guided tour can download the activity sheets for schools.

Perhaps the most fun of all is the Whispering Gallery, where the acoustics simply have to be tested. From there it is a few more steps up to the Stone Gallery for an amazing 360-degree view of London, one of the best vantage points in the city. If you have the energy to make it further up to the Golden Gallery, try to go early, otherwise you could find yourself sandwiched between boisterous teen tourists jostling for space on the cramped balcony.

Down in the airy crypt there are tombs of historical figures, such as Nelson, Wellington and Wren. Florence Nightingale and Lawrence of Arabia are honoured with memorials. At the back is the shop and Crypt Café.

If you want to experience the true spirit of St Paul's, evensong is every day at 5pm and, at only an hour long,

Around Town

isn't too difficult for youngsters to sit through, with lessons and psalms beautifully sung by the all-male choir. *Buggy access. Café. Disabled access: lifts, ramps, toilet. Nappy-changing facilities. Nearest picnic space: garden. Restaurant. Shops.*

St Swithin's Garden

Oxford Court, off Cannon Street, EC4N 5AD (no phone). Monument tube/Bank tube/DLR. **Open** *24hrs daily.* **Admission** *free.* **Map** *p319 Q7.*
This carefully tended walled garden is the burial place of Catrin Glendwr and two of her children. Catrin was the daughter of Owain Glendwr, the Welsh hero whose uprising ended bloodily in 1413. A memorial sculpture is dedicated not only to her, but to the suffering of all women and children in war.
Buggy access.

Tower Bridge Exhibition

Tower Bridge, SE1 2UP (7403 3761/www.tower bridge.org.uk). Tower Hill tube/Tower Gateway DLR. **Open** *Apr-Oct* 10am-6.30pm daily (last entry 5.30pm). *Nov-Mar* 9.30am-6pm daily (last entry 5pm). **Admission** *£6; £3 5-15s; £4.50 concessions; free under-5s; £14 family (2+2).* **Credit** *AmEx, MC, V.* **Map** *p319 R8.*
One of London's most popular sites, Tower Bridge offers stupendous views and a lesson in Victorian engineering. When you step through the entrance, you and yours are whisked on to a stage to have your photo taken. The finished product is ready to pick up on your departure, if you wish, at a rather pricey £10 (for a pack). A lift transports you to the walkway foyer, where there are models of the alternative designs put forward for the bridge and a video re-enacting Victorian opposition to its construction. Visitors have to pass through both walkways to catch the east and west views. Large aerial photographs pinpoint famous landmarks, and there are photo points where you can slide open the windows to get an uninterrupted shot. Occasional school-holiday events, such as storytelling and games, take place here; ring for details.
From the walkways it's a short walk to the south tower and engine rooms for a more thorough explanation of hydraulics. There's an interactive experience called Lifting the Bridge. This, after all, is what every visitor would like to see for real: it happens most often during the summer

(sometimes several times a day). To find out when the next opening is taking place, call 7940 3984.
Buggy access. Disabled access: lift, toilet. Nappy-changing facilities. Nearest picnic place: Potters Field/ Tower of London Gardens. Shop.

Tower of London

Tower Hill, EC3N 4AB (info 0870 756 6060/booking line 0870 756 7070/www.hrp.org.uk). Tower Hill tube/ Tower Gateway DLR/Fenchurch Street rail. **Open** 10am-6pm Mon, Sun; 9am-6pm Tue-Sat (last entry 5pm). **Tours** *Beefeater tours (outside only, weather permitting) every 30mins, all day.* **Admission** *(LP) £16; £9.50 5-15s; £13 concessions; free under-5s; £45 family (2+3). Audio guide £3. Tours free.* **Credit** *AmEx, MC, V.* **Map** *p319 R7.*
This centuries-old fortress, palace, prison and execution place (two of Henry VIII's wives got the chop here) can be insanely crowded in high season, but it's worth braving the mob (and the prices). With so many displays and towers to explore, you can spend a whole day here.
The beautiful vaulted chamber of the Bowyer Tower opened Easter 2007. Legend has it the Duke of Clarence met a grisly fate here in 1478, drowning in a barrel of malmsey (a type of Madeira). The most entertaining way to hear such stories is to follow a Beefeater. These Yeoman Warders, photogenic in their black and red finery, are genial hosts and a mine of information. Special events punctuate the day so check the programme, or the website.
The crown jewels are the Tower's biggest draw, and the permanent exhibition, Crowns and Diamonds, is a must for lovers of sparkle. It includes a model of the uncut, fist-sized Cullinan, the world's largest diamond, and a display of how it was cut into nine stunning cut diamonds – the two largest are now part of the crown jewels. The 2m-wide Grand Punch Bowl gives new meaning to the phrase family silver.
The Medieval Palace, where kings and queens stayed until the reign of Elizabeth I, was recently restored and uses smells and sound effects to whisk you back in time. An exhibition about the palace, which features stories about 13th-century royal life, runs until 1 January 2009.
Outside, on Tower Green, stands the spot where royals were beheaded, including Anne Boleyn and Lady Jane Grey. Battle fans love the armoury in the White Tower (there is usually a half-term event centred on the collection).
Buggy access (Jewel House). Café. Nappy-changing facilities. Nearest picnic place: riverside benches; Trinity Square Memorial Gardens. Shops.

Lunch box

For more recommended restaurants and cafés in the area, *see pp166-168*.
Auberge *56 Mark Lane, EC3R 7NE (7480 6789).*
Barcelona Tapas *1 Beaufort House, St Botolph Street, EC3A 7DT (7377 5111).*
Browns *8 Old Jewry, EC2R 8DN (7606 6677).*
Chez Gerard *64 Bishopsgate, EC2N 4AW (7588 1200).*
Crypt Café *St Paul's Cathedral, Ludgate Hill, EC4M 8AD (7236 4128).*
Gaucho Grill *1 Bell Inn Yard, EC3V 0BL (7626 5180).*
Just the Bridge *1 Paul's Walk, EC4V 3QQ (7236 0000).*

McDonald's *41 London Wall, EC2M 5TE (7638 7787).*
Paul *Paternoster Square, EC4M 7DX (7329 4705).*
Pizza Express *125 Alban Gate, London Wall, EC2Y 5AS (7600 8880); 20-22 Leadenhall Market, EC3V 1LR (7283 5113); 7 St Bride Street, EC4A 4AS (7583 5126).*
Strada *St Paul's Churchyard, EC4M 8AY (7248 7178).*
Tokyo City *46 Gresham Street, EC2V 7AY (7726 0308).*
Wagamama *1A Ropemaker Street, EC2V 0HR (7588 2688).*

Holborn & Clerkenwell

Besuited, bewigged and respectable now, but with a ghost of an unsavoury past.

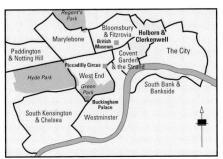

A buffer between the West End's glitz and the City's gravitas, Holborn is predominantly characterised by modern office blocks along its main routes, although its essence is, in fact, medieval. Two ancient Inns of Court – Gray's Inn and Lincoln's Inn – are at Holborn's heart, and they're tranquil, tree-bordered quadrangles that house the 'chambers' (offices) of barristers. Lincoln's Inn (7405 1393, www.lincolnsinn.org.uk) is the most impressive of the four inns of court. Its Old Hall dates back to 1422 and its buildings are a blend of various styles – Gothic, Tudor and Palladian. The other two surviving Inns, south of the western end of Fleet Street, are the Inner and Middle Temples, which were named after the Knights Templar, who owned the site for 150 years, and the maze of courtyards and fine buildings makes for some interesting wandering. Lincoln's Inn Fields is London's largest garden square, and it's flanked by a series of historic buildings. First up, one of London's weirdest attractions, the Hunterian Museum. Then there's Sir John Soane's Museum, a real cabinet of curiosities. Talking of which, south-west, on Portsmouth Street stands the Old Curiosity Shop, supposedly the oldest extant shop in London (now selling shoes).

It is also worth seeking out the **Temple Church** (Kings Bench Walk, 7353 3470, www.templechurch. com); consecrated in 1185, it is the last remaining round church in London. It's the setting for some of the action in the 2005 film *The Da Vinci Code*. On the Strand, **Temple Bar** marks the boundary between the borough of Westminster and the City of London; it's guarded by a bronze griffin mounted here in 1878 to replace Wren's archway. Nearby the **Royal Courts of Justice** are open to the public, of course, but only children over 14 are allowed in. While London's judicial heart are the Royal Courts of Justice, its veins and arteries spread over all the area – as well as the Inns of Court, there are the legal wig shops on Chancery Lane, not to mention the pubs that have refreshed lawyers for centuries.

In Fleet Street, **St Dunstan in the West** (No. 186A, 7405 1929, www.stdunstaninthewest.org) – was once next door to the shop of the murderous barber-surgeon Sweeney Todd.

A few churches of note in the area include **St Clement Danes**, restored after the Blitz, and St Mary le Strand (free lunchtime recitals, Wed-Fri).

Going towards Clerkenwell, the **Museum & Library of the Order of St John** has an ancient crypt that pre-dates even the 13th-century example at nearby **St Ethelreda's** on Ely Place.

Hunterian Museum. *See p58.*

Around Town

There is also a gatehouse from the original priory of St John of Jerusalem, dating to 1504.

Further towards Clerkenwell and Farringdon, there are echoes of the area's long tradition of arts and crafts: the **Clerkenwell Green Association** provides studios for tradespeople in the area in St John's Square and Clerkenwell Green. Elsewhere in Clerkenwell, Hatton Garden is the centre of the British diamond trade (look out for some striking display windows). Nearby Leather Lane market – a good place for bargain hunters – is a vivid contrast.

Hunterian Museum

Royal College of Surgeons of England, 35-43 Lincoln's Inn Fields, WC2A 3PE (7869 6560/www.rcseng.ac.uk). Holborn tube. **Open** 10am-5pm Tue-Sat. **Admission** free; donations appreciated. **Credit** *Shop* MC, V. **Map** p318 M6.

John Hunter (1728-93) was a pioneering surgeon and anatomist, appointed physician to King George III. Through his life he amassed a huge collection of many thousands of medical specimens. After he died, the collection was enhanced and expanded by others; today it can be viewed in this museum housed at the Royal College of Surgeons. Among the quirkier exhibits are Winston Churchill's false teeth and the freakish skeleton of 'Irish Giant' Charles Byrne, who reached 2.2m (7ft 7in) in his socks. Children can peruse drawings using the art materials on site, peruse the concise library of books at hand or perhaps try on the skeleton suit and test their knowledge of the human anatomy with the textile body-part game. A programme of workshops aimed at school groups and families is set to expand, with the introduction of more actor-based events, such as the popular Barber Surgeon, with his grim array of real-life tools of the trade. Tours take place every Wednesday at 1pm, often led by a knowledgeable retired surgeon. A grant received in 2007 from the Heritage Lottery Fund will be used to fund Exhibiting Difference, a one-year programme of events, including an exhibition to mark the bi-centenary of the Parliamentary abolition of the transatlantic slave trade. *Buggy access. Lift. Nearest picnic place: Lincoln's Inn Fields. Shop.*

Museum & Library of the Order of St John

St John's Gate, St John's Lane, EC1M 4DA (7324 4005/www.sja.org.uk/museum). Farringdon tube/rail/ 55, 63, 243 bus. **Open** 10am-5pm Mon-Fri; 10am-4pm Sat. Closed 24 Dec-2 Jan, bank hol weekends (phone to check). *Tours* 11am, 2.30pm Tue, Fri, Sat. **Admission** free; suggested donations for tours £5; £4 concessions. **Credit** MC, V. **Map** p318 O4.

St John Ambulance treated 5,054 people in soaring heat at the 2007 Flora London Marathon. This museum marks the

Ghouls, greens and ghastly goings-on

Charles Dickens described Clerkenwell as a 'decidedly unsavoury and unattractive locality': the notorious rookeries of Saffron Hill were depicted in *Oliver Twist*; in *Little Dorrit*, the Plornish family lived in a house in Bleeding Heart Yard. This courtyard owes its name to a myth surrounding a brutal murder in 1626, cobbled together from various unrelated events and people of the time. One version of this tale tells of a ball being interrupted at the stroke of twelve by the appearance of the Devil himself, who then spirited away society belle Elizabeth Hatton and danced with her all night long. The next morning her body was found in the yard, torn limb from limb, her heart ripped out yet still pumping blood – *Cinderella* as written by Clive Barker. Today, the yard is home to a wine bar and French bistro.

A short walk from here, via the Green (once an execution site with a pound, pillary and Watch House), is Clerkenwell Close. All manner of unexplained phenomena and sightings have been reported by locals – phantom footsteps, the 'heartrendering sobs' of an unseen small girl, an apparition of a lady in Victorian dress, an old woman wandering the streets seemingly in search of something or someone. The Hugh Myddleton School building, now converted into apartments, stands on the site of the 'Tench' as it was known in Dickens' time; underground lies a surviving labyrinth of corridors housing transportation cells, a laundry, a kitchen and ventilation tunnels. There had been a prison on this site since 1616 and in 1845 the entire area was re-built as the Clerkenwell House Of Detention. In 19th century London, over 10,000 prisoners a year passed through the doors of this remand prison, its subterranean design making escape near impossible. People would be clapped in irons here for begging, attempting suicide or even 'stealing two grapes'; in the mid-1860s it became a radical pen, housing Fenians. The Fenian Society, in attempting to free prisoners, bombed a prison wall in 1867 and destroyed many of the houses in nearby Corporation Row. Children were also imprisoned at the Tench – the motto of 'look on and despair all ye who enter here' speaks of their terrible anguish and suffering in those dank, dark and freezing corridors. Three storeys originally stood above ground, all demolished in 1890. During the Second World War some of the underground cells were used as air raid shelters; others were sealed off at the time of demolition and were only recently excavated. The House of Detention re-opened in 1983 as a museum, displaying a collection of sinister torture weapons (the 'tongue-tearer', the 'throat-catcher') and prisoner records. The BBC filmed part of *Great Expectations* here in 1998 and it has also appeared in an episode of Living TV's *Most Haunted*. Closed down in 2000 by Customs and Excise for non-payment of VAT by management, the House of Detention remains empty today, save for the ghosts of some of its more unfortunate inhabitants.

Around Town

Old Curiosity Shop. *See p57.*

beginnings of this life-saving organisation. The order began with the crusaders in 11th-century Jerusalem. It has been dealing with disease and pestilence ever since, and this museum gives an insight into the history of both the order and medicine. Exhibits are divided between a static collection of antiques (from holy relics to full suits of armour) and a brighter, more interactive room that showcases the order's medical history. Here surgical models and tools of the trade are displayed, as well as a primitive wooden ambulance (essentially a wheelbarrow). The museum is set beside St John's Gate, a Tudor stone edifice, part of the original priory. If you take the grand tour, you'll see the extant 12th-century crypt. There's an annual roster of temporary exhibitions, as well as year-round activity trails for younger groups. Those wanting to get some hands-on experience can become a member (depending on their age) of the Badgers (5-10) or Cadets (10-18) – membership is free (you only pay for the uniform), and the young lifesavers receive first-aid training. *Buggy access (not tours). Shop.*

Prince Henry's Room

17 Fleet Street, EC4Y 1AA (www.cityoflondon.gov.uk). Blackfriars tube/rail/11, 15, 172 bus. **Open** *from Sept 2007* 11am-2pm Mon-Fri. **Admission** free; donations appreciated. **Map** p318 N6.

This ornate and atmspheric oak-panelled room is one of few in central London to have survived the Great Fire of 1666. Originally used by lawyers of Prince Henry, eldest son of King James I, the room was built in 1610 – the same year that the 14-year-old Henry became Prince of Wales. Four years later he died of typhoid, and it was his brother who succeeded to the throne as Charles I. The rest of the

---

✕✕ Lunch box

For more recommended restaurants and cafés in the area, *see pp162-84.*

Al's Bar *11-13 Exmouth Market, EC1R 4QD (7837 4821).*

Bank Aldwych *1 Kingsway, WC2B 6XF (7379 9797).*

Bierodrome *67 Kingsway, WC2B 6TD (7242 7469).*

Fryer's Delight *19 Theobald's Road, WC1X 8SL (7405 4114).*

Gallery Café *basement of the Courtauld Institute Gallery, Somerset House, Strand, WC2R 1LA (7848 2526).*

McDonald's *152-153 Fleet Street, EC4A 2DQ (7353 0543).*

Pizza Express *99 High Holborn, WC1V 6LF (7831 5305).*

Spaghetti House *20 Sicilian Avenue, WC1A 2QD (7405 5215).*

Strada *8-10 Exmouth Market, EC1R 4YA (7278 0800).*

Terrace Restaurant *Lincoln's Inn Fields, WC2A 3LJ (7430 1234).*

Wagamama *109 Fleet Street, EC4A 2AB (7583 7889).*

Yo! Sushi *95 Farringdon Road, EC1R 3BT (7841 0785).*

---

building – now an office – was once a tavern called the Prince's Arms, which happened to be a favoured haunt of the diarist Samuel Pepys. So that is why cases in Prince Henry's Room display a range of Pepys memorabilia, including original portraits, newspaper clippings and – of course – extracts from his chronicle of 17th-century life. Children already predisposed towards this particular portion of history will enjoy it, but don't expect the place to inflame younger imaginations.

St Ethelreda's

14 Ely Place, EC1N 6RY (7405 1061/www.stetheldreda. com). Chancery Lane tube/Farringdon tube/rail. **Open** 8am-6pm daily; phone to check. **Admission** free; donations appreciated. **Map** p318 N5.

Built by Bishop Luda of Ely in the 13th century, it's the oldest Catholic church in Britain and serves as London's only standing example of Gothic architecture from that period. It survived the Great Fire of London thanks to a change in the wind. These days the upper church – rebuilt after damage caused by the Blitz – is used for services. The crypt is dark and atmospheric, untouched by the noise of nearby traffic.

Despite its postcode, Ely Place is, through a quirk of legal history, under the jurisdiction of Cambridgeshire. It is even subject to its own laws and precedents. This is where David Copperfield meets Agnes Wakefield in the Dickens novel. The strawberries grown in the church gardens receive commendation in Shakespeare's *Richard III*; in past years there has been a fair to celebrate the fruit, but not in 2007. *Buggy access. Café (noon-2pm Mon-Fri).*

Sir John Soane's Museum

13 Lincoln's Inn Fields, WC2A 3BP (7405 2107/ education officer 7440 4247/www.soane.org). Holborn tube. **Open** 10am-5pm Tue-Sat; 10am-5pm, 6-9pm 1st Tue of mth. Closed bank hol weekends. *Tours* 2.30pm Sat. **Admission** free; donations appreciated. *Tours* £3; free concessions, under-16s. **Credit** *Shop* AmEx, MC, V. **Map** p315 M5.

The son of a bricklayer, John Soane was able to indulge his passion for collecting unusual artefacts after he married into money. But it was a passion he then indulged relentlessly and without prejudice. Far from confining himself to relics of a specific period, he filled his home with everything from an Ancient Egyptian sarcophagus to paintings by his near-contemporary, renowned satirist William Hogarth. The latter's *Rake's Progress* is on display in a room that also contains several of Soane's own architectural plans, all nestled together in an elaborate and utterly charming series of folding doors and walls. It is such touches of ingenuity that elevate this museum from a mere cabinet of (admittedly extraordinary) curiosities to something more beguiling. Soane turned his house into a museum to which 'amateurs and students' should have access, and that is the way it has been ever since.

The museum has recently been extended, which means there is now a floor devoted to educational workshops for families and schools. Check the website for details of forthcoming events. On the first Tuesday of every month, you can visit it in the evening (6-9pm) when the house is candlelit after dark. You do have to book ahead however, and at other times be prepared to queue, as the delicate fabric of the house cannot cope with the huge upsurge in this museum's popularity. Note that buggies cannot be accommodated. The next big exhibition here is A Passion for Building: The Amateur Architect in 18th-Century England (until 1 September 2007). *Nearest picnic place: Lincoln's Inn Fields. Shop.*

Bloomsbury & Fitzrovia

With plenty of play space, it's not all academic.

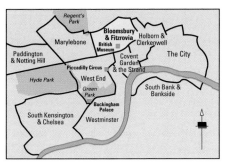

As far as visitors are concerned, the central beacon of this area is the **British Museum**. The museum's bookish brother, the **British Library**, is just to the north at King's Cross. Separated from Bloomsbury by Tottenham Court Road, Fitzrovia lacks for sights but it makes up for it with a bohemian past – it was a cauldron of creativity in the 1930s and '40s. But young people will be more keen to ogle the Egyptian mummies at the British Museum. During half-terms and holidays, Egyptology-related activities are often organised, both here and at the **Petrie Museum of Egyptian Archaeology**.

The Petrie, part of University College London's campus, is one of half a dozen small venues of cultural interest in the area. Also part of UCL is Grant Museum of Zoology (Gower Street, WC1, www.ucl.ac.uk/museums/zoology), the only remaining university zoological collection in London. The Grant, founded in 1827, houses around 32,000 specimens. It's packed full of skeletons, mounted animals and specimens preserved in fluid. It's open 1-5pm Monday to Friday and runs occasional family workshops – see the website for details. Most appealing is the **Foundling Museum**, a memorial to London's abandoned children, which opened in 2004 and was nominated for the Gulbenkian Prize for Museum of the Year. Its location is child-friendly, too: adjacent to the extensive inner-city park **Coram's Fields** (named after benefactor Thomas

Coram). And just a stone's throw from the British Museum you'll find the **Cartoon Museum**, dedicated to collecting and preserving British cartoons, caricatures, comics and animations.

Other prominent names in local history are those of the fourth Earl of Southampton, who built **Bloomsbury Square** around his house in the 1660s (none of this architecture remains), and the Russells – or Dukes of Bedford – who intermarried with the Southamptons and developed this rural area into one of London's first planned suburbs. It was during the 18th and 19th centuries that the lovely Georgian squares and elegant terraces here were built in an easy-to-navigate grid style.

In stark contrast, opposite Russell Square tube is the **The Brunswick**. Hailed as the future of community living when it was built in the 1960s, this concrete complex of high-density housing has just undergone a major revamp befitting its Grade II-listed building status. It provokes strong feelings: denounced by some as Bloomsbury's carbuncle, it's loved by fans of Modernism.

Fitzrovia is less well defined than Bloomsbury. Its highlight, Fitzroy Square, is disappointingly paved over, although its main visitor attraction, **Pollock's Toy Museum**, is a gem for collectors, and has a wonderful shop.

An eclectic mix of transitory students, hospital staff and happily entrenched locals populate the streets to the east of Tottenham Court Road, home to London University and various medical buildings. At their heart is **Senate House**, Malet Street's towering and forbidding monolith, which inspired George Orwell's Ministry of Truth in *1984* and housed the Ministry of Information during World War II. It was a particular favourite of Adolf Hitler: he had planned to make his headquarters there if Germany had won the war.

British Museum

Great Russell Street, WC1B 3DG (7323 8000/7323 8299/www.thebritishmuseum.ac.uk). Holborn, Russell Square or Tottenham Court Road tube. **Open** *Galleries* 10am-5.30pm Mon-Wed, Sat, Sun; 10am-8.30pm Thur, Fri. *Great Court* 9am-6pm Mon-Wed, Sun; 9am-11pm Thur-Sat. **Tours** *Highlights* 10.30am, 1pm, 3pm daily;

Around Town

phone to check. *Eye Opener* frequently; phone to check. **Admission** free; donations appreciated. *Temporary exhibitions* prices vary; phone for details. *Highlights tours* £8; £5 under-11s, concessions. *EyeOpener tours* free. **Credit** *Shop* AmEx, DC, MC, V. **Map** p317 K5.

London's most popular tourist attraction, this gargantuan museum was founded in 1753, an embodiment of the Enlightenment concept of all of the arts and sciences being interconnected. The world-famous collections are best appreciated in bite-sized chunks. The Great Court, London's largest covered public square, makes an impressive starting point for exploring the Egyptian antiquities (the Rosetta Stone, imposing statues, mummies) and ancient Greek treasures, including the Elgin Marbles, but do make time (or plan a return visit) for its less famous prehistoric, ethnographic, Asian and European collections. Here are artefacts as diverse as Japanese suits of armour, Mexican Day of the Dead papier-mâché figures and the Lindow Man, garotted in 300 BC Britain and preserved in peat ever since. The restored King's Library was built in the 1820s, and its Grade I-listed interior is widely considered to be the finest neoclassical space in London. Its exhibition, Enlightenment: Rethinking the World in the 18th Century is a 5,000-strong collection examining that formative period of the museum.

Sampler tours of its top treasures (starting from the information desk) and EyeOpener tours, which concentrate on specific aspects of the collection, such as Africa, the Americas or the classical world are run by volunteer guides; check the website for details of free special family EyeOpeners, run twice daily during half-terms and irregularly through the school holidays (book at the information desk), or pick up a family backpack (deposit required) from the Paul Hamlyn Library on the ground floor to navigate the galleries independently. The Roman Britain, Mexico, Africa, Greece and Egypt trails contain hands-on activities. Young Friends of the British Museum (£20 per year for children aged eight to 15) receive a welcome pack, 10% discount in the shop and magazines three times a year. Young Friends can also book – way ahead! – a museum sleepover with the mummies (£27.50). Membership also entitles children to half-term activities. The Paul Hamlyn Library is doing the work of the central Reading Room, which is being prepared for the big Exhibition (13 September 2007– 6 April 2008), entitled The First Emperor: China's Terracotta Army. This is a once-in-a-lifetime exhibition of one of the greatest archaeological discoveries of the 20th century. On the Lower Ground Floor, the Clore Educational Centre and the Ford Centre for Young Visitors are dedicated family areas… there's space for picnics, nappy changing, rest and recuperation.
Buggy access. Cafés. Disabled access: lift, toilet. Nappy-changing facilities. Nearest picnic place: Russell Square. Restaurant. Shops.

Cartoon Museum

35 Little Russell Street, WC1A 2HH (7580 8155/ www.cartooncentre.com). Holborn or Tottenham Court Road tube. **Open** 10.30am-5.30pm Tue-Sat; noon-5.30pm Sun. **Admission** £3; £2 concessions; free under-18s, students. **Credit** *Shop* MC, V. **Map** p315 L5.
Housed in a former dairy, this museum is dedicated to collecting and preserving the best of British cartoons, caricatures, comics and animations. The ground-floor displays are arranged chronologically, with Hogarths and Gillrays leading on to well-known World War II political cartoons, Thelwell's playful countryside images, and satirical works by revolutionary artists Ralph Steadman

and Gerald Scarfe. Both the permanent displays and temporary exhibitions rotate every three months or so. The first-floor gallery is the most engaging for children, detailing the history of British comics and cartoon strips from 1884. Here you'll see favourite childhood characters close up: 1920s Rupert, Desperate Dan from the 1940s, Dennis the Menace, Dick Tracy, Tank Girl and Judge Dredd. Check the website for details of family fun days (every second Saturday) and activities. Everyone is encouraged to create their own art for the Young Cartoonists Gallery.

The Cartoon Art Trust runs the Young Cartoonist of the Year competition, awards for which are presented at the Cartoon Awards each year (check the website for this year's closing date for entries). The exhibition for 2007 is Heath Robinson's Helpful Solutions, his daft but genial solutions for the world' (5 July–7 October 2007).
Buggy access (ground floor). Nearest picnic place: Russell Square. Shop.

Charles Dickens Museum

48 Doughty Street, WC1N 2LX (7405 2127/www. dickensmuseum.com). Russell Square tube. **Open** 10am-5pm Mon-Sat; 11am-5pm Sun. **Admission** £5; £4 concessions; £3 5-15s; free under-5s; £14 family (2+5). **Credit** AmEx, DC, MC, V. **Map** p317 M4.
Charles Dickens's miserable childhood – his father was sent to Marshalsea Prison for debt and, at 12, Charles had to leave school and work in a shoe-polish factory – shaped his personality and literary career. After the publication and success of *The Pickwick Papers* in 1836, Dickens left his poverty-striken past and cramped chambers in Holborn and moved to Doughty Street, at that time a private street sealed at both ends with gates and manned by porters. *Oliver Twist* and *Nicholas Nickleby* were written here. This is the author's only surviving London residence, but he lived here only for three years. The museum on these premises is filled with memorabilia and artefacts; its passageways are decorated with paintings of Dickens characters, among them Little Nell, Uriah Heep and Little Dorrit. Dickens's personal effects are all over the place. Displays include personal letters, original manuscripts and the desk on which he wrote *Oliver Twist*. In the basement, visitors can see a 25-minute film on Dickens's life in London. Children's handling sessions, in which kids get to grips with quill pens, first editions and Dickens family photographs, are held most Tuesdays and Wednesdays (11am-4pm, call ahead as these are volunteer-run).

There are two mini-trails for children, using Dickens's best-known stories such as *Oliver Twist* and *A Christmas Carol*. Trails for primary-school children are picture-based; older kids get a multiple-choice questionnaire. Check the website for details of occasional Victorian craft workshops.
Buggy access (ground floor). Disabled access: ramp (ground floor only). Nearest picnic place: Coram's Fields/Russell Square. Shop.

Coram's Fields

93 Guilford Street, WC1N 1DN (7837 6138). Russell Square tube. **Open** *May-Aug* 9am-7pm daily. *Sept-Apr* 9am-dusk daily. **Admission** free. **Map** p317 L4.
Famous long before it became one of young Londoners' favourite parks, this site dates back to 1747, the year Thomas Coram established the Foundling Hospital for abandoned children (site of the Foundling Museum, *see right*). After the orphanage was demolished in the 1920s, a campaign to turn the site into a children's play area kept the

British Museum. *See p61.*

developers at bay; the park finally opened in 1936. There are spacious lawns, sandpits and slides, a paddling pool, an AstroTurf football pitch, a basketball court, a wooden climbing tower, swings, a helter-skelter chute and an assault-course pulley. There's also a city farm, with goats, geese, a duck pond, rabbits, guinea pigs and an aviary. Occasionally during the summer, bands and circus performers entertain picnicking families; under-fives fun days are often held. Activities for the summer holidays include sports and arts workshops; ring for details. A small veggie café (closed Mon in winter) provides healthy fuel for all that active play.

Parents love the park because it's safe. It's permanently staffed, and adults are admitted only if accompanied by children. Sports such as football, basketball, aerobics and trampolining are all available free (call for details). In the Band Room and play centre, a range of classes are offered; call for details. A youth centre has free IT courses for 13- to 19-year-olds. There are toilets and shower rooms in the sports area (including facilities for wheelchair-users) and a drop-in playgroup (7837 6611). The nursery, after-school and holiday play centres are run by Camden Council (7837 0255). All activities are dependent on funding, so do make a donation or spend some money in the café.
Buggy access. Café. Disabled access: toilet. Nappy-changing facilities.

Foundling Museum

40 Brunswick Square, WC1N 1AZ (78413600/ www.foundlingmuseum.org.uk). Russell Square tube. **Open** 10am-6pm Tue-Sat; noon-6pm Sun. **Tours** by arrangement. **Admission** £5; £4 concessions; free under-16s. **Credit** AmEx, MC, V. **Map** p317 L4.
Retired sea captain Thomas Coram spent 17 years relentlessly campaigning to improve the lots of the babies and children abandoned in 18th century London. He established his Hospital for the Maintenance and Education of Exposed and Deserted Children in 1739, the first foundlings being admitted in 1741. During the life of the hospital (it finally closed in 1953), more than 27,000 abandoned infants were taken in and cared for until they were of apprentice age.

The Foundling Museum, which stands in a restored building adjacent to the original site of the hospital, tells the story of those children – and the adults who campaigned for them. Most prominent of these were William Hogarth, whose support and gifts of paintings caused the Foundling Hospital to become established as Britain's first public art gallery, and George Frederic Handel, whose manuscripts and ephemera are displayed on the top floor of the museum. Handel was a Governor and benefactor of the Foundling Hospital, and annual performances of his Messiah provided a sources of income for the institution.

More poignant, however, is the array of humble items left by mothers as a keepsake for their children – a key, buttons, a piece of shell engraved with the child's name and date of birth, a scrap of poetry. Sadly, to keep the mother's identity anonymous, the foundlings were never given these tokens. Children and families can explore the museum through activity packs, audio games, story books and special events throughout the year. These include artistic workshops, drop-in family fun days on Saturdays as well as Tuesdays and Thursdays in the school hols, concerts and author visits. Call ahead or check the website for details of other regular events.
Buggy access. Café. Disabled access: lift. Nappy-changing facilities. Nearest picnic place: Brunswick Square/Coram's Fields. Shop.

Petrie Museum of Egyptian Archaeology

University College London, entrance through DMS Watson Library, Malet Place, WC1E 6BT (7679 2884/www.petrie.ucl.ac.uk). Goodge Street or Warren Street tube/29, 73, 134 bus. **Open** 1-5pm Tue-Fri; 10am-1pm Sat. Closed Easter hols; 24 Dec-2 Jan.
Admission free; donations appreciated. **Map** p317 K4.
Named after Flinders Petrie, an inexhaustible excavator of ancient Egyptian treasures, this museum was set up in 1892 by traveller and diarist Amelia Edwards. It contains the pieces that made up the minutiae of Egyptian life: cosmetic pots, the remains of a child's rag doll, painted tile

PETRIE MUSEUM OF EGYPTIAN ARCHAEOLOGY

UCL's Petrie Museum houses c.80,000 objects, and is one of the greatest collections of Egyptian and Sudanese archaeology in the world. It gives a unique insight into how people have lived and died in the Nile Valley from prehistory to Islam.

PUBLIC OPENING HOURS

Tuesday to Friday 13.00–17.00
Saturday 10.00–13.00
Admission is FREE

The Petrie Museum of Egyptian Archaeology
University College London,
Malet Place, London WC1E 6BT

Tel: 020 7679 2884
email: petrie.museum@ucl.ac.uk

www.petrie.ucl.ac.uk

fragments and, most famously, the world's oldest piece of clothing (a dress worn by a teenager in 2800 BC). Some of the collection might be heavy-going (the room filled with broken pots is a bit off-putting), but there are items to rouse interest: a collection of ancient toys, jewellery, painted coffin cases, a rat trap and a mummy head, with eyelashes and eyebrows still intact. The maze-like journey to this tucked-away museum (there are plans to rehouse the collections in purpose-built galleries in 2009) and its gloomy surroundings give the place a spooky, *Indiana Jones*-like atmosphere. Pick up a free torch from reception and explore the dusty aisles and the thousands of items crammed into the dimly lit cases. Children can work through the Rock Trail worksheet, a themed journey around the collection. There's also a Petrie Family Pack archaeology kit, with free postcards and replica objects or painted papyrus (depending on availability). For activities and events contact the Education Officer on 7679 2151, or encourage your kids' teachers to visit the website and order packs aimed at seven- to 11-year-olds (school visits 10am-1pm Tue, Wed; free).
Buggy access. Disabled access: lift, toilet. Nearest picnic place: Gordon Square. Shop.

Pollock's Toy Museum

1 Scala Street (entrance on Whitfield Street), W1T 2HL (7636 3452/www.pollockstoymuseum.com). Goodge Street tube. **Open** 10am-5pm Mon-Sat. **Admission** £3; £2 concessions; £1.50 3-16s; free under-3s. **Credit** MC, V.
Formed from two adjacent houses (one dates from the 1780s, the other a century later), and named after Benjamin Pollock, the last of the Victorian toy theatre printers, this appealingly ramshackle museum is run by the founder's grandson and has been on this site for over 36 years. The upper floor consists of a warren of atmospheric rooms, with creaking floorboards, period fireplaces and sloping walls. These rooms house treasures gathered from nurseries across the world. The oldest item is a 4,000-year-old Egyptian clay toy mouse; among the other curiosities are well-loved teddy bears, dolls, Chinese shadow puppets and 19th-century magic lanterns. The first-floor toy theatre room houses English and European examples; look for

photographs of Mr Pollock (in his Hoxton shop, bombed in 1944) in the alcove. Adults are more likely to appreciate the nostalgia value of old board games and playthings; they won't mean much to kids – but there's hands-on fun to be had in the museum shop: reproduction cardboard theatres, wind-up music boxes, animal masks and tin robots are sold alongside modern items such as tubs of fluorescent, maggotty green slime, and jumping spiders. *Nearest picnic place: Crabtree Fields, Colville Place. Shop.*

Around King's Cross

A fast-changing part of town (it's looking a bit like a war zone, what with all the roads in chaos and buildings boarded up), King's Cross is enduring the mother of all makeovers. The redevelopment will make this a major transport hub, with six underground lines, high speed connections to Kent via Stratford, thence to France. Once all the building work is done, the gaping badlands to the north of St Pancras and King's Cross stations (not a very nice place to linger, traditionally) will have been transformed into a mixed-use nucleus called King's Cross Central. Until then there are still reasons to pick your way through the rubble (not least the fact that Harry Potter goes to King's Cross station to board the Hogwarts Express). The British Library is a big landmark, Camley Street Natural Park is a green one, and the London Canal Museum is a nostalgic one.

Camley Street Natural Park

12 Camley Street, NW1 0PW (7833 2311/www.wild london.org.uk). King's Cross tube/rail. **Open** *May-Sept* 10am-5pm (or dusk) Thur-Sun; 10am-5pm daily during school holidays. Closed 20 Dec-1 Jan. **Admission** free. **Map** p315 L2.

Stuff to consider

Ours is a nation famed and ridiculed for its devotion to domestic pets, but consider the attitude of the Ancient Egyptians. At the British Museum (*see p61*), several family trails lead visitors past bestial relics with a religious twist (see www.thebritishmuseum.ac.uk/compass). It's not that the Egyptians worshipped animals; but they did believe many of their gods had special animals. All cats, for example, were thought to belong to the goddess Bastet, and so live cats were naturally sacrificed and made into animal mummies as gifts for her. There are mummies of snakes, fish, mice, gazelles, beetles and even eels in the Museum's galleries, but the cat mummy is among the most appealing, since it has a recognisable clay cat head. Other specimens are disappointingly turd-like in shape; apparently the embalmers took very little care over animals, often binding up just a few bones and feathers. The slap-dash approach has its

merits, however: with so little expertise involved, you can let the kids have a go with a few leftover chicken bones when you get home.

These days it's much harder to find designated ground for the burial of animals and the lack of space in London leads many pet owners to come up with more creative memorials. Taxidermy is favoured by some; it's not as expensive as you might imagine to have your cat or dog preserved in three dimensions (from £300-400; rather less than some vets' bills). At the wonderfully old-fashioned Get Stuffed on Essex Road, Islington, N1 (7226 1364, www.thegetstuffed. co.uk; open by appointment only) you can gaze at any number of antique exemplars, from butterflies and tiny birds (£30-40) to snarling wolves and snarling lions (several thousand pounds) – though quite apart from the cost, you would have to think carefully about where you could display the 10ft head and neck of a giraffe.

Right in the heart of noisy London, perched on the banks of Regent's canal, this two acres of wild green space constitutes the London Wildlife Trust's flagship reserve. Tiny by national standards, the reserve combines woods, ponds, marshes and flower meadows creating a haven for birds, bees, butterflies, amphibians and a rich variety of plant life. Every Saturday and Sunday the Park runs special free activities for families: there's pond dipping, insect hunting, nature trails and arts and crafts sessions with a wildlife theme. It's a peaceful place for a family breather. *Buggy access. Disabled access: toilets. Nappy-changing facilities.*

London Canal Museum

12-13 New Wharf Road, N1 9RT (7713 0836/ www.canalmuseum.org.uk). King's Cross tube/rail. **Open** 10am-4.30pm Tue-Sun, bank hol Mon. Last entry 3.45pm. **Admission** (LP) £3; £2 concessions; £1.50 8-15s; free under-8s. **Credit** MC, V. **Map** p315 M2.
This small shrine to life on Britain's canals is a charmer. Apart from panels of text relating the historic importance of the waterways, there is a real narrowboat to explore, complete with recorded domestic dialogue; a children's corner with canal-themed books and lots of pictures of Rosie and Jim to colour in; a life-size 'horse' in its stable; and videos showing life afloat in all its grimy grimness. A touch-screen display introduces visitors to the life and times of one Carlo Gatti. Gatti, sometime owner of the warehouse at 12 New Wharf Road, was an Italian-Swiss immigrant who rose from humble chestnut seller to wealthy ice-cream manufacturer, simply by importing ice blocks from the frozen lakes of Norway. The ice was stored in two deep, circular ice wells below the warehouse – throw in pennies to appreciate the drop. The displays relating to the commercial history of ice-cream are also fascinating. The shop has some lovely artefacts with curious child appeal, from enamelware painted with 'castles and roses' to lace-and-ribbon plates. Regular craft sessions in the school holidays often involve recreating such items. Check out the 'what's on' section of the museum's website for information on temporary exhibitions and activities, such as arty fun for the Big Draw weekend in October and spooky goings on for Hallowe'en. *Buggy access. Disabled access: lift, toilets. Nappy-changing facilities. Nearest picnic place: museum terrace/canal towpath. Shop.*

British Library

96 Euston Road, NW1 2DB (7412 7332/Learning 7412 7797/www.bl.uk). Euston or King's Cross tube/rail. **Open** 9.30am-6pm Mon, Wed-Fri; 9.30am-8pm Tue; 9.30am-5pm Sat; 11am-5pm Sun, bank hols. **Admission** free; donations appreciated. **Credit** *Shop* MC, V. **Map** p317 K3.
Each year the library receives a copy of everything that is published in the UK and Ireland, including maps, newspapers, magazines, prints and drawings. Once part of the British Museum but rehoused (20 years behind schedule) in these state-of-the-art premises in 1997, the Library's burgeoning collection of 150 million-plus items is staggering – spread over 388 miles (625km) of shelves in 112,000sq m (1.2m sq ft) of space. It's mostly of interest to serious researchers but casual visitors can glimpse the King's Library: the 60,000-volume collection of George III, given to the nation in 1823 and housed in a six-storey, glass-walled tower that is the centrepiece of the building. The John Ritblat Gallery is a treasure trove: where you can admire (under glass) the Magna Carta of 1215, Leonardo da Vinci's notebook and the Lindisfarne Gospels of AD 721.
The rare old manuscripts have to be kept in dimly lit surroundings, but Turning The Pages digital kiosks let you virtually explore original manuscripts, such as *Alice In Wonderland*. Archive recordings on jukebox headphones are fun to hear – Kalahari bushmen performing a healing dance, Bob Geldof at Live Aid or the quavery voice of Florence Nightingale recorded in 1890. Other items of interest include The Beatles' scribbled lyrics alongside recordings of their songs. The long wall flanking the ground floor café holds the philatelic collection – over 80,000 stamps from around the world on view in pull-out cases.
During the summer months the Library stages a variety of events in its open-air piazza area – a haven from the thunderous thoroughfare that is the Euston Road. At other times there are regular free demonstrations of, for example, bookbinding, printing and calligraphy for children. During holidays, workshops, activities and storytelling sessions are organised for children aged five to 11 and their families. To join the free Learning mailing list, write to the address above, or call 7412 7797 or check the website. (For dates and details of all events, call the information line on 7412 7332).
Buggy access. Café. Disabled access: lift, toilet. Nappy-changing facilities. Nearest picnic place: St James' Gardens. Restaurant. Shop.

 **Lunch box**

For recommended restaurants and cafés in the area, *see p169*.
Apostrophe *216 Tottenham Court Road, W1T 7PT (7436 6688).*
Busaba Eathai *22 Store Street, WC1E 7DF (7299 7900).*
Ciao Bella *86-90 Lamb's Conduit Street, WC1N 3LZ (7242 4119).*
Cigala *54 Lamb's Conduit Street, WC1N 3LW (7405 1717).*
Coram's Fields Café *Coram's Fields WC1N 1DN (7837 6138).*
Court Café *British Museum, Great Russell Street, WC1B 3DG (7636 1555).*
Fryer's Delight *19 Theobald's Road, WC1X 8SL (7405 4114).*

Goodfellas *50 Lamb's Conduit Street, WC1N 3LH (7405 7088).*
Navarro's *67 Charlotte Street, W1T 4PH (7637 7713).*
Pizza Express *30 Coptic Street, WC1A 1NS (7636 3232).*
Sheng's Tea House *68 Millman Street, WC1N 3EF (7405 3697).*
Spaghetti House *20 Sicilian Avenue, WC1A 2QD (7405 5215).*
Wagamama *4A Streatham Street, WC1A 1JB (7323 9223).*
Wagamama *14A Irving Street, WC2H 7AF (7839 2323).*
Yo! Sushi *myhotel, 11-13 Bayley Street, WC1B 3HD (7636 0076).*

Covent Garden & the Strand

Entertainment replaced the vegetables in the Piazza long ago – and what kid wouldn't be grateful for that?

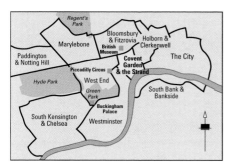

A tourist honeypot, for sure, but this attractive area of central London is a heady mix for everyone, with its cor blimey Eliza Doolittle associations sitting happily alongside bling Opera House ones. Its beautiful central piazza throngs with crowds; strolling around the central market on a bright day, one is reminded of the European café culture – the central square's original design was based on the classical Italian style.

The name Covent Garden is most likely drawn from the 'convent garden' surrounding the historic abbey on the original site. The land that belonged to the Convent of St Peter at Westminster was handed over by the Crown to John Russell, the first earl of Bedford following the dissolution of the monasteries. In the 1630s, the earl commissioned master architect Inigo Jones to design a series of Palladian arcades. These tall terraces, opening on to a central courtyard, constituted the first public square in the country and proved popular with wealthy tenants, until the fruit and vegetable market expanded on to their patch. This forced the well-to-do to move further west, in search of more fragrant lodgings, and the market came to dominate the main square. Covent Garden soon became a hangout for artists, literary and theatrical folk. In 1973 the vegetable market moved south to Vauxhall – the congested streets of central London were unsuitable for market traffic. When the traders moved out the property developers loomed large, but the area was saved from office-block ignominy through demonstrations. Now its residential community thrives alongside shops, bars and street artists – comedians, musicians etc – who perform in front of the portico of St Paul's or in the square. Every summer there are open-air operatics courtesy of the Royal Opera House. The area's oldest theatre is the Theatre Royal Drury Lane (Catherine Street, WC2B 5JF, 7494 5000); its largest is the Coliseum (St Martin's Lane, WC2N 4ES, 7632 8300), home to the English National Opera.

Covent Garden, especially around Neal Street, is dominated by pricey boutiques. Yet more fashion can be found in the trendy Thomas Neal Centre (which has a café, plus toilets with nappy-changing facilities – see security for the key). The alternative enclave of Neal's Yard is integral to the area. A lively clutter of veggie cafés, New Age crystal shops, herbalists and skate-wear emporia, the Yard remains blissfully eccentric.

Families visiting Covent Garden have been missing the terrific **Transport Museum** (Covent Garden Piazza, WC2E 7BB, 7379 6344, www.ltmuseum.co.uk) since it closed for an £18m refurbishment in August 2005.

Covent Garden

The good news is that it's opening in autumn 2007, with more exhibition space and a revitalised collection. Families will be able to explore a new learning zone, there's a bright and cheerful play area for the under-5s and all sorts of fantastic interactives throughout the Museum. Other revamped facilities will include a two-storey shop, a café overlooking the Piazza and a 120-seat theatre. The LTM's famously imaginative gift shop has, until the museum's reopening, relocated to No.26 in the nearby Covent Garden Market.

Phoenix Garden

21 Stacey Street (entrance on St Giles Passage), WC2H 8DG (7379 3187, www.phoenixgarden.org). Tottenham Court Road tube. **Open** dawn-dusk daily. **Admission** free; donations appreciated. **Map** p315 K6.

This Phoenix rose from the site of a car park, proving that all is not lost in the war against urban decay. Its peaceful crooked pathways, trellises and fragmented statues are a delightful surprise (tucked away behind the Odeon cinema on Shaftesbury Avenue). Rather handily, its entrance is right next to the playground in the garden of St Giles-in-the-Fields. The garden's planting is designed to encourage wildlife and children love the nature sanctuary in the recently extended back area of the garden. The area has new plants and flowers, boxes for birds and insects, plus benches for visitors. It's a grand spot for an urban picnic.

The garden and staff rely on volunteers; call for details of how you can help or visit on Wednesdays from 11am for the 'Clean Sweep Group' to help with duties such as weeding. Support the garden and receive invitations to activities by signing up for the quarterly newsletter. Membership forms can be picked up at the garden. The annual membership fee is £18 per household (£12 individuals, £5 concessions) and will give you advance notice of events organised for children around Hallowe'en, Bonfire Night and Christmas. Check the website for details. *Buggy access. Kiosk.*

Royal Opera House

Bow Street, WC2E 9DD (7240 1200/box office 7304 4000/www.royaloperahouse.org). Covent Garden tube. **Open** *Box office* 10am-8pm Mon-Sat. *Tours* 10.30am, 12.30pm, 2.30pm Mon-Sat (times may vary, book in advance). **Tickets** *Tours* £9; £7 9-16s, students, OAPs. **Credit** AmEx, DC, MC, V. **Map** p317 L6.

The ROH is anything but stuffy: its great glass ceilings make it a bright and airy space; regular free recital tasters are given (1-2pm Mon, pick up a ticket from the box office from 10am on the day), and the upstairs café offers terraced seating with fantastic views over the thronging crowds and street entertainments in Covent Garden. Previous hits have included *Wind in the Willows*, *Clockwork*, based on Philip Pullman's short story and *Pinocchio*. Child-friendly Christmas shows are usually planned for the 2007/8 festive season. Guided tours (no under-nines) allow curious kids a glimpse into working dressing rooms and rehearsal halls. Over-16s keen to rack up some invaluable hands-on stage experience and administration skills should apply to the ROH's education department, which runs an unpaid work-experience scheme.

Buggy access. Disabled access: lift, toilets. Nappy-changing facilities. Nearest picnic place: Covent Garden Piazza/St Paul's churchyard. Restaurants. Shop.

St Paul's Covent Garden

Bedford Street, WC2E 9ED (7836 5221/www.actors church.org). Covent Garden tube. **Open** 8.30am-5.30pm Mon-Fri; 9am-1.00pm Sun. *Services* 1.10pm Wed; 11am Sun. *Choral evensong* 4pm 2nd Sun of mth. Closed 1 Jan, bank hols. **Admission** free; donations appreciated. **Map** p317 L6.

Dominating the west side of the Piazza, St Paul's is the last extant section of Inigo Jones's original Palladian squares, and its peaceful interior offers respite from the carnival of tourists outside. It's still influenced by the theatrical heritage of its surroundings, though: the consecrated 'Actors' Church' has walls adorned with plaques commemorating the legends of screen and stage, including Charlie Chaplin, Noel Coward and Vivien Leigh. The first known victim of the plague, Margaret Ponteous, is buried in the churchyard. The church has served as a backdrop for several cameos in the history of theatre: on 9 May 1662 Samuel Pepys described being 'mighty pleased' after witnessing the first recorded Punch and Judy show here, an event marked by the annual May Fayre & Puppet Festival (held on the second Sunday in May; *see p30*), and George Bernard Shaw set the opening to *Pygmalion* under the ornate portico. That same portico is most notable today as a performance site for street entertainers. At 11am on the first Sunday of each month, Junior Church meets; under-10s can try storytelling, drama and art activities, then rejoin their parents after the service. The church also hosts regular concerts and festivals: the Royal Theatrical Fund Midsummer Fayre takes place in the church grounds on 22 July 2007, a harvest festival usually takes place in October. This event will be visited by pearly kings and queens. Moving on to Christmas, each year more than 30 carol services are held at the church, so it's all very festive.

Buggy access. Disabled access: ramp. Nearest picnic place: churchyard.

The Strand & Embankment

In the 14th century, the Strand was a residential street with desirable waterside homes. All this changed when the overflow from Covent Garden threatened to overwhelm this hitherto narrow strip. By 1600 the wealthy folk had run away, and the Strand held a reputation for poverty and bawdiness, rather like Bankside across the river. It was at this time that Sir Christopher Wren suggested the creation of a reclaimed embankment to ease congestion and house the main sewer.

At the eastern end of The Strand is the Aldwych, a grand crescent that dates to 1905, although the name 'ald wic' (old settlement) has its origins in the 14th century. On its south side is the splendidly regal Somerset house, with its courtyard attractions and art galleries. On sinister Strand Lane, reached via Surrey Street, you'll find the architecturally contentious 'Roman' Baths (7641 5264, www.nationaltrust. org.uk), another spot frequented by Dickens (he liked to take a cold plunge). They can be viewed only through a window, unless you've made an appointment with Westminster City Council.

You can feel the history in your bones at **Benjamin Franklin House**.

There's little else among the Strand's collection of overbearing office blocks and underwhelming restaurants on the Strand to really fire the imagination. Richard D'Oyly Carte's Savoy Theatre, however, which pre-dates the famous hotel by eight years, gives some indication of how the area's fortunes began to change once again after the reinforced concrete Embankment was completed.

The Embankment can be approached down Villiers Street. Cut down Embankment Place to Craven Street, where, at No.36, Benjamin Franklin lived from 1757 to 1775. Continuing down to the river you reach the embarkation point for a number of riverboat tours with on-board entertainment. Embankment Gardens is a tranquil park with an annual programme of free summer music played out on its small public stage. Near the gardens stands Cleopatra's Needle. This stone obelisk was first erected in Egypt under Pharaoh Tothmes III c1500 BC, and underwent truly epic adventures (not least of which was its being abandoned and then rescued after a storm in the Bay of Biscay in 1877) before being repositioned on the Thames in 1878.

Benjamin Franklin House

36 Craven Street, Covent Garden, WC2N 5NF (information 7930 9121/bookings 7930 6601/ www.benjaminfranklinhouse.org). Embankment tube/Charing Cross tube/rail. **Open** *11.45am-4.15pm daily.* **Admission** *£7; free under-12s, OAPs,£7. Tours noon, 1pm, 2pm, 3.15pm, 4.15pm Wed-Sun. Pre-booking essential.* **Credit** *MC, V.* **Map** *p317 L7.*

'Early to bed, early to rise, makes a man healthy, wealthy and wise.' So said Benjamin Franklin, and he should know. Not only did he coin a number of pithy phrases ('fish and visitors stink after three days' is another favourite), but this 18th-century overachiever also discovered electricity and was one of the Founding Fathers of the United States. This renaissance man – he was a scientist, inventor, philospher and diplomat – also happened to be resident of this house from 1757 to 1775. The world's only remaining home of Benjamin Franklin, it opened on 17 January 2006 – Franklin's 300th birthday – as a museum and educational facility. Visitors and school parties can embark on the Historical Experience, which uses the rooms where so much took place as staging for a drama. This 'museum as theatre' approach is highly entertaining, taking as its main character Polly Hewson, the daughter of Franklin's landlady. Polly speaks to her guests – assuming they are there to see Franklin – before he sets off back to America as the War of Independence looms.

The activities for schools here are designed to support elements of the National Curriculum and stimulate inquisitiveness, creativity and critical thought through enjoyable play-based workshops. The house incorporates the Medical History Room, where the emphasis is on the medical research work of William Hewson, Polly's husband, who operated an anatomy school at 36 Craven Street. In the Discovery Room, children are challenged to identify various objects or artefacts, to explain their function and to suggest how they are used or work. Items are set in both a historical and scientific context.

Café (at New Players Theatre). Nearest picnic place: Victoria Gardens, Embankment.

Courtauld Institute Gallery

Somerset House, Strand, WC2R ORN (7848 2777/ recorded information/Learning Centre 7420 9406/ www.courtauld.ac.uk/gallery). Covent Garden or Temple tube (closed Sun)/Charing Cross tube/rail. **Open** *10am-6pm daily (last entry 5.15pm). Tours*

Around Town

phone for details. **Admission** £5; £4 concessions; free under-18s, UK students, registered unwaged. Free to all 10am-2pm Mon (not bank hols). **Credit** MC, V. **Map** p317 M7.

The fabulous permanent collection here comprises a huge body of Impressionist and post-Impressionist paintings (including a major group of paintings by Cézanne), works by Renaissance artists and a 20th-century section including Matisse and Kandinsky. The Learning Centre brings exhibits across all three galleries at Somerset House (the Courtauld Institute, the Gilbert Collection and the Hermitage Rooms) to life. For more details, *see p217.*
Buggy access. Café. Disabled access: lift, toilet. Nappy-changing facilities. Shop.

The Gilbert Collection

Somerset House, Strand, WC2R ORN (7420 9400/ www.gilbert-collection.org.uk). Covent Garden or Temple tube (closed Sun)/Charing Cross tube/rail. **Open** 10am-6pm daily (last entry 5.15pm). *Tours* phone for details. **Admission** £5; £4 concessions; free under-18s, UK students, registered unwaged. **Credit** AmEx, MC, V. **Map** p317 M7.

These extensive displays from the collection of the late British-born property magnate Sir Arthur Gilbert were given to the nation in 1996. The jewelled curios, gleaming silverware and decorative boxes are so resplendent that families would do well to don sunglasses before entering. Ring for details of hands-on activities.
Buggy access. Café. Disabled access: lift, toilets. Nappy-changing facilities. Shop.

The Hermitage Rooms

Somerset House, Strand, WC2R ORN (7845 4630/ www.hermitagerooms.co.uk). Covent Garden or Temple tube (closed Sun)/Charing Cross tube/rail. **Open** 10am-6pm daily (last entry 5.15pm). **Admission** £5; £4 concessions; free under-18s, UK students, registered unwaged. **Credit** MC, V. **Map** p317 M7.

A window into one of the world's greatest museums – St Petersburg's State Hermitage Museum – the Rooms exhibit works from the Old Master, Impressionist and post-Impressionist collection of its Russian progenitor.
Buggy access. Café. Disabled: lift. Nappy-changing facilities. Shop.

St Clement Danes

Strand, WC2R 1DH (7242 8282). Temple tube (closed Sun)/1, 171, 172 bus. **Open** 9am-4pm Mon-Fri; 9am-3pm Sat, Sun. Closed bank hols. **Admission** free; donations appreciated. **Map** p318 M6.

No longer believed to be the church namechecked in the popular nursery rhyme 'Oranges and Lemons', St Clement's nonetheless does have bells – they ring four times daily (9am, noon, 3pm, 6pm) as well as in an annual ceremony that involves children from the local primary school choosing from a mountain of citrus fruit. The bells were silenced when the church, rebuilt by Christopher Wren (a fourth incarnation since the ninth century), was gutted by air raids in 1941. After the war, it was restored and on 19 October 1958 St Clement's was reconsecrated as the Central Church of the RAF. Spitfires may not get young pulses racing anymore, but there is a wealth of RAF memorabilia on display. The statue of Arthur 'Bomber' Harris, the man behind the RAF's brutal raids on Dresden, arouses mixed feelings.
Buggy access.

Somerset House

Strand, WC2R ORN (7845 4600/www.somersethouse.org.uk). Covent Garden or Temple tube (closed Sun)/Charing Cross tube/rail. **Open** 10am-6pm daily (last entry 5.15pm). *Courtyard & River Terrace* Apr-Sept 8am-6pm daily (extended hours apply for restaurant). **Tours** 1.30pm, 2.30pm, 3.45pm 1st Sat of mth; free. **Admission** *Parts of South Building, Courtyard & River Terrace* free. *Exhibitions* prices vary; phone for details. **Credit** MC, V. **Map** p317 M7.

One small step into the courtyard of Somerset House is one giant leap into the 18th century. The elaborate stone edifices that surround the stately courtyard shut out all but a whisper of traffic from the Strand. Erected on the site of a long-demolished Tudor palace, this grand exercise in neoclassical architecture – originally designed to house public offices – is home to three of the UK's finest galleries: the Courtauld Institute Gallery, the Gilbert Collection and the Hermitage Rooms (*see above*). Somerset House is a family destination in and of itself, most notably throughout December and January, when the courtyard becomes an attractive ice rink that, vast crowds notwithstanding, is idyllic at Christmas (but be warned: you must book well in advance to get a ticket). Equally inspired is the big square fountain in the centre, which entertains even with waterjets that dance in formation. On hot summer days, children love running down the brief corridors of water – even more so when the corridors collapse and everyone gets a soaking. The courtyard also provides a stage for events during the summer holidays, and the Family Free Time Festival takes place in July.
Buggy access. Cafés. Disabled: lift, toilet. Nappy-changing facilities. Restaurant. Shops.

☒ Lunch box

For recommended restaurants and cafés in the area, *see reviews pp170–172.*

Café Pasta *2-4 Garrick Street, WC2E 9BH (7497 2779).*
Café Rouge *34 Wellington Street, WC2E 7BD (7836 0998).*
Christopher's *18 Wellington Street, WC2E 7DD (7240 4222).*
Great American Bagel Factory *18 Endell Street, WC2H 9BD (7497 1115).*
Papageno *29-31 Wellington Street, WC2E 7DB (7836 4444).*
Pizza Express *9 Bow Street, WC2E 7AH (7240 3443); 147 Strand, WC2R 1JA (7836 7716).*
Ponti's Central Market Buildings, *Covent Garden Market, WC2E 8RA (7836 0272).*
Spaghetti House *24 Cranbourn Street, WC2H 7AB (7836 8168).*
Strada *6 Great Queen Street, WC2B 5DH (7405 6293).*
Wagamama *1 Tavistock Street, WC2E 7PG (7836 3330).*
West Cornwall Pasty Company *1 The Market, WC2E 8RA (7836 8336).*
World Food Café *1st Floor, 14 Neal's Yard, WC2H 9DP (7379 0298).*

West End

Come on foot and shop your socks off.

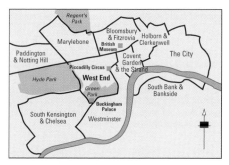

Oxford Street, Regent Street & Soho

Big spender central, Oxford Street attracts more than 200 million visitors in a year. Ironically, it is also one of the city's least-loved streets. Anyone who's ever trailed children along it will agree this is not a pleasant place to be, particularly on a Saturday afternoon, although that's all set to change (*see p72* **Hit the shops**). Yet when only a department store will do, Oxford Street still has the pick of the bunch, even if the commanding presence of John Lewis, Selfridges and Debenhams serves only to underline the tawdriness of the surrounding shops.

South of Oxford Street is Soho, with a red-light district and gay neighbourhood that may provoke some challenging questions from intrigued infants. Be careful which streets you walk down.

Running south to Piccadilly Circus, Regent Street was designed to separate the working class population from the royals at St James's Park. The Portland stone arcades were designed by John Nash, but children are likely to be more impressed by Hamleys (*see p208*). On the popular Family Day (2 September 2007), the whole of Regent Street is closed off for a Victorian-style funfair.

There may be some mileage in the West End's Chinatown, settled in the 1970s by migrants from Hong Kong. Pedestrianised Gerrard Street has gaudy street decorations, shops selling Asian produce, and Chinese New Year celebrations that usually take place in mid February.

The **Trocadero**, a former theatre converted into a giant amusement arcade, is generally loathed by big people and loved by little ones.

Handel House Museum

25 Brook Street (entrance at rear), W1K 4HB (7495 1685/www.handelhouse.org). Bond Street tube. **Open** 10am-6pm Tue, Wed, Fri, Sat; 10am-8pm Thur; noon-6pm Sun. **Admission** £5; £2 6-16s; £4.50 concessions; free under-6s. **Credit** MC, V. **Map** p316 H6.

The great German composer lived in this Georgian townhouse from 1723 to his death in 1759, while the American axeman Jimi Hendrix lived at No. 23 from 1968 to 1969. Handel's old home now contains a modern museum with whose agenda is to spread enjoyment of classical music to the next generation. As well as recitals of baroque music every Thursday, the museum has a programme of weekend concerts and Talking Music events. Saturdays are best for families, when there are all manner of story-telling, live music, dressing up, art and music activities. The main exhibition space has displays on the life and music of Handel, including letters and scores and a reproduction of Handel's harpsichord. The child-friendly ethos extends to numerous trails, quizzes and activities to go with the displays. *Buggy access. Disabled access: lift, toilet. Nappy-changing facilities. Nearest picnic place: Hanover Square. Shop.*

Handel House Museum

Around Town

Trocadero

Coventry Street, W1D 7DH (7439 1791/www. londontrocadero.com). Piccadilly Circus tube. **Open** 10am-midnight Mon-Thur, Sun; 10am-1am Fri, Sat. **Admission** free; individual attractions vary. **Credit** varies. **Map** p317 K7.

Most of the interior of this pulsating indoor complex is given over to Funland – a vast arcade of coin-in-the-slot video games that eat money faster than the purple people- eater eats people; as well as simulator rides and dance machines. The noise and disorientating lights are a fast track to tantrums and migraines.

There's a seven-screen cinema on the first floor. Other facilities include a dodgem track, a ten-lane Brunswick bowling alley, (Central London's only one) and various fast-food outlets as well as 'proper' sit-down restaurants, including child-pleasers such as the jungle-themed Rainforest Café and rowdy Planet Hollywood (*see p170 for both*). The sports bar is adults only.

Buggy access. Cafés. Disabled access: lift, toilet. Nappy-changing facilities. Nearest picnic place: Leicester Square; Trafalgar Square. Restaurants. Shops.

Piccadilly & Mayfair

Piccadilly Circus, the geographical centre of the West End, was designed in the 1820s by architect John Nash as a harmonious circle of curved frontages to mark the intersection of two most elegant streets, Regent Street and Piccadilly. It hasn't quite panned out that way, with its tacky neon billboards and traffic ruckus, but it's a landmark all the same – quite a circus. The central statue is of the Angel of Christian Charity, placed there in honour of child-labour abolitionist Earl Shaftesbury, but everyone decided it was Eros, so Eros it has stayed. It was once a gold image, but it was replaced by a less tempting lead one.

Just east of Piccadilly Circus is Leicester Square, where the latest movie blockbusters have their UK premières. Hollywood stars sometimes put in an appearance if they have a film to

Hit the shops

The West End has always been a magical place for children, with all-year treats like Hamleys (*see p208*) and seasonal specials such as the Christmas grotto at Selfridges (*see p200*), but in recent years many mums and dads have failed to be enchanted. So severe was the exodus that the Great London Authority (GLA) commissioned a survey to get to the bottom of it. The conclusion? Families have retreated en masse to the relative calm of suburban shopping centres. Armed with the reasons why, Westminster Council has vowed to woo them back.

It's no easy task luring busy parents away from the likes of Bluewater, in Kent, which they can pop to in the car, where shopping is mercifully smog-free and the loudest din is likely to be the kids themselves. Room for a buggy or two is also a condition hard to replicate on the West End's streets, but with the spotlight on London for the Olympics there was never a better time to welcome families back to the centre.

A VIP (Very Important Pedestrians) day was held in December 2006 to test the survey's conclusions and see if parents with youngsters could be persuaded back. Bingo! Families turned out in droves to shop and stroll through traffic-free streets, enjoy loads of free entertainment, goody bags and special offers. Westminster knew it was on the right track – now it was time to plan the great family comeback.

More pavement space was priority number one. Oxford Street has the busiest footfall in London, carrying almost four times the number of pedestrians estimated to be able to share its pavement space in comfort. Pickpockets' heaven it might have been, but for families with young, darting children, it was hell.

So this is the plan. Pavements along the length of Oxford Street are to be dramatically widened.

The tarmac space will have to be radically reduced to achieve this, a measure that should banish two other shoppers' gripes' simultaneously – traffic pollution and noise. At the moment the din on Oxford Street reaches over 70 decibels, making normal conversation a battle. Despite the planned traffic reduction, more buses will run through the area to relieve overstretched services. There's no magic involved; they will simply be diverted to streets around the main route.

Why was nothing done sooner? Unlike shopping centres, the West End never had a single decisive managing body to respond to requests; implementing basic improvements – like the provision of more public toilets – was fraught with red tape. None of the retail businesses was prepared to take the initiative if the others could piggy-back on the benefits for free. Cue the New West End Company (NWEC), a collective of businesses and organisations in the area set up to get everybody working together on solutions.

For visitors from out of town, a day's shopping in the West End is likely to include a spot of sightseeing. Opportunities to rest tired feet and refuel after all this frenzied activity are few and far between around here. St Christopher's place and Heddon St are examples of the little pockets of café culture around the West End's main arteries, but these, too, are full to bursting. The NWEC has planned more 'oases' around Oxford Street, which will double up as performance spaces.

The West End's principal streets will get a much-needed designer makeover with modern lighting and some arty touches – a huge illuminated halo-shaped sculpture hovering over Oxford Circus is one dramatic proposal. With work already underway on pedestrianising Marble Arch, a new family-friendly West End could be nearer than you think.

The famous statue of Eros (or is it the Angel of Christian Charity?) overlooks **Piccadilly Circus**.

promote; there's a small walk of fame with the handprints of the stars.

Piccadilly is lined with exclusive shops catering mostly for the well-heeled – **La Maison Du Chocolat** (45-46 Piccadilly, 7287 8500) may attract with its cocoa smells and the glorious **Fortnum & Mason** department store, with its top ice-cream sundaes, is generally very appealing. Designed to protect shoppers from the mud of horse-drawn Victorian London, Burlington Arcade is apparently patrolled by beadles in top hats and tails who ensure that nobody breaks the centuries-old ban on 'singing, humming or hurrying' in the arcade.

Piccadilly continues along the top of Green Park to Hyde Park Corner, with a cluster of memorials to heroes of the British Empire. On the far side of Green Park is St James's Park and **Buckingham Palace**, the most touristy place in London. **St James's** is an über-posh area bordered by Green Park, Piccadilly, Haymarket and The Mall, and does not get many visitors. St James's Palace was originally built for Henry VIII in the 1530s and has remained an official sovereign residence since then despite the fact that the monarchs have always lived in Buckingham Palace. It is now used by the Princess Royal (Anne) and not open to the public, although it's possible to attend services at the Chapel Royal here on the first Sunday of the month. Adjacent to St James's Palace sits Clarence House (The Mall, SW1A 1AA (7766 7303, www. royalcollection.org.uk), which is open from August

to mid October. This was the home of the late Queen Mother; Prince Charles and his two sons moved in after she died.

Mayfair was first developed by the Grosvenor and Berkley families in the 1700s, and most of the townhouses are set aside for diplomats and the English gentry. Children may want to pay their respects at the Animals at War memorial on Park Lane (*see p94*), commemorating the donkeys, horses, dogs, camels, elephants, carrier pigeons and canaries that died during World War I and World War II.

The Faraday Museum at the Royal Institute on Albemarle Street is closed until December 2007 for refurbishment. It will re-open with interactive displays on the miracle of electricity and a programme of science-based lectures and events for families and school groups. Contact the Royal Institute (7409 2992, www.rigb.org) for the latest developments.

Apsley House: The Wellington Museum

149 Piccadilly, Hyde Park Corner, W1J 7NT (7499 5676/www.english-heritage.org.uk). Hyde Park Corner tube. **Open** *Apr-Oct* 10am-5pm Tue-Sun. *Nov-Mar* 10am-4pm Tue-Sun. Also opens Mon bank hols. **Tours** by arrangement. **Admission** (EH) £5.10 (includes audio guide if available); £2.70 5-16s; £3.90 concessions; free under-5s. *Joint ticket with admission to Wellington Arch* £6 adults; £4.20 5-16s; £3 concessions; free under-5s; £15 family (2+3). *Tours* phone for details. **Credit** MC, V. **Map** p316 G8.

This stately Portland stone mansion was the family home of Arthur Wellesley, the first Duke of Wellington, who helped crush Napoleon at Waterloo. His descendants still live in the building, but some of it has been given over to a museum about Wellington, his campaigns and his extravagant taste in tableware. The address of Apsley House used to be No. 1 London, this being the first house seen after passing through the Knightsbridge tollgate. Considering who lived here, it seems quite appropriate.

The Regency lifestyle displayed here include the duke's settings, used for formal dinners with heads of state. The artworks add to a sense of hushed reverence, although Goya's portrait of the Iron Duke after he defeated the French in 1812 conceals a secret. X-rays revealed that Wellington's head had been brushed over that of Joseph Bonaparte, Napoleon's brother. A basement room contains Wellington's medals, death mask and boots – so named after the victory at Waterloo.

Families can pick up a 'Wellington Boot' pack with activity sheets and puzzles for children aged five to 11. Special talks and storytelling sessions for children take place on Thursdays throughout the year. Probably the most exciting time to visit is during the Waterloo Weekend in June (check the website for 2008 dates) when activities are laid on for the Waterloo memorial celebrations.
Buggy access. Lift. Nearest picnic place: Hyde Park. Shop.

Buckingham Palace & Royal Mews

SW1A 1AA (7766 7300/www.royalcollection.org.uk). Green Park or St James's Park tube/Victoria tube/rail. **Open** *State Rooms* 28 July-25 Sept 2007 9.45am-3.45pm daily. *Royal Mews* Mar-Oct 11am-3.15pm Mon-Thur, Sat, Sun (last entry 4.15pm when palace is open); 26 July-24 Sept 10am-5pm daily (last entry 4.15pm). *Queen's Gallery* 10am-4.30pm daily. Closed during Ascot & state occasions. **Admission** (LP) £15; £8 5-17s; £13.50 concessions; free under-5s; £38.50 family (2+3). *Royal Mews* £7; £4.50 5-17s; £6 concessions; free under-5s; £18.50 family (2+3). *Queen's Gallery* £8; £4 5-17s; £7 OAPs, students; free under-5s; £20 family (2+3). **Credit** AmEx, MC, V. **Map** p316 H9.

The seat of the British monarchy is one of the showpieces of the London tourism industry, pulling in millions of visitors a year. The royal stables and the state rooms are thrown open in the summer, when the Queen retires to her Scottish castle at Balmoral. Buckingham Palace has belonged to the royal family since 1762 but it became the official royal residence in 1837. It used to be smaller, but Queen Victoria moved the Marble Arch to the end of Park Lane to make way for extensions. The famous balcony, scene of many a party of waving royals, was added in 1913.

The Queen's Gallery, open year round, has collections by Rembrandt, Canaletto, Dürer, Rubens and Van Dyck as well as some exquisite Fabergé eggs and the diamond-studded diadem worn by HM on British postage stamps and coins. The big exhibition that runs until 20 January 2008 is The Art of Italy, which brings together 90 paintings and 85 drawings from royal palaces and residences across Britain.

There's a nature trail for children in the gardens and a family activity room, open throughout August. At the Royal Mews, children can watch horses being groomed, fed and exercised and examine the ostentatious Gold State Coach, last used for the 2002 Golden Jubilee.
Buggy access (baby slings supplied in State Rooms, Royal Mews). Disabled access: lift, toilet (Buckingham Palace). Nappy-changing facilities (Buckingham Palace). Nearest picnic place: Green Park. Shop.

Guards Museum

The Guards Museum

Birdcage Walk, SW1E 6HQ (7414 3430 www.theguards museum.com). Victoria tube/rail. **Open** 10am-4pm daily (last entry 3.30pm) **Admission** £3; £2 OAPs; £1 ex-military; free under-16s. **Map** p316 J9.

Displays in these small museums include all sorts of military relics – flags, medals, uniforms, drums and weapons – covering every major campaign fought by the Scots, Irish, Welsh, Grenadier and Coldstream Guards. Children will get the most out of it as a follow-up to seeing the Changing of the Guard at nearby Buckingham Palace (*see above*). There are some extremely rare and important pieces in here and the cabinets are carefully arranged so that plenty of exhibits are visible to children.

Worksheets (aimed at eight- to 14-year-olds) help children get the most out of their visit. Highlights on display include Wellington's funeral book, rare examples of 18th-century soldiers' tunics, the bearskin belonging to the 'Grand Old Duke of York', who had commanded while there were no battles to be fought – hence the nickname and nursery rhyme, a ball outfit worn by Wellington on the night before the Battle of Waterloo and a display of World War I items. Other notables include Florence Nightingale's cup, a scarf knitted by Queen Victoria for a soldier, military tunics worn by a 16-year-old Queen Elizabeth II, medical instruments used by Victorian military surgeons and the mounted head of Jacob, the pet goose of the Coldstream Guards. Staff let kids try on the 'one-size-fits-all' bearskin hats and regimental tunics they keep hidden behind the counter – they can have their photo taken for £5. The museum shop's impressive collection of toy soldiers covers just about every campaign in British military history (the toys were originally made out of lead, but these days, they're cast from metal for safety reasons).
Buggy access. Disabled access: lift, ramps. Nearest picnic place: St James's Park. Shop (closed Fri).

Royal Academy of Arts

Burlington House, Piccadilly, W1J 0BD (7300 8000/ www.royalacademy.org.uk). Green Park or Piccadilly Circus tube. **Open** *Temporary exhibitions* 10am-6pm Mon-Thur, Sat, Sun; 10am-10pm Fri. *John Madejski*

Fine Rooms 1-4.30pm Tue-Fri; 10am-6pm Sat, Sun. Opening times can vary for exhibitions. **Admission** *Fine Rooms* free. *Exhibitions* vary; free under-7s. **Credit** AmEx, DC, MC, V. **Map** p316 J7.

Housed in a fabulous 17th-century mansion, with gorgeously ornate rooms, the Royal Academy was Britain's first art school. Works by Constable, Reynolds, Degas and others are drawn from the Royal Academy's holdings and are on permanent display – free to view – in the John Madejski Fine Rooms. The main focus is on extravagant temporary exhibitions, however. The schedule for 2007 includes the Impressionists by the Sea and Making History: Antiquaries In Britain, 1707–2007. Most popular is the annual Summer Exhibition (11 June-19 Aug 2007). For more than two centuries, this exhibition has drawn from works entered by the public – anyone can submit work to the show. Some 12,000 pieces are submitted each year by hopefuls (about ten per cent make it past the judges).

Talks and activities for school groups are often programmed; activity sheets for 'art detectives' are available at reception. Interactive family workshops and gallery talks are part of the Summer Exhibition. Usually there are a few extra workshops during the school half-terms to match the current exhibition; check the website for details. *Buggy access. Café. Disabled: lift, ramp, toilets. Nappy-changing facilities. Nearest picnic place: Green Park; St James's Square. Restaurant. Shop.*

St James's Church Piccadilly

197 Piccadilly, W1J 9LL (7734 4511/www.st-james-piccadilly.org). Piccadilly Circus tube. **Open** 8am-6.30pm daily (phone for details of evening events). **Admission** free. **Map** p316 J7.

A rare piece of medieval history, St James's Church has quite a pedigree. It was designed by Christopher Wren; Grinling Gibbons carved most of the details, and Haydn, Handel and Mendelssohn were all resident organists. An unusual

Lunch box

For recommended restaurants and cafés in the area, *see pp164-186.*
Chocolate Society *32-34 Shepherd Market, W1J 7QN (7495 0302).*
Fortnum & Mason *181 Piccadilly, W1A 1ER (7734 8040).*
McDonald's *There are seven along Oxford Street from Tottenham Court Road to Marble Arch.*
Miso *66 Haymarket, SW1Y 4RF (7930 4800).*
Pâtisserie Valerie *44 Old Compton Street, W1D 4TY (7437 3466).*
Pizza Express *29 Wardour Street, W1D 6PS (7437 7215); 10 Dean Street, W1D 5RW (7437 9595); 20 Greek Street, W1D 4DU (7734 7430).*
Satsuma *56 Wardour Street, W1D 4JG (7437 8338).*
Sofra *18 Shepherd Street, W1Y 7HU (7493 3320).*
Spiga *84-86 Wardour Street, W1D OTA (7734 3444).*
Zoomslide Café *The Photographers' Gallery, 5 Great Newport Street, WC2H 7HY (7831 1772).*

outdoor pulpit was added in 1902 so that rectors could preach to the shoppers. There's a programme of evening choral performances – call for the latest schedule. From Tuesday to Saturday, there's a small but colourful market in the courtyard. Tuesday is set aside for antiques, while the rest of the week it's Covent Garden-style bric-a-brac. *Buggy access. Café. Disabled: ramp. Nearest picnic place: St James's Square; church gardens.*

St James's Park

SW1A 2JB (7930 1793/www.royalparks.org.uk). St James's Park tube/3, 11, 12, 24, 53, 211 bus. **Open** 5am-midnight daily. **Map** p317 K8.

Pelicans have lived in St James's Park ever since the Russian ambassador donated two live pelicans to King Charles II as a gesture of Anglo-Russian friendship in 1662, and their daily feeding on Duck Island is probably the most child-friendly spectacle in the West End.

The current pelicans on Duck Island, this Royal Park's most delightful location, come from Eastern Europe and America and they loiter about on an artificial skerry on the lake until 3pm, when it's feeding time at the shingled, *Hansel and Gretel*-style Duck Island Cottage. At certain times of year, park staff run guided tours of the island, with visits to nests and roosts – once dates are confirmed, they go on the park website.

If you can't time your visit to coincide with pelicans' tea, you can feed more familiar birds at stations dotted around the shore of the lake. The range of birds includes dozens of varieties of ducks, geese and seagulls, black and white swans, coots, moorhens, teals, grebes, smews…You name it, St James's has it. The honking, quacking cacophony has to be heard to be believed. Don't overlook the park squirrels – they're tame enough to take food from your hand. Duck Island is the headquarters of the London Historic Parks & Gardens Trust (7839 3969, www.londongardenstrust.org), which aims to promote and enhance London's parks and green spaces for families and young people. *Buggy access. Disabled access: toilet. Kiosk. Nappy-changing facilities. Restaurant.*

Wellington Arch

Hyde Park Corner, W1J 7JZ (7930 2726/www.english-heritage.org.uk). Hyde Park Corner tube. **Open** Apr-Oct 10am-5pm Wed-Sun. Nov-Mar 10am-4pm Wed-Sun. **Admission** (EH) £3.20; £1.60 5-16s; £2.40 concessions; free under-5s. *Joint ticket with admission to Apsley House* £6.90; £5.20 concessions; £3.50 under-16s; £16.30 family (2+3). **Credit** MC, V. **Map** p316 G8.

Built in 1828 to honour the Duke of Wellington, the monument was originally topped by a bronze statue of the duke on horseback but it was taken down and replaced by the more aesthetically pleasing Quadriga, a bronze triumphal chariot. The arch used to stand by the northwest corner of the roundabout but was moved in 1883 to reduce horse-drawn traffic congestion. The main lure for kids is the chance to get up on to the viewing deck for views out over Hyde Park Corner and the surrounding area. There's also an interesting photographic display on arches around the world that puts the monument into context. On the lower floors there are displays on the casting of the Quadriga, some delightful satirical cartoons about the ill-fated first statue, and a room where children can nominate various contemporary public figures for a commemorative blue plaque. The best way to visit is on a joint ticket with the Apsley House Museum (*see p73*). *Buggy access. Lift. Nearest picnic place: Hyde Park. Shop.*

Around Town

Marylebone

Once a felon's last view, the village by the bourne is now to die for.

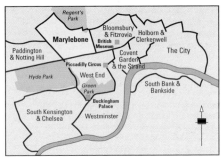

Marylebone takes its name from two sources: St Mary's Parish Church (on Marylebone Road, in various forms, since around 1400) and the Tyburn (an ancient stream, or bourne, hence Marylebone). Back in the 14th century, when the name first appeared on a map, the manors of Tyburn and neighbouring Lileston were best known for their criminal population. Tyburn, in fact, was the site of a gallows. The first execution recorded at Tyburn took place in 1196 in a place next to the stream, but in 1571 the 'Tyburn Tree' was erected near Marble Arch. The 'Tree' was a form of gallows supported by three legs, from which several felons could be hanged at once. On 23 June, 1649, as many as 24 prisoners were hanged simultaneously.

The squares leading off Marylebone High Street are serene places to walk. Treasures to admire are the glorious gilded **Wallace Collection**, whose appearance belies an accommodating attitude to children. The Gothic Roman Catholic church of St James, Spanish Place (22 George Street, W1, 7935 0943) is another inspiring place for a sit-down. Keep strolling in a northerly direction for busy Marylebone Road, which you have to negotiate if you want to manhandle celebs in top tourist destination, **Madame Tussauds**.

London Central Mosque

146 Park Road, NW8 7RG (7724 3363/www.iccuk.org). Baker Street tube/13, 82, 133 bus. **Open** *9.30am-6pm daily.* **Admission** *free.*
Offices around a large courtyard accommodate the Islamic Cultural Centre, bookshop and information booth. Visitors must remove their shoes; women should wear a headscarf. *Buggy access. Café. Disabled access: ramp, toilet. Nappy-changing facilities. Nearest picnic place: Regent's Park. Shop.*

London Zoo

Regent's Park, NW1 4RY (7722 3333/www.zsl.org). Baker Street or Camden Town tube then 274 or C2 bus. **Open** *Mar-late Oct* 10am-5.30pm daily. *Late Oct-Feb* 10am-4pm daily. Check website for any changes. **Admission** £14.50 (£16 with voluntary contribution); £13 concessions; £11.50 3-15s; free under-3s; £48.50 family (2+2 or 1+3). **Credit** AmEx, MC, V. **Map** p314 G2.
One thing that hasn't changed about the Zoological Society of London (aka London Zoo) since its inception in 1826 is its ability to 'interest and amuse the public' (Sir Stamford Raffles, Founder). Today the interest and amusement is finely balanced with the charity's ethical concerns: conservation, education, eco-tourism to name just three. The main thrust of the zoo is to keep its inhabitants content and dignified: in recent years millions of pounds have gone into more naturalistic enclosures and 'bringing down the bars' to render the animals more visible to the viewing public. A case in point is Gorilla Kingdom (*see p77* **Kingdom Kong**). Habitat work continues apace. Visitors have also been treated to walk-through monkey and bird enclosures and the brilliant Butterfly Paradise – an inflatable butterfly tunnel shaped like a caterpillar and filled with hundreds of free-flying tropical butterflies and moths. Then there's the chance to go face-to-face with a pack of African hunting dogs and eye-to-eye with a giraffe via a high-level viewing platform in Into Africa. Don't miss BUGS (the biodiversity centre with its ant empire and cockroach quarters).

Don't be a-llama-ed. It's **London Zoo**.

The Animals in Action talk in the amphitheatre give you a chance to meet destinked skunks and jolly kinkjou to meet. Feeding time for the penguins now takes place in a more naturalistic enclosure near the shop, as the famous listed Lubetkin pool doesn't suit them. The meerkats, the otters, the children's zoo and the Activity Centre are much loved by small visitors.

There are eating places all over the park, or bring a picnic. Blindfold the children near the bouncy castles, carousel and huge shop to save your wallet.
Buggy access. Café. Disabled access: ramps, toilet. Nappy-changing facilities. Nearest picnic space: zoo grounds. Restaurant. Shop.

Madame Tussauds
Marylebone Road, NW1 5LR (0870 400 3000/www. madame-tussauds.co.uk). Baker Street tube/13, 27, 74, 113, 159 bus. **Open** 9.30am-6pm daily (last entry 5.30pm). Times vary during holiday periods. **Admission** *9.30am-5pm Mon-Fri, 9.30am-6pm Sat, Sun* £23.99; £20.99 concessions; £19.99 5-15s. *5-5.30pm daily* £15; £13 concessions; £10 5-15s. Internet booking only for family tickets. **Credit** AmEx, MC, V. **Map** p314 G4.
Tourist attraction extraordinaire Madame Tussauds has its roots in the 18th century and Marie Tussaud (1761-1850), who made wax death masks during the French revolution. When she came to London in 1802, she brought a

Kingdom Kong

Opened by the HRH the Duke of Edinburgh in March 2007, Gorilla Kingdom is ZSL London Zoo's biggest project in 40 years. The development cost £5.3 million to build – prime real estate for three pampered primates called Bobby, Zaire and Effie. The enclosure is designed to look as much like the African rainforest as possible for the gorillas, who look less than chuffed at having their privacy compromised by the larger colony of fellow primates in fleeces and jeans wielding camera phones on the other side of the glass walls of the indoor enclosure. (Note to visitor: researchers have warned against looking at gorillas straight in the eye, they take offence.) Not that the gorilla trio are unused to the attention. None of them has much experience of the wild. Bobby (Bongo Junior) was born in Guinea but captured for the circus as a baby; since then he's been a zoo man, on loan from Rome in order to mate with the females in the colony – his wild birth makes him genetically important for breeding purposes. His older girlfriend, Zaire (Ziggy) was born in Jersey Zoo, and is destined for the role of spinster aunt, entertaining any offspring Bobby might produce with Effie, the young elegante introduced from Leipzig Zoo, whose slim build has inspired her keepers to describe her as the Kate Moss of the gorilla colony.

The Gorilla Kingdom environment certainly looks attractive as it is, with its planting carefully researched to make it look like a forest clearing in Gabon, its moat, 'enriching' gym and indoor quarters, not to mention the outdoor areas filled with a group of Colobus monkeys, fast-moving little black and white numbers. Walking around the special Gorilla Trail in the kingdom, admiring the jungly bits, you're reassured that animal husbandry has come a long way. The main test of the new enclosure, however, will be whether Effie and Bobby show the need to breed, a sure sign that they feel at home.

The most famous gorilla ever to have groomed himself in the public eye was Guy. He was a year old when he came to London Zoo from Paris Zoo in exchange for a tiger on Guy Fawkes Day of 1947. His early friends were a young chimpanzee

and an orang-utan. One of the most popular animals in the history of the Zoo, Guy was given a mate, Lomie, in 1969, but they did not breed. In those days, the animals' enclosures were basic and rather boring, and visitors were not prevented from feeding the animals with inappropriate treats. Guy was given too many sweets and chocs, and his teeth deteriorated. It was while under anaesthetic to deal with his decayed gnashers that the poor chap died. He was just 32. Today a healthy diet plays a major part in a celebrity gorilla's lifestyle. Effie, as we have heard, watches her figure and Bobby drinks litres of herbal fruit tea every day. He wouldn't touch a Mars Bar for all the fruit tea in Holland & Barrett, thank you very much.

Around Town

collection of masks left to her by her teacher Dr Philippe Curtiius, one of which was of Marie-Jeanne du Barry, Louis XV's mistress. A cast of that mould is the oldest work currently on display as the reclining figure of a breathing, animatronic Sleeping Beauty.

Today's Madame Tussauds is a flurry of crowds and interactives. Figures are constantly being added and updated. Kylie Minogue and the Queen have been recast four times (the latest Kylie smells of her new scent). Kate Moss joined the A-list in February 2007, not long after Christina Aguilera earned herself a wax figure and interactive singing experience. Elsewhere, children adore the *Pirates of the Caribbean* display set in the hull of the *Black Pearl*, with Keira, Orlando and, of course Johnny. The World Stage hall is a fully interactive room split into various zones for sports, culture, politics and current music, royals and history. Holographic imagery and touch screens provide hands-on action, although nobody stops the public from snogging, hugging and pinching stars' bottoms.

Once you've muscled your way through celebsville, been terrified witless in the Chamber of Horrors (parents, don't let young children go through the 'live' experience) and everyone has enjoyed their time-travel ride – The Spirit of London, which takes you through 400 years of London life in a taxi pod – there's the Stardome. This used to be the Planetarium show; now it's an Aardman show of breathtaking banality called The Wonderful World of Stars. *Café. Disabled access: lift, toilet. Nappy-changing facilities. Nearest picnic place: Regent's Park. Shop.*

Regent's Park

The Store Yard, Inner Circle, Regent's Park, NW1 4NR (7486 7905/boating lake 7724 4069/www.royalparks. gov.uk). Baker Street, Camden Town, Great Portland Street or Regent's Park tube. **Open** 5am-30mins before dusk daily. **Admission** free. **Map** p314 G3.

One of London's most treasured green spaces, Regent's Park, as the name suggests, had right royal beginnings. It was Henry VIII's hunting land, then landscaped in 1811 for use as a private residential estate. The park finally opened its gates to the great unwashed in 1845 – for two days a week – during the reign of Queen Victoria; even then, it was only for two days a week. Today, however, we're allowed in, 365 days a year, to admire the planting

schemes in the flower beds, the heronry on the lake, the wonderful café (*see p182*) and the open-air theatre (*see p229*) and the free concerts in the bandstand.

Sporty types appreciate the park for the Hub, the name given to the biggest outdoor sports facility in central London; it boasts tennis and netball courts, an athletics track, football and hockey pitches and a new sports pavilion. Check the website for an energetic programme of school holidays sports courses and events – sessions that may include cricket, footie, TAG rugby and rounders cost just 50p each and are suitable for ages six to 13.

There are four playgrounds, each with a sandpit and toilets. The shallow boating lake is one of the nicest places to spend a summer's afternoon, with rowing boats available for hire by the hour (£6.50/hr adults, £4.40 children), but there is also a small, circular lake for children who want to mess about in pedalos. These cost £3 for 20 minutes and the youngsters must pass a height test to use them. *Buggy access. Cafés. Disabled access: toilets. Nappy-changing facilities.*

Sherlock Holmes Museum

221B Baker Street, NW1 6XE (7935 8866/www. sherlock-holmes.co.uk). Baker Street tube/74, 139, 189 bus. **Open** 9.30am-6pm daily (last entry 5.30pm). **Admission** £6; £4 6-16s; free under-6s. **Credit** AmEx, MC, V. **Map** p311 F4.

Children look a bit bewildered when you explain that this is the home of Britain's most famous detective, who in fact never existed. Such is the blurring between fact and fiction that pilgrims visiting this, Sherlock Holmes's faithfully constructed home, often ask where the great man was buried. When the famous books were written, No.221 was a fictional address: Baker Street didn't extend that far. Now, however, it does, and by some bizarre coincidence, the building on the real 221 Baker Street is being developed into luxury flats by a company called Baskerville Estates. Fans of the books delight in the care with which fictional detail has been faithfully reproduced. The house is set up as if the master detective and associate are in situ, complete with affable housekeeper Mrs Hudson, who can tell you all you need to know about the detective, whose chair can keep warm in his study. Upstairs is the room belonging to his sidekick Watson. The

---

✖ Lunch box

For recommended restaurants and cafés in the area, see reviews pp164-86.

ASK 56-60 Wigmore Street, W1U 2RZ (7224 3484).
Caffè Caldesi 118 Marylebone Lane, W1U 2QF (7935 1144).
Carluccio's Caffè St Christopher's Place, W1U 1AY (7935 5927); 8 Market Place, W1W 8AG (7636 2228).
Eat & Two Veg 50 Marylebone High Street, W1U 5HN (7258 8595).
Garden Café Inner Circle, Regents Park, NW1 4NU (7935 5729).
Giraffe 6 Blandford Street, W1U 4AU (7935 2333).
Golden Hind 73 Marylebone Lane, W1U 2PN (7486 3644).
Honest Sausage Broadwalk, off Chester Road,

Regent's Park, NW1 4NU (7224 3872).
La Spighetta 43 Blandford Street, W1U 7HF (7486 7340).
Le Pain Quotidien 72-75 Marylebone High Street, W1U 5JW (7486 6154).
Oasis Café London Zoo, Regent's Park, NW1 4RY (7722 3333).
Pâtisserie Valerie at Sagne 105 Marylebone High Street, W1U 4RS (7935 6240).
Paul 115 Marylebone High Street, W1U 4SB (7224 5615).
Pizza Express 13-14 Thayer Street, W1U 3JS (7935 2167).
Tootsie's Grill 35 James Street, W1M 5HX (7486 1611).
Wagamama 101A Wigmore Street, W1U 1QR (7409 0111).

The **Sherlock Holmes Museum**, I deduce.

third-floor exhibit rooms contain a new arrangement of wax models of scenes from the stories. Sherlock Holmes and Professor Moriarty can be seen in the same room. The lumber room in the attic, where the lodgers used to store their trunks and luggage, is also open to visitors, who then rush downstairs to browse the extensive range of Sherlockian merchandise in the shop.
Nearest picnic place: Regent's Park. Shop.

Wallace Collection

Hertford House, Manchester Square, W1U 3BN (7935 0687/www.wallacecollection.org). Bond Street tube/ 2, 10, 12, 30, 74, 113 bus. **Open** 10am-5pm daily. Closed 1 Jan, Good Fri, 1 May, 24-26 Dec. **Admission** free. **Credit** *Shop* MC, V. **Map** p314 G5.
A collection of beautiful rooms full of priceless paintings, furniture, and, of most interest to children, armour, swords and daggers. The largest part of the collection was amassed by the Fourth Marquess of Hertford, a great Francophile who had bought it for safekeeping from the ravages of the French Revolution; he left it to his son Sir Richard Wallace, hence the name. Visitors' facilities include a lecture theatre and a dedicated education room for schools. Café Bagatelle in the central courtyard is a splendid place for a light lunch, and they have a children's menu. The Study and Oval Drawing Rooms are recreated in the style of Marie Antoinette's Versailles boudoir and include objects once housed in her royal palaces.

Prize paintings in the main collections include Frans Hals's *Laughing Cavalier* and Fragonard's *The Swing*. On the first Sunday of every month there is 'The Little Draw,' during which families can pick up art materials and a drawing board and get sketching with help from the gallery's in-house artist. The armour workshops (check the website for the next one) let kids discover how heavy the armour and weapons are, letting them handle items like 3,000-year-old bronze swords and oriental daggers decorated with jade and gold. Check the website for daily events. *See also p233* **Drawing on the experience**. *Buggy access. Disabled access: lift, toilet. Nappy-changing facilities. Nearest picnic place: grounds. Restaurant. Shop.*

St John's Wood

Walking up from Baker Street, keeping Regent's Park to your right, you pass Dorset Square, which bears a plaque marking it out as the birthplace of Marylebone Cricket Club (Thomas Lord staged his first MCC match here in 1787). A new rural ground, formerly a duck pond, was found for the MCC in 1814 and **Lord's Cricket Ground** has been there ever since. The area round here is upmarket and residential. The grounds of St John's Wood Church (Lord's Roundabout, NW8 7NE, 7586 3864), with its picnic tables, wildlife walk, meadow ground and play area, are a useful stopping-off point before or after visiting the cricket museum. St John's Wood High Street is well thought of for its high-class traditional purveyors of organic and free-range foods, a variety of smart children's and women's boutiques and a pleasant, villagey atmosphere.

Further north is **Abbey Road**, home of the recording studios and immortalised on the cover of the Beatles album of the same name.

Lord's Cricket Ground & MCC Museum

St John's Wood Road, NW8 8QN (7616 8500/tours 7432 1033/www.lords.org). St John's Wood tube/13, 46, 82, 113, 274 bus. **Open** *Tour* Oct-Mar noon, 2pm daily. *Apr-Sept* 10am, noon, 2pm daily. Closed 1 Jan, 25, 26 Dec, all major matches & preparation days; phone to check. **Admission** *Tour* £10; £7 concessions; £6 5-15s; free under-5s; £27 family (2+2). **Credit** MC, V.
Tours of Lord's let visitors go behind the scenes at MCC's historic ground, taking in the Long Room, in the heart of the Pavilion, which is both a cricket-watching room and a cricket art gallery, then on to the MCC Museum, where paintings, photographs and artefacts, covering 400 years of cricket history, reveal the game's development. Eccentric exhibits include a stuffed sparrow and cricket ball (the bird was killed by the ball in 1936 – a truly freak cricketing accident). The Museum's most precious exhibits include the Wisden Trophy and the delicate Ashes urn (yes, we have it, even though the Aussies destroyed England in the 2006 series). Other attractions include the Tennis Court, where Real Tennis (one of King Henry VIII's favourite pastimes) is still played, and the MCC Indoor Cricket School with their 100mph bowling machines. Cricket kit and equipment for children and adults is available for purchase. *Buggy access. Disabled access: toilets. Lifts. Nappy-changing facilities. Nearest picnic place: St John's churchyard playground. Shop.*

Westminster

The city's historic pin-ups lined up.

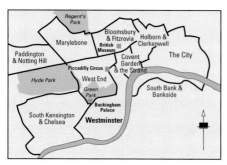

Around Town

Top of most tourists' sightseeing agenda, central Westminster is anchored by the country's powerhouse – the Houses of Parliament – but its beating heart is Trafalgar Square, scene of mass civic gatherings. This area of London became pivotal almost 1,000 years ago, when Edward the Confessor built his church, West Minster, on marshy Thorney Island, to the west of the established city. The minster stood on the site now occupied by Westminster Abbey. Today, the Abbey competes with Charles Barry's neo-Gothic Palace of Westminster for prominence on Parliament Square. The only surviving fragment of the original medieval palace of Westminster is the Jewel Tower, which has a permanent exhibition dedicated to the development of Parliament. In the central garden of Parliament Square, laid out in 1868, statues of great British Prime Ministers Benjamin Disraeli and Winston Churchill are soon to be joined by a statue of Nelson Mandela – a vote in the South African's favour was announced in April 2007.

Running from this square to the much more public one, the long, gentle curve of Whitehall is named after Henry VIII's palace, which burned down in 1698. It's lined by grandiose buildings that you're not allowed into, but Whitehall is most memorable (for children at least) for the steely-eyed Horse Guards standing outside their building, which stands opposite Banqueting House. Downing Street itself holds little interest for children: you can't get anywhere near numbers 10 or 11 as you used to before Mrs Thatcher stepped up security with iron railings. Nearby, the Cenotaph is Edward Lutyen's memorial to the

dead of both world wars. A few hundred feet away stands the busier bronze memorial to the women of World War II, which features 17 sets of work clothes hanging on pegs (when the war was over women were told to give up their work outside the home). At the end of King Charles Street sit the Cabinet War Rooms – Winston Churchill's operation centre during air raids on London.

Behind many of the grand buildings of Westminster there are numerous secluded spaces to discover among the hubbub. Within walking distance of Parliament Square is St James's Park (see p75), Westminster Abbey College Garden and the less well-known Victoria Tower Gardens (off Millbank), whose small playground occupies a riverside space next to Parliament. A stroll along Victoria Street leads you to Westminster Cathedral, whose viewing gallery at the top of the Campanile Bell Tower is a must.

Trafalgar Square is London's centrepiece. Children clamber gleefully over the lions guarding the 52-metre (170-foot) testament to Britain's most celebrated military commander, Lord Nelson, but the ban on pigeon feeding by Mayor Ken in 2001 has meant a steady decline in the number of fat feathered Londoners in the square. The Fourth Plinth project features one piece of contemporary sculpture every other year to occupy the empty plinth on the north-west corner of the square (the others are fairly starchy bronze busts). The current winner (Marc Quinn's gentle *Alison Lapper Pregnant*) will be replaced by German artist Thomas Schütte's refractive perspex colourscape, *Hotel for the Birds*, later in 2007.

The Summer in the Square festival of outdoor performances, dance and music runs every year and is organised by the office of the Mayor of London; visit www.london.gov.uk for more information. Overlooking the square is the National Gallery, first of Westminster's world-class trio of treasure troves. The smaller but equally impressive National Portrait Gallery is tucked behind it on St Martin's Place. The third artistic giant can be found on Millbank, which runs along the river from Parliament to Vauxhall Bridge. Tate Britain occupies the former site of the Vauxhall Penitentiary, one of Victorian London's more ghastly prisons, eventually demolished in

Houses of Parliament. Big Ben is the bell inside the tower. *See p82.*

1890. They say the ghost of a past inmate haunts the cellars of a pub (the Morpeth Arms) nearby.

Trafalgar Square's eastern edge is overlooked by St Martin-in-the-Fields (Trafalgar Square, WC2N 4J; 7766 1100,www.stmartin-in-the-fields.org), the parish church for Buckingham Palace (*see p74*), whose crypt is home to the London Brass Rubbing Centre and a great café. It's closed for renovations until September 2007; check the website for details.

Banqueting House

Whitehall, SW1A 2ER (0870 751 5178/ www.hrp.org.uk). Westminster tube/Charing Cross tube/rail. **Open** 10am-5pm Mon-Sat (last entry 4.30pm). Sometimes closes at short notice; phone to check. **Admission** £4.50; £3.50 concessions; £2.25 5-15s; free under-5s. **Credit** MC, V. **Map** p317 L8.
On 30 January 1649, outside Banqueting House, King Charles I gave his cloak to the presiding Bishop and lay down with his head on a low block. With one blow the executioner severed his head from his body. 'A groan as I never heard before, and desire I may never hear again' went up from the watching crowd. This was not the sort of state occasion architect Inigo Jones had had in mind for his magnificent building, which had opened with much jollification 27 year before. Its regicidal associations may pull in today's tourists (the Sealed Knot Civil War Re-enactment Society plays out the execution one Sunday each January), although the building is a sight to see quite apart from its

bloodstained history. Rubens's original ceilings are still in place, despite extensive fire damage in 1698 and removal for their own safety during World War II. Audio guides (included in the ticket price) bring the scene to life for children. The Hall is also a venue for regular lunchtime classical concerts throughout the year. These are primarily aimed at adults, but there's a lighter Christmas concert in December (check the website for the date). *Buggy storage. Disabled access: toilets. Nearest picnic place: St James's Park. Shop.*

Churchill Museum & Cabinet War Rooms

Clive Steps, King Charles Street, SW1A 2AQ (7930 6961/www.iwm.org.uk). St James's Park or Westminster tube/3, 12, 24, 53, 159 bus. **Open** 9.30am-6pm daily (last entry 5pm). **Admission** £11; £9 concessions; free under-16s (prices incl audio guides). **Credit** MC, V. **Map** p317 K9.
Churchill's secret underground HQ in World War II, the Cabinet War Rooms resembles a time capsule, sealed against the intervening years. The same maps chart progress on the same walls; the same steel beams – hurriedly erected to reinforce the building against bombs – still line the low ceilings. It's an atmospheric and effective installation guaranteed to bring the period to life for kids, who can take advantage of a number of activities. An expanded programme of family workshops runs in the school holidays; ring for details.

The Churchill Museum has as its centrepiece an enormous digital Lifeline (essentially a flat-screen monitor the length and breadth of a banquet hall table), in which is stored, chronologically, thousands of Churchill-related documents and images. There's also a wooden mock-up of his family home in Chatsworth, Kent. The big event for 2007 is Dig for Victory, which takes place both here and in St James Park (*see p75*). Spin-off summer specials include Green City Week (23-27 July 2007) and Healthy Living Week (27-31 August 2007). *See also p83* **Dig for Victory**. *Buggy access. Café. Disabled access: lift, toilets. Nappy-changing facilities. Nearest picnic place: St James's Park. Shop.*

Houses of Parliament

Parliament Square, SW1A 0AA (Commons info 7219 3000/Lords info 7219 3107/tours 7219 4206/ www.parliament.uk). Westminster tube. **Open** (when in session) *House of Commons Visitors' Gallery* 2.30-10.30pm Mon, Tue; 11.30am-7.30pm Wed; 10.30am-6.30pm Thur; 9.30am-3pm Fri. Closed bank hols. *House of Lords Visitors' Gallery* from 2.30pm Mon, Tue; from 3pm Wed; from 11am Thur, Fri. Check website for debate times. *Tours* summer recess only; phone for details for other times. **Admission** *Visitors' Gallery* free. *Tours* £12; £5 5-15s; free under-5s, disabled; £30 family (2+2). **Credit** *Tours* MC, V. **Map** p317 L9.
The Palace of Westminster became a permanent home for Parliament in 1532, when Henry VIII relocated to Whitehall. These days, the only parts of the original palace still standing are Westminster Hall, where the Queen Mother's body lay in state before her funeral in 2002, and the Jewel Tower (*see below*); the rest was destroyed by fire in 1834. The building we see today was rebuilt by Charles Barry and Augustus Pugin. Children are usually satisfied by the mere proximity of the big old bell known as Big Ben (the tower is St Stephen's). UK residents can visit Parliament to watch laws being made, attend debates, committees or judicial hearings, use the Archives, tour the estate and climb the Clock Tower. Public committee sessions – meetings take place Monday to Thursday most weeks when Parliament is sitting – are open to everyone. Visitors queue on the day, as places cannot be booked in advance. Tickets from your MP or a Lord are necessary to secure entrance to Question Time and Prime Minister's Question Time in the House of Commons. Everyone aged from 11 can climb the Clock Tower to have a closer look at Big Ben, but note that the tower will be closed between 28 August-7 October 2007 for maintenance.
Buggy access. Disabled access: lifts, toilets. Nappy-changing facilities. Nearest picnic place: Victoria Tower Gardens. Shop.

Jewel Tower

Abingdon Street, SW1P 3JY (7222 2219/www. english-heritage.org.uk). Westminster tube. **Open** *Apr-Oct* 10am-5pm daily. *Nov-Mar* 10am-4pm daily. (last entry 30mins before closing). **Admission** (EH) £2.90; £2.20 concessions; £1.50 5-16s; free under-5s. Phone to check prices for special events. **Credit** MC, V. **Map** p317 L9.
Emphatically not the home of the Crown Jewels (you'll see those at the Tower of London (*see p56*), this tower was the 'King's Privy Wardrobe', originally built to house the private treasures of Edward III. It's one of the two parts of medieval Westminster Palace still standing. Since being built, the tower has served as a repository for parliamentary records and a Board of Trade testing centre for weights and measures, but these days English Heritage keeps it open to the public – winding staircases, unrestored

Trafalgar Square. *See p80.*

ribbed vault and all. A Parliament Past and Present exhibition looks at the development of today's parliamentary structure. Upstairs there are illustrated panels depicting the history of this significant little scrap of a building. Take the kids to see the ancient sword on display in the on-site shop. It dates back to around AD 800 and looks like something on loan from Middle Earth.
Nearest picnic place: surrounding green. Shop.

National Gallery

Trafalgar Square, WC2N 5DN (information 7747 2885/www.nationalgallery.org.uk). Charing Cross tube/rail/24, 29, 176 bus. **Open** 10am-6pm Mon, Tue, Thur-Sun; 10am-9pm Wed. *Tours* 11.30am, 2.30pm daily; additional tours 6pm, 6.30pm Wed, 12.30pm, 3.30pm Sat. **Admission** free. *Temporary exhibitions* prices vary. *Tours* free. **Credit** *Shop* MC, V. **Map** p317 K7.
It started with just 38 paintings, but now our national collection has more than 2,000 Western European pieces. There are masterpieces from virtually every school of art, but the national treasure would mean little to younger guests if it weren't for the accessibility of the place. If you have a buggy to push, enter via the impressive Getty Entrance for step-free access from Trafalgar Square. Pick up a plan at the info desk opposite the door and make for the Impressionists (room 45), where you'll find a wall of Van Goghs. There's also an atmospheric Monet, *London at Westminster*, painted in 1871. The unmissable *Bathers*

at *Asnières* by Seurat is in the next room. The famed *Execution of Lady Jane Grey* is in room 41 – children are fascinated by Lady Jane, who was queen for nine days in 1553 and beheaded at just 17 years old at the Tower of London. The long gallery (room 34) has many celebrities: Stubbs's fabulous painting of the stallion Whistlejacket hangs opposite Constable's *Hay Wain* and Turner's *The Fighting Temeraire*. Young ones after something gory will like room 24, where there's the impressive *Two Followers of Cadmus Devoured by a Dragon* by Cornelis van Haarlem, and, in the Sainsbury Wing galleries, an image of David holding the head of Goliath and Paolo Uccello's *Saint George and the Dragon*.

There are listening posts offering headphone commentaries on more than 1,000 pieces from the collection. ArtStart computer terminals in the Espresso Bar on Level 0 allow visitors to personalise and print out their own themed tour, free. The National's online facilities are an excellent resource for use in the gallery, or when you get home to look up the history of a favourite painting. There are also audio tours and paper trails (A Right Royal Tour, for example, in which you're led by journalists Tania Fawningely Grovel and Jimmy Snoop on the hunt for royal figures in paintings). The laid-back children's workshops include the Magic Carpet storytelling sessions, aimed at under-fives, which run on weekdays during school holidays, and the Second Weekend workshops, led by a contemporary artist. All materials are provided, and the hour-long sessions take place at 11.30am on Saturdays and Sundays (repeated at 2.30pm). The remaining three weekends of the month bring staff talks, starting at 11.30am.

Check the gallery website for details of holiday workshops for families and teenagers. Forthcoming free exhibitions include Scratch the Surface (20 July-4 November 2007), which commemorates the 200th anniversary of the abolition of slavery and Work Rest & Play (26 July-14 October 2007) which explores changing attitudes to hard graft and leisure time from the 16th century to the present day. The big exhibition coming up (with an admission charge) is Renaissance Siena: Art for a City (24 October 2007-13 January 2008). The Oliver Peyton restaurant here is just fabulous (*see p172*).
Buggy access. Café. Disabled access: lift, toilets. Nappy-changing facilities. Nearest picnic place: Leicester Square/Trafalgar Square. Restaurant. Shop.

National Portrait Gallery

2 St Martin's Place, WC2H 0HE (7306 0055/ tours 7312 2483/www.npg.org.uk). Leicester Square tube/Charing Cross tube/rail/24, 29, 176 bus. **Open** 10am-6pm Mon-Wed, Sat, Sun; 10am-9pm Thur, Fri. *Tours* times vary, phone for details. *Temporary exhibitions* prices vary. *Audio guide* £2. *Tours* free. **Credit** AmEx, MC, V. **Map** p317 K7.

Awarded Best Large Visitor Attraction at the Visit London awards, the NPG is a unique treat for all ages. The collections are concerned with history, not art, gathering together a pantheon of those who have contributed to creating British society. A short wander around its halls will turn up faces as far removed as William Shakespeare (the only known contemporary portrait of the bard) and Benny Hill (not quite such a rarity), captured in a variety

Dig for Victory

Contrary to popular belief, World War II did not result in the creation of allotments – areas of unused urban land given over to private gardening. But the conflict certainly turned what was already a worthy feature of city life into a national cause. Suddenly Great Britain noticed that three-quarters of her food was imported and easily cut off by a few U-boats. So the cry went up: 'Grow your own!' and local councils dug up the royal parks and even the moat round the Tower of London and marked out neat plots of land measuring 30m by 9m (100ft by 30ft), which they rented to anyone who applied for them for a peppercorn sum per year.

In memory of this inspiring call to self-sufficiency, an allotment-sized portion of St James' Park has now been fenced off by the royal park keepers, fertilised with royal manure from the royal horseguards' horses and planted with the sort of market garden vegetables suitable for a sturdy, rich, indeed royal, ration-era broth. The idea belongs to the marketing and education departments at the Cabinet War Rooms museum (*see p81*), situated in the very bunker beneath the Treasury from where Churchill directed the Allied campaign. (Look at the Map Room. How evocative! Oh, and that's where Churchill slept and that's his potty.) An exhibition of propaganda photographs – featuring ordinary joes at their hoes, 'Dig For Victory' posters and

documents (ration books etc) – begins in the museum and continues at the allotment, itself a five-minute walk away across the road, surrounded by deckchairs in the park.

The allotment is divided into two beds with paved paths around each. One is planted as it would have been in the war, the other as it might be today. This will enable comparison between, say, the different potato varieties, 'Home Guard' and 'Sharp's Express'. The wartime one, apparently, was more prolific but less tasty.

The contemporary allotment has a raised bed (so that seniors don't have to bend down) and is planted with herbs – ginger, chives, lemon grass, fennel, basil, and coriander. The war one has an Anderson Shelter, a thick corrugated iron hut which Londoners were encouraged to buy at £7 each (free to the very poor), half-bury in their gardens and repair to at the sound of the air-raid siren, although how many actually left comfortable beds in the middle of the night for a cold, dank plank in the garden is not recorded.

Entry to the allotment is free (the museum has an admission charge) and it already has a programme of school and community group visits for the summer. Cookery sessions – how to make wartime carrot cake – are planned, as is a secular harvest festival at the end. It's a temporary allotment and will probably be grassed over again in October 2007. We think they should keep it.

of media (paintings, photographs, sculptures) by artists ranging from medieval illuminators to celebrity snappers like Mario Testino. The permanent collection is organised by period, so you can select an area, such as the Elizabethans, Victorian portrait photography or British portraits from 1990, to peruse. Upcoming exhibitions include Four Corners (until 5 August 2007), which celebrates through portraiture London's many different cultures, the BP Portrait and Travel Award (14 June to 16 September 2007) and the Photographic Portrait Prize 2007 (8 November 2007-24 February 2008). To help children fathom the exhibitions, there are family rucksacks – lent on a first-come, first-served basis – which correspond to one of three galleries: Tudor, Victorian and 20th century. Each rucksack is stuffed with activities (for three- to 12-year-olds) from jigsaws and dressing-up items to paper trails. There are also regular holiday workshops. Log on to the website to join the e-list and receive monthly information on family events, exhibitions and talks. Free trails are available from the information desk. Monthly Are You Sitting Comfortably storytelling sessions are for under-fives and Small Faces art activities for over-fives are usually held on the third Saturday of each month, but check before visiting.
Buggy access. Café. Disabled access (Orange Street entrance): lifts, ramps, toilets. Nappy-changing facilities. Nearest picnic place: Leicester Square/Trafalgar Square. Restaurant. Shops.

Tate Britain

Millbank, SW1P 4RG (7887 8008/www.tate.org.uk). Pimlico tube/88, 77A, C10, bus. **Open** 10am-5.50pm daily; late opening 6-10pm first Fri of mth. *Tours* 11am, noon, 2pm, 3pm Mon-Fri; noon, 3pm Sat, Sun. **Admission** free. *Temporary exhibitions* prices vary. *Tours* free. **Credit** MC, V. **Map** p317 L7.
Big sister to the Modern one (*see p46*), this Tate collection of British fine art from 1500 to the present day unites artists from Blake to Bacon. As well as the permanent exhibition, regular temporary shows are staged in several large halls. Until 27 August 2007 there's the Turner-shortlisted Mark Wallinger: State Britain, a dramatic installation comprising peace campaigner Brian Haw's Parliament Square protest. Until 21 October 2007, the special display, 1807: Blake, Slavery and the Radical Mind marks the anniversary of the abolition of the slave trade and focuses on William Blake (1757-1827). Best of all is the Tate's ongoing effort to help younger audiences engage with and enjoy the art on display. The time-honoured Art Trolley is wheeled out every Saturday and Sunday and at weekends (11am-5pm), and it is packed with a wide range of make-and-do activities. The Spot the Circle Discovery Trail, available anytime during gallery hours, invites you to find a variety of delicious and strange circles around the gallery. Check the website for special events for children and their families, as well as practical workshops designed for teenagers (check website for dates). There's also a number of themed workshops during half-term and holiday breaks. Tate Britain offers buggy storage, baby change facilities and healthy meals for children in its café and restaurant. You can nip swiftly to Tate Modern for another art fix via a trip on the Damien Hirst-decorated Tate-to-Tate boat. It runs every 40 minutes and it takes about 20 minutes to get from Millbank to Bankside, with a stop at the London Eye in between (£4.30, £2.15 under-16s £10.80 family, discounts for Travelcard holders). The annual, headline-grabbing Turner Prize exhibition for contemporary artists runs from October to January.
Buggy access. Café. Disabled access: lift, ramps, toilets. Nappy-changing facilities. Nearest picnic place: lawns (either side of gallery)/Riverside Gardens (by Vauxhall Bridge). Restaurant. Shop.

Westminster Abbey

20 Dean's Yard, SW1P 3PA (7222 5152/tours 7654 4900/www.westminster-abbey.org). St James's Park or Westminster tube/11, 12, 24, 88, 159, 211 bus. **Open** *Nave & Royal Chapels* 9.30am-3.45pm Mon, Tue, Thur, Fri; 9.30am-6pm Wed; 9.30am-1.45pm Sat. *Abbey Museum & Chapter House* 10.30am-4pm daily. *Cloisters* 8am-6pm daily. *College Garden* Apr-Sept 10am-6pm Tue-Thur; Oct-Mar 10am-4pm Tue-Thur (last entry 1hr before closing). *Tours* phone for details. **Admission** £10; £7 11-15s, concessions; free under-11s with paying adult; £24 family (2+2). *Chapter House* free. *Abbey Museum* free (audio guide £4). *Tours* £5. **Credit** AmEx, MC, V. **Map** p317 K9.
Edward the Confessor just lived to see the building of his church – it was consecrated eight days before he died – but at least there was no question as to where his final resting place should be. His body remains entombed in the abbey, although where, exactly, is unknown: it was removed from its elaborate shrine and reburied at an unmarked location during the Reformation. Almost every coronation since 1066 has taken place here and many crowned heads (and bodies) are interred here, including Elizabeth I (although

---

 Lunch box

For recommended restaurants and cafés in the area, *see reviews pp164-186.*

Bank Westminster 45 Buckingham Gate, SW1E 6BS (7379 9797).
Cathedral Kitchen Westminster Cathedral, Victoria Street, SW1P 1QW (7931 6023).
Gallery Café National Gallery, Trafalgar Square, WC2N 5DN (7747 2885).
Inn The Park St James's Park, SW1A 2BJ (7451 9999).
Jenny Lo's Tea House 14 Eccleston Street, SW1W 9LT (7259 0399).
Laughing Halibut 38 Strutton Ground,

SW1P 2HR (7799 2844).
McDonald's 155 Victoria Street, SW1E 5NA (7828 6911).
Pizza Express 85 Victoria Street, SW1H 0HW (7222 5270); 25 Millbank, SW1P 4QP (7976 6214).
Ponti's Café 127 Victoria Street, SW1E 6RD (7828 7242).
Portrait Restaurant National Portrait Gallery, St Martin's Place, WC2H 0HE (7312 2490).
Prêt à Manger 62-65 Cockspur Street, WC2N 5DS (7932 5350).
Texas Embassy Cantina 1 Cockspur Street, SW1Y 5DL (7925 0077).

Art comes alive in the **National Portrait Gallery**. *See p83.*

her father was buried in Windsor) and Mary Queen of Scots. Poets' Corner is the final resting place of Geoffrey Chaucer; you can also see the graves of Charles Dickens, Dryden, Samuel Johnson, Browning and Tennyson. Several 20th-century martyrs (including Martin Luther King Jr) have been immortalised in 15th-century niches above the west door. The extraordinary nave – the highest roof in Britain at 31m (101ft) – is a seemingly endless sea of stained glass. Escape the crowds in the 900-year-old College Garden, one of the oldest cultivated gardens in Britain. The Abbey Museum (Broad Sanctuary; free if you have a ticket to the Abbey, £1 otherwise) is in the vaulted area under the former monks' dormitory in one of the oldest parts of the Abbey. There you'll find a collection of effigies and waxworks of British monarchs, such as Edward II and Henry VII wearing the robes they wore when alive. The Queen's Coronation robes are also on show. The Choir School is the only school in Britain exclusively for the education of boy choristers from eight to 13 (voice trials are held twice a year; see the website for details). Check the website in October 2007 for details of the magnificent Christmas services. Next door, St Margaret's Church (free to visit) is where the weddings of diarist Samuel Pepys and Winston Churchill (in 1655 and 1908 respectively) took place. Sir Walter Raleigh is buried here.

Buggy access. Café. Disabled access: toilets. Nearest picnic place: college gardens (10am-6pm Tue-Thur)/ St James's Park. Shop.

Westminster Cathedral

Victoria Street, SW1P 1QW (7798 9055/tours 7798 9064/www.westminstercathedral.org.uk). St James's Park tube/Victoria tube/rail/11, 24, 211, 507 bus. **Open** 7am-7pm Mon-Fri, Sun; 8am-7pm Sat. *Campanile* Apr-Nov 9.30am-12.30pm, 1-5pm daily. Dec-Mar 9.30am-12.30pm, 1-5pm Thur-Sun. *Tours* by arrangement; phone for details. **Admission** free; donations appreciated. *Campanile* £5; £2.50 concessions; £11 family (2+2). *Tours* £2.50. **No credit cards. Map** p316 J10.

London's Catholic cathedral is a bit of an upstart compared to Westminster's other religious edifices, because its neo-Byzantine exterior was completed only at the beginning of the 20th century. The interior, dominated by a huge cross hovering over the altar, remains a work in progress. When the Cathedral architect, John Bentley, died in 1902, he left no finished mosaics in the Cathedral and few mosaic drawings and designs, so it was left to future architects, donors and designers to decide on the art work. It has been a long-running effort, raising funds to commission and create new mosaics, and to provide the money required to decorate the high ceiling, which remains black with candle smoke. Tourists are welcome (although they're respectfully asked not to break the reverie); the shop sells a neat little workbook that leads kids on an activity trail around the building, and the Cathedral Cafeteria is on hand to provide half-time refreshments.

If you have a head for heights, the newly refurbished 83m (273ft) Campanile Bell Tower is topped by a four-sided gallery with spectacular views across London; there's a lift all the way to the top. The tower is dedicated to St Edward the Confessor. It has one bell, named Edward, which was the gift of the Duchess of Norfolk, in 1910. Inscribed on the bell are the words: 'While the sound of this bell travels through the clouds, may the bands of angels pray for those assembled in thy church. St Edward, pray for England'.

Consult the cathedral's website for details of choral and music recitals.

Buggy access. Café. Disabled access: ramp. Shop.

Paddington & Notting Hill

Bohemian no longer, this area sends estate agents into rhapsodies.

Bayswater & Paddington

There's a small statue of a bear in a hat on Paddington Station. He is, of course, Michael Bond's furry post-war refugee, whose South American name was too complicated for the kindly family that took him in to pronounce. He will always be Paddington, and this station will forever be connected with him.

It is appropriate that Paddington should have these connotations, as the area has long served as a home to refugees and immigrants. It was a country village until the 19th century, when the grand Junction Canal turned it into the linking point between London and the Midlands. The coming of the railway sealed its destiny as a place of arrivals and departures. The current station was built in 1851 to the specifications of the great engineer Isambard Kingdom Brunel; its beautiful triple roof of iron and glass is a tribute to Victorian engineering.

Today, the Paddington Basin development project is restoring land on either side of the Grand Union Canal with futuristic offices, arty bridges, waterside housing and a range of amenities and entertainments. Free walking tours (7313 1011,www.inpaddington.com) get this fascinating area into perspective for visitors. One of them, starting at the Paddington Bear's statue and heading over to Peter Pan's in Hyde Park, is aimed at children.

Further south, the Bayswater Road skirts the north side of Hyde Park. This road is worth a stroll on Sundays, when the metal gates are adorned with a mile of paintings by aspiring artists. Queensway, towards the road's western end, was named after Queen Victoria; the main target for kids is Queens, the bowling alley and ice rink (see p265).

Whiteley's shopping centre (7229 8844, www. whiteleys.com) is a three-floor retail nirvana that retains its Edwardian charm (marble floors, sculpted water features, a glass domed ceiling) despite holding the unfortunate honour of being Hitler's favourite London building (he intended to make it his headquarters following victory in Europe). It boasts an eight-screen UCI cinema and a Gymboree Play and Music Centre. The area is also dotted with an array of Oriental and Middle Eastern cafés and restaurants.

Alexander Fleming Laboratory Museum

St Mary's Hospital, Praed Street, W2 1NY (7886 6528/www.st-marys.nhs.uk). Paddington tube/rail/ 7, 15, 27, 36 bus. **Open** 10am-1pm Mon-Thur; other times by appointment. Closed bank hols. **Admission** £2; £1 concessions, 5-16s; free under-5s. **No credit cards. Map** p313 D5.
In the era of the superbug, this shrine to antibiotics is either increasingly relevant or a relic from a simpler time. The museum recreates the lab where Alexander Fleming discovered penicillin back on 3 September 1928. Displays and a video celebrate Fleming's life and the role of penicillin in fighting disease. Staff run tours for family and school groups; other visitors get a guided tour as part of the fee. *Disabled access: toilets (in hospital). Nearest picnic place: Hyde Park. Shop.*

Notting Hill

Once known for great antiques and bohemian charm, Notting Hill is these days characterised by swanky celebrity residents, spiralling house prices and a proliferation of Starbucks-style coffee shops and smart bars and restaurants. In keeping with its hip reputation, it's one of the most media-centric kids' fixtures in the capital, with weekly script-writing classes for 14- to 18-year-olds at the Gate Theatre (7229 5387, www.gate theatre.co.uk) and the Youth Culture TV centre (8964 4646, www.yctv.org), which gives 11- to 20-year-olds a head start in television.

Not that things have always been so fancy. In the 1950s, Notting Hill was a reluctant hub for racial tensions between working-class whites and the unwelcome influx of Afro-Caribbean immigrants. In August 1958, there were four days of race riots – Britain's first – centred on Pembridge Road, where West Indian homes were attacked by white gangs, many of them bussed in especially. The following August, the first Notting Hill Carnival took place as an assertion of cultural identity and solidarity. The carnival remains the area's defining event. Portobello Road – the 'street where the riches of ages are stowed' immortalised in *Bedknobs and Broomsticks* – is one of the quirkiest markets on earth, filled with unexpected treasures, although prices seem to be rising as rapidly as the surrounding residences. It's still a glorious retro experience. In fact, the new **Museum of Brands, Packaging and Advertising** may reduce nostalgic parents to jelly with its images of yesteryear.

There's an excellent range of sporting and recreational facilities beneath the A40, which bisects Ladbroke Grove. The Westway Sports Centre (1 Crowthorne Road, W10 6RP, 8969 0992, www.westway.org/sports) has London's finest indoor (and outdoor) climbing wall, the Westway Stables (20 Stable Way, Latimer Road, W10 6QX,

Lunch box

For recommended restaurants and cafés in the area, see reviews *p173*.
Alounak Kebab 44 Westbourne Grove, W2 5SH (7229 0416).
Ask 145 Notting Hill Gate W11 3LB (7792 9942).
Costa's Fish Restaurant 18 Hillgate Street, W8 7SR (7727 4310).
Fresco 93 Praed Street, W2 1NT (7402 0006).
McDonald's Notting Hill Gate South (7792 4151).
Ottolenghi 63 Ledbury Road, W11 2AD (7727 1121).
Pizza Express 137 Notting Hill Gate W11 3GQ (020 7229 6000).
Satay House 13 Sale Place, W2 1PX (7723 6763).
Tea Palace 175 Westbourne Grove, W11 2SB (7727 2600).
Tom's Delicatessen, 226 Westbourne Grove, W11 2RH (7221 8818).

8964 2140, www.westwaystables.co.uk) organises riding lessons and pony-based birthday parties. Then there's the awesome Bay Sixty6 Skate Park (*see p264*). Kensington Leisure Centre, just across the way (Walmer Road, W11 4PQ, 7727 9747), has sporting facilities and something for the tinies in the form of Bumper's Back Yard, a littler version of **Bramley's Big Adventure**.

Local green lungs include Avondale Park, which has a playground, although parents are swayed by the proximity of Kensington Gardens. An eerie ramble can be enjoyed at Kensal Green Cemetery, north of the Grand Union Canal. A Victorian graveyard with a Greek Revivalist chapel and catacombs (over-12s only), it's the final resting place for many, including Isambard Kingdom Brunel and the author William Thackeray.

Bramley's Big Adventure

136 Bramley Road, W10 6TJ (8960 1515/www. bramleysbig.co.uk) Latimer Road tube. **Open** *Term-time* 10am-6pm Mon-Fri; 10am-6.30pm Sat, Sun. *Holidays* 10am-6.30pm daily. **Membership** £15/yr. **Admission** *Members* £2/£2.50 under-2s; £3.50/£4 2-5s; £4/£4.50 over 5s. *Non-members* £3/£3.50 under-2s; £4.50/£5 2-5s; £5/£5.50 over-5s (Mon-Fri/Sat, Sun). Under-1s free with older child. **Credit** AmEx, MC, V.
Silence is unheard of at this, the largest indoor playground in central London. For a start, it's under the Westway fly-over. The real noise comes from the interior, where a giant three-level playframe with slides, ball pools, swings, climbs, spooky den, giant balls, sound effects makes it tot paradise. There are separate under-five and baby areas, and the café does a good line in organic and healthy grub. Ask about children's parties, which include meals and party bags. Parents can catch up on some work while the children run wild; there's free Wi-Fi for their lap tops. *Café. Disabled access: toilets. Nappy-changing facilities. Shop.*

Museum of Brands, Packaging and Advertising

2 Colville Mews, Lonsdale Road, W11 2AR (7908 0880/www.museumofbrands.com) Ladbroke Grove or Notting Hill Gate tube/23 bus. **Open** 10am-6pm Tue-Sat; 11am-5pm Sun (last entry 1hr before closing). **Admission** £5.80; £2 7-16s; £3.50 concessions; free under-7s. £14 family (2+2). **Credit** MC, V.
Calling all nostalgia freaks. If you go weak at the knees when confronted by original boxes of Bassett's Liquorice Allsorts or Rowntree's Black Magic, this is the museum for you. It all started when consumer historian Robert Opie filed a Munchies wrapper when he was 16. His collection grew, and this museum – opened in 2005 – charts the evolution of consumer society over 200 years. It covers Victorian leisure pursuits, the advent of the radio, the chipper thrift of the wartime 1940s and the liberal revolution of the swinging '60s. The displays are geared towards nostalgic adults, but historically minded children may be amused by the antiquated toys, magazines and comics on show – not to mention old versions of their favourite chocolate wrappers. Maltesers looked quite different, you know. *Buggy access. Café. Disabled access: toilet. Nappy-changing facility. Shop.*

Around Town

South Kensington & Chelsea

Don't try covering this lot in one day – your brain might explode.

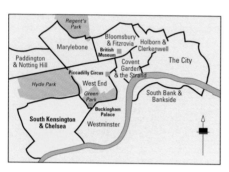

South Kensington is the busiest end of the Royal Borough of Kensington & Chelsea, as far as cultural and academic institutions are concerned. With three of London's most heavyweight museums, a royal palace and swathes of lovely parkland, there's plenty to keep a family occupied. Tops on the 'grand day out' itinerary is the world-renowned **Natural History Museum**, for dinosaurs and other animals. The **Science Museum** shows how science touches all aspects of life and the **Victoria & Albert Museum** is a stunner. These three form an oasis of learning envisaged by Prince Albert, who bought the land on which they stand with the profits of the 1851 Great Exhibition (the princely sum of £185,000) to build institutions 'to extend the influence of Science and Art upon Productive Industry'. They've certainly been productive in terms of London's tourist industry. Three great colleges also benefit from the area once known as Albertopolis: Imperial College, the Royal College of Art and the Royal College of Music. The latter forms a unity with the **Royal Albert Hall**, the great, rotund performance space inaugurated in 1871 and used for boxing bouts, pop concerts, motor shows, Miss World and the Eurovision Song Contest, but most importantly, for the Proms (*see p222*). Looking out across Kensington Gore from the Hall gives a great view of the golden tribute to the royal benefactor, the **Albert Memorial**.

Hyde Park is a fine public space for picnics and sports. You can barely take a step in neighbouring **Kensington Gardens** without happening upon some tribute or other to the late Diana Spencer, as a leisurely stroll following the Diana, Princess of Wales Memorial Walk will reveal. The Diana, Princess of Wales Memorial Playground is terrific for kids, and the Diana, Princess of Wales Memorial Fountain is an aptly controversial paddling pool that attracts hordes of visitors on warm summer days. Stroll on for the oldest boating lake in the capital, the Serpentine, and Kensington Palace, birthplace of Queen Victoria in 1819 and home to the late princesses Diana and Margaret.

Baden-Powell House
65-67 Queen's Gate, SW7 5JS (7584 7031/www.scout base.org.uk). Gloucester Road or South Kensington tube. **Open** 7am-10pm daily. Closed 22 Dec-3 Jan. **Admission** free. **Credit** MC, V. **Map** p313 D10.
Robert Baden-Powell's memorial hostel was opened in 1961 and it provides accommodation for about 300,000 people from 30 different countries each year, with family rooms for visitors with children. There's an exhibition on the ground floor about the Chief Scout's life. Special events to celebrate the centenary of Scouting (Aug 2007) are taking place throughout the year. Be prepared: check the website for more information.
Buggy access. Café. Disabled access: toilet. Nappy-changing facilities. Nearest picnic place: Natural History Museum gardens. Shop. Nappy-changing facilities. Nearest picnic place: Kensington Gardens.

Hyde Park & Kensington Gardens
W2 2UH (7298 2117/www.royalparks.gov.uk). Hyde Park Corner, Knightsbridge, Lancaster Gate or Marble Arch tube/2, 8, 10, 12, 23, 73, 94 bus. **Open** 5am-midnight daily. **Map** p311 E7.
Hyde Park is the largest of London's Royal Parks and was the first to be opened to the public. Year-round, the park's perimeter is popular with skaters, cyclists and horse-riders (there are riding schools near Rotten Row, part of the wide riding track around Hyde Park). If you're cycling, stick to the designated tracks; only children under ten are allowed to cycle on the footpaths. At the west side of the park is the Serpentine, London's oldest boating lake, with its complement of wildfowl. You can rent rowing boats and pedalos from March to October. The Serpentine's swimming club is renowned for ice-breaking winter swims.

That's entertainment: there's rarely a dull moment at the **Royal Albert Hall**.

Across the road from the Serpentine Gallery is an innovative water feature, the Diana, Princess of Wales Memorial Fountain, which was designed by American architect Kathryn Gustafson as a Cornish granite channel filled with running water.

At the park's eastern end, near Marble Arch, is Speakers' Corner, the world's oldest platform for public speaking, which takes place every Sunday. Every morning at 10.30am (9.30am Sun), the Household Cavalry emerge smartly from their barracks on South Carriage Drive and ride across the park to Horse Guards Parade, prior to the Changing of the Guard.

Kensington Gardens covers 260 acres and meets Hyde Park at the Serpentine. It is home to the Diana Princess of Wales Memorial Playground, as well as the Albert Memorial, with its huge statue of Prince Albert, picked out in gold and seated under a 55m (180ft) spire and canopy (for guided tours ring 7495 0916). By Long Water, the park's lake, there's a bronze statue of Peter Pan, built by Sir George Frampton in 1912 to honour his creator, JM Barrie. Kensington Gardens is also home to what surely must be the poshest park café in the capital: the Orangery, which has a children's menu and high chairs.
Buggy access. Cafés. Disabled access: toilet. Nappy-changing facilities.

Diana, Princess of Wales Memorial Playground

Near Black Lion Gate, Broad Walk, Kensington Gardens, W8 2UH (7298 2117/recorded info 7298 2141/www.royalparks.gov.uk). Bayswater tube/12, 148, 390 bus. **Open** *Summer* 10am-7.45pm daily. *Winter* 10am-6.45pm (or 1hr before dusk, if earlier) daily. **Admission** free. All adults & over-12s must be accompanied by a child. **Map** p310 C7.

This commemorative play area is a wonderland for little ones. The focal point is a pirate ship, run aground in fine, white sand. Children enjoy scaling the rigging to the crow's nest and adore the ship's wheel, cabins, pulleys and ropes. During the summer months, the mermaids' fountain and rocky outcrops are fab for water play. Beyond these ship-shape glories lies the tepee camp: a trio of wigwams, each large enough to hold a sizeable tribe. The tree-house encampment has walkways, ladders, slides and 'tree phones'. The area's connection with Peter Pan's creator JM Barrie is remembered in images from the story etched into the glass in the Home Under the Ground. Many of the playground's attractions appeal to the senses: scented shrubs, whispering willows and bamboo are planted throughout. Much of the equipment has been designed for use by children with special needs, including those in wheelchairs. There's plenty of seating for parents, and the café has a children's menu. During the school summer holidays there's a programme of free entertainment, such as visits by clowns or storytelling sessions; check the website for details. Unaccompanied adults aren't allowed in, but they can view the gardens between 9.30am and 10am daily.
Buggy access. Café. Disabled access: toilet. Kiosk.

Kensington Palace

W8 4PX booking line, 0870 751 5170/www.hrp.org. uk). Bayswater or High Street Kensington tube/9, 10, 49, 52, 70 bus. **Open** *Mar-Oct* 10am-6pm daily. *Nov-Feb* 10am-5pm daily. Last entry 1hr before closing. **Admission** (LP) incl audio guide £12; £10 concessions; £6 5-15s; free under-5s; £33 family (2+3). **Credit** MC, V. **Map** p310 B8.
William III and his wife Mary came to live in this Jacobean mansion in 1689, when Kensington was still a country village. They moved from Whitehall Palace to escape the

smoggy air, which played havoc with William's asthma, having commissioned Sir Christopher Wren to alter the existing house into a palace. Since then, many royals have called it home. Queen Victoria, born and baptised here, enjoyed living in Kensington so much that she awarded the borough its 'Royal' status. The Duke and Duchess of Kent have apartments in the palace. The palace is open for tours of the State Apartments (which you enter via Wren's lofty King's Staircase), the King's Gallery and the Queen's Apartments, where William and Mary lived quite simply. The most popular part is the Royal Ceremonial Dress Collection, which includes outfits worn by Princess Diana. An exhibition of photographs of Diana, Princess of Wales by Mario Testino will be on display until 31 December 2007. Princess Line – the Fashion Legacy of Princess Margaret runs until 30 September 2007.
Buggy access. Disabled access: toilet. Nappy-changing facilities. Restaurant. Shop.

Natural History Museum

Cromwell Road, SW7 5BD (information 7942 5725/ switchboard 7942 5000/www.nhm.ac.uk). South Kensington tube. **Open** 10am-5.50pm Mon-Sat; 11am-5.50pm Sun. **Admission** free; charges apply for special exhibitions. **Credit** AmEx, MC, V. **Map** p313 D10.
Greeted by the massive 150-million-year-old Diplodocus skeleton, visitors can only feel impressed. You'll never be able to see every one of the 70 million plants, fossils, rocks and minerals stashed here, but grab a free map from one of the information desks at the entrances and, with the help of an army of staff, you'll soon be navigating with ease.

The museum is split up into zones – the blue zone is always a winner with kids – and here you'll find the enormous model blue whale (three buses long) and many impressive dinosaur skeletons. In the red zone you'll be able to explore our planet in detail – including an earthquake simulation which never fails to put smiles on faces. In the green zone kids can discover how to calculate a whale's age by its teeth, look a (stuffed) dodo in the eye, and learn how humans evolved. The orange zone includes the famed Darwin Centre that houses around 22 million specimens. Free behind-the-scenes tours take place daily in the centre, allowing visitors to meet the scientists and have a closer inspection of the collections. Book your place on the tour on arrival (children have to be over 8). Darwin Centre Phase Two is due to open in 2009.

To really get the most out of your visit take advantage of the kids' packs available at the entrance. If you're entertaining under-sevens, pick up a free (£25 deposit needed) Explorer Backpack; each one comes with an explorer hat and binoculars and is filled with drawing materials and activities. Or for under a quid you can buy a themed Discovery Guide which are suitable for children up to the age of 16. Ring nearer the time to check whether the ice rink and fair will take place again this winter.
Buggy access. Cafés. Disabled access (Exhibition Road entrance): lift, toilet. Nappy-changing facilities. Nearest picnic place: indoor eating area/museum grounds. Restaurant. Shops.

Oratory Catholic Church

Thurloe Place, Brompton Road, SW7 2RP (7808 0900/ www.bromptonoratory.com). South Kensington tube/ 14, 74 bus. **Open** 6.30am-8pm daily. **Services** 7am, 10am, 12.30pm, 6pm Mon-Sat; 7am, 8am, 9am, 10am, 11am, 12.30pm, 4.30pm, 7pm Sun. **Admission** free; donations appreciated. **Map** p313 E10.

Science Museum

The second-largest Catholic church in the city (Westminster Cathedral occupies the top slot) is full of marble and mosaics. Many of the internal decorations are much older than the building itself: Mazzuoli's late 17th-century statues of the apostles, for example, once stood in Siena Cathedral. This church was used by Russian spies as a dead letter box during the Cold War. The Oratory's Junior Choir sings Mass at 10am on Sunday, and Schola, the boys' choir of the London Oratory School in Fulham (a reason many parents of secondary-transfer children in London discover popish associations), performs Mass on term-time Saturday evenings.
Buggy access. Disabled access: ramp. Shop.

Science Museum

Exhibition Road, SW7 2DD (7942 4454/booking & information line 0870 870 4868/www.sciencemuseum. org.uk). South Kensington tube. **Open** 10am-6pm daily. **Admission** free; charges apply for special exhibitions. **Credit** AmEx, MC, V. **Map** p313 D9.
Children find the Science Museum a thrilling day out. The vast collection includes landmark inventions such as Stephenson's Rocket, Arkwright's spinning machine, Whittle's turbojet engine and the Apollo 10 command module. The collections are enlivened through imaginative interactive displays. Children can spend hours learning through play at one of the museum's six play zones. Under-sixes dig the Garden area in the basement, where they can discover the principles of science by playing in the three multi-sensory zones: water, construction and sound and light. On the ground floor, in the Wellcome Wing, the Patter Pod introduces under-eights to patterns and repetition in the natural world.

The Launch Pad is the museum's largest and most popular interactive gallery, with a wide range of amazing hands-on exhibits covering subjects such as light, sound, energy and electricity. If you need help with an exhibit look out for an Explainer – a member of staff in a bright orange

One day out and a Family Railcard could pay for itself.

(How many other big days out will you enjoy?)

% off kids' fares, adults save $1/3$

y a Family Railcard for £20, and you could easily
er the cost the first time you use it.

a family journey that normally costs £60, for
mple, you'd more than make your money back.

Up to 4 adults and 4 children can travel on one card, and
they don't even need to be related. So get your card now,
and look forward to great savings for a whole year!

• **New! Buy online at www.family-railcard.co.uk**
• **Pick up a leaflet at your nearest staffed train station**
• **Or call 08457 48 49 50 for your local Train Company number**

National Rail

Family Railcard

shirt. Explainers also present 20-minute shows throughout the day – the subject could be bubbles, bridges, rockets or explosions. The shows, which tie in to the National Curriculum, are suitable for all ages, and they're free.

Until October 2007 you'll be able to visit The Big Bang, a sneak preview into a revolutionary experiment. In school holidays, look out for the museum's free educational events and workshops – they can't be booked in advance so turn up early on the day and check out their website for advanced details. Science Night sleepovers are held once a month (£30 eight- to 11-year-olds, in groups of five or more), with an evening of activities that might include creating slime or making balloon-powered buggies. You have to book as much as two months ahead (24hr information line 7942 4747). The Science Museum is currently undergoing a ten- year revamp – first of the improvements to open is the Exploring Space Gallery, which celebrates British participation in space explorations.

Buggy access. Cafés. Disabled access: lift, toilet. Nappy-changing facilities. Nearest picnic place: Hyde Park (outdoor); museum basement & 1st floor (indoor). Restaurant. Shop.

Serpentine Gallery

Kensington Gardens (nr Albert Memorial), W2 3XA (7402 6075/www.serpentinegallery.org). Lancaster Gate or South Kensington tube. **Open** 10am-6pm daily. **Admission** free; donations appreciated. **Credit** AmEx, MC, V. **Map** p311 D8.

It may be housed in a 1930s tearoom, but this lovely, light gallery is a cutting-edge space for contemporary art. Its programme includes family days, artist-led workshops and trails relating to the current exhibitions; check the website for dates or to sign up for the email newsletter. Keeping its high profile in the art world, the gallery has a rolling two-monthly programme of exhibitions and an annual Serpentine Pavilion commission, which enlists an internationally renowned architect to design and build a new pavilion. This year it's a Scandinavian duo: Danish architect Olafur Eliasson and Norwegian Kjetil Thorsen.

Buggy access. Disabled access: toilets. Nappy-changing facilities. Nearest picnic place: Hyde Park. Shop.

V&A: the perfect place for rainy days.

Victoria & Albert Museum

Cromwell Road, SW7 2RL (7942 2000/www.vam. ac.uk). South Kensington tube. **Open** 10am-5.45pm Mon, Tue, Thur, Sun; 10am-10pm Wed & last Fri of mth. *Tours* daily; phone for details. **Admission** free; charges apply for special exhibitions. **Credit** *Shop* AmEx, MC, V. **Map** p313 E10.

Crammed with beautiful displays of ceramics, fashion, paintings, sculpture, and textiles, the V&A's halls are tailor-made for whiling away the hours. To amuse potentially restless children, however, try one of the many laid-on free activities. On Saturdays and during school

✖ Lunch box

For recommended restaurants and cafés in the area, see reviews *pp172-175.*

ASK *222 Kensington High Street, W8 7RG (7937 5540).*
Benihana *77 King's Road, SW3 4NX (7376 7799).*
Café Crêperie *2 Exhibition Road, SW7 2HF (7589 8947).*
Carluccio's Caffè *1 Old Brompton Road, SW7 3HZ (7581 8101).*
Ed's Easy Diner *362 King's Road, SW3 5UZ (7352 1956).*
Gelateria Valerie *9 Duke of York Square, SW3 4LY (7730 7978).*
Giraffe *7 Kensington High Street, W8 5NP (7938 1221).*
Great Escape Café *National Army Museum, Royal Hospital Road, SW3 4HT (7730 0717).*
Green Fields Café *13 Exhibition Road,*

SW7 2HE (7584 1396).
Manicomio *85 Duke of York Square, SW3 4LY (7730 3366).*
The Orangery *Kensington Palace, Kensington Gardens, W8 2UH (7376 0239).*
Oratory *234 Brompton Road, SW3 2BB (7584 3493).*
Pâtisserie Valerie *215 Brompton Road, SW3 2EJ (7823 9971); 27 Kensington Church Street, W8 4LL (7937 9574).*
Pâtisserie Valerie *Left Wing Café, 81 Duke of York Square, SW3 4LY (7730 7094).*
Paul Boulangerie *41 Thurloe Street, SW7 2LQ (7581 6034).*
Pizza Express *The Pheasantry, 152-154 King's Road, SW3 4UT (7351 5031).*
Pizza Organic *20 Old Brompton Road, SW7 3DL (7589 9613).*
Wagamama *26 Kensington High Street, W8 4PF (7376 1717).*

Free entry

Open your mind

We're open every day from 10am – 6pm
⊖ South Kensington • www.sciencemuseum.org.uk • Telephone 0870 870 4868

Open your eyes to 3D cinema

⊖ South Kensington • www.sciencemuseum.org.uk/imax • To book call 0870 870 4771
The Science Museum is free to enter but charges apply for the IMAX 3D Cinema   IMAX is the registered trademark of Imax Corporation

Monumental sacrifice

As you walk east across Hyde Park toward Speakers' Corner, there's no shortage of animals. Pause to admire the pampered ponies trotting along Rotten Row, watch the spoilt spaniels chasing balls across the grass, and throw the end of your ice-cream cornet to the portly pigeons outside the café. But soon you'll come to a monument dedicated to animals that weren't quite so lucky as the creatures living a peaceful park life. Just east of Rotten Row, on Park Lane stands David Backhouse's magnificent sculpture *Animals in War*, inspired by Jilly Cooper's book of the same name. Eight million horses, as well as countless pack mules, donkeys, carrier pigeons, dolphins and even glow-worms died in the service of their country in the First World War. This piece, a testament to their sacrifice, is also a graphic comment on mankind's uneasy relationship with animals. In the wretched posture of the mule, weighed down by artillery; in the passage of the sinewy bronze creatures through an opening in the stone frieze to an imagined battlefield beyond, Backhouse draws attention to the plight of animals in war. They were not, he notes in the inscription, volunteers.

At the same time, many animals aim to please their owners and are capable of astonishing acts of bravery. The exhibition, Animals in War has now moved to the Imperial War Museum North in Manchester, but some exhibits remain in the First World War galleries on Lambeth Road (Imperial War Museum, London, *see p126*. They include a messenger pigeon in a parachute and the stuffed remains of Edith Cavell's dog. Cavell (there is a statue to her memory across the road from the National Portrait Gallery on St Martin's Place; *see p83*) was a nurse who helped many Allied soldiers escape from occupied Belgium during the First World War. She was shot for her troubles by a German firing squad in 1915. Her dog, Jack, was brought back to England after her death, where he worked tirelessly for charities established in tribute to Cavell. Another four-legged friend honoured in the Galleries is Tirpitz the Pig, whose perfectly preserved head is mounted on a plaque in the Museum for all to admire. This German porker was the sole surviving crew member of the cruiser SMS *Dresden*, which was sunk by HMS *Glasgow* and HMS *Kent* in 1915. British sailors dived in to save the pig, which was subsequently made into the ship's mascot and decorated with an Iron Cross for standing by his sinking ship. Tirpitz did one other great thing: he raised £1,785 for the Red Cross when auctioned off for pork a few months later.

It does not follow, however, that the Edwardians were less sentimental about animals than we are. Two pet cemeteries in Greater London testify to the esteem in which many pets were held in the 19th and 20th centuries. Sadly, the one at Chester Gate at Hyde Park (Bayswater Road) is now largely obscured from view, since the residents of the gatehouse erected a wooden fence around their property. (You can just glimpse the Lilliputian charm of the tiny headstones through an opening next to the garden gate.) But the good news is that the PDSA cemetery in Ilford, Essex, which is the resting place of more than 3,000 animals, has been awarded a restoration grant. When the work is completed in November 2007 this will be a fascinating place to visit, with an information point and boards telling the animals' life stories. At least a dozen were First World War heroes and received the PDSA Dickin medal — the animals' equivalent of the Victoria Cross. See the veterinary charity's website www.pdsa.org.uk for details.

holidays, children from five to 12 years old can borrow themed back-packs full of hands-on activities, puzzles and stories. For younger children there are activity sheets that complement each backpack. On Sundays and during holidays look out for the Activity Cart; it's suitable for over-threes and can be found in different areas on different days. Your child could soon be designing a kimono or even making a samurai helmet. There are also many interactive exhibits dotted around the museum; most of them can be found in the British Galleries and they're available at all times. In the Victorian Discovery Area, for example, there are corsets and crinolins to try on and you can have a go at building a model Crystal Palace or a chair. The 18th century Discovery Area has children making domestic objects, and there's a tapestry to weave and armoury to try out in the Tudor and Stuart Discovery Area. A great way for families to explore the museum is to follow one of the tailor-made trails; for instance the Picnic Trail invites you to plan the perfect picnic as you journey through South Asia, the Middle East and East Asia Galleries.

The V&A is undergoing a ten-year refurbishment – one of the most recent completed renovations is the fantastically stylish Central Hall Shop, where there are some equally eye-catching (if pricey) toys for children. Following the demise of the performance-themed Covent Garden wing of the V&A (the Theatre Museum), the V&A will be developing a new performance display.

Buggy access. Café. Disabled access: lift, ramps, toilets. Nappy-changing facilities. Nearest picnic place: Pirelli Gardens, museum garden & basement picnic room. Restaurant. Shop.

Chelsea

In the early 15th century, **Chelsea** was a fishing village, then from the late 18th until the early 20th century the area became popular with artists and writers – Dante Gabriel Rossetti and TS Eliot were among the creatives who lived here. During the '60s, it had a bohemian air and in the '70s the Kings Road became a punk hangout. Nowadays, the area is synonymous with wealth, style and culture. Sloane Square, home to the acclaimed Royal Court Theatre, is the place to start a tour of Chelsea. The **Duke of York Square** nearby hosts a wintertime ice rink, fountains in summer and several upmarket cafés, including Gelateria Valerie for truly scrumptious ice-creams. The **National Army Museum** and the Chelsea Royal Hospital, where the Chelsea Flower Show is held, are a short walk away.

Also in the neighbourhood is the **Chelsea Physic Garden**. It can be reached via Flood Street, one of the many attractive side roads branching off King's Road. The prettiest is Glebe Place, which has a very picturesque little nursery school, tucked sweetly in the corner. The western end of King's Road is known as World's End. If you've walked all the way from the Royal Court you deserve to rest your tired legs in **Cremorne Gardens**, which has fine views over the river.

Chelsea Physic Garden

66 Royal Hospital Road (entrance on Swan Walk), SW3 4HS (7352 5646/www.chelseaphysicgarden.co.uk). Sloane Square tube/11, 19, 239 bus. **Open** *Apr-Oct noon-5pm Wed; 2-6pm Sun. Tours times vary, phone to check.* **Admission** £7; £4 5-16s, concessions (not incl OAPs); free under-5s. *Tours free.* **Credit** *Shop* AmEx, MC, V. **Map** p313 F12.

The garden was set up in 1673, but the key phase of development was under Sir Hans Sloane in the 18th century. Its beds contain healing herbs and rare trees, dye plants and medicinal vegetables; plants are also sold. Public opening hours are restricted – because this is primarily a centre for research and education. That said, the education depar tment organises activity days with interesting botanical themes over the Easter and summer holidays. Activity days should be pre-booked, and are suitable for seven- to 11-year-olds (although there are some for four- to six-year olds and nine- to 13-year-olds) and cost £5 per child per day. Phone or email education@chelseaphysicgarden. co.uk for a list of 2007 dates. Educational visits and teacher-training days can be arranged.

Buggy access. Café. Disabled access: ramp, toilet. Nappy-changing facilities. Shop.

National Army Museum

Royal Hospital Road, SW3 4HT (7881 2455) www.national-army-museum.ac.uk). Sloane Square tube/11, 137, 239 bus. **Open** 10am-5.30pm daily. Closed bank hols. **Admission** free. **Credit** *Shop* AmEx, MC, V. **Map** p313 F12.

Don't be put off by the rather severe modern exterior. Some eccentric exhibits and displays, together with an exciting programme of family events, make this friendly museum dedicated to the British Army's 500-year history far more entertaining than you would think. Sure, there are a number of dry displays of regimental items – old uniforms, kit bags and the like – but there are also fascinating highlights: the Road to Waterloo, a version of the battle starring 75,000 toy soldiers; the skeleton of Napoleon's beloved mount, Marengo; and Florence Nightingale's lamp. Children love the bizarre exhibits, such as the frostbitten fingers of Major 'Bronco' Lane, conqueror of Mount Everest. The Redcoats Gallery starts at Agincourt in 1415 and ends with the redcoats in the American War of Independence; The Nation in Arms covers both World Wars, with reconstructions of a trench in the World at War (1914-1946) exhibition, and a D-Day landing craft. There's more military hardware, including a hands-on Challenger tank simulator, up in The Modern Army exhibition. A new exhibition, opening 19 October 2007, is Special Forces, focusing on the British Army's elite teams, such as the SAS. Themed weekend events (check the website for details), which usually involve costumed interpreters and craft activities, have gone a long way to broadening the museum's appeal, as has the Kids' Zone – a free interactive learning and play space. It's the sort of place you can bring all your troops to, as its attractions include construction, reading, art activity and board-game areas all tailored for under 10s, including a soft-play area for babies. It can be booked by the hour for birthday parties.

Buggy access. Café. Disabled access: lift, ramps, toilet. Nappy-changing facilities. Nearest picnic place: benches outside museum/Chelsea Hospital grounds. Shop.

Around Town

North London

Bijou high streets, picture-book parks and a treasured heath – it's glam up north.

Camden Town

One of the busiest places in the capital, Camden is also one of the scruffiest and buzziest; it's a haven for the fashionable middle class (Camden School for Girls, the trendy successful state school and Emma Thompson's alma mater, is a bastion of cut-glass accents). In spite of the area's long-standing reputation for hedonism, drugginess and badly behaved teens, gentrification's relentless march now threatens to take the spirit out of it. Proposals to develop a substantial part of the famous market have met with resistance from residents and visitors, who fear that rents will go up and the independent traders who thrive on Camden's weird and wacky vibe will be forced out by homogeneous high street chains.

Other developments in Camden have been met with more equanimity. The council has spent £24 million on a Boulevard Project (to make the district safer, and more attractive for walkers and cyclists). However, plans have stalled on the famously chaotic tube station (the present Camden Town tube is horribly overcrowded at weekends, and there's no disabled access).

Like everywhere else in London, it was all fields round here once. Camden has come a long way. Even in the 18th century, it had a reputation for being dangerous, and frequented by highwaymen. With a little imagination, children can picture the gibbet that stood by the Mother Red Cap inn (now the World's End by the tube station), where highwaymen and other criminals of the day would be displayed, post-hanging, for public viewing.

Camden Market

The major attraction today, especially for teenagers, is bound to be the market at Camden Lock (*see p208*), which draws more than 100,000 shoppers at the weekends. The newly restored **Roundhouse** on Chalk Farm Road (*see p98*) should also prove popular. The canal gives blessed relief. Watch the lock in action as boats pass through, or catch a ride on one of the narrowboats that offer a passenger service up to Little Venice – a trip that could be combined with a visit to the excellent **Puppet Theatre Barge** (*see p225*). Boats heading west pass through London Zoo and some allow you to hop off there for a visit. The 45-minute one-way trip passes elegant terraces with gardens backing on to the canal, willow-fringed towpaths and converted warehouses.

Jewish Museum, Camden

Raymond Burton House, 129-131 Albert Street, NW1 7NB (7284 1997/www.jewishmuseum.org.uk). Camden Town tube. **Open** 10am-4pm Mon-Thur; 10am-5pm Sun. Closed public hols, inc 25 Dec, Jewish festivals. **Admission** (LP) £3.50; £2.50 OAPs; £1.50 5-16s, concessions; free under-5s; £8 family (2+2). **Credit** MC, V.

Although it's undoubtedly of interest to students of history and world religions, this museum, which covers the history of one of Britain's oldest immigrant communities, is neither too dry nor too academic for the young. Monthly activities are run for children (pre-booking essential), with storytelling, puppet shows and craft workshops. Permanent exhibits include a jewelled breastplate depicting the 12 tribes, a silver scroll case in the shape of a fish, and a coconut-shell kiddush cup. The museum will be closing on 2 September 2007 for 18 months or so while a major refurbishment takes place. Until then, temporary exhibitions include the pugilistic 'Ghetto Warriors: Minority boxers in Britain'.
Buggy access. Disabled access: lift, toilets. Nearest picnic place: Regent's Park. Shop.

Primrose Hill

Primrose Hill's reputation as an outpost of villagey smartness has been enhanced by the numerous famous folk who have opted to live – and bring up their kids – here. Separated from its brasher neighbour Chalk Farm only by a railway footbridge, the district's high street (Regent's Park Road) is café heaven. Trojka (101 Regent's Park Road, NW1 8UR, 7483 3765, www.trojka.co.uk), with its preponderance of matryoshki dolls and its Russian violinist (on Friday and Saturday

Around Town

Round Camden way

Pop? Hip-hop? Indie? Drama queen? Whatever their passion, North London's young are lucky to have a top-of-the-range creative outlet in the **Roundhouse**. Many a (mature) local has a story to tell about this historic landmark. Whether it was sneaking into early gigs by Jimi Hendrix, moshing to Motorhead or participating in the wacky experimental stage shows of the Living Theatre – a generation of Camdenites grew up around the Roundhouse. Now it's back, providing an avant-garde programme of music, theatre and arts with a twist. Many of the activities are specifically aimed at children.

The Roundhouse started life in 1846 as a railway engine shed. When, in the late 19th century, locomotives became too large for the shed to handle, it was briefly used as a store for gin makers, but no real purpose was found for it until 1966, when the then Greater London Council bought the freehold and turned the place into an arts venue. Hendrix, The Doors and Pink Floyd all famously played here, but the building's progress as an arts forum called Centre 42 floundered in the 1980s and it was shut down again for 16 years. The Roundhouse's next incarnation as a venue lasted from 1996 until 2004 when it was shut for a refurb that cost £32 million. Its new look was unveiled to gasps of pleasure in 2006.

Backed by the Arts Council, the studios at the Roundhouse are open to creative-minded youngsters from anywhere in London, seven days a week. Aspiring performers can rent rehearsal space and studio time at reduced rates; newcomers can join weekly courses and one-off projects designed to develop the creative skills of young people – after school, at weekends, and during school holidays.

Creative courses also encompass modern music, experimental drama, live jams, singing and rap, beat poetry, contemporary dance, film and television, digital photography, sound engineering, recording, production, podcasting, computer game design... there are even presenter slots on Roundhouse Radio, broadcasting live youth content over the internet. This being Camden, all the courses have one thing in common: they're up-tempo and upbeat.

The studios place strong emphasis on peer-to-peer education and youth interaction. Young people aged 13 or over can join volunteer projects in the local community, and over-16s have the opportunity to visit schools to mentor other young artists. Enthusiastic amateurs are as welcome as child stars. There are courses for beginner, intermediate and advanced performers, and the studios can arrange vocational internships for kids who want to turn their hobbies into a career.

Most courses run on a weekly basis during school term time, and participation costs just £1 to £3 a session – that's professional arts training for the price of a fruit smoothie. Courses and workshops are laid on during the school holidays, often linked to events on the main stage. The hook for the 2007 summer term is 'Circus Front', a celebration of modern circus from around the world. Brochures and enrolment forms for each term's activities can be downloaded from the Roundhouse website, but sign up early; courses fill up fast. *See also p223* **Arts & Entertainment**.

Roundhouse

Chalk Farm Road, NW1 8EH (7424 9991/ www.roundhouse.org.uk). Chalk Farm tube.

evenings), is an inexpensive and entertaining eastern European contribution to the mix – try the Hungarian chocolate torte. Just off the main drag is Manna (4 Erskine Road, NW3 3AJ, 7722 8028, www.manna-veg.com), a spacious vegetarian restaurant where the cooking is good enough for children not to notice they're being asked to eat a plateful of healthy stuff.

As well as attractive cafés, restaurants, pubs and shops alongside the park, Primrose Hill has some of the prettiest houses in North London, making it well worth an ogle, especially en route to nearby **Regent's Park** and **London Zoo**. Primrose Hill itself is a smallish park, with a nice play area that is secure for small children, and a big sand pit. The hill is ideal for flying kites and offers views over the parkland.

Back over the railway footbridge in **Chalk Farm** is the **Roundhouse** (*see above*).

Hampstead & around

In times of plague, Londoners retreated to hilly Hampstead, and today its heath is still a prime destination for a restorative rural wander when the city gets too much. The narrow streets and graceful, period architecture have a village feel to them, although the busy high street is somewhat blighted by traffic. A short walk along East Heath Road takes you to North London's pride, Hampstead Heath. Willow Road joins the heath at Hampstead Ponds. You can take a break in the playground opposite No.2 Willow Road (7435 6166, www.nationaltrust.org.uk). This modernist house was built by Ernö Goldfinger in 1939. Artworks by Henry Moore, Max Ernst and others are contained within, and there's a newly expanded exhibition on the Goldfinger family. You get a good view of many rooms while pushing a swing in the playground. It's amusing to think that James Bond's creator, Ian Fleming, hated the architect so much he named a villain after him.

Up in the village itself are legions of cafés (though none, perhaps, so atmospheric as Louis Pâtisserie at 32 Heath Street, NW3 6TE, 7435 9908) and the pedestrian-only lanes make for peaceful shopping.

Hampstead was always a favourite roosting place for artists and authors – witness Keats House (Keats Grove, NW3 2RR (7435 2062/ www.cityoflondon.gov.uk/keats and the Freud Museum (20 Maresfield Gardens, NW3 5SX, 7435 2002, www.freud.org.uk). Neither of these historic homesteads is going to be top of a child's must-see list, but do note that that the latter is closed for refurbishment until summer 2008.

Hampstead also boasts some of the finest dwellings in town. Modern artists get a kick out of the superbly refurbished **Camden Arts Centre** (*see p217*). **Burgh House** (New End Square, NW3 1LT, 7431 0144, www.burghhouse.org.uk), a Queen Anne house containing a small museum about the area's history, also has a pleasant café and garden. **Fenton House** is *rus in urbe* perfection. Climb further up Hampstead Grove to reach the Hampstead Scientific Society Observatory (8346 1056,www.hampsteadscience.ac.uk), a registered charity that opens its doors to the celestially inclined – especially if they're well behaved – between September and mid-May on clear Friday and Saturday evenings (8-10pm) and Sunday mornings (11am-1pm). A whole lot of educational activities go on during science week in March; phone for details.

The daylight pleasures of **Hampstead Heath** – running wild, cycling, gathering conkers and climbing trees – are without doubt the major attraction of the area. A good combination might be a walk through the Vale of Health (spot the blue plaque for DH Lawrence) to the top of Hampstead, then down the hill to the village for refreshment (there are several well-known chain restaurants here). If you want to continue on the high road, North End Way takes you to a barn of a pub formerly known as Jack Straw's Castle and now rejoicing under the name of **Jack & Lulu's** (*see p178*). Child friendly doesn't begin to describe it. Walking south on the heath to **South End Green** and the car park will bring you to **Polly's** (55 South End Road, NW3 2QB, 7794 8144), a nice place for tea. Alternatively, move on to the 'heath extension', or **Golders Hill**, where the park café (*see p183*), smooth, winding paths, playground, fallow deer and an aviary of exotic birds await.

Fenton House

3 Hampstead Grove, NW3 6RT (7435 3471/ information 01494 755563/box office 01494 755572/ www.nationaltrust.org.uk). Hampstead tube/Hampstead Heath rail. **Open** *Mar* 2-5pm Sat, Sun. *Apr-Oct* 2-5pm Wed-Fri; 11am-4.30pm Sat, Sun, bank hols. *Tours* phone for times. **Admission** (NT) £5.20; £2.40 5-15s; free under-5s; £12 family (2+2). **No credit cards**.

This late 17th-century house has a beautiful garden and contains the Benton Fletcher collection of early keyboard instruments as well as Peter Barkworth's 19th- and early 20th-century English paintings. Children enjoy the orchard, vegetable garden and lawns, and are fascinated by the harpsichords, clavichords, virginals and spinets indoors. There's also a porcelain collection that includes a 'curious grotesque teapot' and several poodles. Apple Day in October is celebrated in the orchard, and musical families love the fortnightly summer concerts utilising instruments in the collection.

Baby slings for hire. Buggy access. Disabled access: ramp. Nappy-changing facilities.

Hampstead Heath

NW5 1QR (8348 9908/www.cityoflondon.gov.uk/ openspaces). Kentish Town tube/Gospel Oak or Hampstead Heath rail/214, C2, C11 bus. **Open** dawn-dusk daily.

An undulating swathe of grass, woods and lakes that measures an impressive 800 acres (320 hectares). Toil up Parliament Hill to fly a kite, or gaze over the city for miles and miles. Stay at the bottom of the hill to play tennis, bowls or boules; to feed the ducks on the first lake, or admire the model boats (occasionally noisy) on the second.

The heath is maintained by the Corporation of London. In recent years, the various ponds, which are fed by an underground stream thought to be the old River Fleet, have been cleaned up. Bathing is segregated, and since the Ladies Bathing Pond is located in a secluded enclosure, entry is barred to all males and to girls under eight. Consequently, family bathing is probably best undertaken in the lido close to Gospel Oak station. The playground here has free access to a shallow paddling pool during the summer months. The adventure playground behind the athletics track has challenging timber-framed equipment.

Clowns, magicians, storytellers and puppeteers perform in various locations each week (pick up a leaflet from the Parliament Hill information office). There are also tennis courses, learn-to-fish days, bat walks and nature trails. More accessible these days is a children's 'secret garden' and wildlife pond, near the tennis courts; call at the information centre to gain entry. No wonder the heath has a Green Flag Award (given to top-quality parks). Check the website and local press for more news of the Hampstead Heath consultation and management plan, and to check that family events are going ahead as expected.

Buggy access. Cafés. Disabled access: toilets. Nappy-changing facilities.

Kentish Town City Farm

1 Cressfield Close, off Grafton Road, NW5 4BN (7916 5421/www.ktcityfarm.org.uk). Chalk Farm tube/Kentish Town tube/rail/Gospel Oak rail. **Open** 9am-5.30pm daily. Closed 25 Dec. **Admission** free; donations appreciated.

Founded in 1972, this is London's oldest city farm. It stretches way beyond the farmyard into precious pasture and well-tended vegetable gardens by the railway line.

Livestock includes farmyard ducks, goats, pigs, horses, cows, chickens, a cat, dogs and sheep. A pond with a dipping platform is full of frogs, and a riding school (home to the Camden Pony Club) is the scene of weekend pony rides (1.30pm Sat, Sun, weather permitting, £1). A new farm centre, toilet block and classroom have appeared this year where a plethora of inventive craft and play sessions take place through the week. The energetic education officer welcomes school visits from all boroughs, and anyone can come to the May Day celebrations, Easter egg hunt, Apple Day (October) and so on.

Buggy access. Disabled access: ramp, toilet. Nappy-changing facilities. Nearest picnic place: on the farm.

Kenwood House/Iveagh Bequest

Hampstead Lane, NW3 7JR (8348 1286/www.english-heritage.org.uk). Hampstead tube/Golders Green tube then 210 bus. **Open** *Apr-Oct* 11am-5pm daily. *Nov-Mar* 11am-4pm daily. **Tours** by appointment. **Admission** (EH) free; donations appreciated. *Tours* £3; £2 concessions; £1.50 under-16s. **Credit** MC, V.

Strike out across Hampstead Heath from almost any direction and a path will lead you to Kenwood House. Hot chocolate and cream teas in winter, or classy lemonade and ice-creams in summer, persuade small feet that the trek is worthwhile – the Brew House café (*see p182*), set in the old kitchens, is the best catering venue for miles around. The house is a white stucco mansion, built in the classical style for the Earl of Mansfield by Robert Adam in 1767-69 and bequeathed to the nation in 1927. It houses the Iveagh Bequest, a collection of paintings with works by Reynolds, Turner, Van Dyck, Rembrandt, a rare Vermeer (*The Guitar Player*), Hogarth, Guardi and Bouche. There's also a vast library. From 24 May to 2 September 2007 there will be an exhibition on the 200th anniversary of the abolition of slavery. Of special interest to children are the annual Easter egg hunt, St George's Day 'dragon trails', kite-making workshops and spooky Hallowe'en storytelling days.

Volunteer group Heath Hands also has its office here. It plans family events throughout the year, mostly to do with improving the look of the heath and the estate gardens; phone for details or pick up a leaflet at the visitors' centre in the Kenwood House Estate Office. Left to their own devices, most youngsters will find ample amusement in the vicinity: running through the Ivy Arch, hiding in the vast rhododendron bushes, or rolling down the grass slopes in front of the house.

Buggy access. Café. Disabled access: ramps, toilets. Nappy-changing facilities. Shop.

Highgate & Archway

Legend has it that the young Dick Whittington was walking away from the city at the foot of Highgate Hill when he heard the Bow bells peal out 'Turn again Whittington, thrice Mayor of London'. The event is commemorated on the Whittington Stone, near the hospital, and there's a little statue of his famous cat there too.

Today, Highgate village is bursting with rummage-worthy shops, child-friendly pubs – and lucky residents who greatly treasure the sylvan backdrop. One of the main reasons to bring children here is **Highgate Wood**, which

has a delightful setting, a well-designed play area and a pleasant café. Waterlow Park, donated to Londoners by the low-cost housing pioneer Sir Sydney Waterlow in 1889, and containing **Lauderdale House**, is also gorgeous.

Next door, beautiful **Highgate Cemetery** (Swains Lane, N6 6PJ, 8340 1834, www.highgate-cemetery.org) is on the visiting list of many a tourist, although the Friends of Highgate Cemetery prefer to play down the visitor pull of their historic patch. Youngsters are discouraged from visiting unless they're coming to see the grave of a relative, but if you long to pay respects to Karl Marx, Mary Ann Evans (aka George Eliot), Max Wall or any of the other admired figures who now repose in the Eastern Cemetery, you can bring children to this delightful boneyard, as long as they behave well. The Western Cemetery is out of bounds to casual visitors (adults and kids aged eight and over can pay £3 for a guided tour, which brings the departed to life and affords a chance to see the eerie catacombs).

A little further down the hill from the tube station is Shepherd's Close, from where you can access the Parkland Walk (which runs to Finsbury Park). Hornsey Lane, on the other side of Highgate Hill, leads you to the **Archway**, a Victorian viaduct spanning what is now the A1 and offering views of the City and the East End. Jackson's Lane arts centre (269A Archway Road, N6 5AA, box office 8341 4421, www.jacksonslane.org.uk) is a lovely old landmark, although it was closed through storm damage as we went to press and concerns are growing for its future.

Highgate Wood/Queen's Wood

Muswell Hill Road, N10 3JN (8444 6129/www.cityof london.gov.uk/openspaces). Highgate tube/43, 134, 263 bus. **Open** 7.30am-dusk daily.

These 70 acres are some of the last remaining ancient woodlands in London. The wood has been tended by the Corporation of London and its trusty team since 1886, when the Lord Mayor declared the wood 'an open space for ever'. Carpeted with bluebells and wild flowers in spring and dappled with sunlight filtered by the trees, this corner of London really doesn't feel like London at all.

The wood is carefully managed: trees are traditionally coppiced; areas are fenced off to encourage new growth; boxes are provided for owls, bats and hedgehogs to live in; and everything that moves is chronicled. The bird population has increased dramatically in recent years, both in species and numbers. You can pick up leaflets about the wildlife in the visitors' information hut beside the café, or join one of the bird identification walks, bat walks or nature trails. Last spring's Big Brother bird watch, during which a camera was installed into a bird box, showed the blue tit fledglings growing via a monitor near the playground.

The award-winning, newly resurfaced children's playground has been carefully planned to allow wheelchair-users and their more mobile friends to play together. The bridge and tower structure is accessible to

Hampstead Heath. *See p99.*

buggies and wheelchairs, the swings are designed to be used by children who need more support, and there are Braille noticeboards. In front of the café is a football and cricket field, and exercise equipment has been placed among the trees.

Buggy access. Café. Disabled access: toilet. Nappy-changing facilities.

Lauderdale House

Highgate Hill, Waterlow Park, N6 5HG (8348 8716/restaurant 8341 4807/www.lauderdale.org.uk). Archway tube/143, 210, 271, W5 bus. **Open** 11am-4pm Tue-Fri; 1.30-5pm Sat; noon-5pm Sun; phone to check weekend openings. *Restaurant* 10am-dusk Tue-Sun. Closed 24 Dec-mid Jan. **Admission** free. **Credit** (Café) MC, V.

The pretty, 16th-century Lauderdale House, once home of Nell Gwynne, is the centrepiece of Waterlow Park. A favoured venue for wedding receptions and other bashes, it's sometimes closed to the public. Saturdays, however, are sacrosanct, because that's when children come for their morning shows (*see p229*). In the summer, weather permitting, the parkland surrounding the house hosts open-air shows. Whatever's on, it's lovely to sit on the terrace of the café and admire the view over a coffee and ice-cream or an Italian meal; book ahead if you fancy having Sunday lunch here. The Grade II-listed park, with its lakes and toddler playground, has a 17th-century terrace garden whose depot building contains an activities room and toilets.

Buggy access (ground floor only). Café/restaurant. Disabled access: toilets (ground floor). Nearest picnic place: Waterlow Park.

Islington

Looking at this smart and fashionable area, it's hard to believe that for more than a century and a half it went into a decline, when the opening of the busy Regent's Canal brought with it industrial slums in the 1820s. Creeping gentrification, starting in the late 1970s, has over the decades resulted in a very trendy Islington, with smart Georgian squares and Victorian terraces. The district is characterised by its mix of modish bars, shops, and flourishing arts centres – many of which have plenty to offer children.

Islington has 11 theatres and is home to the Anna Scher Theatre School, where many *EastEnders* cast members learned their trade; it has a five-year waiting list. In a pretty square off Cross Street, the old-established **Little Angel Theatre** (*see p225*) is a celebrated, purpose-built puppet theatre.

Highbury Fields has a smashing playground, where the equipment is challenging but extremely crowded on sunny days. Footie fans of the Gunner variety are proud of Arsenal's swish new 60,000-capacity Emirates Stadium down the road. Occasional 75-minute guided tours, which end at the museum, take place at the £390 million ground (call 7704 4504 to book).

Kentish Town City Farm.
See p100.

Question time: North London

Where can we play?

Our favourite playgrounds up north are, in order of preference, at Highgate Woods (for the birds; see p100), in Highbury Fields (for the zip wires; see p103) and in Alexandra Park (for the height; see p105).

What can we learn?

Jewish history, where else but at the Jewish Museums (see p97 and p106); Early Music at Fenton House (see p99); entomology at Abney Park Cemetery (see p104); zoology at Clissold Park (see p104) and aeronautics at the RAF Museum (see p107).

Whom might we meet?

Sadie Frost is bringing up her four in Primrose Hill; Fiona Shaw is also a resident. Richard Branson flies his helicopter greenly over his Hampstead pad, and Thierry Henry and family lead a quieter life in the same desirable village.

Where should we eat?

The Islington branch of Giraffe (see p103) is always a good bet, as is the S&M Café (see p180) almost opposite. The best kebabs in the world come from Mangal II in Stoke Newington (see p178) and our favourite place in London for pasta, with ice-cream to follow, is Marine Ices (see p178). For a real blowout, however, Banners (see p175) is hard to beat.

What can we buy?

The shopping is easy for teens at Camden Market (see p208), but parents with small children to entertain and kit out are better off trying Igloo (see p202) and Route 73 Kids (see p212). There are fairies galore at Mystical Fairies (see p209) and fantasy cakes at Ottolenghi (see p179). Fortis Green is never knowingly short of books and toys; head to the Children's Bookshop (see p189) and Never Never Land (see p212).

The other big park in the area is the rather sprawling **Finsbury Park**, for which the borough of Islington shares responsibility with the boroughs of Haringey and Hackney. It's a sprawling green space currently in the hands of an outfit called Finfuture (www.finfuture.co.uk), which is busying itself with the long-promised park regeneration. There's no shortage of sporting facilities, notably the **Michael Sobell Leisure Centre** (see p265) with its climbing walls, trampolining, table tennis, squash and badminton, and mini ice-rink. Nearby, on Green Lanes, the **Castle Climbing Centre** (07776 176007, www.castle-climbing.co.uk) is one of London's top climbing venues, but, unfortunately, is always oversubscribed. You'll find it in a Grade II-listed Victorian folly (previously a water tower) modelled on Stirling Castle.

Those who crave the scent of the countryside can commune with pigs at **Freightliners City Farm** or learn about green activities at the **Islington Ecology Centre**. The taste of the country can be sampled every Sunday from 10am to 2pm at the Islington Farmers' Market (William Tyndale School, Upper Street, N1, 7833 0338). Look out for happily picnicking families sampling their farmers' market goodies on the green. These folk are sensible: most eating places on Upper Street are expensive. The Turkish restaurants are great value, however, and very friendly. The three branches of the highly popular Gallipoli (102 Upper Street, N1 1QN, 7359 0630, www.cafegallipoli.com; Gallipoli Again, No.120,

N1 1QP, 7359 1578; Gallipoli Bazaar, No.107, N1 1QP, 7226 5333) also serve hearty English breakfasts. On nearby Essex Road, the **S&M Café** (see p180) is another affordable option, as is **Giraffe** (No. 29, 7359 5999).

Chapel Market (on the street of the same name) is a gloriously downmarket bargain bin of fruit and vegetables, linen, partyware, toys and not-always durables, presided over by rowdy costers. It has to endure competition from the N1 Shopping Centre. The centre has reliable childrenswear chains, restaurants such as Wagamama and Yo Sushi!, and an eight-screen cinema. The Islington Museum, in the Town Hall on Upper Street (7527 2837), is closed until February 2008.

Freightliners City Farm

Paradise Park, Sheringham Road, off Liverpool Road, N7 8PF (7609 0467/www.freightlinersfarm.org.uk). Caledonian Road or Holloway Road tube/Highbury & Islington tube/rail. **Open** *Summer* 10am-4.45pm Tue-Sun. *Winter* 10am-4pm Tue-Sun. Closed 25 Dec-1 Jan. **Admission** free; donations appreciated.
A stone's throw from Pentonville Prison, thisfarmteems with life. There are rabbits, cows, sheep, goats, cats, geese and pigs, as well as all kinds of poultry. The animals, many of them rare breeds, are impressive. Giant Flemish rabbits are the biggest you'll see anywhere; guineafowl run amok in other animals' pens; exotic cockerels with feathered feet squawk in your path; bees fly around their hives. You can buy hen and duck eggs of all hues, plus own-grown veg and plants when in season. There's an organic market on Saturdays. Playschemes run in summer and are popular. *Buggy access. Café. Disabled access: toilets. Nappy-changing facilities. Nearest picnic place: farm picnic area. Shop* .

Around Town

Highbury Fields

Highbury Crescent, N5 1RR (7527 4971). Highbury & Islington tube/rail/19, 30, 43, 271 bus. **Open** *Park* 24hrs. *Playground* dawn-dusk daily.

Islington's largest outdoor space repays careful exploration. Hidden behind Highbury Pool and a series of high bushes is an unusual playground that combines old-fashioned thrills (such as a circular train demanding passenger propulsion *Flintstones*-style, and an excitingly long and steep slide) with more recent additions, like the flying fox and giant, web-like climbing frames. The outdoor tennis courts have been refurbished and are used by the excellent Islington Tennis Centre. A stroll across Highbury Fields can take you from busy UpperStreet past imposing period terraces to Highbury Barn, a trendy enclave boasting several excellent food shops, restaurants and child-friendly cafés.

Buggy access. Café.

Islington Ecology Centre

Gillespie Park Nature Reserve, 191 Drayton Park, N5 1PH (7354 5162/www.islington.gov.uk). Arsenal tube. **Open** *Park* 8am-dusk Mon-Fri; 9am-dusk Sat; 10am-dusk Sun. Closed Arsenal FC home matches. *Centre drop-in sessions* varies; phone to check. **Admission** free; donations appreciated.

Islington's largest nature reserve was fashioned from derelict railway land. It has woodland, meadows, wetland and ponds, and the Ecology Centre is its educational heart. Staff are endlessly enthusiastic and helpful on the subject of all natural things in the borough. An events diary is published biannually, listing events suitable for families: from moth evenings to junk modelling. Nature-themed workshops run in the holidays.

Buggy access.

Stoke Newington

Nestled between Islington and Hackney, 'Stokey' has, it is averred, more buggies per square mile than anywhere else in London. Still pleasantly bohemian, the heart of the area is Church Street, host to North London's best street festival every June. Visit on a usual weekend and you'll find a heap of great little independent shops, an organic farmers' market, antique yard, a few good second-hand bookshops, and one of the best toy shops around – all on the same street. There's no shortage of child-friendly places to grab a bite, but if the weather's good pick up a picnic from a suitable deli and wander along the road to dear old **Clissold Park**. Parents denied proper park action by wet weather might opt for the over-excitement encouraged by the large and jolly adventure play centre, **Zoomaround**.

Around the corner from Church Street is the contrasting High Street with its array of Turkish cafés and grocers. Keep heading south and you get to Stokey's rough-and-ready neighbour, Dalston, which has the biggest street market for miles around, Ridley Road, full of Afro-Caribbean and Turkish ware, alongside the traditional costers.

Abney Park Cemetery & Nature Reserve

Stoke Newington High Street, N16 0LN (7275 7557/ www.abney-park.org.uk). Stoke Newington rail/73, 106, 149, 243, 276, 349 bus. **Open** dawn-dusk daily. *Visitors' centre* 9.30am-5pm Mon-Fri. **Admission** free.

A decayed Victorian cemetery, the winsomely antiquated Abney Park is a hub of conservation activity. There's an environmental classroom at the Stoke Newington High Street entrance, which is the scene of many free workshops for children and adults (check the website for current events). Go on a mini beast hunt and examine beetles and bugs at close quarters or take a tree tour and learn about the hundreds of different varieties on site. The visitors' centre doubles as a shop for guides to green London and other such environmentally aware literature. While still plainly part of a burial ground, the decaying monuments – draped urns, angels, Celtic crosses, saints and shepherds – add romantic interest to a local nature reserve where trees and plants are now in the ascendancy.

Buggy access. Disabled access: toilet (visitors' centre). Shop.

Clissold Park

Stoke Newington Church Street, N16 5HJ (7923 3660). Stoke Newington rail/73, 149, 329, 476 bus. **Open** *Park* 7.30am-dusk daily. **Admission** free.

There's much to discover on a pleasant amble around Clissold Park. Stroll over the river bridge and peek through the fences at some surprisingly friendly deer, rabbits, birds and goats. You'll also find several ponds supporting various waterfowl, an outdoor stage for children to cavort on whenever it's not in use by bands, and tennis courts that carers could use while kids are in the adjoining well-kitted-out playground. The courts are home to the Hackney wing of the City Tennis Centre (7254 4235); ring for details of its programme (family tennis evenings, coaching, and junior clubs and tournaments are all available). The playground is lovely, with modern equipment and shady picnic tables. Clissold House and Park have been given a £4.5 million grant for restoration work, so the future looks even more beautiful round here.

Buggy access (in park, steps at café). Café. Disabled access: toilets (in front of café). Nappy-changing facilities (on request).

Zoomaround

46 Milton Grove, N16 8QY (7254 2220/ www.zoomaround.co.uk) Highbury & Islington tube/ rail then 393 bus/73, 476, 141, 341, 236 bus. **Open** 10am-6.15pm daily. **Admission** £2 under-1s; £3.50 1-3s; £4.50 over-4s; free siblings (under-1s). **No credit cards.**

This huge multi-level play frame is filled with ball ponds, slides, rope swings, climbing nets and tunnels – all made of brightly coloured, padded plastic. Bouncing, crawling and climbing (up, down, across, inside and out) are the order of the day. Toddlers have their own separate area and carers can either squeeze through the child-size nooks and crannies in hot pursuit of little ones, or sit and look on with some cake and a cappuccino from the café. There's a fine-weather garden too.

Buggy access. Café. Nearest picnic place: Butterfield Green.

Crouch End & Muswell Hill

Crouch End and Muswell Hill have become the settlements of choice for North Londoners looking for more space to breathe. Architecturally, they are blessed with a wealth of unspoilt Victorian and Edwardian housing (check out the scenery, pre-1890s building boom, at the **Bruce Castle Museum** – *see p107*). This, together with decent primary schools, has made both districts popular with young families, and many of the shops and cafés reflect the trend.

The area's best-known attraction is **Alexandra Park & Palace**, but there are plenty of other green spaces. Priory Park off Middle Lane is great for cycling, rollerskating and football, and has a paddling pool, formal gardens, tennis courts and the excellent Rainbow Café, right next to the paddling pool (and thus convenient for beady-eyed nannies/mummies). The park is the venue for an annual fun run organised by the YMCA: a huge event every May for runners and families (it includes children's races where doughnuts, T-shirts and such like are given away).

Stationers Park, between Denton Road and Mayfield Road, contains a decent adventure playground, a pre-school children's play area and (free) tennis courts. Park Road Pools has both indoor and outdoor swimming pools, though the latter gets packed in fine weather. Hidden tracts of greenery off Park Road allow ample space for the North Middlesex Sports Club, plus various other tennis and cricket clubs; these are the venues

for sport-related holiday playschemes and useful after-school coaching.

There are so many family-oriented restaurants in Crouch End, you'd stumble into one if you were blindfolded and spun around three times. **Banners** (*see p175*) is probably the most popular.

Alexandra Park & Palace

Alexandra Palace Way, N22 7AY (park 8444 7696/ information 8365 2121/www.alexandrapalace.com). Wood Green tube/Alexandra Palace rail/W3, 144 bus. **Open** *Park* 24hrs daily. *Palace* times vary depending on exhibitions. **Admission** free.

The Ally Pally has had some bad luck. It burnt down twice – once in 1863, just weeks after opening, and once in 1980 – only to rise like a veritable phoenix on each occasion as a grandiloquent place of public entertainment. The place was still upright last time we went ice-skating (*see p264*) although sadly the boating lake has closed indefinitely. Outside, the children's playground is a well-equipped and wholesome place to take the air. In all, the palace on the hill and its environs have much to offer, some crumbliness notwithstanding. Chief interest for children is the glorious ice-skating rink, along with (in summer) the pitch-and-putt course. Walking around the park affords breathtaking views of London, and there's plenty of space for picnics. In bad weather, try the café in the garden centre. Bonfire Night in November is the best night of the year, with lots of room for spectators and pyrotechnics that can be seen for miles around.

Buggy access. Disabled access: lift, ramps, toilets. Nappy-changing facilities (ice rink). Nearest picnic place: picnic area by boating lake.

Finchley

A popular, sprawling London suburb, Finchley has a settled Jewish and Japanese community and a general air of peace and prosperity. Three tube stations make the district handy for commuters into town. A preponderance of family-friendly leisure facilities (parks, playgrounds, leisure centres and retail parks) mean that Finchley's youth are quite well-served – until they reach an age when the lure of London's meaner streets takes them on the Northern line southward.

A short way south of Finchley Central tube station – at the heart of what was once a village and is now a cluster of small shops and cheap Turkish and Chinese restaurants – is **Avenue House** and its beautifully landscaped gardens, which were given to the nation in 1918. A five-minute walk north from the station gets you to Victoria Park, just off Ballards Lane between Finchley Central and North Finchley; here you'll find a bowling green, playground and tennis courts. In July the park also provides a venue for the Finchley Carnival.

For indoor entertainment, the **Great North Leisure Park** (Leisure Way, High Road, N12)

Zoomaround

Around Town

Alexandra Park & Palace – plenty to see, lots to do. *See p105.*

is an ugly but useful US-style entertainment complex. The cinema, Finchley Warner Village (0871 224 0240, www.myvue.com), has a Saturday morning kids' club. There's also a swimming pool kitted out with a vigorous wave machine and swirling currents. The Hollywood Bowl bowling alley (Leisure Way, High Road, N12 0QZ, 8446 6667, www.hollywoodbowl.co.uk) contains a bar and burger restaurant; adjacent to it is an amusements arcade.

East Finchley's Phoenix Cinema (52 High Road, N2 9PJ, 8883 2233, www.phoenixcinema.co.uk) holds children's screenings on Saturdays. The Old Manor House, on East End Road, is now a cultural centre, which includes ritual baths, a school and the absorbing **Jewish Museum, Finchley**.

Should you decide to get away from it all en famille, try the **Dollis Valley Green Walk** (www.ramblers.org.uk), which forms part of the London Loop encircling the city. This links green spaces from Moat Mount, near Mill Hill in the north, to Hampstead Garden Suburb in the south. Setting off with a map is advisable, as the way isn't very well signposted.

Avenue House

17-19 East End Road, N3 3QE (8346 7812/www. avenuehouse.org.uk). Finchley Central tube/82, 125 bus. **Open** *Ink Museum* 2-4pm Tue-Thur. **Admission** free; donations appreciated.
Built in 1859, this handsome country pile was bought in 1874 by Henry Charles ('Inky') Stephens, whose father invented blue-black ink. He was a Member of Parliament but inherited a keen interest in writing fluids from his father, installing a laboratory in the house when he refurbished it. Stephens died in 1918, bequeathing Avenue

House to the people of Finchley. The one-room Ink Museum commemorates Stephens father and son (Stephens' ink factory was on the site of the Islington Ecology Centre, *see p104*). The rest of Avenue House is open to view only on certain days of the year – phone for details – but some rooms can be hired for parties. Fundraising is still continuing to build a tearoom; with luck it will open by the end of 2007. Otherwise, the grounds are open free of charge from 7am until dusk, and offer a pleasantly situated playground and buggy-accessible tree trail.
Buggy access. Café (Mar-Sept). Disabled access: toilet. Nappy-changing facilities. Nearest picnic place: Avenue House grounds. Shop.

Jewish Museum, Finchley

Sternberg Centre, 80 East End Road, N3 2SY (8349 1143/www.jewishmuseum.org.uk). Finchley Central tube/143 bus. **Open** 10.30am-5pm Mon-Thur; 10.30am-4.30pm Sun. Closed bank hols, Jewish hols, Sun in Aug. **Admission** (LP) £2; £1 concessions, 12-16s; free under-12s. **No credit cards.**
The northerly branch of the informative Jewish Museum (*see p97*) focuses on Jewish social history. Like its Camden sibling it is also due to close in September 2007 for an 18-month refurbishment. Until then, the displays in the main gallery include several hands-on areas, such as tailor's and cabinetmaker's workshops, where you can test the weight of a flat iron and find out how a suit is made. There's also a Treasure Trail, suitable for ages seven to 11. Upstairs, an exhibition traces the life of Leon Greenman, a British Jew (now aged 96) who survived Auschwitz. The Holocaust Exhibition may be considered too upsetting for young children, but staff leave it to the discretion of parents; the images are more likely to be understood by those of at least secondary school age. Temporary exhibitions include 'The Last Goodbye: The Rescue Of Children From Nazi Europe', which tells the story of 10,000 unaccompanied children rescued from Nazi Europe on the Kindertransport.
Buggy access. Café (lunch Mon-Thur). Nearest picnic place: museum garden/Avenue House gardens. Shop.

Further north

The neighbourhoods of Tottenham and Harringay have sizeable Greek Cypriot, Turkish Cypriot and Kurdish communities. The influence of these cultures is most noticeable on Green Lanes, where food-related business success is evident in the kebab shops, supermarkets and bakeries.

Spurs fans willingly make the pilgrimage to the frozen north and White Hart Lane, the home of **Tottenham Hotspur Football Club**, but for ordinary folk a good reason for heading north is **Bruce Castle**, an island of stateliness in run-down surroundings.

Further west, the North Circular (an escape route or a vehicle trap, depending on traffic) leads to **Brent Cross Shopping Centre** with its large range of chains and a handy crèche, thence to IKEA, purveyor of affordable flatpacks and always a good bet for a plate of meatballs and a play in the ball pond.

Away from the shopping and west of the M1, there's blessed peace to be had around Cool Oak Lane and its extensive reservoir and attendant countryside. The Welsh Harp Reservoir is a major watersports centre as well as a Site of Special Scientific Interest. The informative environmental centre makes a good starting point for nature trips. Leafy waterside areas provide space for games pitches, tennis courts, playgrounds and picnics.

In Hendon proper, the **Royal Air Force Museum Hendon** is a lavish tribute to the history of flying machines and the magnificent men who piloted them.

Bruce Castle Museum

Lordship Lane, N17 8NU (8808 8772/www.haringey. gov.uk). Wood Green tube then 123 or 243 bus/Seven Sisters tube/rail then 123 or 243 bus/Bruce Grove rail. **Open** 1-5pm Wed-Sun. **Admission** free.
This local museum, set in an unexpectedly beautiful 16th-century manor house and holding the entire collections of the borough of Haringey, is a lively place appreciated for its weekend and holiday children's activities. Sunday afternoons (2-4pm) always see some craft session or other in progress; this leaves adults free to peruse the photographs of local streets in Victorian times undisturbed (Muswell Hill as a muddy cart track; quaint shopfronts on North London high streets; rolling green pastures now filled with housing). The building itself was owned by successive generations of the Coleraine family and is said to be haunted by one of them still. More concrete is the lasting influence of Rowland Hill, a progressive schoolmaster on this site and subsequently a postal reformer; his ideas led to the formation of the Penny Post. Hill is featured in a room devoted to local inventors, which has plenty of buttons to push and pull. Other displays, highlighting the war years, are popular with grandparents. The museum's archives may be visited by appointment; if you live in Haringey borough, there's every chance your own street

will be featured in a historic photo that may be copied to take home. Outside, the 20 acres (8 hectares) of grounds make for good picnicking; there's a playground and a collection of antique postboxes.
Buggy access. Car park (in Church Lane, free). Disabled access: lift, toilet. Nappy-changing facilities. Shop.

Royal Air Force Museum Hendon

Grahame Park Way, NW9 5LL (8205 2266/ www.rafmuseum.org). Colindale tube/Mill Hill Broadway rail/303 bus. **Open** 10am-6pm daily. Closed 24-26 Dec, 1 Jan. *Tours* daily; times vary, phone for details. **Admission** free. *Tours* free. **Credit** MC, V.
There has been an airfield at Hendon since 1910, hence its claims to be the birthplace of aviation in Britain. These days the Aerodrome houses more than 80 historic aircraft, among them a Camel, Tempest, Gypsy Moth, Mosquito and Harrier – all parked at ground level or hung in dog-fight poses from the rafters of the ultra-modern Milestones of Flight building. As you take a break in the café, helicopter blades jut out above your head. A little further on, miniature parachutists go up and down in a tube or drop off a wire into the hands of kids eager to learn about the laws of gravity. More interactive games are available in the Aeronauts gallery, many in the guise of pilot aptitude tests. Only the flight simulator (over-eights only) carries an extra charge; everything else is gloriously free, so although a comprehensive tour is exhausting, you can come as often as you like. More low-key than the Milestones of Flight gallery are the atmospheric and dimly lit Battle of Britain building, and the restored Grahame-White Aircraft Factory.

Activities for children and adults take place all year. The ever-popular workshops (book ahead) include hot-air balloon making, rocket science, and Search and Rescue role-playing. Quizzes, Pulsar Battlezone interactive laser games, face-painting, aircraft displays and giant garden games are also on the cards. The Summer High Fliers month (1-31 August 2007) will have a Roald Dahl theme, and an exhibition of other famous people who served in the Royal Air Force. The Wings restaurant now includes a corner for kids with books a playstation, beanbags and other toys.
Buggy access. Café. Disabled access: ramps, toilets. Lift. Nappy-changing facilities. Nearest picnic place: on-site picnic area. Restaurant. Shop.

Tottenham Hotspur Football Club

Bill Nicholson Way, 748 High Road, N17 0AP (8365 5000/ticket office 0870 420 5000/www.spurs.co.uk). White Hart Lane rail. **Open** *Tours* 11am, 1pm non-match Sats. **Admission** *Tours* £8; £5 under-16s, OAPs. **Credit** (advance only) MC, V.
Tours of the pitch-side, the tunnel, changing rooms, boardrooms and press rooms take place regularly, but the Saturday tours tend to be booked up well in advance. Note that they cannot take place on a match day, nor the day before; indeed their regularity depends on a minimum number of customers, so don't turn up on spec. Tours last about 60-90 minutes, depending on how chatty the punters are. Finish in the megastore, where you can blow £35 on a home shirt and £1.99 for a sticker pack.
Buggy access. Disabled access: toilet. Shop.

Around Town

East London

Relax or run wild in the rough-and-tumble East End.

Spitalfields & around

It may be within what was recently pronounced in a survey as London's sickest borough (Tower Hamlets), but Spitalfields, right on the City's doorstep, is rude with health. It's best approached from Liverpool Street Station via Brushfield Street. Once you are confronted by the huge bulk of Christ Church Spitalfields, you know you're on the right track. Crispin Place, a chichi courtyard shopping area with a sail-like curved awning is part of the continuing development of the huge, covered market at Spitalfields (*see p208*).

The streets surrounding the market – once home to Huguenot families, whose skills in the silk-weaving trade supported their flight from religious persecution in France – are a delight. Among them is Folgate Street, where you'll find **Dennis Severs' House**. Architectural merit won't mean much to the children – so lure them to the area with promises of lunch in a Brick Lane curry house, or a burger at Bubba's pit barbecue inside the market (Arkansas Café, *see p180*).

Sunday is the busiest day of the week in this neighbourhood. Thankfully, the sprawl of market stalls that extended at one point to Shoreditch High Street, petering out into pitiful bundles of cast-offs laid on the pavement, has been pruned back. Now the place to start is the northern end of **Brick Lane** and surrounding streets. Here, in front of boutiques selling lifestyle products, chic baby clothes and vintage paraphernalia, you'll find cheap children's footwear, sports gear, leather jackets, DVDs and so on.

Off elegant Fournier Street (which runs alongside Christ Church towards Brick Lane), you'll find the minor jewel that is **19 Princelet Street**; unfortunately, it is open only occasionally.

Dennis Severs' House

18 Folgate Street, E1 6BX (7247 4013/www.dennis severshouse.co.uk). Liverpool Street tube/rail. **Open** 2-5pm 1st & 3rd Sun of mth; noon-2pm Mon (following 1st & 3rd Sun of mth); Mon evenings (times vary; booking required). **Admission** £8 Sun; £5 noon-2pm Mon; £12 Mon evenings. No under-10s. **Credit** MC, V. **Map** p319 R5.
Dennis Severs (1948-1999) is not the man you come to see in this fully restored Huguenot house close to Spitalfields, but his mark is on everything. Severs was an American who came to the UK to study law but fell in love with the

18th century, and lived in his house *sans* bathroom, modern cooking facilities or even electricity. During his lifetime he narrated tours in which each room – from the cellar, kitchen, dining room, smoking room and upstairs to the bedrooms – was the scene of a different drama, covering eras from 1724 to 1914.

Making your way around the house in silence, you seem to chance upon the everyday activities and belongings of a fictitious family of Huguenot silk-weavers. You may hear their voices; you certainly feel the warmth of their log fires, the scent of their pomanders, the gorgeous sheen of their heavy silk drapes. It's as if the inhabitants only deserted these rooms a moment before. The house is still lived in, and no museum could provide an experience quite like it, though it's a bit dry for children under ten.
Nearest picnic place: Broadgate Circus (Liverpool Street station) or Elder Street Gardens. Shop.

19 Princelet Street

19 Princelet Street, Spitalfields, E1 6QH (7247 5352/ www.19princeletstreet.org.uk). Aldgate East tube/ Liverpool Street tube/rail. **Open** check website or phone for occasional open days. **Tours** groups by appointment. **Admission** free; donations appreciated. **Map** p319 S5.
This Grade II-listed building makes an unusual museum. First, it's the only one in Europe dedicated to immigration and cultural diversity. Second, the opening hours are infrequent, to say the least (just a few days in 2007, including every day in Refugee Week, 17-24 June), to preserve the fragile building until trustees raise the £3 million required to mend it. Still, it's worth making an effort to join in on one of its rare open days, as they give you a rare opportunity to see inside this crumbly silk merchant's home and hidden Victorian synagogue. No.19 was home to Huguenot silk weavers – you can still see a big bobbin hanging above the door – then to Irish dockers. In 1869 the house was a synagogue and, in the 20th century, it hosted English lessons for Bangladeshi women. Check the website for details of opening dates and special events.
Buggy access. Nearest picnic place: Christ Church grounds.

Whitechapel

Not one of London's prettier parts, this district takes its name from the white stones used to build a long-demolished church. The main Whitechapel Road is pretty anonymous, so it comes as a surprise to see any tourists here at all, until you realise they're mostly in the East End for a Jack the Ripper Walking Tour (Original London Walks, *see p32*). A brighter spot would be **Whitechapel Art Gallery** (80-82 Whitechapel High Street, E1 7QX, 7522

7888/www.whitechapel.org), except it's closed for 2007 for a refurb – check the website for details.

The **Women's Library** (London Metropolitan University, Old Castle Street, E1 7NT, 7320 2222/ www.thewomenslibrary.ac.uk), a former wash house, holds free exhibitions (9.30am-5.30pm Mon-Wed, Fri; 9.30am-8pm Thur; 10am-4pm Sat), as well as workshops and family activities in the summer holidays. The library holds the best collection relating to women's history in the country. The bright, contemporary Wash House Café on the first floor is a useful pit-stop, even for those with only a cursory interest in gender issues. The striking, rectangular **Idea Store** (321 Whitechapel Road, E1 1BU, 7364 4332/ www.ideastore.co.uk) is one of several Idea Stores, a flagship project of Tower Hamlets council. Its ultra modern interior offers a café and state-of-the-art learning and information services – among them a children's library and classrooms.

The **Whitechapel Bell Foundry** runs tours for over-14s. Pop into the foyer to see the huge frame of Big Ben surrounding the door. The **Royal London Hospital Archives & Museum** has more macabre attractions. And in the unprepossessing backstreets behind the hospital, scientists are busy growing tuberculosis and the like (not just for fun – they're researching new cures) in brand-new laboratories. If you think medical research is boring, think again: see the labcoats in action at Centre of the Cell (*see p111* **Thinking outside the pod**).

Shoreditch & Hoxton

Now one of London's most vibrant and dynamic social centres, these areas were once colonised by impoverished artists (hard to believe that former residents Tracey Emin and Damien Hirst fitted into that humble category) because studio rents were cheap. They didn't leave a whole heap of family entertainment with them, however. The **Geffrye Museum** is a gem, and provides a cultural impetus to visit Kingsland Road, whose other main asset is its plethora of inexpensive Vietnamese restaurants.

Hoxton Square, formerly Hoxton Fields, was where playwright Ben Jonson killed Gabriel Spencer in a duel in 1598. Fearless children will surely be interested in the possibility of a Sunday morning course in tightrope walking, trapeze work and so on at nearby **Circus Space** (*see p259*).

Geffrye Museum

136 Kingsland Road, E2 8EA (7739 9893/www. geffrye-museum.org.uk). Liverpool Street tube/rail, then 149, 242 bus/Old Street tube/rail, then 243 bus.

Open 10am-5pm Tue-Sat; noon-5pm Sun, bank hol Mon. Closed 1 Jan, Good Fri, 24-26 Dec. **Admission** free; donations appreciated. *Almshouse £2; £1 concessions; free under-16s. Under-8s must be accompanied by an adult.* **Credit** (restaurant, shop) MC, V.

This attractive, U-shaped building was constructed around a deep, lawned courtyard as almshouses in 1715. In 1914 the place was converted into a furniture and interior design museum. Now rooms represent different periods in history, from the Elizabethan era to the present day, and visitors walk past in a roped-off corridor, admiring the changing tastes and styles of succeeding generations. What keeps the children occupied is a thoughtful programme of activities. For example, on weekend afternoons there's an art trolley and a quiz desk.

In spring and summer, emphasis is placed on outdoor fun in the award-winning Herb Garden. The airy restaurant that overlooks it is a pleasure year-round (and serves children's portions). Summer Sundays take place once a month in June, July and August, typically involving the making of lavender potions and so on, with live music and plant sales.

The second, newer, half of the museum has space for changing exhibitions downstairs. In winter, the Christmas Past exhibition is always a hit, with each room decorated for the festive season according to its period. The museum also stages a Twelfth Night ritual (6 January), when a Christmas tree is burned to the accompaniment of cheers and mulled wine.

Buggy access. Disabled access: lift, toilet. Nappy-changing facilities. Nearest picnic place: museum grounds. Restaurant. Shop.

Royal London Hospital Archives & Museum

St Philip's Church, Newark Street, E1 2AA (7480 4823/www.brlcf.org.uk). Whitechapel tube. **Open** 10am-4.30pm Mon-Fri. Closed 24 Dec-2 Jan, bank hols & adjacent Tue. **Admission** free.

Along a backstreet and down some barely noticeable steps is the entrance to this fascinating museum, located in the former crypt of a late 19th century, early English style church, designed by Arthur Cawston. The museum chronicles the history of the hospital on parallel Mile End Road, once the biggest general hospital in the UK. The 1934 X-ray control unit could have been created by a mad inventor from a sci-fi B-movie, but the museum is mostly a serious-minded affair. The development of nursing and childcare is traced through displays of starchy uniforms such as those worn by Florence Nightingale and war heroine Edith Cavell; there's a replica of the hat former patient Joseph Merrick (the 'Elephant Man') wore and a forensics case with a copy of Jack the Ripper's notorious 'From Hell' letter. Most entertaining, however (and providing a welcome moment of rest if you have been dragging children about on foot all day), are the plummily-narrated documentaries shown on a video screen, which date from the 1930s to the 1960s. We see children kitted out in pilot's goggles gratefully receive doses of ultra-violet light after the London smog prevented the natural synthesis of vitamin D, leading to rickets. In the footage, keen young nurses talk passionately of their vocations as they cast down their eyes before the great male doctors in white coats. Priceless.

Buggy access. Café (in hospital). Disabled access: lift, ramp, toilet. Nappy-changing facilities (in hospital). Shop.

Spitalfields City Farm

Weaver Street, off Pedley Street, E1 5HJ (7247 8762/ www.spitalfieldscityfarm.org). Whitechapel tube. **Open** *Summer* 10am-4.30pm Tue-Sun. *Winter* 10am-4pm Tue-Sun. Closed 25 Dec-1 Jan. **Admission** free; donations appreciated.

This is a particularly well-run community farm, always spick and span. It was established in 1978 after local allotments were lost to property developers. Having reorganised some of its land to make way for the East London Line extension, the farm currently has geese honking about, a daily goat-milking demo, mice and rabbits for stroking, and a full complement of cows, pigs and sheep. Poultry, gardeners and all the livestock produce free-range eggs, seasonal vegetables and manure (in that order). Keen eight-to 13-year-olds can join the Young Farmers Club, which runs a play scheme on Saturdays; there's also a jolly parent and toddler group for under-fives (Tue, Sun). The Coriander Club, where local Bangladeshi women grow vegetables and teach how to cook them, is a very popular community class. Young visitors can often enjoy donkey rides (£1) if the donkeys are up for it, and special annual events include various open days, the Spitalfields Show in September and Apple Day in October.
Buggy access. Disabled access: toilets. Nappy-changing facilities. Nearest picnic place: Allen Gardens. Shop.

Whitechapel Bell Foundry

32-34 Whitechapel Road, E1 1DY (7247 2599/www. whitechapelbellfoundry.co.uk). Whitechapel tube. **Open** 9.30am-4.30pm Mon-Fri. *Tours strictly by appointment* 10am, 2pm Sat. No under-14s. **Admission** free. *Tours* £8. **Credit** MC, V.

Even if you have no interest in church bells, you'll be impressed by the foundry – Britain's oldest manufacturing company. It has been in continuous production since 1570; its most famous product was the 13.7 tonne Big Ben, cast in the 19th century. Anyone can pop in during office hours to see the little exhibition that illustrates the bell-founding process with miniature figures. A shop can set you up with handsome doorbells, and a handbell room introduces children to the techniques of producing music in a group with hand chimes. Tours of the foundry are open only to those aged 14 and over, but friendly staff are always willing to explain their techniques and terminology. 'Clappering', 'change ringing', 'five-tone peals' and so on are soon understood; just as the meaning of popular expressions like 'ringing the changes' is suddenly enhanced.
Disabled access: ramp (ground floor only). Shop.

Bethnal Green to Hackney

The old-style East End begins to reassert itself along the Bethnal Green Road, which is a market street, even on weekdays. Amid the many fast-food eateries, the lovely little caff E Pellicci (No.332, 7739 4873) is worth a visit. A sign in the window may say 'no buggies', but they are often accommodated in its general atmosphere of Italian bonhomie. **Columbia Road Flower Market** (between Gosset Road and the Royal Oak pub, 8am-2pm Sun) makes a lovely morning excursion; if the garish colours of tightly packed plants fail to impress, there is the banter of the traders and the

assortment of increasingly smart shops and cafés. **V&A Museum of Childhood** is the biggest draw here, though.

Hackney has been the subject of plans for improved transport links for well over a decade, and now that the London's Olympic preparations are in full swing, the East London Line is on its way. However you get here, there's stuff worth seeing. The centre of Hackney is Town Hall Square on Mare Street, where you'll find the well-preserved old Hackney Empire (*see p228*), the cornerstone of Hackney's 'cultural quarter', which includes the **Hackney Museum**, housed in the Central Library opposite.

For somewhere with such a definitively urban reputation, Hackney has a surprising number of green spaces – surprising, that is, until you learn that as late as the 19th century it was almost entirely rural. Adjoining the brilliant **Hackney City Farm**, **Haggerston Park** (Audrey Street, off Goldsmith Row, E2 8QH, 7739 6288) has pretty gardens beside a large pond, as well as places for ball games and BMX riding, and a wood-built playground. Head north up Goldsmith's Row, cross Regent's Canal and you're on **Broadway Market**. The chichi establishments along this strip include chic but friendly gastropub the Cat & Mutton (No.76, 7254 5599, www.catandmutton. co.uk), the Argentinean grill (Santa Maria de Buen Ayre, No.50, 7275 9900) and Holistic Health (64 Broadway Market, E8 4QJ, 7275 8434, www. holistic-health-hackney.co.uk), specialists in holistic therapies for tots. The area's sleek incomers buy their organic fruit and vegetables at the Saturday market (www.broadwaymarket.co.uk), which has a dedicated Brat Park Corner. There's a play area with hopscotch, chess and draughts marked out on the ground, and storytelling and face-painting for under-sevens (12.30pm); the Broadway Knitters Club meets monthly, supplying special giant needles so that children can have a bash. London Fields (Westside, E8) is right at the top of the market. This attractive open space is now a major destination, thanks to the opening of the lovely lido in late 2006. *See p268*.

Further east, across the River Lee, lie 300 acres (120 hectares) of Hackney Marshes, a great place to take the air. It's fine kite-flying country and provides a muddy home for English Sunday League, American and Gaelic football, rugby and cricket. North up the river you'll find the very pretty Springfield Park, which looks east past the narrow boats of Springfield Marina and out over breezy Walthamstow Marshes. Refreshments are available at the child-orientated Springfield Park Café (www.sparkcafe.co.uk), in the White Lodge at the top of the park's steep hill.

Thinking outside the pod

The front of the imposingly Victorian Royal London Hospital gives little hint that something unprecedented is happening in the back streets beyond. Centre of the Cell, due to open in spring 2008, is a multimedia experience located bang in the middle of a busy, cutting-edge medical research facility. Some of the laboratories around it are so important they're designated Category 3 – sealed-off, in other words, so that scientists can work with brutally infectious diseases like TB, an illness of growing significance in modern-day Tower Hamlets.

The fun is focused on 'the pod' (*pictured*). Suspended above the labs, the pod is accessed by a glass-walled walkway from which you can peer down on scientists beavering away in their white coats. Once everyone's inside, a film is projected on to the surrounding walls, introducing children to the amazing work going on all around them. Film over, a silver lozenge pulsating with light opens to reveal interactive games. Through this linked sequence of alternating audiovisual projections and interactives, the visitors can explore all sorts of biomedical science.

They will get to compare the size of a cell to a five-pence piece (it's a quarter of the size of one of the little dots around the edge), trace the progress of growth of an embryo (ending with a picture of a child with the watching child's face superimposed on top), see the ultramagnification of their own hands, and guess how many cells there are in a mouse, a person, then an elephant.

Other interactives are based on ultra-advanced medical research – showing how drugs can help regrow someone's damaged spinal cord at the site of an accident, perhaps, or creating real, new skin with hair for grafting on to burns victims. It just depends what the scientists have discovered, since everything in the pod is based on the work of the white-coated folks you spied on as you walked above their labs. Even better, the format of the pod experience ensures it can be regularly updated to keep abreast of current developments.

There are even (oooer!) real body organs in the exhibition – something the exhibition organisers found, during their three years of extensive research and development in local schools, that parents and teachers were far more squeamish about than their charges. The experience is rounded off by considering the impact of biomedical research on your own life.

The whole experience lasts around 90 minutes but – given the intimate space (no more than 40 people fit into the pod), the setting and the theatricality of the presentation – young 'uns should remain entertained throughout. Hardly aware, in fact, that they're busy boning up on the scientific enquiry, investigation and applied science aspects of Key Stages 2 to 4, and all the while learning that scientists aren't all white, middle-aged – 'and mad', as audience researcher Katie Chambers says, with a distinct twinkle in her eye.

Sneaky people, these scientists.

Centre of the Cell

64 Turner Street, E1 2AB (7882 2562/ www.centreofthecell.org). **Open** *Sessions* 10-11.30am, noon-1.30pm, 2-3.30pm, 4-5.30pm, 6.30-8pm.
Sessions are open to the general public during weekends, evenings and school holidays. Visitors are encouraged to book a timeslot in advance online or by phone.

Clowns International Gallery & Museum

All Saints Centre, Haggerston Road, E8 4HT (office hours only 0870 128 4336/www.clowns-international.co.uk). Dalston Kingsland or London Fields rail, then 38, 149, 236, 243 bus. **Open** noon-5pm 1st Fri of mth; other times by appointment. **Admission** free; donations appreciated.

Next to a church – where the annual Joseph Grimaldi memorial service is held in February – is this one-room gallery devoted to the history of clowns. Manned by members of Clowns International, the gallery holds displays of pottery eggs painted with famous clowns' faces; sequinned and harlequin costumes; original artworks, vintage posters and endlessly tumbling automata. The plethora of clown images is thought-provoking as well as jolly. 'Clown doctoring' proves to be the art of modern laughter therapy in

Around Town

hospitals; an old wooden 'slap-stick' shows you just how clowns were able to make comic slapping noises without inflicting pain. For details of the summer Clown Social or other events, check the website; the 'find a clown' section also allows you to find local member clowns and junior clowns. To arrange a workshop or school event, phone Mattie Faint on the listed number.
Buggy access. Disabled access: toilet. Nearest picnic place: Stonebridge Common (opposite). Shop.

Hackney City Farm

1A Goldsmiths Row, E2 8QA (7729 6381/www. hackneycityfarm.co.uk). Cambridge Heath rail, then 26, 48, 55 bus. **Open** 10am-4.30pm Tue-Sun & bank hol Mon. Closed 23 Dec-3 Jan. **Admission** free; donations appreciated.

The scent of manure, plus a muted cacophony of clucking, quacking, honking and squeaking are bound to make nature lovers smile, while occasional flower shows, weekly Indian head massage, children's pottery classes and other wholesome entertainments ensure the venue is lively summer and winter. The animals are nicely varied: turkeys, geese, ducks, donkeys, rare breed pigs (including Bella the Saddleback), cattle, rabbits and guinea pigs are housed around the courtyard or swish their tails in the fields. The award-winning organic café, Frizzante, is a homely meeting place for not-very East End mummies and babies every lunchtime. Outside, the well-established farm garden, with a plant nursery attached, is lovely to sit in during summer. Many fitness and craft activities take place at the Farm in the evenings and are aimed at parents; children's workshops run throughout the holidays. Keen over-12s can also join the Young Farmers' Club, with activities every second and fourth Saturday of the month. The meeting room is available for children's parties.
Buggy access. Café. Disabled access: ramp, toilet. Nappy-changing facilities. Nearest picnic place: gardens. Shop.

Hackney Museum

Technology & Learning Centre, 1 Reading Lane, off Mare Street, E8 1GQ (83563500/www.hackney.gov.uk). Hackney Central rail. **Open** 9.30am-5.30pm Tue, Wed, Fri; 9.30am-8pm Thur; 10am-5pm Sat. Closed bank hols. **Admission** free.

Occupying a sizeable chunk of Hackney's modern, light and glassy library, the museum is wonderfully accessible to children, who often wander in after school. Hackney's history certainly extends back 1,000 years, but instead of dreary pieces of flint, there's an Anglo-Saxon log boat sunk into the floor and, beside it, a replica to load up with plastic fruits and pretend you're paddling off to market. Much is made of the borough's ethnic diversity, with one area devoted to shows put on by different community groups. A Jewish print shop, a traditional eel and pie shop and an air-raid shelter are all part of the permanent displays. There are also free Explorer Pads, full of activities, available at the entrance. Phone or check the website for details of exhibitions and the changing programme of drop-in events.
Buggy access. Café (Fab Food, next door). Disabled access: toilets. Nappy-changing facilities. Nearest picnic place: benches in square/London Fields. Shop.

Kidzmania

28 Powell Road, E5 8DJ (8533 5556). Clapton rail. **Open** 10am-6pm daily. **Admission** £4 4-12s; £3.50 under-3s. **No credit cards.**

An indoor adventure centre perfect for use as a children's party venue and activity centre. Kidzmania has full on-site catering (special party menus can be prepared). There are ball rooms, slides and bouncy castles.
Buggy access. Café. Nearest picnic place: Hackney Downs.

Sutton House

2 & 4 Homerton High Street, E9 6JQ (8986 2264/ www.nationaltrust.org.uk). Bethnal Green tube, then 106 bus/Hackney Central rail. **Open** 12.30-4.30pm Thur-Sun (last entry 4pm). Closed 23 Dec 2006-31 Jan 2007. **Admission** (NT) £2.70; 60p 5-16s; free under-5s; £6 (2+2). *Tours* free, phone for details. **Credit** MC, V.

This handsome, child-friendly National Trust property offers a lot more than oak panelling and august portraits, though these are also splendid. Built of brick at a time when most houses were wattle and daub (1535), it was originally know as 'The Bryk Place'. Down some rickety steps in the cellar is a fascinating little exhibition explaining how bricks were made locally from 'brickearth', and the sediment whipped up by winds at the end of the last Ice Age. At the top of the house is an archive room where youngsters can access pictures of Hackney on computer, play with period toys and games and read panels about the Tudors, Georgians and so on. In between are nicely differentiated rooms with harpsichords, tea sets, scratched drawings behind secret panels, spot-the-difference carvings and paintings of mythical beasts. To help families enjoy these rooms, a free activity pack, designed for children aged three to 11, can be booked out from the Sutton House shop. The café is Hackney's best-kept secret and looks out through conservatory windows on to a school playground, so the entertainment at lunch is all skipping and hopping. Free family activity days on the last Sunday of each month feature music, arts and crafts.
Café. Disabled access: toilet. Nappy-changing facilities. Nearest picnic place: St John's churchyard. Shop.

V&A Museum of Childhood

Cambridge Heath Road, E2 9PA (8983 5200/recorded info 8980 2415/www.vam.ac.uk/moc). Bethnal Green tube/rail. **Open** 10am-5.45pm daily. **Closed** 1 Jan 24-26 Dec. **Admission** free. Under-12s must be accompanied by an adult.

The UK's biggest collection of toys and childhood paraphernalia re-opened after a long refurbishment in December 2006 with a considerably more child-friendly look to it. There are more new spaces, including a basement complex of activity rooms and a screening room. The main hall's mezzanine is configured to house touring exhibitions (Feel the Force, 28 Jul-11 Nov 2007, a science exhibition exploring the forces of nature; and Lost in Space, 24 Nov 2007-June 2008, an astronomical extravaganza featuring Star Wars toys, are two biggies coming up). There's a lot more that's hands-on and interactive now, but some things remain the same. The museum's star items – breathtakingly detailed dolls houses, ancient teddy bears and children's clothes through the ages – are fascinating but hands off. A fantastic innovation has been the Benugo café, which is tasteful and cheering; and a pleasant picnic lunch space in the basement (where there are always activities and workshops going on in the school hols). Every effort has been made to inspire children and there's lots of room to run around without causing much damage.

V&A Museum of
Childhood. *See p113*.

Buggy access. Café. Disabled access: lifts, ramps, toilet. Nappy-changing facilities. Nearest picnic place: museum grounds. Shop.

Mile End to West Ham

The nondescript council estates that gather around the arterial Mile End Road are not exactly enticing, but Mile End has two impressive parks: **Victoria Park** and **Mile End Park**, with the additional attraction of the **Ragged School Museum** nearby. Towards town, you'll also find **Stepping Stones Farm**, with Stepney Green's bijou playground practically next door.

Further east is Bow, named in the 12th century after a bow-shaped bridge, built because Queen Mathilde (Henry I's wife) almost drowned trying to cross the River Lee. Here you'll find industrial heritage that predates the Victoriana – grain was being unloaded from boats for grinding at Three Mills as early as the 11th century – and then the new-look Stratford, the focal point for Olympian regeneration plans for east London. Gerry Raffles Square provides both a cinema and the Theatre Royal Stratford East (8534 0310, www.stratfordeast.com). On the other side of the bus station lies Stratford's only die-cast kids' attraction: **Discover**. West Ham Park provides breathing space; there's a museum at **West Ham United Football Club**; and the stalls at Queen's Market (Tue, Thur-Sat) give Green Street a bit of zing.

Discover

1 Bridge Terrace, E15 4BG (8536 5563/www.discover. org.uk). Stratford tube/rail/DLR. **Open** *Termtime* 10am-5pm Tue-Sun. *School hols* 10am-5pm daily. **Admission** *Garden* free. *Story Trail* £3.50; £3 concessions; free under-2s; £11 family (2+2). **Credit** MC, V.

In an area strikingly devoid of greenery or playspaces, this community-driven children's centre is an unexpected delight. Developed from a piece of wasteland in collaboration with local children and artists, Discover is an interactive 'story trail' that encourages the under-eights to give their imagination free rein. Outside, the Story Garden is a handsomely designed playground with monster's tongue-slide, raised stream, wooden playship and futuristic space vehicle. Inside, the principal character is a baby space monster called Hootah; children are told she is visiting from the faraway planet, Squiggly Diggly, on a mission to collect new stories and take them home. To this end, kids are invited to stand in various Hootah 'cones', a sort of hairdryer affair that plays example stories and records any that the user cares to invent. In an atmosphere that is calm and fun, children go on a trail involving a Lollipopter, an indoor river full of twinkling lights and a wooden footbridge that shouts 'Trip', 'Trap', baas like a sheep and gobbles like a troll. Inside the low, softly lit 'caves' are machines that allow you to hear your own echo, manipulate string puppets or appear onscreen in a film shot in the garden. Craft activities include making

puppets with wooden spoons. Regular weekend drop-in activities include Stories in a Bag, during which children and a Story Builder create a tale using a random selection of objects, while bookable events for half-terms and holidays may include mask-making and home-made puppet shows. Discover also does parties for a gratifyingly low price of £6.50 per head.

Buggy access. Disabled access: ramp, toilet. Nappy-changing facilities. Nearest picnic place: ground-floor area. Shop.

Mile End Park

Locksley Street, E14 7EJ (7364 4147/children's park 7093 2253). Mile End tube. **Open** 24hrs daily. **Admission** free.

Mile End Park is for many the quintessential modern urban park. The south end of the park has a great playground (funded by HSBC to the tune of £2m), with rope slide, scrambling wall, complicated climbing frame, swings and see-saw, as well as a dedicated area for under-fives. New apparatus installed in the playground is designed especially to appeal to children with disabilities as well as their able-bodied playmates, with a huge bird-nest style swing and a ramped bridge. The interactive play structure is made from a forest of uprights with hooks and catches, so that children can attach ropes, canvases and scramble nets. There's a refreshments kiosk and toilet, and the Play Pavilion hosts 'stay and play' sessions (phone for details). A little to the north, the go-kart track provides thrills and spills for older children. School holidays offer structured, themed events for children.

Buggy access (ground floor only). Disabled access: toilet. Nappy-changing facilities. Nearest picnic place: Mile End Park. Shop.

Olympic Park

Stratford, E15 (www.london2012.org). Stratford tube/rail/DLR/West Ham tube/rail/Pudding Mill DLR/Hackney Wick rail.

London is gearing up to host the 2012 Olympics, having pipped Paris with its bid in 2005. Different venues will be used across London, but the main events will take place at the new Olympic site in Stratford, currently under construction. The Olympic Park will eventually include an 80,0000-capacity stadium, an aquatic centre, a velopark, a hockey centre and the Olympic village, located east of Victoria Park, around the western fringe of Stratford.

You can get a feel for the enormous scale of the project by walking around the area with the aid of a free 'Walk the Bid' guide produced by Newham Council. There are two circular routes, one starting at Leyton tube station and taking in the sites for the Olympic Village, hockey centre, velopark and multi-sport arenas. The other tour starts and finishes at Stratford station and includes the Olympic Stadium and Aquatic Centre. To get a copy, either email walkthebid@newham.gov.uk or download a PDF from the official website at www.london2012.org. Go East London has been running an occasional Routemaster bus tour of the Olympic sites from Stratford; check www.goeast london.co.uk for details of any upcoming tours.

Ragged School Museum

46-50 Copperfield Road, E3 4RR (8980 6405/www. raggedschoolmuseum.org.uk). Mile End tube. **Open** 10am-5pm Wed, Thur; 2-5pm 1st Sun of mth. *Tours* by arrangement; phone for details. **Admission** free; donations appreciated.

Ragged schools were an early experiment in public education: they provided tuition as well as food and clothing for destitute children. The Copperfield Road Ragged School was the largest in London, and it was here that the famous Dr Barnardo taught. It's now a fascinating museum that contains a complete mock-up of a ragged classroom, where historical re-enactments are staged for schoolchildren, as well as an Edwardian kitchen. There are also displays on local history and industry in a downstairs room. *Buggy access. Café. Disabled access: toilet. Nappy-changing facilities. Shop.*

Stepping Stones Farm

Stepney Way (junction with Stepney High Street), E1 3DG (7790 8204). Stepney Green tube. **Open** 10am-4pm daily all year round incl. bank hols. **Admission** free; donations appreciated.

Punctuated by ruined walls and a hillock on which sheep graze, this sprawling farm is part allotments, part animal enclosures – and there are lots of animals. The larger ones come in twos, ark-style. A couple of donkeys grace the entrance opposite a toddlers' play area full of plastic tractors; two cows stand in a big field on the other side. Smaller animals are to be found in a pleasing muddle: long-eared rabbits sitting among bantams, ferrets and stoats standing up to look at you from inside their hutches, chickens and pigs amiably eating together. It's not the tidiest of farms, but old railway carriages full of straw bales look poetic and, just opposite, St Dunstan's Church makes a lovely antique backdrop. There's also a wildlife pond and picnic area, and the activities room is stocked with arts and crafts materials. Annual events include an Easter egg hunt, Christmas on the Farm and ever-popular summer weekend activities; phone for details. *Buggy access. Café. Disabled access: toilet. Nappy-changing facilities. Shop.*

Three Mills Island

Lea Rivers Trust, Three Mill Lane, E3 3DU (River Lee Tidal Mill Trust 8980 4626/schools programmes 8981 0040/www.leariverstrust.co.uk). Bromley-by-Bow tube. **Open** *House Mill* May-Oct 1-4pm Sun. Phone to check other times. *Funday Sundays* Mar-Dec 11am-5pm 1st Sun of mth. **Admission** *Mill £2; free under-16s (incl tour).* **No credit cards.**

The House Mill, built in 1776, is the oldest and largest tidal mill left standing in Britain. It was used to grind the grain for gin distilling. Taken over in 1989 as part of a big restoration project by the Tidal Mills Trust, it now has a visitors' centre that provides a history of the area, maps for walkers, a little souvenir shop and a café. Outside, Riverside Green and Three Mills Green are pleasant for picnicking and strolling. The first Sunday of the month is Funday Sunday (usually Mar-Dec, phone to confirm), during which children are able to take part in a variety of workshops, often with some sort of an environmental theme. The Christmas Fayre (early December) usually attracts huge numbers of people. *Buggy access. Café. Disabled access: lift, toilet (in Tesco if House Mill is closed). Nearest picnic place: Riverside Green/Three Mills Green.*

Victoria Park

Old Ford Road, E3 5DS (8985 1957/www.tower hamlets.gov.uk). Mile End tube/Cambridge Heath or Hackney Wick rail/8, 26, 30, 55, 253, 277, S2 bus. **Open** 6am-dusk daily. Closed 25 Dec.

Victoria Park was opened in 1845 after demands for more public space were met with an extraordinarily generous £100,000 in donations. With wide carriageways, lamp-posts and wrought-iron gates, the park was conceived as the Regent's Park of the East End, and is the largest area of formal parkland this side of town. Poverty-stricken locals made good use of the park's two lakes as baths, but somehow there are still fish in the Western Lake (you can help deplete the stock by getting a free fishing licence); Britain's oldest Model Boat Club convenes around the other lake, near Crown Gate East, every second Sunday. There's a fallow deer enclosure on the east side, tennis courts and a bowling green, plus football, hockey and cricket pitches. Stop off for refreshments at the Lakeside Pavilion Café and watch the geese, swans and ducks play under the fountain. *Buggy access. Café. Disabled access: toilets. Nappy-changing facilities.*

West Ham Park

Upton Lane, E7 9PU (8472 3584/www.cityoflondon. gov.uk). Stratford tube/rail/104, 238 bus. **Open** 7.30am-30mins before dusk daily.

Voted best park in the South East in 2005's Britain's Best Park competition, West Ham Park is an East End treasure. Opened in 1874, it is still neat and civilised as ever, with pretty ornamental gardens and lovely trees; it's one of the few London parks to have its own plant nursery and full time parkies (attendants). The playground has some impressive climbing apparatus, a wooden prairie locomotive to clamber on and a Wendy house corner. There are 12 tennis courts (the annual tennis clinic is held in June), three cricket nets (Essex CCC run free training for under-16s in July), two match-quality cricket tables, two football pitches (one all-weather), a running track and a rounders area. The pre-war paddling pool (late May-Aug) is another attraction. From late July to August there are children's events on Monday and Friday afternoons; a bouncy castle arrives each Wednesday; and there are occasional Sunday concerts. An ice-cream van lingers tantalisingly close to the playground (from noon daily, Easter to Oct) but it also has healthy snacks, such as fresh fruit and sandwiches. *Buggy access. Disabled access: toilet. Nappy-changing facilities.*

West Ham United Football Club

Boleyn Ground, Green Street, E13 9AZ (8548 2748/ www.whufc.com). Upton Park tube. **Open** *Museum* 9.30am-5pm Mon-Sat/shop 9.30am-5pm Mon-Sat; phone to confirm. Closed 25 Dec. **Admission** *Museum free. Tours £10; £5 concessions, 5-16s; free under-5s.* **Credit** MC, V.

Scarily close to the bottom of the Premiership as we went to press, West Ham United harks back to the glory days via its museum. This tells the story of the club from its origins in 1895 as the Thames Iron Works FC through happy times under Ron Greenwood to the ups and downs of the present. Those who aren't fans of the claret and blue go for the Champions Collection: it includes the World Cup winners' medals of Sir Geoff Hurst, Bobby Moore and Martin Peters. Book in advance if you're visiting on a match day. With the refurbishment in progress, opening times may be erratic, and admission prices are also under review. Visitors are advised to phone first. *Bars. Buggy access. Disabled access: toilet. Shop.*

Docklands

Fundamental to the prosperity of the British Empire, London's docks employed thousands of people in their 19th-century heyday. By the 1960s, however, the business had moved east: modern cargo containers demand the sort of huge ships that could not fit in the city docks. The work moved out to Tilbury and the London docks shut up shop. The London Docklands Development Corporation (LDDC) was set up in 1981 and spent £790m of public money on redevelopment during the following decade. Then there was a recession. In the decades since, however, Docklands has become a rather chipper destination. More than just the modern alternative to a City address for financiers, this part of London now has plenty of entertainment options.

The best way to get around Docklands is on the Docklands Light Railway (DLR; 7363 9700, www.tfl.gov.uk/dlr). With various extensions over the years, the DLR now reaches from Bank in the

Discover. *See p115.*

City to Beckton in the east, and from Lewisham south of the Thames (it will be all the way to Woolwich by 2008) to Stratford to the north. The real beauty of the network is that much of it runs on raised tracks, making the journey a sightseeing pleasure. Pick quiet times (weekdays after 10am and before 5pm) and the kids can sit in the front windows of the train and pretend to drive.

To take things a step more touristy, and make the most of this riverside destination, snap up a **Rail & River Rover ticket** (£10.50 adult, £5.25 children, free under-5s, £26 family), which combines travel on the DLR with trips on City Cruises sightseeing boats. Disembark at Tower Pier to check out the marina of St Katharine Docks, with its flashy yachts and Thames barges. Then stroll the ten minutes past **Tower Bridge** and the **Tower of London** to the DLR station at Tower Gateway. Alternatively, stay on board and enjoy the views until you reach Greenwich Pier (for Greenwich's numerous attractions, *see p133*), then take the DLR back under the river for more sightseeing on the Isle of Dogs. If you want to dock at Canary Wharf itself, there's a fast commuter service.

The westernmost point to fall under the Docklands banner is Wapping (the name derives from Wapol, old English for marsh). It's now very des res, but until well into the 19th century, convicted pirates were brought at low tide to Execution Dock (at Wapping New Stairs), hanged and left in chains until three tides had washed over them. A rather new-looking noose dangles from the 16th-century Prospect of Whitby pub (57 Wapping Wall, E1, 7481 1095), which has a riverside courtyard. A couple of pirate ships (sadly, you can't board either) reside in dry docks at the deserted Tobacco Docks mall. Between Wapping and the Isle of Dogs is Limehouse, so called because medieval lime kilns once stood here. A century ago this was a commercial port; now it's a marina with yachts and jolly narrowboats, surrounded by luxury flats. The lofty white church north-east of the basin, St Anne's Limehouse, was designed by Hawksmoor between 1712 and 1724 and has a man-sized pyramid in the north-west corner of the churchyard. The basin is a starting point for canal walks: head north up Regent's Canal for Mile End Park (*see p115*), or take a longer walk north-east on Limehouse Cut to Three Mills Island (*see p116*).

The Isle of Dogs is the pre-eminent destination for visitors. You can explore all the area's history, as well as such arcane areas of debate as to whether the Isle of Dogs is an island and what dogs have to do with it (answers: not really, not much), at the excellent **Museum in Docklands**.

Mudchute City Farm

It stands in a row of converted warehouses, most of them cafés of one sort or another, on a cobbled quayside overlooking the water – lovely in bright weather, if a little windy. The museum is across the bouncing bridge (it's supported on floats) from Cabot Square, which looks up at Canary Wharf.

The impact of Cesar Pelli's 244-metre-high (800-foot) monster edifice, actually called One Canada Square, may have been diminished by the duller buildings that now surround it, but it's still a stunner. Tables outside Carluccio's Caffè (Reuters Plaza, E14 5AJ, 7719 1749) provide a good vantage point if you're peckish. The kids might enjoy finding artworks along Canary Wharf's public sculpture trail (click the 'Lifestyle' link at www.canarywharf.com or phone 7418 2000 for a map). They include bits of floor or wall or more impressive pieces like Pierre Vivant's *Traffic Light Tree*. The fountain in Cabot Square is lovely, and there are benches, but the Japanese Garden beside the Jubilee Line tube station is the best place to picnic. There are chain shops in the mall and when you see how peaceful the pristine Docklands shopping malls are at weekends, you may well wonder why you don't patronise them instead of your local shopping centre; the contrast is wonderfully relaxing.

A south-bound DLR ride from Canary Wharf takes you to Mudchute, once just a dump of silt dug out of Millwall Dock. In the 1970s locals fought off property developers to ensure the place

afternoon) weekends only in term time and, during school hols, a shop for cannily selected model farm toys and riding accessories. The farm is also a charming site for a 64-place nursery (10am-5pm Wed-Sun), along with a garden centre specialising in plants for urban gardens.
Buggy access. Café. Disabled access: toilet. Nappy-changing facilities. Shop.

Museum in Docklands

No.1 Warehouse, West India Quay, Hertsmere Road, E14 4AL (0870 444 3857/recorded info 0870 444 3856/www.museumindocklands.org.uk). Canary Wharf tube/West India Quay DLR. **Open** 10am-6pm daily. Closed 1 Jan, 24-26 Dec. **Admission** (annual ticket, allows for multiple visits) £5; £3 concessions; free under-16s. **Credit** MC, V.

Housed in a Grade I-listed Georgian warehouse overlooking the cobbled quayside, this three-floor museum tells the story of the Thames, the port of London and its people, from Roman times to the Docklands redevelopment. There are models of London Bridge and a reconstructed quay. The business of importing goods by boat over the centuries is illustrated everywhere with reconstructed coffee and tea offices, vast weighing machines, coils of rope, model ships and computer diagrams of the lock systems. Sailortown is an alleyway depicting the Victorian sailors' murky milieu, complete with pub and poky front room. The Docklands at War gallery is as moving as it is vivid – much helped by period black and white footage. The reward for taking in so much information is surely the Mudlarks Gallery, which is so popular that (free) entry is by timed ticket. There are soft-play bricks, cargo games and the wonderfully messy Foreshore Discovery Box, with its archaeological treasures buried in gravel and flowing water. A permanent gallery explores links between the slave trade and sugar imports, with particular attention to the role of West India Dock. In October 2007 the Museum will open a new permanent gallery – London and the Slave Trade – in recognition of this terrible heritage.

Events include dramatic narratives from costumed actors and half-term craft and handling events; check the website for details or to join the mailing list.
Buggy access. Café. Disabled access: lift, toilet. Nappy-changing facilities. Nearest picnic place: quayside benches, refectory. Restaurant. Shop.

SS Robin Gallery

SS Robin Trust, West India Quay, Hertsmere Road, E14 4AE (7538 0652/www.ssrobin.org). West India Quay DLR. **Open** during exhibitions Wed-Fri; 1-4pm Sat. **Admission** free. **Credit** AmEx, MC.

A registered arts, educational and heritage charity housed on board the newly restored cargo hold of the *SS Robin* – the world's oldest complete steamship. World-class documentary photography exhibitions take place here (Feb-Nov). The forecastle is now a classroom, and restoration work continues on the rest of the vessel.
Bookshop. Café. Nearest picnic place: Cabot Square.

East of Docklands

The DLR splits after Westferry station: one branch goes south via Island Gardens station to Lewisham in south-east London (*see p137*), the other east via Poplar to Beckton. At the end of

was preserved as an unlikely park and natural habitat, with lovely **Mudchute City Farm** the principal result. You can walk to Island Gardens (cross the main road from the eponymous station) with its unbeatable view of Greenwich over the Thames. There's also the spookily drippy and echoing Victorian foot tunnel under the river; the attendant-operated lifts (7am-7pm Mon-Sat, 10am-5.30pm Sun) are large enough for a fleet of buggies. From here you can stroll through to the Cutty Sark (*see p134*). You're not allowed to cycle through the tunnel.

Mudchute City Farm

Pier Street, Isle of Dogs, E14 3HP (7515 5901/ www.mudchute.org). Crossharbour, Mudchute or Island Gardens DLR. **Open** 9am-4pm daily. Closed 25 Dec-1 Jan. **Admission** free; donations appreciated.

Mudchute offers what is surely East London's most surreal experience: standing in a vast meadow full of cattle, while taking in the New York-style skyscrapers of Canary Wharf. By far the largest of the city farms, Mudchute is perhaps best approached from Mudchute station, where you are obliged to walk on a raised path past parkland and allotments, spying the llamas only sporadically through the trees as you trudge. The closer you get, the more audible the sounds of farm animals such as ducks, chickens and pigs, goats, donkeys and horses. There's also a serious equestrian centre: local kids can join the pony club or Young Farmers Club over-12s midweek, and everyone, wherever they live, can enjoy summer arts and crafts workshops and play schemes. There's a small aviary and petting corner for cuddling guinea pigs and bunnies, a volunteer-run café (usually open mid morning to early

Around Town

2005 a new spur of the network opened, which runs directly from Canning Town via London City Airport and the **Thames Barrier Park**.

To the south, **North Woolwich Old Station Museum** is next to the North Woolwich Silverlink station, near the tidy Royal Victoria Gardens. A foot tunnel to the south bank takes you to **Firepower** (*see p139*), but the free Woolwich ferry (8921 5968, www.greenwich.gov.uk), which takes pedestrians and cars across the river every 10 minutes daily, is always fun.

Eastbound, Beckton is the last DLR stop. Lovers of the outdoors are well served by Docklands Equestrian Centre (2 Claps Gate Lane, E6 7JF, 7511 3917), the little **East Ham Nature Reserve** and **Newham City Farm**. Otherwise, Beckton is mainly new builds and retail parks.

East Ham Nature Reserve

Norman Road, E6 4HN (8470 4525). East Ham tube/ Beckton DLR. **Open** *Nov-Feb* 10am-5pm Tue-Fri; 1-4pm Sat, Sun. *Mar-Oct* 10am-5pm Mon-Fri; 2-5pm Sat, Sun. Closed bank hols. **Admission** free.

The East Ham Nature Reserve combines a little museum with the largest churchyard in London, with beguilingly shaggy nature trails. The museum comprises a small room dotted with stuffed birds and mammals, all looking a bit weary, plus a case each of beetles and butterflies. *Buggy access. Disabled access: toilet. Nearest picnic place: grounds.*

Newham City Farm

Stansfeld Road, E16 3RD (7474 4960/recorded info 7476 1170). Royal Albert DLR/262, 300, 376 bus. **Open** *Summer* 10am-5pm Tue-Sun, bank hols. *Winter* 10am-4pm Tue-Sun. Closed 1 Jan, 25 Dec. **Admission** free; donations appreciated.

The farmyard animals (a shire horse, cows, Kune Kune pigs, sheep, goats, poultry) take centre stage, but there are also littler chaps (rabbits, guinea pigs, a ferret) and a twittering house of finches, a kookaburra and, last time we visited, a buzzard. The farm's school programme is well established, and there are plans to improve the facilities for casual visitors. There are picnic areas and, depending on volunteer availability, refreshments. Fun days offer the likes of sheep-shearing demonstrations, rides on a shire-horse-drawn cart and felt-making. *Buggy access. Café. Disabled access: toilets. Nearest picnic place: grounds.*

North Woolwich Old Station Museum

Pier Road, E16 2JJ (7474 7244/www.newham.gov.uk). North Woolwich rail/101, 473, 474 bus. **Open** *Jan-Nov* 1-5pm Sat, Sun. *Newham school holidays* 1-5pm daily. **Admission** free. **No credit cards.**

The museum contains carefully preserved old engines, timetables, signs and other relics from the age of steam travel. There's an old ticket office and plenty of models and information, but the children will probably tire of that and clamour to rush round to the back and poke around Coffee Pot (a Victorian commuter train from the 1890s) and Pickett (from the 1940s). They can climb all over Dudley the Diesel, which will sometimes even be able to

Museum in Docklands. See p119.

take them for a gentle spin. There's outside play equipment and, indoors, a Brio layout, a computer running a Thomas the Tank Engine programme, and the Hornby Virtual Railway. The museum's small shop sells souvenirs and snacks. During school holidays, jolly drop-in Wednesday afternoon arts and crafts sessions keep fledgling railway buffs amused.

Buggy access. Disabled access: ramps, toilets. Nappy-changing facilities. Shop.

Thames Barrier Park

Barrier Point Road, off North Woolwich Road, E16 2HP (7511 4111/www.thamesbarrierpark.org.uk). Canning Town tube/DLR, then 474 bus. **Open** dawn-dusk daily. **Admission** free.

With its sleek landscaping and view over the silver shoe-shapes of the Thames Barrier, this park is an unexpected delight. The Barrier's visitor centre is actually on the south side (*see p139*), but that hardly matters as long as you know how it works and can enjoy the river breezes. On one side of the park is a concrete and granite channel the width of a small motorway. Called the Green Dock, it is filled with fragrant honeysuckle and wavy yew hedges, giving it excellent hide-and-seekability – with the two pedestrian bridges overhead adding a whole extra dimension to the game. At the riverfront is the Pavilion of Remembrance, which commemorates those who lost their lives in the Blitz. It is made of undulating beechwood, with similarly shaped granite benches below that make excellent skateboard ramps. The flat lawns are beautifully manicured, perfect for picnics and games. There's a playground packed with apparatus; a basketball hoop and five-a-side court and plenty of ducks, geese, swans and oyster catchers picking around the gleaming mudflats. The park is fantastic for

waterfowl watching: herons feed along the shore at low tide and large numbers of teal, shelduck and cormorants enjoy the river's bounty.

The tea pavilion serves the best coffee in Docklands, for a low price. It's a great refuge from the wind on chilly days; you can even hide inside and watch your kids play through the massive plate-glass windows.

Buggy access. Café. Disabled access: toilet. Free parking. Nappy-changing facilities.

Walthamstow & Wanstead

Five minutes' walk east of Walthamstow Central (the last stop north on the Victoria line) you'll find yourself in curiously rural Walthamstow Village. Around St Mary's Church the atmosphere may be villagey, but the history is grisly: Vinegar Alley was once a trench full of the stuff, intended to prevent pestilence spreading from the mass graves of Black Death victims in the churchyard. The half-timbered Ancient House opposite predates the Plague, although the current incarnation is a painstaking 1934 restoration designed to look authentically saggy. Pamphlets recounting such history are available at the **Vestry House Museum**. Orford Road boasts the Village Kitchen (No.41, 8509 2144) and the Village pub (No.31, 8521 9982). The rest of Walthamstow is as busy as the Village is quiet, especially the street market, open Tuesday to Saturday; see p209.

Lloyd Park, on Forest Road, lies to the north, with the **William Morris Gallery** at the southern entrance, near a scented garden, an aviary of budgies and cockatiels, and a lake with strangely black water. At the far end of the park is a play area and skate park. Across the North Circular Road the art deco façade of **Walthamstow Stadium** is worth a look; this greyhound track runs family race days, and its restaurant, the Stowaway Grill, does dogs' dinners in a good way. The Walthamstow Marshes are at the end of Coppermill Lane (you might prefer to cycle or drive there: it's a good 15-minute walk from St James Street rail station). Ideal for picnics and walks by the River Lee, the marshes are where doughty Sir Edwin Alliot Verdon Roe made the first all-British powered flight on 23 July 1909 in his triplane *Yellow Terror*, flying roughly 300 metres (900 feet). The marshes employ a low-tech method of horticultural maintenance: a herd of cows is let loose in July to munch the grass until it's all gone, usually by January the following year. East of Walthamstow, Wanstead is another urban village. There's another St Mary's church, Grade I listed and dating to 1790, but the attraction for visitors, especially those with kids, is Wanstead's greenery: Wanstead Flats and, notably, **Wanstead Park**.

Around Town

Vestry House Museum

Vestry Road, E17 6HZ (8509 1917/www.lbwf.gov.uk).
Walthamstow Central tube/rail. **Open** 10am-1pm,
2-5.30pm Mon-Fri; 10am-1pm, 2-5pm Sat. **Closed**
1 Jan, 25, 26 Dec, bank hols. *Tours* groups only, by
prior arrangement. **Admission** free.
At different times a home, a police station and a
workhouse, this lovely little museum has displays that are
thoroughly engaging, even for children. One room is
devoted entirely to attractive vintage toys and games;
another is got up as a Victorian parlour; on the ground
floor you can see a reconstructed police cell, complete with
amusing waxen figures dressed as village bobby and
arrested drunk. Other displays are pleasingly domestic:
carpet beaters, meat mincers and knife sharpeners survive
as quaint relics of the housewife's former lot. An airy
space has been created to house a reconstructed Bremer
Car, London's first petrol-driven vehicle.
Buggy access (ground floor only). Disabled access:
toilets (ground floor only). Nappy-changing facilities.
Nearest picnic place: museum garden (closed 1-2pm).
Shop.

Walthamstow Stadium

Chingford Road, E4 8SJ (8531 4255/www.wsgrey
hound.co.uk). **Admission** free Mon, Fri; £3-£6 Tue,
Thur, Sat. Free under-15s. **Racing** from 2.15pm Mon;
from 11am Fri; from 7.30pm Tue, Thur; from 7.30pm
Sat. **Credit** *Restaurant* MC, V.
'Going to the dogs' on Saturday night remains a
popular family outing hereabouts. It's fun – and even
educational if you consider that gambling is a part of
everyday life, for its costs may be learned here for low
stakes. But first, the know-how. If you pass through the
Popular entrance you only pay £3, whereas the Main
Enclosure costs £6 (for adults; children go free). The difference is crucial: in the latter, you are close to the start and
finish, while in the former you only glimpse a sort of canine
streak as six dogs hurtle after an orange fluorescent 'rabbit'. For this reason the atmosphere in the main enclosure
tends to be jollier. Under-11s are often riveted. Bets may
be placed for as little as 10p at the Microtote, so eking out
pocket money over an evening should pose no problem
(although only the over-18s in the party are allowed to
place bets). All this, plus the anthropological interest of
excited punters, po-faced tic-tac men and many bags of
chips, and the interesting fact that a young David Beckham
used to work here as a £10-a-night glass collector on race
nights – what more could you want?.
Buggy access. Disabled access: ramps, toilets. Nappy-
changing facilities. Restaurant.

Wanstead Park

Warren Road, E11 (8508 0028). Wanstead tube.
Open dawn-dusk daily. **Admission** free.
Managed by the City of London as part of Epping Forest
(*see p124*) this is a heavily wooded London lung, with several beautiful water features (the Ornamental Water and
the three ponds – Perch, Heronry and Shoulder of Mutton).
At the fenced-off end of the Ornamental Water is a ruined
grotto, built in the early 1760s with a boathouse that is now
all tumble-down romantic. The other important ruin in the
park is the Temple, once a fancy summerhouse, which has
the park toilets to one side. Both (the grotto and Temple,
not the toilets) are Grade II listed, but the children will probably get far more excited by the ball-throwing and kite-
flying possibilities on the extensive grassy area between

the Temple and the tea stall. The park's Wildlife Group
(www.wrengroup.fsnet.co.uk) is a good point of contact. In
the summer of 2007, there'll be outdoor Shakespeare performances, community operas and various Open Temple
weekends, with guided walks. For more details contact the
Epping Forest Visitor Centre (8508 0028).
Buggy access. Café. Disabled access. Free parking.

William Morris Gallery

Lloyd Park, Forest Road, E17 4PP (8527 3782/
www.lbwf.gov.uk/wmg). Blackhorse Road tube, then
123 bus. **Open** 10am-1pm, 2-5pm Tue-Sat; 1st Sun of
mth. Closed 25, 26 Dec, 1 Jan, bank hols. *Tours* phone
for details. **Admission** free; donations appreciated.
This handsome, moated building on Forest Road was artist
and wallpaper exponent William Morris's childhood home.
The rooms are now kept as galleries, showing as many
artefacts by Morris's friends and collaborators as by the
man himself. Paintings by Edward Burne-Jones contain
wildly romantic depictions of angels and damsels; those of
Frank Brangwyn are full of incident and colour. Kids will
doubtless find the furniture dull as ditchwater, but there's
consolation in the trails, which encourage them to examine ceramic tiles narrating such stories as *Beauty and the
Beast*. To the rear of the house, invisible from the road, is
Lloyd Park, with its aviary, hillock and moat.
Buggy access. Disabled access: ramp (ground floor).
Nearest picnic place: Lloyd Park. Shop.

Lee Valley Regional Park

Starting east of Hackney (*see p110*) and heading
north-east all the way into Hertfordshire, Lee
Valley Regional Park is a network of lakes,
waterways, parks and countryside areas that
covers a vast area on either side of the River
Lee. There's plenty to do, though a gentle guided
walk is a good way to start. The park's ideal for
picnics, walking or fishing; it's well signposted
and open year-round.
It's also a nature lover's paradise. There are
said to be 32 species of mammals making their
home in the park, not to mention 21 species of
dragonfly. Waymarked walks, some providing
easy buggy access, take you to see orchids,
grasshoppers and water lilies. The birdwatching
is excellent: winter brings 10,000 migrant
waterbirds from chillier climes, and summer
is the time to enjoy the kingfishers. Other
attractions include the Lee Valley Riding
Centre (71 Lea Bridge Road, E10 7QL, 8556
2629). The erstwhile Lee Valley Cycle Circuit
has been handed over to the Olympic builders
to become a velopark in time for 2012. Lee Valley
Boat Centre (Old Nazeing Road, Broxbourne,
Herts EN10 6LX, 01992 462 085, www.leevalley
boats.co.uk) hires boats by the hour and organises
narrowboat holidays. The fascinating town of
Waltham Abbey has plenty of cafés and shops
and an Augustinian abbey, founded in 1060 by
King Harold. Once one of the largest in the

The river east

Twenty years ago, nobody would have considered a family stroll east from the Isle of Dogs. The disused docks between Canning Town and Barking were so decayed by the 1980s that Stanley Kubrick used them as a stand-in for war-torn Vietnam in *Full Metal Jacket*. How things change – the area around Silvertown and Royal Victoria Dock is being dramatically redeveloped with luxury apartments, parks, nature reserves, watersports centres, marinas, conference venues, a post-modern university campus and London's City airport.

The logical starting point for a stroll east is the East India Dock Basin bird sanctuary, a calm pond visited by ducks, gulls and cormorants, just around the corner from East India Dock DLR. A short walk east along industrial Orchard Place is Trinity Buoy Wharf (www.trinitybuoywharf.com), site of the only lighthouse in London. Built in 1864, the old lighthouse station has been converted into artists' studios, some housed in surreal towers of shipping containers, with windows and balconies added on. There's a rusting lightship, informative billboards and the dockside offers the best view of the Millennium Dome in London. Rewards for good behaviour are available from Fatboy's Diner (64 Orcard Place, E14 0JW, 7987 4334), a perfect facsimile of a 1940s American snackbar.

There's no smooth path to Silvertown, so jump back on the DLR to Canning Town, then amble down to Royal Victoria Dock, a millpond-calm expanse of water surrounded by some of Docklands' plushest developments. Giant cranes stand like monster robots around the wet dock and jets roar overhead on take-off from City airport. For a pilots' eye view of the runway, take the lift to the top of the futuristic Royal Victoria Dock Footbridge (open 5am-1am), which rises over the dock like a hovering airship. There are small shops on either side of the bridge selling ice-lollies and cold drinks.

Dominating the north side of the dock, Excel (7069 5000; www.excel-london.co.uk; One Western Gateway) is London's largest exhibition venue. Most events are a bit dull for kids, but there are occasional gems like the Star Wars Celebration (July 2007) and the London Boat Show (January 2008). At weekends, cadets and sailing clubs take out sail boats from the Royal Victoria Dock Watersports Centre (7511 2342; Tidal Basin Road) while rowers practise strokes at the Regatta Centre (7511 2211; www.london-regatta-centre.org.uk; Dockside Road), just east on Albert Dock.

Exploring north of the dock, a footbridge over Royal Albert Way takes you into Beckton District Park (Stansfeld Road, E6 5LT, 8430 2000 ext 23639), which has a wildflower meadow and woodland walk, plus a good-sized lake at its northern end. The Millennium Tree Trail takes you past 50 trees from five different continents and there are various play and sports areas. The best space to play, however, is south of the Royal Victoria Dock, on the river. Cut through the Britannia Village development to North Woolwich Road and duck into Thames Barrier Park (7511 4111; www.thamesbarrierpark.org.uk; North Woolwich Road), a lovely green haven overlooking the silver cocoons of the Thames Barrier and consider the next big thing to hit Silvertown. A whale, perhaps? The redevelopment of Newham is an ongoing process; the Zoological Survey of London is overseeing the construction of Europe's largest aquarium in Silvertown Quays – Biota! (7449 6363; www.zsl.org/biota) – set to open in 2009.

Until that watery attraction comes along, the main sights around here are firmly centred on dry land. If you still have energy to burn, duck into a DLR train and visit the Old Station Museum (*see p121*), Newham City Farm (*see p120*) or East Ham Nature Reserve (*see p120*).

country, the abbey had its own farm, fishponds and brewery; only the gateway, a few walls and a stone bridge remain, but the gardens contain a variety of public artworks, and there's a Sensory Trail highlighting the natural history of the area. The exciting **Royal Gunpowder Mills** and **Epping Forest** are but a ten-minute drive from the town.

Lee Valley Park Farms

Stubbins Hall Lane, Crooked Mile, Waltham Abbey, Essex EN9 2EG (01992 702 200/www.leevalley park.org.uk). Broxbourne or Waltham Cross rail. **Open** *Mar-Oct* 10am-4pm Mon-Fri; 10-5pm Sat, Sun. Closed Nov-Feb. **Admission** £4.50; £4 concessions; £3.50 3-16s; £17 family (2+3); free under-3s. **Credit** MC, V.

Hayes Hill Farm is a rare-breeds centre, with a 'Tudor Barn' for sheltered picnics, a restored gypsy caravan and an adventure play area. Visitors can watch the milking of cows (from 2.30pm daily) at the nearby commercial farm, Holyfield, and talk to the farmer via an intercom. Livestock includes sheep, goats, cows, llamas and even water buffalo. There's also the Pet Centre, where you'll meet all manner of little furry and scaly things. There are guided tours for school parties as well as tractor-trailer rides (1.45pm weekends, school holidays, Apr-Oct, weather permitting).
Buggy access. Café. Disabled access: ramps, toilets. Nappy-changing facilities. Shop.

Royal Gunpowder Mills

Beaulieu Drive, Waltham Abbey, Essex EN9 1JY (01992 707 370/www.royalgunpowdermills.com). Waltham Cross rail, then 213, 250, 251 bus.

Around Town

Question time: East London

Where can we play?

Eastern playgrounds combine imagination and challenge for all ages and abilities. Mile End park's playground is great for climbers and scramblers (see p115); Discover is a bright spot for the under eights, and has indoor and outdoor facilities (see p115). Of all the parks in all the east, however, the Thames Barrier Park has to be the most unusual (see p121).

What can we learn?

All about the history of London's docks and the colourful characters that worked them at the Museum in Docklands (see p119); agriculture, self sufficiency and growing your own at Spitalfields Farm (see p110); how to ride (ponies) and the finer points of llama husbandry at Mudchute City Farm (see p119); pyrotechnics at the Royal Gunpowder Mills (see below); basic economics at Walthamstow Stadium (see p122).

Whom might we meet?

Gandalf (Sir Ian McKellen) in Limehouse. Dannii Minogue and The Queen (Helen Mirren) in Docklands (not together, probably); Graham Norton (possibly) in Wapping; Gilbert & George (artists) and any number of celebrity shoppers around Spitalfields.

Where should we eat?

The ultimate barbecue is Bubba's, in Spitalfields Market (see p180); super sandwiches at Story Deli (see p181) and brilliant bagels at the Brick Lane Beigel Bake (No. 159, 7729 0616); for dim sum by the water go to Royal China in Docklands (see p181) and for that sense of wholesomeness that can only come from eating in a farmyard kitchen, try Frizzante @ City Farm (see p180).

What can we buy?

Great logo T-shirts for children and babies and luvverly grub in Spitalfields Market (see p208); cool togs and toys for tots at Bob & Blossom and flowers, plants and trees from the Columbia Road Sunday Market it sits on; toys that last from Play (see p211); browsable books at Victoria Park Books and good fashions, second time around, from Merry Go Round (see p203).

Around Town

Open *Apr-Oct 2006* 11am-5pm Sat, Sun (last entry 3pm), bank hols; 10.30am-2.30pm daily for school groups. **Admission** £6; £5 concessions; £3.£5.50 5-16s; free under-5s; £19 family (2+3). **Credit** MC, V.

The Royal Gunpowder Mills were involved in the making of explosives for more than 300 years. Few of the 20 historic buildings on the 175-acre site have been renovated, in a deliberate attempt to convey their long and complex past. The Visitors Centre runs an introductory film, as well as having a hands-on exhibition that concentrates on the human story behind gunpowder. You can explore the extremely dangerous process of nitroglycerine manufacture, try on workers' boots or put cannon balls into a chute. A 'guided land train' (a tractor and trailer) takes visitors on a woodland tour (£1.50; £1 children). Explorer programmes cover everything from nature walks to the making of air-powered paper rockets. Costumed re-enactments (such as the Guy Fawkes Experience, 29-30 Sept 2007) usually involve some kind of live firing.
Buggy access. Café. Disabled access: lift, ramps, toilets. Nappy-changing facilities. Nearest picnic place: on site. Shop.

Epping Forest

The biggest public space in London, Epping Forest (www.cityoflondon.gov.uk/openspaces) is a gift for walkers, riders and cyclists, not to mention wildlife fans. It is 19 kilometres long and 35 kilometres across (12 miles by 22 miles) and was saved from development by the Corporation of London in 1878. Commoners still have grazing rights and, each summer, English Longhorn cattle can be seen chewing the cud. The forest contains Iron Age earthworks and two listed buildings – the Temple in Wanstead Park (see p122) and the fully restored, 16th-century Queen Elizabeth's Hunting Lodge (Rangers Road, E4 7QH, 8529 6681; under-16s must be accompanied by adults). The latter has a quiz trail, weekend craft activities and Tudor-themed dressing up; in the kitchen area, you can smell food made from 400-year-old recipes – ring for details. If you're coming to Epping Forest by public transport, be prepared for some exercise. Chingford railway station gives access to the Hunting Lodge and some lovely strolls. Loughton and Theydon Bois (Central Line) are the forest's nearest Tube stops, though it's a two-mile (three-kilometre) uphill walk from both. The best advice is to get a map and plan your route in advance – or use the car. At High Beech car park there's a small tea hut, as well as the Epping Forest Information Centre (High Beech, Loughton, Essex IG10 4AF, 8508 0028, www.eppingforest.co.uk, May-Sept 10am-5pm Tue-Sat, 11am-5pm Sun, bank hols; Oct-Apr 11am-3pm Wed-Fri, 10am-4pm Sat, 11am-4pm Sun, bank hols), with a children's area, disabled toilet and shop. For a real back-to-nature feeling, between May and September you can pitch your tent at the Debden House campsite (Debden Green, Loughton, Essex IG10 2NZ, 8508 3008; £7/night, £3.50/night children) and listen to the owls hoot.

South-east London

A collection of curiosities with a royal riverside edge.

Kennington & the Elephant

A short walk from the tourist havens of Westminster Bridge and the South Bank, the **Imperial War Museum** is the main draw to this district for visitors. The rather dilapidated environs of Elephant & Castle aren't pleasant to wander around, but we're assured they will be by 2014, when a £1.5 billion regeneration scheme has transformed the area. A brief walk south of the museum takes you to Kennington. Once owned by the Duchy of Cornwall, Kennington Common (now known as Kennington Park) had a less than regal function as a major place of execution. Today, it's a little more enticing, being home to the Charlie Chaplin Adventure Playground (Bolton Crescent, SE5 0SE, 7735 1819). This fine community park for children with disabilities was named after the little clown who was born in Kennington; contact the playground in advance if you plan to use it. Also in Kennington Park, the Kennington Play Project (Bolton Crescent, SE5

0SE, 7735 7186) is an excellent resource, with a pool table, table tennis and a pretty good zip line. Not far from here Walworth Garden Farm (Manor Place, Braganza Street, SE17 3BN, 7582 2652) runs Nature Explorer clubs on the first Saturday of the month, for eight to 12 year olds, for details see www.walworthgardenfarm.org.uk.

When Kennington Common became a park, local cricketers had to play elsewhere, so they founded the Oval Cricket Club, now known as the **Brit Oval**. The home of Surrey County Cricket, the Oval runs first-rate youth initiatives, *see below*.

Brit Oval

Kennington Oval, SE11 5SS (ticket office 7582 7764/ tours 7820 5750/www.surreycricket.com). Oval tube. **Open** *Ticket office 9.30am-4pm Mon-Fri. Tours* by arrangement; phone for details. **Admission** varies; depending on match. **Credit** MC, V.
The Brit Oval is a world-renowned cricket venue. The £24 million LCS stand, with its swanky aerofoil roof, was unveiled in 2005. Membership of the new under-18s Holioake Club – named in honour of ex-Surrey captain Adam Holioake and his late brother Ben – costs £15 for

Around Town

Architectural digest: the view from **Greenwich Park** takes in skyscrapers and museums. *See p135.*

the season, including free entry to all games (the last domestic match of 2007 starts on 23 September). The Oval offers Outreach coaching for 250 London schools, as well as school tours, educational workshops and tournaments (including a girls-only series). The club also has a second community cricket ground (used for training by Kennington United) at Kennington Park.
Buggy access. Café. Disabled access: ramps, toilets. Nappy-changing facilities. Shops.

Imperial War Museum

Lambeth Road, SE1 6HZ (7416 5000/www.iwm. org.uk). Lambeth North tube/Elephant & Castle tube/rail. **Open** 10am-6pm daily. **Admission** free; donations appreciated. *Exhibition* prices vary. *Audio guides* £2.50-£3. **Credit** MC, V.

Fascinating and disturbing, this monument to conflicts from World War I to the present – especially those involving Britain and the Commonwealth – is housed in what was Bethlehem Royal Hospital ('Bedlam'). Exhibits range from tanks, aircraft and big guns to photographs and personal letters. The lower-ground floor contains both the smelly World War I Somme trench experience and the teeth-chattering Blitz Experience. Between the two galleries there's a countdown clock-face, whose minute hand ticks off the number of people killed in war. The 'Children's War' exhibition (open until 1 Mar 2008) explores the conflict of 1939-45 through the eyes of children, and features a 1940s house with interactive exhibits such as boxes full of wartime treasures and dressing-up clothes. There's also a 200-seat cinema showing footage of conflicts through history. The Holocaust Exhibition, on the third floor, traces the history of anti-Semitism and the rise of Hitler. Unsuitable for children under 14, it comprises a heartbreaking collection of salvaged shoes, clothes, spectacles and other mementoes, as well as testimonials from survivors. On the fourth floor, 'Crimes against Humanity' (over-16s only), covering genocide and ethnic violence in our time, leaves you in no doubt about the pointlessness of war. Temporary exhibitions include 'Camouflage' (until 18 Nov 2007), which explores the impact of camouflage on warfare and its adoption into popular culture. 'The Falklands War' (until 31 Dec 2007) is based on the experiences and memorabilia of those involved. 'Posters of Conflict' (4 Oct 2007 to 30 Mar 2008) is constructed around 300 posters from the Museum's international collection, dating from 1914 to the Iraq War demonstrations. The museum's busy educational programme offers audio guides, workshops and talks by costumed actors, especially during school holidays.
Buggy access. Café. Disabled access: lifts, ramps, toilets. Lifts. Nappy-changing facilities. Nearest picnic place: Geraldine Mary Harmsworth Park. Shops.

Camberwell & Peckham

Camberwell Green was once rural enough to have a species of butterfly named after it (the Camberwell Beauty, first identified here in 1748), but today it's better known for having one of South London's busiest crossroads. There's a popular playground close by, but for a breath of fresher air, locals tend to retreat to nearby Burgess Park or the more bosky Ruskin Park. The bus junction at Camberwell links Kennington,

Elephant, Peckham and points south-east. Head east and you pass the enormous St Giles's Church, designed by Sir George Gilbert Scott, on your way to Peckham and the Camberwell College of Arts and the South London Gallery. The streets between Peckham Road and the southern edge of Burgess Park have been transformed over the last seven years. The impetus for regeneration round here was tragedy. The murder of 11-year-old Damilola Taylor sent the community into shock but much has been done to create something good out of the boy's horrific death. The Damilola Taylor Centre (1 East Surrey Grove, SE15 6DR, 7703 9996) is a well equipped sports club for 11 to 25-year-olds near the site of the notorious, now mostly demolished, North Peckham Estate. Further north, the Grove Children & Family Centre (Towermill Road, SE15, 7701 6629) is the first of 12 superb centres with weekly breastfeeding cafés, health advice, toy and book libraries, soft play and gardens across Southwark Borough, whose provision for young families is legendary in south London.

You know you've hit Peckham's centre when you see its distinctive library, a 2000 RIBA award-winner by Will Alsop. Next door, the Peckham Pulse health club (7525 4999, www.fusion-lifestyle.com) has swimming pools, classes and healthy living advice. Peckham High Street, diverse though it is, holds a grubby mix of bargain warehouses and butchers. The best thing along here is the Peckham Multiplex Cinema (0870 042 0299, www.peckhamplex.com) which has gratifyingly cheap seats before 7pm (all £4.50). Peckham Rye Common has been spruced up with gravelled paths, reshaped gardens and a skateboard park. Less sculpted but more sublime is nearby **Nunhead Cemetery**.

North of Nunhead lies New Cross. Goldsmith's College, part of the University of London, occupies several sites along here. The Ben Pimlott Building, a dramatic glass and steel construction, with a metal sculpture that sits astride the fifth-floor terrace, is another Will Alsop creation. The main source of fun in these parts is located away from the traffic, on the airy slopes of Telegraph Hill Park. The park takes its name from a semaphore telegraph, placed on the summit by the Admiralty Board. News of the victory of the Battle of Waterloo was passed to London via this station. Redeveloped in 2005, the park has been awarded a Green Flag (given in recognition of a green space's all-round excellence). Highlights include a terrific slide, a One O'Clock club and a farmers' market that runs twice on the third Saturday of each month. For news and events in the park, log on to www.thehill.org.uk.

Burgess Park

Albany Road, SE5 0RJ (7525 500/www.southwark. gov.uk). Elephant & Castle tube/rail then 12, 42, 63, 68, 171, 343 bus. **Open** 24hrs daily. **Admission** free.
Planned in 1943, the construction of this park involved demolishing terraced housing and uprooting many residents, who were relocated to the notorious Aylesbury Estate. In an area sorely needing community initiatives, Burgess Park holds attractions for all ages. For young tearaways, there's a busy little kart track (7525 1101), an adventure playground, an indoor games room and a BMX track. Then there is Chumleigh Gardens (home to Southwark Rangers football team) which has a great little café for fry-ups, salads, jazz and atmosphere. Various garden styles – English country, a fragrant Mediterranean, a meditative Islamic, and a flamboyant Caribbean – are explored in a lovely series of interconnecting plots. The Heart Garden is a fruit and vegetable patch planted, tended and harvested by those with long-term illnesses. On Wednesdays and Thursdays throughout the year, the Peckham Sure Start programme organises creative outdoor games and activities for families with young children (phone for information). Festivals include Southwark Youth Carnival, a parade of 200 young people to begin the annual Vibrations festival (4 Aug 2007); and Carnaval del Pueblo (5 Aug 2007), the UK's largest Latin American celebration.
Buggy access. Café. Disabled access: toilets.

Livesey Museum for Children

682 Old Kent Road, SE15 1JF (7639 5604/www. liveseymuseum.org.uk). Elephant & Castle tube/rail then 53 bus. **Open** 10am-5pm Tue-Sat (last entry 4.30pm). Closed bank hols. **Admission** free.
The first library in Camberwell (opened in 1890), the Livesey was converted into a museum and reopened in 1974 by Poet Laureate, Sir John Betjeman. It has since developed into an interactive children's museum, showing temporary exhibitions for under-12s, their families, carers and teachers. There's an agreeable little courtyard for play, together with regular holiday workshops that centre on current exhibitions. The 'Magnificent 12' exhibition runs until 25 August 2007. It's a colourful journey through numbers 0 to 12, with all sorts of hands-on and interactive games and puzzles, plus displays about symmetry and pattern, music and measurement, as well as masses of fantastic number facts. The museum closes over the summer holidays; phone for details of new exhibitions and events.
Buggy access. Nappy-changing facilities. Nearest picnic place: museum courtyard.

Nunhead Cemetery

Limesford Road or Linden Grove (entrances), SE15 3LP (information 7732 9535). Nunhead rail. **Open** *Summer* 8.30am-7pm daily. *Winter* 8.30am-4pm daily. **Tours** 2pm last Sun of mth. **Admission** free; donations to FONC appreciated.
A Victorian cemetery with a restored chapel at its heart, ths pretty place charms with broken statues and stone monuments that have been upturned over time by roots of trees and ivy. Plot clearance is carried out with a view to keeping Nunhead's overgrown charm. The tree-filled cemetery is a nature reserve, and from its highest points offers some fine views of the city. The Friends of Nunhead Cemetery (FONC) runs guided tours on the last Sunday of each month, meeting at the Linden Grove gates at 2pm. An annual open day takes place in May; phone for details.
Buggy access.

Peckham Library

122 Peckham Hill Street, SE15 5JR (7525 0200). Peckham Rye or Queen's Road rail/12, 36, 63, 171 bus. **Open** 9am-8pm Mon, Tue, Thur, Fri; 10am-8pm Wed; 10am-5pm Sat; noon-4pm Sun. **Admission** free.
Family activities that take place inside Will Alsop's funny-looking library include creative baby and toddler sessions and the Sure Start reading group for under-fives. At both, kids are encouraged to make use of the wide selection of children's books on the fourth floor. Mondays and Fridays ring in the Homework Club (4-7pm), and craft sessions are held on Tuesdays after school. In addition, there are monthly meetings of the Teenage Reading Group. An extended programme of holiday workshops is also run. For details of clubs, ring the library. The square outside hosts a farmers' market on Sundays (9.30am-1.30pm).
Buggy access. Disabled access: toilets. Lift. Nappy-changing facilities.

South London Gallery

65 Peckham Road, SE5 8UH (7703 6120/www.south londongallery.org). Peckham Rye rail/12, 36, 171, 345 bus. **Open** noon-6pm Tue-Sun. Closed bank hols. **Admission** free.
Work displayed in this gallery tends towards the cutting edge. Artists including Tracey Emin and Bill Viola have exhibited here, and the gallery has a forward-thinking approach and futuristic atmosphere. Family workshops tie in with current exhibitions. For details, check the website.
Buggy access. Disabled access: lift, ramp, toilets. Nappy-changing facilities. Nearest picnic place: gallery garden (during summer).

Dulwich & Herne Hill

Rusticated streets, upmarket amenities and an abundance of wide open spaces make Dulwich Village one of the most pleasant places to raise children. Many parents settle here with one eye on their offspring and the other on Dulwich College, with its stately brick campus, bulletproof reputation for rugger and formidable roster of literary alumni (Michael Ondaatje, Raymond Chandler, PG Wodehouse). The affiliated Edward Alleyn Theatre (8299 9232, www. dulwich.org.uk/drama) named after the founder of the College – has a busy programme of drama. **Dulwich Picture Gallery** offers an artistic education at a less eye-watering price than the public school's fees. Every May, the Dulwich Festival (www.dulwichfestival.co.uk) brings the village to life for young ones. There's also a small skateboard park in Belair Park, opposite West Dulwich station. Sydenham Hill Wood, on the other side of the A205, is a rambler's paradise, comprising one of the last remaining tracts of the old Great North Wood that once stretched from Deptford to Selhurst.

Neighbouring East Dulwich isn't quite so sylvan, but remains a popular destination for young parents thanks to the number of child-

Around Town

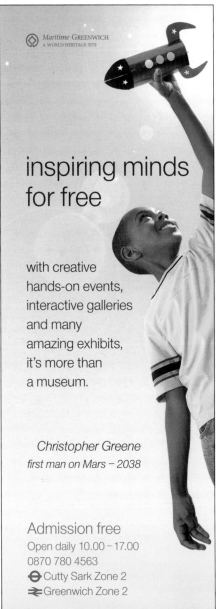

friendly pubs, restaurants and cafés on Lordship Lane – gentrified almost beyond recognition in the last few years. The northernmost end has a children's playground on Goose Green, All Fired Up, the ceramic painting café (7732 6688, www.allfiredupceramics.co.uk) and the East Dulwich Community Centre (8693 4392). Around the middle you'll find such delights as Soup Dragon (*see p214*), the Family Natural Health Centre (*see p214*), and Hope & Greenwood (*see p191*) the nostalgic sweetie purveyor written about in glowing terms by every yummy mummy in the media (of which there are many round here). Further west, Herne Hill has a range of family-friendly shops, pubs and restaurants on Half Moon Lane, as well as Brockwell Park, a slightly grittier, hillier alternative to **Dulwich Park**.

Dulwich Park

College Road, SE21 7BQ (park ranger 8693 5737/ www.southwark.gov.uk). North Dulwich or West Dulwich rail. **Open** 8am-dusk daily.

The park was formally landscaped in 1890, but had served as a scenic retreat long before that. Queen Mary was a regular visitor (one of the park's four gates is named after her). Visitors today are treated to the exceptionally child-friendly Pavilion Café, a super playground, boat hire on the lake, novelty bike hire from London Recumbents (8299 6636, www.londonrecumbents.com) and a number of gardens (including the original American Garden, home to one of London's largest collections of rhododendrons and azaleas, as well as herons, cormorants and the occasional kingfisher). Boats can be rowed on the central pond at a hire price of £5.25 per half hour during the summer. The playground is one of the best in the area, with loads of web-like climbing structures, swings, slides and, since March 2007, the Ability Whirl, a safe, robust roundabout that can be used equally by able-bodied and disabled children. A community officer runs a programme of children's activities from the Francis Peek Centre, housed in the cricket pavilion (phone for details).

Buggy access. Café. Disabled access: ramps, toilets. Nappy-changing facilities (café).

Dulwich Picture Gallery

Gallery Road, SE21 7AD (8693 5254/www.dulwich picturegallery.org.uk). North Dulwich or West Dulwich rail/P4 bus. **Open** 10am-5pm Tue-Fri; 11am-5pm Sat, Sun, bank hol Mon. Closed 24-26 Dec, 1 Jan, Good Friday. **Tours** 3pm Sat, Sun. **Admission** £4; £3 concessions; free under-16s. *Tours* free. **Credit** MC, V.

Soane's bijou neo-classical gallery houses an outstanding collection of work by European Old Masters and offers a fine introduction to the baroque era through pieces by Rembrandt, Rubens, Poussin and – batting for the home team – Gainsborough. The programme of children's activities is consistently praised. The after school art club for 11 to 14 year-olds takes place on Thursdays (4.30-6pm); seven to ten year-olds learn a range of techniques on Saturdays (10.30am-1pm). Students aged between 15 and 18 can attend Tuesday art clubs (5-6.30pm). Courses cost £50-£60 per term, and there are school-holiday courses and workshops (Art in the Garden takes place on Wednesdays during the summer hols and costs £2 per child). Free,

drop-in Art Play afternoons (first Sunday of the month, 2-3.30pm) let parents and children (aged over four) engage in artist-led activities across a range of subjects and creative media. Check the website for details and fees of all courses and classes; booking is essential.

The big exhibition for 2007 is 'The Changing Face of Childhood: British Children's Portraits and their Influence in Europe' (1 Aug to 4 Nov), which takes in 1630's depictions of children as loveable, innocent pets, to the portrayal of children as more independent in the Age of Enlightenment. The autumn and winter show takes you to the 'Age of Enchantment', with Beardsley, Dulac and their contemporaries (28 Nov 2007 to 17 Feb 2008). These illustrators, along with Arthur Rackham, created a whimsical, pastel-toned world of childish delights as exhibited in the pages of familiar fables and classic children's tales.

Buggy access. Café. Disabled access: ramps, toilets. Nappy-changing facilities. Nearest picnic place: gallery gardens. Shop.

Horniman Museum

100 London Road, SE23 3PQ (8699 1872/ www.horniman.ac.uk). Forest Hill rail/122, 176, 185, 312, P4 bus. **Open** 10.30am-5.30pm daily. **Admission** free; donations appreciated. **Credit** *Shop* MC, V.

Frederick J Horniman's assembly of curiosities was first housed in his Forest Hill home and later in this art nouveau building. The Natural History gallery contains skeletons, pickled animals, stuffed birds and insect models in glass cases – all presided over by an overstuffed walrus on a central plinth. The World Cultures exhibition offers 80,000 objects. In the Music Room walls are hung with hundreds of instruments, with touch screens on tables for you to hear their sound and a 'Hands On' room where visitors can bash away on Thai croaking toads and an Irish bodhrán. There's also an under-fives book zone, cases of exotic reptiles and an observation beehive in the Environment Room. Outside, the delightful gardens have an animal enclosure, a conservatory and superb views. The café is a welcome pit stop in colder weather.

The terrific Horniman aquarium reopened in summer 2006 after a £1.5 million overhaul and was this year short-listed for the Gulbenkian prize. More than 200 species of aquatic animal and plant are housed in seven separate zones. The aim is to explain challenges faced by the world's delicate ecosystems. The British Pond Life Zone, for example, wows kids with its viewing den located inside a hollow willow tree, and features an interactive learning area. Elsewhere there's a hypnotic display of jellyfish suspended in a dramatically lit cylindrical tank; it is accompanied by a game where participants can learn about the challenges facing species in the open seas.

The big exhibition, on until 4 November 2007, is a blockbuster linked to the BBC's *Walking with Beasts*. From the early periods there's the Phorusrhacos, known as the terror bird, and the vegetarian Doedicurus, which looks something like an armadillo. A huge woolly mammoth dominates the room. All the magnificent beasts are displayed as life-size models, courtesy of the BBC, and they're supplemented by glass cases of skeletons, carved icons, fossils and a selection of early weapons found on digs throughout the world. Interactives, such as touch-screen computers, give visitors the chance to put themselves in a prehistoric landscape via blue-screen technology.

Buggy access/storage. Café. Disabled access: lift, ramps, toilets. Nappy-changing facilities. Nearest picnic place: Horniman Gardens. Shop.

London Wildlife Trust Centre for Wildlife Gardening

28 Marsden Road, SE15 4EE (7252 9186/ www.wildlondon.org.uk). East Dulwich rail. **Open** 10.30am-4.30pm Tue-Thur, Sun. **Admission** free.

The London Wildlife Trust has for more than 20 years been reclaiming derelict land for nature reserves. This centre – created on a disused bus depot – is one of its best, with areas of wildlife-friendly woodland, marshland, a herb garden, a pond area and a nursery for plants and trees. Local families fill their own gardens with the greenery raised here, giving a donation to the LWT. For children, there's a play area, sandpit and parent-and-toddler group, and the visitors' centre has tanks of fish and stick insects. Inspired children should join the LWT's Wildlife Watch Club for eight to ten year-olds (£15 per year), which runs all sorts of outdoor activities, like pond-dipping and bat-walking. *Buggy access. Disabled access: toilets. Nappy-changing facilities. Nearest picnic place: wildlife garden. Shop.*

Crystal Palace

In 1852, when Joseph Paxton moved his enormous glass centrepiece from the Great Exhibition in Hyde Park to a hilltop estate in Sydenham's Great North Wood, he turned a quiet London suburb of London into a cultural hub. The building was a showcase for world creative and industrial achievements and could be seen for miles. Its surroundings blossomed as a result; new houses, amenities and transport links were built to accommodate the influx, and Crystal Palace looked set to redefine London's cultural heritage – until 1936, that is, when it was destroyed in the country's largest peacetime fire of the 20th century.

These days, the crumbling remains of the park's heyday – statuary, graffitied stone stairs to nowhere, a motley collection of bizarre dinosaurs – lend it the otherworldly air of a lost civilisation. Yet recent refurbishments, including a dinosaur makeover in 2003, mean this is still a pleasant park to visit. The Crystal Palace National Sports Centre does its best to drag the place into the 21st century (hosting various national athletics championships, and the odd concert), but its grim mid-1960s architecture – Grade II listed it may be – isn't easy on the eye. The Centre's days as the home of British Athletics are numbered in any case; the Olympic Stadium planned for Stratford for 2012 will see to that. Another landmark is the 222-metre (728-feet) television transmission tower, which dominates the south London skyline. This area's proud history is celebrated by the Crystal Palace Foundation (www.crystalpalace foundation.org.uk), which runs an annual Victorian weekend (30 June and 1 July 2007).

Crystal Palace Museum

Anerley Hill, SE19 2BA (8676 0700/www.crystal palacemuseum.org.uk). Crystal Palace rail. **Open** 11am-4.30pm Sat, Sun. *Tours* noon 1st Sun of mth. **Admission** free.

To find out more about the majestic exhibition hall that gave this area its name, pop into this friendly museum, housed in the old engineering school where John Logie Baird invented the television. Hours are limited as the museum is run entirely by volunteers, but school groups are welcome on weekdays provided teachers book a few weeks ahead. The 'exhibition of an exhibition' includes Victorian artefacts from the original Hyde Park production, as well as video and audio presentations about the great glass building. A small Logie Baird display marks the birth of home entertainment; from June 1934 the Baird Television Company had four studios at Crystal Palace. *Nearest picnic place: Crystal Palace Park. Shop.*

Crystal Palace Park

Thicket Road, SE20 8DT (Park Rangers Office 8778 9496/www.crystalpalacepark.net). Crystal Palace rail/ 2, 3, 63, 122, 157, 227 bus. **Open** 7.30am-dusk daily. **Admission** free.

A stop-start redevelopment programme means that the Crystal Palace Park reality, and the information on the Bromley Council website, are at odds. Much of the historic park has been replanted and spruced up, but there's still a lot to be done. The boating lake is unlikely ever to reopen and the architecturally impressive children's farm is still without animals. The rangers say that Capel Manor horticultural college is intending to restock and run the farm, but nothing was happening when we last visited. Until the work is finished, or restarted, the decaying ruins of Joseph Paxton's enterprise make the park a highly atmospheric place. The 'monsters' (the remains of a Victorian prehistoric theme park created by Benjamin Waterhouse-Hawkins), restored in 2003, stand majestically around the freshly landscaped tidal lake, the hornbeam maze was recently replanted and the main playground is a great favourite with south London children. The National Sports Centre has a busy programme of events for all ages and abilities, as well as one of London's few Olympic-sized (50m/160ft) pools. *Buggy access. Café. Disabled access: toilets. Nappy-changing facilities.*

Rotherhithe

A shipbuilding village for centuries, Rotherhithe had a less edifying role in the 18th century, when it was the centre of London's whaling trade. The area relinquished its links with whaling in 1864, but the old wharves, warehouses and ancient seafarers' pubs still have an air of the salty sea dog about them. One pub, the Angel, on Bermondsey Wall East, contains a smugglers' trapdoor. Another, the Mayflower, recalls the Pilgrim Fathers, who sailed from here in 1620.

Most visitors to this history-steeped area call in at **St Mary's Rotherhithe** (St Marychurch Street, SE16 4JE, 7231 2465), a church built by local sailors in 1715. Many are disappointed to find they have to glimpse its treasures – including

Horniman Museum. *See p129.*

Around Town

On the right track: **Brunel Engine House & Tunnel Exhibition.**

a communion table made from timber from the Battle of Trafalgar gunship *Temeraire* – through a vandal-proof glass partition. Come for a Sunday service to get closer. Nearby, the **Brunel Engine House & Tunnel Exhibition** celebrates the world's first underwater tunnel.

The Norwegian Church and Seaman's Mission lies at the mouth of the Rotherhithe car tunnel. There are several Scandinavian churches around here. Their presence harks back to Nordic sailors and their Viking ancestors who settled in the area. Across Jamaica Road lies **Southwark Park**. South of here, and across the London Bridge-bound railway tracks, is South Bermondsey – Millwall FC territory. The streets around the stadium are in line for a £100 million facelift from regeneration groups with their eyes on the 2012 Olympics prize.

Heading east from Southwark Park brings you to the Surrey Quays Shopping Centre and attendant leisure activities, including a massive cinema, a branch of Hollywood Bowl (7237 3773) and Surrey Docks Watersports Centre (*see p270*).

Wild green spaces nestle uneasily among the urban new-build. Lavender Pond and Nature Park (Lavender Road, SE16 5DZ) was created from a dock inlet in 1981. The Pumphouse Educational Museum (7231 2976, www.thepumphouse.org. uk) is used by schools. Other parks, promoted by the Trust for Urban Ecology include Russia Dock Woodland and Stave Hill Ecological Park.

Brunel Engine House & Tunnel Exhibition

Brunel Engine House, Railway Avenue, SE16 4LF (7231 3840/www.brunelenginehouse.org.uk). Rotherhithe tube. **Open** 10am-5pm daily. **Admission** £2; £1 concessions, free 5-16s; £5 family (2+2). **No credit cards.**
The Brunels, father and son (Sir Marc and Isambard Kingdom), worked together from 1825 until 1843 to create the world's first underwater tunnel, with Isambard nearly drowning in the process. The story of what the Victorians hailed as 'the Eighth Wonder of the World' is told in this museum in the original engine house. The tunnel is now used by the East London tube line. It was Isambard's first project and this well-run paean to it is fascinating history is worth a visit. To get the most out of your visit, join a guided tour (check the website for details). There's plenty for children, not least the popular summer play-scheme in the sculpture garden 30 July-10 August 2007). The giant Brunel figure owned by the museum is always (and literally) a big player in the Bermondsey (7 July 2007) and Rotherhithe (15 July, 2007) carnivals. Excitingly, the museum was just putting finishing touches to plans a splendid new café overlooking the river, as well as a new schools and activity room, making this Thameside treasure even more of a delight to visit.
Buggy access/storage. Nearest picnic place: museum gardens & riverbank. Shop.

Discovery Planet

1st Floor, Surrey Quays Shopping Centre, Redriff Road, SE16 7LL (7237 2388/www.discovery-planet.co.uk). Canada Water tube. **Open** 10am-6pm Mon-Sat; 11am-5pm Sun. **Admission** *2-10yrs* £3.99 Mon-Fri; £4.99 Sat, Sun. *Under-2s* £3.49 Mon-Fri; £4.49 Sat, Sun. **Credit** (over £10) MC, V.

This huge indoor area filled with brightly coloured tubes, tunnels, ball ponds and slides gives children two hours of climbing, sliding, bashing and throwing themselves about. Check the website for party information.

Southwark Park

Gomm Road, SE16 2UA (art gallery 7237 1230). *Canada Water tube.* **Open** *Park* 8am-1hr before dusk daily. *Gallery* (during exhibitions) *Summer* noon-5pm Wed-Sun. *Winter* 11am-4pm Wed-Sun; phone ahead to check. **Admission** free.

The Metropolitan Board of Works first opened Southwark Park to the public in 1869, making it London's oldest municipal park. In 1998 the Park was given a new bandstand, bowling pavilion and children's play area, and nine years later the whole place is still looking spruce, thanks to the efforts of the energetic Friends of Southwark Park and the vandal-busting wardens. The park is surrounded by art galleries, the most accessible being the Café Gallery Project, which holds frequent exhibitions and a Saturday morning DIY family art club; check www.cafegalleryprojects.com for details of this and the summer Children's Exhibition and winter Open Exhibition. Parkside Café & Bar, just across from the Gallery, is a useful place for lunch, with sandwiches and hot pasta meals costing from about £3. Children's parties are also hosted in the park. *Buggy access. Café. Disabled access: toilet. Nappy-changing facilities (in gallery).*

Surrey Docks Farm

Rotherhithe Street, SE16 5EY (7231 1010/www. *surreydocksfarm.org). Canada Water tube then 225, 381 bus.* **Open** *Farm* 10am-5pm Tue-Sun. *Café* 10am-5pm Wed-Sun. **Admission** free (except for school parties & playschemes); donations appreciated.

A riverside location, a yard patrolled by over-friendly goats and sheep (buy a bag of grain in the café then try fending them off), paddocks and loose boxes filled with donkeys, cattle and various poultry breeds, a yurt, gardens and a resident blacksmith who runs metalwork courses – all combine to make this city farm a favourite of ours. Café Nabo is a haven of healthy eating, with hot snacks and meals, herbal teas and Fair Trade flapjacks. The raised beds by the riverside yield organic vegetables and herbs, some of which are for sale (along with bought-in organic veg) outside the café. Honey, fresh eggs and compost are also sold when available. Outside, the wonderful river walk beckons. Children enjoy sitting on the bronze donkey that stands among the animal sculptures just outside the farm. Can you spot the mouse? *Buggy access. Café. Disabled access: ramps, toilets. Nearest picnic place: riverside. Shop.*

Deptford & Greenwich

The 2012 Olympics promise much for both these riverside enclaves, but five years before that, the sporting folk of Deptford and Greenwich will be out in force for the Grand Départ of the Tour de France 2007. On Sunday 8 July, the cyclists will stream through from Bermondsey, across Deptford Creek, through Greenwich town, past the Millennium Dome and on to Woolwich and Erith en route for Kent.

Stellar sporting events aside, the regeneration of Deptford continues. The famously diverse High Street full of independent shops and cafés – bisected in part by the old established market, where some traders come from a long line of Cockney costers – runs parallel to the more trafficky Church Street. The area's multitude of artists and indie bands foregather along Creekside, to the east. Deptford's Creek is the tidal reach of the river Ravensbourne at the Thames. The shoreline here, known as Greenwich Reach, is also undergoing a massive regeneration project. Take time on your way to the river to admire St Nicholas's Church on Deptford Green; known as the sailors' church, it dates from 1697 and has timber-shivering skulls and crossbones carved on the gate piers. If you walk along Creekside to the point it joins the Thames you'll see the striking Laban dance centre (*see p234*) to your right. Non-dancing visitors are allowed into the reception area, café and grounds. Just beyond the railway bridge lies the Creekside Centre (14 Creekside, SE8 4SA, www.creeksidecentre.org.uk) that gives you access to almost a mile of the muddy, stony bottom of Deptford Creek when the tide falls each day. The staff here run guided walks along the river bed, as well as regular weekend wildlife-watching activities for families. The Ha'penny Hatch footbridge, which crosses the Creek, opened in 2002. To the right, the sewage pumping station is part of Sir Joseph Bazalgette's system of the 1860s. Picturesque Albury Street, with its early 18th-century houses (Nelson and Lady Hamilton allegedly lived here) is worth a detour.

East of Deptford lies historic maritime Greenwich, a UNESCO World Heritage Site. It has a wealth of attractions, all listed below, as well as one of the most wonderfully sited parks in London. For two centuries (between around 1450 and 1650), England's principal royal palace, the Palace Of Placentia, stood in Greenwich. It was the birthplace of King Henry VIII and the Queens Mary and Elizabeth I. In the late 17th century the palace was torn down and replaced by Sir Christopher Wren's **Old Royal Naval College** (*see below*). Remains of the palace's chapel were discovered in 2006.

River trips to Greenwich (Thames Cruises, Catamaran Cruises; *see p292*) take you to Greenwich Pier, just by the weathered old tea clipper currently undergoing renovations, the **Cutty Sark**. The Docklands Light Railway (DLR) offers sightseers the Rail & River Rover (www.dlr.co.uk), a family pass that is also valid on City Cruises. Not far from the pier is **Greenwich Crafts Market** (*see p208*).

From the riverside it's a ten-minute walk (or you can take the park's shuttle bus) up the steep slopes of Greenwich Park to the **Royal Observatory**. This building looks all the more stunning at night thanks to its bright-green Meridian Line Laser (*see p136* **Walk the line**).

From Greenwich the Thames Path can take you to the Greenwich Peninsula, dominated by the structure formerly known as the Millennium Dome, now rechristened the O_2. Owned by American billionaire Philip Anschutz, this is the world's largest single-roofed structure, 365 metres (around 1,200 feet) in diameter – and the largest white elephant, according to its many critics. Mr Anschutz's lofty plans for the arena suffered a serious set back in February 2007 when it was announced that the country's new 'super casino', which was hotly tipped to be established within the old Dome premises, would instead be built in Manchester. Nonetheless, there are still exciting events scheduled for the arena. A whole lot of dib-dobbing will be going on if, as promised, the structure is used for LIVE 07, a Festival of Scouting on 24 November 2007. Two epic shows are planned to mark 100 years of scouting by creating a 'scouting theme park', with circus activities, bands and other performers. There's also talk of the O_2 being the venue for the last

ever departure from Egypt of the treasures of King Tutankhamun. In addition, the structure is due to host the 2009 World Gymnastics Championships.

The area around the O_2 is being regenerated too. Work has begun on the construction of Millennium Square, all part of the plan to make this once-derelict stretch of the riverscape a new haven and offshoot of Olympics 2012 action. The peninsula is also home to the **Greenwich Peninsula Ecology Park** (*see below*), a pleasant riverside walk from the O_2.

Cutty Sark

King William Walk, SE10 9HT (8858 3445/www. cutty sark.org.uk). Cutty Sark DLR/Greenwich DLR/ rail. **Open** *Pavilion and Tours* ring for details. **Admission** £2; free under-5s; £12 family (2+3). *Tours* free. **Credit** MC, V.
Launched in 1869 from Dumbarton on the Clyde, the *Cutty Sark* took tea to China and wool to Australia. Now a museum, and the world's only Grade I-listed ship, the vessel has the builders in – but she's still entertaining visitors. Work isn't due to be finished until October 2008. During the £25 million, two-year restoration the ship has been suspended 3m (10ft) off the ground for visitors to see shipwrights and their trainees at work. You can visit an exhibition centre that details the history and revamping of the ship. Hard-hat tours are available on request. Tea tasting is also available. Once reopened 1.5m (5ft) from the ground, the ship will have a new keel and main deck, accessed by lift, with

Royal Observatory courtyard. *See p137.*

a small auditorium. Below will be an exhibition space and gallery for Robert Burns memorabilia (his poem gave the ship her name) and the famous figurehead collection. *Buggy storage. Nearest picnic place: Cutty Sark Gardens. Shop.*

Fan Museum

12 Crooms Hill, SE10 8ER (8305 1441/www.fan-museum.org). Cutty Sark DLR/Greenwich DLR/rail. **Open** 11am-5pm Tue-Sat; noon-5pm Sun. Closed 25 Dec, 1 Jan, Easter. **Admission** £3.50; £2.50 concessions; free under-7s, OAPs, disabled 2-5pm Tue. **Credit** MC, V.

Over-tens with artistic leanings admire the exhibition of hand-held fans: the world's most important single collection of wafters, housed in a pair of restored Georgian townhouses. There are more than 3,000 in the collection (only a proportion is on display at any one time). A new temporary exhibition is mounted every four months or so. Come on a Tuesday or Sunday afternoon and you'll be able to take tea in the Orangery Café. Check the website for exhibition dates and details of fan-making workshops.
Buggy access. Disabled access: lift, toilet. Nearest picnic place: Greenwich Park. Shop.

Greenwich Park

Blackheath Gate, Charlton Way, SE10 8QY (7706 7272/www.royalparks.org.uk). Cutty Sark DLR/Greenwich DLR/rail/Maze Hill rail/1, 53, 177, 180, 188, 286 bus/riverboat to Greenwich Pier. **Open** 6am-dusk daily.

The best park in London, we reckon. Greenwich, a Green Flag flier, has it all – fab views, teeming wildlife, roly-poly hills, an observatory at the top and a museum at the bottom, an excellent café, playgrounds, boating and entertainments. It's the oldest Royal Park, whose proud connections go back to Tudor times. Henry VIII hunted here and there's an ancient husk of an old oak tree, which the monarch is said to have danced around with his then paramour, Anne Boleyn. The dead tree has a more vigorous neighbour: a new oak planted on the site by Prince Philip to mark his wife's Golden Jubilee.

A grassland enclosure near the Flower Garden serves as a sanctuary for deer, foxes and birds. It's home to the Greenwich Park Secret Garden Wildlife Centre, where a hide has been built to let kids get close-up views of wild red and fallow deer that live in Greenwich Park. Just outside the top gates, across Charlton Way, a group of donkeys give rides to children on sunny weekends – fitting for a park that's going to host the equestrian events at 2012's Olympics. Free fun for under-tens is provided by the Royal Parks' summer entertainments programme, including alfresco theatricals, plus circus skill and craft workshops *Buggy access. Cafés. Disabled access: toilets. Nappy-changing facilities.*

Greenwich Peninsula Ecology Park

Thames Path, John Harrison Way, SE10 0QZ (8293 1904/www.urbanecology.org.uk). North Greenwich tube/108, 161, 422, 472, 486 bus. **Open** 10am-5pm Wed-Sun. **Admission** free.

A pond-dipping, bird-watching haven run by the Trust for Urban Ecology for English Partnerships. The park is reserved for schools on Mondays and Tuesdays. The rest of the week, you'll have the place all to yourself. A wetland area with woodland, marsh, meadow, lakes and streams,

it supports frogs, toads, dragonflies, and many bird species. The park also hosts a wide variety of children's entertainment. Children are plied with various quizzes and trails to follow as they explore. Regular activities involve pondlife, mud and gumboots. The centre's open day takes place every June and the Frog Day is usually held on the first weekend in March. A summer play event runs from the end of July to early September.
Buggy access. Disabled access: toilets. Nappy-changing facilities. Nearest picnic place: southern park.

National Maritime Museum

Romney Road, SE10 9NF (8858 4422/information 8312 6565/tours 8312 6608/www.nmm.ac.uk). Cutty Sark DLR/Greenwich DLR/rail. **Open** July-Aug 10am-6pm daily. *Sept-June* 10am-5pm daily. *Tours* phone for details. **Admission** free; donations appreciated. **Credit** *Shop* MC, V.

The nation's seafaring history is covered in style at this bright, lively museum on three floors. At weekends and during school holidays, amiable staff invite children to take part in various maritime-themed artistic endeavours, trails, games and storytelling sessions. But just wandering around the place is a lark. More recent additions include, on Level 2, Your Ocean, which shows how we are dependent on the health and survival of the world's oceans. Also on this level, in Gallery 15, is Nelson's Navy, which displays more than 250 objects drawn from the Museum's collection of naval memorabilia from this period (including the coat worn by Nelson at the Battle of Trafalgar), plus weaponry, artefacts and art. The very hands-on Alls Hands and The Bridge galleries are on Level 3. Children can play with several exhibits, including Morse code machines, ships' wheels and a cargo-handling model. In The Bridge, young hopefuls can play ship's captain and manoeuvre a vessel into port using the bridge simulator – good navigation scores points.

Elsewhere in the museum, 'Explorers' is devoted to pioneers of sea travel (there's a small but spooky Titanic exhibition here); 'Passengers' is a paean to glamorous old ocean liners; and 'Maritime London' relates the capital's nautical history through old prints and model ships. 'Seapower' covers naval battles from Gallipoli to the Falklands, and the 'Art of the Sea' is the world's largest maritime art collection. No young pirate can leave without plundering the gift shop, which runs the vaguely nautical gamut from dolphin water pistols to models of HMS *Victory*.
Buggy access. Café. Disabled access: lifts, ramps, toilets. Nappy-changing facilities. Nearest picnic place: Greenwich Park. Restaurant. Shop.

Old Royal Naval College

King William Walk, SE10 9LW (8269 4747/tours 8269 4791/www.greenwichfoundation.org.uk). Cutty Sark DLR/Greenwich DLR/rail. **Open** 10am-5pm daily (last entry 4.15pm). *Tours* by arrangement. **Admission** free. **Credit** *Shop* MC, V.

Built by Wren in 1696, these buildings were originally a hospital, then a naval college and are now part of the University of Greenwich. The public can admire the rococo chapel and Painted Hall, a tribute to William and Mary that took overworked and underpaid artist Sir James Thornhill 19 years to complete. In 1806 the Upper Hall was draped in black for three days as the body of Lord Nelson was laid in state here for thousands to pay their respects. In the chapel free organ recitals take place on the first Sunday of each month.

The Greenwich Gateway Visitor Centre (a council-run tourist information office, 0870 608 2000) is in the Pepys Building, where there's also an exhibition on 2000 years of Greenwich history, the story of the Royal Hospital for Seamen and information on other Greenwich attractions; school holiday activities take place here; check the website for details. Make a date to skate: the courtyard will be iced over as usual to form a seasonal rink from December 2007. *Buggy access. Café. Disabled access: toilet. Nappy-changing facilities. Nearest picnic place: Naval College grounds. Restaurant. Shop.*

Queen's House

Romney Road, SE10 9NF (8312 6565/www.nmm. ac.uk). Cutty Sark DLR/Greenwich DLR/rail. **Open** 10am-5pm daily (last entry 4.30pm). *Tours* noon, 2.30pm. **Admission** free; occasional charge for temporary exhibitions. *Tours* free. **Credit** (over £5) MC, V.

Designed in 1616 by Inigo Jones, this house is now home to the National Maritime Museum's art collection. An exhibition on the ground floor charts the house's former life as a boarding school for the sons of sailors. The Queen's House is also home to a ghost, famously captured on film by a couple of Canadian visitors in 1966 but spotted as recently as 2002 by a gallery assistant. Until 2 September 2007, Art for the Nation brings together 200 of the Museum's finest works by famous artists such as Gainsborough, Lely, Hogarth, Reynolds and Turner. A colonnade connects the building to the National Maritime Museum (*see above*). Check website for family events. *Buggy access. Disabled access: lift, ramps, toilets. Nappy-changing facilities. Nearest picnic place: Greenwich Park.*

Ranger's House

Chesterfield Walk, SE10 8QX (8853 0035/www.english-heritage.org.uk). Blackheath rail, Greenwich DLR/rail/53 bus. **Open** *Apr-Sept* 10am-5pm Wed-Sun & bank hols. *Oct-Dec* group bookings only. Closed Jan, Feb. **Admission** (EH) £5.50; £4.10 concessions; £2.80 5-16s; free under-5s. **Credit** MC, V.

This Georgian villa, which dates back to 1723, was from 1815 the residence of the Greenwich Park Ranger, a post held by George III's niece Princess Sophia Matilda. It now contains the collection of treasure amassed by millionaire diamond-trader Julius Wernher. Wernher died in 1912. His priceless collection of 19th-century art, including jewellery, bronzes, tapestries, furniture, porcelain and paintings, is highly unusual. Displayed in 12 elegant rooms, it shows what Britain's richest man spent his dosh on: enamelled skulls, miniature coffins and jewel-encrusted reptiles. *Buggy storage. Disabled access: lifts, toilets. Nearest picnic place: Greenwich Park. Shop.*

Walk the line

East meets west in London. The line that divides the world into hemispheres runs through Greenwich. It was chosen for this honour by astronomers and scientists with top hats and mutton chop whiskers at the International Meridian Conference of 1884, whose purpose was to agree the position of a fixed line (the Prime Meridian) from which all points east and west on the earth could be measured. Greenwich was the obvious choice because of its maritime and astronomical credentials but this didn't stop Paris, as usual, being irritated. The French pointedly kept their own *méridien d'origine* until well into the 20th century.

The line was especially useful for people at sea. In past times, sailors had been unable to estimate exactly how far they would have to travel before crashing into the coast of America. Indeed, the government of the day was so keen to find a solution to this perennial problem that they offered a reward of £20, 000 to whoever could provide it.

The line divides the capital not as the boroughs do. Hence there are places in the west which are actually in the east of London, and London's East End is situated in the west. Some local councils have taken pains to mark the course of the line with bollards and plaques. In Coney Hall, Bromley, it cuts across playing fields enabling footballers to shoot in the east and score in the west. In Waltham Forest, where meridian plaques are plentiful, it divides houses causing families to eat breakfast at opposite ends of the earth and in Stratford it runs through the Olympic site.

Nowhere is the line more celebrated than at Greenwich itself, however, where it is embedded in the paving stones at the Royal Observatory in Greenwich Park. It has become a particular thrill for visitors to straddle the line or hop from one side to the other while their friends video the event on mobile phones. Daily from dusk until midnight the line becomes a laser pointing at the North Pole. It is visible from as faraway as Royston near Cambridge if the sky is clear.

In fact the exact position of the line has varied over the years according to which Observatory window successive Astronomers Royal set up their telescopes in. Flamsteed's line is different from Halley's which is different from Airy's which is where today's is as you can see in the Observatory's cobbled courtyard. It's not the only attraction here. A costumed actor explains the physics of navigation by the stars and the significance of the Prime Meridian. There too you can visit Flamsteed's Apartments where the first Astronomer Royal lived. In his dining room he shares a punishing loaf of 17th-century bread with his friend Samuel Pepys. In the study his quill, his lunettes and a jug of claret summon his ghost. In the basement, a permanent exhibition tells the story of the sometimes desperate competition to win the government's twenty grand by solving the longitude problem. One entrant suggested longitude could be measured and the Prime Meridian fixed by a dog barking at sea. Apparently, the top-hatted astronomers, unused to cranks and time-wasters, actually tried out the theory before discarding it.

The future is in the stars. How the new Planetarium will fit in at the **Royal Observatory**.

Around Town

Royal Observatory

Greenwich Park, SE10 9NF (8312 6565/www.rog. nmm.ac.uk). Cutty Sark DLR/Greenwich DLR/rail. **Open** 10am-5pm daily (last entry 4.30pm). *Tours* phone for details. **Admission** free. *Planetarium shows* £6; £4 under-16s. **Credit** MC, V.

Following the £15 million Time and Space refurbishment, completed in May 2007, it's all change at the Observatory, built for Charles II by Wren in 1675. As well as four new Astronomy galleries whose hands-on exhibits help to explain recent developments in modern astronomy, there are the Time galleries. These chart the development of timekeeping since the 14th century. The Observatory has a dome housing Britain's largest refracting telescope – and the eighth largest in the world. In the courtyard is the Prime Meridian Line: star of a billion snaps; you can pay £1 to receive a certificate marking your visit. The new 120-seater Peter Harrison Planetarium contains an advanced digital laser projector. This unique building has a shape that reflects its own astrological position; a semi-submerged, bronze-clad cone tilts at 51.5 degrees, the latitude of Greenwich, so it points to the north star and its reflective disc is aligned with the celestial equator. The planetarium shows are presented by a Royal Observatory astronomer and special shows are available for children daily (suitable for children aged from six; shows for kids aged three to six than this takeplace at weekends and school during holidays; check the website).

Buggy access (courtyard only). Nappy-changing facilities. Nearest picnic place: Greenwich Park. Shop.

Blackheath & Lewisham

The flat common land against whose southern edge **Blackheath** village nestles, was where Wat Tyler assembled his revolting peasants in 1381, and where Henry VIII met Anne Of Cleves in 1540, shortly before finding her revolting in

a different way. Today, the wide-open spaces are banded on all sides by incessant traffic, but this is still a place of huge importance for sporting types, from kite fliers to ball whackers. Blackheath is home to three historic sports clubs: the Royal Blackheath Golf Club (established 1745), the Blackheath Hockey Club (1861) and the Blackheath Football Club (1862), which plays rugby union. The village is a fashionable mix of independent and small-chain shops and cafés (think Neal's Yard and Café Rouge). Blackheath Halls (*see p232*) is the area's arts focus. A farmers' market (10am-2pm Sun) takes place in Blackheath station car park.

South-west of here the tone lowers considerably. **Lewisham**, more than ready for its promised makeover, has a rowdy market, a good library and Tourist Information office, an uninspiring shopping centre and a heavy police presence outside McDonald's at school chuck-out time.

If you keep walking down Lewisham Promenade you'll end up in Catford, with its landmark black-and-white cat over an ugly shopping centre, its art deco **Broadway Theatre** and its trees lit up by blue light bulbs. Lewisham Borough's saving grace is its many parks, the best of which are the stunning Sydenham Wells Park (Wells Park Road, SE26) and **Manor House & Gardens**. **Mountsfield Park** (Stainton Road, SE6) hosts People's Day (14 July 2007), an annual festival. There's an indoor playground called Kids Korner (8852 3322) at the Hither Green end. East of here, Staplehurst Road is a pleasant enclave by Hither Green station, with a bohemian café, flower shop and knitting club called You Don't Bring Me Flowers (8207 2333, www.you dontbringmeflowers.co.uk) and Education Interactive (*see p191*).

Age Exchange Reminiscence Centre

11 Blackheath Village, SE3 9LA (8318 9105/ www.age-exchange.org.uk). Blackheath rail. **Open** 10am-5pm Mon-Sat. **Admission** free. Groups must book in advance, for a small charge. **Credit** MC, V. You're treated to a low-key, cosy, living-history experience here. The charity Age Exchange aims to improve the quality of life for older people by emphasising the value of memories. A mock-up of a grocer's shop from about 60 years ago features drawers of comestibles. An old-fashioned sweetie shop stocks classics like rosy apples, and a sitting room circa 1940 contains nostalgic toys, a stove, old-style furnishings and crockery. There's also a little café and theatre space at the back. The Centre's programme of exhibitions is also based on older people's memories. Check the website for dates of future attractions.
Buggy access. Café. Disabled access: toilets. Nearest picnic place: centre gardens. Shop.

Manor House & Gardens

Old Road, SE13 5SY (8318 1358/www.lewisham. gov.uk). Hither Green rail. **Open** *Café & park* 9am-dusk daily. *House & library* 9.30am-5pm Mon, Sat; 9.30am-7pm Tue, Thur. **Admission** free.
This 1772 manor house, once the home of George Baring the illustrious banker, is now one of London's grandest local libraries. Visit on a Tuesday morning with your pre-schoolers for the parent-and-toddler session. The gardens and park are lovely. The central lake has a raised platform, with flocks of wildfowl to feed. The handsome play area, made of natural materials, includes rocks, wooden seesaws, balance bars, climbing frames and swings. On one side of it is a wildlife garden; on the other is the child-friendly Pistachios park café with its menu of simple, own-made hot meals, ice-cream, drinks and snacks. A farmers' market takes place here on the first Saturday of the month.
Buggy access. Café. Disabled access: toilets.

Charlton & Woolwich

Until 1872 **Charlton** was famous for the rowdy Charlton Horn Fair – a gift to the people from King John as recompense for seducing a local miller's wife. This once well-to-do area still retains villagey charm around the church and remnants of the green. **Charlton House** is the main attraction if you're not an Addicks fan (the Valley, Charlton Athletic's ground, is just down the hill from here). Its terrace looks out north over a grim-looking Charlton Park. **Maryon Wilson Park**, across the road, is more pleasant. It has a small farm (organised tours only, phone 8319 4253 for details). The park's northernmost edge leads to Woolwich Church Street and the river, spanned by London's life-line, the **Thames Barrier**.
This section of riverside London is at long last

to be connected to the rest of civilisation courtesy of the Woolwich Arsenal DLR extension, which will run under the Thames from King George V station at North Woolwich to Woolwich Arsenal. The line should be finished in 2009. Add to that the Thames Gateway Bridge plan to connect Thamesmead and Beckton north of the river, and it looks as if this area's days as a backwater are numbered. Commuters also use Thames Clippers (www.thamesclippers.com) for a high-speed service to Canary Wharf.

Looking at the high street, though, it's hard to imagine Woolwich ever becoming upmarket. The street's claim to fame is as the venue for the first ever UK McDonald's (in 1974, trivia fans).

Come to Woolwich for **Firepower**, the artillery museum, located in the old buildings of the Woolwich Arsenal. Established in Tudor days as the country's main source of munitions, by World War I, the Arsenal stretched 32 miles (51 kilometres) along the river, had its own internal railway system and employed 72,000 people. Much of the land was sold off during the 1960s, but the main section, with its lovely Georgian buildings, has been preserved. South of here, the Royal Artillery Barracks has the longest Georgian façade in the country. For more on the Arsenal, visit the **Greenwich Heritage Centre**. Another Woolwich highlight is the free **Woolwich Ferry** (8921 5786), earliest references to which date from the 14th century. Today the two ferries are diesel-driven monsters that take pedestrians and cars across the river every 10 minutes through the day. The ferry to the north shore lands you by **North Woolwich Old Station Museum** (*see p119*) and Royal Victoria Gardens. By the ferry terminal on the south bank is the **Waterfront Leisure Centre** (*see p267*).

Charlton House

Charlton Road, SE7 8RE (8856 3951/www.greenwich gov.uk). Charlton rail/53, 54, 380, 422 bus. **Open** *Library* 2-7pm Mon, Thur; 10am-12.30pm, 1.30-5.30pm Tue, Fri; 10am-12.30pm, 1.30-5pm Sat. *Toy library* 10.30am-12.30pm, 1.30-3.30pm Mon, Tue, Fri. **Admission** free.
One of Britain's finest examples of Jacobean domestic architecture, this handsome house was built between 1607 and 1612 by Sir Adam Newton. These days it's a community centre and library, but glimpses of its glorious past can be seen in the creaky oak staircase, marble fireplaces and ornate plaster ceilings. The library within has a good children's section (activities take place 10.30am Mon) and is home to the Charlton Toy Library (8319 0055). Outside, the venerable mulberry tree, dating from 1608, still bears fruit that sometimes finds its way into crumbles, cakes and chutneys sold here in the Mulberry Café. Charlton House has two walled gardens, one a Peace Garden with rose beds, benches, sculpture and a Japanese peace pole. A programme of events, organised to mark Charlton House's

400th anniversary in 2007, will include concerts, quizzes, children's workshops and tea parties, art events and a Jacobean feast. On 17 June 2007 the historic Horne Fayre will take place here. See the website for more anniversary events. Visit at 1pm on a Friday and you'll be treated to a free concert by musicians from the Trinity College of Music, which also puts on a soaring Christmas concert. *Buggy access. Café. Disabled access: ramps, toilets. Lifts. Nappy-changing facilities. Nearest picnic area: Charlton House grounds.*

Firepower
Royal Arsenal, SE18 6ST (8855 7755/www.fire power.org.uk). Woolwich Arsenal rail. **Open** *Apr-Oct* 10.30am-5pm Wed-Sun (last entry 4pm). *Nov-Mar* 10.30am-5pm Fri-Sun (last entry 4pm). **Admission** (LP) £5; £4.50 concessions; £2.50 5-16s; free under-5s; £12 family (2+2 or 1+3). **Credit** MC, V.
The Gunners commemorated here are the soldiers of the Royal Artillery, not the North London Premiership team, whose new Emirates Stadium has a couple of guns from this collection gracing its entrance. Why? The footie team has its roots in Woolwich – in 1886 a group of workers in the armaments factory had a kickabout – and the rest is Arsenal FC history. There are plenty of guns left to admire in this thrilling museum, which occupies a series of converted Woolwich Arsenal buildings close to the river. It's a popular destination for children and their families during the school holidays. The first site to explore has the Gunnery Hall, bristling with preserved artillery pieces, some centuries old. An introductory cinema presentation in the Breech Cinema tells the story of the Royal Artillery. This leads on to Field of Fire, where four massive screens relay archive film and documentary footage of warfare. Smoke fills the air, searchlights pick out artillery surrounding you, and the sound of exploding bombs shakes the floor. After this, you can repair to the Real Weapons Gallery to fire ping-pong balls out of (mini) cannons and take part in all sorts of other militaristic activities. The Gun Pit café, which has hot dishes of the day and decent coffee as well as great value children's picnic boxes, is also on this site.

Across the courtyard (where during the hols children can join a drill class run by a barking sergeant in combats) is another building containing a huge collection of trophy guns and the Cold War gallery, which focuses on the 'monster bits' (ginormous tanks and guns used in military conflict from 1945 to the present). Of most interest to children, however, is the first-floor Command Post, where £1.50 buys you a go on the brilliant Rolling Rock climbing wall, or a paintball target session. Both activities are supervised by staff/soldiers in fatigues. Special events take place throughout the year. Camouflage party packages for little birthday soldiers are available too (for details phone 8312 7103).
Buggy access. Café. Disabled access: ramps, toilets. Lift. Nappy-changing facilities. Nearest picnic place: riverside. Shop.

Thames Barrier Information & Learning Centre
1 Unity Way, SE18 5NJ (8305 4188/www.environ ment-agency.gov.uk). North Greenwich tube/Charlton rail/riverboats to & from Greenwich Pier (8305 0300) & Westminster Pier (7930 3373)/177, 180 bus. **Open** *Apr-late Sept* 10.30am-4.30pm daily. *End Sept-Mar* 11am-3.30pm daily. Closed 24 Dec-2 Jan. **Admission** *Exhibition* £2; £1.50 concessions; £1 5-16s; free under-5s. **Credit** MC, V.
The Barrier, spanning the 1700ft (520m) Woolwich Reach, is the world's largest adjustable dam. It was built in 1982 at a cost of £535 million; since then it has saved London from flooding at least 67 times. The small Learning Centre explains how it works and has a map that shows which parts of London would be submerged if the barrier stopped working. Every September there's a full-scale testing (9 Sept 2007), with a partial test closure once a month (ring for dates). The best way to see the structure is from the river: Campion Cruises (8305 0300) runs trips from Greenwich (Mar-Oct only). Another interesting vantage point is on the other side of the river, in Thames Barrier Park, easily reached on the DLR to Pontoon Dock station. *Café. Shop.*

Around Town

Question time: South-east London

Where can we play?
There's no shortage of top playgrounds, but our favourites are in Dulwich Park (*see p129*), where the equipment's well maintained, and Greenwich Park (*see p135*), where there are summer entertainments and a next-door boating lake should the play equipment pall.

What can we learn?
Wartime history, at the Imperial War Museum (*see p125*); astrology and physics at Greenwich's new Time & Space Project (*see p137*); and botany at the LWT London Wildlife Garden Centre (*see p129*).

Whom might we meet?
Laurence Llewelyn Bowen, Jools Holland, Jenny Eclair, Helen Lederer and Timothy Spall are all South-east Londoners.

Where should we eat?
Try the lovely Joanna's in Crystal Palace (*see p183*). TGI fans (*see p173*) should note there's a branch near Croydon, with the usual crayons and balloons for kids and free Heinz baby food for the tykes. Fish and chip nippers might like Sea Cow in East Dulwich (*37 Lordship Lane, 8693 3111*) or Olley's in Herne Hill (*see p183*). Great grub for all age groups is served up at The Green in East Dulwich (*see p181*). Dim sum dumpling delights are produced all day at Walworth Road's new Dragon Castle (*see p181*).

What can we buy?
Fantastic sweets at Hope & Greenwood (*see p191*); the best picture books at Tales on Moon Lane (*see p190*); top togs at Biff (*see p201*) and crafts, clothes and candy at Greenwich Crafts Market (*see p208*).

Further south-east

Watling Street, the pilgrims' way out of London en route to Canterbury, is now the A207. The villages it passed through have become London suburbs, such as Bexleyheath, where the National Trust's Red House (13 Red House Lane, Bexleyheath, Kent DA6 8JF, 01494 755588), once the home of William Morris, attracts an arty crowd.

Between Bexleyheath and Welling, huge Danson Park contains an 18th-century Palladian villa (8304 9130), but lively children may be more interested in the grounds, which include woods, lakes and a terrific watersports centre. Danson Park's Festival takes place on 24 June 2007.

More delightful parkland and a stunning Tudor mansion can be enjoyed at Hall Place (Bourne Road, Bexley, Kent DA5 1PQ (01322 526 574, www.hallplaceandgardens.co).

The area around Eltham and Bexley is dotted with meadows and woodlands. **Oxleas Wood** across the Shooters Hill Road is an 8000-year-old piece of woodland, dating from the Ice Age. The wood was to be uprooted in the mid-1990s – until a campaign stopped the bulldozers. Its paths link with the Green Chain Walk (www.greenchain.com), a 40-mile (64-kilometre) network starting near the Thames Barrier (*see p121*) and ending at Crystal Palace. The Oxleas Wood path starts at Erith and takes in the remains of 12th-century **Lesnes Abbey**, a fine picnic place with towerblock views.

Organic **Woodlands Farm** lies just off Shooters Hill (the name of this area of Kent, as well as the road that leads to it from near Blackheath). Across the A20, the village of **Chislehurst** has its very own Druids' caves.

Further west, beyond Bromley, Croydon is one of London's busier southern suburbs. It's no oil painting, but it's worth visiting for its trams, the Whitgift Centre for shopping and the cash-strapped but feisty Warehouse Theatre Company (www.warehousetheatre.co.uk) and the Croydon Clocktower (www.croydon.gov.uk/clocktower) for the arts. Croydon Council has some lofty plans up its sleeve. A planned 29-storey classroom and apartment block for Croydon College, if it is approved, will be one of London's tallest buildings.

If you're prepared to venture out to Orpington, try to visit Downe House or Darwin House (Luxted Road, Downe, 01689 859119, www.english-heritage.org.uk). The latter is the former home of Charles Darwin. Downe, the scientist's home for 40 years, is open Wednesday to Sunday only, ring for details.

Chislehurst Caves
Old Hill, Chislehurst, Kent BR7 5NB (8467 3264/ www.chislehurstcaves.co.uk). Chislehurst rail. **Open** 9am-5pm Wed-Sun. *Tours* hourly from 10am-4pm Wed- Sun. **Admission** £5; £3 under-16s, OAPs. **Credit** MC, V.
Druids carved these spooky caves out of the hillside in order to get chalk and flint. They also came to make grisly human sacrifices. Later, the Romans extracted chalk from here. More recently, the caves were used as a World War I ammunition dump and, in the 1930s, a mushroom farm. It was in World War II, however, that the caves gained fame as Britain's largest bomb shelter. The 45-minute tour covers less than a mile (1.6km). It's not strenuous, but isn't for the claustrophobic. You could even have a birthday party in the café here.
Café. Nappy-changing facilities. Shop.

Eltham Palace
Court Yard, off Court Road, SE9 5QE (8294 2548/ www.elthampalace.org.uk). Eltham rail. **Open** Apr-Oct 10am-5pm Mon-Wed, Sun. *Nov-Mar* 10am-4pm Mon-Wed, Sun. Closed 22 Dec-31 Jan. **Admission** (EH) *House & grounds* (incl audio tour) £7.90; £6.75 concessions; £4 5-16s; free under-5s; £19 family. *Grounds only* £4.90; £2.50 concessions; £2.30 5-16s; free under-5s. **Credit** MC, V.
The palace, acquired by Edward II in 1305, was a royal home right up until Henry VIII's heyday, before falling out of favour. Its Great Hall, the most substantial surviving medieval hall outside the Palace of Westminster, was used as a barn for many years. It wasn't until 1931 that Stephen Courtauld, a patron of the arts, commissioned a thoroughly modern house to stand among the relics of the old palace. The Great Hall with its stained glass and hammerbeam roof was pressed into service for glamorous society parties, concerts and banquets. The interior is all polished veneer and chunky marble, and the Courtaulds incorporated the latest technological gadgetry then available, such as concealed lighting, under-floor heating and a room-to-room vacuuming system. Even the family's beloved pet ring-tailed lemur, Mah-Jongg, lived the life of Riley in his special lodgings. The grounds are beautifully restored and the tearoom and shop have a distinctly 1930s flavour.
As well as free quiz sheets and trails for children, various family-friendly events are laid on for visitors. Check the website for details.
Buggy storage. Café. Disabled access: lift, toilets. Nappy-changing facilities. Nearest picnic place: palace grounds. Shop.

Woodlands Farm
331 Shooters Hill, Welling, Kent DA16 3RP (8319 8900/www.thewoodlandsfarmtrust.org). Falconwood rail/89, 486 bus. **Open** 9.30am-4.30pm daily. **Admission** free; donations appreciated.
This community farm straddles the boroughs of Greenwich and Bexley and is a thriving organic enterprise, with a lovely cottage garden, wildlife garden, orchards and meadows. Livestock includes some noisy geese, hens, a flock of sheep, a cow, a goat and a Shetland pony called Bob. Volunteers are welcome to don their gumboots and help out. The farm hosts educational group visits, giving lessons on farm-animal care, conservation, composting, and the history of farming. Keep an eye on the events diary to see what's in the offing.
Buggy access. Nearest picnic place: farm grounds. Shop.

South-west London

Park life and animal magic.

Vauxhall & Stockwell

In the 13th century the area known as Vauxhall was dominated by a manor owned by a soldier loyal to King John called Falkes de Bréauté. Falkes' Hall was gradually worn down to Fox Hall, then Vauxhall. There's no grand manor house now, but the area is impressively well connected, transport wise, and has an eye-catching monolith watching over it in the form of the riverside 'Spy Central', the MI6 headquarters flanking Vauxhall Bridge.

Vauxhall is plagued by round-the-clock heavy traffic, exacerbated by the fruit and flower wholesalers of New Covent Garden Market. Happily, though, there's a fine selection of green spaces for families to enjoy – admittedly, these are less exotic than the 18th-century local hotspot Vauxhall Pleasure Gardens (the plain Spring Gardens is all that remains).

Vauxhall Park (junction of South Lambeth Road and Fentiman Road, SW8) has a One O'Clock Club and a model village. A rural aspect comes from **Vauxhall City Farm**. Neighbouring Stockwell has Slade Gardens Adventure Playground (Lorn Road, SW9, 7737 3829) and Larkhall Park (Courland Grove, SW8). Stockwell Bowl Skatepark, nearer Brixton, has been popular with local kids since the '70s.

The local Portuguese community is reflected in the cafés and shops along South Lambeth Road. Overall, community spirit is a mark of this part of town – take the housing co-operatives of Bonnington Square, where residents created a 'secret garden' from a former bombsite. Oasis Children's Nature Garden (*see p239*) is run by local residents and has a variety of plants and flowers, a kart track and a cycle centre.

Vauxhall City Farm

165 Tyers Street, SE11 5HS (7582 4204). Vauxhall tube/rail/2, 36, 44, 77 bus. **Open** 10.30am-4pm Wed-Sun. Closed 1wk in late summer, phone to check. **Admission** free; donations appreciated.

Battersea Park Children's Zoo. See p143.

Around Town

Bag a bargain at **Brixton Market**.

Founded on derelict land in 1977, and run by a team of staff and volunteers, Vauxhall City Farm attracts around 12,000 visitors a year. The sociable livestock reared in its grassy paddocks – against a backdrop of big city buildings – include cows, pigs, sheep, poultry, donkeys and horses. Various education, refugee and gardening groups meet at the farm; it also runs Sunday art classes and offers subsidised riding lessons for local children. Phone for updates on the after-school club and summer holiday play scheme – as we went to press these were under threat of closure due to funding problems.
Buggy access. Disabled access: toilet. Nappy-changing facilities.

Brixton

Culturally rich Brixton has transformed itself from its 19th-century roots as a prototype suburb into South London's buzziest residential area. With a rough-around-the-edges charm, it's most famous for its nightlife and live venues such as Brixton Academy (accompanied under-18s are admitted to some gigs). Still, there's plenty to do before dark – such as exploring the cheap 'n' cheerful Brixton Market; dating back to 1870, its stalls now offer everything from Afro-Caribbean food to children's clothes. The street running alongside is Electric Avenue, so-called because it was one of London's first streets to be

lit by electricity; it is namechecked by Eddy Grant's single. The handsome Ritzy Cinema (*see p223*) runs Saturday clubs for kids. For a hot summer day, few attractions could beat Brockwell Lido – as most of South London seems to agree.

Brockwell Park

Dulwich Road, SE24 0PA (7926 0105). Herne Hill rail.
Open 7am-dusk daily.
Part of Herne Hill but most valued by the people of built-up Brixton, Brockwell Park is a little piece of paradise in the midst of the concrete jungle. The pastoral landscape even comes with its own manor house – Brockwell Hall, which opened to the public in 1892. Plus points include play facilities for a broad age range (playgrounds, a multi-sports pitch, tennis courts, and a BMX trail is currently under construction), duck ponds and an increased live entertainment schedule, including music festivals and a free fireworks display around 5 November. The annual Lambeth Country Show (21-22 July 2007) is a hit with families, with entertainment such as farmyard displays, live music, knights jousting, a miniature railway, food stalls and the delightfully dotty Vegetable Animal Competition.

The art deco, shiveringly unheated Brockwell Lido (*see p267*) comes into its own during a hot summer; there's also a paddling pool for water babies. A proactive users' group (www.brockwelllido.com) ensures that there is plenty going on despite funding difficulties.
Buggy access. Café. Disabled access: toilets. Nappy-changing facilities.

Streatham

Ever since Roman Londinium, this part of town
has been a major thoroughfare; today, traffic-
choked Streatham High Road is reviled for its
famously ill looks. Still, it is a well-used hive of
weekend activities for active youngsters. Its buses
and three railway stations make access easy, too.
The Streatham Ice Arena (see p266) has long been
an essential destination, and there's also fun to be
had at the Streatham Megabowl (see p269) and
Playscape Pro Racing (see p262). Streathamites
call the combined attractions of rink, track and
bowling lane the Streatham Hub and they
campaigned for improvements to the facilities
here, with particular concern for the future of
the ice rink, as Streatham has had one since 1931.
Everyone's holding their breath in the hope that
Tesco will honour their commitment to fund a
new top-flight rink with swimming pool in
exchange for putting a supermarket in the area;
for more details check Streatham Ice Skating
Action Group's website (www.sisag.org.uk).

Streatham's welcome designation as a
conservation area has drawn more attention
to local green sites. Streatham Common includes
woodlands, a wild flower area and a sweet
'secret' garden known as the Rookery, and
hosts such lively annual events as 'Kite Day'
(www.streathamkiteday.org.uk) and Streatham
Festival's arty entertainment programme (7-15
July 2007, www.streathamfestival.com).

Battersea

Clapham Junction station, Britain's busiest
railway station, is the main gateway to Battersea.
It's not the most child-friendly introduction to
the district: numerous steps and no lift mean it's
tricky to negotiate with a pushchair. It's worth
persevering, however, as a plethora of family-
friendly pursuits await (they don't call this
general area of Wandworth 'Nappy Valley'
for nothing). Northcote Road, with its fine
shops and market, is just a stroll away from
the station. Walk in the other direction for
Battersea Arts Centre (see p226), the jewel in
the area's crown. Sporty children may prefer
the Latchmere Leisure Centre (see p267), which
also has a popular line in birthday pool parties.

Battersea Park is a year-round delight to
explore, and to the east of this beauty hulks the
beast – handsome in its way – Battersea Power
Station (see p144). A major commercial/cultural
project is planned here, but the site looks dormant
still. Proposals to demolish the famous chimneys
have provoked a fierce debate.

Battersea Dogs & Cats Home

*4 Battersea Park Road, SW8 4AA (7622 3626/
www.dogshome.org). Vauxhall tube/rail then 44
bus/Battersea Park or Queenstown Road rail/344
bus.* **Open** *Viewings* 1-4pm Mon-Fri; 10.30am-4pm
Sat, Sun. Closed 1 Jan, Good Friday, 25, 26 Dec.
Admission £1; 50p 5-16s, concessions; free
under-5s. **Credit** *Shop* MC, V.
Hardly a conventional tourist attraction, but this world-
famous sanctuary for canines and felines (opened in 1860)
is open to casual visitors as well as potential adopters.
Diligent staff here vet all candidates to ensure they're right
for the pet they're paying to rescue, and it should be point-
ed out that many of rescue dogs are for child-free homes
only. Still, visiting animal lovers enjoy the souvenir and
accessory shop, café and the collection of tributes to dogs
and their owners. The Home offers workshops on how to
choose and train your puppy or kitten, and kennels can
also be 'sponsored' via their bright website.
*Buggy access. Café. Disabled access: lift, ramp, toilet.
Nearest picnic place: Battersea Park. Shop.*

Battersea Park Children's Zoo

*Queenstown Road, Battersea Park, SW11 4NJ
(7924 5826/www.batterseazoo.co.uk). Sloane
Square tube then 19, 137 bus/Battersea Park
or Queenstown Road rail/156, 345 bus.* **Open**
10am-6pm daily. Last admission 5pm. **Admission**
£5.95; £4.50 3-15s; free under-3s; £18.50 family
(2+2). **Credit** MC, V. **Map** p313 F13.
A zoo of small, sweet things, whose new owners (who also
run an otter sanctuary in the New Forest) have pitched it
just right for small children. The most entertaining residents are the playful otters, whose antics – playing with
pebbles and chasing each other in and out of the stream –
drew large crowds on a freezing January day. Children
have lots of fun with the meerkats; little ones can actually
pop their heads up in their enclosure – their heads are protected by see-through plastic viewing bubbles. We also
loved the mouse house, especially all those little mice living it up in their own doll's house. Other friendly creatures
include talking mynah birds and parrots, cuddlesome
sheep and goats, bossy turkeys, wide-eyed monkeys,
Shetland ponies and loads more. The shops's strong on
pocket-money-priced toys; there's plenty of space for a picnic if you don't fancy the Lemon Tree café. *Photo p141.*
*Buggy access. Café. Disabled access: ramps, toilets.
Nappy-changing facilities. Shop.*

Battersea Park

*SW11 4NJ (8871 7530/www.wandsworth.gov.uk).
Sloane Square tube then 19, 137 bus/Battersea Park
or Queenstown Road rail.* **Open** 8am-dusk daily.
Map p313 F13.
The marshy fields that this park was built on were
originally used for market gardens, and more
excitingly, for duelling. The Duke of Wellington fought
an (abortive) duel at Battersea Fields in 1829. The
riverside park laid out here in 1858 has been splendidly
restored. Facilities range from water features (a boating
lake, elegant fountains and riverside promenade) to its
state-of-the-art sporting facilities and play areas,
including a toddlers' playground and a challenging
adventure playground for children aged eight to 15
(8871 7539). Tennis coaching is available to anyone
over eight on the floodlit courts, a range of cycles can
be hired from London Recumbents (7498 6543; open Sat,

Battersea Power Station. *See p143.*

Sun, bank holidays, school holidays), and open fishing is available from mid June to mid March (for permit information, contact 8871 7530). Battersea Park is also home to a rich array of wildlife, the London Wildlife Trust runs nature reserves within its grounds.

The Gondola al Parco café (7978 1655) has tables overlooking the boating lake and live music during summer evenings. The loveliest landmark is the lofty Peace Pagoda, donated in 1985 by Japanese monks and nuns to commemorate Hiroshima Day. It stands serenely opposite the Children's Zoo, in the centre of the park's northern edge. *Buggy access. Café. Disabled access: toilets. Nappy-changing facilities.*

Clapham & Wandsworth

Posh during the 18th and 19th centuries, when the upwardly mobile could afford to seek their rural idyll in its pleasant pastures, the area suffered a grimy setback with the coming of the railways. Noise and large numbers of working class folk chased the nobility away. Today, however, the well-to-do are all back and the streets skirting both Clapham Common and Wandsworth Common are hugely desirable. Both districts (the latter is the prettier) have great recreational features – playgrounds, ponds, cafés, courts and numerous summer events. The most northerly tip of Wandsworth Common is home to the excellent Lady Allen Adventure Playground (Chivalry Road, SW11 1HT (7228 0278, www.kids-online.org.uk) a well-designed playground for children with special needs who are Wandsworth residents. The district between the Commons has earned the nickname 'Nappy Valley.' The claim that it has the highest birth rate in Europe may be hard to verify, but a quick stroll around the pleasant streets provides plenty of empirical evidence: au pairs push buggies; mummies lunch with offspring in tow; swathes of spruced-up schoolchildren fill the streets.

The Nappy Valley effect has brought artisan bakers, frou-frou boutiques (for parents and children) and upmarket child-friendly cafés to the area hubs of Northcote Road and Bellevue Road. Clapham Old Town, north-east of the common, also has an upmarket high street, with plenty of places to eat out and the excellent Clapham Picture House (*see p144*).

Wandsworth's formerly grim shopping centre, the Southside mall (Wandsworth High Street, www.southsidewandsworth.com), includes a multiplex cinema. Alongside, King George's Park has seen better days, but it remains popular for its playgrounds and sports facilities, including the **Kimber BMX/Adventure Playground** and the football pitches and indoor play area at Wandle Recreation Centre (Mapleton Road, SW18 4DN, 8871 1149, www.kinetika.org), on the banks of the River Wandle.

The River Wandle, which flows out of ponds at Carshalton and Beddington in Surrey, bisects the meadowland around **Morden Hall Park** (*see p147*) and flows towards Wandsworth. The 15-kilometre (nine-mile) Wandle Trail (www.wandle trail.org) runs alongside the river between Wandsworth and Carshalton, passing through grim industrial landscape and newly regenerated wildlife havens. Towards Earlsfield, down Magdalen Road, lurks It's a Kid's Thing.

It's a Kid's Thing

279 Magdalen Road, SW18 3NZ (8739 0909/www. itsakidsthing.co.uk). Earlsfield rail. **Open** 9am-6pm daily. **Admission** £5 over-2s; £4 under-2s; £1 siblings under 18mths. *Activities* prices vary; check website for details. **Credit** MC, V.

An award-winning family-run indoor adventure play centre, with a two-tier playzone and a cuddly soft play area. Parents can keep a watchful eye from the café, which offers nursery food for all ages, or bury themselves in the complimentary daily papers. There's also an imaginative programme of activities (such as capoeira for five- to seven-year-olds) and a party room. It's a popular spot, so book ahead to avoid tantrums. *Photo p147.*

Buggy access. Café. Disabled: toilets. Nappy-changing facilities. Nearest picnic place: Wandsworth Common.

Kimber BMX/Adventure Playground

King George's Park, Kimber Road, SW18 4NN (8870 2168). Earlsfield rail then 44 or 270 bus. **Open** *Termtime* 2.30-7pm Tue-Fri; 11am-6pm Sat. *Holidays* 11am-6pm Mon-Sat. **Admission** free.

Aimed at under-16s, Kimber has all the usual variously challenging platforms, ropes, tyres and ladders, big swings, little swings and monkey bars, plus the added attractions of a basketball court and a compact BMX track. If kids don't have their own bike to skid around on, they can usually hire one at the playground (though do phone ahead to check availability). For showery days there's an indoor games room. The five ramps of the skateboard park are open to all; helmets are essential. If you're not bringing your own, they may be hired for a princely 30p.

Buggy access. Disabled access: ramp, toilet. Shop.

Wandsworth Museum

The Courthouse, 11 Garratt Lane, SW18 4AQ (8871 7074/www.wandsworth.gov.uk). Clapham Junction rail then 39, 77A, 156, 170, 337 bus/Wandsworth Town rail/28, 37, 44, 220, 270 bus. **Open** 10am-5pm Tue-Fri; 2-5pm Sat, Sun. Closed bank hols. **Admission** free. **Credit** *Shop* MC, V.

A tiny museum whose exhibits reflect the area's long history by way of Ice Age treasures, such as the fossilised skull of a woolly rhino, and more modern displays: a model of Wandle Mills, a World War II air-raid shelter and a Southfields chemist's shop. Downstairs there's an Iron Age sword and scabbard, cooking and farming tools from Wandsworth's Roman period and sundry weaponry from the medieval villages of Batricesage (Battersea), Baelgeham (Balham), Puttenhythe (Putney) and Totinge (Tooting). Interactive exhibits let children make a brass rubbing of a Putney knight or get their hands on an ancient flint hand-axe or a Roman helmet. Some activities for schoolchildren are connected with the exhibitions, others link in with nationwide events, such as Black History Month and The Big Draw (both in Oct). Summer 2007

marks the passing of Young's Brewery from Wandsworth with an exhibition called Last Orders: Memories of Young's Brewery, which runs from 14 August to 23 September. *Buggy access. Disabled access: toilet. Nappy-changing facilities. Nearest picnic place: King George's Park/Old Burial Ground. Shop.*

Tooting

Rooting in Tooting's history uncovers a Roman beginning, when its high street connected London with Chichester. Nowadays it's an even more popular commuter base with a healthy countryside scene evoked by Tooting Common with its famous Lido, Europe's biggest open-air pool (*see p267*) and a heady urban buzz along the high street, where the well-established Asian community does good business. During festivals such as Eid or Diwali, illuminations are strung along Tooting High Street and Upper Tooting Road. There are some excellent South Asian restaurants here too – these might not offer kids' menus, but the atmosphere is reliably family-orientated.

Wimbledon

The annual Lawn Tennis Championships that put Wimbledon on the world map take place every June. They started here in 1877, and their history is documented in the entertaining Wimbledon Lawn Tennis Museum. Racquet sports apart, this is an accessible and family-friendly suburb. Many amenities are based in the Centre Court shopping centre adjoining the station; an Odeon multiplex cinema is just across the road, and, further along the Broadway, there's entertainment to be had at Wimbledon Theatre and the superb Polka Theatre for Children (*see p145*). Southbound, towards Colliers Wood, there's the vast Tiger's Eye indoor adventure playground for boisterous under-nines.

Outdoor pursuits are always well served, thanks to Wimbledon Common's lovely nature trails, horse rides, cycle paths, sports facilities – and resident Wombles, according to Elisabeth Beresford's classic books. A wealth of green spaces includes Wimbledon Park, which has a boating lake, and the stately Morden Hall Park, which has meadows, wetlands and waterways. At the south of the common, Fishpond Wood & Beverley Meads nature trail (entrance near Beverley Meads car park at the end of Barham Road, SW20) is open at all times. The trail comprises oak avenues, coppiced hazel woodland and bluebells aplenty in springtime. Seasonal ponds have plenty of amphibians and dragonflies.

The best guides to enjoying London life

(but don't just take our word for it)

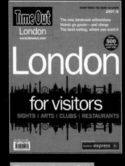

'More than 700 places where you can eat out for less than £20 a head... a mass of useful information in a geuinely pocket–sized guide'

Mail on Sunday

'Extremely useful'

The Times

'I'm always asked how I keep up to date with shopping and services in a city as big as London. This guide is the answer'

Red Magazine

'Get the inside track on the capital's neighbourhoods'

Independent on Sunday

'Armed with a tube map and this guide there is no excuse to find yourself in a duff bar again'

Evening Standard

Rated 'Best Restaurant Guide'

Sunday Times

Available at all good bookshops and
timeout.com/shop from £6.99

100% Independent

Venture further south from Wimbledon, or alternatively follow the Northern Line to the bitter end, and you will be rewarded with **Morden Hall Park**, a former deer park on the River Wandle.

Deen City Farm & Community Garden

39 Windsor Avenue, SW19 2RR (8543 5300/www. deencityfarm.co.uk). Colliers Wood tube then 200 bus. **Open** 10am-4.30pm Tue-Sun, bank hol Mon. **Admission** free; donations welcome.

Founded in 1978, this community farm has pigs, goats, rabbits and poultry alongside rare breeds, which include Jacob sheep, fluffy alpacas Kimby and Milo, and Derek the white peacock. Deen City works as an educational resource for all ages, with volunteer schemes for those who fancy getting their hands dirty; it now boasts a successful parent and toddler group. Children's activities include Young Farmer days for eight to 13 year-olds, who can learn to feed, groom and clean out the animals during the school holidays. The riding school has facilities for the disabled and runs Own a Pony days (bookings on 8543 5858; it is advisable to book well ahead, as the days are popular). *Buggy access. Café. Disabled access: toilet. Nappy-changing facilities. Shop.*

Morden Hall Park

Morden Hall Road, Morden, Surrey, SM4 5JD (8545 6850/www.nationaltrust.org.uk). Morden tube. **Open** 8am-6pm daily. Closed 1 Jan, 25-27 Dec. **Admission** free. **Credit** *Shop* AmEx, MC, V.

This is 125 acres of National Trust-owned parkland of uncommon beauty. The Morden Hall of the name is run as a private restaurant, so you have access only to meadows, woodland, a network of waterways from the River Wandle and a stunning rose garden. The renovated Snuff Mill Environmental Centre, housed in one of several historic buildings in the park, includes children's activities every Thursday during school holidays at Snuff Mill Environmental Centre. Craftspeople, furniture restorers and artists occupy many of the old estate buildings, and the Riverside Café is a beautiful place from which to admire the surrounds while having tea. *Buggy access. Café. Disabled access: toilets. Nappy-changing facilities. Shop.*

Tiger's Eye

42 Station Road, SW19 2LP (8543 1655/www. tigerseye.co.uk). Colliers Wood or South Wimbledon tube. **Open** *Termtime* 10am-6pm Tue-Sun. *Holidays* 10am-6pm daily. **Admission** £5.50 over-6s; £4.99 2-5s; £2.50 under-2s. Height limit 4ft 9 inches. **Credit** MC,V.

This vast and exciting, jungle-themed indoor play centre for children up to the age of ten has ball ponds, nets, soft play and slides. Children's parties are a speciality. *Buggy access. Café. Disabled access: ramps, toilets. Nappy changing facilities.*

Wimbledon Lawn Tennis Museum

Centre Court, All England Lawn Tennis Club, Church Road, SW19 5AE (8946 6131/www.wimbledon.org/ museum). Southfields tube/39, 93, 200, 493 bus.

The day will go by in a blur at **It's a Kid's Thing**. *See p145.*

Around Town

Open 10.30am-5pm daily. *During championships* spectators only. *Tours* Phone/see website. **Admission** *Museum* £8.50; £7.50 concessions; £4.75 5-16s; free under-5s. *Museum & tour* £14.50; £13 concessions; £11 5-16s, free under-5s. **Credit** AmEx, MC, V.

Still glowing from its triumph in Visit London's Large Visitor Attraction of the Year Award (2006), this museum has reaped the benefits of a multi-million pound refit. It has some wow-factor interactives now, but keeps a sense of tradition in its displays of tennis memorabilia.

The wows include Court on Camera, derived from the filming of Centre Court's 2005 Wimbledon Championships, when a 200° camera with five separate lenses was used to capture the match between Maria Sharapova (Russia) and Nuria Llagostera (Spain). The recordings in the museum can be frozen and the image is shown in 3-D. Other, more conventional footage includes recordings of past finals from 1970 to 1999. Another attraction is a 3-D John McEnroe 'ghost' shown walking through the 1980s gents'-dressing room. The champ is seen opening lockers and reminiscing about the good old days. Other donations from top players are more tangible: Roger Federer's cream jacket and winning tennis outfit; Amélie Mauresmo's dress and Andre Agassi's distinctive baggy ensemble. The Wimbledon Tour is led by Blue Badge guides and there's an extensive education programme. Family activities happen throughout the year; see the website for details.
Buggy access. Café. Disabled access: lift, toilet. Nappy-changing facilities. Shop.

Wimbledon Windmill Museum

Windmill Road, Wimbledon Common, SW19 5NR (8947 2825/www.wimbledonwindmillmuseum.org.uk). Wimbledon tube/rail. **Open** *Apr-Oct* 2-5pm Sat; 11am-5pm Sun, bank hols; school groups by appointment only. **Admission** £1; 50p under-16s, concessions. **No credit cards.**

Built in 1817, this is believed to be the only remaining example of a hollow-post flour mill in this country, and its restored interior is now a museum, full of display cases containing working models of many other types of windmill. Other hands-on exhibits feature various pieces of grain-grinding equipment, including pestles and mortars and hand querns (grinding stones). Such items are put to good use during occasional children's workshops. Dioramas, tool and machinery displays, videos, and a small Robert Baden-Powell exhibition (the founder of the Scout movement wrote *Scouting For Boys* here in 1908) make up the rest of the museum.
Buggy access (ground floor). Café. Car park. Shop.

Putney & Barnes

Quiet (except in late March, when thousands turn up to watch the Varsity Boat Race that starts at the University Stone, near Putney Bridge, www.boatrace.org), Putney's riverside has a rural look. This is in contrast to the busy high street, and Putney Exchange Shopping Centre nearby.

Putney Heath, a lengthy stretch of rugged beauty that eventually adjoins Wimbledon Common, was once the haunt of highwaymen, but it's quieter nowadays. The riverside King George's Park is better for entertainments,

though, as it features playgrounds, tennis courts and a good line in November fireworks.

Neighbouring Barnes has an upmarket, village-like atmosphere, although its outskirts are well known to glam rock devotees, who visit the shrine of musician Marc Bolan, killed in a car crash near Barnes Common in 1977. That might have a limited appeal – not so the highly recommended **WWT Wetland Centre**, where all age groups find something to delight them.

Eddie Catz

68-70 High Street, SW15 1SF (0845 201 1268/www.eddiecatz.com). Putney Bridge tube. **Open** 9.30am-6.30pm Mon-Sat; 10am-5pm Sun. **Admission** £5.50 over-3s; £5 under-3s; £3.50 under-2s. **Credit** MC, V.

This first-floor play centre and café is a big, bright, clean space, bordered by windows and mirrors, where the admission charge buys excited children access to interactive video games, table ice-hockey and a themed adventure play frame. There's an innovative programme of workshops such as 'Mad Science', which gave kids a chance to build rockets and robots; themes vary, so check the website for upcoming bookings. The central café area is where adults can wallow unmolested, with the newspapers.
Buggy access. Café. Disabled access: lift, toilets. Nappy-changing facilities. Shop.

WWT Wetland Centre

Queen Elizabeth's Walk, SW13 9WT (8409 4400/ www.wwt.org.uk). Hammersmith tube then 33, 72, 209 (alight at Red Lion pub) or 283 (Duck Bus direct to Centre) bus. **Open** *Summer* 9.30am-6pm daily. *Winter* 9.30am-5pm daily (last entry 1hr before closing). *Tours* 11am, 2pm daily. *Feeding tours* 3.30pm daily. **Admission** £8.75; £6.60 concessions; £4.95 4-16s; free under-4s; £21.95 family (2+2). *Tours* free. *Feeding tours* free. **Credit** MC, V.

Since it opened in 2000, this, the London outpost of of the Wildfowl & Wetlands Trust, has morphed into a brilliant family day out. Just 6.5km (four miles) from the West End, it's accessible by public transport (including the 283 Duck Bus from Hammersmith tube) and has a free car park and bike park. The main point of the wetlands is to support 170 species of bird, as well as all manner of insects and amphibians, bats and butterflies. It does this with ingenuity: the acres are divided into World Wetlands, with areas like North America, Hawaii, East Asia Rice Paddy, all carefully recreated, with hides and trails. Then there are the reedbeds, lagoons, marshes, a field lab and two large hides all arranged around a central lake. If the weather's good, you can bring a picnic and enjoy the peaceful vibe.

Grotty weather brings no problems for visitors with children, as there is a fantastic Discovery Centre and Wet Lab, where children can play boisterous or educational games. In good weather leave a long time for children to enjoy the Explore playground. Here too there are plenty of opportunities to get wet and run off some energy. Parents should make a note to come back without the infants to eat a pleasant three-course dinner in the posh Water's Edge restaurant (although child helpings are available), above the more tot-friendly café of the same name, where the food is of high quality. Our last visit coincided with an Easter duckling event, with workshops and a treasure hunt, but there's an

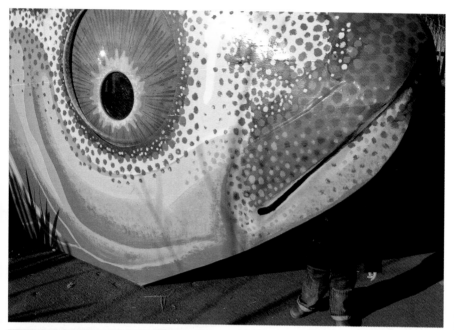

WWT Wetland Centre

excellent programme of activities for children year round. Summer bat walks are immensely popular, so book ahead. *Buggy access. Café. Car park. Disabled access: lifts, toilet. Nappy-changing facilities. Shop.*

Richmond & Kew

This strikingly scenic borough is beloved of royalty. Henry VII built Richmond Palace in 1501 (its remains can be found on Richmond Green). And Elizabeth I resided here in her senior years (she died at Richmond Palace in 1603). Older celebs (Pete Townshend, Jerry Hall) like it too. It's also perfect for families thanks to its expansive open spaces, and is well-connected to London, via rail and tube. Indoor entertainment can be found at Richmond Theatre, a beautiful, Victorian venue that offers children's shows and musicals (The Green, Richmond, Surrey, TW9 1HH, 0870 060 6651, www.richmondtheatre.net). There's no better way to enjoy a sunny day on Richmond Green than with a cornet from Gelateria Danieli (16 Brewers Lane, Richmond, Surrey TW9 1HH, 8439 9807) in one hot little hand. They make 30 flavours of ice-cream in this hole-in-the-wall parlour – the best in the south-west (of London).

One westbound stop along on the District Line, Kew is world-famous for its majestic **Royal Botanic Gardens**, while the town itself is a pleasant, sedate place for a family stroll.

East Sheen Common Nature Trail
East Sheen Common, Fife Road, SW14 7EW (8876 2382/Borough Ecology Officer 8831 6125). Hammersmith tube then 33 bus/Mortlake rail, then 15min walk. **Open** dawn-dusk daily. **Admission** free.
This nature trail runs through 13 areas of woodlands, ponds and streams marked with orange posts. A wildlife-watching leaflet tells you about the animals and insects that live around here. You'll be lucky if you see the badgers, but visit in spring and you should hear frogs croaking and woodpeckers tapping. Summer brings butterflies to the meadow flowers and woodland floor; autumn provides berries for the birds. Contact the ranger for details of children's activities and guided walks.

Museum of Richmond
Old Town Hall, Whittaker Avenue, Richmond, Surrey TW9 1TP (8332 1141/www.museumofrichmond.com). Richmond tube/rail. **Open** 11am-5pm Tue-Sat. Closed public hols. **Admission** free.
Richmond's museum parades its regal history, detailing the lives of silver-spooned former residents, from the 12th-century Henry I to Elizabeth I four centuries later. There are permanent and temporary displays including local art,

Question time: South-west London

Where can we play?
South-west London's legendary leafiness means you're never far away from a decent acreage of greensward. For our money (ie none), the best free playgrounds are at Battersea Park (*see p143*) and Wandsworth Common (*see p144*); the best playgrounds that make learning fun (although you'll have to cough up for the playdate) are in Kew Gardens (*see p151*) and the Wetland Centre (*see p148*), where there are lots of indoor activities too. If the weather's beastly, indoor playgrounds and activity centres worth noting include Eddie Catz (*see p148*) and It's a Kids Thing (*see p145*).

What can we learn?
Tudor history comes alive at Hampton Court (*see p152*); family history history can be uncovered at the National Archives (*see p151*); Botany for tots is fun at Climbers & Creepers (*see p151*); ornithology for infants is the business of the Wetland Centre (*see p148*).

Whom might we meet?
Jack Dee is bringing up his four in Wandsworth; Tommy Steele resides in Richmond; Balham boy Ainsley Harriot and family; 'Mayor of Balham' Arthur Smith; Gordon Ramsay, another father of four, resides in Battersea; John McEnroe, looking like a shadow of his former self in the Wimbledon Lawn Tennis Museum (*see p147*), where his ghost appears in 3D, wandering through the dressing room and reminiscing about his glory days on the grass courts of SW19.

Where should we eat?
Every quality restaurant chain that was ever invented seems to have a family-friendly branch in Northcote Road, but Boiled Egg and Soldiers (*see p184*) and Crumpet (*see p184*) are sweeter. For outdoor eating look no further than Common Ground (*see p182*); for over-the-top eating make an entrance at the Blue Elephant (*see p183*); for hamburger-and-hot dog fanatics, Dexter's Grill (*see p184*) hits the spot, as do the posh patties at Gourmet Burger Kitchen (*see p184*).

What can we buy?
Loads of lovely stuff in Northcote Road, where farmyard names like Trotters (*see p202*) and Quackers (*see p202*) specialise not in animal feeds but unusual gear for kids. Honey from the bees in the Hive Honey shop (93 Northcote Road, SW11 6PL, 7924 6233, www.thehivehoney shop.co.uk); nursery furnishings from Putney's artfully swish Chic Shack (*see p194*) and reading matter from the best little bookshop in the south, the Lion & Unicorn (*see p190*).

and the broad programme of children's activities includes workshops for pre-schoolers. Harry the Herald's Saturday Club, for six- to 11-year-olds, takes place on the third Saturday of every month (10-11.15am, £2 per child). An under-fives club, Mini-Heralds, takes place on the third Wednesday of every month (2-2.40pm, £1 per child). Free trails and drop-in activities change with the museum's various exhibitions, so consult the website for details. *Buggy access. Disabled access: lift, toilets. Nearest picnic place: Richmond Green/riverside. Shop.*

National Archives

Kew, Richmond, Surrey TW9 4DU (8876 3444/ www.pro.gov.uk/education). Kew Gardens tube then 10min walk/65, 391 bus, then 5min walk. **Open** 9am-5pm Mon, Wed, Fri; 10am-7pm Tue; 9am-7pm Thur; 9.30am-5pm Sat. *Tours* 11am, 2pm Sat (booking necessary). **Admission** free. *Tours* free.

As custodian of the records of 1,000 years of central government and the law courts, the Archives has a surprisingly good line in family-friendly activities at its Education and Visitor Centre. Sadly, the museum, which spans British history from the Domesday Book to the Festival of Britain, is closed for refurbishment until Spring 2008. Check the website's excellent online resources for details or call the interpretation department on 8392 5202. The Learning Curve, a free online teaching and learning resource, following the History National Curriculum from Key Stages 2 to 5, is well worth a look.

Buggy access. Café. Disabled access: lifts, toilet. Nappy-changing facilities. Nearest picnic place: National Archives grounds. Shop.

Richmond Park

Holly Lodge, Richmond, Surrey TW10 5HS (8948 3209/www.royalparks.gov.uk). **Open** *Summer* 7am-30mins before dusk. *Winter* 7.30am-30mins before dusk. **Admission** free.

Extensive Richmond Park, 13km (eight miles) across at its widest point, is the biggest city park in Europe and, along with Epping Park, the nearest London gets to wild countryside. Herds of red and fallow deer roam freely, a source of much fascination to children (don't get too close). The park is also home to numerous varieties of bird, fish and, 1,000 species of beetle. Tucked away in the middle is the Isabella Plantation, a tranquil woodland garden with streams, ponds and bridges. Home to camellias, azaleas and rhododendrons, it is best seen in all its glory in early summer or late September. There are also plenty of benches and grassy glades where you can picnic. The park's Petersham Gate has a playground. From the top of nearby King Henry VIII's Mound, you'll have a spectacular view right across London. Alternatively, you could stroll along Terrace Walk, a Victorian promenade that stretches all the way from the philosopher Bertrand Russell's childhood home, Pembroke Lodge (now a licensed café, and a good lunch spot), and beyond the park to Richmond Hill.

A well-kept cycle path rings the perimeter. It's possible to hire bikes from Roehampton Gate (07050 209249/7581 1188). Adult bikes with tag-alongs or children's seats and children's bikes are available.

Between June and March, fishing is available at Pen Ponds by paid permit from Holly Lodge (child concessions available); for details, call 8948 3209. Like all the Royal Parks, Richmond hosts a summer events programme for families, see the notice at the gate lodge or check website. *Café.*

Royal Botanic Gardens (Kew Gardens)

Richmond, Surrey TW9 3AB (8332 5655/information 8940 1171/www.kew.org.uk). Kew Gardens tube/rail/ Kew Bridge rail/riverboat to Kew Pier. **Open** *Apr-early Sep* 9.30am-6.30pm Mon-Fri; 9.30am-7.30pm Sat, Sun. *Early Sep-late Oct* 9.30am-6pm daily. *Late Oct-early Feb* 9.30am-4.15pm daily. *Early Feb-late Mar* 9.30am-5.30pm daily (last entry 30mins before closing). **Tours** 11am, 2pm daily. **Admission** (LP) £12.75; £10.25 concessions, late entry (4.45pm); free under-17s. **Credit** AmEx, DC, MC.

These gardens, split into 47 areas, constitute a massive amount of ground to cover – but small visitors will always make a beeline for the Climbers & Creepers adventure playground. Kids aged three to nine have great fun climbing into a giant flower, clambering through an illuminated blackberry tangle, and digging for 'fossilised plants', while real insects buzz through see-through habitats; all the while, the kids learn about the importance of plant and animal relationships. Climbers & Creepers is the base for Midnight Ramble sleepovers, which give eight- to 11-year-olds and their guardians the chance to track local wildlife like badgers and bats, and earn prizes; scheduled dates for 2007 are 8 Sept, 22 Sept, 13 Oct, 27 Oct, 10 Nov (£40 per head, booking subject to availability; check the website).

If you're exploring the gardens on foot, pick up a free map at the ticket office. Little legs might prefer to ride the Kew Explorer people-mover, which plies a circular route around the gardens (£3.50; £1 concessions, under-17s).

This extraordinary collection of monuments, gardens, buildings and landscapes are arranged into more than half a square mile. We love the 1848 Palm House, which has exotic plants from Africa, Asia and America, and a series of spiral staircases that allows you to view them all from a gallery. Resident record-breakers enjoying old age here include the oldest pot plant in the world and the tallest palm under glass. The £800,000 Alpine House, designed by Wilkinson Eyre Architects, opened in spring 2006 and is another must-see. The Pagoda's 253 steps lead to stunning views over London (it is currently closed but will reopen in 2009). The Riverside Zone, which runs alongside the Thames, contains the newly opened Kew Palace and the 17th-century-style Queen's Garden.

There are cafés and restaurants dotted throughout Kew Gardens, but on a fine day you can't beat a picnic. Art exhibitions and live music during the summer, and a winter ice rink in front of the Temperate House (check website for dates) ensure that this place is a year-round treat. Junior Kew fans might like to escort their parents to the gift shop, to purchase a copy of *Kids' Kew: a children's guide* (£3.95), a new guide book full of games, crosswords, photographs, stickers, a fold out map, and information describing all that Kew has to offer for children.

Buggy access. Cafés. Disabled access: ramps, toilets. Nappy-changing facilities. Nearest picnic place: grounds. Restaurants. Shop.

Further south-west

Stunningly scenic greenery and historic splendour are all within easy reach of the capital; hop aboard a south-bound train from Clapham Junction station, or just follow the undulating Thames into Surrey. Nearby Kingston-upon-Thames has pretty riverside paths alongside its busy pedestrianised

Around Town

shopping hub, while Richmond and sporty Twickenham offer an increasingly tranquil, genteel ambience.

The pretty southern reaches of the river towards well-to-do Twickenham are lovely spots for bike riding, and there's the Thames Path for walkers. Way out on the westerly reaches of Twickenham, pretty Crane Park Island (entrance on Ellerman Avenue, TW1, 8755 2339, www.wildlondon. org.uk) is one of the London Wildlife Trust's staffed reserves. It used to be the old Hounslow Gunpowder Mills, but is now a peaceful haven surrounded by the River Crane, where woodland, scrub and reedbeds provide a home for the increasingly scarce water vole. Work is now in progress to turn the tower, an imposing relic of the old mills, into a nature study centre.

The area has a number of gracious historic buildings. Overlooking the river from Marble Hill Park, **Marble Hill House** is a perfect example of a Palladian villa. Neighbouring **Orleans House** (Riverside, Twickenham, Middx TW1 3DJ, 8831 6000, www.richmond. gov.uk) was built in 1710 for James Johnston, William III's secretary of state for Scotland, but later it became home to the exiled Duke of Orléans – hence the name. **Ham House** is another favourite: a handsome, red-brick, riverside mansion with a beautiful garden. Carrying on along the river past Twickenham, you'll eventually come to the **Museum of Rugby** inside Twickenham Stadium.

From Twickers, the river passes by the busy shopping centre of Kingston-upon-Thames, then curves around to **Hampton Court Palace**. Once the country seat of Cardinal Wolsey, the palace was taken over by Henry VIII, who liked it so much he spent three honeymoons here.

For a real day-trip retreat, try Box Hill (www.nationaltrust.org), where cyclists and ramblers take in the lovely woodland and chalk downs, which helped to inspire Jane Austen's 1815 novel *Emma*. The views from its summit make for a memorably great outdoors experience.

Ham House

Ham Street, Ham, Richmond, Surrey TW10 7RS (8940 1950/www.nationaltrust.org.uk). Richmond tube/rail then 371 bus. **Open** *House* mid Mar-Nov 1-5pm Mon-Wed, Sat, Sun. *Gardens* 11am-6pm or dusk Mon-Wed, Sat, Sun. Closed 1 Jan, 25, 26 Dec. *Tours* Wed (pre-booking essential). Phone for membership details & prices. **Admission** (NT) *House & gardens* £9; £5 5-15s; free under-5s; £19 family (2+2). *Gardens only* £4; £2 5-15s; free under-5s; £9 family (2+2). **Credit** AmEx, MC, V. Built in 1610, this lavishly restored riverside mansion was originally home to the Duke and Duchess of Lauderdale, and it was occupied by the same family until 1948. Today

the interiors boast exemplary original furniture, paintings and textiles. The landscaped grounds include the Cherry Garden, with a central statue of Bacchus, the South Garden and the maze-like Wilderness, beside an Orangery with a terrace café. Alfresco theatre takes place in the garden in the summer, and there are egg trails for Easter, art and craft open days for the August bank holiday weekend, spooky tours for Hallowe'en and all manner of carols, feasts and art and craft events for Christmas. *Café (high chairs). Disabled access: lift, toilets. Nappy-changing facilities. Parking (free). Shop.*

Hampton Court Palace

East Molesey, Surrey KT8 9AU (0870 751 5175/ www.hrp.org.uk). Hampton Court rail/riverboat from Westminster or Richmond to Hampton Court Pier (Apr-Oct). **Open** *Palace* Mar-Oct 10am-6pm daily. Nov-Feb 10am-4.30pm daily (last entry 1hr before closing). *Park* dawn-dusk daily. **Admission** *Palace, courtyard, cloister & maze* £13; £10.50 concessions; £6.50 5-15s; free under-5s; £36 family (2+3). *Gardens only* £4; £3 concessions; £2.50 5-15s; free under-5s; £13.50 family. *Maze only* £3.50; £2 5-15s; free under-5s; £10 family. **Credit** AmEx, MC, V. 'Magnificence-upon-Thames' is a very apt name for this most lavish of palaces. This sumptuous 1514 monument is a testimony to the rule of Henry VIII and a focal point in English history: Elizabeth I was imprisoned in its tower by her elder sister Mary I; Shakespeare performed here; and after the Civil War, Oliver Cromwell went against the puritanical grain and moved in. Little wonder, then, that there's so much to explore. The imposing buildings span over six acres, with costumed guides adding a lively dimension to its state apartments, courtyards and cloisters. On selected bank holidays and weekends, Tudor cookery demonstrations take place in the impressively vast kitchens, where children love the bubbling cauldrons and game bird carcasses. The gardens are a draw in their own right; Hampton Court's famous maze is a family favourite. The oldest maze in the land, it was planted between 1689 and 1694, and is pretty easy to get lost in. Special events run throughout the year – blockbusters to look out for include the Hampton Court Palace Music Festival (June-July) and the Hampton Court Flower Show (July). Themed activities during the school holidays include fun outdoor activities that once delighted Henry VIII, including jousting, archery, hunting, shooting and laughing at jesters. For about six weeks from the beginning of December to mid January (call or check the website for 2007-8 dates) the west front of the palace is iced over for a scenic skate rink. *Buggy access. Café. Car park. Disabled access: lift, toilets. Nappy-changing facilities. Nearest picnic place: palace gardens/picnic area. Restaurant. Shops.*

Marble Hill House

Richmond Road, Middx TW1 2NL (8892 5115/ www.english-heritage.org.uk). Richmond tube/rail/ 33, 90, 290, H22, R70 bus. **Open** *Apr-Oct* 10am-2pm Sat; 10am-5pm Sun. *Tours* noon, 3pm Tue, Wed. **Admission** (EH, LP) £4.20; £3.20 concessions; £2.10 5-15s; free under-5s; £10.50 family (2+2). Price includes tour. **Credit** MC, V. This stunning Thameside villa, once home to Henrietta Howard, mistress of King George II, was built in the 1720s with an £11,500 cash present from the king. The property is filled with Georgian objects and paintings, but the star of the decorative show is the Honduran mahogany aircase. Marble Hill House hosts events throughout the ear, including Easter trails and open-air concerts. Guided urs can be taken of the house and its surrounding park- nd, and the house is connected by ferry to Ham House ist across the river. *afé. Nearest picnic place: Marble Hill Park. Shop.*

Museum of Rugby/ wickenham Stadium

wickenham Stadium, Rugby Road, Twickenham, Middx TW1 1DZ (0870 405 2001/www.rfu.com/ microsites/museum). Hounslow East tube then 281 us/Twickenham rail. **Open** *Museum* 10am-5pm Tue- at; 11am-5pm Sun (last entry 30mins before closing). Tours 10.30am, noon, 1.30pm, 3pm Tue-Sat; 1pm, 3pm

Sun. Closed 1 Jan, Easter Sun, 24-26 Dec, Sun after match days. **Admission** *Combined ticket* £10; £7 concessions; £34 family (2+3). Advance booking advisable. **Credit** AmEx, MC, V.

On non-match days there are tours of the stadium, during which visitors can walk down the players' tunnel, look at the England dressing room and drop in on the Members' Lounge, the President's Suite and the Royal Box. The World Rugby Room tackles the game on an international level, and regular exhibitions reveal the history of such leg- endary teams as the All Blacks. Fans can admire sporting memorabilia dating back to 1871. Rugby in the Frame, an exhibition of art relating to the World Cup, features scenes from important matches, plus an interactive play area for children (the show runs until 4 November, 2007).

Buggy access. Disabled access: toilet. Restaurant. Shop

Royal haunts

Look at any map of London's countrified south- western reaches and you will notice its wealth of courtly residences and houses, their attendant gardens and the royal parks of Richmond and Bushy. This is hardly surprising when you consider that the river Thames here connects the royal domain of Greenwich to Windsor Castle (*see p279*) via Westminster, Kew (*see p151* and Hampton Court (*see p152*).

A visit to **Hampton Court Palace** (*see p152*) confirms that royal families were as mobile in Tudor times as they are today. King Henry VIII and his entourage could move as much as eight times in six months, from Greenwich to Whitehall to Eltham. And Henry also had the habit of dropping in on his courtiers along the way, an occasion they scarcely relished, given the colossal cost of hosting the king.

Ghosts and gardens are bewitching features of many of the area's regal residencies. The Haunted Gallery at Hampton Court, for example, is so called because Catherine Howard, the fifth wife of King Henry VIII, placed under house arrest for adultery, escaped from her guards and came tearing down the gallery looking for the King to plead for her life. She was caught and dragged back to her room screaming. In due course she was executed at the Tower of London. The famous maze in the garden is immortalised in Jerome K Jerome's *Three Men in a Boat* ('It's absurd to call it a maze. You keep on taking the first turning to the right. We'll just walk round for ten minutes, and then go and get some lunch.' The chaps are lost for hours, then have to be rescued).

Ham House (*see p152*), the 17th-century home of King Charles I's pal William Murray, is said to be one of the most haunted houses in Britain (receiving ghostly visitations from William's daughter, the Duchess of Lauderdale, and her pet dog). Regular family events include entertaining Ghost Tours (suitable for over-fives; a torch-lit adult version is also available) to make the most of its spritely reputation. The Stuart gardens, like

the house, have changed little in the past 300 years and contain the oldest orangery and thorn bush in the country.

Kew Palace (*see p151*) is surrounded by 300 acres of flowerbeds and shrubberies as well as having its own nosegay parterres directly outside. The sound recordings and visual projections inside the palace conjure up the life of Queen Charlotte (who died here) and the ailing King George III more effectively than a display could.

Overlooking Kew on the left bank is **Syon House** (Syon Park, Brentford, 8560 0883, www.syon park.co.uk) built on the site of a medieval abbey which was brutally dissolved by Henry VIII. As if by divine retribution, his coffin was later brought to Syon in transit to Windsor Castle. During the night it mysteriously burst open and the king's corpse was found being unceremoniously licked by dogs. It was also here that the doomed Lady Jane Grey reluctantly accepted the crown and became queen for nine days. Renowned for its collection of rare trees, Syon Park was the set for *The Madness of George III* while the television drama *Elizabeth* was filmed nearby at Ham House.

The embodiment of an Arcadian idyll, **Marble Hill House** (*see p152*), which stands opposite Ham, became a retreat for both king and court and was the home of Henrietta Howard, King George II's mistress.

Many more palaces have not endured, often destroyed by the next in line. The White House in Kew Gardens, its location now marked by a sundial, was where George III was incarcerated during painful bouts of Porphyria. Richmond Lodge – the hunting outpost for King James I in 1615 – was demolished by Queen Charlotte in 1772. The embarrassing white elephant of the Castellated Palace – erected as a fantasy world for King George III but never completed – was taken down by George IV, who needed no reminder of his father's extravagances. Today, these past palaces exist only in prints and paintings, a testimony to the dreams of kings – and what can happen to them.

Around Town

West London

Upwind and upriver from the heaving masses – or so West Londoners think.

Kensington & Holland Park

Now synonymous with good breeding, Kensington was called Chenesit in medieval times, which sounds a little lumpen. It was a rural, apple-cheeked distant cousin of London for some 800 years, but gradually the city's wealthy inhabitants began to build their country retreats on Kensington's bosky pastures and by the early 19th century the link with the metropolis had been forged. Over the next 100 years, the Victorians built their railways, and transformed the district; by the turn of the 20th century, the population had increased twenty-fold.

It's still exclusive and posh around here. If you've the cash to indulge yourself, Kensington High Street is a shopper's paradise. It is surrounded by handsome 19th-century streets; further west the exclusivity remains, but there are more trees. Holland Park, both a fine green space and a residential area, was once the grounds of Holland House: built in 1607 and the scene of many society parties courtesy of its 19th-century hostess, Lady Holland. The building was bombed in World War II (only the east wing was saved; it is now the most refined youth hostel in the capital), but its remains are to be found in the heavily wooded, well-equipped park.

Another local building worth an ogle is **Leighton House** (12 Holland Park Road, W14 8LZ, 7602 3316, www.rbkc.gov.uk), formerly the live-in studio of the Victorian artist and president of the Royal Academy, Frederic Leighton. It was built at a time when Leighton and his peers were struggling to found an 'artists' colony'. Tracking down other buildings from this period (William Burges's medieval folly, the Tower House, on 29 Melbury Road, W14; and the Peacock House on Addison Road, W14, which hosts a craft fair every December) makes for a highly amusing architectural history trail. For Victorian grandeur, however, you should take a tour of **Linley Sambourne House**.

Holland Park

Ilchester Place, W8 6LU (7471 9813/www.rbkc. gov.uk/Ecology Centre 7471 9809). Holland Park tube/9, 27, 28, 49 bus. **Open** 8am-dusk daily. **Map** p314 A9.

A series of paths through this prodigiously forested park takes you past imperious peacocks and plenty of squirrels and rabbits. The Ecology Centre provides site maps, nets for pond-dipping and information on local wildlife. It also hosts half-term and holiday activities and meetings of the local Wildlife Watch group, the junior branch of the Wildlife Trust (www.wildlondon.org.uk). Elsewhere there's a smart Italian café and an open-air theatre. The peaceful Japanese Garden has a pond full of koi carp, which fascinate children, and the adventure playground keeps the over-fives entertained. Of most interest to youngsters is Whippersnappers (7738 6633, www.whippersnappers.org) for weekly musical and puppet workshops. Also in the park are tennis courts and two art spaces, the Ice House and the Orangery. The lovely North Lawn is busy with families and picnickers throughout the summer. *Buggy access. Café. Disabled access: toilets. Nappy-changing facilities. Restaurant.*

Linley Sambourne House

18 Stafford Terrace, W8 7BH (7602 3316 ext 300 Mon-Fri/7938 1295 Sat, Sun/www.rbkc.gov.uk/linley sambournehouse). High Street Kensington tube. **Tours** 11.15am, 1pm, 2.15pm, 3.30pm Sat, Sun; other times by appointment only. Maximum of 12 on each tour. Pre-booking essential. **Admission** £6; £4 concessions; £1 under-18s. **Credit** MC, V. **Map** p314 A9.

Edward Linley Sambourne was a Victorian cartoonist famous for his work in *Punch*. His house, which contains almost all its original fittings and furniture, can be visited only on one of the terrific and slightly eccentric tours. These are guided by costumed actors (especially popular with children is gossipy housekeeper Mrs Reffle, who provides a cheeky insight into Victorian family life and tells a few jokes along the way). There's a visitors' centre where children can participate in craftwork sessions relating to objects in the house. *Shop.*

Maida Vale, Kilburn & Queen's Park

The westerly outpost of the London Borough of Westminster, Maida Vale is a pleasant residential area, home to the BBC's recording studios. Its picture postcard highlight, however, is **Little Venice,** where the Grand Union and Regent's canals meet. Every May Day weekend, narrowboats from across the country travel here for the lovely **Canalway Cavalcade** (*see p30*). The Cavalcade also heralds a special performance from the unique 50-seat **Puppet Theatre Barge** (*see p225*), one of London's treasures, which spends the winter here. From Little Venice, it's

Splendour in the past: **Leighton House**.

possible to follow the canal all the way to Camden Lock, stopping for refreshments along the way at Café Laville (Little Venice Parade, W2 1TH, 7706 2620), and taking in sights such as the infamous 'Blow Up Bridge' (originally destroyed when a barge, loaded with gunpowder, detonated beneath it; evidence of the blast can still be seen on a neighbouring tree) or, further up, **London Zoo** (see p76). Little legs not up to the walk can board a London Waterbus (www.londonwaterbus.com); these narrowboats chug between Little Venice, Camden Lock and London Zoo (via a private water gate), and through the creepy Maida Vale Tunnel.

At Meanwhile Gardens, on the other side of the canal, there's a concrete skateboard bowl for aspiring Z-Boys; make sure they wear a helmet. The area's largest official outdoor space, however, is Paddington Recreation Ground (Randolph Avenue, W9, 7641 3642). Roger Bannister trained here before breaking the four-minute mile in 1954. These days, the park is home to a cricket ground, bowling green, gym and various tarmac courts for tennis, basketball and football.

Further north, **Queen's Park** is a real beauty. Nearby Kilburn has a crowded, uninspiring high street littered with chainstores and cafés, but is rescued from obscurity by the delightful **Tricycle Theatre & Cinema** (see p217).

Queen's Park

Kingswood Avenue, NW6 6SG (park manager 8969 5661/info@queenspark.gov.uk). Queen's Park tube/rail. **Open** 7.30am-dusk daily. **Admission** free.

Keeping its hard-earned Green Flag flying, this Corporation of London park is a godsend to the people of Brent. It boasts an excellent playground with giant sandpit, a summer paddling pool, a small animal enclosure, and patrolling wardens. At the northern end is a wild, overgrown area; here a nature trail displays pictures of the mini beasts you might encounter. The pleasant café is great for own-made cakes and local Disotto's ice-cream. For exercise, there's a pitch-and-putt area, pétanque enclosure and six tennis courts. Lively kids' entertainment takes place at the bandstand during the summer holidays. The annual Queen's Park Day, which in 2007 is on 9 September, involves fancy dress competitions, face-painting, a dog show and plenty of 'He's behind you' puppeteering. *Buggy access. Café. Disabled access: toilet. Nappy-changing facilities.*

Earl's Court & Fulham

There were, in fact, two earls involved in the old court, so the area is Earls' Court by rights (notice the difference, grammar fans?). It was once a rural hamlet, and the site of the courthouse of the Earls of Warwick and Holland. However, the rumbling arrival of the Metropolitan line in the 1860s put paid to any exclusivity the district might have

Fulham Palace & Museum

njoyed. Today its grand buildings are all flats nd bedsits, housing a large transient population nce, many of them were Antipodeans, so arl's Court gained the nickname Kangaroo 'alley; now it's mostly eastern Europeans and outh Americans).

The huge exhibition centre synonymous with arl's Court was erected in 1937; before that, ne site was used as a funfair and show ground, rith Buffalo Bill's Wild West show of 1891 roving to be a big draw. These days, the 18,000-apacity venue hosts regular trade shows, awards eremonies and conferences, plus the occasional ock concert, despite echoey acoustics. The egendary coffee house, the Troubadour (263-67 Old Brompton Road, SW5 9JA, 7370 1434, rww.troubadour.co.uk), is a major venue for nusic, poetry and comedy – mostly appealing o grown-ups, but on the ground floor is a lovely eli and gallery. In its heyday the Troubadour osted Jimi Hendrix, Joni Mitchell and Bob Dylan.

There's a paucity of open spaces around here, ut the rambling, overgrown Brompton Cemetery Fulham Road, SW10 9UG, 7352 1201, www. oyalparks.gov.uk) provides a last resort in nore ways than one. Most parents retreat to lammersmith or Fulham for their fresh-air fixes. An abundance of greenery along the riverside, nost notably the picturesque Bishop's Park off Bishop's Park Road, SW6) – with its boating ake, teahouse and a popular One O'Clock Club – nakes it splendid for a walk. Neighbouring Fulham Palace has been on the receiving end f a £3 million lottery refit. No less hallowed rounds can be found at Craven Cottage, the iverside stadium of Fulham Football Club Stevenage Road, SW6 6HH, 7384 4777, www. ulhamfc.com) and the rather more plush tamford Bridge, manor for the millionaires f Chelsea FC (Fulham Road, SW6 1HS, 0870 03 0005, www.chelseafc.com). Guided tours f both stadiums run throughout the year. Well-off families can make use of the grounds and ports facilities at the exclusive Hurlingham lub (Ranelagh Gardens, SW6 3PR, 7736 8411, rww.hurlinghamclub.org.uk) but it's free to rheel the tots around Hurlingham Park Hurlingham Road, SW6), where rugby and ootball pitches, tennis courts and a running rack take pride of place.

The Fulham Broadway end of the Fulham Road aters for the entertainment needs of the many amilies living in the Parsons Green urban village. There's a **Pottery Café** (*see p241*) and a nine-creen Vue cinema in the Fulham Broadway hopping centre (Fulham Road, SW6 1BW, 385 6965, www.fulhambroadway.co.uk).

Fulham Palace & Museum

Bishop's Avenue, off Fulham Palace Road, SW6 6EA (7736 3233/www.fulhampalace.org). Hammersmith or Putney Bridge tube/220, 414, 430 bus. **Open** times vary, phone to check. **Admission** *Museum* free; under-16s must be accompanied by an adult. *Tours* £5; free under-16s. **No credit cards.**

The official residence of the Bishops of London from 704 until 1973, Fulham Palace has some buildings dating back to 1480, although the main house is 16th century. Refurbishment work that continued throughout 2006 has left the East Quandrangle looking beautiful – the café is a particularly pleasant place to sit in. The new-look museum opened in April 2007 with new exhibits displayed (the mummified rat is still there), plenty of new interactives, lots more room to show treasures dug up in the grounds over the years, as well as a brand new programme of workshops and exhibitions for families. These were being finalised as we went to press, but details are listed on the website. Leave time to admire the lovely grounds (also getting ready for a refurb) planted with rare trees, which provide sanctuary from busy Fulham Palace Road. The walled kitchen garden is full of herbs and rare plants.

Buggy access. Disabled access: toilet (in palace). Shop.

Shepherd's Bush & Hammersmith

Urbanisation took hold of these sheep-grazing grounds by around 1900. Today, Shepherd's Bush Common is little more than a glorified roundabout with a grungy look to it. In contrast, White City, to the north, is undergoing a multi-million-pound development that promises facelifts all around, improved transport links and the largest shopping centre in Greater London (150,000 square metres/ 37 acres).

The unpolished nature of Shepherd's Bush gives it a rock 'n' roll allure bolstered by the number of rock legends bred here (members of The Who, the Sex Pistols, the Bush and – more recently – Pete Doherty), not to mention the gigs held at the Empire, one of London's greatest venues. Future rockers should enrol at the **Music House for Children** at **Bush Hall** (*see p239*).

Nor are the Bush's entertainment ties merely musical; until 1991, the BBC broadcast many shows from the Empire (*Wogan, Crackerjack* and *This Is Your Life*, among others). You can still take backstage tours of the BBC studios at nearby Wood Lane (minimum age nine years; book tickets on 0870 603 0304). Those seeking an induction into the dramatic arts are better off in Hammersmith, where the Dramatic Dreams Theatre Company (8741 1809, www.dramatic dreams.com) runs children's workshops at the Riverside Studios (Crisp Road, W6 9RL, 8237 1111, www.riversidestudios.co.uk). The biggest local draw for pint-sized Pinters, however, is the **Lyric Theatre** (*see p229*).

Around Town

Children who support **Queens Park Rangers FC** (*see p271*) are on to a good thing. The club's Loftus Road headquarters is a hub of community football for young people, and the soccer schools and party packages are great value.

Ravenscourt Park

Ravenscourt Road, W6 0UL (www.lbhf.gov.uk). **Ravenscourt Park** *tube.* **Open** 7.30am-dusk daily. **Admission** free.
In summer the packed paddling pool is the most popular attraction here. But this family-friendly park also has three play areas, including a pre-school (for two to five year-olds, 8748 3180) offering a Fathers' Club (2-4pm Sat) for bonding between babes and their overworked old men (a Grandparents' Club is expected to be up and running by summer 2007). A One O'Clock Club operates during half terms and holidays. There's a big pond, a nature trail and a scented garden for the visually impaired. Kids with spare energy can use the skateboarding ramp or enjoy a gam of tennis. The café is open all year and is conveniently pos tioned for the playground. There's a flower show and chi dren's fair in July, and an annual Play Day, with bounc castles and face-painting (1 Aug 2007).
Buggy access. Café. Disabled access. Nappy-changing facilities.

Chiswick

All that you could wish from a London suburb – great transport links (tube, M4, Heathrow), amenities and pretty riverside walks – make Chiswick one of the most desirable places to bring up families. The popularity isn't a recent phenomenon; prehistoric tools found in the grounds of **Syon House** suggest this was one of London's first human settlements. William

The river west

Looping through Hammersmith, then arching down to Chiswick before rising again at Kew, the western reaches of the Thames curve through moneyed residencies with waterside gardens, past a scattering of aits and islands and a wooded nature reserve, before moving on to Isleworth, Richmond and Twickenham.

Between the 14th and 17th centuries, this stretch of the river was the route used by the monarchy travelling from palace to palace. The area remains a retreat for the wealthy; even the houseboats are palatial. Here nature has room to breathe; the skies are immense, barely brushed by the lines of poplar and alder trees. From Chiswick Pier, look across the pontoons to the colourful boats that push by, and spot the waterfowl roll-called on the information board downstream grey herons, Canada geese, coots and tufted ducks. The flashes of green and gold are goldfinches and parakeets zipping across the sky.

On a fine day, this is pushchair country, with the Thames pathway abuzz with mums and buggies stopping off at the benches, the children's playground and family-friendly pubs along the way. At the Dove pub near Hammersmith (19 Upper Mall, W6 9TA, 8748 540) – sadly no children are allowed here, Thomas Arne found inspiration in liquid refreshment and river views to compose the music for 'Rule Britannia' in 1740.

An annual fixture here is the University Boat Race, which takes place every spring (29 March 2008) along the Championship Course, roughly between the bridges of Putney and Chiswick. The race, which was first run in 1829, is between two teams drawn from the country's oldest universities, Oxford and Cambridge, who battle it out in a furious assault on the water. Cambridge won in 2007.

For young rowers, Chiswick Pier Canoe Club (07933 276792, www.chiswickcanoeclub.co.uk) meets every Sunday between 10.30am and 1pm and provides boats and training for all abilities from the age of eight. The Chiswick Pier Trust (8742 2713, www.chiswickpier.org.uk) exists to promote and preserve the river; it organises waterborne family events throughout the year including a party on the pier in July and a pageant of traditional boats past Chiswick Pier in September. The Pier House is also home to the Chiswick Sea Cadets (www.sea-cadets.org), a maritime club for local kids aged ten to 18. And if you're looking to hold a children's party with river views, the Pier House can again oblige.

During late afternoons at the weekend the river banks are busy with the rowing fraternity dismantling boats and snacking on tea and cakes. There are also joggers to watch out for along the Thames pathway. To dodge them both, bear right from Chiswick pier and you'll come to the green expanse of Dukes Meadow, with its bandstand and golf club (8994 3314, www. golflessons.co.uk), which offers junior group coaching on Saturdays. Cricket pitches, tennis courts and boathouses abound, but you can always stray from the river path; **Chiswick House** (*see p160*) is ten minutes' walk away and hosts a weekend farmers' market. The 18th-century gardens are a solace from the horrors of the nearby A4 and you can picnic between the conifers and urns or ride the stone sphinx that overlooks the waterfall and lake.

Refreshments are available over the iron bridge at Tanya's fish and chip shop (39B Barnes High Street, SW13 9LN, 8878 4750) on the quaint high street, or alternatively, continue along the river to Annie's café (162 Thames Road, W4 3QS, 8994 9080) to take a break and take stock.

Around Town

Strand on the Green

ogarth, the 18th-century painter, engraver
nd social commentator, had a country retreat
n Chiswick (Hogarth's House, Hogarth Lane,
reat West Road, W4 2QN, 8994 6757), when
e traffic was somewhat calmer than today.
Away from the Great West Road, Chiswick's
illagey attractiveness is embodied by its many
arks and traditional high streets. Turnham
reen, for example, is surrounded by shops,
ld houses and the town hall, with a small
hurch at its centre. Acton Green Common –
e site of a confrontation between the cavaliers
f King Charles I and the forces of the Earl of
ssex in 1642 – makes for an idyllic spot to
retch out and watch the cricket in summer.
icnic materials are available from the delis
n adjoining Turnham Green Terrace; cheese-
aking may have been Chiswick's forte in the
8th century, but these days you'll also find
nart butchers and traditional fishmongers.
orth of Turnham Green station lies the
racious acreage of London's first suburb,
edford Park, laid out in a rural setting in
375 by Jonathan Carr.
The lion's share of Chiswick's charm can be
und by the river. A leisurely stroll along its
anks reveals all manner of wholesome outdoor
ctivities for families (*see p158* **The river west**).

Continue beyond Chiswick Bridge to the
picturesque Strand-on-the-Green, a former
fishing community; these days it is more
congested with buggies than boats, as walkers
descend on the family-friendly pubs lining the
river, and muddy their boots frolicking on the
banks at low tide.

The area has enough entertainments and
educational diversions to engage kids all year.
As well as the **Kew Bridge Steam Museum**,
there's the fantastic Musical Museum (399 High
Street, Brentford, Middx TW8 0BD, 8560 8108,
www.musicalmuseum.co.uk), which should
reopen in September 2007 after a painstaking
move; don't miss its world-class collection of
(often self-playing) oddities, including player
pianos, orchestrions, Wurlitzers and a 'therem
in' (an early producer of eerie sci-fi soundtracks).
The riverside arts venue Watermans (40 High
Street, Brentford, Middx TW8 0DS, 8232
1010) has an eclectic programme of children's
entertainment covering drama, puppetry and
musical workshops.

The **Brentford Fountain Leisure Centre**
(*see p267*) is an excellent local resource for
water babies. Further north, the private Park
Club (East Acton Lane, W3 7HB, 8743 4321,
www.theparkclub.co.uk) runs sporting activities

and workshops for children, and is home to both the Ark in the Park crèche and childcare centre as well as Urban Parx, a place for children and young people aged 11 and over.

More historical adventures await in the grounds of **Syon House**, where there's all manner of child-friendly amusements. Regular animal-encounter sessions take place at the Tropical Forest, and there's a motorised bike track and an indoor adventure playground.

Also at Syon Park, the London Butterfly House has wowed generations with its tropical hothouse of creepy crawlies and exotic birds; it might close down on 31 October 2007 – catch it while you can. Gunnersbury Park (Popes Lane, W3 8LQ, 8992 1612) has a nature reserve, two playgrounds, a Gothic folly, a miniature golf course and the Gunnersbury Park Local History Museum (open Apr-Oct 11am-5pm daily; Nov-Mar 11am-4pm daily), which runs local-interest exhibitions and regular tours, talks and workshops. Nearby, the **Kids' Cookery School** (*see p238*) has been turning on children to good home cooking with unusual or unfamiliar ingredients for years – long before the heroic Mr Oliver put them off their turkey twizzlers.

Chiswick House

Burlington Lane, W4 2RP (8995 0508/www.english-heritage.org.uk). Turnham Green tube then E3 bus to Edensor Road/Hammersmith tube/rail then 190 bus/Chiswick rail. **Open** *Apr-Oct* 10am-5pm Wed-Fri, Sun; 10am-2pm Sat. Last entry 30mins before closing.

Closed Nov-Mar. *Tours* by arrangement; phone for details. **Admission** (EH, LP) incl audio guide £4.20; £3.20 concessions; £2.20 5-16s; free under-5s. **Credit** MC, V.

Walking through the gardens of Chiswick House, you fee as if you've stepped into a classical landscape painting There are obelisks hidden among the trees, a dome Palladian temple, a lake and a cascading waterfal Families come here in summer for a picnic. You can tak a jaunt along the river too, which is only a stone's throw away. Also in the grounds is beautiful Burlington's Café there are plans to give it a refurb. A multi-million-poun restoration of the grounds looks likely to go ahead; Stag 2 proposals to the Heritage Lottery Fund are being sub mitted in Sept 2007. For news on plans, see the Chiswic House and Gardens Trust's website, www.chgt.org.uk English Heritage stages activity days and re-enactment here; check its website for details.

Buggy access. Café. Disabled access: stairlift, toilet. Nearest picnic place: Chiswick Park. Shop.

Gunnersbury Triangle Nature Reserve

Bollo Lane, W4 5LW (8747 3881/www.wildlondon. org.uk). Chiswick Park tube. **Open** *Reserve* 24hrs daily. *Information* June-Sept 10am-4.30pm Tue-Sat. Oct-May 10am-4.30pm Tue, Sun. **Admission** free.
Run by the London Wildlife Trust, this expanse of wood land, marsh and meadow, enclosed by railway tracks, i the scene of much ecological endeavour. Practical conser vation workshops are supplemented by free, drop-in activ ities for youngsters: craft workshops, mask-makin sessions, and mini beast safaris. When the small informa tion cabin is open (throughout the summer, but only o Tuesdays and Sundays in winter), you can pick up tra leaflets, find out about guided tours and hire a net fo pond-dipping.
Buggy access.

Question time: West London

Where can we play?

For sporting variety, great paddling, good food and loads of family clubs, you can't beat Ravenscourt Park (*see p158*), although Holland Park is prettier and greener in every sense, having its own Ecology Centre (*see p154*). For an exciting, and potentially wallet-draining fun day, head for Syon House (*see p158*).

What can we learn?

Find out about water, the stuff of life, and the Victorian engineering that brought it to us, at Kew Bridge Steam Museum (*see p159*); discover more Victorians, this time in a chatty domestic setting, at Linley Sambourne House (*see p154*); experience RE in its most colourful incarnation at the Shri Swaminarayan Mandir Temple (*see p162*).

Whom might we meet?

Ant & Dec, Bill Bailey, Al Murray, Davina McCall and Elton John all seem to reckon west is best.

Where should we eat?

Tootsies Grill in Holland Park is a family favourite (*see p186*) and great if your kids like burgers: varied patties include lamb & rosemary, pork and apple to Thai chicken; the Bush Garden Café (*see p186*) is one of the best things about Shepherd's Bush; and Chiswick's High Road Brasserie (*see p186*) offers all-day treats.

What can we buy?

You're never far from a farmers' market or chi-chi deli in the posher bits of the west, but for non-grub-related treasures (toys) strike out for Snap Dragon in Turnham Green terrace (*see p212*). Just across the road is the repository of extremely trendy designer labels, Tots (*see p200*). The best shoe fitting service for miles around is carried out by the staff of Stepping Out (*see p205*), but if you really, really want a pony, save up your pennies and go to Southall Market (*see p161*) on a Wednesday. Chickens are on Tuesdays, poultry fans.

ew Bridge Steam Museum

*reen Dragon Lane, Brentford, Middx TW8 0EN
*568 4757/www.kbsm.org). Gunnersbury tube
en 237 or 267 bus/Kew Bridge rail/65, 391 bus.
pen 11am-5pm Tue-Sun, bank hol Mon. Closed
-26 Dec, Good Friday. Tours times vary; phone
check website, book in advance. **Admission**
on-Fri £5; £4 concessions; free under-16s. *Sat,
n £7; £6 concessions; free under-16s. Under-16s
ust be accompanied by an adult. **Credit** MC, V.

Classic Award winner in the 2006 Museums and
*eritage Awards for Excellence, this Victorian riverside
*imping station is 'all systems go' every weekend, when
*eam engines burst into life (check the website for details).
*n Sundays (Mar-Nov), children can ride the working nar-
*ow-gauge steam locomotive, *Cloister*. During the school
*id bank holidays, family activities are run. The fasci-
*iting Water for Life Gallery saturates you with facts
*oout the history of water supply and usage in London,
*overing cholera, toshers (sewer scavengers), domestic
*iter usage, the city's ring main and much more. 'Down
*elow' takes you down the sewers to learn about the work
*' Bazalgette and modern-day underground heroes. Have
*look for the memorial to dear old Boulton, the Museum's
*iendly cat named after the Boulton & Watt engine. He
*ient a happy life here, charming the visitors, but died in
ebruary 2007.

*uggy access. Café (Sat, Sun). Disabled access: lift,
*imps, toilet. Nappy-changing facilities. Nearest picnic
ace: Kew Green. Shop.

yon House

*yon Park, Brentford, Middx TW8 8JF (8560 0881/
*ondon Butterfly House 8560 0378/Tropical Forest
*347 4730/Snakes & Ladders 8847 0946/www.
*onpark.co.uk). Gunnersbury tube/rail then 237, 267
us. **Open** *House* mid Mar-late Oct 11am-5pm Wed,
*hur, Sun, bank hol Mon (last entry 4.15pm). *Gardens*
*lar-Oct 10.30am-5pm daily. Nov-Feb 10.30am-4pm
*aily (last entry 45min before closing). *Tours* by
*rangement; phone for details. **Admission** *House &
ardens £8; £7 concessions, 4-16s; free under-4s; £17
*mily (2+2). *Gardens only* £3.75; £2.50 concessions, 5-
*5s; free under-4s; £9 family (2+2). *Tropical Forest* £5;
*3.75 3-15s; free under-3s; £15 family (2+3). *Butterfly
ouse £5.25; £4.25 concessions; £3.95 3-16s; free under-
*s; £16 family (2+2). *Snakes & Ladders* £3.50 under-2s;
*4.50 under-5s; £5.50 over-5s; free over-16s. Reduced
*ite after 4pm. **Credit** *Shop* MC, V.*

*his turreted Tudor mansion grew out of a building ded-
*ated to the Bridgettine Order. Following the Dissolution
*' the Monasteries, it became dedicated to providing Henry
*III with another country seat. Each room seems more
*npressive than the last, from the grand Roman hallway
*) the Red Drawing Room, with its crimson silk walls and
*oman statues. In the gardens on Sundays, a wooden mini
*:eam railway travels through the trees and around the
*owerbeds. Family-friendly workshops include demon-
*trations and re-enactments, such as 'Syon and the Battle
f Brentford' (28 October 2007).

*Most children find more thrills in the other attractions
*it out in the grounds. The London Butterfly House has
*een granted a stay of execution by the Duke of
*Iorthumberland, because plans for a hotel have been put
*ack. Hurray! The warm and fluttery experience can be
*njoyed until 31 October 2007. As well as the butterflies,
*iere's a Tropical Forest that has regular 'animal encoun-

ters' sessions. Children yearn for Snakes & Ladders, an
indoor adventure playground designed like a castle, with
three tiers of play areas, including slides, hanging ropes
and enormous ball pools. There's also an indoor motorised
bike track (£1 a ride) and a café. Bring a picnic in summer,
as the best eating locations are outside, although the café
has a junior menu.

*Café. Nappy-changing facilities. Nearest picnic place:
Syon House Gardens/Syon Park. Shop.*

Further west

At the western end of the District line, Ealing
has many open spaces including Ealing Common
(close to the congested Uxbridge Road) and
Horsenden Hill in Sudbury. The latter, the site
of a Stone Age settlement, is the highest point
in the borough, offering stunning views and
great kite-flying opportunities.

London's Transport Museum in Covent Garden
opens in autumn 2007 (*see p68*), but its Acton
Depot, on Gunnersbury Lane, will be closed until
March 2008 when it will once again run tours
(see www.ltmuseum.co.uk for details).

Petrolheads can also marvel at the collection
of hogs and choppers at the London Motorcycle
Museum (Oldfield Lane South, Greenford, Middx
UB6 9LD, 8575 6644, www.motorcycle-uk.com)
in Greenford's Ravenor Park, where there is also
a playground and an annual carnival.

The banks of the River Brent provide a cheerful
picnic spot in clement weather, with pleasant
riverside walks in either direction. Don't miss
the Hanwell Flight of Locks on the Grand Union
Canal, seven locks in close succession just north
of Osterley Park. This park is now bisected by
the M4, but stately **Osterley House** remains
a great place to visit. The best seasonal family
entertainment, however, is provided at Walpole
Park (off Mattock Lane, W5), which hosts much
of the Ealing Summer Festival (13-29 July 2007;
8579 2424, www.ealing.gov.uk). Nearby, Questors
Theatre (12 Mattock Lane, W5 5BQ, 8567 0011,
www.questors.org.uk) runs a great term-time
youth theatre for children (aged six to 16).

There are numerous sporting facilities in
Ealing; the most interesting is the Gurnell Leisure
Centre (Ruislip Road East, W13 0AL, 8998 3241,
www.gll.org), which boasts a 50-metre swimming
pool. Riders tack up at **Ealing Riding School**
(*see p263*), while those wanting to swing a club
should head for the Brent Valley Golf Course
(Church Road, W7 3BE, 8567 1287), which is
good for beginners.

Southall, west of Ealing, has London's largest
Asian community. Its market, housed in a scruffy
yard behind the high street, is a cross between a
traditional London street market and a trip to the

Around Town

Punjab. The goods sold vary from day to day: on Tuesdays it's a poultry market, where you can buy live birds for the pot; Wednesday is devoted to the buying and selling of horses (really) and the odd goat (for around a fiver); Friday will remind you of *Steptoe and Son*; and Saturday is when it all comes together and looks like downtown Delhi – the range of goods is astonishing. Unsurprisingly, fine curries are served in the restaurants around here.

The Sri Guru Singh Sabha Gurdwara (Alice Way, Hanworth Road, Hounslow, Middx TW3 3UA, 8577 2793, www.sgss.org) is the largest Sikh temple outside India, second in size only to Amritsar's Golden Temple. The **Shri Swaminarayan Mandir Temple**, to the north, is a monument to Hinduism.

The refurbished Heathrow Airport Academy (Newall Road, Uxbridge, Middx UB3 5AP (www.baa.com) is open at weekends, bank holidays and some half-terms for talks and educational activities; phone for updated information. Nearby, **Hounslow Urban Farm**, and, further out, Hounslow Heath nature reserve (450 Staines Road, Hounslow, TW4 5AB), explore the glories of terra firma.

Brent Lodge Park

Church Road, W7 3BL. Hanwell rail/E1, E2 bus. **Open** 7.30am-dusk daily. *Maze & animals* May-Aug 10.30am-6pm daily. Apr, Sept, Oct 10.30am-5pm daily. Nov-Mar 10.30am-4pm daily. **Admission** £1; 50p concessions, 3-16s; free under-3s. **No credit cards**.
Walk up the hill from the Millennium Maze, planted in 1999, for the hub of activities in this sweet and well-maintained local park, There's a café and a playground with an animal centre, housing a handful of primates as well as reptiles, amphibians, birds and domestic pets such as bunnies and guinea pigs. The centre organises children's activity days in summer; phone for details.
Buggy access (no access to animal area). Café. Disabled access: toilet.

Hounslow Urban Farm

A312 at Faggs Road, Feltham, Middx TW14 0LZ (8751 0850/www.hounslow.info/urbanfarm). Hatton Cross tube then 20min walk or 90, 285, 490 bus. **Open** 10am-4pm daily. **Admission** £4; £3.75 concessions; £3 2-16s; free under-2s; £13 (2+2) family. **No credit cards**.
London's largest community farm has plenty to see. There are pigs, goats, numerous varieties of duck, Exmoor ponies and more, with feeding time at 3.30pm daily. The farm has a conservation programme; endangered and historic breeds of domestic livestock are reared here. Turn up at the right time of year and you could be lucky enough to see brand-new lambs, goats or even a litter of piglets. Orphan lambs need to be bottle-fed and children are sometimes allowed to help. There's a playground (with pedal tractors), a picnic area and a refreshment kiosk.
Buggy access. Café. Disabled access: toilet. Nappy-changing facilities.

Osterley House

Osterley Park, off Jersey Road, Isleworth, Middx TW7 4RB (8232 5050/recorded information 01494 755 566/www.nationaltrust.org.uk/osterley). Osterley tube. **Open** *House* late Mar-Oct 1-4.30pm Wed-Sun, bank hols Mon. *Park* 8am-7.30pm daily. *Tours* by arrangement; minimum 15 people. **Admission** (NT) *House* £5.10; £2.50 5-15s; free under-5s; £12.80 family (2+3). *Park* free. **Credit** *Tearoom/shop only* MC, V.
Once a fine manor in the heart of the countryside, Osterley is now a welcome National Trust retreat in the heart of the western suburbs. It was built for Sir Thomas Gresham (founder of the Royal Exchange) in 1576, but came into the hands of Sir Francis Child, the head of Child's Bank, as result of a mortgage default. He had it altered by fashionable architect Robert Adam in the 18th century. Mrs Child's flower garden, set out at that time, is still delightful. The splendour of the state rooms alone makes the house worth a visit, but the still-used Tudor stables, the vast parkland walks and the resident ghost – said to lurk in the basement – add to Osterley's allure. Visitors can buy home-grown produce in a farm shop. Regular events include historic tours of the house, bluebell walks, bay walks, outdoor performances and the annual free Osterley Day (15 July 2007) full of arts and fun. In October 2007, a special exhibition in the Garden Gallery marks the bicentenary of the abolition of the slave trade.
Baby slings for hire. Buggy access (not when busy). Café. Car park (£3.50/day, NT members free). Disabled access: lift, toilet. Nappy-changing facilities. Nearest picnic place: front lawn/picnic benches in grounds. Shop.

PM Gallery & House

Walpole Park, Mattock Lane, W5 5EQ (8567 1227/ www.ealing.gov.uk/pmgallery&house). Ealing Broadway tube/rail/65 bus. **Open** *May-Sept* 1-5pm Tue-Fri, Sun; 11am-5pm Sat. *Oct-Apr* 1-5pm Tue-Fri; 11am-5pm Sat. Closed bank hols. **Tours** by arrangement; phone for details. **Admission** free. *Audio guide* £1.
Ealing's flagship cultural centre is Pitzhanger Manor, beautiful Regency villa rebuilt 1801-3 by Sir John Soane. Among the exhibits is the Hull Grundy Martinware pottery collection, and there's an art gallery where contemporary exhibitions are held, plus a lecture and workshop programme for all ages. Outside is Walpole Park, the borough's rose-scented pride and joy, which hosts jazz and comedy festivals in summer.
Buggy access. Disabled access: lift, ramp, toilet. Nearest picnic place: Walpole Park.

Shri Swaminarayan Mandir Temple

105-119 Brentfield Road, NW10 8LD (8965 2651/ www.swaminarayan.org). Wembley Park tube then BR2 bus/Neasden tube, then 15min walk. **Open** 9am-6pm daily. **Admission** (LP) free. *Exhibition* £2; £1.50 6-15s; free under-6s. **Credit** AmEx, MC, V.
Built in 1995, this beautiful Hindu temple is an extraordinary structure, intricately carved by master sculptors. Much of the stone was sent to India to be carved, then brought back to Neasden: at a cost of more than £10 million. An inspirational place to visit, the temple also has a permanent exhibition (with a video) called Understanding Hinduism – especially useful for children in Years 6 and 7 studying world religion.
Buggy access. Café. Disabled access: lift, toilet. Nappy-changing facilities. Shop.

Consumer

Features

Eating

Consumer

You can almost forgive him the supermarket ads. St Jamie of Kidbrooke (aka Mr Oliver MBE) has had an impressive impact on the food now offered to children in schools. Nevertheless, this transformation is only just starting to get under way in London's restaurants. Too often, children's menus are still packed with the worst kind of junk food – cheap, industrially produced fodder full of fat, sugar and salt. In an age where children's well-being is paramount in every other aspect of life, it's astonishing we should expect our younger generation to stomach such stuff.

It's easy to be prissy about the subject, however, and trying to force children to eat what they don't like will only harm their education in the delights of food and restaurant-going. Fortunately, there are now several venues in London that offer wholesome, appetising children's menus – and many more that serve high-quality food and are happy to offer smaller portions of it to kids at a reduced price. We've listed the best of them here.

Burger and chips isn't necessarily junk food, and London is now blessed with an ever-increasing number of 'gourmet burger' restaurants offering prime beef. US-style restaurants in general are well-represented on these pages, simply because so many of them sport excellent child-friendly credentials. Chains like **Tootsies** and **TGI Friday's** pay at least as much attention to kids' entertainment as their food.

From spaghetti bolognese to potato gnocchi, pasta is nearly always a popular choice among children, and pizza was practically invented for kids, so you'll find find several decent Italian restaurants here too. However, it's worth broadening a child's culinary horizons – what about dim sum (**Royal China** offers some of the best), or a plate of noodles (at **Wagamama** or **Sông Quê**), or even a curry (try **Masala Zone**)?

Children's food can be inexpensive, without being of a debased quality. M Manze's, the century-old pie and mash shop (87 Tower Bridge Road, SE1 4TW, 7407 2985, www.manze.co.uk) will sell a 'baby bowl' of proper mashed potatoes, for just 65p (though you might want to go easy on the accompanying 'liquor' – a salty, parsley-based gravy). Add a couple of quid and you can have cherry pie and custard for pud.

But to improve the general quality of children's menus, it's simply a case of supply and demand. If no-one orders chicken nuggets or their illegitimate offspring, turkey twizzlers, they will slither off restaurants' lists and forever be consigned to the mechanically recovered meat bin of history.

For handy places to eat while sightseeing in a particular area of central London, look for the **Lunch box** round-ups in the **Around Town** section (*see pp31-162*).

South Bank & Bankside

Cantina del Ponte
Butlers Wharf Building, 36C Shad Thames, SE1 2YE (7403 5403/www.danddlondon.com). Tower Hill tube/ London Bridge tube/rail. **Dinner served** 6-11pm Mon-Sat; 6-10pm Sun. **Main courses** £9-£16.50. **Credit** AmEx, DC, MC, V.
Italian
Although this former-Conran riverside Italian restaurant is smart, children always seem to get a warm welcome. The close-up view of Tower Bridge is truly breathtaking, and when not too busy the terrace (with heated canopy) is ideal for youngsters. On our last visit, potato gnocchi with basil pesto was overwhelmed by a heavy-handed use of the sauce. Much better was a juicy roast guinea-fowl breast with grilled fennel. Children can choose from several rice and pasta dishes in junior helpings (£4-£4.50). *Buggy access. Tables outdoors (20, terrace).*

fish!
Cathedral Street, Borough Market, SE1 9AL (7407 3803/www.fishdiner.co.uk). London Bridge tube/rail. **Meals served** 11.30am-11pm Mon-Thur; noon-11pm Fri, Sat; noon-10.30pm Sun. **Main courses** £9.95-£22.95. **Credit** AmEx, MC, V. **Map** p317 M8.
Fish
The child in our party was fed with alacrity and a smile at fish!. This gleaming, glass and steel fish restaurant is surrounded by London at its most grimy and Dickensian, but it does very well out of the affluent food shoppers of Borough Market. A large noticeboard informs diners of the provenance of their dinner (the cod's Icelandic, the salmon organic, and the veg is from across the road). For starters, toasted cheese-topped smoked haddock was a savoury treat. Next, lovely crunchy batter surrounded nice firm cod chips were golden and chunky – but the dish cost £13.95. The children's menu gives a choice of goujons of fish and chips or chicken and chips, with a soft drink and ice-cream. *Buggy access. Children's menu (£6.95). Crayons. High chairs. No-smoking tables. Tables outdoors (24, pavement).*

Giraffe. *See p166.*

Giraffe

Units 1&2, Riverside Level 1, Royal Festival Hall, SE1 8XX (7928 2004/www.giraffe.net). Waterloo tube/rail. **Open** 8am-11pm Mon-Fri; 9am-11pm Sat; 9am-10.30pm Sun. **Main courses** £7.95-£10.95. **Set meals** (5-7pm) £6.95 2 courses. **Credit** AmEx, MC, V. **Map** p317 M8.

Brasserie

Always full of families sheltering from river breezes on weekend strolls, this branch of the ever expanding Giraffe chain is large and busy, but that has not compromised the trademark cheerfulness of its young staff. The balance of the global food menu is just right – with plenty for vegetarian children, discreetly placed salad and veg and yummy favourites, such as burgers and chicken and toast and jam alongside healthier falafel, noodles and salmon. Smoothies, juices, shakes and strawberry sorbets can be the sweet course, or you can extend the treat and go for cola, lemonade, ice-cream and chocolate chunk brownie. Everyone's happy, especially the adults after a couple of delicious mango lime daiquiris. *See p165.*

Balloons. Buggy access. Children's set menu (£5.50 noon-3pm Mon-Fri). Crayons. Disabled: ramp, toilets. High chairs. Nappy-changing facilities. No smoking. Tables outdoors (20, terrace). Takeaway service. **Branches:** throughout town. Check website for details.

Konditor & Cook

10 Stoney Street, SE1 9AD (7407 5100/www.konditorandcook.com). London Bridge tube/rail. **Meals served** 7.30am-6pm Mon-Fri; 8.30am-5pm Sat. **Main courses** £2-£5. **Credit** AmEx, MC, V. **Map** p319 P8.

Café

Locals flock here for a daily changing selection of appealing lunches: soups and salads, well-filled sandwiches, frittata, spinach and ricotta tartlets, plus hot meals and daily specials (gnocchi in fresh tomato and basil sauce with black olives, for example). Children will doubtless be unable to take their eyes off the cakes; try the heavenly orange lavender slab cake, or the Curly Whirly double-layer chocolate cake with real vanilla bean frosting.

Buggy access. No smoking. Tables outdoors (1, pavement). Takeaway service. **Branches:** 22 Cornwall Road, SE1 8TW (7261 0456); 46 Gray's Inn Road, WC1X 8LR (7404 6300); 99 Shaftesbury Avenue, W1D 5DY (7292 1684).

Roast

Floral Hall, Borough Market, Stoney Street, SE1 1TL (7940 1300/www.roast-restaurant.com). London Bridge tube/rail. **Breakfast served** 7-9.30am Mon-Fri; 8-10.30am Sat. **Lunch served** noon-2.30pm Mon-Fri; noon-3.30pm Sat. **Brunch served** noon-5.30pm Sun. **Dinner served** 5.30-10.30pm Mon-Fri; 6-10.30pm Sat. **Main courses** £13.50-£25. **Credit** AmEx, MC, V. **Map** p318 P8.

British

Gastro-destination Borough Market's fine-dining experience does not leave children out of the mix, offering a good kids' menu. The views might not be the most beautiful in the world, but they're great for market bustle and trains. The menu is wonderfully British, with, for example, Lincolnshire sausages for breakfast, Cornish new potatoes to accompany Welsh lamb for Sunday lunch and splendid dinners of roast hake or pan-fried halibut for a really special dinner. The children's menu offers boiled organic eggs with soldiers, fish and chips and meaty little chipolatas. *Children's menu (£6 main courses).*

Tamesa@oxo

Second floor, Oxo Tower Wharf, Barge House Street, SE1 9PH (7633 0088/www.oxotower.co.uk). Blackfriars or Waterloo tube/rail. **Lunch served** noon-3.30pm **Dinner served** 5.30-11.30pm Mon-Sat. **Meals served** noon-6pm Sun. **Main courses** £11.50-£15.75. **Set meal** (lunch 5.30-7pm Mon-Fri) £12.50 2 courses, £15.50 3 courses. **Credit** AmEx, MC, V.

Brasserie

An intimate view of the Thames without, bright aqua rear wall, neat red chairs, white tables within. The wide-ranging menu (hot-and-sour and hoi sin, niçoise and caesar, a spot of pub grub, a bit of Italian) is cooked and presented nicely. Main courses might include new season lamb with green beans with shallots and rosemary. The children's menu (£5.50) gives a choice of penne pasta with tomato and parmesan, minute steak with chips, or fish and chips, followed by ice-cream and chocolate sauce. *Children's menu; crayons; high chairs.*

Tas/EV Restaurant Bar & Delicatessen

The Arches, 97-99 Isabella Street, SE1 8DA (7620 6191/www.tasrestaurant.com). Southwark tube/ Waterloo tube/rail. *Bar* **Open/meze served** noon-11.30pm Mon-Sat; noon-10.30pm Sun. **Meze** £3.55-£8.95. *Deli* **Open** 7.30am-10pm Mon-Sat; 9am-10pm Sun. *Restaurant* **Meals served** noon-11.30pm Mon-Sat; noon-10.30pm Sun. **Main courses** £5.45-£12.45. **Set meal** £8.25 2 courses, £18.25 3 courses per person (minimum 2). **Set meze** £8.25-£10.25 per person (minimum 2). *All* **Credit** AmEx, MC, V.

Turkish

Restaurants of the upmarket Tas chain have many features in common, despite being called variously Tas, Tas Café, Tas Pide and EV. Fittings are lush. Set in three old railway arches, EV has a large bar next to an equally capacious restaurant, plus a bakery/deli. Though there are no obvious trappings of child-friendliness, there's ample space and family groups often eat here. Much of the menu will appeal to little ones: from dips such as houmous and hot meze like borek (little filo parcels stuffed with feta cheese) to pasta with tomato sauce. Adults might enjoy such innovative dishes as grilled chicken with orange and mustard sauce. Booking advisable Tue-Sat. *Disabled: toilet. Entertainment: guitar 7.30pm Mon-Sat. No smoking. Tables outdoors (50, pavement). Takeaway service. Vegetarian menu. Vegan dishes.* **Branches:** throughout town. Check website for details.

The City

Shish

313-319 Old Street, EC1V 9LE (7749 0990/www.shish.com). Old Street tube/rail. **Meals served** 11.30am-11.30pm Mon-Fri; 10.30am-1.30pm Sat; 10.30am-10.30pm Sun. **Main courses** £5-£9. **Credit** AmEx, MC, V. **Map** p309.

International

The good-value, wholesome children's menu is a major attraction of this small chain. Food hails from points east, from Turkey to China and Japan. On the kids' menu this translates as a choice of salmon and herb fish cakes, Mediterranean chicken, falafel and houmous wrap,

wagamama

**delicious noodles | rice dishes | freshly squeezed juices
wine | sake | japanese beers**

positive eating + positive living

wagamama.com

chicken in pandan leaves, or three of the meze, followed by own-made ice-cream or sorbet, all for £4.25. Adult main courses are centred on kebabs, which are made fresh with good meat, though occasionally can taste bland. Fresh juices are another forte of this canteen-like restaurant. *Buggy access. Children's menu (£4.25). Disabled access: toilet. High chairs. Nappy-changing facilities. No smoking. Takeaway service.*
Branches: 71-75 Bishops Bridge Road, Bayswater, W2 6BG (7229 7300); 2-6 Station Parade, Willesden Green, NW2 4NH (8208 9290).

Smiths of Smithfield
67-77 Charterhouse Street, EC1M 6HJ (7251 7950/ www.smithsofsmithfield.co.uk). Farringdon tube/rail. **Meals served** *Ground-floor bar/café* 7am-4.30pm Mon; 7am-5pm Tue-Fri; 10am-5pm Sat; 9.30am-5pm Sun. **Main courses** £3.50-£8.50. **Credit** AmEx, DC, MC, V. **Map** p318 O5.

Café
One of London's most ambitious eating and drinking projects of the past decade has developed into an unstoppably successful operation, over four floors of converted warehouse. The best option for families is the ground floor

café/bar, especially at weekends (City workers dominate during the week). Highlights of the breakfast and brunch menu include smoothies such as Monkey Business (apple, banana, peanut butter and vanilla ice-cream), milkshakes, brunches (corn beef hash, spinach and fried egg) and breakfasts (waffles with maple syrup, porridge, and fry-ups). *Buggy access. Disabled access: lift, toilets. High chairs. Nappy-changing facilities. Tables outdoors (6, pavement). Takeaway service.*

Holborn & Clerkenwell

Ambassador
55 Exmouth Market, EC1R 4QL (7837 0009/www. theambassadorcafe.co.uk). Angel tube/Farringdon tube/rail/19, 38 bus. **Meals served** 9am-11pm Mon-Fri; 11am-11pm Sat, 11am-4pm Sun. **Main courses** £9.50-£17. **Set lunch** (noon-3pm Mon-Fri) £12.50 2 courses, £16 3 courses. **Credit** AmEx, MC, V.

Modern European
Weekend brunch is the favoured time for families at this easy-going incarnation of a bistro. The children's menu might be limited to bangers and mash, and banana and

Eating posh

'I don't blame the schools, I blame the parents,' says London restaurateur and TV celeb Oliver Peyton. He's talking about children and food. Restaurants have a tough time trying to please all age groups. Establishments that offer children's menus characterised by chicken nuggets and chips are merely following the path of least resistance. Irish-born Peyton, whose restaurants include the child-friendly Meals at Heal's department store, 196 Tottenham Court Road, W1, 7580 2522), the **National Dining Rooms & Café** (at the National Gallery; *see p173*) and **Inn the Park** (in St James's Park; *see p183*), among more grown-up establishments, doesn't offer children chicken nuggets. He doesn't 'believe in bad food' and he doesn't want children to have it. On the kids' brunch menu at Meals, therefore, you will find 'organic boiled eggs and soldiers' and 'macaroni cheese' but also 'steamed cod fillet, broccoli and new potatoes' and 'roasted corn-fed chicken, roast potatoes, green beans and gravy'. Such dishes cost £5 to £6.

This will be music to the ears of all sane parents who feel they must battle against the sheer convenience and cost advantages of junk food when they go out. Look around, however, and it's clear that good food is available – at a fair price – in the most unexpected places.

French chef and new father, Alexis Gaulthier, was shocked to discover the British divide between adult and child eating habits. 'I went to lunch at a friend's house and was disappointed not only that all the children were seated at a separate table, but that the food they were given was so boring,' he says, adding, 'After about ten minutes they all went upstairs to play computer games.' Gaulthier has since instituted a

children's menu at his rather grand, award-winning restaurant, **Roussillon** (*see p175*). Entitled 'Mini-gastronomes', it offers seven courses of such delights as 'jerusalem artichoke soup, truffle ravioli, warm camomile tea' and 'smoked eel, scrambled eggs, almond milk'. It costs £15 per child, but on the first and third Wednesday lunchtimes of every month – mon Dieu! – it is free. Too ambitious? So far, say waiting staff, the experiment is going well, probably because the little gourmands are suitably impressed with the sense of occasion.

Another classy joint offering adventurous children a free dining experience is **Le Cercle** near Sloane Square (*see p175*). No messing: the 'Petits Gourmets' dégustation menu is six courses selected from the weekly-changing main menu. Dishes range from pumpkin cream with star anise emulsion, through roast quail with sweet potato purée and lemon sauce, to chocolat fondant. The menu is available without charge every week, Tuesday to Saturday, for children aged from four to 11, with an accompanying paying adult.

These offers are remarkable, it must be said. But parents who trouble to eat with their children at home, teaching them good manners and acceptance of a wide variety of flavours, are in a great position to take them out to eat. And since children are hungry for supper around 6pm, and many London restaurants offer great deals (also known as pre-theatre menus) before 7.30pm, this could work out less expensive than you might think. Pay 20 quid for a night's babysitting, or order two children's meals? The choice is yours.

Consumer

chocolate milkshake (£5.25 the pair), but there's also such temptations as waffles, muesli with yoghurt, pork belly sandwich with caramelised onions, wild mushroom omelette, and warm chocolate pudding. Service is friendly. Tables spread on to the street in summer. *Children's menu and children's portions on request. High chairs. Toys.*

Bloomsbury & Fitzrovia

Carluccio's Caffè
8 Market Place, W1W 8AG (7636 2228/www. carluccios.com). Oxford Circus tube. **Meals served** 7.30am-11pm Mon-Fri; 10am-11pm Sat; 9am-10.30pm Sun. **Main courses** £4.95-£12.95. **Credit** AmEx, MC, V. **Map** p314 J6.
Italian
This is the original branch of the now-widespread chain of New York-style Italian deli-cafés. It wins our plaudits for having plenty of outdoor tables away from the traffic. The light airy interior can be noisy. Food is of a high quality and service is impeccable – by café standards. Snacking or picnicking is half the deal here, with soups, antipasti, salads and pasta dishes leading the way by deploying classic combinations. Then there are the wonderful breads, olives and breadsticks that children enjoy nibbling on. Daily specials supplement the fixed menu. Desserts are notable, including a scrumptious lemon tart. *Buggy access. Children's menu (£4.95 incl drink). Crayons. Disabled access: toilets. High chairs. Nappy-changing facilities. No smoking. Tables outdoors (15, pavement). Takeaway service.*
Branches: throughout town. Phone or check website.

North Sea Fish Restaurant
7-8 Leigh Street, WC1H 9EW (7387 5892). Russell Square tube/Euston or King's Cross tube/rail/68, 168 bus. **Lunch served** noon-2.30pm, **dinner served** 5.30-10.30pm Mon-Sat. **Main courses** £7.95-£17.95. **Credit** AmEx, MC, V. **Map** p315 L3/4.
Fish & chips
This chippy's salmon velvet chairs, dark-wood tables and threadbare carpet give the place a near-comical look in such an up-and-coming district. Starters of own-made fish cakes are definitely worth trying, as is the fish soup. The 'normal sized' portions of battered cod and haddock are massive, the chips are of golden hue, and the tartare sauce (made in-house) has quite a kick. For pudding, go for sherry trifle or apple crumble and custard. Adjust your belt. *Buggy access. High chair. Children's menu (£5-£6). No-smoking tables. Takeaway service.*

Wagamama
4A Streatham Street, WC1A 1JB (7323 9223/www. wagamama.com). Tottenham Court Road tube. **Meals served** noon-11pm Mon-Sat; noon-10pm Sun. **Main courses** £5.95-£9.95. **Credit** AmEx, DC, MC, V.
Oriental
The Wagamama chain has stood the test of time well. The minimalist interior of this original branch still looks contemporary, and the business still provides wholesome oriental fast food at a fair price. The menu is more extensive than in the beginning, when it focused on Japanese-style noodle dishes with South-east Asian flavours. You can now follow the filling main courses with desserts such as tamarind and chilli pavlova. For children, there's chicken

katsu (chicken breast fried in breadcrumbs) with dipping sauce, rice and shredded cucumber, or vegetarian or chicken noodle dishes for just £3.50. The gyoza (steam-fried dumplings) are usually a hit with kids too. To drink there's saké, raw juices and free green tea. *Buggy access. Children's menu (£2.95-£4.25). Disabled access: toilets. High chairs. Nappy-changing facilities. No smoking. Takeaway service.*
Branches: throughout town. Check website for details.

West End

Cibo
Mamas & Papas, 256-258 Regent Street, W1 (01484 438476/www.mamasandpapas.com). Oxford Circus tube. **Open** 10am-8pm Mon-Wed, Fri; 10am-9pm Thur; 9.30am-8pm Sat; noon-6pm Sun. **Main courses** £6.75-£9.95. **Credit** AmEx, MC, V. **Map** p314 J6.
Italian
On the first floor of the Mamas & Papas flagship store, this Italian café is a symphony in coffee and cream. Staff are amenable, and Cibo's menu is tailored to the needs of pregnant people and small children. The appealing breakfast section offers organic yoghurts, muesli, fruit, smoked salmon and scrambled eggs; then there are lunchtime smoothies, sandwiches, salads and hot meals. Children's dishes include raw vegetables and dips, organic beans on toast, pizza, organic hamburgers and ice-creams. We sampled the organic salmon fish cakes from the children's menu and made short work of the golden-brown patty stuffed with pink fish, potato and parsley. *Children's menu (£3.25-£4.50).*

Fairuz
3 Blandford Street, W1H 3AA (7486 8108/8182). Baker Street or Bond Street tube. **Meals served** noon-11.30pm Mon-Sat; noon-10.30pm Sun. **Main courses** £10.95-£18.95. **Set meals** £18.95 meze; £26.95 4 courses. **Cover** £1.50. **Credit** AmEx, V. **Map** p314 G5.
Middle Eastern
Its fold-back frontage, pavement seating and Mediterranean-flavoured interior, are sufficiently welcoming to make this casual Lebanese restaurant constantly busy. The menu, encompassing some 50 hot and cold meze dishes, is a hit with children, and staff are usually accommodating to youngsters. The quality of food is consistently excellent. Standouts include light, fluffy falafel that come with a little pot of tahina, and houmous strongly flavoured with tahina and decorated with diamonds of red pepper. The mains are unusually good too. 'Knuckle of lamb' was more like a fist of the most tender meat. *Booking advisable. High chairs. No-smoking tables. Tables outdoors (4, pavement). Takeaway service.*

Hard Rock Café
150 Old Park Lane, W1K 1QR (7629 0382/www. hardrock.com). Hyde Park Corner tube. **Meals served** 11.30am-12.30am Mon-Thur, Sun; 11am-1am Fri, Sat. **Main courses** £8.45-£15.95. **Credit** AmEx, DC, MC, V. **Map** p316 H8.
North American
This is a classic example of the Hard Rock chain, with rock memorabilia covering the walls, music blasting at impressive levels and the hamburgers, nachos and salads piled high on plates carried by wafer-thin waitresses in teeny-

Consumer

tiny uniforms. It's ideal for children, as nobody can hear them scream, and the ice-cream sundaes are excellent. Further attractions include face-painting at certain times, a Lil' Rocker children's menu with pizza, pasta and burgers, plus occasional themed activities.
Buggy access. Children's menu (£5.95). Crayons. Disabled access: toilet. Entertainment: face-painting Sat, Sun. High chairs. Nappy-changing facilities. No-smoking. Tables outdoors (10, pavement).

Hong Kong
6-7 Lisle Street, WC2H 7BG (7287 0352). Leicester Square or Piccadilly Circus tube. **Dim sum served** noon-5pm daily. **Meals served** noon-11.30pm Mon-Thur; noon-midnight Fri, Sat; 11am-11pm Sun. **Main courses** £5.50-£10.50. **Set lunch** £10 3 courses. **Credit** AmEx, JCB, MC,V. **Map** p317 K7.
Chinese
Dim sum is usually a hit with children. There's ample choice, and the dumplings make perfect comfort food. Hong Kong is a decent Chinatown practitioner of the genre. The menus are plasticky, the style tacky, and the photographs of dim sum titbits amuse the kids. Service comes with a smile, and children are usually made a fuss of. Steamed dumplings stuffed with prawn and chives are nicely done.
Buggy access. High chairs. Takeaway service.

Planet Hollywood
13 Coventry Street, W1D 7DH (7287 1000/www. planethollywoodlondon.com). Piccadilly Circus tube. **Meals served** 11.30am-1am daily. **Main courses** £10.45-£21.95. **Credit** AmEx, DC, MC, V. **Map** p317 K7.
North American
The Hollywood version of the Hard Rock, with movie memorabilia floor to ceiling, swinging klieg lights (just like in LA) and blasting film soundtracks. It's ideal for open young minds, eager to be inculcated into the Hollywood cabal. The food is slightly more adventurous than at the Hard Rock: fewer burgers, more rôtisserie chickens, fajitas and steaks and there's plenty for the kids to choose from.
Balloons. Booking advisable (weekends; limited reservations Sat). Buggy access. Children's menu (£7.95 incl drink & ice-cream). Crayons. High chairs. Nappy-changing facilities. No-smoking tables.

Rainforest Café
20 Shaftesbury Avenue, W1D 7EU (7434 3111/ www.therainforestcafe.co.uk). Piccadilly Circus tube. **Meals served** noon-10pm Mon-Thur; noon-8pm Fri; 11.30am-8pm Sat; 11.30am-10pm Sun. **Main courses** £10.50-£17.50. **Credit** AmEx, MC, V. **Map** p317 K7.
International
The ultimate themed restaurant, designed to thrill children with animatronic wildlife, cascading waterfalls and jungle sound effects. The Rainforest's menu has plenty of family-friendly fare, from 'paradise pizza', and 'Bamba's bangers' for kids to a host of amusingly named dishes for grown-ups. The children's menu is £10.95 for two courses. Organic spaghetti with tomato sauce could be followed by fresh fruit salad and ice-cream. Burger and chips could precede 'jungle jelly' with ice-cream and Smarties. To keep the bill down, order a small adult dish and polish off what the kids don't eat. Unlimited refills of sodas for £1.95.
Bookings not accepted Sat. Buggy access. Children's menu (£10.95 incl dessert). Crayons. High chairs. Nappy-changing facilities. No smoking.

Royal Dragon
30 Gerrard Street, W1D 6JS (7734 1388). Leicester Square or Piccadilly Circus tube. **Dim sum served** noon-5pm daily. **Meals served** noon-midnight daily. **Main courses** £6.50-£10. **Credit** AmEx, MC, V. **Map** p317 K7.
Chinese
The interior at Royal Dragon verges on the trendy, with comfy seating, exposed air-conditioning tubes and plentiful dark wood. The menu includes such culinary delights as minestrone soup, cheese burgers, mixed sausage spaghetti, and bubble teas – popular with Chinese yoof. Otherwise the list offers plenty of scope to sample authentic Cantonese food (pan-fried pork chop with salted fish, for instance), as well as a wide choice of dim sum dumplings. We like the shredded chicken cheung fun: a good, slithery rice roll packed with succulent chicken, shredded carrot and coriander. The black-clad staff are cool, efficient and kind to children.
High chair. Takeaway service.

Tamarind
20-22 Queen Street, W1J 5PR (7629 3561/www. tamarindrestaurant.com). Green Park tube. **Lunch served** noon-3pm Mon-Fri, Sun. **Dinner served** 6-11.30pm Mon-Sat; 6-10.30pm Sun. **Main courses** £14.50-£26. **Set lunch** £16.95 2 courses, £18.95 3 courses. **Set meal** (6-7pm, 10-11pm) £24 2 courses. **Credit** AmEx, DC, MC, V.
Indian
The Sunday lunch deal at this classy Indian restaurant is an attractive proposition if you're dining with children. For every adult ordering the £24 tasting menu, a child under ten can sample the children's menu for free. So while the grown-ups are tucking into delicacies like lamb patties with dal, followed by supreme of corn-fed chicken, the youngsters can be sampling the likes of pan-fried potato cakes with split lentils, ginger, toasted cumin and spinach stuffing, followed by battered tilapia fish then vanilla ice-cream with fresh seasonal fruits. Watch the highly skilled chefs at work in the open kitchen.
Children's menu (£12.95 3 courses).

Ten Ten Tei
56 Brewer Street, W1R 3PJ (7287 1738). Piccadilly Circus tube. **Lunch served** noon-3.30pm Mon-Fri; noon-4pm Sat. **Dinner served** 5-10pm Mon-Sat. **Main courses** £5.80 **Credit** over £10 MC, V.
Japanese
For generously proportioned, well-made sushi at a streetwise price, this functional diner is hard to beat. It has the look of a backstreet noodle bar, with its plain wooden tables ready-loaded with napkins, chopsticks, toothpicks, pepper pots, togarashi sprinkles, soy and tonkatsu sauce. Children love all the accessories and the sweet service meted out to My First Sushi novices.

Covent Garden & the Strand

Abeno Too
17-18 Great Newport Street, WC2H 7JE (7379 1160/ www.abeno.co.uk). Leicester Square tube. **Meals served** noon-11pm Mon-Sat; noon-10pm Sun. **Main courses** £6.95-£22.80. **Set lunch** £7.80-£12.80. **Credit** AmEx, DC, JCB, MC, V.
Japanese

Bodean's

Local workers and Japanese regulars populate this neat little provider of okonomiyaki (like Spanish omelette), which is cooked on hot-plates set into the window tables and the main counter. It's fun for children to see their food being prepared, and the bill won't break the bank. Rice and noodle dishes are also on the menu.
Bookings not accepted. Disabled: toilet. Takeaway service.
Branch: 47 Museum Street, WC1A 1LY (7405 3211).

Bodean's
10 Poland Street, W1F 8PZ (7287 7575/www. bodeansbbq.com). Oxford Circus or Piccadilly Circus tube. **Lunch served** noon-3pm, **dinner served** 6-11pm Mon-Fri. **Meals served** noon-11pm Sat; noon-10.30pm Sun. **Main courses** £8-£16. Service 12.5%. **Credit** AmEx, MC, V.
North American
It's a bit noisy, what with all the ice hockey/baseball on the wide screens around the place, but this basement restaurant, with its tartan carpets and general air of bonhomie, is so welcoming that families can't help but feel at home. It does, of course, help if they are not vegetarians, as Bodean's 'signature' trough is a mighty rack (or half rack for wusses) of baby back ribs. Non-meat eaters can choose a barbecued tuna steak (a meaty fish) or a griddled pepper ensemble, but most people go for the carnivorous options: juicy ribs, steaks, burgers and fiery chicken wings. Children eat free (options include baby back ribs, bbq chicken breast or slices of smoked beef, turkey or ham with fries or mash, with ice-cream to follow) between noon and 5pm at the weekend when accompanied by an adult. At other times the children's menu costs £5. Kindly touches,

such as jugs of iced tap water delivered without demur, and extra scoops of ice-cream for older siblings, make us love this place all the more.
Children's area. Children's menu (£5 incl ice-cream). Children eat free at the weekend. High chairs. Nappy-changing facilities. No-smoking tables. Takeaway service.
Branches: 4 Broadway Chambers, Fulham Broadway, SW6 1EP (7610 0440); 169 Clapham High Street, SW4 7SS (7622 4248).

Hamburger Union
4 Garrick Street, WC2E 9BH (7379 0412/www. hamburgerunion.com). Leicester Square tube. **Meals served** 11.30am-10pm Mon; 11.30am-10.30pm Tue-Sat; 11.30-9.30 Sun. **Main courses** £3.95-£8.95. **Credit** MC, V. Map p317 L7.
North American
No doubt the hamburgers come from happy cows here; they're certainly made from well-textured beef, cooked medium and served in a good-looking bun. The chips are properly chunky too. The Union is a clean and attractive place to have lunch, and there are chicken and vegetarian choices (including chargrilled halloumi) for the beef-avoiders. To finish, it's hard to keep children away from the malts (vanilla, chocolate, strawberry or banana).
Buggy access. High chairs. No smoking. Takeaway service.
Branches: 25 Dean Street, W1D 3RY (7437 6004); 341 Upper Street, N1 0PB (7359 4436); 1 South End Road, NW3 2PT (7794 7070); 64 Tottenham Court Road, W1T 2ET (7636 0011); Leicester Square, WC2E 0HA (7839 8100).

Eat your way around the world

Remember the not-so-nonsensical rhyme by Walter de la Mare?

'It's a very odd thing-
As odd as can be-
That whatever Miss T eats
Turns into Miss T'

Nearly all children like this poem, which makes it useful for a) entertainment purposes (after all, 'cooked-to-order' can never mean 'ready-right-now') and b) admonition (the thought of metamorphosing into a plate of chips may prove unattractive to even the greediest child).

Most parents who dine out with their kids worry less about over-indulgence, however, than sulky rejection. Will the five-year-old eat raw fish? Will the pre-teens be bored if the service is slow? Will the baby sleep long enough for the adults to bolt down their food? Often all these issues can be solved, or soothed, by entertaining distractions. At the determinedly British restaurant, **Roast** (*see p166*), the view of Borough Market below, with its bustling crowds and opera-singing costermongers, may be entertainment enough, but in any case junior diners are routinely greeted with breadsticks in recognition of the childish hunger that requires satisfaction NOW. Then there is a two-course menu (£6.50) featuring, for example, chipolata sausages and mash, roast chicken and chips and steamed treacle pudding. Another great British institution, fish and chips, received a lift in Spring 2007 when Notting Hill's famous chippy, **Geale's** (*see p177*) – a stalwart since 1939 – reopened under new ownership. Fish and chips have long been a meal many people recall with nostalgia, but fear to eat. Geale's, with its glamorous gingham cloths and wood panelling, its offerings of champagne as well as ginger beer, and its perfect rendering of a dish so often ruined by rancid fat, may well restore it to a favourite family outing. Other restaurants score with children in terms of sheer exoticism. The **Benihana** brand (*pictured*, and *see p171*) has won a market for (Americanised) Japanese food with its showy food preparation (knifemanship, sizzling flames) but it's pricey and these days kids will kill for sushi with or without the theatre. On Soho's Brewer Street, among the Japanese grocery stores you'll find several noodle shops offering soup in bowls the size of crash helmets, and others with great value sushi on conveyor belts - much cheaper than the ubiquitous Yo!Sushi (www.yosushi.com). Try **Ten Ten Tei** (*see p170*) if your kids, like many we know, are capable of hoovering up plate after plate of sushi with cheerful disregard for the cost.

Lebanese restaurants are another wholesome possibility for family dining. The **Maroush** (*see p175*) chain typifies the appeal: child-friendly chefs behind glass counters groaning with fresh fruit, meat and vegetables. Aromas of char-grilling

Benihana.

stimulate the tastebuds; views of Arab visitors smoking shisha pipes on the pavement add to a holiday atmosphere. A smaller chain, **Shish** (*see p166*), offers mezze and mains of kebabs which are also clean-tasting and healthy; the pandana leaves filled with marinated chicken are fun to unwrap; free activity packs can be a godsend. The grilled-meat theme is also done well in myriad Turkish eateries around town. There are several on Green Lanes, N4; wander into any one that takes the kids' fancy.

If you like meat and fancy somewhere more upmarket, **Butcher & Grill** (*see p184*), next to Battersea Park, is a novel conjunction of proper butcher and restaurant. Dishes come with sides such as aioli and Béarnaise; the kids' menu (£5.25) includes a roast of the day on Sundays.

Of all the cosmopolitan treats in London, Scandinavian cuisine (unless you count lunch at IKEA) has been sadly forgotten until recently. The opening of Islington's **Upper Glas** (First Floor, The Mall, 395 Upper Street, N1 0PD (7359 1932) aims to set this straight. Owned and run by the self-styled ambassador for all things Swedish, Anna Mossesson, it encapsulates laidback Swedish charm. The traditional menu includes meatballs, venison, salmon, and herring dishes aplenty. You can select a smörgåsbord of small plates or go for the standard course-by-course option. Afternoon tea, known here as 'fika', features biscuits, cakes and savouries on all sorts of themes. The meal is often accompanied by recitals on the piano, or storytelling.

Consumer

Rock & Sole Plaice

47 Endell Street, WC2H 9AJ (7836 3785). Covent Garden or Leicester Square tube. **Meals served** 11.30am-10.30pm Mon-Sat; noon-9.30pm Sun. **Main courses** £8-£20. **Credit** MC, V. **Map** p315 L6.

Fish & chips

Sturdy wooden tables, fairy-lights on trees, and a maître d' dressed in Bavarian garb: these are the characterful ingredients that give Rock & Sole Plaice the feel of a beer garden. Yet this is supposedly London's oldest surviving chip shop, dating back to 1871. Tourists and suit-wearers beat a path here, ready to wait for the super-sized fish suppers. Chips, fried fish and mushy peas are all present and correct. Finish off with spotted dick or sticky toffee pudding – just £2.50. The toilets are in the basement, as is a splendid fish and whale mural.

Buggy access. Tables outdoors (10, pavement). Takeaway service.

Smollensky's on the Strand

105 Strand, WC2R 0AA (7497 2101/www. smollenskys.co.uk). Embankment tube/Charing Cross tube/rail. **Meals served** noon-11pm Mon-Wed; noon-11.30pm Thur-Sat; noon-4.30pm, 6.30-10.30pm Sun. **Main courses** £8.95-£21.95. **Credit** AmEx, DC, MC, V. **Map** p317 L7.

North American

The new look in this basement steakhouse is cool and modern, with candles glittering everywhere. Despite the hip new surroundings, the food is as straightforward as ever. The emphasis is still on steaks, which arrive with good chips and a choice of sauces. The children's menu is divided into two sections: one category for under-sevens (who are deemed only to want fried food – burgers, chicken, fish – apart from a vegetarian pasta dish) and one for 'mini adults' (who are treated to the likes of jambalaya or steak). Food can be variable, but we've no complaints about the puddings: moreish chocolate mousse, and memorable Mississippi mud pie. Children's entertainment (a clown, a magician, Punch and Judy and a face painter) takes place every weekend lunchtime (noon-3pm), when there's also a playing area with a TV and play station, balloons on the tables and party bags.

Booking advisable. Buggy access. Children's menu (£3.95-£7.95). Crayons. Entertainment: clown, magician, Nintendo games, face-painting (Sat, Sun lunch). High chairs. No smoking. Play area (under-7s).

TGI Friday's

6 Bedford Street, WC2E 9HZ (7379 0585/www. tgifridays.co.uk). Covent Garden or Embankment tube/Charing Cross tube/rail. **Meals served** noon-11.30pm Mon-Sat; noon-11pm Sun. **Main courses** £7.45-£17.95. **Credit** AmEx, MC, V. **Map** p317 L7.

North American

The most child-centred of all the US chains, despite the entire restaurant being focused on a noisy bar. Kids are decked out with balloons, given crayons, and generally encouraged by cheery waiters. The food is varied, with an emphasis on sticky barbecues and tasty Tex-Mex dishes, as well as the inevitable burgers and fries. The children's menu (main courses £2.95) has all the fried regulars too, but also a batch of pasta dishes, and fruity sundae for pudding – or dirt and worm pie, for chocolate and fudge fiends. Free Heinz baby food is provided for babes accompanying a dining adult.

Balloons. Buggy access. Children's menu (£2.95).

Crayons. Disabled access: lift, toilets. Entertainment: occasional face-painting (noon-5pm Sat, Sun). High chairs. Nappy-changing facilities. No smoking. **Branches**: throughout town. Check website for details.

Westminster

National Dining Rooms & Café

Sainsbury Wing, National Gallery, Trafalgar Square, WC2N 5DN (7747 2525/www.nationalgallery.co.uk). Charing Cross tube/rail. *Bakery* **Snacks served** 10am-5pm Mon, Tue, Thur-Sun; 11am-8.30pm Wed. *Restaurant* **Lunch served** noon-3pm daily. **Dinner served** 5-7pm Wed. **Main courses** £13.50-£18.50. **Set meal** £22.50 2 courses, £27.50 3 courses. **Credit** AmEx, JCB, MC, V.

Café

Fine British food in a modern setting at reasonable prices is what you'll find at the National Gallery's new eaterie – especially in the café area, where a raised pork pie is £4.50 and scones with Cornish clotted cream cost £3.50. The restaurant menu has heritage tomato salad followed by roast beetroot and wensleydale tart on mustard leaves and, to finish, wonderful eccles cakes with Lancashire cheese. The children's menu includes boiled eggs with soldiers, and macaroni cheese. *See p168* **Eating Posh**.

Children's menu (£2.50-£6.50). High chairs. Booking advisable.

Texas Embassy Cantina

1 Cockspur Street, SW1Y 5DL (7925 0077/www. texasembassy.com). Embankment tube/Charing Cross tube/rail. **Meals served** noon-11pm Mon-Wed; noon-midnight Thur-Sat; noon-10.30pm Sun. **Main courses** £7.50-£25.95. **Credit** AmEx, DC, MC, V. **Map** p317 K7.

North American

A big, boisterous barn of a restaurant, the Texas Embassy is brazenly staked out at the edge of Trafalgar Square. This tourist favourite is loud, and the noise is, ahem, enhanced by the twangs of country music. The children's menu goes beyond the usual burgers and hot dogs (though these are available) to include enchiladas, nachos and tacos. Round things off with apple pie, ice-cream and a rousing 'yee haw!'

Balloons. Buggy access. Children's menu (£4.75 incl drink). Crayons. High chairs. Nappy-changing facilities. No smoking. Tables outdoors (8, pavement).

Kensington & Chelsea

Big Easy

332-334 King's Road, SW3 5UR (7352 4071/www. bigeasy.uk.com). Sloane Square tube then 11, 19, 22 bus. Meals served noon-11.15pm Mon-Thur, Sun; noon-12.15am Fri, Sat. Main courses £8.85-£27.50. Set lunch (noon-5pm Mon-Fri) £7.95 2 courses. Credit AmEx, MC, V. Map p313 E12.

North American

With the raucous conviviality of its namesake city (New Orleans), Big Easy packs in crowds every night. Apart from the fun-loving atmosphere, the draw consists of huge steaks, vast seafood platters and racks of ribs. Things can get boozy at night, so lunchtime is the preferable option for young families. Steaks are tender and well priced, Alaskan king crab and lobster are house specialities, side

Consumer

dishes are carefully done. The children's menu offers the likes of burgers, hot dogs and chicken dippers, all served with chips and a drink (ice-cream sodas, fresh juices, milk). *Balloons. Buggy access. Children's menu (£6.95 main courses, dessert £2.95-£4.75). Crayons. High chairs. Nappy-changing facilities. No-smoking tables. Tables outdoors (5, pavement). Takeaway service.*

Blue Kangaroo
555 King's Road, SW6 2EB (7371 7622/www.the bluekangaroo.co.uk). Fulham Broadway tube/Sloane Square tube then 11, 19, 22 bus. **Meals served** 9.30am-7.30pm daily. **Main courses** £9.50-£12.50. **Credit** AmEx, MC, V. Map p312 C13.
Brasserie
Oft praised for its sterling service in the field of children's dining – and children's parties – the Blue Kangaroo has a winning formula. The basement playground is the main attraction for under-eights. You can eat alongside it, but the crisper upstairs restaurant has less taxing noise levels. Food is well presented, and children are served first. The minors' menu consists of tasty, own-made burgers, chicken goujons, scrambled eggs (meat, poultry and eggs are organic), spaghetti carbonara or penne pasta, or splendid salmon fish cakes. Adult portions (from £9.50) are large and arrive with salads or vegetables. Choices include chicken breast, fish cakes, pumpkin risotto or specials such as tagliatelle with beef ragù. You wouldn't come here without children, but if you fancy lingering *en famille* over a decent meal with wine, not whine, the Kangaroo will do. *Buggy access. Children's menu (£5.45 incl drink). Disabled access: toilet. High chairs. Nappy-changing facilities. Play area. No smoking.*

Le Cercle
1 Wilbraham Place, SW1X 9AE (7901 9999). Sloane Square tube. Bar **Open/snacks served** noon-midnight Tue-Sat. *Restaurant* **Lunch served** noon-3pm. **Tea served** 3-6pm. **Dinner served** 6-11pm Tue-Sat. **Set lunch** £15 3 dishes incl tea or coffee, £19.50 4 dishes. **Set dinner** (6-7pm Tue-Sat) £17.50 3 dishes incl tea or coffee, £21.50 4 dishes. **Tapas** £4.50-£16. **Credit** AmEx, JCB, MC, V.
French
Le Cercle has the air of a well-kept secret. A discreet entrance hidden among mansion blocks leads you down into this smart, airy basement restaurant. The menu, divided into unconventional categories such as 'terroirs' (French farmhouse dishes) and 'plaisirs' (foie gras and other luxuries), offers small and appealing dishes, tapas-style. For children, the 'Petits Gourmets' dégustation menu includes six courses selected from the weekly-changing main menu. Dishes range from pumpkin cream with star anise emulsion, through roast quail with sweet potato purée and lemon sauce, to chocolat fondant. The menu is available without charge every week, Tuesday to Saturday lunchtimes, for children aged from four to 11, with an accompanying adult. *See p168* **Eating Posh.**

Roussillon
16 St Barnabas Street, SW1W 8PE (7730 5550/ www.roussillon.co.uk). Sloane Square tube. **Lunch served** noon-2.30pm Mon-Fri. **Dinner served** 6.30-10.30pm Mon-Sat. **Set lunch** £35 3 courses incl half bottle of wine, coffee. **Set dinner** £48 3 courses. **Set meal** £60-£70 tasting menu. **Credit** AmEx, MC, V.
French

Does the chic, stylishly decorated Roussillon serve one of the best-value top-quality lunches in town? A few brightly coloured paintings have been added to this long-time favourite, and a new children's menu was introduced in 2006, which seems to have been a success with smart Chelsea families. (We heard a precocious eight-year-old say, 'Daddy, I've finally managed to tackle eight courses.') This 'Mini-gastronomes', menu offers six courses of such quality as 'jerusalem artichoke soup, truffle ravioli, warm camomile tea' and 'smoked eel, scrambled eggs, almond milk'. It costs £15 per child, but on the first and third Wednesday lunchtimes of every month is free. Service is exemplary too. *See p168* **Eating Posh.**
Children admitted; children's menu.

Paddington & Notting Hill
Geale's
2 Farmer Street, W8 7SN (7727 7528/www.geales. com). Notting Hill Gate tube. **Lunch served** noon-3pm Tue-Sat. **Dinner served** 6-11pm Tue-Sat. **Main courses** £9-£18. **Credit** AmEx, MC, V.
Fish & chips
More than just your average chippie, Geale's has class, with its tablecloths and fresh flowers. Grown ups adore the crab and leek tarts and own-made fish soup, but most people are here for the ginormous portions of fish and chips, all golden and crunchy and moist and flaky where it matters. They do a wicked sticky toffee pudding and a children's menu to boot.
Children's menu. Takeaway and delivery available.

Maroush
68 Edgware Road, W2 2EG (7224 9339/www. maroush.com). Edgware tube. **Open** noon-midnight daily. **Main courses** £12.95-£16. **Credit** AmEx, DC, MC, V.
Lebanese
Marouf Abouzaki's Maroush chain is a big player in Lebanese dining in the capital. In all the branches, the menu is meze-strong, with about 60 options (tabouleh, fatoush, falafel, sambousek are favourites) as well as mixed grills, with plenty of good bread for dipping and lovely, sweet baklava and ma'amul to eat with coffee.
Branches throughout town. Check website for details.

North London
Banners
21 Park Road, Crouch End, N8 8TE (8292 0001/ booking line 8348 2930/www.bannersrestaurant.co.uk). Finsbury Park tube/rail then W7 bus. **Meals served** 9am-11.30pm Mon-Thur; 9am-midnight Fri; 10am-4pm, 5pm-midnight Sat; 10am-4pm, 5-11pm Sun. **Main courses** £9.25-£14.75. **Set lunch** £6.95 soup or salad & side dish. **Credit** MC, V.
Brasserie
A crazy cartoon-painted wall greets you outside this lively venue. A daytime crèche-like atmosphere gives way to a hipper, mellower feel after 7pm. You'll find much that kids will love to eat. The 'world food' encompasses Mexican, Greek, Thai and particularly Caribbean cuisines (jerk being a favourite sauce). Cornmeal-coated calamares with own-made tartare sauce is excellent, so is the tender venison steak. A massive portion of the daily crumble –

Consumer

Brilliant Kids Café & Arts Centre

pineapple and passionfruit smothered in custard – is a rib sticker. The children's menu lists sausage and mash, chicken and chips, burgers, beans on toast and pasta. There's also a £1.95 baby meal of cheesy mash and baked beans. *Buggy access. Children's menu (£4.95). High chairs. No smoking (9am-7pm Mon-Fri).*

Belgo Noord
72 Chalk Farm Road, Chalk Farm, NW1 8AN (7267 0718/www.belgo-restaurants.com). Chalk Farm tube. **Lunch served** noon-3pm Mon-Fri. **Dinner served** 6-11pm Mon-Thur; 6-11.30pm Fri. **Meals served** noon-11.30pm Sat; noon-10.30pm Sun. **Main courses** £8.95-£17.95. **Set lunch** £5.95 1 course incl drink. **Credit** AmEx, DC, JCB, MC, V.
Belgian
Descend into Belgo Noord's expansive cellar-like basement, and you'll find a fine selection of steamed mussels, crisp french fries and one of London's best Belgian beer lists. This is a popular spot with office workers and families with kids; two kids eat free when accompanied by an adult ordering from the à la carte menu. The children's menu includes *stoemp* and wild boar sausages (a Belgian version of bangers and mash), roast chicken with tarragon sauce, and, of course, plenty of chips. Service is swift and friendly. Despite the occasional slip, the food's generally decent. *Children's menu. Colouring books. High chairs.*
Branches: Belgo Bierodrome, 44-48 Clapham High Street, SW4 7UR (7720 1118); Belgo Bierodrome, 67 Kingsway, WC2B 6TD (7242 7469); Belgo Bierodrome, 173-174 Upper Street, N1 1XS (7226 5835); Belgo Centraal, 50 Earlham Street, WC2H 9LJ (7813 2233).

Benihana
100 Avenue Road, Swiss Cottage, NW3 3HF (7586 9508/www.benihana.co.uk). Swiss Cottage tube. **Lunch served** noon-3pm Mon-Sat. **Dinner served** 5.30-10.30pm Mon-Sat; 5-10pm Sun. **Set lunch** £11.50-£33.75 4 courses. **Set dinner** £17-£58 6 courses. **Credit** AmEx, DC, MC, V.
Japanese
Prawns, chicken breast, squid, salmon and other family favourites fly on to the central hotplate and are eaten (after starters of sushi rolls, salad and onion soup) with little bowls of rice. The performance is all, but the food, seasoned with mustard and ginger dips, doesn't take a back seat. It's healthy and delicious – not cheap at about £17 for a modest tuck-in without pudding, and, except for Sundays at lunchtime, there's no children's menu, but it's great for a treat. Lunchtime bento boxes and special deals are more affordable. When the performance is over, however, you're increasingly aware of the corporate nature of this place. As we left, our table was already filling up with new clientele. Nevertheless, Benihana won the Best Family Restaurant category at the 2006 *Time Out* Eating & Drinking Awards. *Buggy access. Children's menu (£10.50-£13.50 6 dishes incl ice-cream, noon-3pm Sun). Disabled access: toilets. High chairs. No-smoking tables. Takeaway service.*
Branches: 37 Sackville Street, W1S 3DQ (7494 2525); 77 King's Road, SW3 4NX (7376 7799).

Brilliant Kids Café & Arts Centre
8 Station Terrace, NW10 5RT (8964 4120/www. brilliantkids.co.uk). **Open** 8am-6pm Mon-Fri; 9am-2pm Sat; phone for details Sunday. *Birthday parties* 2-5pm Sat. **Main courses** £6.50 **Credit** MC, V.
Café

Brilliant is a crisp, bright café, with airy art rooms at the back. It exudes friendliness – of the child- and environmental variety. Food is locally sourced. Baked goods, such as croissants, cakes and breads, come from various artisan bakeries nearby. The big porky sausages, chicken and other meats (all free range, and mostly organic), are sourced from the Devon Rose farm, and other local contacts. The menu may also include tomato and mozzarella quiche, or delicious balsamic chicken with lentils. Finish with chocolate brownie or ice-cream. *See p176.* *Buggy access. High chairs. No smoking.*

Camden Arts Centre Café
Corner of Arkwright Road & Finchley Road, NW3 6DG (7472 5516). Finchley Road or Hampstead tube/Finchley Road & Frognal rail. **Meals served** 10am-5.30pm Tue, Thur-Sun; 10am-8.30pm Wed. **Main courses** £3.95-£7.95. **Credit** MC, V.
Café
This serene café located off the main hulk of the Camden Arts Centre is a great place to sit, relax and bask in the surroundings. Staff are quick to recommend items from a menu that consists mainly of sandwiches, salads and soup of the day. This is one of the most pleasant cafés in north London, especially if you're able to dine outside in the gardens. It's also a family-friendly spot: children's portions of the daily special are offered. *Buggy access. Disabled access: ramps, toilets. High chairs. No smoking. Reduced portions for children. Tables outdoors (10, garden). Takeaway service.*

Gracelands
118 College Road, NW10 5HD (8964 9161/www. gracelandscafe.com). Kensal Green tube. **Open** 8am-6pm Mon-Fri; 9am-5pm Sat; 9.30am-3pm Sun. **Main courses** £4.50-£7. **Credit** MC, V.
Café
For local parents, Gracelands is almost too good to be true. Children can entertain themselves in a play corner (which has a book corner, a home corner and a squashy sofa) while parents drink coffee and take advantage of the wireless internet connection. There's a friendly local feel, highlighted by a noticeboard where people give away outgrown baby stuff and look for childcare. The food is healthy and delicious. Creative quiches (goat's cheese and sweet potato is a favourite combination) and salads show a loving touch. A good selection of sandwiches, panini and breakfasts is boosted by heftier daily specials such as meatballs. Staff are a tad chaotic, in a charming way. Children's and adult workshops are available. *Buggy access. Children's menu. High chairs. No smoking. Tables outdoors (4, pavement; 3, garden). Takeaway service. Toys.*

Haché
24 Inverness Street, Camden Town, NW1 7HJ (7485 9100/www.hacheburgers.com). Camden Town tube. **Meals served** noon-10.30pm daily. **Main courses** £4.95-£10.95. **Credit** AmEx, DC, MC, V.
North American
A posh burger bar, Haché resembles a bijou modern bistro with its fairy lights and fey art. The dishes also take a slightly more sophisticated approach: the Ayrshire steaks are chopped (*haché*, in French) and seasoned before being grilled medium, or cooked as requested. The toppings are excellent: bacon dry-cured in brine, proper cheese, huge mushrooms. Chips are frites-style, skinny or fat. Non-beef

Consumer

burgers include tuna steak, chicken, and three vegetarian variations. Crêpes have recently been added to the dessert options. Although this is a stylish place, it is still very friendly and welcoming to children.
Buggy access. High chairs. Takeaway service.

Lansdowne
90 Gloucester Avenue, NW1 8HX (7483 0409). Chalk Farm tube/31, 168 bus. **Lunch served** noon-3pm Mon-Fri; 12.30-3.30pm Sat; noon-4pm Sun. **Dinner served** 7-10pm Mon-Sat; 7-9.30pm Sun. *Restaurant* **Lunch served** 1-3pm Sat, Sun. **Dinner served** 7-10pm daily. **Main courses** £10-£16.50. **Credit** MC, V.
Gastropub
Getting a table isn't easy in the downstairs bar of this perennially popular pub. The scrawled blackboard menu contains a short, gutsy list that's not afraid to indulge in premium ingredients. Sunday roasts are top-notch. Near the bar you'll find other possibilities including pizzas (a very popular choice, with a kid's-sized margherita for £4.95) and bar nibbles. Lamb chops came with grainy tabouleh and harissa dressing to make a satisfying main course; whole red snapper with sausage, tomato and romanesco was even more generously proportioned and the fish beautifully cooked. To finish: chocolate biscuit cake with cashew cream, apple crumble with custard. No wonder families bring children and grandparents here: there's something for everyone.
Disabled: toilet. High chairs. Tables outdoors (5, pavement).

Mangal II
4 Stoke Newington High Street, Dalston, N16 8BH (7254 7888). Dalston Kingsland rail/76, 149, 243 bus. **Meals served** noon-1am daily. **Main courses** £7-£12. **No credit cards**.
Turkish
Popular with a broad spectrum of locals, including many Turkish families, service here is friendly and efficient. For mains, an adana kebab, juicy kebab, alternating patties of minced lamb and slices of aubergine grilled on a skewer are all excellent. Children love the grilled chicken and *pide* and *saç* bread.
Buggy access. High chairs. Takeaway service.

Marine Ices
8 Haverstock Hill, Chalk Farm, NW3 2BL (www. marineices.co.uk 7482 9003). Chalk Farm tube/31 bus. **Meals served** noon-3pm, 6-11pm Mon-Fri; noon-11pm Sat; noon-10pm Sun. **Main courses** £5.20-£9.60. **Credit** MC, V.
Italian
Designed on a naval theme (hence the name) over 70 years ago, this gelateria/eaterie has been run by the same family since its inception. Marine occupies a soft spot in the heart of many locals of Chalk Farm and Camden, particularly families who bring successive generations to continue dearly held traditions. You'll want to join in with the uninhibited nippers screaming for ice-cream – the frozen treats here are so good they come with their own menu. The pizza and pasta main courses aren't gourmet by any means, but are immensely hearty, as our tomato and cream gnocchi and chilli scampi linguine coated in fluoro-orange sauces attested. Its location is handy for Camden Market, the London Zoo and Regents Park, not to mention shows at the Roundhouse across the road.
Buggy access. High chairs. No smoking. Takeaway service.

Masala Zone
80 Upper Street, Islington, N1 0NU (7359 3399/ www.realindianfood.com). Angel tube. **Lunch served** 12.30-3pm, **dinner served** 5.30-11pm Mon-Fri. **Meals served** 12.30-11pm Sat; 12.30-10.30pm Sun. **Main courses** £6.50-£9. **Thalis** £7-£11.55. **Credit** MC, V.
Indian
'We serve more customers than any other Indian cuisine restaurants within the M25,' boasts Masala Zone. Certainly on our visit, this branch was abuzz. It's a spacious venue decorated with colourful tribal-style murals, an open kitchen, outside seating and, in fine weather, a barbecue at the front. Children will find much to please, both in the location and the menu, which is ideal for sharing. Start with crisp and savoury Bombay beach snacks, then move on to meal-in-one plates, properly prepared curries and thalis.
Buggy access. Children's menu (£3.75 incl ice-cream). High chairs. No smoking. Takeaway service.
Branch: 9 Marshall Street, W1F 7ER (7287 9966); 147 Earl's Court Road, SW5 9RQ (7373 0220).

Ottolenghi
287 Upper Street, Islington, N1 2TZ (7288 1454/ www.ottolenghi.co.uk). Angel tube/Highbury & Islington tube/rail. **Meals served** 8am-11pm Mon-Sat; 9am-7pm Sun. **Main courses** £7.50-£25. **Credit** MC, V.
International
Ottolenghi's long white room looks stunning. The entrance area doubles as a bakery and deli, with puffy meringues, colourful salads and sublime breads to take away or eat in.

Marine Ices

Choose from breakfast dishes (granola or pastries), cakes, sandwiches and other savouries. In the evening, the place shifts emphasis from café to restaurant, with a daily changing menu of small dishes 'from the counter' or 'from the kitchen' (the latter served hot). There's a Mediterranean slant in dishes like fried halibut on a dal and sweet potato mash with minted yoghurt and pitta bread, while other dishes defy categorisation – such as pork belly on a potato and salt cod purée.

Buggy access. Disabled access: toilet. High chairs. No smoking. Reduced portions for children (£3.50). Tables outdoors (2, pavement). Takeaway service.
Branches: 63 Ledbury Road, W11 2AD (7727 1121); 1 Holland Street, W8 4NA (7937 0003).

Pick More Daisies
12 Crouch End Hill, N8 8AA (8340 2288/www. pickmoredaises.com). Finsbury Park tube/rail then W7 bus. **Meals served** 9am-10pm Mon-Fri; 10am-10.30pm Sat, Sun. **Main courses** £8-£15. **Credit** DC, MC, V.
North American
During the day, this Californian-style, gourmet burger joint is busy with unhurried, coffee-drinking mummies. A snackette of (very good, soft, boccata) breadsticks with tiny bowls of houmous and aïoli costs £4.25, making mains at around a tenner seem a better deal. The burgers are indeed gourmet and the quality of the steaks is excellent. The free range chicken used in dishes such as the house caesar salad is admirably tender and the American pancakes on the kids' menu (a snip at £4.50 including a main, skin-on fries and a soft drink) go down a treat. Milk shakes, sundaes

and fresh juices make Daisies a prime venue for family meals out. There are pictures to colour in, puzzles to solve, and even the bill comes in a little pot of M&Ms. *See p180. Disabled access: toilet. High chairs. Kids menu*

La Porchetta
141 Upper Street, Islington, N1 1QY (7288 2488/ www.laporchetta.co.uk). Angel tube. **Dinner served** 5.30pm-midnight Mon-Fri. **Meals served** noon-midnight Sat, Sun. **Main courses** £5.10-£7.50. **Credit** DC, MC, V.
Italian
This Islington branch is by far the best, occupying two roomy floors and serving a budget, varied menu. Food is fresh and filling. The pizzas (26 varieties) are good, spilling over the edge of the plate with decent toppings. Pasta dishes (35 of them) are impressive; there are five salads.
High chairs. No-smoking tables. Reduced portions for children (pasta). Takeaway service.
Branches: throughout town. Call or check the website.

S&M Café
4-6 Essex Road, Islington, N1 8LN (7359 5361). Angel tube/19, 38 bus. **Meals served** 7.30am-11.30pm Mon-Thur; 7.30am-midnight Fri; 8.30am-midnight Sat; 8.30am-10.30pm Sun. **Main courses** £2.50-£7.95. **Credit** MC, V.
Café
Ordering at this breezy, friendly café is slick and painless. Choose three key components from a simple menu plus a daily, changing specials board: first your sausage, then

Pick More Daisies.
See p179.

mash, then your gravy. You might end up ordering two pork bangers in cheesy mash with house gravy, or veggie sausages in 'virgin' mash (no butter) with a neapolitan tomato sauce on top. There are other options – a few pies, salads, desserts such as spotted dick – but, unless opting for one of the excellent fried breakfasts, stick to the S&M as it's too good to miss. Children can choose the same, only smaller, on their menu, which also offers chicken nuggets or fish fingers plus a drink. This branch is a treat: the art deco shopfront of bygone greasy spoon, Alfredo's, has been preserved in all its chrome and Vitrolite glory.

Buggy access. Children's menu (£3.50).
Branches: 268 Portobello Road, W10 5TY (8968 8898); 48 Brushfield Street, E1 6AG (7247 2252).

Toff's

38 Muswell Hill Broadway, Muswell Hill, N10 3RT (8883 8656/www.toffsfish.co.uk). Highgate tube, then 43, 134 bus. **Meals served** 11.30am-10pm Mon-Sat. **Main courses** £7.95-£17.50. **Set meals** (11.30am-5.30pm Mon-Sat) £7.95 1 course incl tea/coffee, bread and butter. **Credit** AmEx, DC, MC, V.

Fish & chips

When you first step foot in Toff's you could be forgiven for thinking it was any other chippie. Behind the takeaway counter, staff in white smocks toss chips into sizzling fryers as they cater for the constant queue of customers. But behind the bustling shop front, through a pair of saloon-style swing doors (children love them), a restaurant offers more serenity. Toff's large choice of fish can be ordered in plain batter, matzo-meal batter, or grilled for a healthier

alternative (a rarity in most chippies). Flaky, generously portioned haddock and melt-in-your-mouth chips were highlights of a recent meal. There's also a well-executed menu for children featuring real fish and home-made chips. For those with stamina, puddings include the likes of own-made tiramisu and crème caramel. There's extra seating in the style of a captain's table.

Buggy access. Children's menu (£3.95). Crayons. Disabled access: toilets. High chairs. Takeaway service.

East London

Arkansas Café

Unit 12, Old Spitalfields Market, Whitechapel, E1 6AA (7377 6999). Liverpool Street tube/rail. **Lunch served** noon-2.30pm Mon-Fri; noon-4.30pm Sun. **Dinner served** party bookings only, by arrangement. **Main courses** £5-£14. **Credit** MC, V.

North American

If it's real barbecue you're after, this is where to go. A word of warning: the Arkansas is not stylish. Seating is whatever Bubba – the gregarious Arkansan owner – has put out that week (folding chairs, church pews). And the walls are covered with pictures of farmyard animals. Still, you don't come here for a glamorous meal – just a hearty, lip-smacking one. Steaming plates of well-sourced, freshly grilled meats are what to order. Kids will love watching the barbecue in action. Options to tickle your smoky fancy include huge platters of juicy pork ribs, and tender steaks of Irish beef. All platters are served (on plastic plates) with potatoes, coleslaw, purple cabbage salad, and beans (cooked from scratch). Puddings are unsubtle and gorgeous (pecan pie, chocolate cake and cheesecake); children might like to share a portion after a hefty main course (£2.75). *Buggy access. Disabled access: toilet (in market). No-smoking tables. Tables outdoors (16, terrace inside market, Sun only). Takeaway service.*

Frizzante at City Farm

1A Goldsmith's Row, Hackney, E2 8QA (7739 2266/ www.frizzanteltd.co.uk). Bus 26, 48, 55. **Meals served** 10am-5.30pm Tue-Sun. **Main courses** £4.50-£7.50. **Credit** AmEx, DC, MC, V.

Café

Being situated within Hackney City Farm might explain the noisy 'herd of animals' atmosphere here. Happily, the food is so good you won't care. The oilcloth-covered tables are heaving with parents and their offspring tucking into healthy foods chosen from the blackboard, and made in the open-plan kitchen. There's own-made lasagne, pastas, herb-crusted chicken and Frizzante's big farm breakfasts. Prices are reasonable, portions large. Our juicy burgers came with delicious roasted potatoes and a big salad, while barbecued chicken had a tangy thai dipping sauce. Drinks include smoothies, tea, coffee and juices. And check out the notice-board – there's always something going on. On our visit it was breastfeeding classes, as well as pottery classes. *Buggy access. Children's menu (£2.50-£3.50). Disabled access: toilets. High chairs. No smoking. Tables outdoors (7, garden). Takeaway service. Toys.*
Branch: Unicorn Theatre, 147 Tooley Street, SE1 2HZ (7645 0500).

Royal China

30 Westferry Circus, Docklands, E14 8RR (7719 0888/www.royalchinagroup.co.uk). Canary Wharf tube/DLR/Westferry DLR. **Meals served** noon-11pm Mon-Thur; noon-11.30pm Fri, Sat; 11am-10pm Sun. **Dim sum served** noon-4.45pm daily. **Main courses** £7-£50. **Dim sum** £2.20-£4.50. **Set meal** £30 per person (minimum 2). **Credit** AmEx, DC, MC, V.

Chinese

Lunching here is consistently more congenial than at any other Royal China branch. Perhaps it's the stunning location, on the brink of the glittering Thames. Perhaps it's knowing that even at weekends you rarely have to queue for long. The food is top-notch. Children adore the pasta-like dumplings on the dim sum menu. Seasonal specials on our last visit included batons of juicy cod in marvellously flaky pastry, and delicate grilled dumplings stuffed with watercress. Dim sum from the regular menu were as good as ever: luxuriantly textured turnip paste, and crisp, deep-fried prawn dumplings served with fruity salad cream. Dinner can be pretty good, but it's the dim sum that shines. Staff are all smiles and very friendly towards children whenever we visit. *Disabled access: toilet. High chairs. Nappy-changing facilities. Tables outdoors (23, terrace). Takeaway service.*
Branches: 40 Baker Street, W1M 1BA (7487 4688); 13 Queensway, W2 4QJ (7221 2535); 68 Queen's Grove, NW8 6ER (7586 4280).

Sông Quê

134 Kingsland Road, Shoreditch, E2 8DY (7613 3222). Bus 26, 48, 55, 67, 149, 242, 243. **Meals served** noon-3pm, 5.30-11pm Mon-Sat; noon-11pm Sun. **Main courses** £4-£9.20. **Credit** MC, V.

Vietnamese

You'll find delicious, authentic Vietnamese food at this rather kitsch-looking caff. The overwhelming menu offers over 170 dishes, including a many regional specialities, and roughly 20 variations of phô (noodle soup: a popular, if messy choice for children). Bi cuon were luscious rice-paper rolls with lettuce, vermicelli, mint and chives. Banh xeo (a bright yellow pancake filled with beansprouts, onions, chicken and prawns) is a greasy, tasty treat. *Buggy access. High chairs. No-smoking tables. Takeaway service.*

Story Deli

3 Dray Walk, The Old Truman Brewery, 91 Brick Lane, E1 6QL (7247 3137). Liverpool Street tube/rail. **Meals served** noon-6pm daily. **Main courses** £5-£9. **Credit** AmEx, MC, V. **Map** p319 S5.

Italian

This 100% organic café and pizzeria is furnished with dis-tressed floorboards, huge butcher-block tables (for com-munal dining) and cardboard packing-case seats. The place is constantly packed with trendy types and their offspring, and on tasting the food it's easy to see why. The pizzas are amazing, a cross between classic thin Neapolitan dough and the delicate pastry of Egyptian fatirs, topped with an inventive range of ingredients: prawns and peppers; ham, aubergine and olive; and rosemary and garlic among them. Other dishes are equally good: prawn kebabs laden with fat prawns, steak sandwiches, the Story burger, roasted cod and aïoli chips, and bowls of salad. For afters, there's a nice selection of cakes and first-rate coffee. *No smoking. Reduced portions for children. Tables outdoors (6, pavement). Takeaway service.*

South-east London

Domali Café

38 Westow Street, Crystal Palace, SE19 3AH (8768 0096/www.domali.co.uk). Gypsy Hill rail. **Meals served** 9.30am-11pm daily. **Main courses** £4.50-£10.90. **Credit** MC, V.

Café

Every home should have a Domali to hand. Wide-ranging (and, where possible, free range, fair trade and largely veg-etarian) fare from breakfast to night-time nourishes all-comers, including pram-pushing parents after a mid-afternoon brie BLT, and post-work locals in for cock-tails. On sunny days, families grab one of the garden tables for lunch: toasties, sandwiches, or hot dishes such as Ribollita (a classic Tuscan bean and cabbage stew). Care and detail abound. An indie jangle at conversational vol-ume spreads around the simple, wooden room. A children's menu is available (the likes of scrambled egg on toast, or pasta of the day), and the chunky chips are fabulous. *Buggy access. High chairs. No-smoking tables. Reduced portions for children (£1.90-£3.50). Tables outdoors (10, garden).*

Dragon Castle

100 Walworth Road, Elephant & Castle, SE17 1JL (7277 3388/www.dragoncastle.co.uk). Elephant & Castle tube/rail. **Meals served** noon-11pm Mon-Thur; noon-11.30pm Fri, Sat; 11.30am-10.30pm Sun. **Main courses** £4.50-£90. **Set meals** £13.50-£22.50 per person (minimum 2). **Credit** AmEx, JCB, MC, V.

Chinese

Park cafés

Brew House

Kenwood, Hampstead Lane, Hampstead Heath, NW3 7JR (8341 5384). Bus 210, 214. **Open** *Oct-Mar* 9am-dusk daily. *Apr-Sept* 9am-6pm daily (7.30pm on concert nights). *Credit* (over £10) MC, V.
Set in the beautiful surroundings of Kenwood House, the Brew House is a self-service café with fabulous cakes and a sunny outdoor seating area. *Buggy access. Children's menu (£2.50-£3.95). High chairs. Nappy-changing facilities. Tables outside (400-seat garden). Takeaway service.*

Common Ground

Wandsworth Common, off Dorlcote Road, SW18 3RT (8874 9386). Wandsworth Common rail. **Open** 9am-5.15pm Tue-Fri; 10am-5.15pm Sat, Sun. **Main courses** £3.50-£9. **Unlicensed.** **Credit** MC, V.
A shady patio overlooks a cricket ground. It's a great place to relax with a sandwich, savoury tart or a few cakes. Inside, the parlour has comfy sofas, a play area and toys and a very child-friendly approach. Indulge in a beer while you tempt kids with a babycino and a fairy cake. *Children's menu. High chairs. Toys.*

Garden Café

Inner Circle, Regents Park, NW1 4NU (7935 5729/www.thegardencafe.co.uk). Baker Street or Regents Park tube. **Open** 10am-dusk daily. **Main courses** £4.25-£12.95. **Licensed.** **Credit** MC, V.
The Garden Café – part full restaurant, part service-counter offering sandwiches and salads – has a smashing location in the middle of Regents Park. Ice-cream comes from the estimable Marine Ices, or there are cakes aplenty. *Tables outdoors.*

Common Ground

Located on the ground floor of a smart new development, this Cantonese restaurant sticks out proudly on the Walworth Road. Inside, crystal chandeliers light a vast dining room. The kitchen produces superb food. Wun tun soup comprised large pork and prawn wun tuns and a little pak choi in a flavourful chicken broth. Daytime dim sum is skilfully produced, with much that would appeal to children. Fresh scallops filled the soft and silky cheung fun; har gau (prawn dumpling) included traditional white fungus rather than the common (and cheaper) bamboo shoot. Staff are friendly too.

The Green

58-60 East Dulwich Road, East Dulwich, SE22 9AX (7732 7575/www.greenbar.co.uk). East Dulwich rail/37, 185 bus. **Breakfast served** 10am-noon, **lunch served** noon-5pm, **dinner served** 6-11pm daily. **Main courses** £9.95-£12.95. **Set lunch** £8.50 2 courses; £11.50 3 courses; (Sun) £16.95 3 courses. *Credit* AmEx, MC, V.

Brasserie
The Green (by Goose Green) offers the young families of gentrified East Dulwich breakfast, lunch and dinner in the spacious but anonymous restaurant, and various in-between snacks in the bar. We enjoyed flavourful coriander, ginger and salmon fish cakes served with a zingy chilli jam (usefully, all starters can be taken as mains). The set lunch menu – which includes the likes of mussels marinière and baked salmon fillet – is good value. Better still are the breakfast choices; the generous set menus (continental, full English, vegetarian) all cost around £5.
Buggy access. Children's menu (£2.20-£7.95). Disabled: toilets. High chairs. No-smoking tables.

Joanna's

56 Westow Hill, Gipsy Hill, SE19 1RX (8670 4052/ www.joannas.uk.com). Crystal Palace or Gipsy Hill rail. **Brunch served** noon-6pm Mon-Sat. **Meals served** 10am-11.00pm Mon-Sat, 10am-10.30pm Sun. **Main courses** £9-£18. **Credit** AmEx, MC, V.

Golders Hill Park Refreshment House

North End Road, Golders Green, NW3 7HD (8455 8010). Golders Green or Hampstead tube. **Meals served** *Summer* 9am-dusk daily. *Winter* 10am-dusk daily. **Main courses** £3-£7. **No credit cards.**
Excellent own-made ices, good-value self-service salads, sandwiches and scones, croissants, muffins and a few cakes and flans. Pasta features heavily, and children's portions are available.
Children's menu (£3-£5). High chairs. Nappy-changing facilities. No smoking. Tables outdoors (25, terrace). Takeaway service.

Inn The Park

St James's Park, SW1A 2BJ (7451 9999/ www.innthepark.com). St James's Park tube. **Open** 8am-11pm Mon-Fri; 9am-11pm Sat; 9am-10pm Sun. **Main courses** £11.50-£14.50. **Credit** AmEx, MC, V. Map p317 K8.
A positive idyll near Duck Island. The classic British food is locally sourced and conscientiously produced, with a children's menu of roast chicken leg and chunky chips, sausage and mash or fish cake with veg. The place is the brainchild of foodie du jour Oliver Peyton.
Buggy access. Children's menu (£7.50). Disabled access: toilets. High chairs. No smoking (inside). Tables outdoors (40). Takeaway service.

Pavilion Café

Dulwich Park, off College Road, Dulwich, SE21 7BQ (8299 1383). North Dulwich or West Dulwich rail. **Open** *Summer* 9am-5.30pm (with some late evenings) daily. *Winter* 9am-dusk daily. **Main courses** £3.50-£6.50. **No credit cards.**

Exceptionally child-friendly, this bright, lively café has plenty of tables inside and family inducements such as ice-creams and frozen yoghurts, sensible own-made specials such as baked potatoes and children's specials like shepherd's pie with two veg (£3.50). Breakfasts, hearty sandwiches and unusual own-made cakes are also served. Children's parties (Mon-Fri, about £5.50 a head) are a speciality.
Buggy access. Children's menu (£1.50-£3.50). Disabled access: toilets . High chairs. Nappy-changing facilities. Tables outdoors (11, terrace). Takeaway service. Toys.

Pavilion Café

Highgate Woods, Muswell Hill Road, N10 3JN (8444 4777). Highgate tube. **Open** *Summer* 8am-7pm daily. *Winter* 9am-dusk daily. **Main courses** £6-£8.95. **Licensed. Credit** AmEx, MC, V.
On the edge of the cricket ground in the middle of Highgate Woods, the Pavilion is strong on locally sourced ingredients. There's a wide selection for kids (pasta, fish, chicken goujons), who are made welcome into the evening.
Children's menu (£3.50). Tables outdoors.

Pavilion Tea House

Greenwich Park, Blackheath Gate, SE10 8QY (8858 9695). Blackheath rail/Greenwich rail/DLR. **Open** 9am-5.30pm Mon-Fri; 9am-6pm Sat, Sun. **Main courses** £4.95-£8.50. **Licensed. Credit** MC, V.
This lovely lunch place is sited by the Royal Observatory. A big draw is the enclosed lawn, with its fab views over Docklands. Hot food has a British bent, and includes smoked salmon and scrambled eggs, welsh rarebit and salads, with plenty of options for children.
Children's menu. High chairs. Tables outdoors.

Brasserie
Classy Joanna's has impressed us with great service and a satisfying menu. Booking the railway carriage towards the back is a popular choice for family groups. Brunch is reasonably priced and mixes oriental dishes like salmon teriyaki alongside such solid British fodder as cottage pie and cumberland sausages. The à la carte menu follows a similar theme, embracing several fish dishes and a choice of meaty platters. The traditional roast dinners on Sundays shouldn't be missed. Opt for an ice-cream for dessert; moreish flavours include vanilla bean, coffee and honey.
Buggy access. Children's menu (£4.95-£5.95 incl ice-cream). High chairs. Tables outdoors (5, pavement).

Olley's

65-69 Norwood Road, Herne Hill, SE24 9AA (8671 8259/www.olleys.info). Herne Hill rail/3, 68 bus. **Meals served** 5-10.30pm Mon; noon-10.30pm Tue-Sun. **Main courses** £8.45-£18.45. **Credit** AmEx, MC, V.
Fish & chips

This celebrated chippie attracts a healthy mix of customers. It occupies two old railway arches knocked together. Olley's fried fish never seems to stop winning awards. It includes the likes of mahi mahi and halibut fillet, which can also come steamed or grilled. The creamy mushy peas are the best in London, and the chips also deserve a mention, being blanched before frying. Don't overlook the Neptune's Punchbowl starter: a creamy own-made soup that's something of a luxury lucky dip, packed with various fish. For the children, there's a wide variety from a sea food platter to a mini cod and chips including soft drink
Children's menu (£4). High chairs. Tables outdoors (12, pavement). Takeaway service. Nappy-changing facilities.

El Pirata

15-16 Royal Parade, Blackheath, SE3 0TL (8297 1880). Blackheath rail. **Meals served** noon-midnight daily. **Main courses** £8-£13. **Tapas** £3.20-£4.90. **Credit** AmEx, DC, MC, V.
Spanish

Consumer

Come here after an afternoon's footie or kite flying expedition on Blackheath. Dishes are big enough for two to share quite happily. Patatas bravas, garlicky mushrooms, spicy chorizo and pincho de pollo (chicken skewers) were all enjoyable, although we also had a couple of dud seafood dishes. The staff are quietly friendly, and we've found them kind to children. Puddings are limited to popular staples, such as ice-creams, bombes, banana fritters and crêpes. *Buggy access. High chairs. Tables outdoors (5, pavement).*

South-west London

Blue Elephant
4-6 Fulham Broadway, Fulham, SW6 1AA (7385 6595/www.blueelephant.com). Fulham Broadway tube. **Lunch served** noon-2.30pm Mon-Fri; noon-4pm Sun. **Dinner served** 7pm-midnight Mon-Thur; 6.30pm-midnight Fri, Sat; 7-10.30pm Sun. **Main courses** £9.50-£28. **Set buffet** (Sun lunch) £22, £11 children 4-11 yrs. **Credit** AmEx, DC, MC, V.
Thai
A carnival atmosphere pervades this lavish restaurant. The interior is a rainforest of palms and topiary, with waterfalls and ponds full of koi carp. It's good fun, in a Las Vegas floorshow kind of way. Children like to be fussed over by the staff, and during Sunday brunch (when they eat for half price) are entertained by face painters. The menu is well thought out, though some exotic-sounding items turn out to be Thai favourites dolled up with flashy names. Flavours are well crafted, witness the orange prawn curry (a creamy, tamarind-flavoured concoction full of cherry tomatoes and jackfruit). The platter of classic starters (mostly deep-fried offerings such as spring rolls) is generally popular with children. *Buggy access. Crayons. Delivery service. Disabled access: toilets. High chairs. Nappy-changing facilities. Takeaway service.*

Boiled Egg & Soldiers
63 Northcote Road, Battersea, SW11 1ND (7223 4894). Clapham Junction rail. **Open** 9am-6pm Mon-Sat; 9am-4pm Sun. **Main courses** £4-£10. **Credit cards** AmEx, DC, MC, V.
Café
The name says it all. Slap-up all-day breakfasts here include the usual fried/scrambled favourites as well as less common smoked haddock and poached egg combos, plus boiled egg and soldiers (served in comedy chicken eggcups). The nursery nostalgia theme continues with Marmite on toast, baked potatoes filled with baked beans and grated cheese, lots of ice-cream and tasty cakes. To drink there are smoothies, milkshakes and jugs of Pimm's. It's a small, squashed space with laid-back (well, a bit haphazard) service and bright decor. Battersea's young crowd (and their kids) love it. *Buggy access. Children's menu (£2.25-£4). High chairs. Tables outdoors (3, pavement; 8, garden). Takeaway service.*

Butcher & Grill
39-41 Parkgate Road, Battersea, SW11 4NP (7924 3999/www.thebutcherandgrill.com). Clapham Junction or Queenstown Road rail/49, 319, 345 bus. **Open Bar** 9am-11pm Mon-Sat; 9am-4pm Sun. **Snacks served** 9am-11pm daily. **Lunch served** noon-11pm Mon-Sat; noon4.30pm Sun. **Main courses** £4.95-£9. *Restaurant* **Lunch served** noon-3.30pm Mon-Sat; noon-4.30pm Sun. **Dinner served** 6-11pm Mon-Sat. **Main courses** £8.50-£25. *Both* **Credit** MC, V, Am Ex
British
The retail area opens into a spacious bar, where you can order pastries or a sandwich; the main dining area is up a short flight of stairs, and there are patio tables overlooking the dock here. There are salads and terrines for starters with bread, but the main thrust of dining is choosing great cuts of British-produced meat, such as barnsley chop, sirloin and rib roasts. The children's menu offers sausage and mash, cheese and ham on toast, a mini roast of the day with beautifully fresh veg and roasties and plaice and chips. *Buggy access. High chairs. Tables outdoors (12, pavement).*

Crumpet
66 Northcote Road, Battersea, SW11 6QL (7924 1117). Clapham Junction rail. **Open** 9am-6pm Mon-Sat; 10am-6pm Sun. **Main courses** £3.95-£6.95. **Credit** AmEx, MC, V.
Café
This place is all about children. Bright, airy and uncluttered, it has ample space for buggies, plenty of high chairs, a special play den at the back and a focus on simple, healthy fare. A tempting assortment of old-fashioned cakes is on display, and the menu offers sandwiches, salads, snacks and smoothies. Soft drinks (ginger beer, lemonade) are all organic. There's a children's menu including cottage pie, sausages and nursery specials, as well as wholesome breakfasts of the porridge or muesli variety. Classroom furniture adds to the sensible nature of the place, which is fantastic for families. *Buggy access. Children's menu (£1.45-£3.95). Disabled access: toilets. High chairs. Nappy-changing facilities. Play area (under-5s). Tables outdoors (2, pavement). Takeaway service.*

Depot
Tideway Yard, 125 Mortlake High Street, SW14 8SN (8878 9462/www.depotbrasserie.co.uk). Barnes Bridge or Mortlake rail/209 bus. **Lunch served** noon-3pm Mon-Fri; noon-4pm Sat, Sun. **Dinner served** 6-11pm Mon-Sat; 6-10.30pm Sun. **Main courses** £9.95-£15. **Set meal** (Mon-Thur) £12.50 2 courses; £15.50 3 courses. **Credit** AmEx, DC, MC, V.
Brasserie
The location, in a courtyard by the Thames, is a big draw. But the food is similarly appealing. Expect the likes of charcuterie or asparagus for starters, and grilled swordfish, roast duck leg and lamb chump for mains. The children's menu includes pasta with various sauces; fish cakes, sausage or chicken strips with roast potatoes; and ice-cream for pudding. There's a monthly prize of a free meal in the 'best colouring-in' competition. *Buggy access. Children's menu (£5.50 incl ice-cream). Crayons. High chairs. Nappy-changing facilities. No-smoking café. Tables outdoors (8, courtyard).*

Dexter's Grill
20 Bellevue Road, Wandsworth, SW17 7EB (8767 1858/www.tootsiesrestaurants.co.uk). Wandsworth Common rail. **Meals served** noon-10pm Mon-Fri; 10am-11pm Sat; 10am-10pm Sun. **Main courses** £7.45-£15.95. **Credit** AmEx, MC, V.
North American

This small branch of the Tootsies tree is a good choice for families. For one thing, it's right on the edge of Wandsworth Common, so you can cap off a play session with a meal. What's more, during the day, the spacious dining room is virtually given over to mothers, push-chairs and toddlers. There's a kind of kiddie heaven in the back devoted to sweets and ice-cream. In the evening, the lights dim and the venue becomes more grown up, reflecting the upmarket neighbourhood in which it sits. The menu is basic Americana that veers from the healthy (big mix-and-match salads, where you can add the meat and dressing of your choice), to the unhealthy (burgers and divine ice-creams), via somewhere in between (steaks). The atmosphere is casual and relaxing.

Buggy access. Children's menu (£5.95-£6.25 2 courses incl drink and dessert). Crayons. Disabled access: toilets. High chairs. Nappy-changing facilities. No-smoking tables. Tables outdoors (8, balcony terrace). Takeaway service.
Branches: throughout town. Phone or check the website.

Fine Burger Company

37 Bedford Hill, SW12 9EY (8772 0266/www. fineburger.co.uk). Balham tube/rail. **Meals served** noon-11pm Mon-Sat; noon-10pm Sun. **Main courses** £5.95-£8.95. **Set lunch** (Mon-Fri) £5.95 burger & drink. **Credit** AmEx, DC, MC, V.
North American

No doubt inspired by the success of the Gourmet Burger Kitchen (*see below*), this upstart has brought deluxe patties to Balham. As well as gourmet burgers, this chain now offers unusual variations such as teriyaki sauce or stilton cheese, but you can also order chicken breast six ways, falafel, minced lamb, even a salmon fish cake in a burger bun. The children's menu includes a smaller burger (with or without cheese), a veggie burger, chicken goujons and chargrilled chicken breast – with a scoop of ice-cream for dessert. In our experience the medium-cooked beefburger is just right, the chips are made from real potatoes and are cooked just-so. We're less sure about some of the side orders, though; onion rings are the size of doughnuts.
Balloons. Buggy access. Children's menu (£4.95-£5.50 incl ice-cream). Crayons. High chairs. Nappy-changing facilities. No smoking. Takeaway service.
Branches: throughout town. Phone or check the website

FishWorks

13-19 The Square, Old Market, Richmond, Surrey TW9 1EA (8948 5965/www.fishworks.co.uk). Richmond tube/rail. **Lunch served** noon-3.30pm, **dinner served** 6-10.30pm Mon-Fri. **Meals served** 9.30am-10.30pm Sat, Sun. **Main courses** £9.50-£25. **Credit** AmEx, DC, MC, V.
Fish

The FishWorks chain is growing at a phenomenal rate. Each branch combines fishmonger, restaurant and cookery school; children find it fascinating to view the fresh species before their meal. This is the biggest outlet to date, housed in an ex-market building with a soaring roof and huge skylight: a lovely, casual spot. The menu offers 'classic' dishes (many in starter or main-course sizes), such as smoked salmon, crab, and skate with black butter and capers, along with seasonal crustacea plus daily specials. Children's meals include fish cakes, own-made fishfingers, mussels, and spaghetti with tomato sauce.

Babies and children welcome: children's menu; high chairs. Booking essential Thur-Sat. Cookery school. Disabled: toilet. Fishmonger. No smoking. Tables outdoors (6, terrace).
Branches: throughout town. Check website for details.

Gourmet Burger Kitchen

44 Northcote Road, Battersea, SW11 1NZ (7228 3309/www.gbkinfo.co.uk). Clapham Junction rail. **Meals served** noon-11pm Mon-Fri; 11am-11pm Sat; 11am-10pm Sun. **Main courses** £5.45-£7.40. **Credit** MC, V.
North American

GBK was the first, and remains our favourite, gourmet burger chain. The sesame-flecked buns have firm texture, the tasty fillings are prime quality, and you'll find no finer Aberdeen Angus beef patties. Portions are huge, and the fat chips are golden, and the extras are no-corners-cut. Among the many fabulous variations is the beetroot- and pineapple-layered kiwiburger: much better than it sounds, honest. Children have a couple of smaller options: the junior burger (the beef cooked well-done, with cheese and tomato sauce) and the junior chicken (breast meat with mayonnaise). Service at this (the original) branch is as friendly and welcoming as ever.
Buggy access. Children's menu (£3.95). High chairs. No smoking. Tables outdoors (4, pavement).
Branches: throughout town. Check website for details.

Jo Shmo's

33 High Street, Wimbledon, SW19 5BY (8439 7766/ www.joshmos.com). Wimbledon tube/rail then 93 bus. **Open** noon-11pm Mon-Sat, noon-10.30pm Sun. **Main courses** £6.95-13.95. **Credit** AmEx, DC, MC, V.
North American

Attractive US diner Joe Shmo's positively embraces the onslaught of families at weekends, with a sensible children's menu, high-chairs and a tolerant attitude to roving toddlers. The restaurant is large enough for waiting staff to seat people with children away from the mainstream clientele. The food is good value and substantial. Splendid burgers (scaled down for children) are thick and juicy. Children may also choose proper hot dogs (and are given free rein with the relish tray), salmon steak and salad, pasta or chicken, as well as a drink.
Children's menu (£4.45 incl drink). Disabled access: toilets, children's menu (£4.45 incl drink). No smoking tables. Tables outdoors.

Marco Polo

Eastfields Avenue, Point Pleasant, SW18 (08714 268448/www.marcopolo.uk.net). East Putney tube. **Open** noon-11pm daily. **Main courses** £7.50 £16.50. **Credit** AmEx, MC, V.
Italian

This modish riverside restaurant is perfectly situated for Wandsworth family groups, and there are a whole lot of them, as we have discovered. There's a useful patch of greensward beside the numerous outdoor tables where leisurewear dads can safely play with their children away from speeding 4X4s. Inside, the restaurant is furnished swishly in dark wood, glass and chrome, with a trendy bar. Children are provided for with £5 pasta dishes and large but pleasantly thin pizzas, with a welcome bowl of ice-cream to follow. This isn't just a pizza and pasta venue, however. A grown-up calf's liver on crushed new potatoes was adeptly pink, and our comforting little filler of

crespolini (pancakes with spinach and ricotta) nicely seasoned. Sunday lunch isn't a great time to go if you're allergic to middle-class family groups.
Buggy access. No-smoking area. Tables outdoors. Takeway service.

Mooli
36A Old Town, Clapham, SW4 0LB (7627 1166/ www.moolirestaurant.com). Clapham Common tube. **Lunch served** noon-3pm, **dinner served** 6.30-11pm Mon-Fri. **Tea served** 3-6pm Mon-Sat. **Meals served** noon-11pm Sat; 1-11pm Sun. **Main courses** £12.95-£14.50. **Credit** MC, V.

Italian
Bedecked with comfy cushions and painted in crème brûlée hues, Mooli is a throughly modern trat. The eclectic menu changes frequently. A risotto dish of the day featured radicchio and gorgonzola, among the pasta dishes, fusilli with broccoli and sausage appealed to us. Italian sausages and mash with gravy, and penne napoletana and parmesan, are on the children's menu. Desserts include own-made pâtisserie, gelatis and sorbets. Mooli has introduced a new service for parents: dine here and send a pizza home for the kids and babysitter.
Disabled access. Children's menu (£4-£5 incl ice cream). Outdoor seating and patio heaters.

Tootsies Grill
120 Holland Park Avenue, Holland Park, W11 4UA (7229 8567/www.tootsiesrestaurants.co.uk). Holland Park tube. **Meals served** 9am-11pm Mon-Thur, Sun; 9am-11.30pm Fri, Sat. **Main courses** £6.95-£13.50. **Credit** AmEx, MC, V.

North American
Parents in London sing the praises of the Tootsies chain. Most branches have elements of their decor in common: round wooden tables, bistro-style chairs, lots of windows and light. The menu promises the 'best burger you've ever eaten'. While that might not be the case, the burgers aren't bad, and the selection is massive, ranging from the usual beef and vegetarian versions to thai chicken burgers, pork and apple burgers, and lamb and rosemary burgers. Children, plied with wax crayons and colouring-in while they wait, have a choice of burgers, hot dogs, ribs or organic pasta meals, with drinks and a build-your-own sundae option for pudding. Junior heaven.
Balloons. Buggy access. Children's menu (£4.95-£6.25 incl drink & dessert). Crayons. High chairs. No smoking. Tables outdoors (3, pavement). Takeaway service. **Branches**: throughout town. Phone or check website.

Victoria
West Temple Sheen, East Sheen, SW14 7RT (8876 4238/www.thevictoria.net). Mortlake rail/33, 337 bus. **Breakfast served** 7-9.30am Mon-Fri; 8-10am Sat, Sun. **Lunch served** noon-2.30pm Mon-Fri; noon-3pm Sat; noon-4pm Sun. **Dinner served** 7-10pm daily. **Main courses** £10.95-£19.95. **Credit** AmEx, MC, V.

Modern European
The ultimate Sunday lunch venue, with its windowed ceiling, the place feels enormous and is flooded with light. Service is bend-over-backwards accommodating. The menu takes pride in its seasonality. To start, spanish salad of salt cod, Ortiz white tuna and boquerones was a mouth-watering pile of delicacies, drenched in excellent vinaigrette. Delicious too were the wild boar and apple sausages with mash and onion gravy. Desserts deserve special mention;

the malted chocolate ice-cream is sublime. A safe play area outside is visible from the restaurant. It could be the ultimate Sunday lunch venue.
Buggy access. Children's menu (£4.50-£5.50). High chairs. Nappy-changing facilities. No smoking (dining area). Play area. Tables outdoors (9, garden & play area).

West London

Bush Garden Café
59 Goldhawk Road, Shepherd's Bush, W12 8EG (8743 6372). Goldhawk Road tube. **Meals served** 8.30am-7.30pm Mon-Fri; 9am-5pm Sat. **Main courses** £3.50-£4.60. **Credit** (over £10) AmEx, MC, V.

Café
This wholesome haven is frequented by all types, including mothers and children in need of a treat. Outside is a garden/play area. Standard café fare sits next to more exotic options on the menu, such as the refreshing acerola (a Brazilian fruit) smoothie or the Heidi pie, made with sweet potato, spinach and goat's cheese. The soups are a good bet, and we've also enjoyed scrambled eggs and salmon bagels for breakfast. Own-made cakes are a treat. The bohemian vibe is welcome, as are the heaving shelves of organic produce available to buy.
Buggy access. High chairs. Nappy-changing facilities. No smoking. Tables outdoors (5, garden).

High Road Brasserie
162-166 Chiswick High Road, W4 1PR (8742 7474/www.highroadhouse.co.uk). Turnham Green tube. **Open** 7am-midnight Mon-Thur; 7am-1am Fri; 8am-1am Sat; 8am-11pm Sun. **Main courses** £10-£22. **Credit** AmEx, MC, V.

Brasserie
With its pillars and mirrors, french windows and canopied pavement seats, ithis s a stunning-looking place. You can eat lighter options such as club sandwiches or salads, through a good seafood list, to roasted and grilled meats; most dishes are in the European brasserie mould. The children's menu includes organic chicken, spaghetti and own-made fishfingers. Desserts, from caramelised lemon tart to summer pudding, are tempting too. We found the service professional, attentive and charming.
Children's menu. Crayons. High chairs. Toys. Booking advisablechildren allowed only till 7pm. Disabled: toilet. Tables outdoors heated (14, terrace).

Pacific Bar & Grill
320 Goldhawk Road, W6 0XF (8741 1994). Stamford Brook tube. **Meals served** 11-11.30pm Mon-Sat; noon-10.30pm Sun. **Main courses** £9.95-£16.50. **Credit** AmEx, MC, V.

North American
Choices in this airy space run from New England clam chowder to Californian chardonnay risotto with enoki mushrooms. The children's menu includes fishcake, grilled chicken and penne pasta. A ribeye steak was tender and flavourful, yet the chips seemed flaccid. Cheesecake was a Yank-sized, triangle of tangy creaminess. At weekends the usual menu gives way to brunch dishes such as buttermilk pancakes with bacon, eggs and maple syrup.
Babies and children welcome: children's menu; crayons; high chairs; magician (1-3pm Sun). No smoking. Tables outdoors and heated. (12, terrace).

Shopping

Time to raise their pocket money.

Striking out for the West End, piggy bank in hand, to showy emporia like **Hamley's** (*see p208*) and the **Disney Store** (*see p207*), will certainly be an event for a child – worth it for the spectacle, if not the cost of the goods. Bustle aplenty can also be found at many of the city's street markets. It would be daft not to introduce the nippers to these glories of London life: where the entertainment is free and the prices are often eye-poppingly low. So many of the best ones are surrounded by excellent lunching spots, you can structure a whole day out round a decent market, so we've picked out our favourites on p208.

Bustle isn't always what you want if you've toddlers to control and essential supplies to buy, however, so we've listed our favourite children's fashion, equipment, toy and book retailers around the capital. Many have diversions for the young ones, leaving you in peace to purchase.

Petit Chou.
See p214.

All-rounders

Daisy & Tom
181-183 King's Road, Chelsea, SW3 5EB (7352 5000/ www.daisyandtom.com). Sloane Square tube then 11, 19, 22, 49 bus. **Open** *9.30am-6pm Mon, Tue, Thur, Fri; 10am-7pm Wed; 9.30am-6.30pm Sat; 11am-5pm Sun.* **Credit** *AmEx, MC, V.* **Map** *p313 E12.*

Four times a day there's a call for children to gather at the ground-floor carousel, for a spin on a painted prancing horse or galloping chicken. Rides take place about every hour at busy times of year, every couple of hours at other times. We'd say that was reason enough for charging over to this excellent all-round children's paradise. After the musical ride there's the half-hourly Peter and the Wolf puppet show upstairs in the clothing department, or the delightful book section where browsing is encouraged. For those actually planning to shop, the range of baby equipment has all the fashionable stuff (like the Bugaboo Cameleon with a footboard for the toddler, £599, or the last word in car seats from Apprica), as well as more affordable bestsellers from Stokke, Baby Comfort and Silver Cross. The toy selection is vast (from Geomag and Lego kits to £2,000-plus handmade rocking horses), with plenty of toys around for children to try. Shaggy children can be shorn by the resident hairdresser (*see p188*). The first-floor clothing department carries Daisy & Tom in abundance, Timberland, Elle, Catimini and more. There's also a One Small Step One Giant Leap concession.
Buggy access. Disabled access: ramp, toilet. Hairdressing. Mail order. Nappy-changing facilities. Play area.

Harrods
87-135 Brompton Road, Knightsbridge, SW1X 7XL (7730 1234/www.harrods.com). Knightsbridge tube. **Open** *10am-8pm Mon-Sat; noon-6pm Sun.* **Credit** *AmEx, DC, MC, V.* **Map** *p313 F9.*

The mother of all posh department stores, Harrods isn't devoid of tackiness. Nonetheless, service is usually friendly on the fourth-floor children's universe, which has the brilliant Toy Kingdom (enquiries 7225 6781). Clothes begin with baby-cool pieces from modish labels like No Added Sugar and go through ultra-smart tweedy garb with the Harrods label, to streetwear with school uniforms (22 London schools represented) along the way. Couture 'casualwear' with styles for newborns onwards includes mini togs by Burberry, Christian Dior, Moschino and Armani. The excellent Bunny London (*see p197*) also has a collection here. Footwear includes Start-rite, Naturino and Instep. There's face-painting, haircutting and lots of interactive fun in the holidays and on selected weekends. The nursery department carries all the famous names prams and buggies, cots, beds and high chairs.
Buggy access. Café. Car park. Delivery service. Disabled access: lift, toilet. Hairdressing. Mail order. Nappy-changing facilities.

Shorn of the head

Looking for a place that will mark the occasion of your shaggy toddler's first haircut with due ceremony? Or is your infant in desperate need of a fringe trim and tidy up in time for school? Whatever your child's barnet requirements, there are many shops listed in this chapter whose specialist kiddie crimpers have their scissors and smiles at the ready.

Harrods (see p187) offer the swankiest – and priciest – haircuts. A no-frills job is £20; the first haircut with certificate and photo costs £30. At the branch of **Caramel** on Ledbury Road (see p197) a friendly cutter comes in on Saturdays and Wednesdays and charges £15-£30, depending on the artistry required; first haircuts are marked with the ceremonious handing over of a lock of baby hair. After the trauma, you can have refreshments in the café.

Mini Kin (see p193) also has a children's hairdressing salon, with animal-themed seats and the possibility of mini makeovers. Baby haircuts start at £10.95; the special first haircut, with lots of fuss, a certificate and samples, costs £15.95. Little girlies love to have their long hair especially dressed with plaits and sparkle; ring for details. **Daisy & Tom** (see p187), always a treat to visit, whatever the reason, has a hairdresser who charges £8 for a fringe trim, £14 for a long hair cut and £16 for that tear-jerking first haircut with photo and certificate. Children being shorn at **Trotters** (see p202) have the added calming influence of a huge tank of tropical fish to gaze at (haircuts cost £13 for age three and under; £14 for older children). At the **Little Trading Company** young customers can watch videos and DVDs while Diane attends to

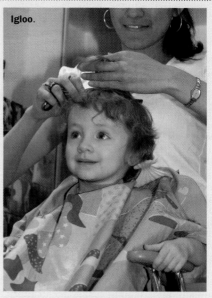

Igloo.

their hairdos (£10.50, Wed, Fri and Sat). Kim comes in to **Their Nibs** (see p200) on a Monday after school, and will cut your child's hair for £10.50. **Little Stinkies** (see p211) offers a good-value first haircut with certificate for £12; ordinary snips are £10, available Tue-Sat. Cheapest of all, however, are the haircuts at **Igloo** (see p202) haircutting station, where £5 buys you a no-nonsense fringe trim.

JoJo Maman Bébé

68 Northcote Road, Battersea, SW11 6QL (7228 0322/www.jojomamanbebe.co.uk). Clapham Junction rail. **Open** 9.30am-5.30pm Mon-Sat; 11am-5pm Sun. **Credit** MC, V.

Best known as a catalogue-based retailer (only a selection of its vast stock of clothing, equipment and furniture is displayed in the shop), JoJo also has several London stores that are popular in areas of high child density. The stores are spacious and attractive; the distinctive Breton-inspired pregnancy and children's wear is relaxed and affordable. A strong code of ethical business practice is exemplified by the well-priced organic cotton baby-clothes range (striped wraparound baby suits from £10). There are many brightly striped fleeces and sweatshirts, as well as easy-wash cottons for comfort, a great range of maternity wear and any number of bright ideas for the nursery, home and people carrier – from packs of muslin squares, to drop-sided cots and car seat accessories. Larger nursery essentials may need to be ordered from the catalogue.
Buggy access. Delivery service. Disabled access. Mail order. Nappy-changing facilities.
Branches: 3 Ashbourne Parade, 1259 Finchley Road, Golders Green, NW11 0AD (8731 8961); 80 Turnham Green Terrace, Chiswick, W4 1QN (8994 0379).

John Lewis

278-306 Oxford Street, W1A 1EX (7629 7711/ www.johnlewis.co.uk). Bond Street or Oxford Circus tube. **Open** 9.30am-7pm Mon-Wed, Fri, Sat; 9.30am-8pm Thur; noon-6pm Sun. **Credit** MC, V.
Map p314 H6.

Recent renovations have given this family favourite a light, bright aspect, thanks to a partly glazed roof that allows a view of seven floors of consumer paradise. Add a spruced-up restaurant on the fifth floor and a fourth floor dedicated to children, and parents agree this is one of the nicest shops for all children's needs. Great for school uniforms, John Lewis is also legendary for well-designed children's-wear, toys, nursery furniture and down-to-earth buying-for-baby advice. The toy department contains a pleasant balance of the latest toys and educational playthings, and many toys are left out for children to test. There's also a car-seat fitting advisory service. The children's shoe department (Clarke's, Start-rite, Kangaroo, Timberland) has a queue-resistant computerised ticketing system, computer games, CBBC on the telly, even free face-painting in those summer-holiday shoe-buying weeks. It's almost preternaturally serene and scores a perfect ten.
Buggy access. Cafés. Delivery service. Disabled access: lifts, toilets. Mail order. Nappy-changing facilities.

Consumer

Little White Company

90 Marylebone High Street, W1U 4QZ (7486 7550/ www.thewhitecompany.com). Baker Street or Bond Street tube. **Open** 10am-7pm Mon-Sat; 11am-5pm Sun. **Credit** MC, V. **Map** p314 G5.

Christian Rucker, one of the founders of the hugely successful White Company, started up the little one, in Chelsea, after she had her own little one, Tom. She'd been looking for affordable, top-quality linen and baby clothes, but hadn't been impressed, so she started sourcing her own. The stock grew, so did her boy, and everyone's happy with the soft furnishing and children's clothes in the dedicated children's shops. With classic boys' T-shirts from £5, long-sleeved seersucker PJs for ages up to ten for £20 and soft cotton nighties and beach dresses from £20 and £16 respectively, this reliable label keeps the prices low. The sweetest, softest white and patterned baby-suits cost from £10. Stylish bedding, including a hand-quilted bedspread with a rocket and planets motif, is £150. Attractive wooden nursery furniture is also sold.

Mamas & Papas

256-258 Regent Street, W1B 3AF (0870 830 7700/ www.mamasandpapas.co.uk). Oxford Circus tube. **Open** 10am-8pm Mon-Wed, Fri; 10am-9pm Thur; 9am-8pm Sat; noon-6pm Sun. **Credit** AmEx, MC, V. **Map** p314 J6.

This swish flagship nursery store promulgates the sort of pregnancy and life-with-baby images you read about in magazines. It seems a thousand miles away from the mewling, puking, sleep-deprived experience of procreation most parents complain about. Still, the cool, idyllic Mamas & Papas look is seductive, and so is this spacious, bright shop. There are more than 2,000 products sold here. As well as the renowned stylish baby travel systems (buggies, prams, car seats and contraptions that provide all three items – priced from about £450), there's tasteful nursery furniture, essentials such as changing mats, all kinds of toiletries and massage oils, baby clothes, pregnancy clothes and gifts. Velvety baby basics cost from £10 for a sleepsuit. The café, Cibo is a soothing place for a healthy lunch. *Buggy access. Café. Mail order. Nappy-changing facilities.*

Mothercare

461 Oxford Street, W1C 2EB (7629 6621/ www.mothercare.com). Marble Arch tube. **Open** 9am-8pm Mon-Sat; noon-6pm Sun. **Credit** AmEx, MC, V. **Map** p314 G6.

This well-equipped three-floored branch of the parents' saviour has everything for that first mad dash before baby arrives (breastpads, wipes, muslins and nappies, high chairs and cots), plus most things you'll need later – not least, a decent range of easy-fold, bus-friendly buggies (from £30) and more elaborate travel systems incorporating carry-cots and car seats (like the gawky looking Quinny Buzz three-wheeler, £330). Prices are fair for all the basics. Newborns' sleep-suits are £12 for three, and T-shirts for boys and girls cost from £6. Although still a bit pink and blue in the respective girl/boy collections, the styles are far less staid than you would imagine, and the Moda maternity wear is very good. This branch was anticipating a relocation further down Oxford Street as we went to press: ring or check the website for details. *Buggy access. Delivery service. Disabled access. Mail order. Nappy-changing facilities.* **Branches**: throughout town. Check website for details.

Educational

Books

Several of the toy shops listed on pp207-214 also stock children's picture books.

Bookseller Crow on the Hill

50 Westow Street, Crystal Palace, SE19 3AF (8771 8831/www.booksellercrow.com). Gypsy Hill rail. **Open** 10am-7pm Mon-Fri; 9.30am-6.30pm Sat; 11am-5pm Sun. **Credit** AmEx, MC, V.

The Crow family's book-filled nest is a local landmark, and Justine Crow's thoughts on literature and domestic dramas are a must-read in *Families South East*. There's a wealth of baby, toddler, child, teen, parent and grandparent literature, alongside modern classics for youth – Rosen, Horowitz, Wilson and Rowling. *Buggy access. Mail order. Play area.*

Bookworm

1177 Finchley Road, Temple Fortune, NW11 0AA (8201 9811/www.thebookworm.uk.com). Golders Green tube. **Open** 9.30am-5.30pm Mon-Sat; 10am-1.30pm Sun. **Credit** MC, V.

This much-loved specialist children's bookshop has cosy spaces for reading. The stock is exemplary – everything is covered. Twice-weekly storytelling sessions for under-fives take place on Tuesdays and Thursdays (2pm), when badges and stickers are handed out and friendships forged. Local authors might drop by for signings. *Buggy access. Disabled access. Mail order.*

Children's Bookshop

29 Fortis Green Road, Fortis Green, N10 3HP (8444 5500). Highgate tube, then 43, 134 bus. **Open** 9.15am-5.45pm Mon-Sat; 11am-4pm Sun. **Credit** AmEx, MC, V.

Quiet, well-stocked and roomy, this is a good atmosphere in which to peruse rows of neatly ordered shelves full of colour and interest. There's a children's corner with picture books at floor level. Book-related events, sch as regular author signings, are publicised in a quarterly newsletter, which also carries reviews of new titles. *Buggy access. Mail order.*

Daunt Books

51 South End Road, South End Green, NW3 2QB (7794 8206/www.dauntbooks.co.uk). Belsize Park or Hampstead tube. **Open** 9am-6pm Mon-Sat; 11am-6pm Sun. **Credit** MC, V.

This friendly branch of the well-loved independent has a cosy, low-ceilinged play area, with stacks of picture books and comics, and mini beanbags to lounge on while reading. There isn't a single children's classic missing. *Buggy access. Mail order. Play area.* **Branches**: 193 Haverstock Hill, NW3 4QG (7794 4006); 83 Marylebone High Street, W1U 4QW (7224 2295); 112-114 Holland Park Avenue, W11 4UZ (7727 7022).

Golden Treasury

29 Replingham Road, Southfields, SW18 5LT (8333 0167/www.thegoldentreasury.co.uk). Southfields tube. **Open** 9.30am-6pm Mon-Fri; 9.30am-5.30pm Sat; 10.30am-4.30pm Sun. **Credit** MC, V.

Consumer

Attractively laid out, with themed cabinets full of, say, fairy favourites, Horrible Histories, Beatrix Potter or Doctor Seuss, this is a spacious treasury for local parents. The central reading area has little tables and chairs, a buggy ramp and enough room for small children to bustle about. There's also plenty of reading matter for teens; authors include Meg Rosoff and Kate Thompson. Parents aren't forgotten either, with books on parenting, coping with family ill health and other such adult preoccupations, not to mention the stand of books about SATS and attendant unpleasantness. Frowning aspirational mums are always buying such publications.
Buggy access. Play area.

Lion & Unicorn
19 King Street, Richmond, Surrey TW9 1ND (8940 0483/www.lionunicornbooks.co.uk). Richmond tube/rail. **Open** 9.30am-5.30pm Mon-Fri; 9.30am-6pm Sat; 11am-5pm Sun. **Credit** MC, V.
'The Roar' is this bookshop's quarterly newsletter. It's invaluable for news about book signings, special events such as the latest, and last, Harry Potter launch (and consequent all-night queuing) and reviews of books. Staff, all specialists, are happy to advise on holiday reading. The reading matter crammed into the various rooms of this exciting shop is certainly diverse, and caters for all ages. Children like to spot their favourite author among the photos pinned up behind the till. The great Roald Dahl was one of the first visiting authors; Jacqueline Wilson and Anthony Horowitz have also popped in for a signing. Displays are broken up into Current Favourites, children's picture books, reads for eight to 12s, and teen books. One wall is devoted to reference books and dictionaries.
Buggy access. Mail order.

Never Ending Story Bookshop
59 North Cross Road, East Dulwich, SE22 9ET (8693 0123/www.theneverendingstorybookshop.com). East Dulwich rail. **Open** 10am-5pm Tue-Fri; 10am-6pm Sat. **Credit** MC, V.
This small, neat bookshop is also headquarters for Future Matters, a family welfare consultancy that covers parenting programmes and play therapy. All the old favourites, from the Mr Men to Jacqueline Wilson, are lined up on the shelves, and there are educational toys and text books for sale. A central rug and toy basket keeps the tinies happy while siblings and parents browse and chat to the helpful proprietor. The shop sees regular book signing events from children's authors, including local wordsmith Gareth Jones.

Owl Bookshop
209 Kentish Town Road, Kentish Town, NW5 2JU (7485 7793). Kentish Town tube. **Open** 9.30am-6pm Mon-Sat; noon-4.30pm Sun. **Credit** AmEx, MC, V.
Children's titles in this general bookshop are sorted by age and interest. There are usually special deals; three for two on picture books is a favourite. The Owl hosts readings by local children's authors and, in term-time, schoolchildren come to listen (join the mailing list for times).
Buggy access. Mail order.

Tales on Moon Lane
25 Half Moon Lane, Herne Hill, SE24 9JU (7274 5759/www.talesonmoonlane.co.uk). Herne Hill rail/3, 37, 68 bus. **Open** 9.15am-5.30pm Mon-Sat; 11am-4pm Sun. **Credit** MC, V.

The window displays in this delightful children's bookshop pull you right in. The range of reading matter is wide, and there are lovely displays of picture books for pre-schoolers. Regular storytelling sessions are very popular (turn up early for a place on the sofa). Local authors Jennie Walters and Garry Parsons are regular visitors. A serious player in Southwark Council's efforts to get local children reading, Tales runs a scheme with the NCT (National Childbirth Trust) whereby each new mum receives a voucher to cover the cost of her baby's first book.
Buggy access. Mail order.

Victoria Park Books
174 Victoria Park Road, Hackney, E9 7HD (8986 1124/www.victoriaparkbooks.co.uk). Bethnal Green tube/rail. **Open** 10am-5.30pm daily. **Credit** MC, V.
This cheery little bookshop has a central space with tables, chairs and toys, where young readers can test the wares while the wallet holder browses. Stock is divided into user-friendly sections: history (plenty of Horrible Histories), art, stories from around the world, dinosaurs, and baby and toddler books, a Ladybird corner and more. Teenagers are well catered for, and there's adult fiction too (plus parenting books). Staff are enthusiastic and author visits are arranged regularly. There's a reading group for under-fives, on Friday morning at 11am.
Buggy access. Delivery service. Play area.

Musical instruments

Chappell of Bond Street
152-160 Wardour Street, W1F 8YA (7432 4400/ www.chappellofbondstreet.co.uk). Bond Street or Oxford Circus tube. **Open** 9.30am-6pm Mon-Fri; 10am-5.30pm Sat. **Credit** AmEx, MC, V.
Map p317 K7.
It keeps the Bond Street in its name, but the long-established Chappell moved to this three-storey shop in autumn 2006. The firm reckons to have the largest range of printed music in Europe for sale here. A Yamaha specialist, Chappell is also renowned for keyboards; many musicians drop in to tickle the ivories. Certain instruments (typically flutes, saxes, clarinets, trumpets) may be available on a rent-to-buy scheme, but quarter- and half-size instruments must be purchased; the child is measured beforehand. Recorders are the most popular instruments for youngsters to begin on; Yamaha sells colourful ones for about £6.
Delivery service. Mail order.

Dot's
132 St Pancras Way, Camden Town, NW1 9NB (7482 5424/www.dotsonline.co.uk). Camden Town tube/Camden Road rail. **Open** 9am-5.30pm Mon-Sat. **Credit** MC, V.
'Dot is the best!' reads an enthusiastic message on this popular music shop's online noticeboard. Run by an experienced music teacher, Dot's sells new instruments – mostly stringed and wind – from, say, £5 for a recorder, £40 for a guitar and £59 for a violin. There's a rent-to-buy scheme too, with hire costs eventually offsetting the purchase price should a child show consistent interest. The great joy here is receiving unpressured advice (and a cup of coffee) in a friendly setting. A notice board holds advertisements for tuition and second-hand instruments, and details about Dot's own recorder club. There's also a repair service.
Mail order.

Dulwich Music Shop

*9 Upland Road, East Dulwich, SE22 9EE (8693 1477).
East Dulwich rail/12, 40, 185 bus.* **Open** 9.30am-
5.30pm Mon, Tue, Thur-Sat. **Credit** AmEx, MC, V.
Rent rises at this shop's previous West Dulwich address
have necessitated the move here, but the operation remains
the same. It still specialises in guitars and string instruments; staff are helpful if you're looking to invest in used
or new instruments and sheet music, and there are various
price lists for wind, brass and string instruments, including hire and buy-back prices. Reeds, strings and cleaning
cloths are also sold, alongside knick-knacks, gifts, CDs and
stationery. There's a repair service, too. Recorders, for
those early days of parent-torture, cost from £5.10.
Buggy access. Mail order.

Northcote Music

*155C Northcote Road, Battersea, SW11 6QB (7228
0074). Clapham Junction rail.* **Open** 10.30am-6pm
Mon-Sat. **Credit** MC, V.
A tiny, friendly place to buy your child's first recorder
(from £4.99) and ask advice about purchasing the big stuff.
Northcote squeezes string, percussion and wind
instruments into the space, as well as brass and digital
equipment. They also carry out minor repairs (specialist
jobs are sent out) and rent woodwind, sring and brass
instruments. A broad spectrum of sheet music is sold too.
Buggy access. Delivery service. Mail order.

Robert Morley Lewisham

*34 Engate Street, Lewisham, SE13 7HA (8318 5838/
www.morleypianos.com). Lewisham DLR/rail.* **Open**
9.30am-5pm Mon-Sat. **Credit** MC, V.
This family firm is reassuring in its dealings with nervous
parents. To see if a child is serious about owning a piano,
Morley's will hire one out, charging £250 to include
delivery, then monthly rental starting from £30. If, after a
year, the child is still keen on the piano, the family can buy
it, and get half their rental payments off the price, plus half
the delivery charge. Morley's also builds pianos, clavichords, harpsichords and virginals.
Buggy access. Delivery service.

Educational toys & games

Education Interactive

*10 Staplehurst Road, Hither Green, SE13 5NB
(8318 6380/www.education-interactive.co.uk).
Hither Green rail.* **Open** 9.30am-5.30pm Mon-Wed,
Fri, Sat; 9.30am-6.30pm Thur. **Credit** MC, V.
High-quality educational resources are the big deal in this
Hither Green and online shop. The idea is to provide games
for children that stimulate thinking through intrigue,
involvement and engagement. The brainchild of
'educationalists in mathematics and in equalities', EI can
also work with teachers and parents to provide low-cost,
high-quality education. Games, puzzles and activities

Something to chew on

We hesitate to recommend them, as tabloids
scream about 14-stone eight-year-olds and Type II
diabetes, but the traditional candy shops that
opened on a wave of nostalgia a couple of years
ago are continuing to make life sweeter on the
high street. For children allowed to blow pocket
money on aniseed twists and jaw-locking toffee
bonbons, the first stop should be the inimitable
Hope & Greenwood, where Miss Hope and Mr
Greenwood dress in vintage clothes to sell sweets
over a marble-topped counter; choose from over
175 jars of cola cubes, acid drops, cough candy,
sarsaparilla tablets and flying saucers. There
are also handmade chocolates, sugar mice, 5p
chocolate eggs and chewy liquorice whips. In
Clapham, **Lollipop** is co-owned by Dani Policane,
who found that his previous venture, a deli, was
selling more confectionery than any other item,
so he sold up and opened this sweet shop. It
stocks 140 classic sweets from around the UK.
Dani, and his partner Virginia Oldani, collect old
toys; a 1960s Pelham puppet presides over the
sherbet pips. Meantime, in Greenwich, David and
Anglea Fireman became so intoxicated by the idea
of proper sweets that they threw in their jobs in
advertising to take on an old family business – a
small, neat, sweet shop in the market called **Mr
Humbug**, where antique shelves are lined with
floral gums, sherbet pips, rosy apples, comfits,
marshmallows, bonbons, gobstoppers and
humbugs, all served in 100g portions in little pink
and white striped bags. Finally, a sweet shop that
isn't so much as traditional as, er, cosmopolitan,

Cybercandy Superette of Brighton and the rest
of the world, and now of Covent Garden, is one
of the best sources of jellybeans, Hello Kitty gum,
chocolate-covered insects, sour fish and unusual
varieties of candy bar we know of. Try getting your
laughing gear round that lot without an emergency
trip to the dentist.

CyberCandy Superette

*3 Garrick Street, Covent Garden, WC2E 9BF
(0845 838 0958/www.cybercandy.co.uk). Covent
Garden or Leicester Square tube.* **Open** 10am-
10pm Mon-sat; 11am-8pm Sun. **Credit** MC, V.

Hope & Greenwood

*20 North Cross Road, East Dulwich, SE22 9EU
(8613 1777/www.hopeandgreenwood.co.uk).
East Dulwich rail/12, 40, 176, 185 bus.*
Open 10am-6pm Mon-Sat; 11am-5pm Sun.
Credit MC, V.

Lollipop

*201 St John's Hill, Battersea, SW11 1TH (7585
1588). Clapham Junction rail.* **Open** 10.15am-
6.30pm Tue-Sat; noon-5.30pm Sun. **Credit** MC, V.

Mr Humbug

*Unit 12, Greenwich Market, Greenwich, SE10 9HZ
(7871 4944/www.mrhumbug.com). Cutty Sark
DLR/Greenwich rail/DLR.* **Open** 11am-5.30pm
Mon-Fri; 10am-5.30pm Sat, Sun. **No credit cards**.

Consumer

high-quality education. Games, puzzles and activities include delights such as Auntie Pasta's Fraction Game, electronic sudoku, amusing Fraction Action snap and the ever-popular Polydron. Phone to check before visiting, as the shop sometimes has to close for complicated mathematical reasons.

Fun Learning

Bentall's Centre, Clarence Street, Kingston-upon-Thames, Surrey KT1 1TP (8974 8900). Kingston rail. **Open** 9am-6pm Mon-Wed, Fri, Sat; 9am-8pm Thur; 11am-5pm Sun. **Credit** MC, V.
Yes, everything's more or less educational, but the breadth of stock (for learning and pure, unalloyed fun) is impressive. Fun Learning covers all types of play: creative, quiet, thoughtful, raucous, and computer-based (harmless games like Shrek are stocked, but most computer games are of an educational bent). Large sections are devoted to puzzles and number games, art and craft activities, and science experiments. Pocket-money-priced items include balloon-making gunk, bouncy balls, puzzles and magnifying glasses. Less affordable are the stunt kites and the tempting Observer 60 Altaz Refractor Astronomical Telescope (£99), which will show you lunar craters, Saturn's rings, Jupiter's moons, star clusters and nebula.
Buggy access. Disabled access.
Branch: Brent Cross Shopping Centre, NW4 3FP (8203 1473).

Equipment & accessories

Baby gifts

Blossom Mother & Child

164 Walton Street, South Kensington, SW3 2JL (0845 262 7500/www.blossommotherandchild.com). South Kensington tube. **Open** 10am-6pm Mon-Sat; noon-5pm Sun. **Credit** MC, V. **Map** p313 E10
This softly scented maternity wear specialist, with its cool green paintwork and pink blossom motif, is a calming place for hot and bothered pregnant mums. Here you can buy Zita West's bump massage oils and Baby's Bliss morning sickness magic. Clothes are designed to flatter the temporarily full-frontal look. There are plenty of things for the baby too. Clothing for infants from birth to one year old includes gift sets of little blankets, trousers, tops and a hat. Angel Baby toiletries, lotions and potions for baby bathing and baby massage, are also sold.
Mail order.

Mini Kin

22 Broadway Parade, Crouch End, N8 9DE (8341 6898). Finsbury Park tube/rail then W7 or 41 bus. **Open** 9.30am-5.30pm Mon-Sat; 10.30am-4.30pm Sun. **Credit** MC, V.
Everything gorgeous, organic, hypo-allergenic and gentle for babies, infants and the healthy pregnancies prior to them, fills the shelves at the front of this smart little venue. Hence you'll find Aviva unguents, SOS toiletries for eczema-traumatised skin, and Burt's Bees salves, creams and lotions for natural healing. Elsewhere, there are carriers by Baby Björn, organic cotton and wool baby clothes, potties, soft leather baby shoes, beakers, and bottles. Mini Kin also has a children's hairdressing salon (*see p188*).
Buggy access. Disabled access. Hairdressing. Nappy-changing facilities. Play area.

The Best On the web: accessories

Aspen & Brown
www.aspenandbrown.com/0870 011 0511.
Quality baby and christening gifts.

Bright Minds
www.brightminds.co.uk/0870 442 2144.
Sparky ideas that make learning fun.

Bump to 3
www.bumpto3.com/0870 606 0276.
Useful products for pregnant mums and suckling babes, plus Grobag sleeping bags. Toys such as wooden boats, and dressing-up sets.

Pedlars
www.pedlars.co.uk/01330 850400.
Eclectic mixture of toys, family games, music, books and more.

Talking Book Shop
www.talkingbooks.co.uk/7491 4117.
An excellent selection of contemporary and classic children's books on tape, CD and MP3.

Urchin
www.urchin.co.uk/0870 112 6006.
Great kids' accessories.

Win Green
www.wingreen.co.uk/01622 746516.
Brilliant handwoven cotton play tents.

Bikes

Chamberlaine & Son

75-77 Kentish Town Road, Camden, NW1 8NY (7485 4488). Camden Town tube. **Open** 8.30am-6pm Mon-Sat. **Credit** AmEx, MC, V.
Hundreds of bikes and accessories are kept here, including reclinable Hamax baby seats (£62.99), Adams trailer bikes (£109) and kids' training bikes from £50. A new child's bike costs about £100; the first service is free.
Buggy access. Delivery service. Disabled access. Mail order.

Edwardes

221-225 Camberwell Road, Camberwell, SE5 0HG (7703 3676/5720). Elephant & Castle tube/rail then 12, 68, 176, P3 bus. **Open** 8.30am-6pm Mon-Sat. **Credit** MC, V.
Bikes for children aged two to 12, including Pro Bike, Bronx and Giant ranges, are supplemented by useful accessories such as bike seats, jolly helmets, trailers and tag-alongs to fix to adult bikes (from £89). Repairs for slipped chains, punctured tyres and damaged wheels are

Consumer

all dexterously carried out by cheery staff. There's often a browseworthy selection of good used bikes of impeccable pedigree lined up outside. Edwardes is also a good place for top-of-the-range bike locks. *Buggy access. Delivery service. Disabled access. Mail order.*

Two Wheels Good

143 Crouch Hill, Crouch End, N8 9QH (8340 4284/ www.twowheelsgood.co.uk). Finsbury Park tube/rail then W7 bus. **Open** 9am-6pm Mon-Sat. **Credit** AmEx, MC, V.
TWG, a very family friendly bike shop, combines the cool side of adult biking with plenty of kids' equipment. The children's versions of Trek, which cost from about £100, are the smartest. There are helmets (by Met, £20) and Adams tag-alongs (from £110, ungeared), plus Hamax child seats (from £50). *Buggy access. Disabled access.* **Branch**: 165 Stoke Newington Church Street, N16 0UL (7249 2200).

Prams & accessories

Babyworld

239 Munster Road, Fulham, SW6 6BT (7386 1904). Fulham Broadway tube then 211, 295 bus. **Open** 10am-6pm Mon-Wed, Fri; 10am-5.30pm Sat. **Credit** AmEx, MC, V.
Although by no means huge, Babyworld displays admirable ingenuity in cramming as much nursery equipment, toys and games for infants as the space allows. Baby transport systems (to buy or order) include the latest in Bugaboo convertible chic, as well as Jane stalwarts, mountain buggies and the last word in dual buggy systems. New in is the buggy pod: a sort of sidecar to attach to the baby's pram, for toddlers who can't decide whether to walk or not, but seem too huge for a pushchair. While browsing, it's tempting to pick up little beauties such as Bobux first shoes, Lamaze soft and educational toddler toys. Great playthings for children under five include the Tomy Aquadraw, a playmat and waterfilled pens to draw with and the Tomy Discovery Dome activity centre. Babyworld also sell indoor trampolines aor rainy days. *Buggy access. Mail order.*

Rub a Dub Dub

15 Park Road, Crouch End, N8 8TE (8342 9898). Finsbury Park tube/rail then 41 or W7 bus. **Open** 10am-5.30pm Mon-Fri; 9.30am-5.30pm Sat; 11.30am-4pm Sun. **Credit** MC, V.
The knowledgeable owner of RDD chooses stock with care and dispenses advice with alacrity – as do her staff. Top baby transport systems are still the ever-popular Bugaboo and the more rugged Mountain Buggy. The Phil and Ted double decker buggy costs from £299. The last word in weather protection is Outlook's Shade-a-babe, a pushchair cover that offers UV protection. For indoors there's the posture-reforming Tripp Trapp high chair (£145), various travelcots, and fun things like wheely bugs in ladybird and bumblebee shapes for whizzing around the house. Every conceivable brand of eco-friendly nappy and bottom cream is stocked. Look out for the always reliable Kooshies and typically green German Moltex nappies: 30% gel, 70% biodegradable and entirely free of bleach. *Buggy access. Delivery service. Disabled access. Mail order. Nappy-changing facilities. Play area.*

The nursery

Chic Shack

77 Lower Richmond Road, Putney, SW15 1ET (8785 7777/www.chicshack.net). Putney Bridge tube then 14, 22 bus. **Open** 9.30am-6pm Mon-Sat. **Credit** MC, V.
A sweet-smelling, aspirational-living sort of place. Selling a dream of faded floral linen, white painted furniture and the New England beach-house look, the Shack isn't one for cheap chic, but the soft furnishings and equipment for nurseries and children's bedrooms smacks of clean living without too much crispness or formality. For babies, the white cots, chests, shelves and wardrobes are sturdy and handsome. There are pink and pale-blue floral or striped linens for children's bedrooms, but nothing is too sugary. Little extras, such as knitted bears and linen bags, quilted covers and cushions, finish the look. *Buggy access. Delivery service. Mail order.*

Dragons of Walton Street

23 Walton Street, Knightsbridge, SW3 2HX (7589 3795/www.dragonsofwaltonstreet.com). Knightsbridge or South Kensington tube. **Open** 9.30am-5.30pm Mon-Fri; 10am-5pm Sat. **Credit** AmEx, MC, V. **Map** p313 E10.
Rosie Fisher's work will always find favour with those who have cash to spend on the baby's room. Dragons is a pleasant place to visit; staff are friendly, the mood relaxed, and personal service is guaranteed. The traditional bunnies, boats and soldiers hand-painted on to sturdy chests of drawers, cupboards and cots have been joined by current fancies for fairy stuff and vintage roses, but customers can come up with their own ideas. Everything for the nursery (curtains, cots, sofas, chaises longues and tiny chairs) is made to order. Expect to pay £2,000 for a special artwork bed, and between £3,500 and £10,000 for a rocking horse. Personalised chairs and prettily-finished quilts are more affordable. Toys include red wooden London buses filled with smiley peg people, tooth-fairy dolls and teddies. *Buggy access. Delivery service. Disabled access. Mail order.*

Lilliput

255-259 Queenstown Road, Battersea, SW8 3NP (7720 5554/0800 783 0886/www.lilliput.com). Queenstown Road rail. **Open** 9.30am-5.30pm Mon, Tue, Thur, Fri; 9.30am-7pm Wed; 9am-6pm Sat; 11am-4pm Sun. **Credit** MC, V.
An extensive one-stop baby shop under the railway arches, Lilliput has a vast range of stock is huge. All the big names in pushchairs and prams are present, from Baby Björn to Stokke. Then there's the baby feeding, baby bathing, baby changing, baby dressing and baby sleeping paraphernalia – not forgetting alarms for baby listening. And before all that kicks off there's the pregnancy (catered for by Crave maternity-wear). Lilliput runs to baby entertainment: toys, mobiles, swimming togs, and Kidorable gumboots and macs (ideal for puddle-splashing tantrums). *Buggy access. Delivery service. Mail order. Nappy-changing facilities. Play area.*

Nursery Window

83 Walton Street, South Kensington, SW3 2HP (7581 3358/www.nurserywindow.co.uk). Knightsbridge or South Kensington tube. **Open** 10am-6pm Mon-Sat. **Credit** AmEx, MC, V. **Map** p313 E10.

Much of the bedlinen, clothes and accessories is good value here, given the quality, but prices are generally high. The Nursery Window Moses basket (£154), with its Swiss lace, voile and linen trimmings, makes a special first bed for the newborn; if this seems excessive, try the bestselling satin-trimmed cotton waffle blankets (£24.95). A cashmere pashmina baby wrap adds luxury for £75. The little bunny-motifed vests and sleep-suits in the softest cotton cost from £14. Nursery furniture comes in two ranges: white-painted pine (cot £380) or solid oak (cot £550). *Buggy access. Delivery service. Mail order.*

Fashion

On the high street, good budget options include **Adams** (www.adams.co.uk), for affordable if slightly uninspiring playwear, babywear and school uniforms, and **H&M** (www.hm.com) – our favourite place to kit out the kids, with its truly covetable, modish and gratifyingly cheap casualwear for babies, children and grown-ups.

A pricier chain option is **Jigsaw Junior** (www.jigsaw-online.com), which has a particularly handsome branch at 190-192 Westbourne Grove, Notting Hill, W11 2RH (7727 0322). Here children can take a silver slide instead of the stairs down to the basement where the clothes for girls are pretty and distinctive. At **Gap Kids** (www.gap.com) there are some smashing looks for babies, boys and girls, with Gap jeans, hooded fleeces and striped tights being favourites. **Zara** (www.zara.com) is another reliable source of clothes for nought to teens. The baby range at **Monsoon** (www.monsoon.co.uk) is very pleasing; the smart/casual clothes for boys and girls are distinctive. The excellent **Petit Bateau** (www.petit-bateau.com) continues to run a tight ship with its classic French baby clothes in trademark *milleraies* stripes. The soft, subtly detailed underwear and separates cater for all lovers of quality cotton.

The Best On the web: clothes

babywit.com
www.babywit.com
American site, with slogans including 'My Mama Drinks Because I Cry' as well as Ramones, Bob Marley and Motorhead rock shirts.

dribblefactory.com
www.dribblefactory.com
Sells designs in flock, puff and glitter prints: 'Evil Dictator'; 'Be Nice – Don't Forget Who Chooses Your Nursing Home'; 'I (heart) Boobies' (£13).

More Tea Vicar
www.moretvicar.com
An online store selling work from a dozen stylish contemporary designers. Lonely hearts ads ('… You had a red balloon, I was on the swings…') from Eat Yer Greens. Celebrities' favourite Jakes and London fashion label Uniform are here too.

Nappyhead
www.nappyhead.co.uk
Sells father-and-child sets ('Who's the Daddy?' and 'Who's the Babby?', £30), and 'Good Cop'/'Bad Cop' Ts for twins (£24).

Nippaz With Attitude
www.nippaz.com
Popular with urban-cool celebrity parents.

No Added Sugar
www.noaddedsugar.co.uk
Vendors of edgy kids' clothes and statement Ts; 'Lock Up Your Daughters!' and 'Future Supermodel' are faves (£15.50-£18.30).

Planet Boo
www.planetboo.co.uk
Band T-shirts for rocker sprogs from £8 come with album-cover images from Blondie, Ramones and The Clash, for example. We also love the classic Top of the Pops logo.

Snuglo
www.snuglo.com
Lisa Quinn's range is typified by hip, grown-up colours and bold lettering: 'I Want Chips, Chocolate and Cake'.

Su Su Ma Ma World Wear
www.susumama.co.uk
Groovy parents click here to kit out their rainbow children for Glastonbury in ethically sourced, tie-dyed and patchwork clothing; for goths, there are pentacle T-shirts - in black, of course.

totsplanet.co.uk
www.totsplanet.co.uk
Stockists of Snuglo's 'My Mummy Rocks' T-shirts, and funky baby socks.

Vinmag
39-43 Brewer Street, W1R 3SD, 7439 8525, www.vinmag.com
Has cult movie posters available as scaled-down T-shirts (£10.99-£12.99).

Woolshed
www.woolshed.co.uk/8444 8529
Hand-knitted children's clothes in a rainbow of fab colours – all machine washable.

Consumer

Designer

Amaia

14 Cale Street, Chelsea, SW3 3QU (7590 0999).
Sloane Square or South Kensington tube. **Open**
10am-6pm Mon-Sat. **Credit** MC, V. **Map** p313 E11.
Amaia and her partner Sergolene's smart Spanish label for
children aged up to eight is notable for simplicity and clas-
sicism; there's no room for mini-me swank here. Hence
you'll find lshift dresses, delicate cardies and skirts for the
girls, and cotton shorts and button-down shirts for boys.
Winter brings in warm, woollen coats and soft woollen
jumpers and cords. Prices are middling to expensive. A cotton dress for a five-year-old costs between £40 and £60.

Bonpoint

*15 Sloane Street, Knightsbridge, SW1X 9NB (7235
1441/www.bonpoint.com). Knightsbridge tube.*
Open 10am-6pm Mon-Sat. **Credit** AmEx, MC, V.
Map p313 F9.
A sophisticated boutique for effortless French holiday
wear, with floral sundresses and denim bib-and-brace
skirts, plus soft cotton shorts and jackets for boys. The
neat little navy macs and smock tops for girls go well with
nicely fitted skirts and trousers. It's all cool European
rather than traditional, and the garments are well made.

Bunny London

7627 2318/www.bunnylondon.com.
The beautiful hand-sewn dresses by make-up artist Debbie
Bunn are well worth the expense, not just because they
are beloved of celebrity sprogs. Distinctive colours, patterns and textures make the limited-edition garments must-
haves among ordinary mortals too. The collection includes
embroidered pieces, coats in vintage fabrics and pretty little blousons. It's available in baby sizes (2-18 months) and
child sizes (2-12 years). The dresses sell from about £60.
Ms Bunn's designs for girls can be seen at Harrods (*see
p197*) Harvey Nichols (109-125 Knightsbridge, SW1X 7RJ,
7235 5000) and Paul Smith (Westbourne House, 122
Kensington Park Road, W11 2EP, 7727 3553).

Caramel Baby & Child

*77 Ledbury Road, Notting Hill W11 2AG (7727
0906/www.caramel-shop.co.uk). Notting Hill Gate or
Westbourne Park tube.* **Open** 10am-6pm Mon-Sat;
noon-5pm Sun. **Credit** AmEx, MC, V. **Map** p310 A6.
This is the newest London branch of the increasingly
appreciated Caramel brand. The firm was started by Eva
Karayiannis, whose distaste for 'mass-produced clothing
covered in logos' led her to open her own shop. She now
also designs togs for children aged 0-12, and the look is
relaxed, not aggressively fashionable but obviously well
finished and fun to wear. Clothes for mini city slickers are
named after London Underground lines (the District, the
Metropolitan and Piccadilly line collections). Boys can have
Bond Street trousers for £59 or Baker Street breeks (long,
cuffed cotton shorts). Gorgeous summer wear for girls
includes the Southfields halter-neck sundress and fine
cotton knits such as the Stratford cardigan. Haircuts are
available on certain days (*see p188*).
*Buggy access (single only). Café. Hairdressing. Mail
order.*
Branches: 259 Pavilion Road, SW1X 0BP (7730 2564).
Caramel 291 Brompton Road, South Kensington, SW3
2DY (7589 7001).

Catimini

*52 South Molton Street, Mayfair, W1Y 1HF (7629
8099/www.catimini.com). Bond Street tube.* **Open**
10am-6.30pm Mon-Wed, Fri, Sat; 10am-7pm Thur;
11am-5.30pm Sun. **Credit** AmEx, MC, V.
Map p314 H6.
The Catimini look is vibrant, colourful, distinctive. Babies
and girls aged one to twelve come off best, with fine shift
dresses and full skirts in florals and sprigs, crocheted cardigans and cotton jackets. For babies, toddlers and school
boys there are sweet baggy shorts and striped T-shirts, as
well as co-ordinating checked cotton shirts. The seasonal
sales are particularly popular.
Buggy access. Disabled access. Mail order. Play area.
Branch: 33 King's Road, Chelsea, SW3 4LX (7824
8897).

Frocks Away

*79-85 Fortis Green Road, Fortis Green, N10 3HP
(8444 9309/www.frocksaway.co.uk). Highgate tube
then 43 or 134 bus.* **Open** 9.30am-5.30pm Mon-Sat.
Credit AmEx, MC, V.
Mother can check out the clothes and lingerie in the grown-
up side of this attractive boutique while her children upend
the toy basket. Staff are relaxed, and very patient when
measuring children's feet at the rear shoe area. Footwear
from Bobux (for new walkers), Geox (sturdy, breathable
shoes), Start-rite (back to school), Timberland and Ricosta
(trendy, trendy) caters for most infants' tastes. The über
cool clothes from Roxy (the Teeny Wahini rain mac in
green and pink florals is a joy), Mim-pi, Balu and others
are good value come sale time. Hosiery is a big thing here;
there are loads of tights and colourful socks from MP and
Catamini. A new branch was opening in Islington as we
went to press.
Buggy access. Disabled access. Play area.

Humla

*13 Flask Walk, Hampstead, NW3 1HJ (7794 8449).
Hampstead tube.* **Open** 10am-6pm Mon-Sat; noon-6pm
Sun. **Credit** AmEx, MC, V.
Best known for its exclusive range of knitwear (a three-
button jumper for a toddler costs about £32), Humla also
stocks designs from Freoli, Albetta, gorgeous D'Arcy
Brown dresses and colourful separates by Molo Kids.
There are also bright wooden toys and bricks for toddlers,
little dolls and those exclusive long, thin clothed bunnies
by Maileg, as well as puzzles and books. It's the knitwear
that catches the eye, however, Humla's wraparound cardigans and stripy tank tops are terribly sweet.

Jake's

*79 Berwick Street, Soho, W1F 8TL (7734 0812/
www.jakesofsoho.co.uk). Oxford Circus tube.* **Open**
11am-7pm Mon-Sat. **Credit** AmEx, MC, V.
Map p314 J6.
Buy a child a hand-printed T-shirt from Soho's Jake and help
make a little lad's prospects brighter. Jake is a boy with
cerebral palsy and a percentage of the profits made on the
clothing for adults and children up to age eight go towards
his future. T-shirts with 'Elvis Loves You', 'California' and
'Lucky Seven' logos look good both on adults and children.
There are some sweet long-sleeved vests for babies too.
Childrenswear also includes sweatshirts, Aran jumpers,
pants, combat trousers and baseball caps.
Buggy access. Disabled access. Mail order.

Consumer

Jakss

463 & 469 Roman Road, Bethnal Green, E3 5LX (8981 9454/www.jakss.co.uk). Bethnal Green tube/rail then 8 bus. **Open** 10am-5.30pm Tue-Sat. **Credit** AmEx, DC, MC, V.

A long-established (since 1977) childrenswear boutique, East End favourite Jakss stocks designer clothes and accessories for newborns to teens in two stores. At No.463, the collections are for babies and children up to six. They include top international labels such as Burberry Kids, Dolce & Gabbana Kids, Diesel Kids, Ralph Lauren Kids, DKNY Kids – there are some gorgeous, fresh floral dresses for little girls in her Summer 2007 range – Miss Sixty Kids, Stone Island Kids, and CP Company Kids. A bright and beautiful Oilily selection adds splashes of colour; yummy mummies who like to mke a statement opt for the flamboyant Oilily chnging bag. All the fun continues for the two to fourteen age group at No.469.
Buggy access. Mail order.

Membery's

1 Church Road, Barnes, SW13 9HE (8876 2910/ www.specialdresscompany.co.uk). Barnes Bridge rail. **Open** 10am-5pm Mon-Sat. **Credit** AmEx, MC, V.

This Barnes landmark, ideally placed near the duck pond, offers special-occasion wear such as bridesmaid and flower girl dresses, cute christening outfits and demure frocks. We adore the 100% white linen, fully lined christening gown and bonnet, delicately emdroidered gown with tiny flowers on the bodice. It's £95 for the set, but carefully cleaned will last generations. Off-the-peg prices are generally fair; white or pastel shaded birds' eye piqué dresses in 100% cotton (machine washable) cost just £34. Most small boys need to be bribed into blue or white linen shorts suits with double-breasted shirts (from £39, all fully machine washable). Designs are by Sally Membery and Frances Johnston Designs. Made-to-measure bridesmaids' dresses are available for all ages.
Buggy access. Delivery service. Play area.

The green scene

Going organic and supporting fair trade will salve your conscience and, more importantly, keep chemicals and toxins away from your baby. Buying unbleached cottons and additive-free toiletries and cleaning products is a positive first step on the long, green road. More of a challenge is opting for washable nappy systems instead of the disposables that clog up our landfill sites. To find out more about taking the environmentally friendly parenting path, check the web, then visit the good green shops listed below.

Bambino Mio (01604 883777, www.bambinomio.co.uk), the Ellie Nappie Company (www.elliepants.co.uk) and Little Green Earthlets (0845 072 4462, www.earthlets.co.uk) sell real nappies. Try Snazzypants (0845 370 8440, www.snazzypants.co.uk) for washable nappies in soft organic cotton. Organic cotton baby-wear, with gift sets (printed cotton body-suit and terry cardi, for example), as well as fab, fairly-traded cotton casuals for children aged up to ten, can be ordered from People Tree (7739 0660, www.peopletree.co.uk).

Born.

Born

168 Stoke Newington Church Street, N16 0JL (7249 5069/www.borndirect.com). Bus 73, 393, 476. **Open** 9.30am-5.30pm Tue-Sat; noon-5pm Sun. **Credit** MC, V.

Specialising in pregnancy products, baby equipment, toys and clothes, Born tries to keep it all organic and fair-trade, where applicable. Other attractions are the organic baby clothes (the Star range by Kate Goldsmith); toiletries and massage oils by Weleda and Tiu Bee Balme; and Born's own brands of pregnancy massage oils. Born is also committed to 'ecologically preferable' nappies (staff will book you in for a free demo) and sanitary products. Easier ways to do the right thing include buying toys made only from renewable materials (by excellent companies such as Heimess), or investing in the attractive Keptin-Jr Organic Comforter. The shop is a joy to visit with lively children. There's plenty of space where they can play, and a comfy sofa for breastfeeding. Trendy baby transport systems include Stokke Xplory, Phil & Ted's Explorer, Bugaboo, Cameleon and Gecko.
Buggy access. Delivery service. Disabled access: ramp. Mail order. Nappy-changing facilities. Play area.

Green Baby

345 Upper Street, Islington, N1 0PD (7359 7037/www.greenbaby.co.uk). Angel tube. **Open** 10am-5pm Mon-Fri; 10am-6pm Sat; 11am-6pm Sun. **Credit** MC, V.

This bright pink little shop attracts yummies, who come for the adorable clothing basics for newborns, such as striped playsuits for summery babies and long, striped baby gowns for wintery ones. Baby clothing is made in South India, as part of a community project that supports the education and employment of young girls. Green

Consumer

Notsobig

31A Highgate High Street, Highgate, N6 5JT (8340 4455). Archway or Highgate tube. **Open** 10am-6pm Mon-Sat; 11am-5pm Sun. **Credit** MC, V.

A little lime-green shop on one of London's loveliest high streets, Notsobig is as cute as a button. It displays some truly covetable children's clothes: delightful separates by Quincy, Cacharel, Braez and Essential Girls (sweet layered skirts, chunky jumpers and plus fours). Gift accessories include boxes of carefully arranged baby socks by Johnny Trumpette (£25) and witty No Added Sugar logo vests to give to new babies. Halfway down the windy stairs hang fancy-dress costumes by Bandicoot Lapin – the French fancy dress specialists, who can kit out your child in full bridal, prince, pirate, fairy, wizard regalia – Notsobig don't have the space to display all the cosues available, but you can order the one you want before the big event, with prices from from £60.

Buggy access. Delivery service. Mail order. Play area.

....

Baby also sells organic sheets, cotton washable nappy systems (and all the gear necessary for same), Tripp Trapp high chairs, the delightful Frog high chair, pop-up baby beds, Huggababy slings and the ever-reliable Baby Björn Active Carrier. Nappy balms and baby lotions based on pure lanolin, sweet almond oil and cocoa butter take up the remaining space. Come here for the Skip-Hop changing bag (£49.99), fab cotton toys and bright, cosy beach wraps. Anything that won't fit in the shop can be ordered from the website or catalogue.

Buggy access. Delivery service. Mail order (0870 240 6894).

Branches: 5 Elgin Crescent, W11 2JA (7792 8140); 4 Duke Street, Richmond, TW9 1HP (8940 8255); 52 Greenwich Church Street, SE10 9BL (8858 6690).

Natural Mat Company

99 Talbot Road, Notting Hill, W11 2AT (7985 0474/www.naturalmat.com). Ladbroke Grove tube. **Open** 10am-6pm Mon-Fri; 10am-4pm Sat. **Credit** MC, V. **Map** p310 A5.

The evidence is compelling that natural fibres are top for sleeping tots, as they allow air to circulate through the mattress keeping the baby at a regular, healthy temperature. The mattresses are non-allergenic, made from tufted wool or mohair on coconut fibre and latex; they are wrapped in unbleached cotton herringbone ticking and conform to all the right safety standards. Infants may safely snooze cuddled up in the organic cotton and wool sheets, blankets, sleeping bags and fleeces sold alongside the mattresses. The giant machine-washable American fleeces make great nursery play-mats. Cots and nursery furniture in painted and natural wood finishes are also sold. Baby clothes, T-shirts and pyjamas in cotton cost from £14.50.

Oilily

9 Sloane Street, Knightsbridge, SW1X 9LE (7823 2505/www.oilily-world.com). Knightsbridge tube. **Open** 10am-6pm Mon, Tue, Thur-Sat; 10am-7pm Wed; noon-5pm Sun. **Credit** AmEx, MC, V. **Map** p313 F9.

The happy colours of Oilily, proudly spotlit in this shiny white store, cannot fail to cheer up a grey London day. The clothes are exuberant gatherings of orange, green, pink and blue with stripes and flowers and little details on full dresses and skirts. Clothing for boys is inevitably less flouncy and more soberly coloured (browns, khakis, blues). Our favourites are the printed canvas holdalls with leather trim for all the infant paraphernalia. There are also prettily detailed sandals, hats and scarves, as well as scent. Expect to pay about £70 for a girl's dress.

Buggy access. Mail order. Play area.

Olive Loves Alfie

84 Stoke Newington Church Street, N16 0AP (7241 4212/www.ollielovesalfie.co.uk). Bus 73. **Open** 9am-5.30pm Mon-Fri; 10am-6pm Sat; noon-5pm Sun. **Credit** AmEx, MC, V.

Determined not to sell anything pink, fluffy, girlie or brainlessly logo-ed, this slightly tweely-named Stokey boutique is a good source of unusual lines for boys and girls up to age eight. Staff are proud of the Lucky Wang NYC kimonos and matching shoes, the hand-printed T-shirts and handsome duffel coats. Dutch designed (Rock-a-bye-Baby) baby suits packaged in record sleeves are bestsellers. Stock includes bold retro-inspired designs from Denmark by Katvig and Story. Conrad Keller wooden toys are also sold, alongside books and games.

Buggy access. Mail order.

Patrizia Wigan

19 Walton Street, Knightsbridge, SW3 2HX (7823 7080/www.patriziawigan.com). Knightsbridge or South Kensington tube. **Open** 10.30am-6.30pm Mon-Fri; 10.30am-6pm Sat. **Credit** AmEx, MC, V. **Map** p313 E10.

Little girls look demure in Patrizia Wigan's carefully smocked dresses; royal princesses have worn such classics in years gone by. For the lads, there are pressed linen shorts, crisp cotton shirts and neat cardies and cable-knits. The look is quintessentially English, and all the more interesting for being designed by a French woman. Big sellers in the successful PW brand are the christening gowns and refreshingly un-naff bridesmaid dresses. Gifts for newborns, such as white cotton presentation gowns (£45) are beautiful and well worth the price, as they'll be heirlooms. Seasonal sales are worth investigating.

Buggy access. Delivery service. Nappy-changing facilities. Play area.

Rachel Riley

82 Marylebone High Street, Marylebone, W1U 4QW (7935 7007/www.rachelriley.com). Baker Street or Bond Street tube. **Open** 10am-6pm Mon-Sat. **Credit** AmEx, MC, V. **Map** p314 5G.

Rachel Riley, a mother of three living in the Loire Valley, has a discerning eye for children's clothes. Her ranges are so gorgeous that parents clamoured for pieces they too could wear – and very elegant these are too. Riley's handsmocked dresses and bloomers for baby girls remain best sellers. Her designs for children go right up to teen style for girls. Young lads (up to 10) will enjoy pulling on the

Consumer

postcard-print open-necked shirts. It's the baby and toddler designs we love best, however. Those smocked gingham baby suits speak of a golden age of 1950s childhood. The price doesn't though; they cost £75.
Buggy access. Delivery service. Mail order.
Branch: 14 Pont Street, SW1X 9EN (7259 5969).

Raisin
50 East Dulwich Road, East Dulwich SE22 9AX (7635 9377). East Dulwich or Peckham Rye rail. **Open** 10am-6pm Mon-Sat. **Credit** MC, V.
As East Dulwich grows ever more precious, along comes the requisite exclusive babywear shop, where small garments are hung and placed on central tables with reverent care. Labels like Oh Baby London (witty T-shirts and tiny, detailed denims), Bonny Baby (from birth to 18 months), Albert (adorable fine-knit body suits) and Baby Caramel (aged from six months to 4 years) cater for trendsetting tots. There are fine hand-sewn cot quilts and blankets, as well as wooden Noah's arks and farmyards that will look arty scattered on one's solid wooden floor.
Buggy access. Mail order.

Ralph Lauren
143 New Bond Street, W1S 2TP (7535 4600/ www.polo.com). Bond Street tube. **Open** 10am-6pm Mon-Wed, Fri, Sat; 10am-7pm Thur; noon-5pm Sun. **Credit** AmEx, DC, MC, V. **Map** p314 6H.
This beautiful shop should be visited even if you're unimpressed by the preppy look of RL clothes. It's all wood panelling and sepia photos. The children's stuff is handsome (although the baby layette gifts, cashmere teddies and matinee jackets seem pricy). The girls' polo shirts and rugger shirts come in a rainbow of colours and wash well; little girls look sporty in the short, flared skirts. Lambswool jumpers, pullovers and striped cardigans, jeans, tennis shoes and windcheatersare well finished and only a little more expensive than similar items in high-street chains.
Delivery service. Mail order.

Roco
6 Church Road, Wimbledon, SW19 5DL (8946 5288) Wimbledon tube/rail. **Open** 10am-6pm Mon-Sat; noon-5pm Sun. **Credit** MC, V.
Luxury brands for children aged from birth to 16 years are sold at Magita Khalouha's shop. There are designer fake fur-trimmed coats from Eliane et Lena, Lili Gaufrette, and for boys, Ollie label vintage polos, IKKS jeans and Timberland jackets. The ten to 16 range is mostly found downstairs, where there's an MTV to distract and a small garden for bored credit-card holders to wait in. The branch in Marylebone is smaller, so carries less teen stuff. Celeb yummies who trick out their progeny here include an awful lot of tennis players. In Marylebone, fragrant mammas Claudia Schiffer and Gwynneth Paltrow have been known to browse with their babes.
Buggy access.
Branch: Coco, 27A Devonshire Street, Marylebone, W1G 6PN.

Selfridges
400 Oxford Street, W1A 1AB (0870 837 7377/ www.selfridges.com). Bond Street tube. **Open** 10am-8pm Mon-Wed, Fri; 9.30am-9pm Thur; 9.30am-8pm Sat; noon-6pm Sun. **Credit** AmEx, DC, MC, V.
Map p314 G6.

Children can gambol around in the spacious third floor Kids' Universe while their parents go label crazy. New for 2007 is Marc Jacobs' kids and teens range, Little Marc: an arresting line of pretty sundresses, denim and caption T-shirts. Another favourite is the Miss Sixty look, cool and quirky for modish girls. Boys and girls aged six to fourteen look casually sporty in Gas wear too. Then there's D&G Junior, Fransa, Burberry and Ted Baker. For babies, there's Absorba, Cacharel, Moschino and Catimini. The atmosphere is quite teenybopperish, with pop on the sound system and white, shiny pods to contain the gear. There are toys, sticker stations, sweetie displays, partywear and fairy frocks. There's also a Buckle My Shoe store. Summer 2007 saw the introduction of the Win Green range of play tents on the third floor. These beautifully embroidered, 100% tents for children include woven cotton castles, gingerbread cottages, and fairy hanging tents. Win Green floor quilts, beanbags and bedlinen are also stocked.
Buggy access. Cafés. Delivery service. Disabled access: lifts, toilet. Mail order. Nappy-changing facilities.

Stardust
294 Milkwood Road, Herne Hill, SE24 0EZ (7737 0199/www.stardustkids.co.uk). Herne Hill rail. **Open** 9.30am-6pm Mon-Sat; 11am-5pm Sun. **Credit** MC, V.
Film star (Monroe, Hepburn, Connery, Bruce Lee) T-shirts and hoodies are among Stardust's wares. The company also produces rompers emblazoned with 'ASBO', 'Drama Queen' and 'The Incredible Sulk'. Baby booties with 'LOVE' and 'HATE' on each foot (£10), and Routemaster vests (£12, age one to three years: perfect for parents pining after London's much-loved bus) make kooky gifts.
Buggy access. Mail order. Play area.

Their Nibs
214 Kensington Park Road, Notting Hill, W11 1NR (7221 4263/www.theirnibs.com). Ladbroke Grove or Notting Hill Gate tube. **Open** 9.30am-6pm Mon-Fri; 10am-6pm Sat; noon-5pm Sun. **Credit** AmEx, MC, V.
Since opening a couple of years ago, Their Nibs has had numerous designs appearing in glossy London lifestyle-with-the-kids mags. No wonder: there are some refreshingly original children's clothes in here. The dresses for little girls (from £38) and traditional striped PJs for boys (£25) plus darling little Nurtured by Nature baby clothes are gorgeous, and there's an amusing vintage rail, on which hang crimplene horrors from the 1970s and 1960s. It's like looking at your childish self in the family photo album. Toys include knitted bears (our favourites) and Heimess pram trinkets from sustainable sources. Children enjoy the large play area, with its blackboard, books and toy basket. Their Nibs also provides haircuts (*see p188*).
Buggy access. Hairdressing. Mail order. Play area.

Tots
39 Turnham Green Terrace, Chiswick, W4 1RG (8995 0520/www.totschiswick.com). Turnham Green tube. **Open** 10am-6pm Mon-Sat; noon-5pm Sun. **Credit** AmEx, MC, V.
A well-loved boutique for babies and children up to about 12, Tots keeps Turnham Green's infants trendy with miniature modes by Catimini, Floriane and Confetti, as well as gorgeous knitwear and coordinates by Miniature. For older children, a sporty, outdoorsy look is achieved by Quiksilver and Timberland. Girlie girls like the zingy designs from Oilily and Ralph Lauren.
Buggy access. Disabled access. Mail order. Play area.

Trendys

72 Chapel Market, Islington, N1 9ER (7837 9070).
Angel tube. **Open** 10am-6pm Mon-Sat; 11am-4pm Sun.
Credit AmEx, MC, V.
It might have the naffest name in Islington, but Trendys is an excellent source of affordable designer wear for babies and children, with frequent sales. On our last visit, Converse All Stars shoes for girls, in a variety of colours, were half price; Diesel jeans were available from £30. For boys, Bench workwear and Timberland boots were well-priced too. Bright summer sandals from a variety of cool Italian designers are a speciality.
Buggy access. Disabled access.

Young England

47 Elizabeth Street, Belgravia, SW1W 9PP (7259 9003/www.youngengland.com). Sloane Square tube.
Open 10am-5.30pm Mon-Fri; 10am-4pm Sat.
Credit MC, V. **Map** p316 G10.
With such a name you wouldn't expect this shop to be full of hoodies and cut-offs, yet it's not all Peter Pan collars and sailor suits either. Some of the made-to-order bridesmaid and pageboy suits can be over-the-top, but Young England's everyday smart stuff is lovely. We adore the lambswool three-button jerseys, the flowerprint blouses, girl's flowery pumps and beach shoes, print frocks, plain woollen jackets for boys of all ages, and good, soft linen shorts. The quality is high, the price middling and the service efficient and friendly.
Buggy access. Mail order.

Mid-range boutiques

Biff

41-43 Dulwich Village, Dulwich, SE21 7BN (8299 0911). North Dulwich rail/P4 bus. **Open** 9.30am-5.30pm Mon-Fri; 10am-6pm Sat. **Credit** MC, V.
Dulwich Village's own children's empire takes up two shop fronts. At No.41 there's a varied choice of shoes and clothes for boys aged two to twelve, with the 14-16 age group catered for at the back. At No.43 it's babies (0-24 months) and girls aged two to twelve. The shoe department has school footwear, trainers and plimsolls, with shoes from Geox and Start-rite, waterproof Crocs as well as more fanciful designs by Lelli Kelly and Umi for girls. Babywear includes Lily Rose, Organics for Kids, Petit Bateau and Framsa. For children up to 16 there's a Quiksilver, Pepe and O'Neill presence, plus shirts by Ben Sherman and Hawk, and separates by Florian.
Buggy access. Disabled access. Mail order. Play area.

Iana

186 King's Road, Chelsea, SW3 5XP (7352 0060/www.iana.it). Sloane Square tube. **Open** 9am-6pm Mon, Tue, Thur, Fri; 9am-7pm Wed; 9.30am-6.30pm Sat; 11am-6pm Sun. **Credit** AmEx, DC, MC, V.
Map p313 F11.
Italian designs for 0-14 years at bargain prices: this is a wonderful find if you don't want your child in high-street fashions, but haven't the budget for designer brands. Girls get pedal pushers, jeans, sundresses appliquéd cotton tops, gingham-frilled denim skirts and bright cords; boys look good in combats and long-sleeved cotton tops. We're impressed by the underwear sets (from £3 for a vest).
Buggy access. Delivery service. Disabled access. Mail order. Play area.

igloo. See p202.

There are great togs to be had at **Sasti**.

Igloo

300 Upper Street, Islington, N1 2TU (7354 7300/ www.iglookids.co.uk). Angel or Highbury & Islington tube. **Open** 10am-6.30pm Mon-Wed; 10am-7pm Thur; 9.30am-6.30pm Fri, Sat; 11am-5.30pm Sun. **Credit** AmEx, DC, MC, V

Igloo is an imaginatively stocked and carefully thought-out one-stop shop that could only have been dreamed up by mothers. And so it was: two of them, with five young children between them. To wear, for babies and children aged up to eight, there are soft and pretty essentials by Petit Bateau, Catimini, Miniature and IKKS, and trendy shirts for boys by His Nibs. Wet weather fashions by Blue Fish are also sold. Toys and games and books line the whole length of the shop. For outdoor play there are items like wig wams and tents, pedal cars and hobby horses. Indoor favourites include some really good educational ideas for bright sparks, such as ant and worm farms, or tripod-mounted telescopes with precision optics to give children a brand new perspective on their surroundings – accompany this with the Night Sky projection kit (a torch and small globe that helps you create the universe on your bedroom ceiling) and you have a mini astronomy lab in the home. There's a cosy curtained-off nook for breast-feeding and notice board reading. You'll also find a big Start-rite shoe corner and a section devoted to quality party tableware and gluey, sticky, glittery art stuff. Igloo also stock stuff for parties, from napkins to goody bags).
Buggy access. Delivery service. Disabled access. Mail order. Play area.

Quackers

155D Northcote Road, Clapham, SW11 6QB (7978 4235). Clapham Junction rail then 319 bus. **Open** 9.30am-5.30pm Mon-Fri; 10am-5.30pm Sat. **Credit** MC, V.

A colourful Battersea favourite, this cheery little store is run by Veronica McNaught, who selects wide ranges of fashions and toys for babies and children aged up to ten. Labels for smart babies include the German brand Kanz and a pretty Portuguese range called Laranjinha as well as Weekend à la Mer. There's a good deal of affordable, individual pieces by Whoopi, with vintage-looking floral pinafores for girls (£24.99), as well as cosy coats and cardies for winter and statement-makers by Toby Tiger. Must-haves for toddlers chilling by the pond on Wandsworth Common include pretty rainwear by Blue Fish and Kidorable ladybird or frog gumboots (£13.50).
Buggy access.

Sasti

8 Portobello Green Arcade, 281 Portobello Road, Ladbroke Grove, W10 5TZ (8960 1125/ www.sasti.co.uk). Ladbroke Grove tube. **Open** 10am-6pm Mon-Sat; 11am-5pm Sun. **Credit** AmEx, MC, V.

If you're looking for out-of-the-ordinary but fairly priced clothes for babies, toddlers and young children, you can't go far wrong with Sasti. Absolutely our favourite thing in here is the cosy fleece all in one, with built-in gloves, feet and hoods for babies on the move. The furry bear design is the most coveted, with little ears on the hood; babies wearing it look good enough to eat. There are dragon versions with dorsal spikes and a tail, tiger or leopard-print designs, and cuddly Friesian cow colours (from £20). Other delights include print skirts, shorts and shift dresses, jolly patterned tights in all hues. Baby toys, themed lunch boxes, hair accessories and books are also sold.
Buggy access. Delivery service. Mail order. Nappy-changing facilities. Play area.

Trotters

34 King's Road, Chelsea, SW3 4UD (7259 9620/www.trotters.co.uk). Sloane Square tube. **Open** 9am-7pm Mon-Sat; 10.30am-6.30pm Sun. **Credit** AmEx, MC, V. **Map** p313 F11.

A bright and busy King's Road landmark, Trotters is the sort of place you never come away from empty handed. There are Trotters children's clothes, a picture book section, a haircutting place (*see p188*), a useful Start-rite concession and lots of toys. The place is always full of children rampaging among the banks of Jellycat soft toys, pocket-money priced playthings and the Dr Seuss collection, while their parents admire the delightful cotton frocks printed with strawberries, cherries and flowers, or the sweet rose-bud-print towelling robes. The lads aren't left out, they get soft checked shirts and logo T-shirts, cargo pants, striped jumpers and cute baggy shorts. There's plenty that would make splendid presents: Beatrix Potter and Maisie crockery; insulated sandwich bags and wheelie suitcases; and accessories such as lamps shaped like rabbits, ducks or toadstools. As well as the Trotters own label there are brands such as Diesel, Bob & Blossom and Osh Kosh.
Buggy access. Delivery service. Hairdressing. Mail order. Nappy-changing facilities.
Branches: 127 Kensington High Street, W8 5SF (7937 9373); 86 Northcote Road, Clapham, SW11 6QN (7585 0572).

Second-hand

Little Angel Exchange

249 Archway Road, Highgate, N6 5BS (8340
8003/www.littleangelexchange.co.uk). Highgate tube.
Open 10.30am-5.30pm Mon-Sat. **Credit** MC, V.
Little Angel's proximity to lofty Highgate Village and
Muswell Hill means it has a ready supply of cleaned,
ironed, nearly new, or (oh joy!) unused clothes, toys and
selected equipment. On our last visit we came across an
unopened Grobag for just £17.95 (as well as quite a few
used, washed ones), miniature wetsuits and UV protective
swimwear, DKNY T-shirt dresses and skirts, Gap jeans
and a rail of fleeces and puffa jackets. Prices go from a few
quid for a mid-range label T-shirt (such as H&M) to a few
more for designer wear. People who want to sell stuff
through the Little Angel can leave it here in the hope of
obtaining half the price if the item sold is over £10, or one
third if it sells for less than £10. After eight weeks in the
shop, the items are given to charity unless claimed back.
Buggy access.

Little Trading Company

7 Bedford Corner, The Avenue, Chiswick, W4 1LD
(8742 3152). Turnham Green tube. **Open** 9am-5pm
Mon-Fri; 9am-4.30pm Sat. **No credit cards.**
Goods crammed into, and displayed outside, this posh little baby stuff exchange are sold on a profit-share or sale-
or-return basis. Among the stock you can find sports kit,
baby accessories and equipment (including car seats),

clothes for all ages, and books, toys, DVDs and videos. The
DVDs and videos may be watched by children who come
in for a haircut (*see p188*). New stuff is also sold,
including shoes by Starchild.
Buggy access. Hairdressing. Play area.

Merry-Go-Round

12 Clarence Road, Hackney, E5 8HB (8985 6308).
Hackney Central rail. **Open** 10am-5.30pm Mon-Sat;
11am-5pm Sun. **Credit** AmEx, MC, V.
This is every green parent's dream. The recycling possibilities provided by the mountains of baby stuff we're
encouraged to buy are fully exploited by this excellent and
unusually large agency. As well as what look like new and
barely used car seats hanging from the ceiling, there are
pushchairs and high chairs, baby-walkers and nursery
equipment. In the basement you'll find clothes and other
items for children aged from two to teenage. Previously
owned clothes are more likely to be Gap than Gucci, but
we saw a few items by Diesel, Ralph Lauren and DKNY.
Buggy access. Nappy-changing facilities. Play area.

Pixies

14 Fauconberg Road, Chiswick, W4 3JY (8995
1568/www.pixiesonline.co.uk). Chiswick Park or
Turnham Green tube. **Open** *Term time* 10am-4.30pm
Mon-Fri; 10am-3pm Sat. *School hols* 10am-4.30pm
Wed-Fri; 10am-3pm Sat. **Credit** AmEx, MC, V.
A clothing and equipment agency full of new and nearly
new clothes, accessories and baby equipment, Pixies can

Consumer

Plenty to plunder at **Trotters**.

A WILD PLACE TO SHOP AND EAT®

Rainforest Cafe is a unique venue bringing to life the sights and sounds of the rainforest.

Come and try our fantastic menu!
With a re-launched healthy kids menu, including gluten free, dairy free and organic options.

15% DISCOUNT
off your final food bill*

Offer valid seven days a week.
Maximum party size of 6.

020 7434 3111

20 Shaftesbury Avenue, Piccadilly Circus, London W1D 7EU

www.therainforestcafe.co.uk

*Please show this advert to your safari guide when seated.
Cannot be used in conjunction with any other offer.

furnish you with quality items such as Stokke high chairs, car seats and pushchairs, buggy boards (these are sold new too), and, for summer, UV bodysuits and swim shoes. The quality clothing is sensibly arranged into school uniforms, babywear and items for older children clearly labelled with age and price. The firm also offers the Babytalk consultation service (£40 per hour), giving advice on equipment and clothing for your new baby.
Buggy access. Delivery service. Disabled access. Mail order.

Shoes

Brian's Shoes

2 Halleswelle Parade, Finchley Road, Temple Fortune, NW11 0DL (8455 7001/www.briansshoes.com). Finchley Central or Golders Green tube. **Open** 9.15am-5.30pm Mon-Sat; 10.30am-1.30pm Sun. **Credit** MC, V.
Calm, spacious, unfussy and a centre of excellence for children's foot-measuring services, Brian's is a sensible place for school-shoe buying (unless you choose to visit on the afternoon before the start of the autumn term, in which case you're barking mad). Staff are highly trained. The shop has been going for about 36 years, and its stock has trendied up over the years with footwear from Diesel and Ricosta as well as the more sober Start-rite and Hush Puppies. Another big draw is the proximity of the excellent Bookworm children's bookshop (*see p189*).
Buggy access. Disabled access.
Branches: throughout town. Check website for details.

One Small Step One Giant Leap

3 Blenheim Crescent, Notting Hill, W11 2EE (7243 0535/www.onesmallsteponegiantleap.com). Ladbroke Grove or Notting Hill Gate tube. **Open** 10am-6pm Mon-Fri; 9am-6pm Sat; 11am-5pm Sun. **Credit** MC, V.
Everything here is beautifully set out, and the range of brands, both fashionable and reliable, is quite astonishing. Babies can have chubby feet encased in Starchild soft leather protectors in a wide range of designs. Then there are Asters from France, with the Dutch are represented by Oilily and Brakkies, the Danish by Ecco and Angulus, the Germans Birkenstocks (of course) and the British by Dunlops and Start-rites. There's also room for trendy Skechers, Puma and Diesel sporty shoes, sturdy Geox and Kickers and many, many more. Prices go from £15 for baby shoes, to £36 for sensible Start-rites and a bit more for the posh continentals. It's so sophisticated there are even magazines for bored parents to flip through while their offspring cogitate.
Buggy access. Mail order.
Branches: throughout town. Check website for details.

Shoe Station

3 Station Approach, Kew, Surrey TW9 3QB (8940 9905/www.theshoestation.co.uk). Kew Gardens tube. **Open** 10am-6pm Mon-Sat. **Credit** MC, V.
The sort of local shoe shop all parents need, the Station (right by Kew station) is run by two women with seven children between them. Children's shoes for every occasion are available, from child's size 2 to adult size 7. Brands include Start-rite (of course), Ricosta, Aster, Naturino, Babybotte, TTY, Giesswein, Mod8, Pom d'Api, Geox, Kenzo, Nike, Puma, Birkenstock, Primigi, Freed and Daisy Roots. Football boots, ballet shoes, slippers and gumboots are also covered. Staff are trained Start-rite fitters.
Buggy access. Play area.

Stepping Out

106 Pitshanger Lane, Ealing, W5 1QX (8810 6141). Ealing Broadway tube. **Open** 10am-5.30pm Mon-Fri; 9.30am-5.30pm Sat. **Credit** MC, V.
A Start-rite agent first and foremost, Stepping Out stocks plenty of Ricosta, Mod8, Lelli Kelly and Geox as well. Experienced assistants specialise in advising on shoes for children with mobility problems, with local GPs often referring kids here; lots of styles provide extra support, but manage to be fashionable too (Babybotte makes good shoes for problem feet, and Le Loup Blanc is perfect for kids with weak ankles).
Buggy access. Play area.

The Red Shoes

30 Topsfield Parade, Crouch End, N8 8QB (8341 9555/www.theredshoes.co.uk). Finsbury Park tube/rail. then W7, 41 bus. **Open** 10am-5.30pm Mon-Sat; noon-4.30pm Sun. **Credit** MC, V.
A fashion-conscious shoe specialist for Crouch End, Red Shoes has a serious selection of children's shoes alongside the women's range. Lelli Kelly designs are going down well, then there are sandals by Elle and Birkenstock, as well as comfortable, breathable Geox, soft Ecco, sensible Start-rite and plenty of footwear and clothing for ballet. Skate shoes and clothes by Heelys are popular lines too.
Buggy access.

Sportswear

Most parents' idea of hell would be to slog down Oxford Street fighting their way through sports emporia looking for child-sized trainers and sports kit. Try instead the pleasant places listed below.

Ace Sports & Leisure

341 Kentish Town Road, Kentish Town, NW5 2TJ (7485 5367). Kentish Town tube. **Open** 9.30am-6pm Mon-Wed, Fri, Sat; 9.30am-7pm Thur. **Credit** AmEx, MC, V.
At Ace you'll encounter walls of footwear for all sports, as well as junior rackets, bats and swimming equipment. Brands include Puma, adidas, Reebok and Nike. There are also small baseball mitts and the latest footballs in mini sizes, children's cricket balls and bats, junior tennis rackets, ping-pong balls in bright colours, tracksuits, swim nappies, goggles, earplugs and nose clips – everything, in fact, to get kids active.
Buggy access. Disabled access.

Decathlon

Canada Water Retail Park, Surrey Quays Road, SE16 2XU (7394 2000/www.decathlon.co.uk). Canada Water tube. **Open** 10am-7.30pm Mon-Thur; 10am-8pm Fri; 9am-7pm Sat; 11am-5pm Sun. **Credit** MC, V.
Parents adore these two vast hangars worth of sports clothing and equipment by Surrey Quays. There's a huge range of gear for young sporty types, including hard hats, jodhs, crops and grooming kits for riders, brilliant snow wear in all sizes for skiers, bikes, fishing rods, walking boots, trainers any which way, footballs, golf equipment, gym wear and more. Decathlon has 12 own brands, including Quechua (affordable and hard wearing, for hiking, mountaineering and snowboarding), and Domyos (for dancewear and fitness equipment). You'll also find the likes of Nike, Reebok and adidas. The young, often French

Consumer

staff are bright and interested and there are loads of bargains. Services include racquet restringing, scuba tank refilling and ski maintenance. Occasional second-hand sales let you trade in unwanted equipment, but not clothes. More than 60 sports are covered.
Buggy access. Disabled access.

Lillywhites

24-36 Lower Regent Street, SW1Y 4QF (0870 333 9600/www.sports-world.com). Piccadilly Circus tube. **Open** 10am-9pm Mon-Sat; noon-6pm Sun. **Credit** AmEx, MC, V. **Map** p317 K7.
Good for mainstream sports gear, Lillywhites concentrates on more urban activities, most especially football. This presumably is because it's now part of the Sports World group. Children's mini football kits, as well as those essential goalie gloves and team socks, are in good supply, and there are plenty of hoodies (in both the human and apparel sense). The layout's a bit chaotic.
Buggy access. Disabled access.

Ocean Leisure

11-14 Northumberland Avenue, Charing Cross, WC2N 5AQ (7930 5050/www.oceanleisure.co.uk). Embankment tube. **Open** 9.30am-7pm Mon-Fri; 9.30am-6pm Sat. **Credit** MC, V. **Map** p399 L8.
This watersports emporium takes up two shops under the arches. One's all sailing and scuba, the other is mostly surfing. Some gear – including wetsuits, Reef sandals and neoprene Aquashoes – comes in very small sizes. There are also baby life jackets, fins, masks and snorkels, and even scuba equipment (from age eight). Swimming equipment, underwater cameras and sea scooters are also sold. Big names in stock include Padi, Aqualung and Scubapro.
Buggy access. Disabled access. Mail order.

Slam City Skates

16 Neal's Yard, Covent Garden, WC2H 9DP (7240 0928/www.slamcity.com). Covent Garden tube. **Open** 10am-6.30pm Mon-Sat; noon-5pm Sun. **Credit** AmEx, MC, V. **Map** p315 L6.

Mystical Fairies. *See p209.*

This is teen heaven, with a range of possibilities for the very small. Skateboard decks, T-shirts, the skate shoes of the moment (the smallest is UK size three), rucksacks and accessories are all sold here. Although there's no stock dedicated to children, most are happy to buy the small Slam City T-shirt and grow into it. The extensive array includes We, Fourstar, Silas, Volcom, Emerica, Etnies and Vans. *Mail order (0870 420 4146).*

Soccerscene

56-57 Carnaby Street, Soho, W1F 9QF (7439 0778/www.soccerscene.co.uk). Oxford Circus tube. **Open** 9.30am-7pm Mon-Wed, Fri; 9.30am-7pm Thur, Sat; 11.30am-5.30pm Sun. **Credit** AmEx, MC, V. **Map** p314 J6.

Scaled-down replica kits are available for most of the popular teams, especially the sainted Arsenal, Man United and Chelsea. Once children have selected their dream shirt and parents have recovered from seeing the price tag (this might be a time to try to interest the kids in vintage shirts – there is a selection), you can have it embossed with name and number for a fee. There are also balls, boots, shin pads, trainers, socks, boxes, scarves and hats. Stocking fillers include little trinkets such as Man U pencil tins and plush teddies. Service is helpful. Rugby kits are upstairs in Rugby Scene.
Delivery service. Mail order.
Branches: 156 Oxford Street, W1D 1ND (7436 6499); 49-50 Long Acre, WC2E 9JR (7240 4070).

Speedo

41-43 Neal Street, Covent Garden, WC2H 9PJ (7497 0950). Covent Garden tube. **Open** 10am-7pm Mon-Wed, Fri, Sat; 10am-8pm Thur; noon-6pm Sun. **Credit** AmEx, MC, V. **Map** p315 L6.

The trusted Speedo brand has traditionally catered for lane swimmers who want comfort and coverage, but it also sells beachwear, towelling capes, sun-tops and knee-length sunsuits (£23) with up to 98% UV protection. The junior range is cool for swimming lessons. There are children's accessories too; come for swim nappies, armbands, snorkels, goggles and caps that match your swimsuit.
Buggy access. Delivery service. Disabled access. Mail order.

Wigmore Sports

79-83 Wigmore Street, Marylebone, W1U 1QQ (7486 7761/www.wigmoresports.co.uk). Oxford Circus tube. **Open** 10am-6pm Mon-Wed, Fri, Sat; 10am-7pm Thur; 11am-5pm Sun. **Credit** AmEx, MC, V. **Map** p314 G6.

London's premier racquet sports specialist is great fun to visit. Disciplines covered include tennis, squash, badminton and more, and there's a 'try before you buy' practice wall, which children love getting to grips with if it's not in use by some hard-bitten hitter. If your child is inspired by Andy Murray, check out the junior stock. Excellent tennis shoes by K-Swiss, adidas, and Nike (£30-£40) are stocked in half sizes from 12 up; shorter racquets (from 50cm/19in; £15-£100) and softer balls are a speciality. Wigmore also sell a range of ball machines for players that never want to be without a partner, although we imagine a large garden would be required for those. The staff here are committed to the tennis cause and can offer some sensible advice to young people who want to imprve their game. There's a concession in Harrods.
Buggy access. Delivery service. Disabled access. Mail order.

Toys & gifts
Fun & games

Cheeky Monkeys

202 Kensington Park Road, Notting Hill, W11 1NR (7792 9022/www.cheekymonkeys.com). Notting Hill Gate tube then 52 bus. **Open** 9.30am-5.30pm Mon-Fri; 10am-5.30pm Sat; 11am-5pm Sun. **Credit** MC, V. **Map** p310 A6.

Friendly, helpful service marks out this small chain of independent toy-sellers as one of our favourites. This branch, the original, has a bookshop in the basement. An enduring bestseller is the beautiful, shaggy rocking sheep for babies and toddlers to ride (£49.99) and the wonderful puppet theatres, with the puppets to perform in them. Smart wooden toys from the Toy Workshop include a fantastic pirate ship. Then there are arty-crafty items such as Hama Beads and knitting sets. Role-play toys are handsome; the adorable wooden kitchen units, standing at around two feet (60cm) high, are highly desirable. Pocket-money toys cost from about £1.99. Fancy-dress outfits are sold too.
Buggy access. Disabled access. Mail order (website only).
Branches: Throughout town. Check website for details.

Disney Store

360-366 Oxford Street, W1N 9HA (7491 9136/ www.disneystore.co.uk). Bond Street tube. **Open** 10am-8pm Mon-Sat; noon-6pm Sun. **Credit** AmEx, MC, V. **Map** p314 J6.

The family film of the moment spawns figurines, stationery, toys and costumes at these most animated of toy shops. Disney has gained a good deal of mileage from the film *Cars*, so there are Lightning McQueen programmable cars, *Cars* ride-ons, *Cars* puzzles and *Cars* cars. *Pirates of the Caribbean* is another moneyspinner. This central London branch has a high turnover for dressing-up costumes (Peter Pan, Snow White, Tinkerbell and Buzz). Children's underwear, nightwear and casuals emblazoned with favourite characters all get shelf space, then there's the tableware, lunch bags and boxes and cuddly toys. Enduring favourites are the character dolls and, of course, the classic DVDs.
Buggy access. Disabled access. Mail order.
Branches: 9 The Piazza, Covent Garden, WC2E 8HD (7836 5037); 22A & 26 The Broadway Shopping Centre, W6 9YD (8748 8886).

Early Learning Centre

36 King's Road, Chelsea, SW3 4UD (7581 5764/ www.elc.co.uk). Sloane Square tube. **Open** 9.30am-7pm Mon-Fri; 9.30am-6pm Sat; 11am-6pm Sun. **Credit** AmEx, MC, V. **Map** p313 F11.

Expect more branches of this excellent chain to appear now it has been bought up by Mothercare. Dedicated to imaginative play for babies and young children, ELC is such a good friend to parents that you miss it when the children grow out of the stuff (from about the age of nine). Everything is sturdy, brightly coloured and reasonably priced. There are some things ELC does extremely well – for example, soft bodied baby dolls, swimming accessories and wooden train sets that link together just like Brio but are cheaper. Other lines include the art materials, play animals and farms, playhouses and pop-up tents, swings, sandpits, paddling pools, picture books and story and song tapes, science sets and craft kits. We particularly like the

Consumer

To market, to market...

...To buy a fat hog. You should find one of these hanging by its trotters at **Borough Market**. Here the traders like to big up their ruddy-complexioned country spiel for us whey-faced Londoners in need of some organic, corn-fed livestock, designer olives or challenging cheeses. Still, for all its celebrity status, this trendy food market is a pleasant assault on the senses, and provides an education in proper food for children.

Of more interest to those stripling teens not bovvered about feeding their faces is **Camden Market**: a mass of clothes, music, collectibles, army surplus, jewellery and incense. Camden is home to six indoor and outdoor interlinked markets – all great places to find offbeat fashion or consider a piercing or a tattoo.

Greenwich Market is in full swing on a Sunday and has a quieter atmosphere on a Thursday, Friday and Saturday. Expect to find plenty of arts and crafts, with a good offering of children's toys and clothing. Typically, there are several international food stalls cooking up a tasty mix of falafel, Thai noodles and fresh juices.

More touristy than trendy these days, but still colourful, **Portobello Road** gets its market into top gear on Fridays and Saturdays. The mile-long procession of busy stalls starts near Notting Hill Gate with antiques, then food and then a flea market strong on vintage clothing and crafts. Do explore the shops and cafés at the market's end near Golborne Road, the Portuguese custard tarts from Lisboa Pâtisserie (57 Golborne Road, W10 5NR, 8968 5242) are legendary.

Regenerated **Spitalfields** is a wrought-iron covered market between the shiny office blocks of the financial district and the curry houses of Brick Lane. The market has scores of stalls selling organic food, funky clothes, especially for children, second-hand retro homewares, fragrant global cuisines and stuff you never thought you needed. Adjacent to the covered market, glittering glass retail units offer designer clothes and make-up, plus snazzy places to eat.

Between Regents canal and London Fields in Hackney **Broadway Market** makes much of its villagey amosphere and history. The farmers style Saturday market has organic meat, fish and veg on its stalls, alongside health products, vintage clothes and crafts. There's a play area with hopscotch, chess and draughts marked out on the ground, and occasional storytelling and face-painting for under-sevens.

Broadway Market.

creative section, which has best sellers like the sturdy Art Centre, an easel that has ith a chalkboard on one side and whiteboard on the other, and ncludes a tray to hold paints and tools, and clips to hold paper. This branch holds play sessions for toddlers on Tuesdays (10am-noon), but not from mid September to early January, when every inch of space is taken up with Christmas stock.
Buggy access. Delivery service. Mail order.
Branches: throughout town. Check website for details.

Hamleys

188-196 Regent Street, W1B 5BT (0870 333 2455/www.hamleys.com). Oxford Circus tube.
Open 10am-8pm Mon-Fri; 9am-8pm Sat; noon-6pm Sun. **Credit** AmEx, DC, MC, V. **Map** p314 J6.
As much a tourist attraction as a ginormous toy shop, Hamley's is an over-exciting experience – and that's just for the parents, who tend to throw tantrums over prices, crowds and queuing at tills. Most must-have toys are here, and attractively displayed to boot, though prices seem to build in a margin for their guaranteed presence (well, almost: Hamley's isn't immune to that pre-Christmas panic when the number one gift toy becomes scarce).

Knowing where to go for stuff helps, so pay attention: the jungle-themed ground floor accommodates most mayhem and a mountain of soft toys; the basement is the Cyberzone, full of games consoles and high-tech gadgetry. The first floor contains items of a scientific bent, plus a lurid sweet factory and a branch of the Bear Factory. On the second floor is everything for pre-schoolers, including more Thomas than you could imagine. Third is pinkly, twinkly perfect girlie heaven: Barbie World, Sylvanian Families and departments for dressing up, make-up and so on. Fourth floor is for hobbies (remote-controlled vehicles, plus die-cast models). Fifth is all about action figures (there's a 10ft/3m Batman in flight), with plenty of Star Wars collectables. Up here, too is baby changing and the reasonably priced café (with cartoons on the telly). Kids can have their birthday party here – typically on a Sunday morning. Check the website for special events.
Buggy access. Café. Delivery service. Disabled access: lift, toilet. Mail order. Nappy-changing facilities. Play areas.

Consumer

At the end of the Victoria line, rather more down-at-heel surroundings are enlivened by **Walthamstow Market**, which rejoices in its reputation as the longest daily street market in Europe. It has 450 stalls touting for business, from Monday to Saturday. What *don't* they sell? Cheap shoes, clothing seconds from high-street stores, low-priced fabrics, cakes, confectionery, fruit and veg – are all yours for a song. Running alongside the thoroughfare there's a number of child-friendly cafés, such as local institution L Manze pie and mash shop (76 Walthamstow High Street, E17 7LD, 8520 2855).

Borough Market

8 Southwark Street, SE1 (74071002/ www.boroughmarket.org.uk). London Bridge tube/rail. **Open** 10.30am-3.30pm Thur; noon-6pm Sat; 9am-4pm Sat.

Broadway Market

Broadway Market, E8 (07709 311869/ www.broadwaymarket.co.uk). London Fields rail.

Camden Market

Camden Market *Camden High Street, junction with Buck Street, NW1 (7278 4444).* **Open** 9.30am-5.30pm daily.
Camden Canal Market *off Chalk Farm Road, south of junction with Castlehaven Road, NW1 9XJ (www.camdenlock.net).* **Open** 9am-6.30pm Fri-Sun.
Camden Lock *Camden Lock Place, off Chalk Farm Road, NW1 8AF (7485 3459/ www.camdenlockmarket.com).* **Open** 10am-6pm daily.
Electric Ballroom *184 Camden High Street, NW1 8QP (www.electric-ballroom.co.uk).* **Open** 10am-6pm Sat, Sun.
Stables *off Chalk Farm Road, opposite junction with Hartland Road, NW1 8AH (7485 5511/ www.camdenlock.net).* **Open** 9.30am-5.30pm daily.
All *Camden Town or Chalk Farm tube.*

Greenwich Market

(www.greenwichmarket.net) off College Approach, SE10/www.greenwichmarket.net). Cutty Sark DLR/Greenwich rail. **Open** *Antiques & collectibles* 7.30am-5.30pm Thur, Fri. *Village Market* Stockwell Street, 8am-5pm Sat, Sun. *Arts & Crafts Market* 9.30am-5.30pm Thur-Sun. *Food Court* 9.30am-5.30pm Sat, Sun.

Portobello Road

Portobello Road, W10, W11; Golborne Road, W10 (www.portobelloroad.co.uk). Ladbroke Grove, Notting Hill Gate or Westbourne Park tube. **Open** *General* 8am-6pm Mon-Wed; 9am-1pm Thur; 7am-7pm Fri, Sat. *Antiques* 4am-6pm Sat.

Spitalfields Market

Commercial Street, between Lamb Street & Brushfield Street, E1 (www.visitspitalfields.com). Liverpool Street tube/rail. **Open** *General market* 10am-4pm Mon-Fri; 9am-5pm Sun. *Food market* 10am-4pm Wed. *Fashion market* 10am-4pm Fri. *Record market* 10am-4pm 1st and 3rd Wed/mth.

Walthamstow Market

Walthamstow High Street, E17. Walthamstow Central tube/rail. **Open** 8am-6pm Mon-Sat.

Mystical Fairies

12 Flask Walk, Hampstead, NW3 1HE (7431 1888/www.mysticalfairies.co.uk). Hampstead tube. **Open** 10am-6pm Mon-Sat; 11am-6pm Sun. **Credit** MC, V.
This is where Angelina, Bluebell, Blossom, Poppy and their gauzy, girlie friends hang out. Literally in fact, because many fairy toys, flower fairies, pixies and elfin toys hang from silver branches above your head. There are around 2,000 fairy products and the atmosphere is overwhelmingly pink and glittery. Quite often the staff are got up in tutus and tiaras too. There's a nod to the lads in the form of a Wizard corner in the dressing-up section. You can buy fairy bedwear (canopies, bed covers, slippers, dressing gowns, pyjamas and duvet covers), fairy and princess books and stickers, and fairy costumes, including various types of wings. Mystical Fairies parties take place in the basement Enchanted Garden, which is also home to Fairy Club and Fairy School.
Buggy access. Mail order. Nappy-changing facilities.
Branch: Bluewater Shopping Centre, Kent, DA9 9SR (01322 624997).

Semmalina-Starbags

225 Ebury Street, Pimlico, SW1W 8UT (7730 9333/www.starbags.info). Sloane Square tube. **Open** 9.30am-5.30pm Mon-Sat. **Credit** AmEx, MC, V. **Map** p316 G11.
A big leap into the wonderful world of party bags has given Semmalina a new lease of life. The neon-lit sweetie selection that catches the eye on entering forms the hub of the party bag productions. The bags (beribboned collections of goodies wrapped in satisfying crackly cellophane and all sorts of sparkles) cost from £2 for the trimmings; the delights that go within (retro sweets, such as flying saucers, liquorice whips and jelly snakes, pocket-money toys, such as googly eyes and bath duckies, twinkly hair accessories and statement-making stationery) cost extra. The choice is yours; the staff just need a week's warning to make them up. There are also all kinds of toys, gifts, clothes and unusual accessories that make sweet baby-welcome presents. In the basement lurks Papillon, a tiny shoe concession with black sensible schoolwear, Hunter wellies, and ballet pumps.
Buggy access. Delivery service. Nappy-changing facilities.

Consumer

Primping and playtime at **Little Stinkies**.

Toys R Us

760 Old Kent Road, Peckham, SE15 1NJ (7732 7322/ www.toysrus.co.uk). Elephant & Castle tube/rail, then 21, 56, 172 bus. **Open** 9am-8pm Mon-Fri; 9am-7pm Sat; 11am-5pm Sun. **Credit** AmEx, MC, V.
The Peckham branch of the chain of spacious toy warehouses, usually found in suburban retail parks, is the most central Toys R Us we know. All branches stock industrial quantities of the toy of the moment. Inexpensive bikes (from £39.99), trikes, ride-on tractors and go-karts. The party paraphernalia is good too: themed paperware, silly hats, balloons and party bags.
Buggy access. Car park. Delivery service. Disabled access: toilet. Nappy-changing facilities.
Branches: throughout town. Check website for details.

Local toy shops

Art Stationers/Green's Village Toy Shop

31 Dulwich Village, Dulwich, SE21 7BN (8693 5938). North Dulwich rail. **Open** 9am-5.30pm Mon-Sat. **Credit** MC, V.
Heaven for the arty and the playful, this pair of shops share the same front door. Veer left if you want paints, pastels, pencils, paper, stationery and craft materials. Continue down the corridor past the elaborate dolls' house for the best in toys: Brio, Sylvanian Families, Playmobil, Crayola, Lego. We're keen on the glove and string puppet selection from Tell a Tale and Puppet Co and are impressed by the enormous pocket money-priced range, which goes from your 25p rubber goldfish to the wonderful £2.25 magnetic car racers. Your party bag troubles are over.
Buggy access.

Fagin's Toys

84 Fortis Green Road, Muswell Hill, N10 3HN (8444 0282). East Finchley tube then 102 bus. **Open** 9am-5.30pm Mon-Sat; 10am-3pm Sun. **Credit** MC, V.
Fagin's is a lovely long space, with a playhouse to hide in, a central table of penny dreadfuls (little toy aliens from 20p) and several shelves of books. Then there are all the outdoor toys (buckets and spades, footballs, frisbees). Come here too for your fuzzy felt play mats, long-sleeve puppets, boxes of games (from Monopoly to Buckaroo) and favourites from Galt, Orchard, Brio, Lego, Playmobil and Sylvanian Families. An art corner has paint, glitter glue, art and craft kits by John Adams, boxes of experiments by Mad Science and magic stuff.
Buggy access. Disabled access. Play area.

Happy Returns

36 Rosslyn Hill, Hampstead, NW3 1NH (7435 2431). Hampstead tube. **Open** 10am-5.30pm Mon-Fri; 10am-6pm Sat; noon-5.30pm Sun. **Credit** MC, V.
Tasteful toys by Jellycat and many wooden toys supplement the boxed items from the consistently adorable and ever-growing Sylvanian Families range, Playmobil and Galt. A Warhammer section with lots of figures and paints draws in prep-school boys on a Saturday morning. We were whisked back in time at the sight of the £24.99 Fuzzyfelt compendium, handsomely packaged in a wooden box. Sturdy painted wooden toys and dollshouse accessories by Plan are stocked and there are also jolly, chunky plastics by Wow Toys.
Buggy access.

Little Rascals

140 Merton Road, Wimbledon, SW19 1EH (8542 9979). South Wimbledon tube. **Open** 9am-5.30pm Mon-Sat. **Credit** AmEx, MC, V.
A friendly, family-run local shop full of unusual wooden toys, clothes and gifts for babies, with Wheelybugs ride-ons in two sizes (£48-£58), Shoo-Shoos baby shoes (all £14), Jellycat toys, Mad Hatter soft toys, those excellent Grobags for babies prone to coverlet-kicking and a variety of toy storage chests.
Buggy access.

Little Stinkies

15 Victoria Grove, South Kensington W8 5RW (7052 0077). Gloucester Road tube. **Open** 9am-6pm Mon-Fri; 10am-6pm Sat. **Credit** AmEx, MC, V.
Funny name for a pretty shop, but Little Stinkies is a pleasure to explore. On our visit it had a highly amusing window display. Jellycat teddies, Manhattan dogs and cats and Maileg bunnies were sharing an afternoon at the beach, accompanied by wind-up fish, Tobarr mini china tea-sets, rubber ducks and the odd fairy. Inside you'll find puppet theatres, dolls' houses, dressing-up costumes, a party bag station with loads of sweets in jars, water-play toys, colouring books and stationery, and role-play items. Everything is rather tasteful, but there are pocket-money priced toys too. Little Stinkies also does haircuts (*see p188*), mini makeovers and hair art; ring for details.
Buggy access. Hairdressing.

Patrick's Toys & Models

107-111 Lillie Road, Fulham, SW6 7SX (7385 9864/ www.patrickstoys.co.uk). Fulham Broadway tube. **Open** 9.30am-5.30pm Mon-Sat. **Credit** MC, V.
A family-run business for more than 50 years, Patrick's is one of London's biggest toy and model shops, and the main service agent for Hornby and Scalextric. The model department specialises in rocketry, planes, cars, military and science fiction, making it popular with little boys. The general toy department has wooden toys, dolls' houses and their accessories. Outdoor sports get a look in with kites, bikes and garden games. TY beanie babies, Barbies and Bratz are also sold and there are many cheap party gifts.
Buggy access. Delivery service (local). Disabled access.

Play

89 Lauriston Road, Victoria Park, E9 7HJ (8510 9960/www.playtoy shops.com). Bethnal Green or Mile End tube/277, 388 bus. **Open** 10am-6pm Mon-Sat; 11am-4pm Sun. **Credit** AmEx, MC, V.
This toy shop on two floors is a pleasure to visit, being in a picturesque part of Hackney. Little girls love the princess themed books, tableware, trinkets and stationery, the Lily Dolls downstairs and the Pintoy dolls' houses, furniture and people. Everyone wants to cuddle the Gund soft toys and play with the Geomag, Galt and Playmobil. There are books and musical instruments by New Classic Toys. There's also a range of dressing-up stuff and messy play products (glitter, glue, dough, beads and paints) alongside trinkets by Jellycat and Lucy Lockett and party paperware.
Buggy access. Play area.

QT Toys

90 Northcote Road, Clapham, SW11 6QN (7223 8637/www.qttoys.co.uk). Clapham Junction rail. **Open** 9.30am-5.30pm Mon-Sat. **Credit** MC, V.

You can find most of the important stuff in a child's life at QT, from tacky plastic waterpistols to Barbie, Bratz, Brio and Lego. Then there's a wall crowded with craft kits, modelling toys, stationery, and educational toys such as a fine times-tables board. Gorgeous Schleich animals include farm and safari park livestock, wildlife and cantering horses. For small children there are dollies, buggies, push-along trucks and pull-along dogs. Outdoor gear includes paddling pools, sandpits, swings and scooters. *Buggy access. Disabled access. Mail order. Nappy-changing facilities. Play area.*

Route 73 Kids

92 Stoke Newington Church Street, Stoke Newington, N16 0AP (7923 7873). Bus 73, 393, 476. **Open** 10am-5.30pm Tue-Sun. **Credit** MC, V.
Take the No.73 bendy to this brightly coloured shop for traditional toys, pocket-money toys, educational toys and children's favourites that aren't toys. Brio trains and track, Plan wooden toys, Galt marble runs and art equipment are in the first category; rubber fish, mini pencils, bubbles and mini cars are in the second; books, puzzles, jigsaws and word games make up the third. Route 73 is strong on crafts and, in summer, it stocks outdoor toys including sandpit toys.
Buggy access. Disabled access.

Snap Dragon

56 Turnham Green Terrace, Chiswick, W4 1QP (8995 6618). Turnham Green tube. **Open** 9.30am-6pm Mon-Sat; 11am-5pm Sun. **Credit** MC, V.
A good general toy shop for big-name brands, where dolls like the pinkly attired Baby Annabell line up against pouty-mouthed Bratz and Smoby sit-and-rides. For imaginative play there are dolls' houses, accessories and figures by Pintoy, as well as sets from Playmobil. Family games include Twister, Buckaroo and Scrabble. Then there are kits, balls, rockets and remote-control cars.
Buggy access. Delivery service (local).

Toy Station

6 Eton Street, Richmond, Surrey TW9 1EE (8940 4896). Richmond tube/rail. **Open** 10am-6pm Mon-Fri; 9.30am-6pm Sat; noon-5pm Sun. **Credit** (over £8) MC, V.
Children are turned saucer-eyed with desire by this old-fashioned, two-storey toy shop. Inside, there's a great display of Schleich and Papo farm animals, wild animals, sea creatures, knights and soldiers. Forts and castles are bestsellers. Elsewhere, there are Nikko remote-control vehicles (Mini Cooper £24.99); dolls' houses and traditional wooden toys by Pintoy and Plan; and dolls, including Baby Annabell. The basement contains Playmobil, along with fancy dress costumes and accessories, and party equipment.
Buggy access. Disabled access.

Word Play

1 Broadway Parade, Crouch End, N8 9TN (8347 6700). Finsbury Park tube/rail then W7, 41 bus. **Open** 9am-5.30pm Mon-Sat; 11am-5pm Sun. **Credit** MC, V.
Children love to peruse Wordplay's pocket-money/party bag selection, which has fripperies from 10p for fortune-telling fish (stretchy aliens and rubbery goldfish – always a useful find in a party bag, we reckon – cost 20p). There's an admirably wide choice of children's books, featuring the likes of Angelina, Alex Rider and Tracy Beaker. Then there are craft supplies and building toys (Bionicles, Geomag). Adorably detailed Schleich toys (little figures like farm animals and soldiers) cost £1.99-£6.99; a castle to keep them in is £69.99. The shop's location in this child-centric area gives it a sociable feel.
Buggy access. Disabled access.

Traditional toys

Benjamin Pollock's Toy shop

*44 The Market, Covent Garden, WC2E 8RF (7379
7866/www.pollocks-coventgarden.co.uk). Covent Garden
tube.* **Open** 10.30am-6pm Mon-Sat; 11am-4pm Sun.
Credit AmEx, MC, V. **Map** p317 L7.

A wonderful, creaky toy shop, Pollock's is best known for
its toy theatres. These cost from £6.95 for the Pollock's
Harlequinade (easy to put together). EReady-assembled
theatres cost about £75; hand-painted ones are £135.
Elsewhere there are all kinds of curiosities, from those fortune-telling fish by the till, to farmyard scenes in match-
boxes, tea sets, marble runs, marionettes, glove and finger
puppets, masks (£1.40) and pocket compasses (£1.99).
Mail order.

Bob & Blossom

*140 Columbia Road, Bethnal Green, E2 7RG (7739
4737/www.bobandblossom.com). Old Street tube/rail/|
55 bus.* **Open** 9am-3pm Sun. **Credit** MC, V.

Danish wooden Noah's Ark sets, toy cars, trademark tiny
T-shirts emblazoned with cheeky mottos, Mexican jump-
ing beans, spinning tops – the selection at B&B is eclectic.
The shop's doing a roaring trade despite being open just
six hours a week, to coincide with Columbia Road's famous
Sunday flower market.
Buggy access. Mail order.

Compendia Traditional Games

*10 The Market, Greenwich, SE10 9HZ (8293 6616/
www.compendia.co.uk). Cutty Sark DLR/Greenwich rail.*
Open 11am-5.30pm Mon-Fri; 10am-5.30pm Sat, Sun.
Credit MC, V.

The ultimate shop for a rainy day, Compendia has the
traditionals – chess, backgammon, dominoes, Scrabble,
Snakes & Ladders – as well as an appealing range of more

obscure games from around the world to suit all ages. Little
ones have fun with Coppit, a wobbly hat game.
*Buggy access. Delivery service. Disabled access.
Mail order.*

Enchanted Forest

*6 Sheen Road, Richmond, Surrey TW9 1AS (0870 420
8632). Richmond tube/rail.* **Open** 9.30am-5.30pm Mon-
Sat; 11am-4pm Sun. **Credit** MC, V.

This shop holds a selection of the extensive Tridias catalogue stock. There are shelves of intriguing chemistry and
science sets, and outdoor toys including croquet, cricket
and swingball sets. Otherwise, expect to find dressing-up
clothes, Brio, tool kits, marble runs, garages and cars,
farms and animals, dolls' houses and accessories, plenty
of educational books and board games. Popular items
include a stage for puppet shows (£34.99), wizard puppets
(£6.99) and an ace wooden rocking horse (£759, including
delivery). For parties, there's some lovely decorated tableware and party-bag gifts.
Buggy access. Mail order (0870 443 1300).

Farmyard

*63 Barnes High Street, Barnes, SW13 9LF (8878
7338/www.thefarmyard.co.uk). Barnes or Barnes
Bridge rail.* **Open** 10am-5.30pm Mon-Fri; 9.30am-
5.30pm Sat. **Credit** MC, V.

Traditional toys and games for newborns to eight year-
olds are corralled into the Farmyard, which has its own
range of wooden toys, models and kits. Small children can't
resist the London bus; the roof slides back to reveal the driver and passengers inside. There are also shelves of
fairy/princess stuff, some dressing-up gear, and keepsake
toys such as personalised piggy banks and jewellery boxes.
Nursery gifts include pram and cot blankets.
Buggy access. Delivery service. Play area.

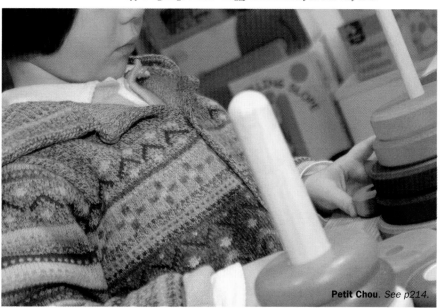

Petit Chou. *See p214.*

Kristin Baybars

7 Mansfield Road, Gospel Oak, NW3 2JD (7267 0934).
Kentish Town tube/Gospel Oak rail/C2, C11 bus. **Open**
11am-6pm Tue-Sat. **No credit cards.**
The faded pink shop-front with grilles over the windows
looks a bit neglected; the signs on the doors ('this is not a
toy shop…') seem forbidding. However, once Ms Baybars
or hr assistant sees you hovering outside she ushers you
in and leaves you to browse, first giving warnings about
what can and can't be touched. Obedient children with an
interest in miniature worlds can have a lovely time – for
this is paradise for anyone with a dolls' house. Many items
are pocket-money priced (tiny Coke bottles, 25p), but
plenty of the dolls' houses are valuable, and for serious
collectors, so very young children aren't encouraged, and
in any case, you couldn't fit a push-chair in here.

Never Never Land

3 Midhurst Parade, Fortis Green, N10 3EJ (8883
3997/www.never-never-land.co.uk). East Finchley tube.
Open 10am-5pm Tue, Wed, Fri, Sat. **Credit** MC, V.
This diminutive shop is crammed with old-world delights,
such as dolls' houses (from £99 in kit form) and their
accessories (from about £1 for plates of food). Other toys
for imaginative play include Baby Safe Dollies with soft
bodies and plaited wool hair, kitchen essentials, such as
little stves with pots and pans to rattle, wooden beads for
jewellery making, Heimess pram toys, tea sets, wooden
firemen and their firestation, soldiers with forts, and cars
with garages. Prices start pretty low; those nostalgic little
gorgeous Chinese purses are 99p.
Buggy access. Mail order.

Petit Chou

15 St Christopher's Place, W1U 1NR (7486 3637/
www.petitchou.co.uk). Bond Street tube.
Open 10.30am-6.30pm Mon-Sat; noon-5pm Sun.
Credit AmEx, MC, V.
This tasteful clothes and toy shop has handcrafted wood-
en toys from all over the world. Especially attractive are
German moorland sheep and wooden ride-on cat walkers.
There are also wooden pull-along toys, such as buses and
dogs, toys to cuddle, knock over, arrange in towers and
knock over again. They're all sturdy and smart. We
particularly like the Jack-in-the-box (you don't see many of
those these days and the funny Peek-a-boo ball.
Buggy access.

Puppet Planet

787 Wandsworth Road (corner of the Chase), Clapham,
SW8 3JQ (7627 0111/07900 975276/
www.puppetplanet.co.uk). Clapham Common tube.
Open 9am-4pm Tue-Sat; also by appointment.
Credit AmEx, DC, MC, V.
A specialist marionette shop, Puppet Planet is run by
Lesley Butler, whose passion for stringed characters
extends to her children's party service. Puppets sold
include classic Pelham characters, Indian and African marionettes, Balinese shadow puppets, and vintage carved and
felt hand-puppets from Germany. Prices go from a couple
of quid for a finger puppet (we love the Red Riding Hood,
Grandma, and Wolf combo) to quite a bit more for the more
expressive models. You can even commission a lookalike
puppet (from £250 for a marionette).
Buggy access. Delivery service. Disabled access. Mail
order.

Rainbow

253 Archway Road, Archway, N6 5BS (8340
9700/www.rainbow-toys.co.uk). Highgate tube.
Open 10.30am-5.30pm Mon-Sat. **Credit** MC, V.
Most small children make straight for the Brio play table
in this friendly , treasure-stuffed shop; older ones check out
the pocket-money priced toys. There are dressing-up
costumes, for would-be pirates and woodland fairies, and
ballet clothes too. Wooden Pin and Plan Toys include
sit-and-rides and tricycles (£30-£50), and you'll also find
painted wooden forts, farms and houses from Le Toy Van,
with wonderfully detailed Papo animals, soldiers, knights
and more. Dolls' houses cost £45-£75. Orchard Toys –
games and puzzles linked to Key Stages in the National
Curriculum and Early Learning objectives – are another
speciality. Puppets are much in evidence, as are Gund
bears and soft, Manhattan cuddlies. Display counters offer
assorted marbles, trinkets kids' jewellery and hair accessories and dolls' house furnishings.
Buggy access. Delivery service. Mail order. Nappy-
changing facilities. Play area.

Soup Dragon

27 Topsfield Parade, Tottenham Lane, Crouch End, N8
8PT (8348 0224/www.soup-dragon.co.uk). Finsbury
Park tube/rail then 41, W7 bus. **Open** 9.30am-6pm
Mon-Sat; 11am-5pm Sun. **Credit** EmEx, MC, V.
With its well-equipped, mini-kitchen play area, big choice
of traditional toys, unusual clothes and quirky baby equipment, the Soup Dragon is a versatile beast. Staff are f
riendly and pleasant to rampaging children. We love the
striped knitted leggings, jumpers and hats for babies (from
about £14) and the more expensive hand knits by Merry
Berry. There are high chairs, slings and Grobag sleeping
bags, but toys are the mainstay. Soft toys for babies come
from LaMaze; fancy dress comes in classic forms like
ballerinas and pirates, as well as cute wild beast outfits
and brave knights. Then there are the soft, bendy fairy
dolls, and pretty dolls' houses (£79 for an impressive
Victorian version, £59 for the Candy Cottage). The noticeboard is excellent. Bargain hunters may leave an email
address to be advised of the warehouse sales. The east
Dulwich branch (*see below*) shares premises with the
Family Natural Health Centre (8693 5515).
Buggy access. Disabled access. Mail order. Play area.
Branch: 106 Lordship Lane, SE22 8HF (8693 5575).

Traditional Toys

53 Godfrey Street, Chelsea, SW3 3SX (7352 1718/
www.traditionaltoy.com). Sloane Square tube then 11,
19, 22 bus/49 bus. **Open** 10am-6pm Mon-Fri; 10am-
6pm Sat. **Credit** AmEx, MC, V. **Map** p313 E11.
This terrific little shop near Chelsea Green fills every nook
and cranny with games, books and toys. Many toys are at
pocket-money prices – such as farm animals, dinosaurs,
bouncy balls, stickers and soldiers. It's the beautiful wood-
en toys that really grab you, however, such as the tell-the-
time clock face and rainbow coloured clown stack. Then
there are the bigger birthday specials, such as painted animal trikes and dolls' houses. Shelves hold Breyer model
ponies, Brio train sets, boats, dolls, teddies (by Steiff, Gund
and the North American Bear Company), wooden Noah's
Arks and much more. The fancy-dress section – sheriffs,
knights, elves and fairies – includes accessories for imaginative games (swords, helmets, hobbyhorses and the like).
Costumes can also be ordered from a catalogue.
Buggy access.

Activities

Features

Arts & Entertainment

Where to gaze and be amazed, and where to create a stir.

Keep your hand in, at the **National Portrait Gallery**. *See p233.*

The best thing about being in a city this immense is the variety of entertainment offered. You could go to a class, a production, a workshop or an exhibition every day if you had the energy. There's so much you can experience at first hand – art, drama, dance, music, languages – that there's no excuse for staying in with the telly. It's true that going to the cinema or theatre is rarely free, but you don't have to be rich to fill your world with art and culture in London. A few pounds buys a day's workshop in one of the world's most beautiful opera houses (**ENO**'s Family Days, *see p223*), a weekend show – at the **Albany** or **Broadway** (*see p226* for both) theatres – or a film and workshop in a cinema (**Clapham Picturehouse**, *see p221*). You can also make art, see concerts and dip ponds for nothing at all. Many galleries (*see p217*), theatres, music colleges (*see p223*) and nature gardens (*see p239*) run free activities in school holidays.

Programmes alter throughout the year – and expand significantly in the school holidays – so get on as many mailing lists as possible and keep an eye on the websites.

Arts centres

Transformation work was continuing on the Southbank Centre (*see p236* **Creative spirit**) as we went to press. The refurbished Royal Festival Hall promises a revamped ballroom and foyer, and improved acoustics, seating and technical design in the main auditorium. For updates, check www.rfh.org.uk. Over in Camden, the historic Roundhouse and its youth-focused Creative Centre is up and running following the relaunch last year.

Barbican Centre

Silk Street, The City, EC2Y 8DS (box office 7638 8891/cinema hotline 7382 7000/arts education programme 7382 2333/www.barbican.org.uk). Barbican tube/Moorgate tube/rail. **Open** *Box office (in person)* 9am-8pm Mon-Sat; noon-8pm Sun, bank hols. *Gallery* 11am-8pm Mon, Wed, Fri, Sat, Sun; 11am-6pm Tue, Thur. **Admission** *Library* free. *Exhibitions, films, shows, workshops* phone for details. **Membership** (BarbicanCard) £20/yr. *Film Club* £7.50/yr/family. **Credit** AmEx, MC, V. **Map** p318 P5.
Twenty five years old this year, the Barbican has a 2007 full of celebratory events, as well as the usual well-organised programme of family-orientated activities

including the weekly Family Film Club with Saturday screenings at 11am, advance ticket prices of £2.50, work-shops, goodies and events. A diverse mix of internation-al movies is screened for kids aged five to 11 and their parents; booking ahead is recommended. The new Baby screening was introduced last year every Monday at noon. Less regularly, the Barbican hosts mini-seasons and events for families, including the annual Animate The World! cartoon-fest in summer, and the London Children's Film Festival in November. The children's classic concerts enchantingly combine music and storytelling.
Buggy access. Café. Disabled access: lift, toilet. Nappy-changing facilities. Restaurants. Shop.

Rich Mix

35-47 Bethnal Green Road, Bethnal Green, E1 6LA (7613 7498/www.richmix.org.uk). Bethnal Green tube/rail. **Open** 9am-11pm daily. **Admission** prices vary; phone for details. **Credit** MC, V.
The Rich Mix building is a vast former garment factory turned cross-cultural arts and media centre, with an artsy, East End flavour. It houses a three-screen cinema; exhi-bition spaces, café and broadcasting centre; recording and music training studios; a 200-seater performance venue; education spaces and workspaces. Trendy events held here include 'Mix the Flavour', East London's only rap and spoken word 'open mic' session for those aged 12 to 25. Rix Mix cinema offers a good-value Sunday family ticket for £12/£16 with free family learning days planned.
Bar. Buggy access. Cafés. Disabled access: lift, ramps, toilet. Nappy-changing facilities.

Southbank Centre

Belvedere Road, South Bank, SE1 8XX (box office 0871 663 2500/www.southbankcentre.co.uk). Embankment tube/Waterloo tube/rail. **Open** *Box office (in person) & Foyer* 10am-8pm daily. **Admission** prices vary; phone for details. **Credit** AmEx, MC, V. **Map** p317 M8.
Down on the South Bank the 3,000-capacity Royal Festival Hall was scheduled to open in June 2007 (information cor-rect as we went to press) after a series of renovations. For more details *see p236* **Creative spirit.**
Buggy access. Café. Disabled access: infrared hearing facility, lift, toilet. Nappy-changing facilities.

Tricycle Theatre & Cinema

269 Kilburn High Road, Kilburn, NW6 7JR (box office 7328 1000/www.tricycle.co.uk). Kilburn tube/ Brondesbury rail. **Open** *Box office* 10am-9pm Mon-Sat; 2-8pm Sun. *Children's shows* 11.30am, 2pm Sat. *Children's films* 1pm Sat. **Tickets** *Theatre* (Sat) £5; £4 advance bookings. *Films* (Sat) £4.50; £3.50 under-16s, concessions. **Credit** MC, V.
A venue with a real community feel, the Tricycle has a programme of children's shows, events, films and workshops hailed by *The Times Educational Supplement* as 'one of the best reasons for living in and around Kilburn'. The inspirational range of children's activities incorporates various after-school classes, covering drama, dance and performance. Half-term and holiday workshops allow kids to get creative with everything from screen printing to producing a play in a day. Details can be found on the website, which also lists the regular Saturday film screenings and stage shows.
Buggy access. Disabled access: lift, ramps, toilet. Nappy-changing facilities. Restaurant.

Art galleries

Many of London's major galleries include free arty activity packs (*see p233*) to enhance the experience for young visitors; it's always worth asking about these. Besides the listings below, check **Around Town** (*p32-162*) for information on children's activities, workshops and all sorts of family events in the South Bank's **Tate Modern** (*see p46*) and **Hayward Gallery** (*see p38*), Westminster's **National Gallery** (*see p81*) and **Tate Britain** (*see p83*), the **Royal Academy of Arts** in Piccadilly (*see p74*), the **Wallace Collection** in Marylebone (*see p78*) and the **Dulwich Picture Gallery** in South-east London (*see p129*).

Camden Arts Centre

Corner of Arkwright Road and Finchley Road, Camden, NW3 6DG (7472 5500/www.camdenartscentre.org). Finchley Road tube/Finchley Road & Frognal rail. **Open** 10am-6pm Tue, Thur-Sun; 10am-9pm Wed. **Admission** free. **Credit** *Shop* MC, V.
Camden Arts Centre's makeover has created more light and space in this attractive building while keeping its lovely entrance arches, terrazzo flooring and tall, stone dressed windows. The three new galleries host exhibitions, a state-of-the-art ceramics studio and a busy programme of courses for adults and children. Typically, half-terms feature two-day courses in, say, clay and mixed media for £46 (£28 concessions). For term-time courses cater on Saturdays for young people of various age groups.
Bookshop. Buggy access. Café. Disabled access: lifts, toilets. Nappy-changing facilities.

Learning Centre

Somerset House, Strand, WC2R 0RN (7836 8686/ recorded information 7848 2526/www.courtauld.ac. uk). Covent Garden, Holborn or Temple (closed Sun) tube/Charing Cross tube/rail. **Open** *Gallery* 10am-6pm daily (last entry 5.15pm); noon-6pm 1 Jan; 10am-4pm 31 Dec. **Tours** pre-booked groups only; phone for details. **Admission** *Gallery* £5; £4 concessions; free under-18s, UK students. Free to all 10am-2pm Mon (not bank hols). **Credit** MC, V. **Map** p317 M7.
Somerset House (*see p70*) is not just a pretty place. Its Learning Centre has an innovative programme of workshops and events. Guided by friendly tutors, family visitors can explore the site and collections and create their own response inspired by the experience. Regular activities include, for six to 12 year-olds and their fami-lies, exploring art, detective trails, and creative writing. Free holiday drop-ins for half terms and school breaks have an emphasis on creative making and play. Free fam-ily trails for five to seven year-olds, and eight to 11s, explore the fabulous building and its history. All day stu-dio days (about £15 for the day) are sometimes run for older (12-16yrs) creative artists during the school holidays. For workshop and learning enquiries, email the Families Programme Coordinator (annette.richardson@somerset-house.org.uk). Make a note of the Free Time festival, which takes place 26-29 July 2007 and promises all sorts of fun for families and young people.
Buggy access. Café. Disabled access: lift, toilet. Nappy-changing facilities. Shop.

Activities

London International Gallery of Children's Art

O2 Centre, 255 Finchley Road, Finchley Road, NW3 6LU (7435 0903/www.ligca.org). Finchley Road tube. **Open** 4-6pm Tue-Thur; noon-6pm Fri-Sun. **Admission** free; donations requested. LIGCA celebrates the creativity of children from around the world. Forthcoming events in 2007 include: 'Magical Buildings from Istanbul' (7 August to 6 October); an exhibition of art by children who have illustrated a book about the aboriginal Australian artist Albert Namatjirra (9 October-8 December); art by children from North Wales (11 December 2007-9 February 2008); and an exhibition of arts and crafts by children in India (12 February-12 April 2008). Free Sunday afternoon art workshops cater for five to 12 year-olds. Arty birthday parties can be booked here too. LIGCA is run by volunteers; so phone before setting out. *Buggy access. Disabled access: lift, toilet. Nappy-changing facilities (O2 Centre).*

Orleans House Gallery

Riverside, Twickenham, Middx TW1 3DJ (8831 6000/ www.richmond.gov.uk). St Margaret's, Richmond or Twickenham rail/33, 490, H22, R68, R70 bus. **Open** *Apr-Sept* 1-5.30pm Tue-Sat; 2-5.30pm Sun, bank hols. *Oct-Mar* 1-4.30pm Tue-Sat; 2-4.30pm Sun, bank hols. **Admission** free; donations appreciated. **Credit** MC, V. Down a secluded riverside path surrounded by woodland, the 18th-century Orleans House resembles a country seat more than a centre for the living arts. The Coach House education centre hosts holiday art workshops using the gallery's art exhibitions as a starting point. There's an upbeat series of year-round activity workshops for kids. Art Club (for five to ten year-olds) and 10:15 (for ten to 15 year-olds) provide after-school art workshops and the Star Club (five to ten year-olds) focuses on performance. For more information, phone to be put on the mailing list. Events for 2007 include Heritage Day (Sunday 16 September); Family Learning Week and the Big Draw. *Buggy access. Disabled access: ramp, toilet. Nappy-changing facilities. Nearest picnic place: Orleans House Gallery grounds, Marble Hill Park or riverside benches. Shop.*

Cinemas

Leicester Square beckons if you're after a blockbuster multiplex blowout. It's home to the (pricey) West End flagships of **Vue** (0871 224 0240, www.myvue.com), the **Odeon** (0871 224 4007, www.odeon.co.uk), and the **Empire** (0871 224 4007). Some of these big boys are however, getting in on the 'watch with baby' act pioneered by the Picturehouse chain (Big Scream! *see p221*). The Odeon's 'newby screenings' take place on Tuesdays in selected branches – check their website. They've a way to go to catch up with Picturehouse, however, whose Saturday Clubs, baby screenings and screenings for autistic people, speak volumes about its all-round good-egg qualities. Many also offer workshops and special events (*see also p216* **Arts Centres**).

Chicken Shed Theatre

An inclusive, dynamic theatre company that devises must-see shows and must-do workshops. *See p226.*

Laban

Runs performance classes that have a dazzling reputation and a lengthy waiting list; book a seat for the junior department's annual show to keep up your spirits while you wait. *See p234.*

London International Gallery of Children's Art

Celebrates children's creativity with its child-centred exhibitions and workshops. *See p218.*

Royal College of Music

Has a highly competitive audition process, but the free performances show you why. *See p223.*

Wigmore Hall

The most beautiful concert hall in town, where Chamber Tots who play their strings right might go on to perform. *See p223.*

BFI London IMAX

1 Charlie Chaplin Walk, South Bank, SE1 8XR (0870 787 2525/www.bfi.org.uk/imax). Waterloo tube/rail. **Open** 12.30-9.30pm Mon-Fri; 10.30am-9.45pm Sat, Sun. **Admission** £8.50; £5 4-15s; £6.50 concessions; free under-4s; add-on film £6 extra per adult, £4 extra per child. **Credit** AmEx, MC, V. This London landmark houses the biggest cinema screen in the UK – over 20m (65ft) high and 26m (85ft) wide. Kids enjoy wearing 3D glasses to watch special IMAX films such as *The Lions of the Kalahari* (purpose-produced documentaries, where storylines are secondary to the fantastic effects that seem to leap from the screen), or popular animated films retooled for 3D. Note that some films could be a bit intense for very young viewers. During the summer, mainstream films are shown here (though rarely in 3D); *Spider-man III* gets the IMAX treatment in 2007. Christmas brings festive entertainment, such as 3D screenings of *The Polar Express*. Ticket prices for these special events are usually higher. *Buggy access. Café. Disabled access: lift, toilets. Nappy-changing facilities.*

BFI Southbank

National Film Theatre, Belvedere Road, South Bank, SE1 8XT (box office 7928 3232/www.bfi.org.uk). Waterloo tube/rail. **Open** Box office phone bookings 11.30am-8.30pm daily. *Personal callers* 5-8.30pm Mon-Thur; 11.30am-8.30pm Fri-Sun. *Film club* times vary; usually Sat, Sun, school hols. **Tickets** *Children* £1 film, £6.25 workshop & film. Prices vary, phone to confirm. *Adults* £7.60 members, £8.20 non-members.

families
Have great days out at Tate

A visit to Tate is child's play...

Let your children's imagination run riot at Tate! Whether it's your first visit with your children or you've been before, there's loads do to for everyone.

Sign up for free families email bulletins to find out more: www.tate.org.uk/bulletins

Tate Britain
Millbank
London SW1P 4RG
⊖ Pimlico or Vauxhall
🚢 Millbank Pier

Open daily 10.00–17.50

BP British Art Displays 1500–2007

Supported by BP

bp

Tate Modern
Bankside
London SE1 9TG
⊖ Southwark or Blackfriars
🚢 Bankside Pier

Open Sunday – Thursday, 10.00–18.00
Friday and Saturday, 10.00–22.00

Opening up art. Tate Modern Collection with UBS

✣ UBS

Call 020 7887 8888
www.tate.org.uk/families

Photo: Richard Eaton

Cinematic city

Film is the pre-eminent creative medium of our age and an essential part of the UK's cultural heritage. The industry in London alone is worth billions. It's only right, then, that the British film industry should invest in its future – the young filmmakers that can ensure Britain's continuing screen successes. Children wishing to take advantage of such investment are spoilt for choice in London. The city is now a perfect location for children – both would-be auteurs and big-screen addicts – to discover filmmaking.

A prime example is **First Light** (www.firstlightmovies.com), the scheme for five to 18 year-olds funded by the UK Film Council. First Light invests over £1 million annually, offering a range of courses across the country via schools and educational groups. Its subsidiary website **Film Street** (www.filmstreet.co.uk) is a user-friendly resource providing a starting point for children exploring filmmaking, while the First Light Awards every February is an inspiring 'mini-Oscars' event, set in London.

Film London (www.filmlondon.com), London's film and media agency, supports projects across the capital. One such venture that represents film education at a local level is East London charitable organisation **The Mouth That Roars** (www.mouththatroars.com), which offers training in video production and gives free membership to under-19s who attend its workshops; the studios and cinema-café are also open to the public. At the other end of the scale, investment can be made in the Young Filmmakers Academy for those aged 14 years and up, a summer course run by the **Metropolitan Film School** (www.metfilm school.co.uk). Practical filmmaking for children aged from seven is the business of the newly rebranded **Young Film Academy** (www.youngfilm academy.co.uk), whose expanding programme of courses, workshops, schools events, parties (*see p249*) and charitable programmes across London has earned it gigs as official workshop provider for the Edinburgh International Film Festival, Encounters (Bristol), Leeds International Film Festival and the London Children's Film Festival (*see below*). The Academy has helped more than 600 young people make their first films. In school holidays its one-to-four-day filmmaking courses for seven to 16 year-olds are based in West London. The four-day courses culminate in a red-carpet première for friends and family in a West End screening room; students on every course receive a DVD copy of their film to keep. Details of YFA work can be found at www.filmfantastic.co.uk.

Children's film festivals offer further opportunities for learning, as well as the chance for families to enjoy lots of films at budget prices. The **London Children's Film Festival**, now in its third year and billed as the biggest family film event in London, is on 17-25 November 2007. The nexus of operations is the Barbican (www.barbican.org.uk), with 15 other cinemas across London involved, presenting new cinema from around the world, a multiplicity of screenings, and hands-on workshops.

To watch films in central London it's worth looking into deals and discounts from West End cinemas and major arts centres. Family tickets giving small savings are offered by most chains including Odeon and Vue; book online for the best deals. Vue West End (www.myvue.com) is introducing Kids AM on weekend mornings; children's tickets cost £1.50 with accompanying adults going free. For the very best screens for Saturday cinema, make a date with the **Barbican** (*see p216*); **BFI Southbank** and **BFI Imax** (for both *see p218*).

Young Film Academy

BFI London IMAX. *See p218.*

Membership £35/yr; £25/yr concession.
Credit AmEx, MC, V. **Map** p317 M8.
All ready for its close-up since relaunching post-facelift in March 2007, the big, bright new film centre is a lovely place to visit, with its arts spaces, installations, comfy café-bar and 4 screens. Bring the family on Saturday mornings, when beautifully remastered junior screenings combine class (*The Railway Children*) and current hits (*Arthur and the Invisibles*). The centre is just across the road from the UK's biggest screen, the BFI IMAX (*see above*).
Buggy access. Café. Disabled access: ramp, toilet. Nappy-changing facilities.

Clapham Picturehouse

76 Venn Street, Clapham, SW4 0AT (0870 755 0061/www.picturehouses.co.uk). Clapham Common tube/35, 37 bus. **Open** *Box office* (phone bookings) 9.30am-8.30pm daily. *Film club* activities 11.15am, screening 11.45am Sat. **Tickets** £3; £2 members. **Membership** £4/yr. **Credit** MC, V.
Kids' film clubs and parent-and-baby screenings were pioneered at this stylish cinema. Parents with infants under one year can bring them to the long-running Big Scream! club at 10.30am every Thursday. Park prams in the bar, and watch a movie from an updated roster of blockbuster and art-house films without having to worry about disturbing the audience. The Kids' Club offers Saturday matinées for three to ten year-olds. Staff organise craft and activity workshops before the show and prize competitions afterwards. Young members can go into the projection room and start the film on their birthday.
Buggy access. Café. Disabled access: toilet (Screens 3 & 4 only). Nappy-changing facilities.

Electric Cinema

191 Portobello Road, Notting Hill, W11 2ED (7908 9696/www.the-electriccinema.co.uk). Ladbroke Grove or Notting Hill Gate tube/52 bus. **Open** *Box office* 9am-8.30pm Mon-Sat; 10am-8.30pm Sun. *Children's screenings* 11am Sat (depending on film length; phone to check). **Tickets** *children's films* £4.50 (all ages). *Workshops* £2.50. **Credit** AmEx, MC, V. **Map** p310 A7.
With its film-star looks, this is one of London's most exclusive cinemas. For membership, you must apply in writing, be accepted by a committee of locals, and then pay up to £250 a year. Membership gives you access to the Electric House's restaurant and private rooms. Another perk is that members receive two free tickets for every Kids' Club screening. These show classic films and preview new releases, with occasional arts activities. Parents and their babies (up to one year) can enjoy special Electric Scream! screenings on Mondays at 3pm (except bank holidays).
Buggy access. Disabled access: lift, toilet. Kiosk.

Gate Cinema

87 Notting Hill Gate, W11 3JZ (08707 550063/ www.picturehouses.co.uk). Notting Hill Gate tube. **Open** *Box Office* 9.30am-8.30pm daily. *Children's screenings* 11am Sat. **Tickets** £4; £3 members. **Membership** £4/yr. **Credit** AmEx, MC, V.
The Gate runs a Saturday Kids' Club with pre-screening activities. Games like pin the tail on the donkey start before the 11am screenings.
Buggy access. Kiosk.

Greenwich Picturehouse

180 Greenwich High Road, Greenwich SE10 8NN (08707 550056/www.picturehouses.co.uk). Cutty Sark DLR/Greenwich rail. **Open** *Box Office* 11am-10pm daily. **Kids' Club screenings** 11.30am Sat. **Membership** £4.50/yr. **Tickets** £3 members; £4.50 non-members, adults. **Credit** MC, V.

The four screener Greenwich branch of the right-on Picturehouse chain has tapas bar attached, as well as a children's club on Saturday mornings and a Big Scream! on Fridays at 11.30am.

Buggy access. Café. Disabled: lift, toilet. Kiosk. Nappy-changing facilities.

Rio Cinema

103-107 Kingsland High Street, Dalston, E8 2PB (7241 9410/www.riocinema.co.uk). Dalston Kingsland rail/Liverpool Street tube/rail, then 67, 77, 149 bus. **Open** *Box office* 2-8pm daily. *Film club* 4.15pm Tue; 11am Sat. **Tickets** £2; £1 under-15s. **Credit** AmEx, MC, V.

The Rio is a fun, friendly place where Kids' Club members are given a card, to be stamped on each visit, and children get a free visit after ten stamps. A parent-and-baby club (under-ones) operates on Tuesdays and Thursday lunchtimes; it costs £5.50 (£4.50 concessions). During the school holidays, they offer daily matinees of a good mix of recent films for 5-15 year olds.

Café. Disabled access: toilet.

Ritzy Cinema

Brixton Oval, Coldharbour Lane, Brixton, SW2 1JG (0870 755 0062/www.picturehouses.co.uk). Brixton tube/rail. **Open** *Box office* 10.15am-9.15pm daily. *Film club* 10.30am Sat. **Tickets** £3; £1 under-14s. **Credit** MC, V.

In the club

Why should children be excluded when adults are having fun? Why indeed – a few clued-up promoters are starting to realise that kids are clubbable too.

After all, clubbing in its late 1980s incarnation was child's play. The dummies, lollipops and smiley accessories beloved of ravers were rooted in a Fisher-Price aesthetic. Rave choons relied on samples from cartoons, helium-style vocals, and even children's safety videos (as in 'Charly' by the Prodigy). Titles too were appropriated from kids' culture ('Rhubarb and Custard' anyone?). Ecstasy itself, originally developed for use in therapy, held the potential to allow users to get in touch with their 'inner child' – even though ultimately that might only amount to lying in front of the *Teletubbies* babbling and dribbling...

Eventually, the first rave generation grew up and rave culture became absorbed into the mainstream, with most aspects becoming commercialised. Even breast-feeding future ravers started to be catered for. **Punk Rock Baby** (www.punkrockbaby.com), a series designed to instil taste into nerdy offspring, gave us lullaby versions of classic tracks; it first appeared in 2002, and includes 'Ibiza Baby'.

Around the same time, many music festivals became a big day out (rather than a night), and evolved further to accommodate families. The free fruity Regent's Park event run by Innocent, (the smoothies people), which has run each year since 2002 (www.innocentdrinks.co.uk), is one such example. Ben & Jerry's **Sundae on the Common** festivals in Clapham is another. Herefordshire's **The Big Chill** (www.thebigchill.net) and the Isle of Wight's **Bestival** (www.bestival.net) attract many London families.

Outside festival season, club events involving children have been more scarce, but there are a few. With its motto music and people of all ages and places, the multifaceted, trance-based **Whirl Y Gig** collective (www.whirl-y-gig.org.uk) has welcomed families to its festival-club events for over 26 years. **Planet Angel**, also with trance roots, has hosted Planet Angel Chilled in north London since 2001: a labour of love with DJs, games and holistic activities. See www.planet angel.net for the next launch. In 2003 duo Lemon Jelly paved the way further with their Jelly Tots live show. The event – featuring bouncy castles, clowns and balloons, with all adults accompanied by a child under 12 – was a sell-out.

In the same year, XFM and Playstation presented the Third Place at Westbourne Studios (stemming from Eddy Temple Morris's radio show) featuring DJing, live music, games, a crèche and restaurant. More recently, 2006 saw the launch of **Disco Loco** at Chat's Palace in Hackney. It's a hip and hugely popular Sunday event underpinned by the belief that adults and children really can enjoy good music together. Food and drink are available too. Music requests for the monthly event can be sent to discoloco@gmail.com.

The baton has also been picked up by **Babygroove** (www.babygroove.co.uk), launched early in 2007. This showcases funky house sounds on Saturdays at Alchemist Bar, Clapham (www.alchemistbar.co.uk), with children's snacks and chill-out areas on hand. Rapturous reactions from families at these events show that kids' clubbing has real mileage. The (dance)floor is now open to promoters in every genre, and every age; there's also a strong under-18s live music and club scene in London, from chart and dance events such as **Rhythm** (www.rhythmparty.com).

Of course, for promoters looking to cash in on steep admission charges to booze- and drug-fuelled all-nighters, catering for under-18s is not a priority. And it's a given that the best clubs are by nature transient and illicit, making for a challenge suited to more imaginative promoters only. However, as long as people continue to make the shift from recreation to procreation, the market is there.

Activities

Opened in 1911, the Ritzy has survived various owners, near demolition and significant development in the 1990s to become one of London's finest. Now it's in the Picturehouse family. Kids' Club films are shown every Saturday at 10.30am. The Big Scream! is on Fridays at 11am, open to parents with under-ones only.
Buggy access. Café. Disabled access: lift, toilet. Nappy-changing facilities.

Stratford East Picturehouse

Theatre Square, Salway Road, Stratford, E15 1BX (0870 7550064/www.picturehouses.co.uk). Stratford tube/rail/DLR. **Open** *Box office* Phone bookings 9am-9pm daily. *Film club* 10.30am Sat. **Tickets** £2 members; £3 non-members. **Membership** £4/yr. **Credit** MC, V.
Attractions for families and children include a film club where creative activities, fun and games take place after a screening. The club is suitable for three to ten year-olds and costs £4 a year, with film tickets costing £2. Kids' Club membership entitles you to the first film free. Members receive a quarterly newsletter and the chance to enter competitions, win prizes, and start the film on their birthday. The sanity-saving Big Scream, for parents who can't escape their babies, is on Tuesdays at 11am, except school holidays (£4.20; no membership fee).
Buggy access. Café. Disabled access: ramps, lifts, toilets. Nappy-changing facilities.

Music venues

English National Opera

The Coliseum, St Martin's Lane, Covent Garden, WC2N 4ES (education 7632 8484/box office 7632 8300/www.eno.org). Leicester Square tube. **Open** *Box office* 10am-8pm Mon-Sat (8pm on performance nights). **Tickets** £16-£85. **Credit** AmEx, DC, MC, V. **Map** p315 L7.
Given the doughty English National Opera's beginnings as an artistic outlet for the poor (thanks to the 19th-century philanthropist Lilian Baylis and her aunt), it seems only right that the institution should have a reputation for sparky accessibility. Central to the outreach work of the ENO Baylis department are the enjoyable Family Days, and its dedicated Clore Education Room. Workshops offer kids aged seven and above, their families and carers, a chance to explore the ENO's current production for just £3 each. Family opera packages are available separately for the matinée performance afterwards. A free crèche is provided for under-sevens, subject to availability. ENO Baylis also runs courses for various age groups, including 'takepart!' a music theatre programme for those aged seven to 18, based at St Marylebone School in central London (7935 9501); check the ENO website for details.
Disabled access: ramp, toilet.

Roundhouse

Chalk Farm Road, Chalk Farm NW1 8EH (7424 9991/Box office 0870 389 1846/www.roundhouse.org.uk). Chalk Farm or Camden Town tube. **Open** *Box office* 11am-6pm Mon-Sat. **Tickets** £10-£25. **Credit** MC, V.
In the 1960s, this former railway engine shed became legendary for staging concerts by the likes of Led Zeppelin and Jimi Hendrix. While not all the shows in its latest, sleek, made-over incarnation are for families, creative opportunities for young people lie at the heart of the Roundhouse Studios (*see p98*).
Café. Disabled access: ramp, toilet. Nappy-changing facilities. Restaurant.

Royal Albert Hall

Kensington Gore, South Kensington, SW7 2AP (7589 8212/www.royalalberthall.com). South Kensington, Knightsbridge tube. **Open** *Box office* 9am-9pm daily. **Tickets** £5-£150. **Credit** AmEx, MC, V. **Map** p313 D9.
This 5,000-capacity rotunda, built as a memorial to Queen Victoria's husband, hosts the BBC Proms from July to September each year. Two annual *Blue Peter* Proms and the outdoor Proms In The Park extend this classical music extravaganza to younger audiences. There's a smart education department, with projects specifically aimed at children and local students. Family-friendly entertainment has included *The War Of The Worlds* musical. Forthcoming programming was due to be announced as we went to press; consult the website for further details.
Buggy access. Café. Disabled access: lift, ramp, toilet. Nappy-changing facilities. Restaurant (booking necessary). Shop.

Royal College of Music

Prince Consort Road, South Kensington, SW7 2BS (7589 3643/www.rcm.ac.uk). South Kensington tube/ 9, 10, 52 bus. **Map** p313 D9.
The RCM'S junior tuition is tailored to students 'of an exceptionally high standard'. Applications (for children aged eight to 17) are by audition and are heavily oversubscribed. Lessons – which run in conjunction with the school term (8am-5pm Sat) – focus almost exclusively on classical instruments. For inspiration, check the website for details of (usually free) performances staged by pupils throughout the year.
Café. Disabled access: lift, toilet.

Wigmore Hall

36 Wigmore Street, Marylebone, W1U 2BP (7935 2141/education 7258 8240/www.wigmore-hall.org.uk). Bond Street or Oxford Circus tube. **Open** *Box office* 10am-8.30pm Mon-Sat; 10.30am-5pm Sun. **Tickets** £10-£25. **Credit** AmEx, DC, MC, V. **Map** p314 H5.
This art deco recital hall has endured a great deal over the years, not least two world wars. Thankfully, the interior remains virtually unaltered, with marble, wooden panelling and plush red seating. There's a programme of family, community and outreach projects. The most famous series is Chamber Tots: music and movement classes for two to five year-olds (£6 children, adults free; maximum of three sessions per child). Every workshop is a sell out. For children five and over, there are two family-themed activity days each term (£3 children, £6 adults). Themed family days such as 'Discover Your Voice' (where renowned choral leader Gillian Dibden teaches vocal techniques to families, through works ranging from African music to modern classical songs) are highly praised. On 1-6 September, 2007, the Wigmore Hall/Kohn Foundation International Song Competition takes place (applications from young songwriters closed in April).
Buggy access. Disabled access: toilet. Nappy-changing facilities. Restaurant.

Activities

Theatre

Puppets

Little Angel Theatre

14 Dagmar Passage, off Cross Street, Islington, N1 2DN (7226 1787/www.littleangeltheatre.com). Angel tube/Highbury & Islington tube/rail then 4, 19, 30, 43 bus. **Open** *Box office* 10am-6pm Mon-Fri; 9.30am-4.30pm Sat, Sun. **Tickets** £8-£9; £6-£7 under-16s. **Credit** MC, V.

Established by John Wright in 1961, this atmospheric little place is London's only permanent puppet theatre. The Little Angel is highly respected for the quality of its puppetry, and for innovative programming, staging productions that use every type of puppet. Themes, styles and stories are drawn from a range of cultural traditions, from fairytales to folk tales. The theatre also plays host to visiting puppet companies. Most productions are aimed at audiences aged five and over, with occasional adaptations for the very young. A Saturday Puppet Club runs over ten weeks, in conjunction with most major productions (£70, £50 concessions). Fundays, on Sundays for families or for unaccompanied children, involve meeting puppets and manipulators, seeing a show and joining a puppet-making workshop. These cost £30 (£25 concessions).
Buggy access. Disabled access: ramps, toilet. Kiosk. Nappy-changing facilities. Shop.

Puppet Theatre Barge

Opposite 35 Blomfield Road, Little Venice, W9 2PF (7249 6876/www.puppetbarge.com). Warwick Avenue tube. **Open** *Box office* 10am-8pm daily. *Children's shows* term-time Sat, Sun; school hols daily. Phone for times. **Tickets** £8.50; £8 under-16s, concessions. **Credit** MC, V.

One of the capital's most enchanting assets, the Puppet Theatre Barge offers a unique combination of puppet shows – courtesy of Movingstage Productions – and unusual location. It's a small and cosy venue (with just 50 seats), moored on the scenic towpath in Little Venice between November and June. A variety of performances are staged, such as *The Town Mouse and the Country Mouse* and various Brer Rabbit tales held on Saturday and Sunday afternoons (3pm). More frequent daytime and evening shows take place during school holidays. Between July and October, the barge floats off on a tour of the Thames, stopping off to perform at riverside towns (Henley, Clifton, Marlow and Richmond). During this period, children's shows take place at 2.30pm and 4.30pm.

Touring companies

These London-based theatre companies are specialists in children's performances and tour all over the country. Their work is innovative, exciting and enchanting. Check their websites for more details.

Kazzum

7539 3500/www.kazzum.org.
Since its inception in 1989, Peter Glanville's Kazzum collective has toured schools, theatres, libraries, parks and festivals. Its diverse projects include works aimed at under-sixes, reworkings of international classics, and interactive installations for under-11s.

Oily Cart

8672 6329/www.oilycart.org.uk.
Oily Cart's forte is in brilliantly innovative, multi-sensory productions conceived to fire the imaginations of two theatrically excluded groups – very young children and children with special needs. The company's work utilises large multi-sensory spaces or 'wonderlands', where groups of children can not only watch, but also become part of the performance. Oily Cart will be bringing back the highly successful *Blue*, a show for young people with complex disabilities, from May to September 2007. The show was inspired by the blues and will also be suitable for some young people with Autistic Spectrum Disorders.

Pop-Up Theatre

7609 3339/www.pop-up.net.
Founded in 1982, the pioneering Pop-Up has made a name for itself creating multimedia theatre for audiences aged under 11. Development projects include Dramatic Links workshops (held at the Robert Blair School in north London), where writers collaborate with schoolchildren to produce relevant scripts. Pop-Up's Equal Voice interactive theatre sessions tour schools, opening up the art form to kids from all backgrounds. In 2007 Pop-Up is to produce a large-scale show for over-sevens in collaboration with a dance company, plus a show for under-eights that will tour schools and theatres. Phone for details.

Quicksilver Theatre

7241 2942/www.quicksilvertheatre.org.
Over 25 years, this collective has developed a rapport with young crowds through its new plays for children, which it tours across the UK. Current projects include a new adaptation of the *Winter's Tale* by Nona Shepphard for children aged from eight, and their families, which will tour from October to December 2007. A three-year work in progress, 'Primary Voices' is a writing project for eight to 11 year-olds. Joining Quicksilver in the scheme are children from Islington and Hackney schools (with the artistic support of Soho Theatre); this should result in a new show which will tour in 2008.

Theatre Centre

7729 3066/www.theatre-centre.co.uk.
Founded in 1953 by the late Brian Way (a pioneering director, educator and writer), Theatre Centre works internationally, in schools, colleges, theatres, arts centres and community spaces. The company has a reputation for excellence and technical invention. It also champions more challenging writing. In 2007, Shakespeare gets the Theatre Centre treatment with *Romeo in the City*, Amber Lone's version for teens. It tours from September to December.

theatre-rites

c/o Battersea Arts Centre, Lavender Hill, SW11 5TN (7228 0504/www.theatre-rites.co.uk).
Founded by the late Penny Bernand, continued by puppet supremo Sue Buckmaster and installation artist Sophia Clist, theatre-rites is a unique and creative company. A reputation for site-specific work was cemented by 1996's astounding *Houseworks*, which took place in a Brixton home. Site specifics are still a speciality; the company has one planned for later in 2007 and 2008, as well as a production in partnership with the Unicorn Theatre (*see p231*).

Venues

London's dedicated children's theatres are a treat – how we love the Polka, the Unicorn, the Colour House and the Half Moon! Nevertheless, much of children's theatre is shoved into the Saturday-morning, school holiday slot and is still a Cinderella of the theatre world – disgraceful when you think that a child turned on to theatre today is tomorrow's bum-on-seat in the 'proper' theatres. *See also p223* **The Roundhouse**.

Albany

Douglas Way, Deptford, SE8 4AG (8692 4446/ www.thealbany.org.uk). Deptford rail/21, 36, 47, 136, 171, 177, 188, 225 bus. **Open** *Box office* 9am-9pm Mon-Fri; 10am-5pm Sat. **Tickets** *Family Sunday* £5; £3.50 under-16s, concessions. **Credit** MC, V.
Serving Deptford since the late 19th century, this now-multimedia arts centre retains a lively neighbourhood focus. Its regular Family Sunday performances (3pm) may include old favourite Strawberry the Clown, specially written pieces, or musical stories with sing-along songs. *Buggy access. Café. Disabled access: lift, ramp, toilet. Nappy-changing facilities.*

artsdepot

5 Nether Street, North Finchley, N12 0GA (8369 5454/ www.artsdepot.co.uk). Finchley Central or Woodside Park tube. **Open** *Box office* 10am-5.30pm Mon-Sat; noon-5.30pm Sun (later during shows).* **Tickets** free-£18. **Credit** MC, V.
The stylish artsdepot houses the 400-seat Pentland Theatre, but most children's performances take place in the smaller 150-seat studio; shows run on Sundays at noon and 3pm. The foyer and public spaces are used for seasonal specials. A learning programme involves all ages from one year-olds to adults, and has courses ranging from drama to visual arts. Depot Youth Theatre (11 years and over) meets on Saturdays at 11am; younger age groups do drama and story making from 2pm. Dance and movement classes for pre-schoolers, as well as terrific Messy Play, take place through the week. Check the website for details of the summer circus school (25-27 July 2007). *Buggy access. Café. Disabled access: lift, ramp, toilet. Nappy-changing facilities.*

BAC (Battersea Arts Centre)

Lavender Hill, Battersea, SW11 5TN (7223 2223/ Puppet Centre 7228 5335/www.bac.org.uk). Clapham Common tube then 345 bus/Clapham Junction rail/77, 77A, 156 bus. **Open** *Box office* 10.30am-7pm Mon-Fri; 4-6pm Sat, Sun. *Puppet Centre* phone for details. **Tickets** £3.50-£15. **Membership** suggested discretionary donation of £30 or £150. **Credit** AmEx, MC, V.
Celebrating 25 years of bold experimentation and community entertainment in 2007, the BAC is threatened with closure, as the local authority has decided to withdraw its funding. This is Wandsworth Council, 3,500 of whose young residents benefit from the BAC's schools programme every year. Shame. As talks between BAC directors and the council go on, so does the ground-breaking theatre. Shows developed here continue to make the leap to the West End. The BAC's Young People's Theatre

groups take those aged 12 to 25, working towards an end-of-term performance (Tue and Wed evenings; £45 per term, £30 concessions) – until 2008, at least. *Buggy access. Café. Disabled access: lift, toilet. Nappy-changing facilities.*

Broadway Theatre

Catford Broadway, Catford, SE6 4RU (8690 0002/ www.lewishamyouththeatre.com). Catford or Catford Bridge rail/75, 181, 185, 202, 660 bus. **Open** *Box office* 10am-6pm Mon-Sat. **Tickets** £3.50-£22. **Credit** MC, V.
Home to the Lewisham Youth Theatre Group (*see p232* **Performance Workshops**), this listed art deco building is Catford's pride and joy. ROAR! is the name given to the Saturday-morning children's show programme, with performances for three to eight year-olds and their families. These usually take place in the intimate 100-seater studio, although the main auditorium (400 seats) has been used for family entertainment such as the rumbustious panto and big school-holiday shows. There are also film screenings on 'dark' nights between shows. *Buggy access. Café. Disabled access: lift, toilet. Nappy-changing facilities.*

Chicken Shed Theatre

Chase Side, Southgate, N14 4PE (8292 9222/ www.chickenshed.org.uk). Cockfosters or Oakwood tube. **Open** *Box office* 10am-6pm Mon-Fri; 10am-5pm Sat. **Tickets** *Workshops* phone for details. **Shows** £4-£18.50. **Credit** MC, V.
Chicken Shed was founded in 1974, on the premise that the performing arts belong to everyone who wants to join in. This inclusive policy has attracted around 700 members from every background. Special groups for the young have been formed, so there's nothing to deter little stars except the waiting lists. Shows take place in one of four creative spaces, including an outdoor amphitheatre in the summer. Chicken Shed's hallmark is the communication between age groups: everyone mucks in. *Bar. Buggy access. Café. Disabled access: lift, toilets. Nappy-changing facilities. Shop.*

Colour House Children's Theatre

Merton Abbey Mills, Watermill Way, Merton, SW19 2RD (8642 5511/www.colourhousetheatre.co.uk). South Wimbledon or Colliers Wood tube. **Open** *Box office* 10am-5pm daily; 1hr before show. **Shows** 2pm, 4pm Sat, Sun. **Tickets** £7. **No credit cards.**
Tucked in amid Abbey Mills' weekend craft market, this bijou riverside venue regularly lends a zany twist to classics, with irresistible titles such as *Robinson Crusoe in Space*. After-show birthday parties with a mini disco can be arranged. Children's theatre workshops and groups are run by the Colour House Theatre School. *Buggy access. Disabled access: toilet. Nappy-changing facilities (in Merton Abbey Mills). Shop.*

Hackney Empire

291 Mare Street, Hackney, E8 1EJ (box office 8985 2424/www.hackneyempire.co.uk). Hackney Central rail/38, 106, 253, 277, D6 bus. **Open** *Box office* 10am-6pm Mon-Sat; 1hr before show on Sun. **Tours** 1st Sat of mth; phone for times. **Tickets** prices vary, phone for details. *Tours* £5; £4 concessions. **Credit** MC, V.

Puppet Theatre Barge. *See p225.*

This East End variety theatre dates back to 1901 – Charlie Chaplin performed here – and was revamped in 2004. The education programme includes workshops run by professionals as well as the Artist Development Programme for 12 to 16 year-olds. Auditions for this programme in 2007 will be on 30 June and 1 July, and the project will take place over the weeks of the summer holidays (fee: £50). *Buggy access. Disabled access: toilet. Nappy-changing facilities.*

Half Moon Young People's Theatre

43 White Horse Road, Stepney, E1 0ND (7709 8900/www.halfmoon.org.uk). Limehouse DLR/rail. **Open** *Box office* 10am-6pm Mon-Fri; 9am-4pm Sat. **Tickets** £4. **Credit** MC, V.

A full season of dramatic events – from weekend children's theatre, to professional and participatory productions for young people – runs at the Half Moon from September to April. Kids are encouraged to participate regardless of race, sex, ability or financial situation; an estimated 32,000 individuals take part. The fully accessible theatre hosts performances for kids from birth right up to 17 years. Most Saturdays there are plays for under-11s with additional seasons of mid-week performances for under-sevens. There are also shows for audiences aged from 11 on Thursday evenings. Children can join one of seven youth theatre groups, which meet weekly during term-time (phone for fee details), working towards a show. The aim is to improve self-expression and confidence. Committed participants often filter into the larger productions. Half Moon has plenty of other creative projects on the go. There are drama workshops for primary school teachers, and a recent foray into the world of film yielded a grand accolade for the company. The 2006 film *Wonderful World* won a Eurobest 2006 award – the European Awards for creative excellence. *Buggy access. Disabled access: ramps, lifts, toilets. Nappy-changing facilities.*

Jackson's Lane

269A Archway Road, Highgate, N6 5AA (www.jacksonslane.org.uk). Highgate tube. **Open** *Box office* 10am-10pm daily. **Tickets** £4.75. **Credit** MC, V.

This arts centre housed in an old church suffered structural damage during storms in January 2007. It is hoped it will open again in autumn; check the website for details. *Buggy access. Café. Disabled access: ramps, toilet. Nappy-changing facilities.*

artsdepot. See p226.

Lauderdale House

Highgate Hill, Waterlow Park, Highgate, N6 5HG (8348 8716/www.lauderdale.co.uk). Archway tube then 143, 210, 271, W5 bus. **Open** *Box office* 30mins before performance; advance bookings not accepted. **Tickets** £4.50; £3 concessions. **No credit cards.**
A manor-house arts centre that backs on to picturesque Waterlow Park. Its programme includes dance and drama courses; the junior versions cater for kids aged three and upwards, as do most of the drawing, painting and music workshops. Popular Saturday shows for children take place at 10am and 11.30am, except over the Easter and summer hols, when there are more seasonal family events. *Buggy access. Café. Disabled access: toilet.*

Lyric Hammersmith Theatre

Lyric Square, King Street, Hammersmith, W6 0QL (0870 050 0511/www.lyric.co.uk). Hammersmith tube. **Open** *Box office* 9.30am-7pm Mon-Sat (until 8pm on performance days). **Tickets** £9-£27; £10 under-16s, concessions; £7 students, 16-25s (restrictions apply). **Credit** MC, V.
The glassy modern façade here belies the antique auditorium, with its gorgeous Victorian proscenium arch. The Lyric remains one of London's most future-focused theatres for children's programming. Lyric Studio, a 100-seater black box space, is home to the Mix: a collection of companies and artists who are making new pieces of work with the Lyric. This studio is also the venue for most children's events: Saturday-morning theatricals, school-holiday workshops and pre-schooler specials during the week. On 7 July 2007 the Lyric stages its Summer Party, a day-long theatre festival for all the family. More details of other festivals are on the website. *Buggy access. Café. Disabled access: lift, toilet. Nappy-changing facilities.*

National Theatre

South Bank, SE1 9PX (box office 7452 3000/information 7452 3400/www.nationaltheatre.org.uk). Waterloo tube/rail. **Open** *Box office* 9.30am-8pm Mon-Sat. **Credit** AmEx, MC, V. **Map** p317 M8.
The three world-class theatres (the Olivier, the Lyttleton and the Cottesloe) making up the National Theatr show primarily adult-orientated material, although a few productions are specifically for families. Occasional half-term shows are supplemented by school holiday specials; summer sees the Word Alive! Storytelling

Activities

festival and the annual free outdoor Watch This Space festival, comprising over 100 world-class shows. The National's Connections programme is designed to encourage schools and youth theatres nationwide to produce new plays, commissioning some of the best playwrights to write specifically for young performers; the culminating event is a week-long festival at the National Theatre (13-18 July 2007). Working in parallel with the Connections programme, the National Theatre Young Company is made up of performers aged 11 to 19, who meet once a week in the theatre. Check the website for details on how to join.

Cafés. Disabled access: lift, toilet. Nappy-changing facilities. Restaurant. Shop.

Nettlefold Theatre

West Norwood Library, 1 Norwood High Street, West Norwood, SE27 9JX (7926 8070/www.lambeth.gov.uk). West Norwood rail/2, 68, 196, 468 bus. **Open** *Box office* 9am-9pm Mon-Fri; 9.30am-6pm Sat. **Tickets** £3.50. **Credit** MC, V.

This 200-seat theatre is built into West Norwood Library and runs one child-orientated show a month (usually on a Saturday at 2pm). Another draw is the Bigfoot Theatre Company (0870 011 4307, www.bigfoot-theatre.co.uk), which runs drama, singing, and dance and movement classes here for eight year-olds and over. These take place between 10am and noon every Saturday during term time. *Buggy access. Disabled access: lift, toilet. Nappy-changing facilities.*

New Wimbledon Theatre

The Broadway, Wimbledon, SW19 1QG (0870 060 6646/www.theambassadors.com/newwimbledon). Wimbledon tube/rail. **Open** *Box office* 10am-6pm Mon-Sat (until 8pm performance days); 10am-5.30pm Sun (during shows). **Credit** AmEx, MC, V.

A glimmer of the West End on a suburban high street, the New Wimbledon Theatre presents a steady flow of touring hits. Family-friendly highlights in 2007 so far include the wacky Scooby Do and the Tweenies live, but we're all saving our pennies for the legendary beauty of *Slava's Snowshow* (18-22 September 2007). The end-of-year panto is always a jolly jape. *Disabled access: lift, toilet. Shop.*

Open Air Theatre

Inner Circle, Regent's Park, Marylebone, NW1 4NU (box office 0870 060 1811/www.openairtheatre.org). Baker Street tube. **Open** *Apr, May* 10am-6pm Mon-Sat. *June-Sept* 10am-8pm Mon-Sat. **Tickets** £8-£32.50; £18 under-16s. **Credit** AmEx, MC, V. **Map** p314 G3.

Reach out and touch, at **Lauderdale House**. *See p229.*

A Midsummer Night's Dream and *Macbeth* are the Shakespeares to be enjoyed in 2007 at this lovely open-air venue. There's nothing to beat hearing Titania hold forth as the surrounding trees rustle their approval on a summer's evening. Children not convinced? OK, the more junior choice this year is Roald Dahl's *Fantastic Mr Fox* (31 July-25 August 2007), adapted by David Wood. If rainy weather stops play, tickets will be exchanged for a later performance – subject to availability – but umbrellas and blankets are always advisable. *Café. Disabled access: toilet.*

Polka Theatre

240 The Broadway, Wimbledon, SW19 1SB (8543 4888/www.polkatheatre.com). South Wimbledon tube/Wimbledon tube/rail, then 57, 93, 219, 493 bus. **Open** *Phone bookings* 9.30am-4.30pm Mon; 9am-6pm Tue-Fri; 10am-5pm Sat. *Personal callers* 9.30am-4.30pm Tue-Fri; 10am-5pm Sat. **Tickets** £5-£10. **Credit** AmEx, MC, V.

This exceptional young person's theatre has earned its place in generations of young hearts since it launched in 1979. Daily shows are staged by touring companies in the main auditorium (10.30am, 2pm), with weekly performances – often puppet-based – taking place in the Adventure Theatre, dedicated to babies and toddlers. There are also in-house productions, workshops and storytelling sessions for families and schools. Book for school-holiday workshops, or enrol at the Polka Youth Theatre (£60 per term, subsidised places available), where in once-a-week sessions children aged from three are taught performance skills and learn to put on their own production with Polka professionals. The wonderful day-long workshops (£30), based on the show in the auditorium (participants see this in the afternoon), are a treat for children in the school holidays. We love the little playground, and the cheerful café is a top place for lunch. Look out for literature events featuring children's authors such as Jacqueline Wilson. Christmas 2007 promises to be gigantic at the Polka with the main theatre show for over-sixes *The BFG* by Roald Dahl, adapted by David Wood and directed by Polka's Roman Stefanski. *Buggy access. Café. Disabled access: lift, toilet. Nappy-changing facilities.*

Shakespeare's Globe

21 New Globe Walk, Bankside, SE1 9DT (7401 9919/tours 7902 1500/www.shakespeares-globe.org). Southwark or Mansion House tube/London Bridge tube/rail. **Open** *Box office* (theatre bookings 4 May-7 Oct 2007) 10am-6pm Mon-Sat; 10am-5pm Sun. **Tours** *Oct-Apr* 10am-5pm daily. **Tickets** £9; £7.50 concessions; £6.50 5-15s; free under-5s; £20 family (2+3). **Credit** AmEx, MC, V. **Map** p318 O7.

Young kids won't be inclined to sit – or stand – through the performances at this reconstructed venue, but older children might like to know that the plays staged in 2007 will be *Othello*, *The Merchant of Venice* and *Love's Labour's Lost*. The building captures the imagination of any age group, and the Globe has a dedicated education department. A huge range of talks, tours and activities – many conducted by staff wearing full period costume – takes place with schools during term time, while holiday workshops and excellent seasonal events open the floor to families. *Café. Disabled access: lift, toilet. Nappy-changing facilities. Restaurant. Shop.*

Unicorn Theatre for Children

147 Tooley Street, Bankside, SE1 2HZ (0870 053 4534/www.unicorntheatre.com). London Bridge tube/rail. **Open** *Box office* 9.30am-6pm Mon-Fri; 10am-6pm Sat; noon-5pm Sun. **Tickets** £9.50-£14 **Credit** MC, V. **Map** p319 R9.

This sleek-looking building is the result of a three-year collaboration with local school children, whose thoughts are incorporated into the £13-million design. The Unicorn's two performance spaces include the 300-seater Weston Theatre and more intimate Clore Theatre; so far they have hosted a vibrant, critically acclaimed programme for audiences aged four and above. Family Days get everybody together for performances and themed workshops, and cost around £24 per person. New productions for 2007 include Billy the Kid, Olga the Brolga, and Baby Balloon. *Buggy access. Café. Disabled access.*

Warehouse Theatre

62 Dingwall Road, Croydon, Surrey CR0 2NF (8680 4060/www.warehousetheatre.co.uk). East Croydon rail. **Open** *Box office* 10am-6pm Mon; 10am-8.30pm Tue; 10am-10pm Wed-Sat; 3-7pm Sun. **Tickets** £6; £4.50 2-16s. **Credit** AmEx, MC, V.

Easy to miss, the Warehouse is tucked into a converted Victorian warehouse behind East Croydon station – but once found, you won't forget it. Theatre4Kidz shows take place every Saturday at 11am (£6; £4.50 children), while a variety of touring shows entertain those as young as two. Croydon Young People's Theatre (CRYPT) offers a creative base for 13 to 16 year-olds; it meets 2-5pm every Saturday during term time, and puts on an annual show in the summer. The fee per term is only £12; application forms are available online. *Disabled access: lift, toilet (bar only).*

West End shows

With the exception of *Billy Elliot*, the shows below are suitable for children of all ages. Less-developed attention spans may find some more suitable than others (many clock in at over two hours). If you've very young children in your party, we'd recommend avoiding the West End and going instead to a more intimate kid-specific venue in another part of town (*see p226*), where plays are shorter, house lights brighter and the bangs less likely to scare.

SOLT, the **Society of London Theatres** (7557 6700, www.officiallondontheatre.co.uk), gives a great introduction to Theatreland with **Kids Week** (www.kidsweek.co.uk), now in its tenth year. Every year during the last two weeks of August, children aged five to 16 can go free to West End shows, provided they are accompanied by a paying adult; up to two additional children can get in at half-price. They can also go backstage, meet the stars and take part in workshops. For more on Kids Week and the best family-friendly theatre information in London, subscribe to the free family bulletin on the SOLT website.

Activities

Billy Elliot

*Victoria Palace Theatre, Victoria Street, Victoria,
SW1E 5EA (0870 895 5577/www.billyelliotthemusical.
com). Victoria tube/rail.* **Times** 7.30pm Mon-Sat.
Matinée 2.30pm Thur, Sat. **Tickets** £17.50-£59.50.
Credit AmEx, MC, V.

The musical version of the BAFTA-winning film, about
the motherless miner's son who discovers a talent for ballet, has 17 songs by Elton John. Its website has a warning
that it contains strong language and scenes of confrontation, which gave the film a 15 rating. Not for under-eights.

Les Misérables

*Queen's Theatre, Shaftesbury Avenue, Soho, W1D 6BA
(0870 890 1110/www.lesmis.com). Leicester Square or
Picadilly Circus tube.* **Times** 7.30pm Mon-Sat. *Matinée*
2.30pm Wed, Sat. **Tickets** £12-£57.70. **Credit** AmEx,
DC, MC, V. **Map** p315 K6.

An enduring musical adaptation of Victor Hugo's tale of
revolution in 19th-century France: 20 years since its
London première, *Les Misérables* is still impressive. The
Les Miz Kids' Club also runs here twice a month, and gives
children aged eight to 15 a chance to tour backstage and
re-enact a scene from the show for £15.

Lion King

*Lyceum Theatre, Wellington Street, Covent Garden,
WC2E 7RQ (0870 243 9000/www.ticketmaster.co.uk).
Covent Garden tube/Charing Cross tube/rail.* **Times**
7.30pm Tue-Sat. *Matinée* 2pm Wed, Sat; 3pm Sun.
Tickets £20-£64.90. **Credit** AmEx, MC, V. **Map**
p317 L7.

Most children are familiar with the film version of this
Disney classic. The beauty of this production lies in the
elaborate staging. Expect awesome set designs, a combination of puppetry and live actors (there are 25 different
animals represented in the show), and a fabulous cocktail
of West End choruses and African rhythms.

Lord of the Rings

*Theatre Royal Drury Lane, Catherine Street, Covent
Garden, WC2B 5JF (0870 890 6002/www.lotr.com).
Covent Garden or Embankment tube/Charing Cross
tube/rail.* **Times** 7pm Mon; 7.30pm Tue-Sat. *Matinée*
2pm Thur, Sat. **Tickets** £15-£60. **Credit** AmEx, MC,
V. **Map** p315 L6.

The long-awaited musical adaptation of the Tolkien epic
is due to open as we go to press. LOTR made its world
stage debut in Toronto in 2006. The show has cost £11.5
million to stage; it's London's most expensive musical.

Mamma Mia!

*Prince of Wales Theatre, Coventry Street, Soho, W1V
8AS (0870 850 0393/www.mamma-mia.com).
Piccadilly Circus tube.* **Times** 7.30pm Mon-Thur, Sat;
8.30pm Fri. *Matinée* 5pm Fri; 3pm Sat. **Tickets** £27.50-
£55. **Credit** AmEx, MC, V. **Map** p317 K7.

It may be thin on story, but what *Mamma Mia!* lacks in
dramatic development it more than makes up for with feel-
good musical numbers.

Mary Poppins

*Prince Edward Theatre, Old Compton Street, Soho,
W1D 4TP (0870 850 9191/www.marypoppinsthe
musical.co.uk). Leicester Square tube.* **Times** 7.30pm

Mon-Sat. *Matinée* 2.30pm Thur, Sat. **Tickets** £15-£59.
Credit AmEx, MC, V. **Map** p315 K6.
Supercalifragilisticexpialidocious! Cameron Mackintosh's
smash-hit stage version of PL Travers's tale of a magic
nanny is closer to the darker original than the sugary
Disney film, but it still has the old sing-along favourites and
spectacular dance numbers, choreographed by Matthew
Bourne. Children under three aren't allowed in, and the website advises against bringing anyone under seven. The
show is booking until the end of September 2007.

Sound of Music

*London Palladium, Argyll Street, Soho, W1F 7TF
(0870 890 0149/www.stoll-moss.com). Oxford Circus
tube.* **Times** 7.30pm Mon, Wed-Sat; 7pm Tue; 2.30pm
Wed, Sat **Tickets** £25-£55. **Credit** AmEx; MC, V.

An old-fashioned musical in which the melodic children are
adorable. The plot might seem a tad absurd in this day and
age, but the spirit of the show is exhilarating. The saccharin
content has been adeptly reduced by director Jeremy Sams.

Stomp

*Vaudeville Theatre, Strand, Covent Garden, WC2R
0NH (0870 890 0511/www.stomp.co.uk). Charing
Cross tube/rail.* **Times** 8pm Tue-Sat. *Matinée* 3pm
Thur, Sat, Sun. **Tickets** £16-£38.50. **Credit** AmEx,
MC, V. **Map** p317 L7.

Kids who like smashing pans together will adore this
hyperactive show. The cast finds music in the most
obscure objects – including the kitchen sink – and the
whole noisy extravaganza is a blast. Just remember to hide
the saucepans and bin lids before you leave home.

Performance workshops

Allsorts

*Office: 34 Pember Road, NW10 5LS (8969 3249/
www.allsortsdrama.com). Classes & locations vary.*
Fees prices vary/1hr class; £90 5-day workshop;
20% sibling discount. **Credit** AmEx, MC, V.

The Allsorts drama school was set up by actresses Melissa
Healy and Sasha Leslie in 1992. Classes bring role playing
and improvisation, rather than song and dance routines,
to the fore (with props kept to a minimum), encouraging
young imaginations to run free. Group sizes are kept small,
and previous drama experience isn't necessary to join up
for Saturday classes and holiday workshops (held at various school venues). It's all about boosting confidence and
communication skills through lively role playing. Ages
range from four years up to 16; bespoke drama workshops
at home can also be booked.

Centrestage

*Office: 117 Canfield Gardens, West Hampstead, NW6
3DY (7328 0788/www.centrestageschool.co.uk).*
Classes 10am-1pm, 2-5pm Sat. **Fees** £260/12wk term.
Credit AmEx, MC, V.

Centrestage (principal, Vicki Woolf) offers Saturday
drama, singing and dance classes for three to 17 year-olds
at its two branches, in Holland Park and Hampstead. The
approach is intensive; kids are encouraged to grasp fundamental skills such as improvisation and diction, before
trying out various performance styles. There are also week-
long workshops during the holidays, concluding in a collective show. Intake is limited: usually between ten and 16
students per class.

Activities

Drawing on the experience

With depressing predictability perhaps, the impulse of most children taken to art galleries and museums is to make a beeline for the shop. But before we brand them as shallow, acquisitive philistines (and that's just the pre-teens) it's as well to consider that exploring by touching things, engaging with colourful displays, and fantasising about ownership are powerful attractants that few art exhibits can compete with.

There's a simple way to redress the balance. It's drawing. Even without the myriad activity packs available from most visitor institutions, you can set your own 'tasks' by allowing kids to choose a postcard image of a painting, then accompanying them on a sort of treasure hunt to find the original. Take some drawing materials and everyone can make an attempt. Hey presto, you have an own-made souvenir to take home, plus the experience of copying from an accomplished artist.

Why draw? It's a good question. Cartoonist and illustrator Gerald Scarfe believes: 'To young children, drawing is as natural an activity as running and playing but, as we grow and develop, in general we drop the drawing – why? It's sad that so many people lose this ability.' His comment is one of many quoted on the website, www.drawingpower.org.uk, the online presence of **The Big Draw** (www.thebigdraw.org.uk), a national campaign 'to get everyone drawing'. Every year in October (1-31 October 2007) Big Draw Day offers a bewildering array of events, including workshops in and around Somerset House (and even in and around the courtyard fountains, in case you've never seen children run through water fully clothed, pen in hand) led by celebrities like Quentin Blake. The events have the exhilarating quality of a festival; there seems no end to the enthusiasm of the general public for drawing,

once they get started. As one art student noted: 'Drawing keeps you sane, really. It's dancing on paper. That's what it is – just dancing on paper.'

Getting started is the thing, then. At **Tate Modern** (see p45), the 'Start' weekend sessions every Saturday and Sunday (11am-5pm) run from jigsaws and card games to drawing. The **Wallace Collection** (see p78) is well-known for its suits of armour, and many boys can be persuaded to visit if they're allowed to try on the pieces. Less well-known are the free, drop-in art workshops held every Sunday (1.30-4.30pm). Entitled 'The Little Draw', these often take inspiration from the 18th-century paintings of the Wallace Collection: a rich seam of rococo frills and flounces.

It can seem that 'family activities' involving drawing are universally available and often free, while more serious art tuition for older kids requires a major investment. Not so. The **Dulwich Picture Gallery** (see p129), for example, runs an award-winning education programme for all ages and abilities at an average cost of £6 an hour (seven to ten year-olds, Saturday mornings, £12; 11 to 14 year-olds, Thursdays after school, £10; 15 to 18 year-olds, Tuesdays after school, £10). There are also free drop-in sessions at Dulwich on the first and last Sundays of the month. The **National Portrait Gallery** (www.npg.org.uk) runs tot-friendly making and pasting sessions as well as more cerebral workshops for young people aged 14 to 21. The **National Gallery** (www.nationalgallery.org) offers art workshops for 12 to 14 year-olds and 15 to 17 year-olds, working with contemporary artists free of charge in the school holidays. The moral, therefore, is to look before you spend; better than any computer game and much more fun than revision, drawing and painting are lifelong skills that can be developed at very little cost.

Dance Attic

368 North End Road, Fulham, SW6 1LY (7610 2055/www.danceattic.com). Fulham Broadway tube. **Fees** *membership £2/day; £40/6 months; £70/year (free under-13s).* **Classes** *£4-£6; children's ballet classes from £50/11wk term.* **Credit** (shop) MC, V.
The variety of classes here is staggering, setting Dance Attic apart from any pretenders. Students must pay for daily/monthly membership besides class fees; reduced rates are available for teens. Children's ballet classes, taught by Laura Snowball, run on Mondays, Wednesdays, Fridays and Saturdays (see website for details). Ballet (for over-threes) goes from beginners to Intermediate Foundation level, with RADA exams at each level. There's also a shop stocking children's dancewear.

Dramarama

Holiday courses: South Hampstead High School, Maresfield Gardens, NW3 5SS. Term-time classes: South Hampstead Junior School, Netherhall Gardens, NW3 5RN (both 8446 0891/www.dramarama.co.uk).

Finchley Road & Frognal rail. **Fees** prices available on request. **No credit cards.**
Jessica Grant's Dramarama organisation, for boys and girls of all abilities, runs a number of Saturday workshops for kids aged three and above. More intensive theatrical tuition leads 11 to 14 year-olds into their LAMDA (London Academy of Music and Dramatic Art) speech and drama exams; these are recognised qualifications in drama and can be converted into university-entrance UCAS points. Half-term and holiday workshops, in which participants devise and perform a play of their own, last five days. Birthday parties for six to 14 year-olds include imaginative games and the chance for children to act in their own mini shows.

Helen O'Grady's Children's Drama Academy

Office: Northside Vale, Guernsey, GY3 5TX (01481 200 250/www.helenogrady.co.uk). **Classes** times vary; phone for details. **Fees** £66/12wk term. **No credit cards.**

Activities

Sound of Music. *See p232.*

Created by a Perth-based drama teacher, the O'Grady Academy opened its first UK school in Croydon in 1994; there are now several in the capital, 47 UK branches overall, not to mention franchises from Malta to Dubai. Children aged five to 17 attend a one-hour workshop each week, with courses spread across three terms. There's no written work and no star system – just an emphasis on high-energy activities and kids together on stage. Skills are developed depending on age: the lower and upper primary groups (five to eight and nine to 11 respectively) learn self-esteem through clear speech and fluent delivery; the Youth Theatre (13 to 17 year-olds) develops more progressive techniques, including improvisation and monologues. A production is performed at the end of every third term.

Hoxton Hall

130 Hoxton Street, Hoxton, N1 6SH (7684 0060/ www.hoxtonhall.co.uk). Angel tube/Old Street tube/rail. **Classes** times vary; phone for details. **Fees** £15/12wk term. **No credit cards.**
In this unique venue – a refurbished Victorian music hall – eight to 11 year-olds can experiment and compose at leisure in the junior music class, working individually or in groups. They can also perform in front of an audience or record their work on CD. The parallel junior arts class encourages fledgling talent by using varied resources and materials. Both the Junior Drama and Youth Drama groups (for eight to 11 year-olds and 11 to 18 year-olds respectively) give young people a free hand in writing and producing a performance for the main hall.

Laban

Creekside, Deptford, SE8 3DZ (8691 8600/www.laban. org). Cutty Sark DLR/Deptford rail. **Classes** times vary; phone for details. **Fees** prices vary; phone for details. **Credit** MC, V.

Performance classes for all ages, as well as contemporary dance and music shows, are on the menu at Laban. Trouble is, the menu is so tasty that the waiting list continues to grow. Once your child is in a class, however, the experience is fantastic. The award-winning building houses 13 studios, where classes cater for all; young children are encouraged to explore inventive movement, and the annual Children's Show (7 July 2007) showcases performance from students aged four to 14. To apply for tickets for this always-impressive show, contact Liz Atkin (8469 9465/l.atkin@laban.org). Touring performances in the theatre are combined with lectures and educational workshops. Laban has mated with Trinity College of Music in Greenwich (*see p239*) to form Trinity Laban, the UK's first conservatoire for music and dance.

Lewisham Youth Theatre

Broadway Theatre, Catford Broadway, Catford, SE6 4RU (8690 3428/www.lewishamyouththeatre.com). Catford or Catford Bridge rail. **Classes** *Junior Youth Theatre* (8-11s, 11-15s) 90 mins Wed, Sat; *Senior Youth Theatre* (14-21s) Oct-Apr Mon 6pm 120 mins. *ROAR! Children's Theatre* Oct-Mar 11.30am Sat (3-8s & families). **Fees** free, £5 refundable deposit. **Tickets** All £4. **No credit cards.**
Driven by the admirable conviction that theatre should be fully accessible (free, with no auditions), LYT's youth programmes have a high standard, and a solid reputation for innovation and variety. All classes work towards full productions. ROAR! Children's Theatre performances are presented to young children and their families on Saturday mornings in this lovely art deco theatre. Junior Youth Theatre is divided into two groups, catering for eight to 11 year-olds and 11 to 13 year-olds, but there's some crossover with the Senior Youth Theatre for young people aged 14 to 21. Most recruitment takes place through schools, but some places are allocated on a first-come first-served basis. Workshops take place after school as well as at weekends.

Activities

London Bubble Theatre Company

5 Elephant Lane, Rotherhithe, SE16 4JD (7237 4434/box office 7237 1663/www.londonbubble.org.uk). Bermondsey, Canada Water or Rotherhithe tube. **Open** Box office 10am-6pm Mon-Fri. **Classes** times vary; phone for details. **Fees** £36/11wk term. **Credit** MC, V.

In October 2005, the London Bubble Theatre Company launched its Everybody's Theatre project, enabling children and adults to boost their performance skills in a collective company. This proved an immediate hit, and continues the company's ethos – to present theatre that's both unusual and accessible. Its wonderfully atmospheric promenade shows have previously toured many unconventional venues, including London parks and woods. Summer 2007 sees The Dong With The Luminous Nose. The company runs Youth Theatre groups for various ages: five to seven year-olds (4.30-6pm Tue; there's a waiting list) and 13 to 17 year-olds, when the Bubble isn't preparing for the summer show (when it is, youth drama members take part in the show – ring for details). Fees can be paid per term (£37.50, £17.50 concessions) or per session (£4, £2 concessions), and the first class is a free 'taster'.

Millfield Theatre School

Silver Street, Edmonton, N18 1PJ (box office 8807 6680/www.millfieldtheatre.co.uk). Silver Street rail then 34, 102, 144 bus/217, 231, W6 bus. **Time** box office 10am-6pm Mon-Sat **Classes** (4-5s) 10.30am-noon (6-7s), 12.30-2pm (8-16s), 11am-2pm Sun; 14-19s), 6.30-9pm Fri. **Fees** (4-5s, 6-7s) £100/10wk term; (8-16s) £185/10wk term; (14-19s) £120/10wk term. **Credit** MC, V.

Millfield Arts Centre presents a regular calendar of musicals, comedies and drama, besides some perky touring children's shows (including many TV adaptations like *Engie Benjy*), in its 362-seat venue. The in-house Millfield Youth

Theatre is divided into three age groups, honing the dramatic instincts of neighbourhood thesps aged from four to 19. Auditions for membership take place in September. The courses run in term time, on Fridays or Sundays, with performances throughout the year, including a panto. Sunday 4 Kidz is on the last Sunday of the month.

National Youth Music Theatre

Head office: 2-4 Great Eastern Street, EC2A 3NW (7422 8290/www.nymt.org.uk) Old Street tube/rail. **Classes** times vary; phone for details. **Fees** prices vary; phone for details. **Credit** MC,V

With alumni like Toby Jones, Matt Lucas and Mica Penniman (Mika of 'Grace Kelly' fame), the NYMT's starring role in the world of youth arts would seem assured, yet it is constantly battling against extinction. Nonetheless, the company continues to audition young hopefuls for its amazing shows; in 2007 the production will be Fiddler On The Roof. Details of auditions and regional workshops are held on the website. Stage-management opportunities appeal to those keen to work behind the scenes.

Perform

49 Charlton St, Euston NW1 1LT (0845 400 4000/www.perform.org.uk). Euston or Kings Crosstube/rail. **Classes** times vary; phone for details. **Fees** £126/10wk term (weekday); £180/10wk term (weekends); free trials. **Credit** MC, V.

Ideal for very young children, Perform was founded in 2000. It concentrates on encouraging the natural potential of four to eight year-olds, with fun, creative workshops encompassing 'Move and Feel', 'Listen, Speak and Sing' and 'Create and Imagine' sections. For even tinier talents, there are 'Mini Ps' classes, which cater for 'Crawlers, Walkers and Talkers' from six months upwards. The workshops take place at more than 100 venues across London and the South East. They're geared towards building up the four Cs: confidence, communication, concentration and coordination. Sessions include movement games, singing and improvisation. A free trial session helps you gauge your child's interest before making a financial commitment. 'Experience' holiday workshops, lasting half a day, three days or a week, with youngsters developing and presenting a mini performance. Check the website for your nearest venue. Phone for details of the children's party service.

Pineapple Performing Arts School

7 Langley Street, Covent Garden, WC2H 9JA (8351 8839/www.pineapplearts.com). Covent Garden tube. **Classes** 1-2pm (8-11s), 2-3pm (12-16s) Sat; 11am-noon (3-4s), 11am-2pm (5-13s), 2-5pm (14-18s) Sun. **Fees** £90/12wk term 3-4s; £295/12wk term over-4s; £5 drop- in session; £160 holiday course. *Trial class £25. Registration fee £30-£35.* **Credit** MC, V. **Map** p315 L6.

A drop-in street-dancing class for young people aged eight to 16 is held here every Saturday. You just turn up, pay a fiver and dance in these legendary Covent Garden studios. Otherwise, children can sign up for a lively sort of Sunday School, which comprises Pineapple Chunks for tiny dancers (three to five years old) rising to junior classes for kids and early teens, and senior classes for 14 to 18 year-olds. Classes fall into three categories: dance, drama and singing, each divided into workshops running over three terms. Week-long Easter and summer-holiday schools in street dance and musical theatre are a fine way to get fit; they're for young folk aged nine to 17 and cost £160.

The Place

17 Duke's Road, Euston, WC1H 9PY (box office 7121 1100/classes 7121 1000/www.theplace.org.uk). Euston tube/rail. **Classes** times vary; phone for details. **Fees** from £85-£95/11wk term; £5 discount for 2nd or subsequent class taken by same student or a sibling. **Credit** MC, V.

Home to both the London Contemporary Dance School and the touring Richard Alston Dance Company, the Place is exemplary in the range of its contemporary dance classes. Parents and children queue up to use the 300-seat dance venue and studios. The prevailing ethos is that anyone can learn to dance; the centre is accessible to all ages, as well as to the disabled. There is, however, a waiting list. The Saturday programme offers classes, accompanied by live music, for five to 18 year-olds, combining imaginative, free-form expression with fundamental dance techniques. The aim is to develop rhythmic, spatial and body awareness, together with concentration, physical skill, coordination and critical appreciation. Shift, an exciting company of young dancers aged between 13 and 19, meets twice weekly during term time (Mondays and Thursdays, 6-8pm) to perform work by a range of choreographers. Auditions are held every September. For more on children's classes, phone or email children@theplace.org.uk.

Royal Academy of Dance

36 Battersea Square, Battersea, SW11 3RA (7326 8000/www.rad.org.uk). Clapham Junction rail. **Classes** times vary; phone for details. **Fees** prices vary; £4.80-£6/class; £48-£132/term.

All sorts of dance styles, from boogie to ballet, are covered at the RAD, whose services are available to children aged from two to 16. They hold summer workshops, private lessons and courses. Activities include West End Jazz for eight to 18 year-olds, tap for nine to 16 year-olds, creative dance for little ones aged five to nine, contemporary for ten to 16 year-olds and an awful lot more.

Stagecoach Theatre Arts

Head office: The Courthouse, Elm Grove, Walton-on-Thames, Surrey KT12 1LZ (01932 254333/www. stagecoach.co.uk). Walton-on-Thames rail. **Fees** *Term-time classes* £295 (£147.50 for 4-7s). **Credit** MC, V.

Creative spirit

Arts-loving Londoners are holding their breath, hoping that the Southbank Centre, one of the city's premier cultural venues, will once again shine after a major renovation. Encompassing three venues, the Royal Festival Hall, Queen Elizabeth Hall and the Hayward Gallery, the Southbank concentrates on four areas of artistic endeavour: music, dance/performance, literature and the visual arts. It is also home to some of the UK's greatest classical orchestras: the London Philharmonic, the Philharmonia, the London Sinfonietta, and the Orchestra of the Age of Enlightenment.

The removal of wraps from the Royal Festival Hall (due to take place in June 2007, as we go to press) comes after a £91 million renovation project. An additional £20 million was pumped into the surrounding area and its facilities. The aim has been to create a leisure destination for people of all ages, along this stretch of the South Bank.

Envisaged as a 'tonic to the nation' in dour post-war Britain, the Southbank was the original venue for the 1951 Festival of Britain. Alongside the **National Theatre** (*see p230*), **Royal Opera House** (*see p67*), Royal Shakespeare Company (in Stratford-on-Avon) and **English National Opera** (*see p223*), it now forms part of the 'big five' flagship arts organisations. The space attracts a range of leading artists from around the world. Addictively danceable African fusion music, awe-inspiring Argentinian tango, emotional classical music renditions – all have taken place in the past here.

Both paid-for and free events are staged at the Centre. Recent programmes have included a series of family music days in conjunction with orchestras and rock bands (such as Dan Zanes' exuberant Brooklyn-based outfit). These brought both hip and soulful music to a child-centred audience and were cool enough for Lou Reed and Debbie Harry to guest at. There's much to entertain a younger audience all year round: spectacular dance shows, musical performances, artist-commissioned fountains, and the animation of outdoor spaces, not to mention the engaging installations and literature events.

Spirit Level, a brand new learning space in the Festival Hall, is also set to open in summer 2007, offering creative opportunities for all ages. The idea is to provide a space where people can learn from each other. Technology is playing a new and exciting role at the Southbank, where children are invited to get stuck in to Spirit Level's technology area to gain hands-on experience in composing music and words, manipulating sounds and creating films.

The Centre is also the home of a gamelan, an Indonesian orchestra of percussive instruments. A special studio here allows enthusiasts to make pleasing and distinctive music in a highly accessible way.

Family taster workshops, as well as more sustained projects (suitable for all ages), are run at the Southbank too. In addition, the education centre's programme of festivals and events includes exploration of various dance styles: from ballroom to hip-hop, and from contemporary to ballet. Children from pre-schoolers through to adulthood can also participate in a range of one-off dance classes.

So, culture in myriad forms is set to manifest itself once again at the Southbank – as soon as the paint dries.

Activities

It's no wonder that families board the Stagecoach with stars in their eyes. This huge, global concern has an attendant performers' agency for children and young people that's now the biggest of its kind in the UK. Of course, this part-time theatre school with 60 branches in London cannot guarantee celebrity, but it does offer a solid grounding in dance, drama and singing, through three hours' tuition a week in small groups. Two performances are given annually. Some students work towards exams in their second or subsequent year. All parents receive a written report twice a year. Third year students may audition for the Stagecoach National Showcase Production, which takes place in London. Half-pints of four to seven years old go on Young Stages courses (three 30-minute classes). School holiday workshops are also organised. Sportscoach is a sister organisation for sporty children (*see p256*).

Sylvia Young Theatre School

Rossmore Road, Marylebone, NW1 6NJ (7402 0673/www.sylviayoungtheatreschool.co.uk). Baker Street tube/Marylebone tube/rail. **Classes** times vary; phone for details. **Fees** *Classes* from £65-£91/13wk term. *Summer school* (10-18s) £275/wk. **No credit cards.**
Sylvia Young's alumni span stage, screen and pop charts (Billie Piper, Matt from Busted and numerous *EastEnders* soap stars). The tuition develops an interest in all aspects of performance art. This is a famously oversubscribed full-time stage school (with around 150 pupils aged ten to 16), as well as a Saturday school (for students aged four to 18); it also runs Thursday evening classes. The holiday school includes a theatre-skills course for eight to 18 year-olds in July and a six-day musical-theatre workshop for ten to 18 year-olds in August.

Workshops & activities

For performance workshops, *see p232*.

Brilliant Kids

7 Station Terrace, Kensal Rise, NW10 5RT (8964 4120/www.brilliantkids.co.uk). Kensal Green tube/Kensal Rise rail. **Open** 9.30am-5pm Mon, Tue, Fri; 8.30am-5pm Wed; 9.30am-6pm Thur; 11am-5pm Sat. **Fees** £5-£7/class. **Credit** MC, V.
This is a sociable little art and activities club with a café (*see p177*), where children aged from 6 months can have fun with painting sessions, cookery clubs, gardening and nature activities and then have a brilliant lunch afterwards. Outside companies put on classes such as Mini Picasso throughout term time. Classes take place every hour.

Maggie & Rose

15a Albert Mews, Kensington, W8 5RU (7581 9344/ www.busykidslondon.co.uk). Gloucester Road or South Kensington tube. **Classes** times vary, phone for details. **Fees** £25-£35 membership; £180/12 wk course. **No credit cards.**
A 'lifestyle members' club' for families that aims to introduce children to a host of exhilarating activities to help build their confidence through play. Activities (term time and holiday) for kids aged from six months to seven years include 'Cheflets Cookery', 'Green Fingered Gardening', 'Messy Masters Art' and 'Film School'. Parties can also be arranged – either here, in the bright double studio, or at the child's home.

Archaeology

Museum of London Archaelogy Service

Mortimer Wheeler House, 46 Eagle Wharf Road, Hoxton, N1 7ED (7410 2200/www.molas.org.uk). Angel tube/Old Street tube/rail. **Fees** £3 membership.
The Museum of London's Archaeology Service (MoLAS) runs various digs and activities for families. Its Young Archaeologists Club, for children aged eight to 16, meets at the Pumphouse Educational Museum, Lavender Pond, Rotherhithe (*see p132*) on the last Saturday of the month and is part of the Council for British Archaeology (CBA) network. Activities include walking the foreshore to collect archaeological objects washed up at low tide on the Thames; identifying animal bones; making Saxon costumes based on reconstructions from archaeological evidence; and mosaic making.

Art

All Fired Up

34 East Dulwich Road, SE22 9AX (7732 6688/ www.allfiredupceramics.co.uk). Peckham Rye rail. **Open** 9.30am-6pm Mon, Tue, Sat; 9.30am-10pm Wed-Fri; 10.30am-4.30pm Sun. **Fees** *Studio fees* £3/day. *Workshops & courses* phone for details. **Credit** MC, V.
A pleasant place to while away a couple of hours creatively, AFU has shelves of plain white ornaments (cartoon characters, animals, fairies), crockery and pots to paint at tables equipped with palettes, sponges, water and brushes. Friendly staff give advice and there's a nice little coffee bar from which to buy salads, sadwiches and pastries. Painted objects are glazed, fired, gift-wrapped and ready for collection within ten days. 'Picasso Birthday Parties' (£10-£12.50 per child) are run for groups of eight or more children aged five to 15.

Art 4 Fun

172 West End Lane, West Hampstead, NW6 1SD (7794-0800/wwww.art4fun.com). West Hampstead rail. **Open** 10am-6pm daily. **Fees** *Studio fees* £5.95/day. *Workshops & courses* phone for details. **Credit** MC, V.
Of the two London branches, this one is the biggest, so is more suited to large groups of children intent on getting creative by painting on to a ceramic, wood, glass, paper or fabric item of their choosing. Mosaic-making is another option. Items for painting cost from £2.50. The studio fee is for the glazing and finishing of a work of art (which is then picked up at a later date). Workshops run throughout the year for kids and adults, and include sand-painting, tie-dyeing and stamp-making. Parties are also a speciality. These friendly places serve refreshments such as hot drinks and cakes, but are quite laid-back about customers bringing in their own snacks.
Branch: 444 Chiswick High Road, W4 5TT (8994 4100).

Art Yard

318 Upper Richmond Road West, Mortlake, SW14 7JN (8878 1336/www.artyard.co.uk). Mortlake rail/33, 337, 493 bus. **Classes** *Term time* 9am-6pm Mon-Fri. *School hols courses* 9.30am-3.30pm Mon-Fri. **Fees** £7/session; £100-£130/term. **No credit cards.**

Activities

After-school art clubs, drop-in sessions for pre-school tinies and school holiday courses for ages five to 11 are all offered at this busy (and pleasingly messy), OFSTED-registered outlet. Many children come for two-day workshops, costing £33, (bring a packed lunch and wear old clothes) during the school holidays, and have great fun creating improvised art works (painting to collage and papier mâché) and listening to music. Five-day workshops at £145 are also available. Themed events include preparations for Easter and Christmas during the relevant school holidays.

Children's Workshops in Clay

Lewisham Arthouse, 140 Lewisham Way, Lewisham, SE14 6PD (8694 9011/www.shirley-stewart.co.uk). New Cross, Deptford or Greenwich rail. **Fees** £55/term; £7 drop-in.
Lewisham Arthouse is a cooperative based in a handsome Grade II listed building with an amazing marble staircase. Artists rent studio space here, and Shirley Stewart is among them. Her throwing and studio pottery workshops for children aged from five are held during term time only, but extra sessions can be arranged for the holidays. Pottery parties are also available at £10 per child, which includes the cost of materials and firings.

Cooking

We're all licking our lips with anticipation about the proposed new food school at **Borough Market** (*see p40*), which promises cookery courses for all ages. Fundraising for this resource continues. Details on www.boroughmarket.org.uk and click on 'Community'.

Kids' Cookery School

107 Gunnersbury Lane, Acton, W3 8HQ (8992 8882/ www.thekidscookeryschool.co.uk). Acton Town tube. **Open** *Office* 9am-5.30pm Mon-Fri. **Fees** *Half-term & school hols* £15/75mins; £30/2.5hrs; £50/5hr incl lunch. **No credit cards**.
A totally inclusive project aimed at promoting culinary skills, healthy eating and food awareness among children of all ages and backgrounds. Events and classes teach kids in a deliciously hands-on way about new ingredients and equipment, encouraging them to touch, smell, taste and feel various foods. Cookery workshops are designed to the young chefs' needs (dietary requirements are catered for); there's a maximum of 12 students in each cookery session, so everyone gets a piece of the culinary action.

Modern languages

Club Petit Pierrot

Head office: 80 Mendora Road, Fulham, SW6 7NB (7385 5565/www.clubpetitpierrot.uk.com). Fulham Broadway tube. **Classes** time and venues vary; phone for details **Fees** vary (from £92 per term).
Children from eight months to nine years old learn with Club PP. Pupils are taught in French by native teachers, with an emphasis on learning through play. The lessons, planned for each age group around diverse themes, include, for the under-fives, songs, rhymes, dances, storytelling, arts and crafts and puppets. Over-fives test their mettle with songs and puppets too, as well as language games, exercises and role-play. Parent and toddler groups (during the week) and holiday clubs come highly recommended.

Easy Mandarin

Lower Belgrave Street, Belgravia, SW1W 0NL (7828 2998/www.easymandarinuk.com). Victoria tube/rail. **Classes** *3-5yrs & 6-8yrs* 9.30-10.30am & 10.30-11.30am Sat; *9-14yrs & 15-18yrs* 11.30am-1pm Sat. **Fees** vary; phone for details. **Credit** MC, V.
As fluent Chinese is apparently going to be a prerequisite for getting on in life, thrusting parents are racing to sign up their children for classes. It's just as well that Miss Jin, Miss Fei and their colleagues run such fun-filled Knightsbridge- and Victoria-based Saturday morning Chinese classes for ages three to 18.

French & Spanish à la Carte

97 Revelstoke Road, Wimbledon, SW18 5NL (8946 4777/www.frenchandspanishalacarte.co.uk). **Classes** phone for details. **Fees** from £115/term 1hr/wk.
This language school gives South London's ambitious two to five year-olds a head start with its weekly playgroups (Tuesday and Thursday, or Wednesday and Friday mornings), involving an hour of activity and an hour of free play while a teacher chats to them in French or Spanish. After-school and holiday courses from £35 per session are offered for older children; adult tuition is also available.

Le Club Tricolore

10 Ballingdon Road, Wandsworth, SW11 6AJ (7924 4649/www.leclubtricolore.co.uk). **Classes** 9-10.30am Sat; 4-5pm Wed. **Fees** from £135/term; £30 membership.
Teresa Scibor and her team of native French speakers teach Tricolore tots (aged three to five) and Tricolore Juniors (five to 12) by means of role-playing or sing-alongs. Classes after school, on Saturday mornings and during school holidays, combine cookery, crafts and treasure hunts in a uniquely French atmosphere. The club operates in venues across London; phone for details of your nearest.

Music

Blackheath Conservatoire

The Conservatoire, 19-21 Lee Road, Blackheath, SE3 9RQ (8852 0234/www.conservatoire.org.uk). Blackheath rail. **Fees** from £91/term. **Credit** MC, V.
There's a whole lot of music going on at Blackheath Conservatoire. Children aged from five can enrol on the Fanfare or Roundabout programmes to learn a musical instrument; they are taught in groups of three or four. Participants receive a free book and CD so they can practise at home, and in their lessons get to make a lot of noise and make friends. Instruments can be hired from the store. School holiday music courses cover all aspects of music-making, and children who like to sing out proud can join the choir. Drama and art courses also take place at Blackheath; see the website for details.

Blueberry

The Contact Centre, 60 Hambalt Road, SW4 9EH (8677 6871/www.blueberry.clara.co.uk. **Fees** from £60/term.
Very young children play, sing and clap along to rousing ditties while their teacher plays guitar. These lovely little music groups take place in many areas across London. They were started by NY-born, Clapham-settled Margo Random, whose desire to bring music into her baby daughter's life gave birth to the business. In the weekly parent-

and-toddler groups (ages nine months to three years), parents have a good sing-song and guide their offspring through the actions. Big Kids Blueberry (two to four year-olds) builds on the singing with more games, but without the aged Ps. For Blueberry birthday parties, *see p243*.

Guildhall

Silk Street, Barbican, EC2Y 8DT (7628 2571/www. gsmd.ac.uk). Barbican tube/Moorgate tube/rail. **Classes** 9am-6pm Sat. **Fees** basic course fee £2,090/term.

On Saturday mornings, this world-class conservatoire runs the coveted Junior Guildhall instrumental training for gifted children. Entry is by audition, and standards are extremely high. A String Training Programme (£1,190) has also been introduced for newcomers aged four to 11, including instrumental training and music appreciation. Talented musicians who can't afford the fee can apply for local authority grants or a Guildhall scholarship funding. The Guildhall's Drama Course (13 to 18 year-olds) involves a more informal audition process and costs £280-£360).

London Suzuki Group

Various venues (01372 720088/www.londonsuzuki group.co.uk). **Fees** from £30/hr. **No credit cards**.

Dr Shinichi Suzuki's belief that talent is inherent in all newborn children inspired a ground-breaking school of music in Japan. This led to the foundation of the London Suzuki Group in 1972; its teachers (covering violin, cello and piano) apply Dr Suzuki's methods to enhance the natural ability of children aged from three. The key is learning through listening, and then playing for pleasure. Classes are held after school and at weekends, and are for members only. A Day Bonanza for kids is available, which includes group lessons and musical games. To find a teacher in your area, check the website.

Musical Express

Southfields Methodist Church, 423 Durnsford Road, Wimbledon Park, SW19 8EE & Wimbledon Rugby Club Barham Road, Copse Hill, Wimbledon, SW20 0ET (8946 6043/www.musicalexpress.co.uk). **Open** times vary; phone for details. **Fees** free first session, then from £5.75 per lesson.

Flautist and music therapist Jenny Tabori's music groups are for babies and pre-schoolers, giving tinies the means to express themselves and develop social skills, with instruments and 'action songs'. Parents and carers stay and share the experience throughout each session, lasting 40-60mins. Musical Jolly Phonics sessions on Wednesday, in which children learn their initial sounds with an accompanying action, are an entertaining way of introducing reading skills in young children.

Music House for Children

Bush Hall, 310 Uxbridge Road, Shepherd's Bush, W12 7LJ (8932 2652/www.musichouseforchildren.co.uk). Shepherd's Bush tube. **Classes** times vary. **Fees** from £45/5 week course; £6/drop-in classes. **Credit** MC, V.

From drop-in music and movement classes for toddlers, to music technology Saturday clubs for teens – with classes in piano, percussion, recorder, violin, guitar and music appreciation in between – the Bush House is a broad musical church. The Music House has over 200 home tutors on its books. Holiday workshops encompass many age groups and interests.

Trinity College of Music

King Charles Court, Old Royal Naval College, Greenwich, SE10 9JF (8305 4444/www.tcm.ac.uk). Cutty Sark DLR. **Classes** Sat. **Fees** £210-£590/term. **No credit cards**.

Junior Trinity, a Saturday School for three to 19 year-olds, was the first junior department of a UK conservatoire to open its doors to schoolchildren on Saturdays, back in 1906. The department encourages the creative aspects of music-making, in improvisation, composition and vocal work. String Time (£60-£120/term), a special programme for young players aged from three to 11, also takes place on Saturday mornings. It's directed by Caroline Lumsden, an experienced violinist and teacher. She has developed a creative approach to music education that enables children to discover for themselves, while gaining a thorough musical understanding. Groups are divided by age into Trinity Teenies, Stepping Stones and Fast Fiddlers. To find out more about applying to Trinity, consult the website. Open Days, in which you can see Junior Trinity in action, take place every term. Auditions are held in March and May.

Wildlife

Oasis Children's Nature Garden

Larkhall Lane & Studley Road, Stockwell, SW4 2SP (7498 2329). Stockwell tube. **Open** *After-school Club* 3.30-5.30pm Tue-Fri. *Term time* 10am-3.30pm Sat. *School hols* 10am-noon, 2-4pm Mon-Fri. **Admission** 25p.

Reclaimed from wasteland, the Nature Garden is one of three projects run by the Oasis Children's Venture (the others are cycling and karting centres). It provides a serene environment in an inner-city area, and has a highly popular after-school club where activities include pond-dipping and gardening, as well as arts and crafts and woodwork. Environmental workshops are run in school holidays or during term time after school.

Roots & Shoots

Vauxhall Centre, Walnut Tree Walk, Lambeth, SE11 6DN (7587 1131/www.roots-and-shoots.org). Lambeth North tube. **Open** *Jan-Apr, Aug-Dec* 9.30am-4pm Mon-Fri. *May-July* 9.30am-5pm Mon-Fri; 10am-2pm Sat. Phone before visiting. **Admission** free; donations welcome.

This half-acre (around 2,000 square-metre) wildlife garden is within sight of the House of Commons, so sometimes the only sound you hear is the distant bong of Big Ben. The Lambeth-based charity has offered vocational training for young people for more than 20 years. Roots & Shoots has introduced the pleasures of tending a simple urban garden to a large number of London's youngsters, many of them children with disadvantages and/or disabilities. The site is also a popular destination for school groups; an outreach worker guides them through the garden's diverse insects, animals and wild flowers, and explains how London honey (some say it's the nicest tasting honey because of the diversity of plants available to the busy little buzzers from a million city gardens) is collected from the resident bees: the centre is also home to the much-loved London Beekeepers' Association.

Activities

Parties

Reach for the gin, it's party time again.

John Humphrys sounded a little bemused during a recent Radio 4 feature on the problem of Competitive Party Syndrome. It was all about a certain set of Londoners with more money than sense, who feel the need to trump their neighbours' efforts at children's parties with ever more elaborate celebrations for their own little darlings.

Thankfully, most sane parents have bigger fish to fry, but all the same it's reasonable to want to make an event of your child's birthday. For working parents, the thought of that 'Sat, 2-5pm' fixture is daunting. Who will entertain 15 five year-olds? What should they eat? Do you have to put up with their parents?

Fear not: help is at hand from the capital's party people, a selection of whom we list below. Personal recommendations are the ideal way of choosing the pick of the bunch, so beyond these listings, simply ask around. With the essential elements – theme, entertainment, venue, food – in place, you'll have the best chance of producing a memorable event.

Whether you go it alone or enlist help, it pays to keep a few party pointers in mind. Many professionals recommend choosing a theme. Sure-fire ideas for fancy dress for infants are princess parties and super-hero parties. A child's favourite film is a safe bet; *Pirates of the Caribbean* springs to mind, and pirate accessories are cheap to buy in costume and toy shops. If you go for professional entertainers, check the age-appropriateness of their set. Some entertainers are best with under-

fives; others like to include an element of danger (sawing Daddy in half could spook young kids, but the over-eights love this hoary old chestnut).

The venue is another consideration. If your home is a white-carpeted Docklands penthouse, consider hiring a church hall, sports centre or hosting the party in the park – for your own sanity. The earlier you book, the better deal you'll get. For decorations, economise by ordering from websites, or visit street markets and pound shops.

As for feeding the hordes – keep it simple. Yes, most children are happy to stuff themselves silly with sugary snacks, but you risk the wrath of other parents by providing entirely traditional party food (such as pink biscuits, sausages on sticks, trifle, crisps and bowlfuls of Smarties). The healthier end of the party food spectrum (meek sandwiches devoid of anything nut- or sugar-related, carrot sticks, rice cakes, raisins and make-your-own fruit smoothies) will be rejected by the kids but will keep fussy parents quiet. You can always go overboard with a spectacular cake, but check with parents about allergies or dietary requirements before you hand out wodges of one of Choccywoccydoodah's finest (*see p244*).

Our party directory lists a wide range of activity organisers, entertainers, cake-makers, partyware and dressing-up shops as well as our favourite London party venues. Where possible, we've given a rough guide to the cost, but as most entertainers and organisers prefer to tailor their service, prices need to be negotiated on application.

Jane Asher Party Cakes

Happy Birthday Philip.

Activities

Activities

Arts & crafts

For more artistic options, *see p237*.

All Fired Up

34 East Dulwich Road, SE22 9AX (7732 6688/ www.allfiredupceramics.co.uk). Peckham Rye rail. **Open** *9.30am-6pm Mon, Tue, Sat; 9.30am-10pm Wed-Fri; 10.30am-4.30pm Sun.*
A ceramic-painting studio in a very family friendly part of town, where children paint their choice from a huge range of crockery and figurines, which are then glazed, fired, gift-wrapped and ready for collection within ten days. 'Picasso Birthday Parties' (£10-£12.50 per child) are run for groups of eight or more children aged five to 15. *See also p237.*

Crawley Studios

39 Wood Vale, Forest Hill, SE23 3DS (8516 0002/www.crawleystudios.co.uk). Forest Hill rail. **Open** *by appointment daily.* **No credit cards.**
Marie-Lou's studio is attached to her home where pottery-painting parties are organised for small groups of children. The cost usually depends on what's to be painted – selections range from popular animal ornaments (around £8) to cups and bowls (£10-£15 including firing charge). Items are ready for collection a week later. Refreshments are provided free (tea and coffee, and hot chocolate for the kids).

Eazi Beadzi

01843 600502/07713 102498/www.eazibeadzi.co.uk. **No credit cards.**
For their jewellery-making parties for six to 12 year-olds, the Beadzi people come along with gems, beads, wire and fixings (tailored to the children's age and ability) and help the party-goers make something to treasure. Prices start at £150 for 90 minutes, plus £6 per child.

Pottery Café

735 Fulham Road, Parsons Green, SW6 5UL (7736 2157/www.pottery-cafe.com). Parsons Green tube/14, 414 bus. **Open** *11am-6pm Mon; 10am-6pm Tue, Wed, Fri, Sat; 10am-10pm Thur; 11am-5pm Sun.* **Credit** MC, V.
Among the first to offer a paint-your-own crockery deal, these studios have added another string to their bow with the Little Toy Shop, selling classic playthings such as puppets, ride-on wheelies, wooden cars and Jellycat cuddlies. Children's parties can be arranged for £17.50 per head, which includes invitations, party food (bring your own cake) and all materials and staff. Alternatively, bring your own sandwiches. You collect the children's works of art after they've been glazed and fired. The café sells fruit juices, Byron Bay cookies, and Union coffee.
Buggy access. Café. Disabled access. Nappy-changing facilities. Shop.
Branch: 322 Richmond Road, Twickenham, Middx TW1 2DU (8744 3000).

Soap & Bubble Company

0845 430 0130/www.soapandbubble.com. **No credit cards**
Looking for a creative party? We like the sound of this squeaky clean one. Children make their own soap, bubble and bath treats to take home. Creations include floating

Top 5 | Party planning ABC

Ask them what they want

Some children prefer a relaxed game of footie and a few pizzas to the full-on party production.

Be age appropriate

Two year-olds don't get magicians, and will scream at clowns; ten year-olds might sneer at tricks eight year-olds adore.

Chat up other parents

Word of mouth is often the best way to find an entertainer.

Don't try to do too much

A bouncy castle, face painter, arts and crafts, not to mention tea and games – all in the space of a few hours – can over-stimulate the children.

Eject the other parents (nicely)

Too much parental involvement can distract the children (and the entertainer), and you don't want to be topping up wine glasses while you sort out the party bags.

duck soap, bath bombs, chocolate lip balm, body glitter and Flower Power bath salt. You can book a (Criminal Records Bureau-checked) photographer to capture all the special moments for an extra fee, so that each party guest will receive a record of the day. The party package (excluding photographer) costs £165 for up to eight children.

Cookery

Cookie Crumbles

8876 9912/www.cookiecrumbles.net. **Credit** MC, V.
Carola Weymouth and her Cookie Crumbles team provide a wide range of cooking activities for young people aged from four to eighteen. They have taught more than 10,000 children to cook since CC was set up just over seven years ago. The well-run cooking workshops offer an enjoyable introduction to food preparation. During the nourishing parties children have a load of fun creating their own celebration tea. Menus have been tailored to suit very little chefs and Ms Weymouth has devised some great ideas for sophisticated teen dinner parties for the 14-18 age range too. A two-hour party starts at £165 (plus VAT) for six kids; the price covers everything, including shopping and mopping up all the flour and sugar children have been crunching underfoot. Bonus!

Gill's Cookery Workshop

7 North Square, Golders Green, NW11 7AA (8458 2608). Golders Green tube. **No credit cards.**
Gill Roberts's parties cater for 12 children (£10 per extra child, up to a maximum of 20). Children can decide on their own themes or menus to make on the day. Gill's two-day holiday classes for six to 13 year-olds cost £90; Saturday morning sessions for three to eight year-olds are £30.

Activities

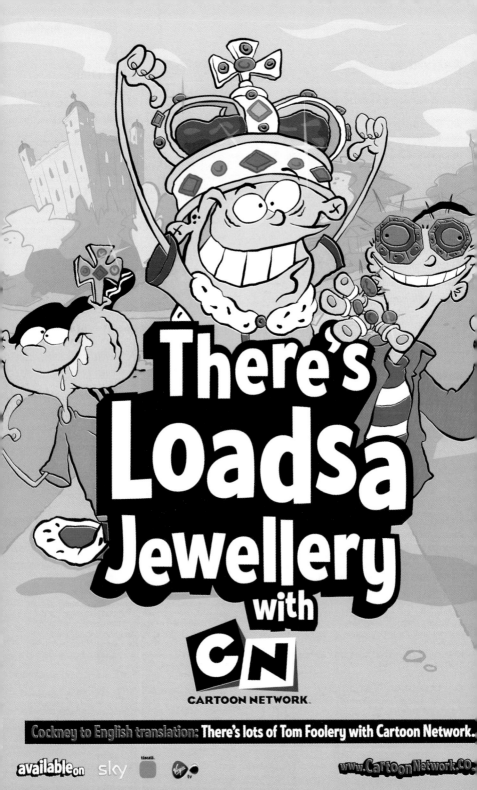

There's Loadsa Jewellery with

CARTOON NETWORK

Face-painting & make-up

Magical Makeovers

01932 244347/07957 681824/
www.magicalmakeovers.com.
No credit cards.

If your party-goers are girly girls (aged six to 16), MM can put at their disposal a friendly beauty therapist with good child skills and a big bag of make-up, nail polishes, hair equipment and endless patience to prettify the celebrants (usually between five and 12 girls). The children are given hair accessories to keep. Prices start at £140 for eight participants (up to two hours). The new spa party package (for ages 11 to 18) offers gentle facials, make-up lessons, manicure and pedicure.

Mini Makeovers

8398 0107/www.minimakeovers.com.
No credit cards.

With a staff-to-child ratio of one to four, hypo-allergenic cosmetics, disco lights and music part of the package, and a pink stretch limo an optional extra – Mini Makeovers provides beauty parties with added bells and whistles. Girls aged ten to 15 can indulge fairy and princess fantasies, or learn dance routines or preening. Guests receive a party bag with hair accessories, bracelet or necklace. Prices start at £160 for eight children. French manicures, a catwalk and a professional photo shoot are also available.

Performance

For more clubs and companies that run term-time music and drama courses, as well as staging parties, *see p237.*

Blueberry Playsongs Parties

8677 6871/www.blueberry.clara.co.uk.
Children aged one to six enjoy 45 minutes of guitar-led singing and dancing. Prices start at £85 for up to 20 children. Bubble machines, puppets, balloons and para-chute games can be arranged, and there's a gift for the birthday child. *See p239.*

Club Dramatika!

8883 7110. **No credit cards.**
Vicky Levy offers fun-packed drama parties for birthday kids with thespian leanings. Parties cost £80 for one hour, £150 for two. Phone for details of after-school sessions in North London for children aged from three.

Dramatic Dreams

8741 1809/www.dramaticdreams.com.
No credit cards.
Arwen Burnett and team send out a questionnaire to find out all about the birthday child. On the day, two actors (for up to 20 children) bring round props, face paints and a script. The children (aged from five) play warm-up games, the actors tell them the plot then everyone acts it out. This costs £350 for two hours. DD also offers after-school and holiday drama workshops in South-west London.

Little Actors Theatre Company

0800 389 6184/www.dramaparties.com. **No credit cards.**

As well as running drama clubs in South-east and East London, Little Actors provides role play, storytelling and games to get the party started for children aged from three. Actors guide the children in activities based around the usual suspects – princesses, pirates, fairy tales, super-heroes – or your suggestions. Little Actors party invita-tions, thank-you cards and stickers come with the booking; party bags cost from £1.50. Parties (London-wide) start at £120 an hour.

Tiddleywinks

8964 5490/www.tiddleywinks.co.uk. **No credit cards.**
Kate Gielgud-Killick's drama parties are action packed (acting's in the blood; she's Sir John's great niece). All the costumes and props are provided for plays that may have James Bond or various supermodels in their plots. Younger children may prefer *Sleeping Beauty* or *Chitty Chitty Bang Bang.* Prices start at £220 for two hours (four to seven year-olds) and £330 for eight to 13s (three and a half hours).

Science

Mad Science

0845 330 1881/www.madscience.org.uk. **Credit** MC, V.
Children of all ages have a blast at these excellent science-based parties. Two mad scientists come to you, bearing a portable laboratory. They entertain the troops with bub-bling potions, indoor fireworks, rocket launchers and other irresistible tours de force. The most popular party is the Platinum (£235), because everyone has a chance to do some cool hands-on experiments. The basic package costs £195 and party bags start at £4.99.

Sport

Campaign Paintball

Old Lane, Cobham, Surrey KT11 1NH (01932 865999/www.campaignpaintball.com). Effingham Junction rail. **Credit** MC, V.
The junior wing of this warlike outfit in the heart of rural Surrey is called Campaign Young Gunz. Paintballing days for 11 to 15 year-olds take place at weekends and school holidays (see the website for details). For £24.95 per child including 300 paintballs (£34.50 for 500 balls) you receive seven to nine games, tuition, a battlesuit, semi-automatic paintball guns, and a barbecue lunch. Campaign trophies and team photographs are handed out after all the fun.

Delta Force

01483 211194/www.paintballgames.co.uk.
Credit MC, V.
Paintball giant Delta Force has several branches near enough to the M25 to be convenient for Londoners (choose from Billericay, Oakwood, Upminster, Reading, Effingham and Sevenoaks). Children have to be over 11 to don their fatigues and participate in the fun. For £12.50 per head, they get 150 paintballs to fire between 9.15am and 4pm, plus a barbecue lunch. If you're planning a large manoeuvre, every 15th person goes free.

League One Sports Academy

8446 0891/www.leagueone.co.uk. **No credit cards.**
Coach Danny Grant and his team organise sporty activi-ties for children aged between three and 12, ranging from basketball, football and cricket to mini Olympics. Varying

skill levels aren't generally a problem, as the coaches will cater for everyone's needs. Prices (phone for details) cover equipment, coaches' fees and a winner's trophy for the birthday child. Venue hire can be arranged for an extra charge. League One also offers after-school, Saturday morning and holiday courses in the Hampstead area. Its partner, Dramarama (*see p233*), runs children's parties of a more theatrical nature.

Pro-Active 4 Parties & Entertainment

0845 257 5005/www.proactive4parties.co.uk.
No credit cards.
Hyperactive coaches keep children (aged from four) jumping, shooting and scoring in sports-theme parties. Prices vary (more children, more dosh), but start at about £200. Activities may include ultimate frisbee and circus skills, depending on the birthday child's proclivities. More sedentary pursuits include makeover and face-painting parties, balloon modelling and 'Who Wants to be a Millionaire'. Pro-Active can set up parties in homes, but most sports events take place in more spacious venues.

Cakes

Amato Caffè/Pasticceria

14 Old Compton Street, Soho, W1D 4TH (7734 5733/www.amato.co.uk). Leicester Square or Tottenham Court Road tube. **Open** 8am-10pm Mon-Sat; 10am-8pm Sun. **Credit** AmEx, DC, MC, V. **Map** p315 K6.
This legendary caffè and cakery can make the bespoke cake of your child's dreams, or dress up one of its renowned chocolate cream numbers (about £20) with a birthday plaque. The marzipan animals are sweet in every sense. *Buggy access. Delivery service.*

Cake Store

111 Sydenham Road, Sydenham, SE26 5EZ (8778 4705/www.thecakestore.co.uk). Sydenham rail. **Open** 8am-5.30pm Mon-Sat. **Credit** MC, V.
The number of artistically iced designs for children in Cake Store's catalogue is mind-boggling. We fell in love with an elaborately coiled viper in lurid colours for £69. Standard 8-inch (20cm) models, decorated with a 'Happy Birthday' and your child's name, cost from £19.95, but you'll doubtless be tempted to go for the more showstopping offerings.

Cakes4Fun

100 Lower Richmond Road, Putney, SW15 1LN (8785 9039/www.cakes4fun.co.uk). Putney Bridge tube/Putney rail/14 bus. **Open** noon-5pm Mon; 10am-5pm Tue-Sat. **Credit** MC, V.
The splendid shop has a section devoted to baking with the children, and making your own sugar-craft delights, but most people order from celebrity cake queen Carolyn and her team. There's a formidable selection of designs to suit all age groups, or you can discuss requirements with the artists. Decorations include sugarcraft figures and flowers, models and edible photos, as well as 2D and 3D cake sculptures. Prices start at £55 for an 8-inch (20cm) round cake. You need to book well ahead for the cake of your child's dreams, however, as this place is popular.

choccywoccydoodah

47 Harrowby Street, Lisson Grove, W1H 5EA (7724 5465/www.choccywoccydoodah.com). Edgware Road or Marble Arch tube. **Open** 10am-2pm, 3-6pm Tue-Fri; 11am-6pm Sat. **Credit** MC, V. **Map** p311 F5.
Crazy name, crazy place to come if chocolate's off the menu, because that's the kind of delicious cake produced here. Choccywoccy cakes are dark, dense moist chocolate sponges layered with chocolate truffle, either sporting the child's name and message, or, if you're minded to have omething really eyecatching, some gorgeous choccy decorations. The smallest-size house cake (£25) yields eight to ten portions. Prices go way higher than that, of course. *Buggy access.*

Tricked out by **Angels**.

Chorak

122 High Road, East Finchley, N2 9ED (8365 3330). East Finchley tube/263 bus. **Open** 8.30am-6.30pm daily. **No credit cards.**
Handmade party cakes embellished with icing versions of cartoon heroes come in two sizes, with the price also depending on whether you opt for a flat cut-out design or a 3D shape. Small cakes contain around 20 portions and cost from £50; large creations (40 portions) begin at £78. *Buggy access. Disabled access.*

Dunn's

6 The Broadway, Crouch End, N8 9SN (8340 1614/www.dunns-bakery.co.uk). Finsbury Park tube/rail then W7 bus/Crouch Hill rail/41, 91 bus. **Open** 6am-6pm Mon-Sat; 9am-4pm Sun. **Credit** MC, V.
Standard sponges cost from £25.30, and feed about 14 children. Personalised ones decorated with your child's photo or Tweenies, Teletubbies etc, cost from £42.35. *Buggy access. Delivery service.*

Activities

Jane Asher Party Cakes

22-24 Cale Street, South Kensington, SW3 3QU (7584 6177/www.jane-asher.co.uk). South Kensington tube/11, 19, 211 bus. **Open** 9.30am-5.30pm Mon-Sat. **Credit** AmEx, MC, V. **Map** p313 E11.
Ever the darlings of the tea-time confectionery world, Ms Asher's team will bake you a cake and decorate it to your spec, or sell you a standard design (there are loads to choose from, costing from £60). Some cake mixes and Jane Asher sugarcraft materials are sold in the shop.
Buggy access. Delivery service. Disabled access. Mail order.

Maison Blanc

102 Holland Park Avenue, Holland Park, W11 4UA (7221 2494/www.maisonblanc.co.uk). Holland Park tube. **Open** 8.30am-5pm Mon, Sun; 8am-7pm Tue-Thur, Sat; 8am-6pm Fri. **Credit** MC, V.
Distinctive, delicious and very French, a Maison Blanc gateau can be rendered birthday-child friendly with elaborate writings, sugarcrafted decorations or by the addition of a pivotal figure, such as Peter Rabbit. They're beautifully presented.
Branches: throughout town. Check website for details.

Margaret's Cakes of Distinction

224 Camberwell Road, Camberwell, SE5 0ED (7701 1940/www.purple-pages.com/margarets). Elephant & Castle tube/rail then 12, 35, 45, 68, 171, 176 bus. **Open** 9am-5pm Mon-Sat.
No credit cards.

Margaret's turns out fairly priced personalised cakes in both Caribbean and English styles. A simple round sponge cake sandwiched with buttercream or jam can be embellished with cute marzipan figurines; it costs from £50.52.
Buggy access. Disabled access.

Primrose Bakery

69 Gloucester Avenue, NW1 8LD (7483 4222/ www.primrosebakery.org.uk). Chalk Farm tube. **Open** 8.30am-6pm Mon-Sat; 10am-5pm Sun. **Credit** MC, V.
Martha Swift and Lisa Thomas, famous for their cupcakes, are top women for beautifully baked children's party creations. They use organic eggs, have a way with sugarcraft and their layer cakes, especially the 70% cocoa versions, can be embellished with delectable edibles. Many parents go for a plateful of personalised cupcakes for the party. Prices are £1.15-£1.75 for cupcakes, or £18 for a simple sandwich sponge.

Sugar Moon

7274 9215/www.sugarmooncakes.co.uk.
Helen's cakes have been roundly admired by South London mothers for their moist, moreish nature and use of entirely organic ingredients. We like them because they don't look mass-produced or suspiciously highly coloured. Top cake for us uses Green and Black's dark chocolate, and is flavoured with orange zest and flecked with white chocolate. For children, we've seen Very Hungry Caterpillars, castles and fairies, but designs can be made up. Prices start at £35 for an 8-inch (20cm) round sponge.

Costumes

Mail order

Hopscotch

01483 813728/www.hopscotchdressingup.co.uk.
Credit MC, V.
From Roman soldiers to disco dollies, Hopscotch can cater for most dressing-up requirements, and provides all the accessories (crowns, fezzes and wands). We adore the dinosaur at £24.95, but serviceable outfits sell from just £7. For parents who want to avoid that nightmare-before-nativity needlework – your Mary, Joseph, kings and shepherds can be tricked out by Hopscotch.

J&M Toys

01274 599314/ www.jandmtoys.co.uk).
Credit MC, V.
Firefighters, lollipop men and ladies, fairies, witches, pirates, cowgirls, Vikings, dragons, police officers, nurses – Jim and Melanie's stock includes over 150 dressing-up costumes, available in age ranges three to five and five to eight. J&M are medieval enthusiasts, so regal robes, Robin Hoods and knights' armour, with wooden swords and shields, are also here. It's all surprisingly cheap; most costumes cost no more than £15, with discounts on group purchases.

Westway – for sport, for fun, for everyone

From Perfect Parties to Training for Excellence plus open after-school and weekend sessions for all!

Climbing age 5 up | Handball – learn Eton Fives – age 8 up
Football age 5 up | Tennis age 3 up (lessons, coaching, open sessions)
Term-time and holiday programmes in all sports

Westway Sports Centre:

England's largest indoor climbing centre, 12 tennis courts, 6 football pitches, 4 Eton fives handball courts, basketball, netball, gym and more.

Westway is an LTA High Performance Tennis Centre with London's leading junior development programme

020 8969 0992
www.westway.org/sports

New at Westway

Westway hosts a number of performance programmes for young people demonstrating sporting promise. The newest of these is the **Frutina Westway Performance Academy**

To find out more about participation, sponsorship or supporting young sportspeople from under-privileged backgrounds call **020 8962 5737**

The Westway Development Trust is registered charity no. 26216

Natural Nursery

0845 890 1665/www.naturalnursery.co.uk.
Credit MC, V.
Some of the most gorgeous partywear for young children we've seen in ages is available on this website. The ladybird and bumblebee tutu-like dresses are adorable, and cost from £17.99. This family-run business specialises in organic, natural, sustainable and eco-friendly materials, so you can dress 'em up with a clear conscience.

Shops

For more toyshops and boutiques with dressing-up gear, *see p207-214.*

Angels

119 Shaftesbury Avenue, St Giles's, WC2H 8AE (7836 5678/www.fancydress.com). Leicester Square or Tottenham Court Road tube. **Open** 9am-5.30pm Mon-Fri. **Credit** AmEx, MC, V.
Angels has costumes, props and make-up for kids and adults, covering many themes. There are angels and fairies, animals and superheroes, witches and skeletons. Prices start at £13.
Buggy access. Disabled access. Mail order (0845 054 8854).

Escapade

150 Camden High Street, Camden Town, NW1 0NE (7485 7384/www.escapade.co.uk). Camden Town tube. **Open** 10am-7pm Mon-Fri; 10am-6pm Sat; noon-5pm Sun. **Credit** AmEx, MC, V.
Dressing-up people for 25 years, Escapade has built a portfolio of wacky outfits for all ages. You can opt for a cuddly bear, rabbit or perhaps a kitten, a comedy vegetable, a Cinderella or perhaps a dandified Prince Charming. Ready-made kits can be bought from around £10; costumes may be hired.
Buggy access. Delivery service. Disabled access. Mail order.

Harlequin

254 Lee High Road, Lewisham, SE13 5PR (8852 0193). Hither Green rail/Lewisham rail/DLR/21, 261 bus. **Open** 10am-5.30pm Mon, Tue, Thur-Sat; 10am-1pm Wed. **Credit** MC, V.
The garb for all the superheroes, from Batman (and Robin) to Spidey (£29.95), is here. Cheaper alternatives come in the form of Indians, pirates, princesses, disco dollies and ninjas or a set of sheriff accessories. The Elvis kid's jumpsuit (£14.95) is a blast.
Buggy access. Disabled access.

Pantaloons

119 Lupus Street, Pimlico, SW1V 3EN (7630 8330/ www.pantaloons.co.uk). Pimlico tube. **Open** 11am-6pm Mon-Wed, Fri; 11am-7pm Thur; 10am-6pm Sat. **Credit** AmEx, MC, V.
A dressing-up and balloon specialist that caters for adults and children, Pantaloons can make sure your party animal looks like an animal, if she should require it, or like a pirate, fairy, soldier, prince, nurse – you name it. Budget costumes cost from £10, but you're more likely to hand over £35 for the full Disney regalia.
Buggy access. Delivery service. Disabled access. Mail order.

Preposterous Presents

262 Upper Street, N1 2UQ (7226 4166). Highbury & Islington tube/rail. **Open** 10am-6pm Mon-Sat.
Credit MC, V.
A quirky shop full of party fripperies, plus jokes of the whoopee cushion, itching powder and fake blood school of humour. Fancy dress includes stage make-up, latex heads, stick-on wizards' beards and junior-sized costumes (expect to pay £10-£22 for a dalmatian or fairy outfit).

Deals on wheels

Party Bus

01753 548822/www.childrenspartybus.co.uk.
A converted coach bedecked with stars is one way of keeping party debris out of the house. It holds up to 24 children (without adults). On-board events (games, magic, disco) are tailored to age group (from four to nine year-olds). The bus parks outside for two hours and costs from £300, including catering (you provide the cake).

Entertainers

More information on the entertainers we've listed can be found on their websites, if they have them, and their prices coaxed out of them by phone.

Ali Do Lali

01494 774300/www.alidolali.com.
The celebrated Do Lali's career spans over 30 years. He has routines to suit all age groups and all situations. He lives in a magic lamp, as would be expected. Prices available on application.

Amigo's Magic

8480 8176/www.amigosmagic.co.uk.
Simple Simon, Magic Circle member and all-round top joker and balloon modeller, is the child-friendly face of Amigo's. Prices start at £125 for an hour (£185 for two).

Billy the Disco DJ

8471 8616/www.billythediscodj.co.uk.
These popular disco parties for ages five to 11 may include limbo contests, temporary tattoos, bubble machines, pop quizzes, dancing competitions and karaoke. Billy costs £150 for a 90-minute do (£170 for two hours) and can take care of your party bag needs for a little bit extra.

Boo Boo

7727 3817/www.mr-booboo.co.uk.
Sean Hampson dons spectacular trousers, steps out of the dry ice and is Boo Boo at parties for three to eight year-olds. His shows include music, balloon-modelling, bubbles, smoke, dancing and lots of comedy. Phone for a quote.

Christopher Howell

7993 4544/www.christopherhowell.net.
A member of the Magic Circle, Howell uses magic, music and storytelling, in which the children play a part. The story is followed by a balloon-model game. Hour-long parties for four to six year-olds start at around £150; £5 of the fee is donated to the Roald Dahl Foundation.

Activities

Foxy the Funky Genie

7692 5664/www.foxythefunkygenie.com.
Foxy is an accomplished magician and balloon modeller and his show gets everyone dancing with balloon limbo, disco and karaoke. He also puts on a puppet show for the under fives. Shows cost from £95 for 45 minutes.

Jenty the Gentle Clown

8527 4855/07957 121764.
Parties for children aged two to 11 include singing, banjo, guitar, magic, storytelling, balloon-modelling, face-painting and limbo dancing. Choose activities to suit your child's tastes. Jenty charges £145 for one hour, £195 for two.

John Styles

8300 3579/www.johnstylesentertainer.co.uk.
Children are enthusiastic devotees of the antique art of ventriloquism as practised by Mr Styles and his team; he also does a Punch and Judy show, balloon modelling and magic.

Juggling John

8938 3218/0845 644 6659/www.jugglersetc.com.
Circus skills (including lots of juggling), action-packed storytelling and all sorts make up the one- or two-hour shows, which cost £125-£180 for an hour, depending on entertainment (one year-olds upwards can be catered for).

Just George

8442 0739/07944 863961.
George McAllister's two-hour parties include parachute games, music, magic and balloon models. All this goes down well with three to eight year-olds. The cost is about £180 at weekends (it's cheaper during the week).

Laurie Temple the Party Wizard

8951 9469/07951 596240/www.thepartywizard.co.uk.
Well-known on the London party circuit, Laurie Temple can wave his magic wand and make the party happen. He and his team of conjurers, jugglers, balloonologists, DJs, puppeteers and magical storytellers can entertain children from as young as two for one or two hours.

Lee Warren

8670 2729/07973 337575/www.sorcery.org.uk.
Lee combines sorcery with audience participation. The hour-long shows – for four to eight year-olds – cost from £110 for a performance in your own home or £120 in a hired hall, and Lee says he's able to deal with nearly any size of audience (eight minimum).

Little Blisters

8392 9093/www.childrensentertainment-surrey.co.uk.
Ava de Souza has created the characters of Flossie Bella the Fairy, Sea Lily the Mermaid and Kitty Willow the Magical Cat for her shows with stories, music and optional face painting. Her productions are for three to seven year-olds and cost from £100 (one hour).

Lydie's Children's Parties

7622 2540/www.lydieparties.com.
Bubbly Lydie has a vast repertoire of themes for boys and girls (from Pocahontas to Batman) and promises to turn your home into a magical, musical world for up to 26 children. Parties cost from £400. Lydie arrives five hours before, to set up for the two-hour show, then, like the trooper she is, stays another two hours to dismantle her set and clear up the house.

Magic Mikey

0808 100 2140/www.magicmikey.co.uk.
Disco, magic, balloon modelling, games and the hyperactive Rocky the Super Racoon make up the two-hour Magic Mikey bash for children up to 12 years old. A seasoned professional, with plenty of cruise ship experience under his magic belt, Magic Mikey is strong on slapstick and high-energy discos. Prices start at £200 for 2 hours within the M25.

Merlin Entertainments

8866 6327/07852 848425/www.merlinents.co.uk.
If you're not sure quite what kind of entertainment you want at the party, talk to Merlin, a one-stop shop for entertainers of all types, from mad scientists to sane clowns. An animal encounters show, Punch and Judy theatres, face painters and makeover artists can also be sought through Merlin. Prices start at £120 for a one-hour performance, or £150 for two hours.

Mr Squash

8808 1415/07939 252241/www.mr-squash.co.uk.
Mr Squash travels all over London with his musical puppet show, balloon tricks, singalongs and funny stories. Well known on the playgroup circuit, he's experienced in engaging the very young (two and three year-olds), but his parties are suitable for children aged up to six. His puppets, performing in a booth, invite audience participation, especially from the birthday child. Mr Squash charges £150-£180 for a one-hour set.

Pekko's Puppets

8575 2311/www.pekkospuppets.co.uk.
Stephen Novy's puppet plays are aimed at children aged three to 12, with shows for under-fives packing in two shorter tales presented by Pekko, a lively and cheerful bird; there's plenty of singing and audience participation. The repertoire for older children includes Celtic folk tales, popular classics, humorous verse and chillers like *Dracula*, all enacted from one of Mr Novy's two mobile booths (from £140 for one hour).

Professor Fumble

01395 579523/www.professorfumble.co.uk.
The Professor can put on a 30-minute balloon modelling party for tinies (aged two to four), an hour-long clowning, slapstick, balloon modelling and circus workshop party, or the two-hour Super Dooper Wizzo with added workshops, prizes and party games galore (and exhausted children guaranteed) for three to eight year-olds. Prices are from £115 for one hour (£160 for two).

Silly Millie the Clown

7823 8329/www.sillymillietheclown.co.uk.
Purple-haired Silly Millie was born in 2001, when Faith Tingle started her training as a special clown working in hospitals with sick children. Cuddly, crazy parties for three to 12 year-olds include magic, balloon animals, singalongs and puppets – all wrapped up in general daftness. Prices start at £85 an hour.

Activities

Shooting party

Sara O'Reilly, *Time Out* magazine's 'Kids' and 'Around Town' editor, invites the MovieParties team round.

When my daughter and her friends signed up for a Young Film Academy MovieParty, they did so without much idea what they were getting into. In the event they had a great time, and they came away with a lasting record of the fun they'd had. True, most of them died – but only on film.

The MovieParty concept – planning, shooting, editing and screening a film in a day – sounds ambitious, but here's how it works. The two-man team behind this enterprise (Ed Boase and James Walker, who run their own small production company, Magma Pictures) arrived at our house at around 9am, lugging their filming and editing equipment and a vast bag of props. By 10am the guests had assembled.

The morning began with a session in which the kids decided on their characters and worked out the plot, having chosen their theme (they opted for a murder mystery, but it could have been James Bond, *Charlie's Angels* or *Lord of the Rings*) in advance. They spent a couple of hours filming before lunch and continued afterwards, with those who weren't acting in the current scene taking it in turns to be responsible for sound, and filming the 'Making of' documentary. Around mid-afternoon Boase and Walker started editing (as requested we'd allocated a room where they could work in relative peace), Boase appearing periodically to grab individual kids to film additional material and reaction shots. Katy and her friends were happy to be left to their own devices at this point; for children who need entertaining, providing a couple of videos would probably be the easiest solution. Around 6pm

(parents' pick-up time if you're dealing with younger children) we broke out the popcorn and the kids settled down for the première.

The formula for MovieParties has been tested at workshops Boase and Walker run during school holidays, at festivals such as Edinburgh and last year's inaugural London Children's Film Festival, and for charities that work with young people who, as Walker puts it, 'have fallen off every rung of the ladder'. Its success boils down to a combination of talent and teamwork. Boase has an exceptional ability to get young people to work with him and each other. He's endlessly encouraging and infectiously positive. He treats the kids like professionals and they respond.

Walker, whose day job is editing news for the BBC, works very, very fast. *Deadline*, the murder mystery Katy and her friends made, is an astonishing 12 minutes long – two or three minutes a day would be considered good going for a drama filmed on location. The speeches are all very short and Boase is skilled at keeping the creative process on track, but the result is very much the kids' film. It's quite dark and wacky, with a sophisticated twist at the end.

Boase and Walker, who made their first film together at school, are passionate about inspiring the next generation of filmmakers. 'We see ourselves as a bit of a one-stop shop for filmmaking for kids of eight to 15,' says Boase. Although the party format can't cover the same ground as the courses, it introduces the language and grammar of film on the hoof.

A MovieParty costs £980, including 12 DVDs of the finished film and 'Making of' documentary. For bookings and details of filmmaking courses run by the company visit www.filmfantastic.co.uk or call 7792 1355. *See also p220.*

Activities

Equipment hire

Disco

Young's Disco Centre

2 Malden Road, Chalk Farm, NW5 3HR (7485 1115/ www.steveyoungdisco.co.uk). Chalk Farm tube.
Open by appointment.
Credit MC, V.
Not just sounds, such as turntables , but sights too – coloured lights, bubbles and smoke into the bargain. Young's will also hire you a DJ and turntables, iPod systems; otherwise, a DIY children's party package with a sound system and disco lights can be hired for £80. *Buggy access. Delivery and set-up service. Disabled access.*

Fairground

PK Entertainments

01344 626789/07771 546676/ www.fairandfete.co.uk. **No credit cards.**
All the fun of the fair (well, village fête) can be hired from PK. If you have the room, it has the hoopla, swingboats, bouncy castles, candy floss and popcorn – even the bucking bronco. PK can also provide clowns, magicians and face painters. See the price list online.

Marquees

Sunset Marquees

Unit 5, Glenville Mews, Kimber Road, Southfields, SW18 4NJ (8741 2777/www.sunsetmarquees.com). Southfields tube. **Open** 8am-6pm daily.
No credit cards.
Hire a tent, fill it with children and protect your home from attack. Sunset supplies mini marquees as well as very large ones (prices from £190 for a weekend). For an extra charge it will also provide lighting, furniture, candy-floss machines, heating and carpeting.

Organisers

Action Station

0870 770 2705/www.theactionstation.co.uk.
This agency's books brim with magical storytellers, face painters, dramatists, cheerleaders, clowns and magicians. Children of all ages are catered for. Prices start at £170 per hour, £258 for two hours.

Top 10 Party venues

Art Yard

Kids choose what they'd like to make (from T-shirt painting to decorating funky bags). Parties cost £16 per child (aged 3-11). *See p238.*

Bramley's Big Adventure

Bramley's parties come in Bronze, Silver and Gold versions. Bronze gives you 75 minutes' play, plus a meal and party bag, from £8 per head). Gold parties cost from £13 a head. *See p87.*

Chislehurst Caves

A private tour of the spooky tunnels, finishing off with a buffet in the Caves Café, costs £60 (maximum 20 kids and four adults), plus £4.50 per child for party food. *See p140.*

Coram's Fields

At weekends, rooms – with kitchen facilities – may be rented, costing from £40 for an afternoon session. Parents provide food and entertainment. *See p62.*

Discover

Follow the Story Trail, then a 'story builder' leads hands-on activities. All for a bargain £6.50-£8.50 per child (minimum 15 children). *See p114.*

Firepower

Camouflage birthday parties cost from £12.50 per head and include dressing up, games and face painting. *See p138.*

London Dungeon

The price (from £17 per head) includes a tour of unspeakable horrors, an hour in the café's games centre, a themed photograph and a well-filled party bag. *See p43.*

Michael Sobell Leisure Centre

Choose from the centre's indoor safari playground facilities (£70-£130), or mixed sports parties with netball, basketball and badminton (£75 for up to 20 kids). Trampolining parties (£90) begin with a lesson; ice-skating parties (£135) come with skates and a lesson. Parents provide the birthday tea and all-important cake. *See p266.*

Playscape Pro Racing

Karting is thrilling stuff for eight-year-olds upwards. The little buggies zip around at speeds exceeding 30 miles per hour. Racing parties give the kids an hour on the track, and cost from £215 for ten drivers, £322.50 for 15 (90 minutes) and £430 for 20 (over two hours). Full training and safety gear are provided, and there's a medal presented to the lucky birthday boy or girl at the end. *See p262.*

Puppet Planet

Lesley Butler's puppet shop is great for parties. Puppets perform favourite tales, then the children can roll up their sleeves to make their own puppets to take home. Get in touch to find out about other puppet-themed parties for all ages. *See p214.*

Activities

Adam Ants

8959 1045/www.adamantsparties.com.
Entertainers, party accessories, including ball ponds and bouncy castles and kid-o-gram characters (from £85), can be hired from Ants. Catering can also be organised.

Boo! Productions

7287 9090/07825 310780/www.booparties.com.
Bespoke parties from Boo! include the entire organisation of your event – all you have to do is discuss your plans. If you only need an entertainer, Boo! will lend you one; prices start at around £170 for two hours.

Mystical Fairies

12 Flask Walk, Hampstead, NW3 1HE (7431 1888/ www.mysticalfairies.co.uk). Hampstead tube. **Open** 10am-6pm Mon-Sat; 11am-6pm Sun. **Credit** MC, V.
Whether you use the mystical basement kingdom – with all its glittering toadstools, flowers, bunting and fairy lights – for your child's sparkling do, or have the fairies come to you, Mystical provides dream parties for the sprite-obsessed. Chaps need not fear, it's not all pinkly perfect: there are pirate and wizard parties too. Young girls in their fairy phase love all the whimsy; for older, more grounded party-goers there are high school musical, disco and fashion-shoot parties. Ring for details. Prices start at about £200 (plus VAT) for a two-hour home party.
Buggy access. Mail order.

Puddleduck Parties

8893 8998/www.puddleduckparties.co.uk.
Puddleduck can put together flexible packages that encompass all those party necessities such as catering (inclusive of tableware), decorations and entertainers. Teddy bears' picnics can be arranged for smaller children; otherwise there's drama, sport or disco parties for all ages, starting from around £200 for two hours of fun.

Splodge

7350 1477/www.planetsplodge.com.
Child-led entertainment is the name of Splodge's game. The actors that make up the team dream up spectacular events, in which kids participate fully. Choose from Splodge specials (themes of Gruffalo, say, or Narnia) and the team of creatives make a party package around it. All ages are catered for, and Splodge is happy to tailor parties for children with special needs. Prices are, of course, subject to your requirements, but Splodge specials start at £470 for two hours (and 20 kids).

Taylor-Made Entertainment

0797 490 1215/www.taylor-madeentertainment.com.
This organisation puts together special party packages aimed at suiting your child's tastes. It will provide discos (with lights, scented smoke, bubbles and karaoke), bang on makeover artists, face-painters, musicians, and party MCs. Supplying entertainment for young and easily bored guests at weddings is another speciality.

Twizzle Parties

8789 3232/www.twizzle.co.uk.
Beloved of London's celebrity parents, Twizzle earned itself the number-one slot in a *Harpers* party survey, and continues to organise glittering children's 'film première' and photo-shoot parties. Themed events for all ages start with simple sing-along parties for toddlers and go quite glamorous with all sorts of pop-starry, street-dancey shenanigans. Twizzle also runs a performing arts school during the holidays. Prices start at about £150 for one hour.

Paraphernalia

Mail order

Baker Ross

Enquiries 8523 2733/call centre orderline 0870 458 5440/www.bakerross.co.uk. **Credit** MC, V.
With its fantastic ideas for craft parties and an inspired range of toys in packs of eight (animal pens, insect fossil paint kits, clockwork bath toys), Baker Ross has a must-see website for those planning their own party.

CYP

01279 444707/www.cyp.co.uk. **Credit** AmEx, MC, V.
Are you in charge of the music for the tot party? Check this firm's selection of party tapes and CDs for traditional games like pass the parcel or musical chairs. The pop party CD costs £4.99.

Party Directory

01252 851601/www.partydirectory4kids.co.uk. **Credit** MC, V.
Themed tableware (cups to tablecloths, ranging from 23p to £2.75), party bags and boxes, plus trinkets, toys and gorgeous little chocolate novelties to put in them, make the Directory a top stop for children's parties. You can even sign up for party-planning email reminders when your your children's big days are looming large on the horizon.

Party Pieces

01635 201844/www.partypieces.co.uk. **Credit** MC, V.
Tableware (from around 25p an item) is themed around the film or programme of the moment (*Cars, Pirates of the Caribbean, Power Rangers*), fairies, football and the like. Then there are party-bag fillers, traditional games (a 'pin the eyepatch on the pirate' version of the donkey's tail original is £2.45), and a whopping range of banners, balloons and assorted decorations.

Your Party by Post

0845 408 4812/www.yourpartybypost.co.uk. **Credit** MC, V.
Stockists of themed children's partyware – everything from Thomas the Tank Engine to Spiderman 3 – as well as gifts for the goody bag: this company can also proivide you with banners, balloons and games to thank-you notes.

Shops

Balloon & Kite Company

613 Garratt Lane, Earlsfield, SW18 4SU (8946 5962/ www.balloonandkite.com). Earlsfield rail. **Open** 9am-6pm Mon-Fri; 9am-5.30pm Sat. **Credit** MC, V.
Balloons in rubber or foil, bearing pictures of any number of favourite screen heroes, or personalised for your child, can be ordered here. There's also themed paper tableware and banners, kites and goody-bag stuff.
Buggy access. Delivery service. Disabled access: ramps. Mail order (balloons & boxes only).

Oscar's Den. *See p255.*

Balloonland

12 Hale Lane, Mill Hill, NW7 3NX (8906 3302/ www.balloonland.co.uk). Edgware tube/Mill Hill Broadway rail/221, 240 bus. **Open** 9.30am-5.30pm Mon-Fri; 10am-5.30pm Sat. **Credit** MC, V.
A super soaraway choice of inflated latex and foil – as well as all sorts of balloon-based services, from helium hire to venue decorating – explains this shop's name, but Balloonland is a fab general party shop too. All the themes in children's tableware and party bags, from Bob (Builder) to Winnie (Pooh) await your offspring's pleasure.
Buggy access. Delivery service. Disabled access. Mail order.

Bouncing Kids

127 Northfield Avenue, Ealing, W13 9QR (8840 0110/ www.bouncing-kids.com). Northfields tube/West Ealing rail. **Open** 9am-5.30pm Mon-Sat. **Credit** MC, V.
Paperware, balloons, fancy dress and party bags fill the shop, but you can also hire bouncy castles, tables and chairs, badge-making machines and parachute games from here. Check the website for details.
Delivery service. Mail order.

Circus Circus

176 Wandsworth Bridge Road, Fulham, SW6 2UQ (7731 4128/www.circuscircus.co.uk). Fulham Broadway tube. **Open** 10am-6pm Mon-Sat. **Credit** AmEx, MC, V.
Staff here can find you caterers, entertainers, and bouncy castle specialists. They'll also show you around what seems like hundreds of themes in tableware and party stationery, a dressing-up department and a whole load of booty for party bags. They've thought of everything.
Buggy access. Delivery service. Disabled access: ramp. Mail order. Play area.

Just Balloons

8560 5933/www.justballoons.com. **Credit** AmEx, MC, V.
You can't have too many helium-filled balloons at a party, we reckon. Just Balloons supplies the wherewithal (including hiring out canisters of helium gas), and also has a lucrative line in balloons emblazoned with messages or photographs (the latter costing £125 for 100). Delivery in central London costs around £15.

Mexicolore

7622 9577/www.pinata.co.uk. **No credit cards**.
Mexicolore makes proper piñatas (not the cheapo cardboard ones you can buy at supermarkets). The decorated papier mâché comes in a number of designs that can be filled by parents with goodies, then hung up ready for frenzied bashing by the children. Prices start at about £20.

Non-Stop Party Shop

214-216 Kensington High Street, Kensington, W8 7RG (7937 7200/www.nonstopparty.co.uk). High Street Kensington tube/10, 27, 391 bus. **Open** 9.30am-6pm Mon, Tue, Thur-Sat; 10am-6pm Wed; 11am-5pm Sun. **Credit** MC, V. **Map** p312 A9.
With eight stores in London and the South East (check website), Non-Stop is a big name in partyware. The balloon services include printing, inflating and decorating party premises. Dressing-up gear, tableware, fireworks and novelties you never knew you needed are also sold.
Delivery service (balloons only). Mail order.

Oscar's Den

127-129 Abbey Road, St John's Wood, NW6 4SL (7328 6683/www.oscarsden.com). Swiss Cottage tube/West Hampstead tube/rail/28, 31, 139, 189 bus. **Open** 9.30am-5.30pm Mon-Sat; 10am-2pm Sun. **Credit** AmEx, MC, V.
It's always fun to visit Oscar's place…and a relief to leave all the arrangements in the hands of the capable staff. They'll take on the whole project if you want them to (they've done so for numerous personalities, not to mention ex Prime Minister Tony Blair). Otherwise, come here for your balloons, bubbles, bouncy castles and super slides, paperware, party tricks, play equipment, fireworks, face paints and fancy dress.
Buggy access. Delivery service.

Party Party

3 & 11 Southampton Road, Gospel Oak, NW5 4JS (7267 9084/www.partypartyuk.com). Chalk Farm tube/Gospel Oak rail/24 bus. **Open** 9.30am-5.30pm Mon-Sat. **Credit** MC, V.
You'll find balloons, banners and decorations at No.3, and a few doors down at No.11, party bags, costumes and tableware. Party Party also has a bespoke piñata service, otherwise their brightly coloured off-the-peg bashables come in number shapes or fashioned into clowns, bees, butterflies, fish and donkeys.
Buggy access. Delivery service.

Party Party

9-13 Ridley Road, Dalston, E8 2NP (7254 5168). Dalston Kingsland rail/30, 38, 56, 67, 76, 149, 236, 242, 243, 277 bus. **Open** 9am-5.30pm Mon-Thur; 9am-6.30pm Fri, Sat. **Credit** AmEx, MC, V.
Unrelated to its Gospel Oak namesake (*see above*), this prince among party shops is a friendly, party-on-a-budget kind of place. One floor is devoted to cake decorating, the other has fancy dress and party accessories. There are plans to expand into the basement – ring before visiting to check the builders have finished.

Party Superstore

268 Lavender Hill, Clapham, SW11 1LJ (7924 3210/ www.partysuperstore.co.uk). Clapham Junction rail/39, 77, 345 bus. **Open** 9am-6pm Mon-Wed, Fri, Sat; 9am-7pm Thur; 10.30am-4.30pm Sun. **Credit** AmEx, MC, V.
The first floor of the glittering Superstore stocks children's party accessories, fancy-dress costumes (from £7.99), eye-masks and novelty hats (from £1.99) and wigs (from £4.99). There are also more than 50 themed tableware collections (many of which are suitable for children), as well as practical jokes, hundreds of balloons in latex and helium, mock jewellery, party-bag fillers, and a collection of cake decorations and candles.
Buggy access. Delivery service. Disabled access. Mail order.
Branch: 43 Times Square, High Street, Sutton, Surrey SM1 1LF (8661 7323).

Purple Planet

8205 2200/www.purpleplanet.co.uk. **Credit** AmEx, MC, V.
Now an internet-only business, Purple Planet stocks party items including helium balloons, streamers, themed tableware and, most importantly, a fine selection of sugarcraft accessories and cookie cutters.

Activities

Sport & Leisure

Olympians of tomorrow, step away from the Xbox and get some exercise.

The prospect of hosting the 2012 Olympic and Paralympic Games has finally pushed sport and physical activity high up the political agenda, so money is at last being spent on improving the health of our children. If you don't already know the acronyms SSCo (School Sport Co-ordinator) and PESSCL (PE, School Sport and Club Links), you soon will: these are major initiatives designed to make a connection between what goes on inside the school gates and the clubs and activities available outside.

The government's aim is for all children to do at least two hours of high-quality PE and sport a week – and about time too. With the demands of children's time from all aspects of the National Curriculum, that still seems a problem for the schools – our experience as parents of a number of children in secondary and primary school is that all too often physical exercise is bumped off the weekly agenda in favour of dreary sedentary demands, comprising an army of ghastly acronyms – SATS, PSHE and extra DT or ITC. Despite this dispiriting trend, it is to be hoped that schools can forge links with clubs, organisations and venues, such as those we list below, to train the Olympians of tomorrow. The aim of this section is to show the wide range of sport and fitness options available in the capital. It's also worth keeping an eye on your local council website for details of affordable, often free, sports camps run for young people during the school holidays. Many independent schools play host to private youth sports organisations that run intensive rugby, football, tennis and cricket coaching when term-time ends. Such courses are more expensive than the council-run ones, but they're well worth it for seriously sporty kids.

Some sporting activities are also covered in the Arts & Entertainments listings starting on *p216*. Stagecoach (*see p237*) has a sporting wing called Sportscoach (www.sportscoach.co.uk), which provides children aged between six and 16 years with three hours of sports training per week. Football, netball, Kwik cricket and hockey are covered, not to mention individual sports such as archery, martial arts and fencing.

Sports to do

Athletics

There are some 18 different sports in track and field. Many children first develop their enthusiasm on the school playing field, then set about joining a local club. Membership usually costs around £25-£40 per year, plus a fee for track use.

Maureen Jones is a senior UK Athletics (www.ukathletics.net) coach who organises Run, Jump, Throw courses during the school holidays in south London for children aged eight to 12.

South of England Athletics Association

4th Floor, Marathon House, 115 Southwark Street, SE1 0JF (7021 0988/www.seaa.org.uk).
The SEAA has details of other clubs around London. There's also a directory at www.british-athletics.co.uk.

The following clubs also have well-established sections for young athletes:

Belgrave Harriers (Battersea)
www.belgraveharriers.com
Blackheath & Bromley Harriers (Bromley)
Duncan Flagg (8300 7894/www.bandbhac.org.uk).
Havering Mayesbrook AC (Hornchurch/Dagenham) *Jean Tierney (01708 341 547/www.havering-mayesbrook.org).*
Newham & Essex Beagles AC (Plaistow)
Jacqui Ramsden (7366 8587/www.neb2005.co.uk).
Shaftesbury Barnet Harriers (Barnet)
8202 6478/www.sbharriers.co.uk.
Thames Valley Harriers (Shepherd's Bush)
Kathy Davidson (01895 676513/www.thamesvalley harriers.com).
Victoria Park Harriers & Tower Hamlets AC (Mile End) *Alf Vickers (07832 251478/ www.vphthac.org.uk).*
Woodford Green AC with Essex Ladies (Woodford) *(8550 9788/www.wgel.org.uk).*

Badminton & squash

Both badminton and squash have excellent junior development programmes and are not saddled with the social preconceptions that bedevil tennis.

Badminton is also easier to learn than tennis, though devotees say it is more taxing to play. For more information, contact:

Badminton Association of England
01908 268 400/www.badmintonengland.co.uk

England Squash
0161 231 4499/www.englandsquash.co.uk.

These clubs have junior badminton and/or squash programmes; phone for prices and times:
Dulwich Sports Club *Burbage Road, SE24 9HP (7274 1242/www.dulwichsquash.com). Herne Hill rail.*
New Grampians Squash Club *Shepherd's Bush Road, W6 7LN (7603 4255/www.newgrampians.co.uk). Hammersmith tube.*
New Malden Tennis, Squash & Badminton Club *Somerset Close, New Malden, Surrey KT3 5RG (8942 0539/www.newmaldenclub.co.uk). Malden Manor rail.*
Southgate Squash Club *Walker Cricket Ground, Waterfall Road, N14 7JZ (8886 8381/www. southsquashclub.co.uk). Southgate tube.*

Wimbledon Racquets & Fitness Club
Cranbrook Road, SW19 4HD (8947 5806/www. wimbledonclub.co.uk). Wimbledon tube/rail.

Baseball & softball

Schemes like Pitch, Hit & Run and Play Ball teach the basics in schools and clubs to children aged from six. For more information, contact:

BaseballSoftballUK
7453 7055/www.baseballsoftballuk.com.

London Baseball Association
www.londonsports.com.

The following clubs have junior programmes:
Essex Arrows (Waltham Abbey)
Phil Chesterton, 07890 280118, www.essex arrows.com.
London Mets Baseball & Softball Club (Finsbury Park) *Neil Warne, 07770 381308/ neil@londonmeteors.co.uk, www.londonmeteors.co.uk.*

The Circus Space. *See p259.*

Basketball

There are basketball clubs all over the capital playing in local leagues, and the sport is extremely well organised at junior level, with competitions right up to national standard. To find out more, contact regional development manager Steve Alexander (8968 0051).

English Basketball Association
0870 774 4225/www.englandbasketball.co.uk.
The following clubs have junior programmes:
Brixton Topcats Brixton Recreation Centre
Station Road, SW9 8QQ (contact Jimmy Rogers 7737 3354/brixtontopcats@hotmail.com). Brixton tube/rail.
Hackney Academy *SPACE Centre, Hackney Community College, Falkirk Street, N1 6HF (7613 9525). Old Street tube rail, 243 bus.*

Boxing

The sport at amateur level has an impressive safety record. Youngsters are simply not powerful enough to inflict serious damage to each other.
To find a local club, contact the London regional secretary on 7252 7008 or the

Amateur Boxing Association of England
www.abae.co.uk.

Circus skills

Thrilling to learn and excellent for physical fitness, circus skills are often popular with children turned off by ball games on muddy

Jump to it

Kilburn's **Moberly Sports Centre** has never seen a class quite like this one. Sure, there are typical aerobics stations involved – balance beams, pommel horses, vaults – but they're being used in ways that are anything but typical, helping participants practise a range of animalistic physical trickery, from cat leaps and kong vaults to safety rolls and wall runs. No sir, step aerobics this most certainly is not.

Yet perhaps the most unusual aspect of **Urban Freeflow**'s (www.urbanfreeflow.com) classes in parkour – the art of traversing an urban environment via a series of freeform movements – are their unprecedented popularity. Participants pack every available square inch of the hall and cover the whole spectrum from kids to wide-eyed adults, from local housing estates to big city law firms and from all corners of not only the capital, but also the country – one guy, Jan, even drove over from Sweden to take part.

It's not hard to account for such enthusiasm: money can't buy the kind of cachet enjoyed by this most counter-cultural of pursuits, a fact that has led to various high-profile appearances. The sport was recently featured in two mainstream films: *Casino Royale* and *Breaking and Entering*, the latter starring members of the Urban Freeflow collective.

If there's a downside to all this media coverage, then it's that the essence of parkour can get eclipsed by the visual pyrotechnics. 'Ultimately, most outsiders are more interested in sheer spectacle,' says class coach Dan Edwardes, 'especially the massive roof jumps, but that's only a tiny part of parkour, and not the hardest part either. We're keen to dispel the myths surrounding parkour and stress the disciplines at its centre, teaching people how to improve themselves – mentally and physically – while overcoming their fears and inhibitions.'

As a result, Dan believes that parkour is the perfect outlet for frustrated city kids. The pursuit has achieved the unthinkable by turning the concrete prisons of housing estates into enormous urban playgrounds for personal expression and development.

'It makes perfect sense,' he says. 'All these kids on estates with no space to move, a "no ball games" policy and no method of expressing themselves, suddenly have a means of learning and playing. It's technically legal – so long as you don't do it on private property – and you don't need any expensive equipment or fancy shoes. Kids can develop a discipline for free while harnessing the urban environment around them, and that's arguably what they've been looking for all along.'

Many parents will recoil at the potential dangers involved in a sport that logically concludes with their offspring hurling themselves off, over or at concrete, but Dan stresses that there's more to it than that.

'All sports contain an element of risk. What parkour teaches you, more than any other, is how to manage that risk through developing coordination and spatial awareness. And that's the key in life – not trying to avoid risk, but learning to minimise it. We actually think it's safer to learn parkour than not to learn it.'

Parkour Academy
Stowe Centre, 258 Harrow Road, W2 (7266 8220/www.urbanfreeflow.com). **Classes** 6.30pm-8.30pm Mon. **Rates** £5 per session. Min age 12. *Moberly Sports & Education Centre, Kilburn Lane, W10 4AE (7641 4807).* **Classes** 7.30-9.30pm Fri. **Rates** £5. Outdoor Academy, various London addresses (www.parkour coaching.com). **Classes** 7-8.30pm Wed, Fri; 10.30am-noon Sun (£5 reservations).

Activities

fields. And in recent years the sport has been growing in popularity. Jackson's Lane Community Circus (www.jacksonslane.org.uk) in Highgate, which was always a fine place to learn your Big Top moves, is unfortunately closed until autumn 2007 pending work to repair storm damage.

Albert & Friends' Instant Circus *Riverside Studios, Crisp Road, W6 9RL (8237 1170/ www.albertandfriendsinstantcircus.co.uk).*
Albert the Clown's Instant Circus workshops teach children skills such as juggling, diabolo, and stilt-, ball- and wire-walking. Many of his students go on to join the Albert & Friends' performing troupe – the UK's largest youth circus theatre, which also tours abroad.

The Circus Space *Coronet Street, N1 6HD (7613 4141/www.thecircusspace.co.uk). Old Street tube/rail.*
There's a Sunday morning 'Little Top' course for eight- to 12-year-olds; older children can choose static and flying trapeze, juggling, trampoline and acrobatics. *Photo p257.*

Climbing

London's indoor centres all cater for children (aged from around eight), with safe sessions run by qualified instructors. For general information on climbing, contact

British Mountaineering Council
0870 010 4878/www.thebmc.co.uk.

Castle Climbing Centre *Green Lanes, N4 2HA (07776 176007/www.geckos.co.uk). Manor House tube.*
Climbing is by private tuition (£40hr plus £10 admission and kit hire) or at a weekend birthday party (£150 for up to six children, £250 for up to 12). Book well in advance.

Mile End Climbing Wall *Haverfield Road, E3 5BE (8980 0289/www.mileendwall.org.uk). Mile End tube.*
This centre runs children's beginner sessions (£6) every Friday evening, with skills sessions on Saturday and Sunday mornings. Birthday parties can be held here and there is a summer holiday programme.

Westway Climbing Complex *Westway Sports Centre, 1 Crowthorne Road, W10 6RP (8969 0992/www.westway.org/sports/wsc/climbing). Latimer Road tube.*
This impressive west London centre caters to all climbing levels. Its big, chunky holds are perfect for kids. There are after-school classes on Mondays and Wednesdays, from 4.30pm-6pm, costing £3.50.

Cricket

Various initiatives to turn children on to cricket include the return of the game to central London. The cricket centre in Regent's Park offers one county-standard and five club-standard pitches, served by a large pavilion. It provides a permanent base for Capital Kids Cricket (www.capitalkids cricket.co.uk) which was set up in 1990 to encourage school-age children to play. For details, contact capitalkids@beeb.net.

There may be a decline in cricket in state schools, but clubs all round the capital have stepped in to develop the game for boys and girls aged from six. Many run junior sections, with 11-year-olds and under playing an adapted form of the game called Terrier Cricket, in which everyone gets an equal chance to bat, bowl and field. All under-16s are required to wear a helmet when batting, wicket-keeping or fielding against a hard ball. Most clubs will provide this, along with the other essential protective equipment, until youngsters buy their own.

Contact the County Board offices to find a club:

Essex (& East London)
01245 254010/www.essexcricket.org.uk.

Hertfordshire
01279 771551/www.hertscricket.org.

Kent
01227 456 886/www.kentsport.org/cricket.cfm.

Middlesex
7266 1650/www.middlesexccc.com.

Surrey
7820 5734/www.surreycricket.com.

For coaching, try the following indoor centres:
Ilford Cricket School *Sussex Close, Beehive Lane, Ilford, Essex IG4 5DR (8550 0041). Gants Hill tube.*
Ken Barrington Cricket Centre *Brit Oval, SE11 5SS (7820 5739). Oval tube.*
MCC Indoor School *Lord's Cricket Ground, NW8 9QN (7432 1014/www.mcc.org.uk). St John's Wood tube.*
Middlesex County Cricket Club *East End Road, N3 2TA (8346 8020/www.middlesexccc.com). Finchley Central tube.*

Cycling

In some European countries, as many as 60 per cent of children cycle to school. In Britain, a mere three per cent do. And a UK cyclist is 12 times more likely to be killed or injured than a Danish one, for example. In response to these worrying statistics, Safe Routes to Schools supports projects throughout the country that encourage young people to cycle and walk to school by improving street design, calming traffic and linking with the 8,000-kilometre (5,000-mile) National Cycle Network. Most local authorities include Safe Routes to Schools schemes in their Local Transport Plans.

Sustrans (www.sustrans.org.uk) is the pressure group that is working to create a safer environment for cycling.

Though the statistics in the UK aren't great, there is hope. Parents who aren't aware of a safe cycle route to their child's school or want to find out more about cycle training or Bike to School Week, can visit www.bikeforall.net for info.

The best guide to family rides around the capital is *The London Cycle Guide* (Haynes, £9.99), published in association with the **London Cycling Campaign** (7234 9310/www.lcc.org.uk).

Cycle Training UK
7582 3535/www.cycletraining.co.uk.
CTUK's instructors offer individual tuition anywhere in Greater London. Accompanied journeys to school are also available. After attending training, 81% of people said they cycled more often and more confidently.

London Recumbents
8299 6636/www.londonrecumbents.co.uk.
London Recumbents has a large range of cycles for hire.

London School of Cycling
7249 3779/www.londonschoolofcycling.co.uk.
Offering private tuition for all ages and abilities, the London School also runs cycle-maintenance workshops.

Cycle sport

Go-Ride is a British Cycling initiative where under-18s can learn track riding, BMX and mountain biking from qualified coaches. It's delivered through a national network of cycling clubs and includes a skills test designed to challenge even the best riders. Clubs involved include Lee Valley Youth Cycle Club (contact Greg Nash on 7553 9494) and Sutton Cycle Club (www.suttoncycling.co.uk). The scheme's website (www.go-ride.org.uk) lets you compare test times.

Herne Hill Velodrome *Burbage Road, SE24 9HE (www.hernehillvelodrome.co.uk). Herne Hill rail.*
The venerable home of track cycling since 1892. Many children begin their cycling careers here.

Hillingdon Cycle Circuit *Minet Park, Springfield Road, Hayes, Middx UB4 0LF (8737 7797). Hayes & Harlington rail.*
Tarmac circuit, good for road racing and tuition. One mile.

Dance
Dance centres
London Dance Network
www.londondance.com.

The network has a directory of other dance venues and organisations. The following centres all offer classes for kids:
Chisenhale Dance Space *64-84 Chisenhale Road, E3 5QZ (8981 6617/www.chisenhaledancespace.co.uk). Mile End tube.*
Danceworks *16 Balderton Street, W1K 6TN (7629 6183/www.danceworks.net). Bond Street tube.*
Drill Hall *16 Chenies Street, WC1E 7EX (7307 5060/www.drillhall.co.uk). Goodge Street tube.*
East London Dance *Stratford Circus, Theatre Square, E15 1BX (8279 1050/www. eastlondondance.org). Stratford tube/rail.*

Greenwich Dance Agency *Borough Hall, Royal Hill, SE10 8RE (8293 9741/www.greenwich dance.org.uk). Greenwich rail.*
Laban *Creekside, SE8 3DZ (8691 8600/www.laban. org). Deptford rail.*
The Place *17 Duke's Road, WC1H 9PY (7121 1000/ www.theplace.org.uk). Euston tube/rail.*
Ravenscourt Theatre School *8-30 Galena Road, W6 0LT (8741 0707/www.ravenscourt.net). Ravenscourt Park tube.*
Rona Hart School of Dance *Rosslyn Hall, Willoughby Road, NW3 1SB (7435 7073). Hampstead tube.*
Tricycle Theatre *269 Kilburn High Road, NW6 7JR (7328 1000/www.tricycle.co.uk). Kilburn tube.*

Fencing

Physically demanding and stylish to boot, fencing is a cool alternative for kids who don't enjoy the usual team games.

Most sessions comprise warm-up activities to develop co-ordination, flexibility and balance, formal work towards the nine fencing grades, followed by free fighting. No-one is allowed to participate without full protective clothing, a mask and the supervision of a qualified instructor.

For a full list of clubs around London, contact

British Fencing Association
8742 3032/www.britishfencing.com.
The following clubs offer regular junior sessions:
Camden Fencing Club *Ackland Burghley School, 93 Burghley Road, NW5 1UJ (www.camden fencingclub.org.uk). Kentish Town tube.*
Finchley Foil Fencing Club *Copthall School, Pursley Road, NW7 2EP (7485 1498/ www.finchleyfoil.co.uk). Mill Hill East tube.*
Haverstock Fencing Club *Haverstock School, Haverstock Hill, NW3 8AS (07811 077 048/www.haverstock.net). Chalk Farm tube.*
King's College School & Wimbledon High School Joint Fencing Club *Southside Common, SW19 4TT (jonmilner@blueyonder.co.uk). Wimbledon tube/rail.*
Kingston Fencing Club *Coombe Boys School, College Gardens, Blakes Lane, New Malden, Surrey KT3 6NU (secretary Joe Shackell 8393 4255/ www.kingstonfencing.co.uk). Motspur Park rail.*
Streatham Fencing Club *Dunraven Lower School, Mount Nod Road, SW16 2QB (www.streatham fencing.org). Streatham Hill rail.*

Football

At the top level, football is a billion-pound industry with 13 professional clubs in London (*see 271*). Lower down the pyramid, more than 45,000 clubs cater for all standards and ages, and both sexes.

Activities

To find a girls' team, contact the **Football Association** (7745 4545/www.TheFA.com/womens). Clubs with extensive girls' development programmes include **Arsenal** (7704 4140), **Charlton Athletic** (8333 4000), **Fulham** (8336 7578) and **Millwall** (7740 0503).

All the professional clubs in London run Football in the Community coaching courses, fun days and skills clinics. These are suitable for boys and girls aged from about six and are staffed by FA-qualified coaches. Check the club websites below (details are usually listed under the 'Club' or 'Community' headings) for venues and dates:

Arsenal *7704 4140/www.arsenal.com.*
Brentford *08453 456442/www.brentfordfc. premiumtv.co.uk.*
Charlton Athletic *8850 2866/www.charlton-athletic.co.uk.*
Chelsea *7957 8220/www.chelseafc.com.*
Crystal Palace *8768 6047/www.cpfc.co.uk.*
Fulham *0870 442 5432/www.fulhamfc.com.*
Leyton Orient *8556 5973/www.leytonorient.com.*
Millwall *7740 0503/www.millwallfc.co.uk.*
Queens Park Rangers *8740 2509/www.qpr.co.uk.*
Tottenham Hotspur *0870 420 5000/www.tottenhamhotspur.com.*
Watford *01923 496256/www.watfordfc.com.*
West Ham United *0870 112 5066/www.whufc.com.*

A highly rated scheme is run by former Queens Park Rangers goalkeeper Peter Hucker (8536 4141/www.peterhucker-soccer.com). Based in Barking and Wanstead, it offers weekly pay-and-play coaching sessions, matchplay and football parties for ages five to 16. Hucker also founded the **East London & Essex Small-Sided Soccer League**, now run by Joe Long (07961 867501, 01375 650 833, www.eleleague.com). Alternatively, **Powerleague** (www.powerleague.co.uk) runs nine centres around London for weekend coaching sessions and leagues for all ages.

There are many commercial football clinics and camps to choose from, including European Football Camps (www.footballcamps.co.uk) and The David Beckham Academy (East Parkside, Greenwich Peninsula, SE10 0JF, 8269 4620/www.thedavidbeckhamacademy. com) . The latter comprises two huge indoor pitches, highly qualified coaches and an impressive array of Becks memorabilia. The football camps run Monday to Friday during school holidays and follow the same lines as the schools education programme, plus coaching and skills sessions. Courses are non-residential and cost £180 (3 days) or £265 (5 days); all kids receive a package of Adidas kit, including footwear, plus healthy lunches and refreshments. There are also single day and after-school sessions – call or check the website for details.

Parents of football-crazy infants can also try the popular **Little Kickers** programme. The classes, developed by a group of FA-qualified coaches and nursery schoolteachers for pre-schoolers (from age two), are a gentle introduction to football. The programme operates all over London. For details, call 01235 859250 or visit www.littlekickers.co.uk.

Golf

The English Golf Union (see below) has developed Tri-Golf for six- to 12-year-olds and is introducing the game in primary schools. Children can play golf as part of the Duke of Edinburgh's Award.

A driving range is an excellent place to introduce a child to the basics of the game; the course professionals may offer lessons to help get them into good habits early on. The **TopGolf** system (www.topgolf.co.uk) is based on a point-scoring game using golf balls with a microchip inside them. Topgolf is played at its centres in Chigwell (8500 2644), Watford (01923 222045) and Addlestone (01932 858551).

English Golf Union
01526 354500/www.englishgolfunion.org.
Beckenham Place Park
The Mansion, Beckenham Place Park, Beckenham, Kent BR3 5BP (8650 2292). Beckenham Hill rail. Juniors can use this course at a reduced rate all day during the week and after noon on Saturdays (before 12pm the cost is £23). Lessons are held on Saturdays at 10am (£3). It costs £10 for juniors to play a round at weekends, £8 weekdays.

Driving ranges
Chingford Golf Range *Waltham Way, E4 8AQ (8529 2409). Chingford rail.*
Cranfield Golf Academy *Fairways Golf Centre, Southend Road, E4 8TA (8527 7692/www.cga-golf.com). Walthamstow Central tube/rail.*
Croydon Golf Driving Range *175 Long Lane, Addiscombe, Croydon, Surrey CR0 7TE (8656 1690). East Croydon/Elmers End rail.*
Dukes Meadows Golf Club *Dan Mason Drive, off Great Chertsey Road, W4 2SH (8995 0537/www.golf lessons.co.uk). Hammersmith tube, then 190 bus.*
Ealing Golf Range *Rowdell Road, Northolt, Middx UB5 6AG (8845 4967). Northolt tube.*
Nevada Bob's A1 *Rowley Lane, Arkley, Herts EN5 3HW (8447 1411). Elstree & Borehamwood rail.*
World Of Golf *Beverley Way, New Malden, Surrey KT3 4PH (8949 9200/www.worldofgolf-uk.co.uk). New Malden or Raynes Park rail.*

Gymnastics & trampolining

The British Amateur Gymnastics Association's clubs and schools run sessions for four year-olds and under, based around soft-play equipment and

Activities

Ross Nye's Riding Stables.
See p264.

simple games, leading to a series of proficiency awards. There are separate awards for rhythmic gymnastics and sports acrobatics. The Association is also the governing body for the British Trampoline Federation.

Bill Cosgrove, a former national gymnastics coach, created TumbleTots and, later, Gymbabes and Gymbobs. Gymbabes is for babies from six months to the crawling stage, TumbleTots is for walkers, and Gymbobs is for school-aged kids up to seven. For details of centres around the country, call 0121 585 7003 or see www.tumbletots.com. Another useful resource is the Little Gym, an international company whose gym programmes aim to help motor skill development and build confidence. There's a Little Gym franchise in Wandsworth (Compass House, Riverside West, Smugglers Way, SW18 1DB, 8874 6567, www.thelittlegym.co.uk).

British Amateur Gymnastics Association

01952 820330/www.british-gymnastics.org.
The following clubs offer a range of age-appropriate activities, and most offer trampolining as well. Both sports are also available at many public sports centres. Check that any club you choose displays a current certificate of inspection by BAGA or the **London Gymnastics Federation** (8529 1142, www.longym.freeserve.co.uk):

Avondale Gymnastics Club *Hollyfield Road, Surbiton, Surrey KT5 9AL (8399 3386/ www.avondalegymnastics.co.uk). Surbiton rail.*

Camberwell Gymnastics Club *Artichoke Place, SE5 8TS (7252 7353/www.camberwell gymnastics.co.uk). Denmark Hill rail.*

Charisma Gym Club *Dulwich College PE Centre, College Road, SE21 7LD (8299 3663/www.charisma gymnastics.com). West Dulwich rail.*

East London Gymnastics Club *Frobisher Road, E6 5LW (7511 4488/www.eastlondongym.co.uk). Beckton DLR.*

Heathrow Gymnastics Club *Green Lane, Hounslow, Middlesex, TW4 6DH (8569 5069/www. heathrowgymnastics.org.uk). Hatton Cross or Hounslow Central tube/H23 bus.*

Hillingdon School of Gymnastics *Victoria Road, South Ruislip, Middx HA4 0JE (8841 6666). South Ruislip tube.*

Richmond Gymnastics Centre *Townmead Road, Kew, Surrey TW9 4EL (8878 8682/www.richmond gymnastics.co.uk). Kew Gardens rail.*

Karting & motor sports

Karting is thrilling stuff for eight-year-olds upwards. The little buggies zip around at speeds exceeding 30 miles per hour, but parent's needn't have an anxiety attack: safety is always uppermost. Modern karts are easy to drive: there are two pedals (stop and go) and no gearbox to confuse the issue. The venues listed below welcome children and can be booked for parties:

Brands Hatch *Fawkham, Longfield, Kent DA3 8NG (01474 872331/www.motorsportvision.co.uk). Swanley rail, then taxi.*
Brands Hatch has loads of things to do on two and four wheels, including YoungDrive!, which puts your young-ster (aged over 13) in control of a Renault Clio.

Playscape Pro Racing *390 Streatham High Road, SW16 6HX (8677 8677/www.playscape.co.uk). Streatham rail.*
This centre can be booked for children's parties (over-eights only) or for half-hour taster sessions. Those who

Kids aged six to 16 can learn this ultra-cool Brazilian martial art, in which creative play is a strong element.

Moving East *St Matthias Church Hall, Wordsworth Road, N16 8DD (7503 3101/www.movingeast.co.uk). Dalston Kingsland rail.*
Judo and aikido (as well as dance and capoeira) classes for children are held at this friendly centre devoted to Japanese martial arts.

School of Japanese Karate *Chace Comunity School, Churchbury Lane, Enfield, Middlesex, EN1 3HQ. Training takes place at various venues in north London; check website or call for details. (8368 6249/www.sjkkarate.co.uk).*
Karate is the most popular Japanese martial art in this country. David and Lilian Alleyn run this well-established school and teach children aged six and upwards at venues around north London including Southgate, Arnos Grove, Cockfosters, Edmonton and Enfield.

Shaolin Temple UK *207A Junction Road, N19 5QA (www.shaolintempleuk.org). Tufnell Park tube.*
Thirty-forth-generation fighting monk Shi Yanzi and several other Shaolin masters teach traditional kung fu, Chinese kick-boxing, meditation and tai chi. Weekly classes for children are included in the programme.

become addicted can join the Cadet School, of the RAC's Association of Racing Kart Schools, which operates on the first Saturday of each month (8.30am-1pm; £35).

Martial arts

All martial arts impart self-confidence, body awareness, assertiveness and resilience.

Most local sports centres will be home to at least one martial arts club; many more are based in church halls and community centres. Look for evidence of a lively but disciplined atmosphere, with well-organised and age-appropriate teaching. Ask instructors about their qualifications – the grading systems used in judo and karate, for example, help to ensure that teachers are of a suitable standard. Note, however, that a black belt is not a teaching qualification. Also ask for proof of insurance cover: martial arts usually involve physical contact, and accidents can happen.

The following venues offer classes for children in a number of disciplines – call ahead and get the full list before setting off:

Bob Breen Academy *16 Hoxton Square, N1 6NT (7729 5789/www.bobbreen.co.uk). Old Street tube/rail.*
Children aged seven to 16 can learn kick-boxing skills and effective self-defence techniques at this well-known and highly respected academy.

Hwarang Academy *Swiss Cottage Community Centre, 19 Winchester Road, NW3 3NR (07941 081 009/www.taekwondo-london-2012.com). Swiss Cottage tube.*
Youngsters aged four to 12 and over can learn the Korean martial art of tae kwon do, now an Olympic sport, here.

London School of Capoeira *Unit 1-2, Leeds Place, Tollington Park, N4 3RF (7281 2020/www.london-schoolofcapoeira.co.uk). Finsbury Park tube/rail.*

Orienteering

Orienteering is navigating your way around a route using a map (and occasionally a compass), collecting points for every station you visit on the way. There are nine permanent courses in London and more than 40 in the surrounding countryside. The permanent course at Hampstead Heath is particularly enjoyable.
British Orienteering Federation *(01629 734042, www.britishorienteering.org.uk).*

Riding

Riding lessons and hacks must be booked in advance: ask the stables whether they have 'taster' sessions for newcomers. Riders must always wear a hard hat (establishments can usually lend one if you don't have your own) and boots with a small heel, rather than trainers or wellies. Some centres run 'own a pony' days and weeks, and offer birthday-party packages. Most stables are also able to cater for riders with disabilities.

Ealing Riding School *Gunnersbury Avenue, W5 3XD (8992 3808/www.ealingridingschool.biz). Ealing Common tube.* **Lessons** £21/hr (group); £27/hr (individual).
Riders from five upwards can take part in many activities here. Lessons are held in an outdoor manège.

Hyde Park & Kensington Stables *Hyde Park Stables, 63 Bathurst Mews, W2 2SB (7723 2813/www.hydeparkstables.com). Lancaster Gate tube.* **Lessons** £49/hr (group); £65-£85/hr (individual). Discounts available for block bookings.
Children aged five upwards can enjoy an hour-long lesson with patient, streetwise ponies in the glamorous surroundings of Hyde Park – not cheap, though.

Activities

Lee Valley Riding Centre *Lea Bridge Road, E10 7QL (8556 2629/www.leevalleypark.org.uk). Clapton rail/48, 55, 56 bus.* **Lessons** £18.20/hr (group); £12.60/30mins (beginners group; Sat, Sun).
Though gritty Walthamstow doesn't exactly call to mind green pastures, Lee Valley Riding Centre is an exception to the stereotype. The placid ponies enjoy the open spaces of Walthamstow Marshes and delight a devoted band of regulars. Bookings must be made in advance

London Equestrian Centre *Lullington Garth, N12 7BP (8349 1345/www.londonridingschool.com). Mill Hill East tube.* **Lessons** £23 (group); £23-£28 (individual; 30min session, Tue-Sun only).
This yard has 30 assorted horses and ponies. The junior members' club runs informal gymkhanas. Birthday parties can be held here, and the centre can organise pony rides for three- to four-year-olds.

Newham Riding School & Association
Docklands Equestrian Centre, 2 Claps Gate Lane, E6 6JF (7511 3917). Beckton DLR. **Lessons** £15 (group).
This is a much-loved stables, where the 20 horses and ponies have many besotted fans.

Ross Nye's Riding Stables
8 Bathurst Mews, W2 2SB (7262 3791). Lancaster Gate tube. **Lessons** £50/hr (group); £60/hr (individual).
The Hyde Park branch of the Pony Club. Membership gives reduced prices for lessons. Clients aged from six learn to ride in Hyde Park. *Photo p262.*

Trent Park Equestrian Centre
Bramley Road, N14 4XS (8363 9005/www.trent park.com). Oakwood tube. **Lessons** £20-£27/hr (group); £16-£34 (individual).
The leafy acres of Trent Park (£28 per hour for hacking out) and a caring attitude towards young riders (aged from four) make this a justifiably popular place to ride.

Willowtree Riding Establishment
The Stables, Ronver Road, SE12 0NL (8857 6438). Grove Park or Lee rail. **Lessons** from £8 (group); from £16 (individual).
A friendly local venue with more than 40 ponies and horses, some of which are pure-bred Arab.

Wimbledon Village Stables
24A/B High Street, SW19 5DX (8946 8579/www.wv stables.com). Wimbledon tube/rail. **Lessons** £25/ 30mins; £50/hr (individual).
If you're looking for a bucolic, pastoral English scene, this is the place to ride. This centre has a small selection of quiet, safe ponies and a popular holiday scheme (£145 for three afternoons). Riding takes place on leafy Wimbledon Common – a slice of the countryside in the city.

Rugby league

In junior rugby league the emphasis is on running, passing, skills and teamwork rather than crunching tackles and physical contact. The Skolars run three junior clubs for kids: two for under elevens and one for 12-16 year olds.

Rugby Football League
0844 477 7113, www.rfl.uk.com.
Greenwich Admirals *www.greenwichrl.com.*
London Skolars *8888 8488/www.skolars.com.*
South London Storm *www.stormrl.com.*

Rugby union

Rugby clubs cater for boys and girls, with 'minis' for six-year-olds, 'midi rugby' for under-11s, and 'youth rugby' for ages 13 and over. Emphasis is placed on the fun of handling, passing and running; impact arts of tackling, scrummaging and kicking are gradually introduced and controlled. Young children play non-contact 'tag' rugby, using a belt worn around the waist with two 'tags' attached. If an opponent removes a tag, possession switches to the other team. Women's and girls' rugby has made progress in recent years and many clubs are now fully integrated. Contact the RFU for details.

Rugby Football Union
Rugby House, Rugby Road, Twickenham, Middlx TW1 1DS (8892 2000/www.rfu.com). Twickenham rail.

Skateboarding & BMX-ing

Baysixty6 Skate Park *Bay 65-66, Acklam Road, W10 5YU (8969 4669/www.baysixty6.com). Ladbroke Grove tube.* **Membership** free. **Prices** £6/5hrs Mon-Fri, 4hrs Sat, Sun; £3 beginners 10am-noon Sat, Sun.
Sheltered beneath the A40, this enormous park includes a vert ramp, a medium half-pipe, a mini ramp and many funboxes, grind boxes, ledges and rails. Some skaters mutter that it's a bit much having to pay £6 when it's free to skate everywhere else in London – but the high quality of the ramps here goes some way to making up for it.

Harrow Skatepark *Peel Road (behind the leisure centre), Wealdstone, Middx HA3 5BD. Harrow & Wealdstone tube/rail.*
There are clover-leaf and kidney bowls, and a concrete half-pipe remains a monumental challenge for the fearless.

Meanwhile 3 *Meanwhile Gardens, off Great Western Road, W9 (no phone). Westbourne Park tube.*
Here are three concrete bowls of varying size and steepness, but no flatland, so it's not for beginners.

Cantelowes Skatepark *Cantelowes Gardens, Camden Road, NW1 (www.cantelowesskatepark.co.uk).*
This phenomenally popular park reopened in May 2006 as part of a £1.5million redevelopment.

Skating

On ice

In recent years, temporary skating rinks have sprung up around the city at Christmas time. Session times at London's permanent rinks vary from day to day, but venues are generally open from 10am until 10pm.

National Ice Skating Association
0115 988 8060, www.iceskating.org.uk.

Alexandra Palace Ice Rink *Alexandra Palace Way, N22 7AY (8365 4386/www.alexandrapalace.com). Wood Green tube/Alexandra Palace rail/W3 bus.*
Courses for children aged five to 15 run on Saturday mornings and early weekday evenings. *Photo p266.*

Activities

Broadgate Ice Arena *Broadgate Circle, Eldon Street, EC2A 2BQ (Summer 7505 4000/Winter 7505 4068/www.broadgateice.co.uk). Liverpool Street tube/rail.*
This tiny outdoor rink is open from late October to April. It's very child-friendly, not usually as beset with crowds as the other outdoors, so a good place to learn.
Lee Valley Ice Centre *Lea Bridge Road, E10 7QL (8533 3154/www.leevalleypark.org.uk). Clapton rail.*

The disco nights are a big hit at this modern, well-maintained and comparatively warm rink. It's never too busy as it's hard to get to by public transport, and the ice rink is a good size. Lessons are also offfered.
Michael Sobell Leisure Centre *Hornsey Road, N7 7NY (7609 2166/www.aquaterra.org). Finsbury Park tube/rail.*
Children from four upwards are welcome at this small rink, which runs popular after-school sessions and six-week courses. You can also hold parties here.

Blades of glory

Reality TV has plenty to answer for in terms of cultural degradation, but at least its celebrity ice skaters have injected some much-needed kudos into a discipline increasingly ignored by young people obsessed with more 'extreme' sports. And that's no bad thing: beginners' blisters are common currency among first-timers renting antiquated skates, but ice skating is a fantastic way of developing balance and co-ordination, potentially paving the way for success in countless other disciplines.

London has several arenas for pint-sized ice-capades, none of them more aesthetically inspiring than the formidable rink in grade II-listed Alexandra Palace (*see p264; pictured*). Tuition is available both privately or in groups, with week-long children's crash courses operating in the school holidays. The Alexandra Palace Amateur Ice Skating Club (www.apskate.org.uk) also runs hour-long junior sessions for more dedicated skaters every Saturday morning at 8.30am (£6 members; £7 guests), and organises various competitions throughout the year for kids looking to take their new-found skills from the playground to the podium.

More centrally, the Queens Ice Bowl (*see p265*) is smaller and infinitely less subtle but far more popular with young ones, largely as a result of its disorientating light displays (the ice is constantly changing colour), pumping sound system and adjoining bowling alley and amusement arcade. As a result, the place can feel like a refrigerated Trocadero at weekends – the rink itself is occasionally so packed that it would be hard to swing a cat, let alone a supple skating partner –

but the centre nevertheless runs comprehensive six-week coaching programmes for kids of all ages (£55 per child including skate hire).

Those aiming for the big time, however, might be better off in the less flash but infinitely more functional Streatham Ice Arena; *see p265*. Okay, so it's not the sprightliest of rinks (built in 1931 and ageing less than gracefully), but it's arguably the best run and certainly the biggest in the capital (60m by 26m), with six-week courses (from £45) allowing everyone from toddlers to teens to get their skates on. The building is due for demolition to make way for a new Tesco (surprise surprise), but not until the supermarket giant has fulfilled its promise to build an Olympic-standard replacement, due for completion in 2008 – get the little ones in there now and they might even be on form for the Winter Olympics in Vancouver two years later.

Of course, this indoor malarkey is all for nothing if kids don't get a chance to transfer their new talents to the great outdoors, and luckily London offers al-fresco skating options at a number of temporary rinks set up during the Christmas holidays. Some of these are beyond picturesque – those at Somerset House (*see p265*) and the Natural History Museum (*see p89*) will melt even the frostiest of hearts – but their unprecedented popularity means that tickets need to be booked weeks in advance. Less hard to wangle are outdoor skate sessions at Broadgate Ice Rink near Liverpool Street (www.broadgateice.co.uk; *see p264*), small but perfectly formed and — more importantly – staying open from November all the way through to mid-April.

Activities

Queens Ice Bowl *17 Queensway, W2 4QP (7229 0172/www.queensiceandbowl.co.uk). Bayswater or Queensway tube.*
The disco nights on Fridays and Saturdays are legendary, but beginners and families are also well looked after at this well-known ice rink.

Somerset House *Strand, WC2R 1LA (7845 4600/www.somersethouse.org.uk). Holborn or Temple tube (closed Sun).*
Every winter the courtyard here is iced over to become the most attractive rink in London. It will be open from late November 2007-late January 2008.

Streatham Ice Arena *386 Streatham High Road, SW16 6HT (8769 7771/www.streathamicearena.co.uk). Streatham rail.*
This popular rink offers six-week courses for all ages, as well as classes for 'toddlers' aged up to four.

Alexandra Palace Ice Rink. *See p264.*

On tarmac

Citiskate (7228 2999, www.citiskate.co.uk) teaches hundreds of Londoners how to skate in parks, leisure centres and schools. The instructors all hold qualifications from UKISA (United Kingdom Inline Skating Association); lessons are available seven days a week. Citiskate's weekly Sunday Rollerstroll (www.rollerstroll.com) and Battersea Park's Easy Peasy skate on Saturday (www.easy peasyskate.com) are popular group skates around the streets that are ideal for families.

Skiing & snowboarding

Note that if you're thinking of taking a mixed-ability group out to a dry ski slope for an open recreational session, the minimum requirement is to be able to perform a controlled snowplough turn and use the ski lift.

Ski Club of Great Britain
8410 2000, www.skiclub.co.uk.

Bromley Ski Centre
Sandy Lane, St Paul's Cray, Orpington, Kent BR5 3HY (01689 876812). St Mary Cray rail, 321 bus.
Two lifts serve the 120m (394ft) main slope, and there's also a mogul field and nursery slope. Skiing and snowboarding taster sessions cost £17. Booking is essential.

Sandown Sports Club
More Lane, Esher, Surrey KT10 8AN (01372 467 132/www.sandownsports.co.uk). Esher rail.
The 120m (394ft) main slope, 80m (262ft) nursery area and 90m (295ft) snowboarding slope are closed during race meetings. This is a lessons-only venue: tuition is available for under sevens (£24/30mins) and seven-year-olds upwards (£43/hr). Parties available.

Snozone *Xscape, 602 Marlborough Gate, Milton Keynes MK9 3XS (0871 222 5670/www.xscape.co.uk, www.snozoneuk.com). Milton Keynes Central rail.*
This is one of the UK's largest indoor snow domes, with three slopes (in reality they are joined, so they resemble one wide slope): two of 170m (558ft) and one of 135m (443ft), with button lifts running all the way to the top. The place can feel

a bit like a big fridge, but beginners couldn't ask for a better environment in which to find their ski legs. The Alps it ain't – but it's a lot less intimidating than hurtling down those fabled slopes.

Swimming

Most local authority pools run lessons for children, plus parent-and-baby sessions to develop water confidence in those as young as three months. However, these can be oversubscribed and often have long waiting lists. Ask at your local pool for details.

Tuition

Amateur Swimming Association
01509 618 700/www.britishswimming.co.uk.
Dolphin Swimming Club
University of London Pool, Malet Street, WC1E 7HU (8349 1844). Tottenham Court Road tube.

ot only does this club teach children to swim, it helps quaphobic adults to overcome their fear. A course of 11 dividual half-hour lessons costs £81. Note: lessons are eld on weekends only.

eander Swimming Club *Balham Leisure Centre, lmfield Road, SW17 8AN (www.leanderswimming ub.org.uk). Balham tube/rail.*
his programme for children aged seven and above in alham, Tooting, Crystal Palace and Dulwich extends om basic strokes to serious competition.

ittle Dippers *0870 758 0302/www.little ppers.co.uk.*
ourses in water confidence for parents and babies have a ood teacher-pupil ratio. No more than seven babies are in e water at any time, using pools in Wimbledon, ichmond, Chiswick, Swiss Cottage and London Bridge, ll chosen for their warm temperature. An initial six-week urse costs £109, with every subsequent course is £74; eekend courses cost £109.

wimming Nature
870 900 8002/www.swimmingnature.co.uk.
wimming Nature teaches children to swim using a con-olled, progressively hands-on method. Lessons take place Bayswater, Brondesbury, Victoria, Chelsea, Kensington, Iaida Vale, Paddington, Regent's Park, Russell Square, ueens Park and Marylebone.

ools

ere's a selection of our favourites. Most pools are pen daily; phone for times.

arnet Copthall Pools *Champions Way, NW4 1PX 3457 9900/www.gll.org). Mill Hill East tube.*
hree pools and a diving area, with coaching and clubs to in if you fancy taking the plunge.

rentford Fountain Leisure Centre *658 Chiswick igh Road, Brentford, Middx TW8 0HJ (0845 456 935/www.hounslow.gov.uk). Gunnersbury tube.*
eisure pool with a 40m (131ft) aquaslide, underwater ghting and wave machine alongside a teaching pool.

rystal Palace National Sports Centre
edrington Road, SE19 2BB (8778 0131/www.gll.org). rystal Palace rail.
ne of the capital's two current 50m (164ft) Olympic-size ols which, along with its fine diving facilities, now looks have a secure future.

oresbrook Leisure Centre *Ripple Road, agenham, Essex RM9 6XW (8593 3570). econtree tube.*
ountains, cascades and a 60m (197ft) flume combine here ith a small area for length swimming.

ampton Heated Open Air Pool *High Street, ampton, Middx TW12 2ST (8255 1116/ ww.hamptonpool.co.uk). Hampton rail.*
hen the sun's shining, Hampton is hard to beat. It's open ll year round, including Christmas Day.

onmonger Row Baths *Ironmonger Row, EC1V QF (7253 4011). Old Street tube/rail.*
ake a trip back in time at this well-preserved 1930s 30m 8ft) pool and Turkish baths (one of only three remaining London).

ingfisher Leisure Centre *Fairfield Road, ingston, Surrey, KT1 2PY (8546 1042/ ww.kingfisherleisurecentre.co.uk). Kingston rail.*
uper-friendly family centre with a teaching pool and a ain pool with beach area and wave machine.

Latchmere Leisure Centre *Burns Road, SW11 5AD (7207 8004/www.latchmereleisurecentre.co.uk). Clapham Junction rail.*
Lane-swimming main pool, teaching pool and a beach area to laze about in, with a wave machine and a slide.

Leyton Leisure Lagoon *763 High Road, E10 5AB (8558 8858/www.gll.org). Leyton tube/69, 97 bus.*
A flume, slides, fountains, rapids and cascades liven up and bring a splash of colour to this rather drab slice of north-east London.

Northolt Swimarama *Eastcote Lane North, Northolt, Middx UB5 4AB (8422 1176). Northolt tube.*
Three pools, plus a 60m (197ft) slide and diving boards.

Pavilion Leisure Centre *Kentish Way, Bromley, Kent BR1 3EF (8313 9911/www.bromleymytime. org.uk). Bromley South rail.*
A large leisure pool with shallows, flumes and a wave machine, lane swimming and a separate toddlers' pool.

Queen Mother Sports Centre *223 Vauxhall Bridge Road, SW1V 1EL (7630 5522/www.courtneys.co.uk). Victoria tube/rail.*
Three excellent pools in this refurbished centre mean it's always popular with schoolkids.

Spa at Beckenham *24 Beckenham Road, Beckenham, BR3 4PF (8650 0233/www. bromleymytime.org.uk). Clock House rail.*
An award-winning leisure centre with loads of sports facil-ities, two swimming pools, the Space Zone soft-play area for children and a crèche.

Tottenham Green Leisure Centre *1 Philip Lane, N15 4JA (8489 5322). Seven Sisters tube/rail.*
Choose between lane swimming and diving in the main pool or splashing amid the waves and slides in the 'beach pool' at this perennially popular leisure centre.

Waterfront Leisure Centre *High Street, SE18 6DL (8317 5000/www.gll.org). Woolwich Arsenal rail/96, 177 bus.*
Four pools, six slides, waves, rapids and a water 'volcano' keep locals happy in Greenwich's flagship centre.

Open-air swimming

For full details of London's outdoor pools (and to join the campaign to reopen those that have closed), visit www.lidos.org.uk.

Brockwell Lido *Brockwell Park, Dulwich Road, SE24 (www.thelido.co.uk). Herne Hill rail.* **Open** July, Aug; check website for times. **Admission** check website for details.
This wonderful listed 1930s lido has received £500,000 from the Heritage Lottery Fund for renovation, so its future seems at last to be secure.

Charlton Lido *Hornfair Park, Shooters Hill Road, Charlton, SE18 4LX (www.gll.org). Charlton or Eltham rail.* **Admission** check website for details.
The last lido to be built by London County Council in 1939. Check the Greenwich Leisure website or phone 8317 5000 to confirm opening times and prices.

Finchley Lido *High Road, N12 0GL (8343 9830/ www.gll.org). East Finchley tube.* **Open** check website for times. **Admission** check website for details.
There are two indoor pools here, but it's the outdoor pool and sun terrace that make it such a popular draw for locals during the summer.

Hampstead Heath Swimming Ponds & Parliament Hill Lido *Lido: Parliament Hill Fields,*

Activities

Gordon House Road, NW5 1LP. Hampstead Heath
rail. Men & women's ponds: Millfield Lane, N6.
Gospel Oak rail. Mixed pond: East Heath Road, NW3.
Hampstead Heath rail. Both (7485 4491/www.city
oflondon.gov.uk). **Open** check website for times.
Admission Lido £4.20; £2.60 concession; £12.50
family. Ponds £2; £1 concession. Season tickets and
early/late entry discounts available.
Children aged between eight to 15 are only allowed in the
ponds if under the watchful eyes of an adult.

London Fields Lido London Fields Westside E8
3EU (7254 9038/www.gll.org). London Fields rail.
Open times vary; phone for details. **Admission**
£3.85; £2.30 under-16s.
Hackney Council resurrected this lovely lido, which has
proved a major draw for swimmers all over London since
it opened in autumn 2006.

Oasis Sports Centre 32 Endell Street, WC2H
9AG (7831 1804/www.gll.org). Tottenham Court
Road tube. **Open** 7.30am-9pm Mon-Fri; 9.30am-
5.30pm Sat, Sun. **Admission** £3.60; £1.40 5-16s; free
under-5s; £6.75 family.
This 28m (92ft) outdoor pool is open all year round.

Pools on the Park Old Deer Park, Twickenham
Road, Richmond, Surrey TW9 2SF (8940 0561/
www.springhealth.net). Richmond rail. **Open** 6.30am-
10pm Mon-Fri; 8am-9pm Sat, Sun. **Admission** £3.70;
£2.90 concessions; £1.50 seniors; free under-5s. Prices
may vary during peak season.
A 33m (108ft) heated outdoor pool (and one the same size
and temperature inside), plus a sunbathing area.

Tooting Bec Lido Tooting Bec Road, SW16 1RU
(8871 7198/www.slsc.org.uk). Streatham rail. **Open**
Late May-Aug 6am-8pm daily. Sept 6am-5pm daily.
Oct-May 7am-2pm daily (club members only).
Admission £4.30; £2.90 concessions and under-16s;
£11.50 family; free under-5s.
At 94m by 25m (308ft by 82ft), this art deco beauty is the
second-largest open-air pool in Europe.

Water polo

In Aquagoal, the version of this game adapted
for kids aged ten and upwards, you score goals
without touching the side or bottom of the pool.

National Water Polo League
www.nwpl.co.uk.

Table tennis

Twenty weekend junior leagues are now running
in the capital, and there are several clubs offering
coaching for youngsters. One of the best is
London Progress (London Progress
Tournament Centre, Southall Sports Centre,
Southall, Middx, UB1 1DP; 0780 308 2661,
www.londonprogress.com), which has a
competitive system to feed into.

English Table Tennis Association
01424 722 525/www.englishtabletennis.org.uk.

Tennis

Tennis for Free (TFF) is a campaign to give
access without charge to Britain's 33,000 public
courts – and encourage a long-overdue change in
this country's white, middle-class tennis culture.
To find out more, visit www.tennisforfree.com.

Most London boroughs run holiday tennis
courses at Easter and in the summer: contact
your local sports development team for details.
The Lawn Tennis Association publishes free
guides giving contacts for private clubs and
public courts listed by borough or county, along
with contact details for local development officers.
Details of tennis holidays are also available.

Lawn Tennis Association
8487 7000/www.lta.org.uk.

Clissold Park Junior Tennis Club Clissold Park
Mansion House, Stoke Newington Church Street, N16
9HJ (7254 4235/www.hackneycitytennisclubs.co.uk).
Stoke Newington rail/73 bus. **Open** Apr-Sept 10am-
7.30pm Mon-Fri; 9am-7.30pm Sat, Sun. Oct-Mar 10am-
4pm Mon-Fri; 9am-4pm Sat, Sun. **Court hire** £5.50/hr.
Reduced rate available for under-16s, phone to check
availability.
Britain's first City Tennis Centre, where racquets and balls
are free to borrow. The club is active with squads, coaching, club competitions and Middlesex League teams. Other
City Tennis Centres are at Highbury Fields and Eltham
Park South, Greenwich.

David Lloyd Leisure 0870 888
3015/www.davidlloydleisure.co.uk.
There are 5 David Lloyd clubs in the London area, combining tennis with upmarket fitness facilities. All are
family-friendly, if not cheap, and the facilities are excellent.
Check out the website or phone for your nearest venue.

Islington Tennis Centre
Market Road, N7 9PL (7700 1370/www.aqua
terra.org). Caledonian Road tube. **Open** 7am-11pm
Mon-Thur; 7am-10pm Fri; 8am-10pm Sat, Sun. **Court
hire** Indoor non-members £18.50/hr; £8.20/hr 5-16s.
Outdoor £8.70/hr; £4/hr 5-16s.
Developed under the LTA's Indoor Tennis Initiative, this
centre offers subsidised coaching and tennis courses.

Redbridge Sports & Leisure Centre
Forest Road, Barkingside, Essex IG6 3HD (8498
1000/www.rslonline.co.uk). Fairlop tube. **Open** 9am-
11pm Mon-Fri; 9am-9pm Sat; 9am-10pm Sun. **Court
hire** varies; phone for details.
Developed by a charitable trust, this outstanding multi-
sports centre has eight indoor and six 18 outdoor courts
which you can use as a member or 'pay as you play'. There
are holiday activities for six- to 14-year-olds and 'fun play'
sessions. There's also a short tennis club for under-eights.

Sutton Junior Tennis Centre Rose Hill Recreation
Ground, Rose Hill, Sutton, Surrey SM1 3HH (8641
6611/www.sjtc.org). Morden tube. **Open** 7am-11pm
daily. **Court hire** Indoor £17.50; £12.50 5-16s. Outdoor
£7.50-£12.50; £5.50-£8.50 5-16s.
Britain's top tennis school, with high-quality performance
coaches, led by Frenchman Erich Dochterman, who has
taught various ATP and WTA-ranked players. There are
residential courses for players seeking professional status.

nd a scholarship scheme linked with Cheam High School. Children can start at three with Tiny Tots classes, move on to mini tennis, join in holiday programmes and book tennis birthday parties. There are six red clay, ten acrylic and 11 indoor courts. The Centre also has good international credentials: in this country, it is a base for Tennis Australia and the Barcelona Tennis Academy.

Westway Tennis Centre *1 Crowthorne Road, W10 5RP (8969 0992/www.westway.org). Latimer Road tube.* **Open** 8am-10pm Mon-Fri; 8am-8pm Sat; 10am-10pm Sun. **Court hire** *Indoor* £16-£20; £8-£10 5-16s. *Outdoor* £8-£9; £5-£7 5-16s.

Also the product of the LTA's Indoor Tennis Initiative, Westway follows a similar model to Islington (*see p268*) – excellent subsidised coaching, short tennis and transitional tennis. There are eight indoor and four outdoor clay courts - the only ones in London open to the public.

Tenpin bowling

A trip to a local bowling centre makes for a great birthday party or family day out, even the very young can be sure of hitting the target with the aid of ball chutes and bumpers. For youngsters keen to progress, there's a network of regional and national youth tournaments and leagues.

British Tenpin Bowling Association *8478 1745/www.btba.org.uk.*

All the centres listed are open seven days a week, typically 10am to midnight. Admission prices vary, but average around £6 per game – which includes the hire of soft-soled bowling shoes. Phone for details of children's parties.

Acton Megabowl *Royale Leisure Park, Western Avenue, W3 0PA (0870 550 1010/www.megabowl. co.uk). Park Royal tube.*

Airport Bowl *Bath Road, Harlington, Middx UB3 5AL (8759 7246/www.airport-bowl.co.uk). Hatton Cross tube.*

AMF Bowling Lewisham *11-29 Belmont Hill, SE13 5AU (0870 118 3021/www.amfbowling.co.uk). Lewisham rail/DLR.*

Bexleyheath Megabowl *Albion Road, Bexleyheath, Kent DA6 7LS (0871 550 1010/www.megabowl.co.uk). Bexleyheath rail.*

Dagenham Bowling *Cook Road, Dagenham, Essex RM9 6XW (8593 2888/www.namcoexperience.com). Becontree tube.*

Feltham Megabowl *Leisure West Complex, Browells Lane, Feltham, Middx TW13 7EQ (0871 550 1010/www.megabowl.co.uk). Feltham rail.*

Funland *Trocadero, 1 Piccadilly Circus, W1D 7DH (7292 3633/www.funland.co.uk). Piccadilly Circus tube.*

Hollywood Bowl Finchley *Great North Leisure Park, Chaplin Square (off Finchley High Road), N12 0GL (8446 6667/www.hollywoodbowl.co.uk). East Finchley tube, then 263 bus.*

Hollywood Bowl Surrey Quays *Mast Leisure Park, Teredo Street, SE16 7LW (7237 3773/www. hollywoodbowl.co.uk). Canada Water DLR.*

Queens *17 Queensway, W2 4QP (7229 0172/ www.queensiceandbowl.co.uk). Bayswater or Queensway tube.*

Rowans Bowl *10 Stroud Green Road, N4 2DF (8800 1950/www.rowans.co.uk). Finsbury Park tube rail.*

Watersports

The sea may be miles away, but that doesn't stop London kids messing about on the water. Canoes, dinghies or rowing boats can be their vessel of choice, and for the more petrol-headed, there are powerboats down Deptford way.

Amateur Rowing Association
8237 6700/www.ara-rowing.org.

British Canoe Union
0845 370 9500/www.bcu.org.uk.

British Dragon Boat Racing Association
www.dragonboat.org.uk.

Royal Yachting Association
0845 345 0400/www.rya.org.uk.

British Waterski
www.britishwaterski.org.uk.

London Windsurf Association
01895 846707/www.lwawindsurfing.co.uk.

Ahoy Centre *Borthwick Street, SE8 3JY (8691 7606/www.ahoy.org.uk). Deptford rail/Cutty Sark DLR.* This is the place to come for sailing, rowing and powerboating on the Thames, and in Surrey and Victoria Docks. Members help run the centre, an approach that keeps prices down and fosters a strong community spirit.

Albany Park Canoe & Sailing Centre *Albany Mews, Albany Park Road, Kingston-upon-Thames, Surrey KT2 5SL (8549 3066/www. albanypark.co.uk). Kingston rail.* A lively centre for sailing, kayaking and canoeing. Tuition and taster sessions are available.

BTYC Sailsports *Birchen Grove, NW9 8SA (8830 5726/www.btycsailsports.org.uk). Neasden or Wembley Park tube.* Club offering dinghy sailing, windsurfing, with basic training and RYA courses held on the Welsh Harp reservoir.

Canalside Activity Centre *Canal Close, W10 5AY (8968 4500). Ladbroke Grove tube/Kensal Rise rail/ 52, 70, 295 bus.* This centre offers canoeing lessons, as well as water safety classes.

Docklands Sailing & Watersports Centre *Millwall Dock, 235A Westferry Road, E14 3QS (7537 2626/www.dswc.org). Crossharbour DLR.* **Membership** £110 adult; £20 youth; £220 family. Canoeing, dragon-boat racing, windsurfing and dinghy sailing for over-eights who are confident in the water.

Activities

Fairlop Sailing Centre *Forest Road, Hainault, Ilford IG6 3HN (8500 1468/www.fairlop.org.uk). Fairlop tube.*
This Royal Yachting Association- and British Canoe Union-approved centre offers windsurfing, dinghy sailing, canoeing and powerboating courses.
Globe Rowing Club *Trafalgar Rowing Centre, Crane Street, SE10 9NP (www.globe.cwc.net). Cutty Sark DLR/Maze Hill rail.*
Friendly, Greenwich-based rowing club.
Lea Rowing Club *Spring Hill, E5 9BL (club house 8806 8282/www.learc.org.uk). South Tottenham or Stamford Hill rail.*
Runs rowing and sculling classes and holiday courses for kids aged from ten who can swim at least 50 metres.
Royal Victoria Dock Watersports Centre *Gate 5, Tidal Basin Road, off Silvertown Way, E16 1AD (7511 2326). Royal Victoria Dock DLR.*
Membership junior £53-£75/year.
The calm waters of Victoria Dock are a great place to master dinghy sailing and tackle an RYA beginners' course. The centre runs the Youth on H₂O scholarship scheme, which offers free tuition, and a busy holiday programme.
Shadwell Basin Outdoor Activity Centre *3-4 Shadwell Pierhead, Glamis Road, E1W 3TD (7481 4210/www.shadwell-basin.org.uk). Wapping tube.*
Downriver from Tower Bridge, the Shadwell Basin Centre offers fairly priced sailing, canoeing, kayaking and dragon-boating for children aged nine and over.
Surrey Docks Watersports Centre *Greenland Dock, Rope Street, SE16 7SX (7237 4009). Surrey Quays tube.*
Sailing, windsurfing and canoeing for over-eights take place in the sheltered dock in school holidays and half-terms. RYA courses also available.
West Reservoir Centre *Stoke Newington West Reservoir, Green Lanes, N4 2HA (8800 6161). Manor House tube.*
This purpose-built environmental education and watersports centre is a good place to learn the basics of dinghy sailing.
Westminster Boating Base *136 Grosvenor Road, SW1V 3JY (7821 7389/www.westminster boatingbase.co.uk). Pimlico tube.*
Canoeing and sailing for over-tens on the tidal Thames. There's no fixed fee for youth membership; instead, the Base asks for a donation according to personal circumstances.

Row your boat

The following venues for rowing boat hire usually charge by the half hour. Some also have pedaloes.
Richmond Bridge can hire out a rowing boat or skiff for a whole day's messing about on the Thames.
Battersea Park *SW11 4NJ (8871 7530). Battersea Park rail.* During summer months only
Regent's Park *Hanover Gate, NW1 4RL (7724 4069). Baker Street tube.*
Richmond Bridge Rowing Boat Hire *1-3 Bridge Boathouse, Richmond, Surrey TW9 1TH (8948 8270). Richmond tube/rail.*
Serpentine *The Boat House, Serpentine Road, W2 2UH (7298 2100/www.royalparks.gov.uk). Hyde Park Corner tube.*

Yoga

Yoga is good for children, but you need to enrol your child on an approved and registered course. A splendid arrival on the London scene is the Special Yoga Centre. This registered charity is the UK home for Yoga for the Special Child, a US/Brazil-based programme that offers one-to-one work with infants with a range of special needs, including Down's Syndrome, cerebral palsy, spina bifida, autism, epilepsy and ADD/ADHD.
The therapeutic aspect of yoga is also explored at the Yoga Therapy Centre, which runs weekly sessions for children with asthma. The big stretches of some positions help to unknot the chest muscles and assist with controlled breathing and relaxation. Yoga Bugs, created by Fenella Lindsell for three- to seven-year-olds, has also done much to promote yoga for children. There are now more than 200 trained Yoga Bugs teachers working in nursery, prep and primary schools. Classes also run at venues throughout the capital. Details from www.yogabugs.com.
The following centres offer children's classes:
Holistic Health *64 Broadway Market, E8 4QJ (7275 8434/www.holistic-health-hackney.co.uk). London Fields rail.*
Iyengar Institute *223A Randolph Avenue, W9 1NL (7624 3080/www.iyi.org.uk). Maida Vale tube.*
Sivananda Yoga *Vedanta Centre, 51 Felsham Road, SW15 1AZ (8780 0160). Putney Bridge tube, Putney rail.*
Special Yoga Centre *The Tay Building, 2A Wrentham Avenue, NW10 3HA (8933 5475/www.specialyoga.org.uk). Kensal Rise rail.*
Triyoga *6 Erskine Road, NW3 3AJ (7483 3344/ www.triyoga.co.uk). Chalk Farm tube.*
Yoga Junction *Unit 24 City North, Fonthill Road, N4 3HF (7263 3113/www.yogajunction.co.uk). Finsbury Park tube/rail.*
Yoga Therapy Centre *90-92 Pentonville Road, N1 9HS (7689 3040/www.yogatherapy.org). Angel tube.*

Disability sport

The high public profile of Paralympians such as Tanni Grey-Thompson is long overdue. However, the broad term 'disability sport' also encompasses activities for people with learning disabilities. A number of organisations have responsibilities in this area. The **Inclusive Fitness Initiative** (0114 257 2060, www.inclusivefitness.org) is helping to redevelop public sports and fitness facilities to include equipment that is accessible for a broad range of disabled people.
Footballers can join the National Multi-Disabled Football League; for details of clubs and junior squads check out the website www.disability football.co.uk. The **Back-Up Trust** (8875 1805,

Activities

www.backuptrust.org.uk), a charity working with people paralysed through spinal cord injury, runs multi-activity weeks for kids aged 13 to 17. Canoeing, abseiling, wheelchair basketball and rugby are among the sports offered. More programmes are run by **British Blind Sport** (01926 424247, www.britishblindsport.org.uk) and the **British Deaf Sports Council** (www.britishdeafsportscouncil.org.uk). The former English Sports Association for People with Learning Disability is now run by **Mencap Sport** (01924 239955).

London Sports Forum for Disabled People

7354 8666/www.londonsportsforum.org.uk. This is the London wing of the English Federation of Disability Sport (www.efds.co.uk).

Wheelpower

01296 395995/www.wheelpower.org.uk. This is the umbrella body for 17 wheelchair sports, from archery to rugby.

Sports to watch

Basketball

London Towers *Crystal Palace National Sports Centre, Ledrington Road, SE19 2BB (8776 7755/www. london-towers.co.uk).* **Admission** £9; £7 concessions; pre-booked tickets are cheaper.
The Towers are one of the leading teams in the British Basketball League, playing home games in front of enthusiastic audiences at Crystal Palace most weekends from October to April.

Cricket

Short, snappy and fast-moving Twenty20 matches are a stark contrast to the traditional image of cricket, bringing a new, younger audience to the sport. The format is ideal for families, with games played at weekends and in the early evenings. Longer county matches are ideal for keen youngsters to while away a day during the summer holidays; tickets for Test matches are more difficult to obtain since England's thrilling victory over Australia in the 2005 Ashes series.

Brit Oval *SE11 5SS (7582 7764/www.surrey cricket.com). Oval tube.* **Admission** Surrey matches £12-£15; £6-£7.50 under-16s.
The Oval, home to Surrey cricket, is a world-class ground with fewer airs and graces than Lord's (see below).
Lord's Cricket Ground *St John's Wood Road, NW8 8QN (Middlesex 7289 1300/www.middlesexccc.com; MCC 7432 1000/www.lords.org). St John's Wood tube.* **Admission** Middlesex matches £12-£20 adults; £5-£7 children.

Any child who is interested in cricket will have heard of Lords, the home ground of Middlesex; young fans will be thrilled to visit these hallowed grounds. Tours give visitors a sneak peak at the historic ground. You can tour the Long Room, which boasts an art gallery depicting the great and the good of the sport. Fans can also have a look at the Players' Dressing Rooms and the MCC museum, which features photographs and artefacts.

Football

It has become increasingly difficult for young fans to watch Premiership football live rather than on TV. Top clubs may have two or three times as many members as the capacity of their ground, while discounts are few and far between for children who want to attend only occasionally. In the second-tier Coca-Cola Championship and Coca-Cola League, it's far easier to get into games. Indeed, lower-division clubs positively encourage youngsters and families with cheap tickets and special deals: at Leyton Orient, a kids' season ticket costs just over £30, little more than £1 a match.'
The season runs from August to May.

Barclays Premiership

Note that at the time of going to press, West Ham and Charlton's prospects for staying in the premiership were looking increasingly dodgy.

Arsenal *Emirates Stadium, Hornsey Road, N7 6DN (7704 4040/www.arsenal.com). Arsenal tube.*
Charlton Athletic *The Valley, Floyd Road, SE7 8BL (0871 226 1905/www.charlton-athletic.co.uk). Charlton rail.*
Chelsea *Stamford Bridge, Fulham Road, SW6 1HS (0870 300 2322/www.chelseafc.com). Fulham Broadway tube.*
Fulham *Craven Cottage, Stevenage Road, SW6 6HH (0870 442 1234/www.fulhamfc.com). Putney Bridge tube.*
Tottenham Hotspur *White Hart Lane, 748 High Road, N17 0AP (0870 420 5000/ www.tottenhamhotspur.com). White Hart Lane rail.*
West Ham United *Boleyn Ground (Upton Park), Green Street, E13 9AZ (0870 112 2700/www.whufc.com). Upton Park tube.*

Coca-Cola Championship

Crystal Palace *Selhurst Park, Park Road, SE25 6PU (0871 200 0071/www.cpfc.co.uk). Selhurst rail.*
Millwall *The Den, Zampa Road, SE16 3LN (7231 9999/www.millwallfc.co.uk). South Bermondsey rail.*
Queens Park Rangers *Loftus Road Stadium, South Africa Road, W12 7PA (0870 112 1967/www.qpr. co.uk). White City tube.*
Watford *Vicarage Road, Watford, Herts, WD18 0ER (0870 111 1881/www.watfordfc.com). Watford High Street rail.*

Activities

Coca-Cola League

Barnet *Underhill, Barnet Lane, Barnet, EN5 2BE (8441 6932/www.barnetfc.premiumtv.co.uk). High Barnet tube.* Division 2.
Brentford *Griffin Park, Braemar Road, Brentford, Middx TW8 0NT (08453 456442/www.brentfordfc. premiumtv.co.uk). Brentford rail.* Division 1.
Leyton Orient *Matchroom Stadium, Brisbane Road, E10 5NE (0871 310 1881/www.leytonorient. premiumtv.co.uk). Leyton tube.* Division 2.

Greyhound racing

'Going to the dogs' can be a fun and informative outing. The stakes are low enough to save the family from ruination, and children love to pick their winners (form is usually eschewed for the dog's attractive smile or waggy tail). For more information about Walthamstow, *see p122*, for greyhound racing in general, try www.ngrc.org.uk.

Romford Stadium *London Road, Romford, Essex, RM7 9DU (01708 762345/www.trap6.com/romford). Romford rail.* **Admission** *£2-£6; free under-14s* (accompanied by adult). **Racing** evenings Mon, Wed, Fri, phone for details; 2pm-6pm Thur; 7.30pm Sat.
Walthamstow Stadium *Chingford Road, E4 8SJ (8498 3311/www.wsgreyhound.co.uk) Walthamstow Central tube.* **Admission** £1-£6; free under-15s. Racing 7.45pm Tue, Thur; 7.30pm Sat; lunchtime racing Mon & Fri, admission free.
GRA Wimbledon Stadium *Plough Lane, SW17 0BL (8946 8000/www.lovethedogs.co.uk) Wimbledon Park tube; 44, 77, 156 bus.* **Admission** £6; £3 12-17; free under-11s **Racing** 7.30pm Tue, Fri, Sat.

Horse racing

All 59 racecourses around Britain offer a warm welcome to children. Admission for under-16s is free at the majority of meetings, and most racecourses stage special 'family days'. Admission prices stated below are for adults attending regular meetings; children go free.

Ascot *High Street, Ascot, Berks, SL5 7TA (0870 727 1234/www.ascot.co.uk). Ascot rail.* **Admission** £10-£45.
This refurbished course is best known for the 'Royal' meeting, but there are plenty of lower-key race days as well.
Epsom Downs, *Epsom Downs Racecourse, Epsom Downs, Surrey KT18 5LQ (01372 726311/www. epsomdowns.co.uk). Epsom Downs or Tattenham Corner rail.* **Admission** £1-£60.
The grassy Lonsdale Enclosure is ideal for a picnic – though probably not on Derby day, when around 150,000 people are attracted to one of the great occasions in Britain's sporting calendar.
Kempton Park *Staines Road East, Sunbury-on-Thames, Middx TW16 5AQ (01932 782 292/www.kempton.co.uk). Kempton Park rail.* **Admission** £9-£20.

The grandstand includes a food hall with the parade ring and winners' enclosure just behind.
Sandown Park *Esher Station Road, Esher, Surrey, KT10 9AJ (01372 470047/www.sandown.co.uk). Esher rail.* **Admission** £17-£38.
This frequent winner of Racecourse of the Year is attractively sited in a natural amphitheatre.
Windsor *Maidenhead Road, Windsor, Berks SL4 5JJ (0870 220 0024/www.windsor-racecourse.co.uk). Windsor & Eton Riverside rail.* **Admission** £7-£22.
One of Britain's most picturesque courses holds several Sunday Fundays each year and a series of popular summer evening meetings. On a fine day, this place can be a crowd pleaser for the whole family: the kids can watch the horses and the parents can place a few bets.

Rugby league

Harlequins RL *Twickenham Stoop Stadium, Langhorn Drive, Twickenham, Middx TW2 7SX (8410 6000/www.quins.co.uk). Twickenham rail.* **Admission** £12-£30; £6-£15 5-16s.
Family entertainment accompanies games in a season stretching from March to October, with games on Saturday or Sunday afternoons. Season tickets for under-16s are free if they are accompanied by a paying adult.

Rugby union

The top London rugby union clubs have a slew of internationals in their line-ups, and taking the kids to a match is a bargain compared to football. The season runs from September to May.

Guinness Premiership

Saracens *Vicarage Road, Watford, Herts WD18 0EP (01923 475 222/www.saracens.com). Watford tube/Watford High Street rail.* **Admission** £17-£30; £10-£15 5-16s.
Harlequins *Twickenham Stoop Stadium, Langhorn Drive, Twickenham, Middx TW2 7SX (8410 6000/ www.quins.co.uk). Twickenham rail.* **Admission** £12-£35; £6-£15 5-16s.
The Harlequins return to take a place in the Premiership again for the 2007-8 season.

National League

London Welsh *Old Deer Park, Kew Road, Richmond, Surrey TW9 2AZ (8940 2368/www.london-welsh.co.uk). Richmond tube/rail.* **Admission** £12-£17; £6-£8.50 concessions; free under-15s. Division 1.

Stock car & banger racing

Wimbledon Stadium *Plough Lane, SW17 0BL (01252 322920/www.spedeworth.co.uk). Wimbledon Park tube; 44, 77, 156 bus.* **Admission** £11; £5 under-14; prices may vary.
Sunday night meetings at Wimbledon Stadium are great fun for all ages. It's the element of surprise that's key: anything can happen when the stock cars and bangers get out on the track – and it usually does.

Days Out

Features

Days Out

Get out there!

Most of the days out we suggest are accessible by train (some may necessitate a taxi ride from the station). A list of London's main-line rail stations is on *p291*. For an online journey planner, try www.nationalrail.co.uk. A Family Railcard is a great boon if you take the train: it costs just £20 for the year and gives four adults and four children a third off their fares.

Too late for this guide, the new Dickens World in Chatham, Kent, was slated to open at the end of May 2007. The £62million project, Dickens World, takes the great Victorian author, who lived in Chatham, as its theme. It promises a four-acre Victorian London setting (cobbled pavements, dim lighting, chaotic street scenes and Dickensian architecture) and animatronics, novel-inspired rides (the Oliver Twister?) alongside shops, restaurants, and a multiplex cinema. Sounds a blast, visit www.dickensworld.co.uk for more details.

Activities

Go Ape!
The Look Out, Nine Mile Ride, Swinley Forest, Bracknell, Berks RG12 7QW (0870 444 5562/www.goape.co.uk). **Getting there** *By train* Bracknell rail then bus 158, 159 or taxi. *By car* J10 off M4. **Open** *Mar-Oct* 9am-dusk daily. *Nov* 10am-4pm Sat, Sun (groups leave every 30mins). *Feb* Berkshire schools half-term; phone for details. **Admission** £25; £20 10-17s. No under-10s. **Credit** MC, V.
An exciting and challenging adventure course of rope bridges, Tarzan swings and zip slides, located up to almost 11m (35ft) above the forest floor so you can really make like a primate here. Children must be aged over ten and measure at least 1.4m (4ft 7in) to have a go. Pre-booking is essential. This is a most adrenalin-filled walk in the woods, so tinies can't get involved.
Café. Car park (pay/display). Disabled access: toilets. Nearest picnic place: grounds. Shop.

Bewl Water
Lamberhurst, nr Tunbridge Wells, Kent TN3 8JH (01892 890661/www.bewl.co.uk). **Getting there** *By train* Tunbridge Wells rail or Wadhurst rail then taxi. *By car* J5 off M25. **Open** 9am-dusk daily. Closed Concert Day (phone for details), 25 Dec. **Admission** (per vehicle) *Apr-Oct* £5, *Nov-Mar* £2.50 daily. *Concert tickets* phone for details. **Credit** MC, V.
This reservoir, the largest stretch of open water in South-east England, is set in an area of serene beauty. For fishering and water-sports enthusiasts, it's paradise.

Windsurfing tuition for adrenaline junkies is given by qualified RYA (Royal Yachting Association) instructors: all equipment is provided. Rowing and powerboat lessons are also given (phone 01892 890716). For special events (such as autumn's colourful Dragon Boat Festival, sale of ex-hire bikes), check the website.
Café. Car park. Disabled access: toilet. Nappy-changing facilities. Nearest picnic place: grounds. Restaurant. Shop.

Diggerland/The Snow Park
Medway Valley Leisure Park, Roman Way, Strood, Kent ME2 2NU (0870 034 4437/www.diggerland.com/www. thesnowpark.co.uk). **Getting there** *By rail* Strood rail then taxi. *By car* J2 off M2, then A228, then follow signs towards Strood. *Diggerland* **Open** 10am-5pm Sat, Sun, bank hols, school hols, half-terms; check website for details. **Admission** £12.50; £6.25 over-65s; free under-3s. *Snow Park* **Open** *Dec-Mar* see website for details. **Admission** see website for details. **Credit** AmEx, MC, V.
Drivers of all ages can get behind the wheel of heavy plant in this park where the trucks are the stars. Dumper and JCB racing is organised for adults, and themed birthday party packages are available for children. For children who love Bob the Builder, this is a great day out. Other activities include bouncy castles, ride-on toys, a vast sandpit and a land train. During winter (December 2007-Easter 2008), the cold stuff is shipped in and Diggerland becomes a snow park with a 100m (328ft) tubing run, a 50m (164ft) main slope and a large play area for building snowmen and throwing snowballs. An all-day ski/board pass is a reasonable £7.50 (ski and boot hire £10), ski and board lessons are available from £25 per hour, and toddler ski sessions cost from £12.50 per hour. It all adds up to a fun and economical preparation for the family ski holiday.
Buggy access. Café. Car park (free). Disabled access: toilet. Nappy-changing facilities. Nearest picnic place: grounds. Shop.

Xscape
Milton Keynes MK9 3XS (0871 200 3220/www.xscape. co.uk). **Getting there** *By train* Milton Keynes Central rail. *By car* J14 off M1. **Open** 9am-11pm Mon, Tue, Thur-Sat. **Admission** prices vary according to activity. **Credit** AmEx, MC, V.
Sporty children have a fantastic time in this huge complex with showdome, skydiving tunnel and tubing (sliding down an ice luge). This man-made mountain under a snow roof has 1,500 tonnes of real snow, with a 175m (575ft) main slope and 135m (443ft) nursery run. The Airkix skydiving tunnel is the most expensive activity at £34.99 per introductory session for children (cheaper if you book online at www.airkix.com). Après ski, in the form of a 16-screen cinema, pool and video games, adds to the expense but, heck, it's cheaper than a skiing holiday.
Buggy access. Café. Car park. Disabled access. Nappy-changing facilities. Restaurant. Shop.

Bird sanctuaries

Birdworld

Holt Pound, Farnham, Surrey GU10 4LD (01420 22140/www.birdworld.co.uk). **Getting there** *By rail* Farnham rail then taxi or 18 bus. *By car* J4 off M3, then A325 & follow signs. **Open** *Mid Feb-Mid Mar* 10am-4.30pm daily. *Nov-mid Feb* 10am-4.30pm daily. *Mid Mar-Oct* 10am-6pm. **Admission** £11.95; £9.95 concessions, 3-14s; £39.95 family (2+2); free under-3s. **Credit** MC, V.

The feathered residents of Britain's biggest bird park come from all over the world. They live in aviaries; some, like the ostriches, have enclosures big enough to sprint in. There's also a tropical aquarium, and the on-site Jenny Wren farm sustains rabbits, lambs, horses, donkeys and a variety of poultry. Penguin-feeding displays take place at 11.30am and 4pm daily; book in advance for a chance to feed them yourself (£19.95). Special events take place throughout the year, including the Wild West Fun Day in August, and Hallowe'en and festive December specials.

Buggy access. Café. Car park (free). Disabled access: toilet. Nappy-changing facilities. Nearest picnic place: grounds. Restaurant. Shop.

Eagle Heights

Lullingstone Lane, Eynsford, Kent DA4 OJB (01322 866577/www.eagleheights.co.uk). **Getting there** *By rail* Eynsford rail then 1.5-mile walk or taxi. *By car* J3 off M25; J1 off M20. **Open** *Mar-Oct* 10.30am-5pm daily. *Jan, Feb, Nov* 11am-4pm Sat, Sun. Closed Dec. *Flying displays* Mar-Oct noon and 3.30pm daily. *Nov, Jan, Feb* noon and 3pm Sat, Sun. **Admission** £7.50; £6.50 concessions; £4.95 4-14s; free under-4s. **Credit** MC, V.

Eagle Heights has approximately 150 raptors of more than 50 species, many of which can be seen flying in daily demonstrations. The centre provides sanctuary for wild, injured raptors and releases rehabilitated birds back to the wild; there's also a collection of reptiles and mammals. The views over the beautiful Darent Valley are fine. In a bid to be more 'all weather', the Centre puts on indoor flying displays.

Buggy access. Café. Car park (free). Disabled access: ramps, toilets. Nappy-changing facilities. Nearest picnic place: grounds. Restaurants. Shop.

Castles

Arundel Castle

Arundel, West Sussex BN18 9AB (01903 882173/ www.arundelcastle.org). **Open** *Apr-Oct* 10am-5pm Tue-Sun, bank hol Mon. *Aug* 10am-5pm daily. **Admission** *Castle, chapel & grounds* £12; £9.50 concessions; £7.50 5-16s, £32 family (2+5); free under-5s. *Chapel & grounds* £6.50. **Credit** MC, V.

The picturesque icing on the cake of Arundel, the castle was built at the end of the 11th century and has been the family home of the Dukes of Norfolk for more than 850 years. In 1643, during the Civil War, the castle was besieged by General Waller (for Parliament) and the defences were partly demolished. Happily, many of the original features – such as the crenellated Norman keep and part of the Bevis Tower – survived. During the late 19th century, the house was rebuilt. The views of the Sussex countryside from the keep are fab, and the grounds include a kitchen garden, rose garden and the

Fitzalan Chapel. Inside, treasures include the Regency library and restored bedrooms with their original baths and basins.

Buggy access (limited). Café. Disabled access: lifts, toilet. Nappy-changing facilites. Nearest picnic space: castle grounds. Shop.

Bodiam Castle

Nr Robertsbridge, East Sussex TN32 5UA (01580 830436/www.nationaltrust.org.uk). **Getting there** *By rail* Wadhurst rail then 254 bus. *By car* J5 off M25. **Open** *Mid Feb-Oct* 10.30am-6pm or dusk daily. *Nov-mid-Feb* 10.30am-4pm or dusk Sat, Sun. Last entry 1hr before closing. **Tours** groups (min 15 people) by prior arrangement; phone for details. **Admission** (NT) £5; £2.50 5-16s; £12.50 family (2+3); free under-5s. **Credit** AmEx, MC, V.

Built in 1385, Bodiam Castle was ransacked during the Civil War and, until the 20th century, its ruins were visited only by a handful of Romantic artists. There's no roof, but the towers and turrets still offer sweeping views across the Rother Valley. Family activities take place in the school holidays (armour-trying sessions, archery have-a-gos and Family Fun Day on 1 August 2007 with tractor rides, armour and corndolly workshops and a Teddy Doctor).

Buggy access. Café. Car park (£2). Disabled access: toilet. Nappy-changing facilities. Nearest picnic place: castle grounds. Restaurant. Shop.

Hever Castle

Nr Edenbridge, Kent TN8 7NG (01732 865224/ www.hevercastle.co.uk). **Getting there** *By rail* Edenbridge Town rail then taxi, or Hever rail then 1-mile walk. *By car* J5 or J6 off M25. **Open** *Gardens* Apr-Oct 11am-6pm daily (last entry 5pm). Nov 11am-4pm daily (last entry 3pm). *Castle* Apr-Oct noon-6pm daily (last entry 5pm). Nov-Dec 11am-4pm Thur-Sun (last entry 3pm). Mar noon-5pm Wed-Fri (last entry 4pm). **Tours** groups (min 20 people) by prior arrangement. **Admission** *Castle & gardens* £10.50; £8.80 concessions; £5.70 5-15s; £26.70 family (2+2 or 1+3); free under-5s. *Gardens only* £8.40; £7.20 concessions; £5.40 5-15s; £22.20 family (2+2 or 1+3); free under-5s. **Credit** MC, V.

The childhood home of Anne Boleyn, this 13th-century castle is filled with Tudor furnishings; the interiors display waxwork scenes and weaponry, as well as Anne Boleyn's illuminated *Books of Hours*. The main attraction, though, is the great outdoors: during school holidays various events take place, including popular jousting and archery displays in August. There are mazes galore, including a water maze (open April-October) set in a shallow lake with a rocky island.

Buggy access (grounds only). Car park. Disabled access: ramps, toilets (grounds only). Nappy-changing facilities. Restaurants. Shops.

Leeds Castle

Maidstone, Kent ME17 1PL (01622 765400/ www.leeds-castle.com). **Getting there** *By car* J8 off M20/A20. *By rail* Bearsted rail. **Open** *Castle* Apr-Oct 10.30am-6pm daily. Nov-Mar 10.30am-5pm daily. Last entry 3pm. *Gardens & attractions* Nov-Mar 10am-5pm daily. Apr-Oct 10am-7pm daily. **Tours** pre-booked groups only. **Admission** (unlimited re-entry over 1yr except for special events) £14; £11 concessions; £8.50 4-15s; free under-4s. **Credit** MC, V.

An immaculately maintained Norman castle whose magnificent chambers contain historical displays (from the Heraldry Room to the Dog Collar Museum), but it's the outdoor wonderland that we love. Lose yourself in the maze, which boasts a grotto and underground passage. Black swans and peacocks patrol the grounds, and more exotic birds tweet in the aviaries. There are special events, such as jousting and horse shows throughout the year, a Family Fun Weekend (1-2 September 2007) and an October half term event all about horrid Henry VIII – consult the website for details. The Museum of Kent Life (www.museum-kentlife.co.uk) is nearby.

Buggy access. Car park. Disabled access: lift, toilet. Nappy-changing facilities. Nearest picnic place: grounds. Restaurant. Shops.

Mountfitchet Castle & Norman Village

Stansted Mountfitchet, Essex CM24 8SP (01279 813237/www.mountfitchetcastle.com). **Getting there** *By rail* Stansted Mountfitchet rail. *By car* J8 off M11.

Open *Mar-Nov 2006* 10am-5pm daily. *House on the Hill Toy Museum* Feb half term-Nov 10am-5pm daily. **Admission** *includes castle and toy museum* £8.50; £7.50 concessions; £6.50 2-14s; free under-2s. **Credit** MC, V.

The 11th-century Mountfitchet Castle today is reduced to isolated piles of rubble, although an amusing 'working' Norman village has been constructed on the site to give some indication of life 900 years ago. Thus the many buildings date from the 1980s and are populated by wax-work figures. New structures for 2007 include a witches ducking stool and a larger archery target. Tame animals wandering about including fallow deer, Jacob sheep and poultry. Events for families take place throughout the school holidays. The adjoining House on the Hill Toy Museum has more than 80,000 exhibits from the Victorian era onward, and the Haunted Manor stars ghosts that have haunted the site for over 1,000 years.

Café (castle). Disabled: ramps, toilet (castle). Nappy-changing facilities. Nearest picnic place: picnic tables in grounds. Shops.

Coastal stations

Everyone knows that a day at the seaside is a tonic, but if that day is bracketed by several hours in a metal box on steaming tarmac, the health benefits are somewhat reduced. Pick up your bucket and spade and take the train to the coast. You might not be able to manage the windbreaks, sun tents, deck chairs, coolboxes and the rest of the paraphernalia British families insist on filling their SUVs with, but you'll be wiggling your toes in the sand and surf way before the car drivers have found themselves an extortionate parking spot. Arm yourself with a Family Railcard (*see p274*) and choose a destination from our selection of

resorts with seaside stations. If you can't be bothered with the coolbox, lunch off fish and chips and ice-cream. What could be nicer?

The obvious contender for easy access to golden sands straight from the tracks is **Margate** (0870 264 6111). Cross the road from the station and you're on the beach, where donkey rides, a warm tidal pool, oodles of sand, bouncy castles and slides will keep everyone amused until sunset. The train journey takes about two hours from London Bridge (one change).

Just round the coast in **Broadstairs**, the gentle waves of Viking Bay (one of the seven bays here)

Windsor Castle

Windsor, Berkshire SL4 1NJ (7766 7304/www.royal. gov.uk). **Getting there** *By rail* Windsor & Eton Riverside rail. *By car* J6 off M4. **Open** *Mar-Oct* 9.45am-5.15pm daily (last entry 4pm). *Nov-Feb* 9.45am-4.15pm daily (last entry 3pm). **Admission** (LP) £14.20; £12.70 concessions; £8 5-16s; £36.50 family (2+3); free under-5s. **Credit** AmEx, MC, V.
Perennially attractive to tourists, Windsor castle houses a unique collection of art and artefacts, with works by Rembrandt, Gainsborough and Rubens, and a collection of medieval weaponry and armour. The intricate Queen Mary's Dolls' House, created by Sir Edward Lutyens in 1924 on a scale of 1:12, remains perfect, from the working water and electrics to the handmade wool rugs. The Jubilee Garden has St George's Chapel, which contains the tombs of ten monarchs, including Henry VIII and the Queen Mum.
Buggy access/storage. Disabled access: lift, toilet. Nappy-changing facilities. Nearest picnic place: grounds. Shops.

Country estates

Borde Hill

Balcombe Road, Haywards Heath, West Sussex RH16 1XP (01444 450326/www.bordehill.co.uk). **Getting there** *By rail* Haywards Heath rail then taxi. **By car** A272 off A23 off M23. **Open** *Apr-Oct* 10am-6pm or dusk (if earlier) daily (last admission 5pm). **Admission** £6.50; £5.50 concessions; £3.50 3-15s; free under-3s. *Season ticket* £18; £12 3-15s. **Credit** AmEx, MC, V.
This 200 acres of stunning parkland and lakes is good for the soul. As well as rare plants from China, Burma and the Himalayas, the Garden of Allah and nearby Azalea Ring – a traditional English rose garden with woodland walks – there's an extensive adventure playground, with a cowboy fort, pirate ship, swings, slides and an obstacle course. Summer holiday events (1-31 August 2007) include puppet shows, teddy bears' picnics and soccer schools. A pond is set aside for children's fishing classes at weekends and during school holidays. The Borde Hill Country Fair

are a ten minute walk down the High Street from the station. On your way you can visit the Dickens House Museum (2 Victoria Parade, 01843 861232, www.dickenshouse.co.uk). Come to Broadstairs in June and you'll find a goodly proportion of the locals dressed up in crinolines and stovepipe hats for the Dickens Festival. Otherwise, the Blue Flag bays are fun for paddling, swimming, fun-fair rides, ice-creams and everything else that makes a seaside special. Broadstairs is about two hours and ten minutes from London Bridge (one change).
   A much shorter train ride takes you to the most sophisticated seaside town in the country,

Broadstairs

Brighton (London on Sea), where the beach, alas, is shingly but the attractions are legion. There's a pier, loads of beachside restaurants and stalls, sports facilities, a mini train and a whole bucketload of ideas for wallet emptying. Take the train from Victoria or London Bridge, walk down through the town centre to the promenade and save yourself a packet (no parking costs). The journey takes just 50 minutes to one hour from either station, and there are no changes.
   West of here lies two-for-the-price of one in the form of the splendid seaside town of **Littlehampton**, infinitely more family orientated than Brighton. Located at the mouth of the River Arun, Littlehampton has two beaches and a promenade train. West Beach, on the opposite side of the river, has unspoilt sand dunes, rare plants and wildlife protected as a Site of Special Scientific Interest. It's a short walk from the station to the Look & Sea Visitor Centre (63-65 Surrey Street, 01903 718984, www.lookand sea.co.uk), near the East, where you pay just 99p (50p for kids) to go up the tower, take in the sea views and get your bearings. It takes an hour and forty minutes to get to Littlehampton from London Victoria, no changes.
   Southend is London's closest seaside, with Britain's longest pleasure pier and some award winning gardens at Westcliff. This town's heyday was in the 1950s and 60s, when day trippers from London would fill up the trains on sunny days and spend happy times playing the slot machines and eating cockles on the shingle. These days there's imported sand, new funfair rides, fireworks every Saturday night on the end of the pier and paninis on the promenade, but it's still dear old Southend, and just 50 minutes from Liverpool Street station.

Explore Chessington World of Adventures & Zoo!

The place for fun rides, amazing animals and excititng live shows

Facilities include:

- Free easy parking
- Bottle warmers & heating of baby food
- Baby changing & nursing facilities
- Family centre

Embark on a true adventure midweek with our discounted Parent & Toddler voucher by visiting:
www.chessington.com/networkmarketing

Or for a fantastic day of family fun throughout the year, visit our website for great family packages.

WWW.CHESSINGTON.COM
SHARE THE CHESSINGTON ADVENTURE!

takes place on 18 and 19 August 2007 and promises Shire horses, Napoleonic re-enactments and a mini circus. *Buggy access. Café. Disabled access: toilet. Nappy-changing facilities. Nearest picnic place: parkland. Restaurant. Shop.*

Groombridge Place Gardens & Enchanted Forest

Groombridge Place, Groombridge, nr Tunbridge Wells, Kent TN3 9QG (01892 861444/www.groombridge. co.uk). **Getting there** *By rail* Tunbridge Wells rail then 290, 291 bus or taxi. *By car* B2110 off A264 off A21. **Open** *end Mar-early Nov* 10am-5.30pm or dusk (if earlier) daily. **Admission** £8.95; £7.45 concessions, 3-12s; £29.95 family (2+2); free under-3s. **Credit** MC, V.
Laid out in the 17th century, these beautiful formal gardens are supplemented by attractions for children. In the Enchanted Forest they can hobnob with medieval outlaws and vast rabbits, spot dinosaurs around the pool, bustle along a treetop walkway and play on giant swings. Events for the school holidays include summer sheepdog trials and medieval encampments, daily birds of prey flying and Hallowe'en in the Spooky Forest (26, 27 October 2007). *Buggy access (limited). Café. Car park (free). Disabled access (limited). Nappy-changing facilities. Nearest picnic place: grounds. Shop.*

Hop Farm Country Park

Beltring, Paddock Wood, Kent TN12 6PY (0870 027 4166/www.thehopfarm.co.uk). **Getting there** *By rail* Paddock Wood rail then (peak times only) shuttle bus. *By car* J5 off M25, then A21 south. **Open** 10am-5pm daily. Closed 24-31 Dec. **Admission** £7.50; £6.50 concessions, 3-15s; £27 family (2+2); free under-3s. Prices vary on event days. **Credit** MC, V.
Once a working hop farm, now a huge tourist attraction, this Country Park has a museum harking back to the glory days of hop-picking, as well as a giddying number of family-fun possibilities – children's playgrounds and play barns, go-karts, crazy golf, petting corners and rides on dray carts pulled by lofty shire horses. This summer (30 July-29 August 2007) there will be daily Around the World-themed childen's events, with special appearances from Sponge Bob Squarepants and Dora the Explorer. And there's also pumpkin-themed October half-term excitement. Big expansion plans have started with new Children's Zones, featuring indoor and outdoor play areas; a tree-top assault course is planned by Special Forces hero, Colonel Tim Collins, for older children and adults, as well as walking, cycling and orienteering opportunities across the 400 acres. The Hop Farm is also branching into holiday accommodation and is working on a new and improved restaurant. Check the website for details. *Buggy access. Car park (free). Café. Disabled access: toilet. Nappy-changing facilities. Nearest picnic place: grounds. Shop.*

Painshill Park

Painshill Park Trust, Portsmouth Road, Cobham, Surrey KT11 1JE (01932 868113/www.painshill. co.uk). **Getting there** *By rail* Cobham or Esher rail. *By car* J10 off M25, then A3, exit A245. Check website or phone (0870 608 2608) for details of the Surrey Parks & Gardens Explorer bus. **Open** *Apr-Oct* 10.30am-6pm daily (last entry 4.30pm). *Nov-Mar* 10.30am-4pm or dusk (if earlier) daily (last entry 3pm).

Admission £6.60; £5.80 concessions; £3.85 5-16s; £22 family (2+4); free under-5s. **Credit** MC, V.
These 160 acres of subtle and surprising vistas created by Charles Hamilton in the 18th century include a vineyard, Chinese bridge, crystal grotto, Turkish tent, a newly restored hermitage and a Gothic tower. Every third Sunday there is a craft workshop; Painshill also does brilliant outdoorsy parties for children aged 4-12, with themes of treasure Hunt and Wonderland Adventure. *Buggy access. Café. Car park (free). Disabled access: toilet. Nappy-changing facilities. Nearest picnic place: grounds. Shop.*

Farms

Barleylands Farm Centre & Craft Village

Barleylands Road, Billericay, Essex CM11 2UD (01268 532 253/www.barleylands.co.uk). **Getting there** *By rail* Billericay rail. *By car* J29 off M25. **Open** *Farm Centre* Mar-Oct 10am-5pm daily. Nov-Feb 10am-4pm daily. *Craft village* Mar-Oct 10am-5pm Tue-Sun. Nov-Feb 10am-4pm Tue-Sun. **Admission** *Farm Centre* £4; free under-2s. *Craft village* free. **Credit** MC, V.
As well as the vintage agricultural implements displayed in the Farm Centre, there's a craft village showcasing the skills of olde worlde woodturners and blacksmiths. Children, however, are entranced by the animals – chickens, rabbits and turkeys, ponies, cows and pigs. There's also a playground and stables, plus tractor rides, a bouncy castle, giant trampolines and a vast sandpit. The twice-monthly farmers' markets are a draw, as are summer specials involving visits from Noddy and mass Teddy Bears picnics. Many East End folk make a date to attend the busy Essex Country Show – a jamboree of steam engines, heavy horses, rural crafts and fun (8, 9 September 2007). *Buggy access. Café. Car park. Disabled access: toilet. Nappy-changing facilities. Nearest picnic place: grounds.*

Bocketts Farm Park

Young Street, Fetcham, nr Leatherhead, Surrey KT22 9BS (01372 363764/www.bockettsfarm.co.uk). **Getting there** *By rail* Leatherhead rail then taxi. *By car* J9 off M25. **Open** 10am-6pm daily. **Admission** £6.40; £5.95 concessions, 3-17s; £4.75 2s; free under-2s. **Credit** MC, V.
There are plenty of opportunities for small-animal handling on this glorious North Downs farm, as well as the chance to ride ponies, milk goats and watch pigs race. Other attractions include play barns with astroslides and trampolines, sandpits and a children's birthday party service. The café sits in a handsome 18th-century building, but there are loads of places to enjoy a picnic. Come in autumn for the pumpkin harvest, or at Christmas for a home-grown tree and the chance to meet Santa. *Buggy access. Café. Car park (free). Disabled access: toilet. Nappy-changing facilities. Nearest picnic place: grounds. Shop.*

Fishers Farm Park

New Pound Lane, Wisborough Green, West Sussex RH14 0EG (01403 700063/www.fishersfarmpark.co.uk). **Getting there** *By rail* Billingshurst rail then taxi. *By car* J10 off M25. **Open** 10am-5pm daily; phone for times during special events. **Admission** *Nov-Mar* £8.50; £7.50 concessions, 2-12s; under-2s free. *Apr-Oct* £11.50; £10.50 concessions, 2-12s; under-2s free. **Credit** MC, V.

Fishers is consistently voted one of the country's top ten countryside attractions for families, mostly because it's run like clockwork, looks gorgeous and has so much to do. If you're after the classic cuddly animals, the bunnies, dwarf goats and the like are happy to be stroked and adored. And the sheer variety and quality of the rides, giant sandpits, climbing/clambering features and general activities is mind-boggling. Imaginations run riot in the wooden house deep in the woods, while older children can try their luck on the climbing wall or massive lighthouse slide complex. Other activities include pony and tractor rides, a ghost tunnel, bumper boats, pedal karts and a mini adventure golf course. If the weather is hot, have a splash in the pool at 'The Beach'; in less clement weather, children can frolic in the indoor play zone. Toilet facilities are spotless and plentiful. Refreshments in the licensed café are also excellent and reasonably priced. You can even camp in the field next door, enjoy takeaway pub meals under canvas, and spend your whole holiday near Fisher's – which for our young reviewers would be absolutely heaven.
Buggy access. Cafés. Car park (free). Disabled access: toilet. Nappy-changing facilities. Nearest picnic place: grounds. Restaurants. Shops.

Godstone Farm

Tilburstow Hill Road, Godstone, Surrey RH9 8LX (01883 742546/www.godstonefarm.co.uk). **Getting there** *By rail* Caterham rail then 409 bus. *By car* J6 off M25. **Open** 10am-5pm daily. **Admission** £5.65 2-16s (accompanying adult £2); £3.80 under-2s. **Credit** MC, V.
Always good for the small, cuddly end of the agricultural scene, Godstone is particularly rewarding come spring, when wobbly lambs career around the paddocks and fluffball chicks bask in the incubators' glow. The pre-schoolers love it. Children with their hearts set on something profound can chase each other across the adventure playground, the biggest, allegedly, in the South-east, and the little ones lose themselves in the ball pools and on the walkways that make up the play barn. There's also a new slide and a crow's nest to climb on. Godstone has a sister in Epsom, Horton Park (01372 743 984/www.hortonpark.co.uk).
Buggy access. Café. Car park (free). Disabled access: toilet. Nappy-changing facilities. Nearest picnic place: grounds. Shop.

Odds Farm Park

Wooburn Common, nr High Wycombe, Bucks HP10 0LX (01628 520188/www.oddsfarm.co.uk). **Getting there** *By rail* Beaconsfield rail then taxi. *By car* J2 off M40 or J7 off M4. **Open** *Early Feb-lateOct* 10am-5.30pm daily. *Nov-early Feb* 10am-4.30pm daily. **Admission** £6.95; £5.95 concessions, 2-16s; free under-2s. **Credit** MC, V.
Odds Farm was created with small children in mind, so expect plenty of fun activities: feeding the chickens; Rabbit World; farmyard tea-time, and tractor and trailer rides. Some activities depend on the season: sheep-shearing, for example, is between May and July; Easter egg hunts, Hallowe'en pumpkin carving, visits with Father Christmas all take place in the relevant school holidays. Outdoor play areas form focal points for birthday parties; kids amuse themselves there while parents linger over a picnic.
Buggy access. Café. Car park (free). Disabled access: toilet. Nappy-changing facilities. Nearest picnic place: grounds. Shop.

South of England Rare Breeds Centre & Country Farm Park

Highlands Farm, Woodchurch, nr Ashford, Kent TN26 3RJ (01233 861493/www.rarebreeds.org.uk). **Getting there** *By rail* Ham Street rail then taxi. *By car* J10 off M20. **Open** *Apr-Sept* 10.30am-5.30pm daily. *Oct-Mar* 10.30am-4.30pm Tue-Sun. **Admission** £7; free under-3s. **Credit** MC, V.
This woodland farm is run by the Canterbury Oast Trust, a charity dedicated to the care of adults with physical and learning difficulties. There's a breeding programme for once-familiar farm breeds, and you can pet unusual species of goat, cattle and poultry. There's an obligatory play barn for wet weather and piggy-racing activities. Children can tear around the Mysterious Marsh Woodland Adventure playground. On Fun Day on 8 August 2007, the animals will be buffed up and paraded in halters for the show ring.
Buggy access. Café. Car park (free). Disabled access: toilet. Nappy-changing facilities. Nearest picnic place: grounds. Shop.

Tulley's Farm

Turners Hill, Crawley, West Sussex RH10 4PE (01342 718472/www.tulleysfarm.com). **Getting there** *By rail* Three Bridges rail then taxi. *By car* J10 off M23. **Open** *Summer* Shop 9am-6pm daily. Tea room 9.30am-5pm daily. *Winter* Shop 9am-5pm daily. Tea room 9.30am-4.30pm daily. *Maze* 7 July-mid-Sept 2007 10am-6pm daily (last entry 5pm) **Admission** *Farm* free. *Maze* £7; £6 4-14s; £22 family (2+2 or 1+3); free under-4s. **Credit** AmEx, MC, V.
Tulley's makes foraging for your five a day fun. The PYO fruit is ready to plunder from mid June, with bush crops, such as raspberries and gooseberries available through August. Pumpkins can be yours in autumn and children are entranced by the rabbits, guinea pigs and pot-bellied pigs in the farmyard. The famous maize maze – whose closely planted plants, with their thick, dark-green foliage and sturdy stems, create a series of dead-ends and impenetrable walls – runs from 7 July to 3 September 2007. The maze is the highlight of the popular Tulley's summer festival; torchlight maze excursions are a spooky summer treat.
Buggy access. Café. Car park (free). Shop.

Specialist museums

Amberley Working Museum

Amberley, nr Arundel, West Sussex BN18 9LT (01798 831370/www.amberleymuseum.co.uk). **Getting there** *By rail* Amberley rail. *By car* B2139 north of Arundel. **Open** *mid Mar-late Oct* 10am-5.30pm Wed-Sun (last entry 4.30pm). **Admission** £8.70; £7.70 concessions, OAPs; £5.50 5-16s; £25 family (2+3); free under-5s. **Credit** MC, V.
Nestling near the South Downs Way, this 36-acre open air museum comprises more than 30 different buildings and hundreds of exhibits from bygone days, before work became all about screens and keyboards. A wonderful conglomeration of our artisan and industrial history, displays cover transport, print workshops, telecommunications and electricity, and there's a variety of working craftspeople in residence, including a potter, clay-pipe maker and broom-maker. There's also a nature and woodland trail and a children's playground. The museum and grounds are buggy and wheelchair friendly, and you can travel around the site on a vintage bus and narrow-gauge railway. Even if you

Days Out

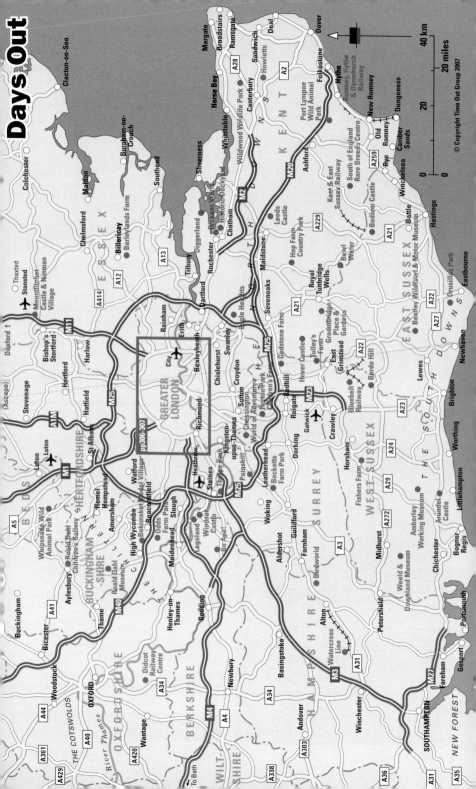

don't partake of refreshments in the sympathetically designed Limeburners Restaurant, pop in to admire its timber frame, artful cedar cladding and clay tiles. Start your visit by watching the introductory video at the Hayloft Theatre, before drawing up a plan of action for the day.
Buggy access. Café. Disabled: toilet. Nappy-changing facilities. Nearest picnic space: museum grounds. Shop.

Bentley Wildfowl & Motor Museum

Halland, nr Lewes, East Sussex BN8 5AF (01825 840573/www.bentley.org.uk). **By rail** Uckfield or Lewes rail then taxi. **By car** A22, then follow signs. **Open** *Summer* 10.30am-5.30pm daily. *Winter* 10.30am-4pm Sat, Sun. House closed during winter. **Admission** £6.80; £5.80 concessions; £4.80 3-15s; £23 family (2+3); free under-3s. **Credit** AmEx, MC, V.
The Duckery and Swan Strip are home to a staggering 125 species of wildfowl. As well as quacking mallards and muscovies, there are rarer Hawaiian geese, black swans and white winged wood ducks. A polished display of Edwardian and vintage cars and motorcycles forms the other part of the attraction. Most children prefer the gorgeous Glyndebourne wood, with its woodworking centre, miniature steam train and adventure playground. Presiding over it all is Bentley House, a Palladian-style mansion restored by Raymond Erith. The Bentley Woodfair (21-23 September 2007) is a timber-based extravaganza.
Buggy access. Café. Car park (free). Disabled access: toilet. Nappy-changing facilities. Nearest picnic place: grounds. Shop.

Chatham Historic Dockyard

Historic Dockyard, Chatham, Kent ME4 4TZ (01634 823800/www.thedockyard.co.uk). **Getting there** By rail Chatham rail. By car J1, 3 or 4 off M2. **Open** *10 Feb-24 Mar* 10am-4pm daily. *25 Mar-28 Oct* 10am-6pm daily. *Nov* 10am-4pm Sat, Sun. Closed Dec, Jan. **Admission** lasts 1yr, not valid on event days) £12.50; £10 concessions; £7.50 5-15s; £32.50 family (2+2 or 1+3; £5 per additional child); free under-5s. **Credit** AmEx, MC, V.
This ancient maritime centre was the starting point of Horatio Nelson's distinguished career in 1771; many buildings from Nelson's time survive. There are tours around both a 40-year-old submarine, HMS *Ocelot*, the last warship to be built at the dockyard, and a World War II destroyer, HMS *Cavalier*. The working ropery is fascinating, as is Wooden Walls, which evokes the sights, sounds and smells of the dockyard of 1758. Interactive displays include a radio-controlled ship-docking exercise and a mock ship fight. Visiting children take part in a family trail around the exhibits, have a go at brass rubbing or play on the outdoor and indoor playgrounds. The Dockyard has frequent steam weekends throughout the summer and a special Smugglers themed family event 26-27 August 2007.
Buggy access. Café. Car park (free). Disabled access: toilet. Nappy-changing facilities. Shop.

Imperial War Museum Duxford

Cambridge CB2 4QR (01223 835000/www.iwm.org.uk). **Getting there** By rail Cambridge rail. By car J10 off M11. **Open** *Summer* 10am-6pm daily (last entry 5.15pm). *Winter* 10am-4pm daily (last entry 3.15pm). **Admission** £14.95; £11.50 concessions; £8.50 16-18s; free under-16s. **Credit** MC, V.
Duxford, a huge aviation and military vehicle museum, has four themed hangars of exhibits, as well as Lord Foster's glass-fronted American Air Museum, and the Land

Warfare Hall, filled with tanks and military vehicles. The complex is so huge that a 'road train' drops people off at the major attractions. The air shows are superb (there are about four each year), and Action Afternoons (check the website for dates), when military vehicles and historic aircraft perform short displays, take place monthly. For terrestrial activities, learn about the Normandy campaign in the Land Warfare Hall. Here, tanks, military vehicles and artillery pieces are shown in battlefield scenes. AirSpace, a 10,000sq m (108,000sq ft) exhibition area displays 30 classic aircraft. During the school holidays staff run craft workshops and other activities.
Buggy access. Cafés. Car park (free). Disabled access: lift, ramps, toilet. Nappy-changing facilities. Restaurant. Shops.

Roald Dahl Children's Gallery

Buckinghamshire County Museum, Church Street, Aylesbury, Bucks HP20 2QP (01296 331441/ www.buckscc.gov.uk/museum). **Getting there** By rail Aylesbury rail. By car J8 off M40. **Open** *see website or phone for details.* **Admission** £4; free under-3s; booking advised. **Credit** MC, V.
The great storyteller's wife, Felicity helped start this tribute to Matilda, James, the Twits et al. Housed in an old coach house, the gallery is decorated with colourful frescoes by Quentin Blake, which introduce different themes based on Roald Dahl's stories. Visitors encounter James and his mini-beast friends inside the Giant Peach, and examine the insect world with the aid of a video microscope. Then there's the Twits' Upside Down Room, a great glass elevator, Willy Wonka's inventions, and Matilda's Library, where you can discover more about Dahl's life and work. Picnic in the walled garden or snack in the café. This gallery complements the Museum & Story Centre, and is suited to the very young. Pre-book in the school holidays.
Buggy access. Café. Disabled access: lift, toilet. Nappy-changing facilities. Nearest picnic place: grounds. Shop.

Roald Dahl Museum & Story Centre

81-83 High Street, Great Missenden, Bucks HP16 0AL (01494 892 192/www.roalddahlmuseum.org). **Open** 10am-5pm Tue-Sun, Mon bank hols. **Admission** £4.95; £3.50 concessions, 5-16s; £16 family (2+3); free under-5s. **Credit** AmEx, MC, V.
Designed to explore the craft of storytelling, this museum furnishes inquisitive young readers (aged 6-12) with a wealth of information about Dahl, his life, his methods and his canon. In the Story Centre, displays and interactive games reveal how contemporary children's authors work. Workshops take place at weekends and in school holidays. Chocolate decorating with local chocolatier Kate Parker of The Chocolate Source takes place on the second Sunday of each month, and there are craft sessions in which children can make, for example, a GFG dream catcher.
Buggy access. Café. Disabled access: lift, ramps, toilet. Nappy-changing facilities. Nearest picnic place: courtyard. Shop.

Weald & Downland Open Air Museum

Singleton, Chichester, West Sussex PO18 0EU (01243 811348/811363/www.wealddown.co.uk). **Getting there** By rail Chichester rail then 60 bus. By car A3, turn off at Millford, A286 to Midhurst & follow signs.

Meet Matilda, James and the Twits at the **Roald Dahl Museum & Story Centre**. *See p283.*

Open *Apr-Oct* 10.30am-6pm daily (last entry 5pm). *3 Jan-18 Feb* 10.30am-4pm Wed, Sat, Sun (last entry 3pm). *19 Feb-25 Feb* 10.30am-4pm daily (last entry 3pm). *28 Feb-31 Mar* 10.30am-4pm daily (last entry 3pm). **Admission** £8.25; £7.25 concessions; £4.40 5-15s; £22.65 family (2+3); free under-5s. **Credit** MC, V. This extraordinary place celebrates a long lost country-side heritage in 50 acres of beautiful Sussex countryside. It's a soothing place to wander through, dotted with about 50 historic buildings dating from the 13th to the 19th centuries, all painstakingly conserved. Some have their own period gardens, showing the herbs, vegetables and flowers of our rural forebears. Visitors can see bread and sweetmeats being prepared in the Tudor kitchen, marvel at the giant water mill where stoneground flour is produced daily, admire the traditional skills of carpenters and watch the heavy horses work the fields. Plenty of other farm animals, including some rare breeds, await inspection, and there are daily craft activities and special events during the school holidays. December features carol singing, tree dressing and fireside storytelling – plus mulled cider for chilly grown-ups.
Buggy access. Café. Car park (free). Disabled access: toilets. Nappy-changing facilities. Shop.

Steam trains

Bluebell Railway

Sheffield Park Station, on A275 between Lewes & East Grinstead, Sussex TN22 3QL (01825 720800/ talking timetable 01825 720825/www.bluebell-railway. co.uk). **Getting there** *By rail* East Grinstead rail then 473 bus. *By car* J10 off M23. **Open** *Easter-Sept* 11am-4pm daily. Phone for details of additional Sat, Sun, school & bank hol openings. **Admission** £9.80; £4.90 3-15s; £28 family (2+3); free under-3s. **Credit** MC, V.
Bluebell is the UK's first preserved standard-gauge passenger railway. It runs along the Lewes to East Grinstead line, with each station the line passes through restored according to a different era: Victorian, the 1930s and the 1950s. Childish delights include summer activities (Punch & Judy shows, quizzes, magic shows and teddy bear hunts), plus a host of specials: Easter, Thomas the Tank Engine, Christmas, plus the popular fish and chip and sausage and mash specials.
Buggy access. Café. Car park (free). Disabled access: toilet. Nappy-changing facilities. Nearest picnic place: grounds. Shop.

Aug 10am-4pm daily. *Nov-Mar* times vary; phone for details. **Admission** £11; £10 concessions; £6 3-15s; £29 family (2+3); free under-3s. **Credit** MC, V.

The antique carriages and engines servicing this railway line were scavenged and restored by enthusiasts, which makes this the most pleasing method of getting from Bodiam (for the castle, *see p275*) to Tenterden. *Buggy access. Café (Tenterden & Northiam stations). Car park (not at Bodiam). Disabled access: carriage (book in advance), toilet. Nappy-changing facilities (Tenterden). Shop.*

Romney, Hythe & Dymchurch Railway

New Romney Station, Kent TN28 8PL (01797 362353/ www.rhdr.org.uk). **Getting there** *By rail* Folkestone Central rail then 711 bus to Hythe. *By car* J11 off M20. **Open** phone or check website for timetable. **Admission** *Romney Rover ticket* £11.20; £5.60 3-15s; £32 family (2+2); free under-3s. **Credit** MC, V.

Racing driver Captain Howley built the 'world's smallest public railway' back in 1927. Nowadays, his locomotives, one-third of the scale of the real thing, puff along a similarly downsized track (it covers 22km or 13.5 miles) between the Cinque Port of Hythe and Dungeness, where the RHDR café can do you a fish and chip lunch. *Buggy access. Café. Car park (50p/day). Disabled access: carriages, toilet. Nappy-changing facilities. Shop.*

Watercress Line

The Railway Station, Alresford, Hants SO24 9JG (01962 733810/talking timetable 01962 733810/ www.watercressline.co.uk). **Getting there** *By rail* Alton rail. *By car* A31 off A3 to Alton or A31 off M3 to Alresford. **Open** *May-Sept* Tue-Thur, Sat, Sun. *Oct, Dec, mid Jan-Feb* Sat, Sun. *Easter hols* daily. Phone or check website for timetable. **Admission** £10; £5 2-16s; £25 family (2+2); free under-3s. Phone for special event prices. **Credit** MC, V.

Beginning in the market town of Alresford, this 16km (ten-mile) railway winds through Home Counties countryside. Londoners can hop on the train at Alton, which has a main-line station for Waterloo. Children love the summer Thomas specials and Santa specials for December. *Buggy access (footbridge at Alton). Café (Alresford). Disabled access: carriages, toilet. Shop (Alresford).*

Theme parks

Bekonscot Model Village

Warwick Road, Beaconsfield, Bucks HP9 2PL (01494 672919/www.bekonscot.com). **Getting there** *By rail* Beaconsfield rail. *By car* J2 off M40. **Open** *Feb-29 Oct-28 2007* 10am-5pm daily. **Admission** £6.90; £4.50 concessions; £4 2-15s; £19 family (2+2); free under-2s. **Credit** MC, V.

This miniature world, stuck in a 1930s time warp, comprises six model villages in a rural landscape, created by Roland Callingham in 1929. A gauge-one model railway stops at each village, and at Chessnade Zoo and a fairground with mini rides. There's also a playground and a newly extended ride-on railway (50p) per person; runs at weekends, bank holidays and local school holidays). *Buggy access. Café. Car park (free). Disabled access: toilets. Kiosk. Nappy-changing facilities. Nearest picnic place: grounds. Shop.*

Didcot Railway Centre

Didcot, Oxon OX11 7NJ (01235 817200/www.didcot railwaycentre.org.uk). **Getting there** *By rail* Didcot Parkway rail. *By car* J13 off M4. **Open** 10am-4pm Mon-Fri; 10am-5pm Sat, Sun (last entry 30mins before closing). Phone to confirm times. **Tours** bank hols (times depend on events; phone for details). **Admission** *Steam days* £7.50; £7 concessions; £6.50 3-16s; £26 family (2+2); free under-3s. *Non-steam days* £4; £3.50 concessions; £3 3-16s; £12 family (2+2); free under-3s. *Special event days* £9.50; £8 concessions; £7.50 3-16s; £29 family (2+2); free under-3s. **Credit** MC, V.

Didcot's steam days involve steam-age activities like 'turning' locomotives and the chance to ride in an original 1930s carriage. The learning centre offers interactive exhibits designed to involve visitors in science and engineering. *Buggy access. Café. Car park. Nappy-changing facilities.*

Kent & East Sussex Railway

Tenterden Town Station, Tenterden, Kent TN30 6HE (0870 600 6074/www.kesr.org.uk). **Getting there** *By rail* Headcorn rail then bus to Tenterden. *By car* J9 off M20. **Open** *Apr-July, Sept-Oct* 10am-4pm Sat, Sun.

Days Out

DISCOVER THE WILDER SIDE OF LONDON

Explore the London Wetland Centre and discover the beautiful wildlife that lives here. Centre includes lakeside restaurant, discovery centre, gift shop and adventure area for children.

Open 7 days a week from 9.30am to 6pm
T: 020 8409 4400   Visit wwt.org.uk/london

WWT London Wetland Centre, Queen Elizabeth's Walk, Barnes, SW13 9WT
Alight at Barnes Station or take the no. 283 Duck Bus from Hammersmith Tube

Registered charity no. 1030884

Chessington World of Adventures

Leatherhead Road, Chessington, Surrey KT9 2NE (0870 444 7777/www.chessington.com). **Getting there** *By rail* Chessington South rail then 71 bus or 10-min walk. *By car* J9 off M25. **Open** *10 Feb-2 Jan 2008.* Check website for timetables. **Admission** £18; £15 under-12s; £51 family (2+2). Check website for details and advance bookings for fast-track entry. **Credit** AmEx, MC, V.
Animal Land, as the fauna part of this 76-year-old theme park is now known, has been given a boost with the opening of some new adventures. Alongside the gorillas, tigers, sea lions and otters, there is now a walk-through squirrel monkey enclosure and a new Monkey and Bird Garden. The 'Zoo Keeper for a day' package lets visitors experience a day in the life of a zoo keeper, going behind the scenes with some of the animals. Chessington is a jollier option for young families. There's Beanoland with Dennis the Menace shenanigans, and Mystic East where you can take a leisurely boat ride with a surprise plunge (height restriction 0.9m; anyone under 1.1m must be accompanied by an adult). Older children can enjoy Land of the Dragons with its thrilling ride, Dragons Fury (height restriction 1.2m). A child gets in free with each paying adult; express tickets promise allotted time slots on the top six rides.
Buggy access. Café. Car park (free). Disabled access: toilets. Nappy-changing facilities. Restaurant. Shops.

Legoland

Winkfield Road, Windsor, Berks SL4 4AY (0870 504 0404/www.legoland.co.uk). **Getting there** *By rail* Windsor & Eton Riverside or Windsor Central rail then shuttlebus. *By car* J3 off M3 or J6 off M4. **Open** *Mid Mar-late Oct* times may vary, check website for timetables. **Admission** *One-day ticket* £31; £24 concessions, 3-15s; free under-3s. *Two-day ticket* £61; £47 3-15s; free under-3s. *Shuttlebus* £3.50; £2 concessions, 3-15s; free under-3s. **Credit** AmEx, MC, V.
Everyone loves Legoland, especially people with young children unburdened by term dates (it pays to avoid the crowds by going outside school hols and turning up way before 10am). It may be basking in its 2007 Tommy's Parent Friendly award, but this park is fab for all ages (teens love this place). With its witty brick-built surprises round every corner and its beautifully landscaped features, it's a treat, astronomical entry fee notwithstanding. New for 2007 is a huge water ride: the impressive Vikings' River Splash. Other rides for the intrepid (although there are no real stomach churners) include Dragon Coaster and Pirate Falls. The London skyline in Miniland features striking replicas of Canary Wharf, the Gherkin, City Hall and the Millennium Bridge. We also love the live action shows and the LEGO driving school. Tots should pester for the Lego Festival (14 July 2007) – it's not Glastonbury but there are live acts to dribble over, including Pingu, Bob the Builder and Barney the purple dinosaur. Rock on. Tips: pack a picnic, because the food is a let-down; check the day before that a) the centre is open (it often closes for random days) and b) the attractions your children are interested in are open.
Buggy access. Cafés. Car park (free). Disabled access: toilet. Nappy-changing facilities. Nearest picnic place: grounds. Restaurants. Shops.

Thorpe Park

Staines Road, Chertsey, Surrey KT16 8PN (0870 444 4466/www.thorpepark.com). **Getting there** *By rail* Staines rail then 950 shuttlebus. By car J11 or J13 off M25. **Open** times vary, check for timetables.

Height restrictions vary, depending on rides. **Admission** £24 adults; £16 under-12s; free under-1m tall. £69-£84 family (2+2 or 2+3). Check the website or phone for advance bookings; allow 24hrs to process advance ticket purchases. **Credit** MC, V.
Stealth, Europe's fastest rollercoaster, was launched last year. In 2007 it is back, all new and improved. Thorpe's mad (sadistic?) scientists have ensured that the rollercoaster is more gut-wrenching than ever – launching riders from 0 to 80mph in under two seconds. In the extreme ride stakes, there's also Colossus, the world's first ten-loop rollercoaster; Nemesis Inferno, where the train mounts a volcano and subjects the body to 4.5 G-Force; or the Vortex, which whirls at great heights above the lake. Slammer – one of only two 'sky-swat' rides in the world (don't ask) – could reduce parents to tears and Rush, the world's largest speed swing, is no walk in the park either. Although Thorpe's more gruesome rides aren't suitable for little ones, there are tamer attractions: swinging seashells, happy halibuts, the Banana Boat ride, and, in 2007, the popular Flying Fish makes a return. In an attempt to unite the family over foot-tapping tunes there's the Top Rockers Show, performed by Billy, Bo and Benny in the Sing Zone. Not one for the Goths and Rude Boys in the family, we fear.
Buggy access. Café. Car park (free-£3). Disabled access: toilets. Nappy-changing facilities. Restaurants. Shops.

Wildlife parks

Drusillas Park

Alfriston, East Sussex BN26 5QS (01323 874100/ www.drusillas.co.uk). **Getting there** *By rail* Polgate or Berwick rail then taxi. *By car* M23, then A23, then A27. **Open** *Apr-Oct* 10am-6pm daily. *Nov-Mar* 10am-5pm daily. Last entry 1hr before closing. **Admission** *Off peak days* £10.70; £9.70 concessions, 2-12s; £18-£45 family; free under-2s. *Standard days* £12.20; £11.20 concessions, 2-12s; £21-£52.50 family (2-2+3); free under-2s. *Peak days* £12.95; £11.95 concessions, 2-12s; £23.90-£59.75 family (2-2+3); free under-2s. Prices vary, check website for details. **Credit** MC, V.
There's tons to do at this zoo, where the focus is on interactive involvement, conservation and fact-finding alongside play. Its naturalistic animal enclosures, innovative design and low-level viewing (most famously demonstrated in the meerkat mound) let you get nose to nose with nature. Animal residents include lemurs, prairie dogs, otters, marmosets, macaques, penguins and crocodiles, snakes, bats and insects. Kids are given animal-spotter books for easy identification, and they can join in activities, such as panning for gold, crazy golf and workshops. There are also playgrounds and a large paddling pool called Explorers' Lagoon. Amazon Adventure is a soft play area. Events include celebrity appearances from Dora, Sponge Bob, Angelina et al. Spider-Man drops in 27 August 2007 and there's a special reptile weekend on 1 and 2 September. Check the website for events. Note that the Safari Train is now a bespoke Thomas, who chuffed in during Easter 2007.
Buggy access. Café. Car park (free). Disabled access: toilet. Nappy-changing facilities. Nearest picnic place: grounds. Restaurant. Shops.

Howletts Wild Animal Park

Bekesbourne, nr Canterbury, Kent CT4 5EL (01227 721286/www.totallywild.net). **Getting there** *By rail* Bekesbourne rail then 30-min walk or shuttle bus available in holidays (consult website or phone for info); Canterbury East rail then taxi. *By car* M2, then A2. **Open** *Summer* 10am-6pm daily (last entry 4.30pm). *Winter* 10am-dusk daily (last entry 3pm). **Admission** £13.95; £10.95 4-16s; £42 family (2+2); £49 family (2+3); free under-4s. **Credit** AmEx, MC, V.

The late John Aspinall set up the parks at Howletts and at Port Lympne, near Hythe, more than 40 years ago to conserve endangered species, with a view to breeding them in captivity to be released into the wild. Enclosures replicate specific environments as closely as possible. Almost 50 gorillas are housed here, as well as African elephants, Siberian tigers and many more; a number of the wolves, tapirs and antelopes are endangered species. In the 'Wood in the Park', you can walk alongside and below a free-roaming family of amazingly agile and lively lemurs. The parks have recently burst into the modern world with web-cam interactivity on the internet and through the BBC children's programme *ROAR!* Launched in 2006, the show goes behind the scenes of the day-to-day running of the park.

Buggy access. Café. Car park (free). Disabled access: toilet. Nappy-changing facilities. Nearest picnic place: grounds. Restaurant. Shop.

Port Lympne Wild Animal Park

Lympne, nr Hythe, Kent CT21 4PD (0870 750 4647/ www.totallywild.net). **Getting there** *By rail* Ashford rail then link bus. *By car* J11 off M20. **Open** *Winter* 10am-dusk daily (last entry 3pm). *Summer* 10am-6pm daily (last entry 4.30pm). **Admission** £13.95; £10.95 4-16s; £42 family (2+2), £49 (2+3); free under-4s. **Credit** AmEx, MC, V.

Even larger than sister site Howletts (*see above*), Port Lympne has room for the African Safari Experience, bounded by 3.2km (two miles) of reinforced steel, which contains the largest breeding herd of Black Rhino outside Africa. The park covers 350 acres of wilderness, where animals coexist in a quasi-game reserve. The easiest way to see everything is on a trailer tour, which takes you through herds of wildebeest, zebra and giraffe. Still, expeditions on foot (a round trip of the park covers five kilometres or three miles) can be more rewarding. Don't miss Palace of the Apes, the largest family gorillarium in the world. Fancy staying over? The Livingstone Safari Lodge lets you sleep near the animals.

Buggy access. Café. Car park (free). Disabled access: toilet. Nappy-changing facilities. Nearest picnic place: grounds. Restaurant. Shop.

Whipsnade Wild Animal Park

Whipsnade, Dunstable, Beds LU6 2LF (01582 872 171/www.whipsnade.co.uk). **Getting there** *By rail* Hemel Hempstead rail then 43 bus from coach station. *By car* J21 off M25, then J9 off M1. **Open** *early Mar-Sept* 10am-6pm daily. *Oct, mid Feb-early Mar* 10am-5pm daily. *Late Oct-early Mar* 10am-4pm daily. Last entry 1hr before closing. Times subject to change; phone to check. **Tours** free bus around the park; phone for times. **Admission** £14.55; £13.20 concessions; £11.40 3-15s; £48 family (2+2 or 1+3); free under-3s. **Cars** £12. **Credit** AmEx, MC, V.

The ZSL (Zoological Society of London), the charity that also operates London Zoo (*see p76*), runs this 600-acre site. There's a small herd of elephants, with a toddler and a newborn among them, plus giraffes, bears, tigers, rhinos (new calf born March 2007), hippos and Lions of the

Serengeti. New for 2007 is In With The Lemurs, an island inhabited by the beautiful ringtaileed variety from Madagascar, they can be reached via a bridge over a moat and featuring a waterfall and raised walkway. Daily activities include birds of prey flying displays, sea lion capers in the Splashzone area, penguins feeding time, cosy chats with chimps and lofty giraffe encounters. There's also a lovely little children's farm with marmosets, goats, alpacas and ponies. The Jumbo Express is named after the biggest elephant ever in captivity, who grew up at London Zoo. There is also an imaginative series of special events during the school holidays.

Buggy access. Café. Car park (£3.50). Disabled access: toilet. Nappy-changing facilities. Restaurant. Shop.

Wildwood Wildlife Park

Herne Common, Herne Bay, Kent CT6 7LQ (01227 712111/www.wildwoodtrust.org). **Getting there** *By rail* Herne Bay rail then 4 bus. *By car* A2, A299 then A291. **Open** 10am-6pm daily (last entry 4.30pm). **Admission** £8-£9; £7 3-15s; £30 family (2+3); free OAPs, under-3s. **Credit** MC, V.

Kent's national woodland discovery park, which lies between Canterbury and Herne Bay, champions the cause of our native furry animals. Visitors can get up close to Britain's furtive little critters that make up Britain's native wildlife, such as otters, dormice, badgers and water voles. Wildwood has also become a safe haven for a host of other creatures – like wolves and wild boar – that no longer exist in the wild in Britain. Several species such as the konik horse and the beaver have been reintroduced to the UK from Europe. More than 300 animals from over 50 species live here, in enclosures that are designed to blend into the landscape. There's also a prettily positioned woodland play area; a Saxon settlement is currently under construction. The aim of Wildwood is to turn more areas of our countryside back into precisely that – a wild wood.

Buggy access. Café. Car park (free). Disabled access: toilet. Nappy-changing facilities. Shop.

Woburn Safari Park

Woburn Park, Beds MK17 9QN (01525 290407/ www.woburnsafari.co.uk). **Getting there** *By car* J13 off M1. **Open** *late Mar-29 Oct* 10am-6pm daily. *30 Oct-late Mar* 11am-4pm Sat, Sun (last entry 3pm). **Admission** £15.50; £13 concessions; £11.50-£13 3-15s; free under-3s. Prices vary during peak season; phone for details. **Credit** MC, V.

Safaris in the Duke of Bedford's Woburn spread let you see the free-ranging elephants, giraffes (with a new calf born to the rare Rothschilds), camels, black bears, monkeys, lions, tigers and wolves, all from the safety of the family jalopy. You can also stretch your legs on a foot safari, taking in demonstrations of birds of prey and talks on penguins and sea lions. At Rainbow Landing (an indoor aviary) you can buy nectar to attract colourful lorikeets to land on your hand to drink – a real thrill for children. Rainbow Landing opens four times a day. The sea lion pool and Land of the Lemurs (red-bellied ones) are also must-sees. In addition, there is the Mammoth Play Ark, a massive indoor adventure play area with slides, ropes, scramble nets and a treetop assault course.

Buggy access. Café. Car park (free). Disabled access: toilet. Nappy-changing facilities. Restaurant. Shop.

Directory

Directory

Getting around

Public transport

The prices listed for transport and services were correct at the time of going to press, but bear in mind that some prices (especially those of tube tickets) are subject to a hike each January.

Public transport information

Details can be found online at www.thetube.com and/or www.tfl.gov.uk, or by phoning 7222 1234.

Transport for London (TfL) also runs Travel Information Centres that provide maps and information about the tube, buses, Tramlink, riverboats, Docklands Light Railway (DLR) and national rail services within the London area. You can find them in Heathrow Airport, as well as in Liverpool Street and Victoria stations.

London TravelWatch
6 Middle Street, EC1A 7JA (7505 9000/www.londontravel watch.org.uk). **Open** *Phone enquiries* 9am-5pm Mon-Fri.
This is the official, campaigning watchdog monitoring customer satisfaction with transport in London.

Fares, Oyster cards & travelcards

Tube and DLR fares are based on of six zones stretching 20 kilometres (12 miles) out from the centre of London. A cash fare of £4 per journey applies across the tube for zones 1-4 (£4 for zones 1-5 or 1-6); customers save up to £1.50 with Oyster pay-as-you-go (see below). Beware of £20 on-the-spot fines for anyone caught without a ticket.

Children aged under 11 travel free on buses, DLR and most tubes. If you are only using the tube, DLR, buses and trams, using Oyster to pay-as-you-go will always be cheaper than a Day Travelcard (see below). If you are using National Rail services, however, the Day Travelcard may best meet your needs (children travelling with you can buy a Day Travelcard for £1). Under-16s travel free on buses.

Travelcards, valid for tubes, buses, DLR and rail services, can be the cheapest way of getting around. Travelcards can be bought at stations, London Travel Information Centres or newsagents.

Day Travelcards

Day Travelcards (peak) can be used all day Mondays to Fridays (except public holidays). They cost from £6.60 (£3.30 for under-16s) for zones 1-2, with prices rising to £13.20 (£6.60 for under-16s) for zones 1-6. Most people use the off-peak Day Travelcard, which allows you to travel from 9.30am (Mon-Fri) and all day Saturday, Sunday and public holidays. They cost from £5.10 for zones 1-2, rising to £6.70 for zones 1-6. Up to four children pay £2 each where accompanied by an adult with a travelcard. New Deal photocard holders aged 5-15 also pay £2.

Oyster card

The Oyster card is a travel smart-card that can be charged with Pre-Pay and/or seven-day, monthly and longer-period (including annual) travelcards and bus passes. Oyster cards are currently available to adults and under-16 photocard holders when buying a ticket. Tickets can be bought from www.oystercard.com, by phone on 0870 849 9999 and at tube station ticket offices, London Travel Information Centres, some National Rail station ticket offices and newsagents. A single tube journey in zone 1 using Oyster to pay-as-you go costs £1.50 at all times (children under 11 go free).

Children

Under-16s can travel free on buses and trams; under-11s travel free on the tube at off-peak hours and at weekends with an adult with a valid ticket. Children aged 14 or 15 need a child – or 11-15 – photocard to travel at child rate on the tube, DLR and trams. Children who board National Rail services travelling with adult-rate 7-day, monthly or longer travelcard holders can buy a day travelcard for £1. An under-16 Oyster photocard is required by children aged 11-15 years to pay as they go on the Underground or DLR or to buy 7-day, monthly or longer period travelcards.

Three-day travelcards

If you plan to spend a few days charging around town, you can buy 3-Day Travelcards. The peak version can be used for any journey that starts between the ticket start date and 4.30am on the day following the expiry date, and is available for £16.40 (zones 1-2) or £39.60 (zones 1-6). The off-peak travelcard, which can be used from 9.30am costs £20. 10 (zones 1-6). Children aged 5-15 and New Deal Photocard holders pay £8.20 for Zones 1-2 (peak and off peak) and £6 (off peak) or £19.80 (peak) for Zones 1-6.

London Underground

The tube in rush hour (8-9.30am and 4.30-7pm Mon-Fri) is not pleasant, so it is best to travel outside these hours with children if possible.

Using the system

Tube tickets can be purchased or Oyster cards topped up from a ticket office or self-service machines. Ticket offices in some stations close early (around 7.30pm), but it's best to keep an Oyster card charged with value. For buying Oyster cards, *see above*.

To enter and exit the tube using an Oyster card, touch it to the yellow reader that will open the gates. Make sure you touch the card when you exit the tube otherwise you may be fined.

There are 12 Underground lines, colour-coded on the tube map for ease of use; we've provided a full map of the London Underground on the back page of this book.

Underground timetable

Tube trains run daily from around 5.30am (except Sunday, when they start later). The only exception is Christmas Day, when there is no service. During peak times the service should run every two or three minutes. Times of last trains vary, but they're usually around 11.30pm-1am daily, and 30 minutes to an hour earlier on Sunday. Debates continue as to whether to run the tube an hour later at weekends. The only all-night public transport is by night bus.

Fares

The single fare for adults within zone 1 is £4 (Oyster fare £1.50). For zones 1-2 it's £4 (Oyster fare £2 or £1.50). The zones 1-6 single fare is £4.00 (Oyster fare £3.50 or £2). The single fare for 5-15s in zone 1 is £1.50 (Oyster fare 50p with a valid Under 14 14-15 or a Child Oyster photocard), £1.50 for zones 1-2 (Oyster fare £1 or 70p) or £2 for zones 1-6 (Oyster fare £1). Children under 11 travel free at off-peak times.

Docklands Light Railway (DLR)

The DLR (7363 9700, www.dlr.co.uk) runs trains from Bank or Tower Gateway, close to Tower Hill tube (Circle and District lines), to Stratford, Beckton and the Isle of Dogs, then south of the river to Greenwich, Deptford and Lewisham. Trains run 5.30am to 12.30am Monday to Saturday and 7am to 11.30pm Sunday.

Fares

The single fare for adults within Zone 1 is £4 (Oyster fare £1.50). For Zones 1-2 it's £4 (Oyster fare £2 or £1.50). The zones 1-6 single fare is £4 (Oyster fare £3.50 or £2). Children under 11 travel free. Children aged 11-15 pay £1.50 (Oyster fare 70p) or £2 for zones 1-6 (Oyster fare £1). One-day 'Rail & River Rover' tickets combine unlimited DLR travel with hop-on, hop off boat travel on City Cruises between Greenwich, Tower, Waterloo and Westminster piers, starting at Tower Gateway. Tickets cost £10.50 for adults, £5.25 for kids and £26 for a family pass); under-5s go free.

Buses

New buses, with low-floors for wheelchair users, and Bendy buses with with multiple-door entry and the 'pay before you board' schemes now make up much of the fleet. Buses in central London require you to have an Oyster card or buy a ticket before boarding from pavement ticket machines.

Using an Oyster card (see p291) to pay as you go costs £1 or 80p depending on the time you travel; the most you will pay a day is £3. Paying by cash at the time of travel costs £2 per trip. A one-day bus pass gives unlimited bus and tram travel at £3.50. Children under 16 and students up to age 18 travel free on buses.

Night buses

Many night buses run 24 hours a day, seven days a week, and some special night buses with an 'N' prefix to the route number operate from about 11pm to 6am. Most services run every 15 to 30 minutes, but many busier routes have a bus around every ten minutes. Travelcards and Bus Passes can be used on night buses until 4.30am on the day after they expire. Oyster Pre-Pay and bus Saver tickets are also valid on night buses.

Green Line buses

Green Line buses (0870 608 7261, www.greenline.co.uk) serve the suburbs and towns within a 40-mile radius of London. Their main departure point is Ecclestone Bridge, SW1 (Colonnades Coach Station, behind Victoria), and they run a 24-hour service.

Coaches

National Express (0870 580 8080, www.nationalexpress.com) runs routes to most parts of the country; coaches depart from **Victoria Coach Station**, a five-minute walk from Victoria rail and tube stations.

Victoria Coach Station

164 Buckingham Palace Road, SW1W 9TP (7730 3466/ www.tfl.gov.uk/vcs). Victoria tube/rail. **Map** p316 H1. National Express, which travels to the Continent as Eurolines, is based at Victoria Coach Station.

Rail services

Independently run services leave from the main rail stations. Travelcards are valid on services within the right zones. The useful Silverlink line (0845 601 4867, www.silverlink-trains.com) goes through north London from Richmond to North Woolwich, via Kew, Kensal Rise, Gospel Oak, Islington, Stratford and City Airport.

If you've lost property on an overground station or a train, call 0870 000 5151; an operator will connect you to the appropriate station.

Family Railcard

This costs £20 and lasts one year. Valid across Britain, it gives travellers with children one year of discounts from standard rail fares (a third off adult fares, 60 per cent off child fares, £1 minimum fare). Under-fives travel free. Up to two adults can be named as cardholders – they do not have to be related. The minimum group size is one cardholder and one child aged five to 15; maximum group size is two cardholders, two other adults and four children. To pick up a form for the Family Railcard, visit your local staffed station.

London's mainline stations

Charing Cross *Strand, WC2N 5LR.* **Map** p317 L7. For trains to and from south-east England (including Dover, Folkestone and Ramsgate).
Euston *Euston Road, NW1 1BN.* **Map** p315 K3. For trains to and from north and north-west England and Scotland, and a suburban line north to Watford.
King's Cross *Euston Road, N1 9AP.* **Map** p315 L2. For trains to and from north and north-east England and Scotland, and suburban lines to north London.
Liverpool Street *Liverpool Street, EC2M 7PD.* **Map** p319 R5. For trains to and from the east coast, Stansted airport and East Anglia, and services to east and north-east London.
London Bridge *London Bridge Street, SE1 2SW.* **Map** p319 Q8. For trains to Kent, Sussex, Surrey and south London suburbs.

Directory

Paddington *Praed Street, W2 1HB.* **Map** p311 D5.
For trains to and from west and south-west England, South
Wales and the Midlands.
Victoria *115 Buckingham Palace Road, SW1W 9SJ.*
Map p316 H10.
For fast trains to and from the channel ports (Folkestone,
Dover, Newhaven); for trains to and from Gatwick Airport,
and suburban services to south and south-east London.
Waterloo *York Road, SE1 7NZ.* **Map** p319 M9.
For fast trains to and from the south and south-west of England
(Portsmouth, Southampton, Dorset, Devon), and suburban
services to south London.

Tramlink

Trams run between Beckenham, Croydon,
Addington and Wimbledon. Travelcards and bus
passes taking in zones 3-6 can be used on trams;
cash single fares cost from £2 (Oyster fare £1 or
50p for 16-to 17-year-old photocard holders). A
one-day bus pass gives unlimited tram and bus
travel at £3 for adults.

Water transport

The times of London's assortment of river services
vary, but most operate every 20 minutes to one
hour between 10.30am and 5pm, with more
frequent services in summer. Call the operators
for schedules, or see www.tfl.gov.uk. Travelcard
holders can expect one-third off scheduled
riverboat fares. Thames Clippers (0870 781 5049,
www.thamesclippers.com) runs a commuter boat
service. Clippers stop at these piers: Savoy (near
Embankment tube), Blackfriars, Bankside, London
Bridge and St Katharine's (Tower Bridge).

The names in bold below are the names of piers.

Embankment–Tower (25mins)–**Greenwich** (40mins);
Catamaran Cruises 7987 1185, www.bateauxlondon.com.
Royal Arsenal Woolwich-Greenwich (15mins)–St
Masthouse Terrace (5mins)–Greenland Dock (4mins)–Canary
Wharf (8mins)-St Katharine's (7mins)–London Bridge City
(4mins)-Bankside (3mins)-Blackfriars (3mins)-Savoy (4mins);
Collins River Enterprises 7977 6892, www.thamesclippers.com.
Westminster–Festival (5mins)–**London Bridge City**
(20mins)–**St Katharine's** (5mins); **Crown River** 7936 2033,
www.crownriver.com.
Westminster–Greenwich (1hr); **Thames River Services**
7930 4097, www.westminsterpier.co.uk.
Westminster–Kew (1hr 30mins)–**Richmond**
(30mins)–**Hampton Court** (1hr 30mins); **Westminster
Passenger Service Association** 7930 2062,
www.wpsa.co.uk.
Westminster–Tower (30mins); City Cruises 7740 0400,
www.citycruises.com.

Taxis

Black cabs

Licensed London taxis are known as black cabs –
even though they now come in a variety of colours
– and are a quintessential feature of London life.
Drivers of black cabs must pass a test called the
Knowledge to prove they know every street in
central London and the shortest route to it.

If a taxi's yellow 'For Hire' sign is switched on,
it can be hailed. If a taxi stops, the cabbie must
take you to your destination, provided it's within
seven miles. Expect to pay slightly higher rates
after 8pm on weekdays and all weekend.

You can book black cabs in advance. Both Radio
Taxis (7272 0272, credit cards only) and Dial-a-
Cab (7253 5000) run 24-hour services for black
cabs (there'll be a booking fee in addition to the
regular fare). Enquiries or complaints about black
cabs should be made to the Public Carriage Office.
(0870 602 7000, www.gov.uk/pco).

Minicabs

Be sure to use only licensed firms and avoid
minicab drivers who tout for business on the
street. There are, happily, plenty of trustworthy
and licensed local minicab firms around, including
Lady Cabs (7272 3300, www.ladyminicabs.co.uk),
which employs only women drivers, and Addison
Lee (7387 8888, www.addisonlee.com). Whoever
you use, always ask the price when you book and
confirm it with the driver when the car arrives.

Driving

Congestion charge

Everyone driving in central London – an area
defined as within King's Cross (N), Old Street
roundabout (NE), Aldgate (E), Old Kent Road (SE),
Elephant & Castle (S), Vauxhall, Chelsea, South
Kensington (SW), Kensington, Holland Park,
North Kensington, Bayswater, Paddington (W),
Marylebone and Euston (N) – between 7am and
6pm Monday to Friday, has to pay an £8 fee.
Expect a fine of £50 if you fail to do so (rising to
£150 if you delay payment). Passes can be bought
from newsagents, garages and NCP car parks; the
scheme is enforced by CCTV cameras. You can
pay by phone or online any time during the day of
entry, even afterwards, but it's an extra £2 after
10pm. Payments are accepted until midnight on
the next charging day after a vehicle has entered
the zone. For information, phone 0845 900 1234 or
go to www.cclondon.com. The Congestion Charge
zone is marked on the Central London by Area
map on p308.

Parking

Central London is scattered with parking meters,
but finding a vacant one can take ages and, when
you do, it'll cost you up to £1 for every 15 minutes
to park there, and you'll be limited to two hours
on the meter. Parking on a single or double yellow
line, a red line or in residents' parking areas
during the day is illegal. In the evening (from 6pm

or 7pm in much of central London) and at various times at weekends, parking on single yellow lines is legal and free. If you find a clear spot on a single yellow line during the evening, look for a sign giving the regulations. Meters are also free at certain times during evenings and weekends.

NCP 24-hour car parks (0870 606 7050, www. ncp.co.uk) in and around central London are numerous but expensive. Fees vary, but expect to pay £10-£55 per day. Among the NCP's central car parks are those at Arlington House, Arlington Street, St James's, W1; Upper St Martins Lane, WC2; and 2 Lexington Street, Soho, W1. Most NCPs in central London are underground, and a few are frequented by drug-users. Take care.

Driving out of town

Check out your route for possible roadworks and delays, and, where possible, avoid the morning and evening rush hour. Try the route-planner service available from the Royal Automobile Association (RAC, www.rac.co.uk).

Cycling

The London Cycle Network (7974 8747, www. londoncyclenetwork.org) and London Cycling Campaign (7234 9310, www.lcc.org.uk) make London better to pedal in. London Cycle Guide maps are available from some stations and bike shops, or the Travel Information Line (7222 1234).

Cycle hire

London Bicycle Tour Company

1A Gabriel's Wharf, 56 Upper Ground, South Bank, SE1 9PP (7928 6838/www.londonbicycle.com). Blackfriars, Southwark or Waterloo tube/rail. **Open** 10am-6pm daily. **Hire** £3/hr; £16/1st day, £8/day thereafter. **Deposit** £1 (or credit card). **Credit** AmEx, DC, MC, V.
Bike, tandem and rickshaw hire, and guided bicycle tours. Chidren's bikes can be hired free. Tours covering major sights in central London start at 10.30am.

Walking

The least stressful way to see London is on foot; it's also the safest way to travel with your head stuck in a map. A selection of street maps covering central London is on *pp308-319* but you'll need a separate map of the city: both the standard Geographers' *A–Z* and Collins's *London Street Atlas* versions are very easy to use.

The Guy Fox London Children's Map puts the power of planning fun excursions straight into the hands of young people. The comprehensive map is packed with colourful illustrations of city icons and landmarks; buy it at www.guyfox.co.uk at £2.95 or bookshops and tourist attractions.

Resources

Councils

Barnet *8359 2000, www.barnet.gov.uk.*
Brent *8937 1234, www.brent.gov.uk.*
Camden *7278 4444, www.camden.gov.uk*
Corporation of London *7606 3030, www.cityoflondon.gov.uk.*
Ealing *8825 5000, www.ealing.gov.uk.*
Greenwich *8854 8888, www.greenwich.gov.uk.*
Hackney *8356 3000, www.hackney.gov.uk.*
Hammersmith & Fulham *8748 3020, www.lbhf.gov.uk.*
Haringey *8489 0000, www.haringey.gov.uk.*
Hounslow *8583 2000, www.hounslow.gov.uk.*
Islington *7527 2000, www.islington.gov.uk.*
Kensington & Chelsea *7361 3000, www.rbkc.gov.uk.*
Lambeth *7926 1000, www.lambeth.gov.uk.*
Lewisham *8314 6000, www.lewisham.gov.uk.*
Merton *8274 4901, www.merton.gov.uk.*
Newham *8430 2000, www.newham.gov.uk.*
Richmond upon Thames *8891 1411, www.richmond.gov.uk.*
Southwark *7525 5000, www.southwark.gov.uk.*
Tower Hamlets *7364 5020, www.towerhamlets.gov.uk.*
Waltham Forest *8496 3000, www.walthamforest.gov.uk.*
Wandsworth *8871 6000, www.wandsworth.gov.uk.*
Westminster *7641 6000, www.westminster.gov.uk.*

Education

Advisory Centre on Education (ACE) *0808 800 5793/ exclusion advice line 7704 9822/www.ace-ed.org.uk.* **Open** 2-5pm Mon-Fri.
Ring the centre for advice about your child's schooling; the advice line is for parents whose children have been excluded from school, or have been bullied, or have special educational needs. School admission appeals advice is also available.
British Association for Early Childhood Education *136 Cavell Street, E1 2JA (7539 5400/www.early-education.org.uk).* **Open** By phone 9am-5pm Mon-Fri.
A charitable organisation that provides information on infant education from birth to eight years. Send an SAE for additional publications.
Gabbitas Educational Consultants *Carrington House, 126-130 Regent Street, W1B 5EE (7734 0161/ www.gabbitas.co.uk).* **Open** 9am-5pm Mon-Fri.
The consultants at Gabbitas give advice on choosing an independent school.
Home Education Advisory Service *PO Box 98, Welwyn Garden City, Herts AL8 6AN (01707 371 854/ www.heas.org.uk).* **Open** By phone 9am-5pm Mon-Fri.
Call for information if you want to educate your child at home. An introductory pack costs £2.50, a year's subscription £15.00.
ISC Information Service London & South-east *7798 1560/www.iscis.uk.net.* **Open** By phone 9am-5pm Mon-Fri.
The Independent Schools Council Information Service works to help parents find out about independent schools.
Kid Smart *www.kidsmart.org.uk.*
Kidsmart is an internet-safety-awareness programme run by Childnet International and is funded by the DFES and Cable & Wireless. Its guide is available to all primary schools.
National Association for Gifted Children *Suite 14, Challenge House, Sherwood Drive, Bletchley, Milton Keynes, Bucks MK3 6DP (0870 770 3217/www.nagcbritain.org.uk).* **Open** By phone 9.15am-4pm Mon, Wed-Fri.
Support and advice on education for parents of the gifted.
Parenting UK *Unit 431, Highgate Studios, 53-79 Highgate Road, NW5 1TL (7284 8389/www.parenting-forum.org.uk).* **Open** By phone 10am-5pm Mon-Fri.
Information about parenting classes and support for parents.
Pre-School Learning Alliance *Units 118 York Way, N7 9AD (7697 2500/www.pre-school.org.uk).* **Open** By phone 9am-5pm Mon-Fri.
The PSLA is a leading educational charity specialising in the early years. It runs courses and workshops in pre-schools around the country for parents of children under the age of five.

Fun & games

Activity camps

Barracudas *Young World Leisure Group, Bridge House, Bridge Street, St Ives, Cambs PE27 5EH (0845 123 5299/ www.barracudas.co.uk).*
School holiday camps based in country schools in outlying countryside. Children aged 5-16 welcome.
Cross Keys *48 Fitzalan Road, N3 3PE (8371 9686/ www.xkeys.co.uk/www.miniminors.co.uk).*
Day camps in Finchley for kids aged 12 or under and rural week-long camps in Norfolk, for children aged up to 17.
eac Activity Camps Ltd *45 Frederick Street, Edinburgh, EH2 1EP (0131 477 7574/www.eacworld.com).*
Day and residential camps for children aged five to 16 in countryside sites across the land.
PGL *Alton Court, Penyard Lane, Ross-on-Wye HR9 5GL (0870 050 7507/www.pgl.co.uk).*
Sport and activity camps for children aged up to 16 in the UK and Europe.
Wickedly Wonderful *Russett Cottage, Itchenor, PO20 7DD (0794 123 1168/www.wickedlywonderful.com).*
A holiday company that runs weekly buses from London down to the beach in the summer holidays.

Health

Asthma UK *Helpline 0845 701 0203/www.asthma.org.uk.* **Open** *Helpline* 9am-5pm Mon-Fri.
Advice and help if you or your child has asthma.
Contact-A-Family *7608 8700/helpline 0808 808 3555/ www.cafamily.org.uk.* **Open** *Helpline* 10am-4pm, 5.30-7.30pm Mon; 10am-4pm Tue-Fri.
Support for parents of children with disabilities.
Family Natural Health Centre *106 Lordship Lane, East Dulwich, SE22 8HF (8693 5515).* **Open** 9.30am-9.30pm Mon-Fri; 9.30am-6pm Sat.
A wide range of alternative therapies, from acupuncture to osteopathy are practised here. French classes, sing and sign classes, children's yoga and art therapy are also offered.
Food for the Brain Foundation *9970 3883/www.food forthebrain.org.*
The Food for the Brain schools project is designed to help parents throughout the UK make the right food choices to help improve their children's brain function, behaviour and intelligence. A downloadable leaflet called the 'Smart Food Smart Kids Shopping Guide' accompanies the scheme.
NHS Direct *Helpline 0845 4647/www.nhsdirect.nhs.uk.* **Open** *Helpline* 24hrs daily.
Confidential information and health advice.

Indoor play

Crêchendo *www.crechendo.com.*
Active play classes for babies and pre-school children.
Gymboree Play & Music *0800 092 0911/ www.gymboreeplayuk.com.*
A parent-and-child play organisation for children aged 16 months to four and a half years.
National Association of Toy & Leisure Libraries *(NATLL) 68 Churchway, NW1 1LT (7255 4600/helpline 7255 4616/www.natll.org.uk).* **Open** *Helpline* 9am-5pm Mon-Fri.
For information on more than 1,000 toy libraries.
Toys Re-united *www.toys-reunited.co.uk.*
Check the website to see if a missing plaything might have been found.
TumbleTots *0121 585 7003/www.tumbletots.com.* **Open** *By phone* 9am-5.30pm Mon-Fri.
Phone to find out about TumbleTot play centres in your area.

Help & support

Bestbear *0870 720 1277/www.bestbear.co.uk.* **Open** 9am-6pm Mon-Fri; 24hr answerphone other times.
Information about childcare agencies.

Childcare Link *0800 234 6346/www.childcarelink.gov.uk.* **Open** *By phone* 8am-8pm Mon-Fri; 9am-noon Sat.
Provides a list of childcare organisations in their area.
ChildLine *0800 1111/www.childline.org.uk.*
Confidential 24-hour helpline for young people in the UK.
Daycare Trust *21 St George's Road, SE1 6ES (7840 3350/ www.daycaretrust.org.uk).* **Open** 9.30am-5.30pm Mon-Fri.
A national charity that works to promote high-quality, affordable childcare.
4Children *7512 2112/info line 7512 2100/www. 4children.org.uk.* **Open** *By phone* 9am-5pm Mon-Fri.
Information on after-school clubs, children's and family services.
Kids *6 Aztec Row, Berners Road, N1 0PW (7359 3635/ www.kids-online.org.uk).* An organisation that seeks to enhance the lives of disabled children.
Kidscape *2 Grosvenor Gardens, SW1W 0DH (7730 3300/ Helpline 08451 205 204/www.kidscape.org.uk.*
The first charity in the UK established specifically to prevent bullying and child abuse. The helpline is for the use of parents, guardians or concerned relatives and friends of bullied children.
Nannytax *PO Box 988, Brighton, East Sussex BN1 3NT (0845 226 2203/www.nannytax.co.uk).* **Open** *By phone* 9am-5pm Mon-Fri.
For £260 a year, Nannytax registers your nanny with the Inland Revenue, organises National Insurance payments and offers advice.
National Family & Parenting Institute *430 Highgate Studios, 53-79 Highgate Road, NW5 1TL (7424 3460/ www.nfpi.org).* Kentish Town tube/rail. **Open** *By phone* 9.30am-5.30pm Mon-Fri; 24hr answerphone other times.
A resource centre that produces factsheets covering all aspects of parenting.
Night Nannies *7731 6168/www.nightnannies.com.*
Night Nannies provides a list of qualified carers who may be able to provide respite from sleepless nights.
Parent Company *6 Jacob's Well Mews, W1U 3DY (7935 9635/www.theparentcompany.co.uk).* **Open** *Bookings* 9am-2.30pm Mon-Fri.
Runs seminars on diverse subjects, from time-management to discipline issues, costing from £45 per session per person.
Parent Courses *Holy Trinity Brompton, Brompton Road, SW7 1JA (7581 8255/www.htb.org.uk).* South Kensington tube. **Open** 9.30am-5.30pm Mon, Wed-Fri; 10.30am-5.30pm Tue.
Runs the Parenting Course for parents with children under the age of 12 and Parenting Teenagers, for parents of children aged 13-18. Each course costs £30.
Parentline Plus *Helpline 0808 800 2222/www.parentline plus.org.uk.* **Open** *Helpline* 24hrs daily.
Organises nationwide courses on how to cope with being a parent. For more details, phone the free helpline.
Parents for Inclusion *Helpline 0800 652 3145/www.parents forinclusion.org.* **Open** 10am-noon, 1-3pm Mon, Tue, Thur.
Organises a series of workshops for parents of disabled children.
The Parent Practice *Bookings 8673 3444/www.theparent practice.org.*
A support group that promises to endow parents with the skills for transforming family life. They also produce CDs (£15.50; £27/pair) that provide harrassed mums and dads with practical strategies to make family life calmer, happier and more rewarding.
Parent Support Group *72 Blackheath Road, SE10 8DA (helpline 8469 0205/www.psg.org.uk).* **Open** *Helpline* 10am-7pm Mon-Fri; 24hr answerphone other times.
As well as the helpline, staff run one-to-one support sessions and offer courses on parenting skills to the parents and carers of adolescents who are acting in an antisocial or criminal manner.
Post-Adoption Centre *5 Torriano Mews, Torriano Avenue NW5 2RZ (7284 0555/Advice Line 0870 777 2197/ www.postadoptioncentre.org.uk)* **Open** *Advice Line* 10am-1pm Mon-Wed, Fri; 5.30pm-7.30pm Thur. Registered charity providing advice, support and information for anyone affected by adoption, including adoptive/foster parents and their children, adopted adults, birth relatives and the professionals who work with them.
Sitters *0800 389 0038/www.sitters.co.uk.* **Open** *By phone* 8am-7pm Mon-Fri; 9am-1pm Sat.
A babysitting agency with locally based nurses, teachers and nannies on its books.

Tourist information

Visit London (7234 5800, www.visitlondon.com) is the city's official tourist information company. There are also tourist offices in Greenwich, Leicester Square and next to St Paul's Cathedral.

Britain & London Visitor Centre

1 Lower Regent Street, Piccadilly Circus, SW1Y 4XT (8846 9000/www.visitbritain.com). Piccadilly Circus tube. **Open** *Oct-May* 9.30am-6.30pm Mon; 9am-6.30pm Tue-Fri; 10am-4pm Sat, Sun. *June-Sept* 9.30am-6.30pm Mon; 9am-6.30pm Tue-Fri; 9am-5pm Sat; 10am-4pm Sun.

London Information Centre

Leicester Square, WC2H 7BP (7292 2333/www.londontown. com). Leicester Square tube. **Open** *By phone* 8am-midnight Mon-Fri; 9am-10pm Sat, Sun. *In person* 8am-11pm Mon-Fri; 10am-6pm Sat, Sun.

London Visitor Centre

Arrivals Hall, Waterloo International Terminal, SE1 7LT. **Open** 8.30am-10.30pm Mon-Sat; 9.30am-10.30pm Sun.

Further reference

Books

Joan Aitken *Black Hearts in Battersea*
Simon comes to London to learn painting with his old friend Dr Field only for to find the doctor has disappeared under mysterious circumstances.
Bernard Ashley *Little Soldier*
The 1999 Carnegie Medal-winning story of Kaminda, a refugee from an African war brought by aid workers to England, where he finds a different kind of warfare on London's streets.
JM Barrie *Peter Pan* (play), *Peter & Wendy* (novel)
Three children in Edwardian Kensington Gardens meet the boy who never grew up.
Ludwig Bemelmans *Madeline in London*
A classic picture book with beautiful illustrations.
Michael Bond *A Bear Called Paddington*
From darkest Peru to 32 Windsor Gardens, the bear wears it well in this and subsequent adventures in London and abroad.
Charles Dickens *Oliver Twist*; *David Copperfield*; *A Christmas Carol*
These three of the master's London-based novels are the best suited to children, but there are plenty more.
Berlie Doherty *Street Child*
A modern classic based on the true story of an orphan who prompted Dr Barnardo to begin his life's work of providing care for homeless children.
Beverley Naidoo *The Other Side of Truth*
The 2001 Carnegie Medal winner, this is the story of two children smuggled to London after the death of their mother.
E Nesbit *The Story of the Amulet*
Robert, Anthea, Cyril and Jane are reunited with the Psammead in a London pet store, and he tells them of the amulet.
Philip Pullman *The Sally Lockhart Trilogy*
A classic adventure set in the Victorian London underworld.
Jonathan Stroud *The Amulet of Samarkand*
Nathaniel, a magician's apprentice, summons up the djinni Bartimaeus in modern-day London.
GP Taylor *Wormwood*
A Gothic tale of sorcery and treachery in 18th-century London.
Jean Ure *Plague*
Three teenagers survive a plague that has killed their parents and left London as a ghost town.

Films

101 Dalmatians (U; 1961)
Disney's masterpiece included that most fabulous of all screen baddies, Cruella de Vil, animated by Marc Davis. It's based on the Dodie Smith story, about two spotted dogs that have an embarrassment of puppies out Regent's Park way.
A Fish Called Wanda (15) dir Charles Crichton (1988)
This madcap smash hit about a London-based plot to commit armed robbery stars John Cleese and Jamie Lee Curtis.
Bedknobs and Broomsticks (U) dir Robert Stevenson (1971)
An apprentice witch, three kids and a conman search for the component to a spell. Look out for a youngish Bruce Forsyth as a surprisingly good gangster.
Finding Neverland (PG) dir Marc Forster 2004
Johnny Depp stars in a tale of magic and fantasy, inspired by the life of Peter Pan author James Barrie.
Mary Poppins (U) dir Robert Stevenson (1964)
The supercalifragilisticexpialidocious magic nanny played by a sparkling Julie Andrews brings joy to an unhappy London family.
My Fair Lady (U) dir George Cukor (1964)
Audrey Hepburn is a luminous Eliza Doolittle in this blockbuster adaptation of George Bernard Shaw's *Pygmalion*.
Notting Hill (PG) dir Roger Michell (1999)
A starry romance blossoms in west London.
Oliver! (U) dir Carol Reed (1968)
A musical adaptation of the story by Charles Dickens in which the late Jack Wilde is the ultimate Artful Dodger, and Oliver Reed is a scarily menacing, brooding Bill Sykes.
One of Our Dinosaurs is Missing (U) dir Robert Stevenson (1975)
Toffs, Chinese spies and feisty nannies run off with a large exhibit from the Natural History Museum.

Websites

BBC London *www.bbc.co.uk/london*.
Children First *www.childrenfirst.nhs.uk*.
Run by Great Ormond Street Hospital and children's charity WellChild, this website has age-appropriate information on all aspects of healthy living, with special sections about going into hospital.
Department for Education and Skills *www.parents centre.gov.uk*.
The DfES website gives parents advice on schools and other aspects of children's education.
Learning Partnership *www.thelearningpartnership.com*.
The Learning Partnership's online guide to parenting, called *Top Tips for Tiny Tots* (www.tt4tt.co.uk), provides new mums and dads with all the information they need about pregnancy, birth, and early development in one easy-to-use downloadable course.
London Active Map *www.uktravel.com*.
Click on a tube station and find out which attractions are nearby.
London Parks & Gardens Trust *www.parkexplorer.org.uk*.
A website designed to help Key Stage 2 children learn more about the parks, gardens and open spaces of London.
London Town *www.londontown.com*.
The official tourist board website, full of information and offers.
London Underground Online *www.thetube.com*.
Meteorological Office *www.met-office.gov.uk*.
The most accurate source of weather forecasts.
The River Thames Guide *www.riverthames.co.uk*.
Shortwalk *www.shortwalk.blog.co.uk*.
A zone 1 underground map adapted by St Martins School of Art students, showing how long it takes to walk between stations on the underground. An eye-opener for visitors.
Simply Childcare *www.simplychildcare.com*.
If you're seeking a nanny, check this website.
Street Map *www.streetmap.co.uk*.
Time Out *www.timeout.com*.
An essential source, of course, with online city guides and the best eating and drinking reviews.
Transport for London *www.tfl.gov.uk*.
The official website for travel information about buses, DLR and river services.
Yellow Pages Online *www.yell.com*.
The best online resource for numbers and addresses.

Advertisers' Index

Please refer to relevant sections for addresses / telephone numbers

Index

Index

Index

Index

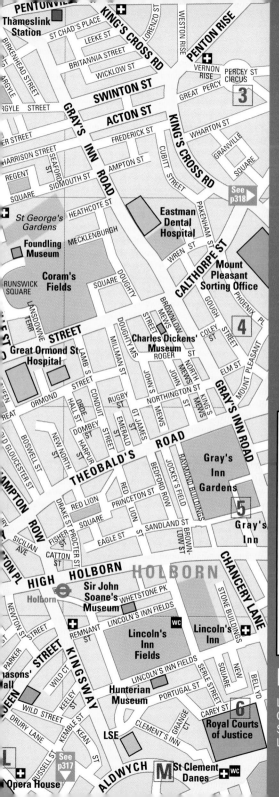

PENTONVILLE
Thameslink
Station
ST CHAD'S PLACE
LEEKE ST
BIRKENHEAD STREET
KING'S CROSS RD
LORENZO ST
WESTON RISE
PENTON RISE
BRITANNIA STREET
WICKLOW ST
ARGYLE STREET
SWINTON ST
ACTON ST
GRAY'S INN ROAD
ER STREET
HARRISON STREET
SEAFORD ST
SIDMOUTH ST
REGENT
SQUARE
FREDERICK ST
AMPTON ST
CUBITT STREET
KING'S CROSS RD
WHARTON ST
GRANVILLE SQUARE
VERNON RISE
PERCEY ST CIRCUS
GREAT PERCY

3

See p318 ▶

St George's
Gardens
Foundling
Museum
HEATHCOTE ST
MECKLENBURGH
RUNSWICK SQUARE
Coram's
Fields
SQUARE
DOUGHTY
LANSDOWNE TERR
WREN ST
CALTHORPE ST
Eastman
Dental
Hospital
PAKENHAM ST
Mount
Pleasant
Sorting Office
GOUGH ST
PHOENIX PL

4

STREET
Great Ormond St
Hospital
LAMB'S CONDUIT STREET
MILLMAN ST
DOUGHTY ST
BROWNLOW MEWS
STREET
Charles Dickens'
Museum
ROGER ST
NORTH MEWS
JOHN'S MEWS
JOHN ST
NORTHINGTON ST
KING'S MEWS
COLEY ST
ELM ST
MOUNT PLEASANT
GRAY'S INN ROAD
RUGBY MEWS
GT JAMES ST
EMERALD ST
ORMOND
HALL ST
ORDE
DOMBEY ST
HARPUR ST
BOSWELL ST
NEW NORTH ST
THEOBALD'S ROAD
RED LION SQUARE
PRINCETON ST
RED LION ST
BEDFORD ROW
JOCKEY'S FIELD
RAYMOND BUILDINGS
Gray's
Inn
Gardens

5

Gray's
Inn
AMPTON ROW
SICILIAN AVE
TON PL
CATTON ST
FISHER ST
PROCTER ST
DRAKE ST
EAGLE ST
SANDLAND ST
BROWN-LOW ST
HIGH HOLBORN
HOLBORN
Holborn ⊖
Sir John
Soane's
Museum
WHETSTONE PK
LINCOLN'S INN FIELDS
CHANCERY LANE
STONE BUILDINGS
NEWTON STREET
REMNANT ST
WC
Lincoln's
Inn
Fields
Lincoln's
Inn
SERLE STREET
SQUARE
NEW SQUARE
BELL YD
PARKER STREET
asons' all
KINGSWAY
WILD CT
KEELEY ST
LINCOLN'S INN FIELDS
PORTUGAL ST
Hunterian
Museum
GRANGE CT
CAREY ST
CLEMENT'S INN

6

Royal Courts
of Justice
QUEEN
WILD STREET
DRURY LANE
KEMBLE ST
KEAN ST
LSE
CLEMENT'S INN
RUSSELL ST
See p317 ▼
Opera House
ALDWYCH
M
St Clement
Danes
WC

Legend:
- Place of interest and/or entertainment . . .
- Hospital or college . . . .
- Railway station . . . .
- Park . . . .
- River . . . .
- Motorway . . . .
- Main road . . . .
- Main road tunnel . . . .
- Pedestrian road . . . .
- Airport . . . . ✈
- Church . . . . ✚
- Synagogue . . . . ✡
- Congestion charge zone . . . . ☻
- Underground station . . . . ⊖
- Area name . . . . SOHO

Maps

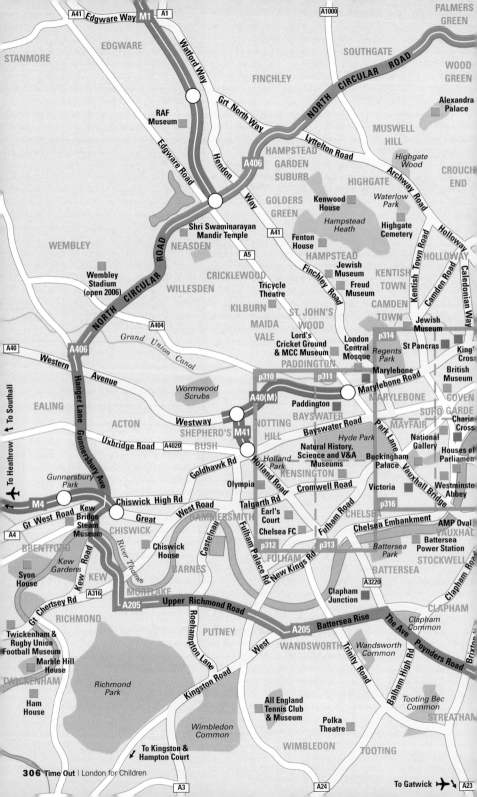

London Overview

Central London
by Area

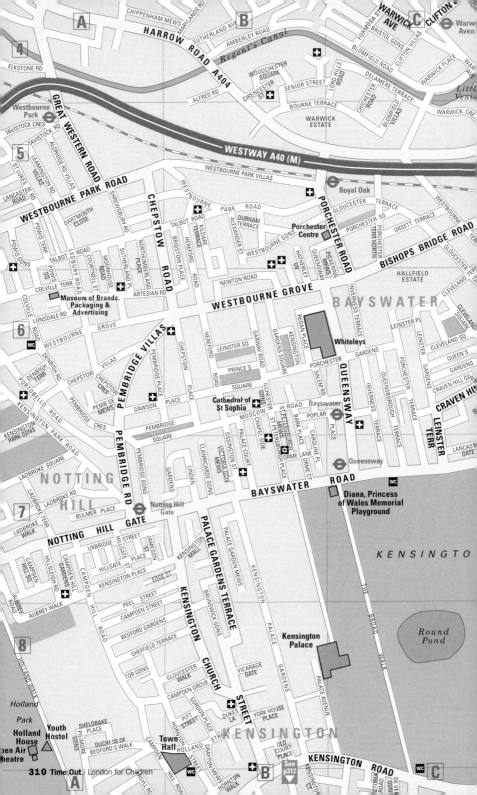

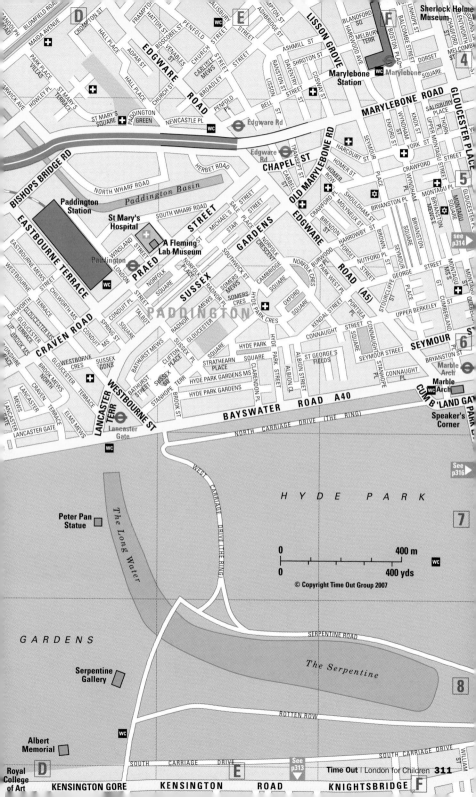

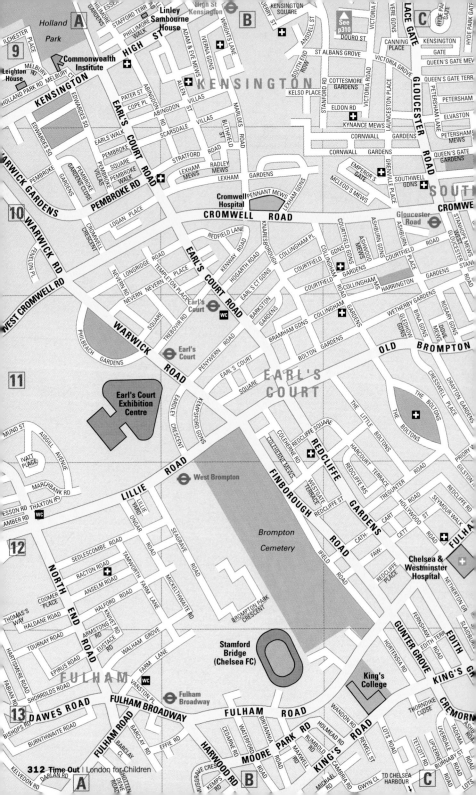

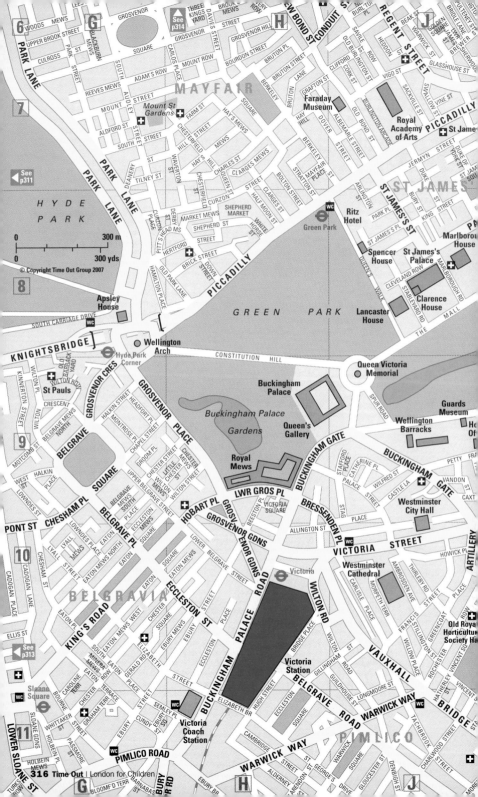

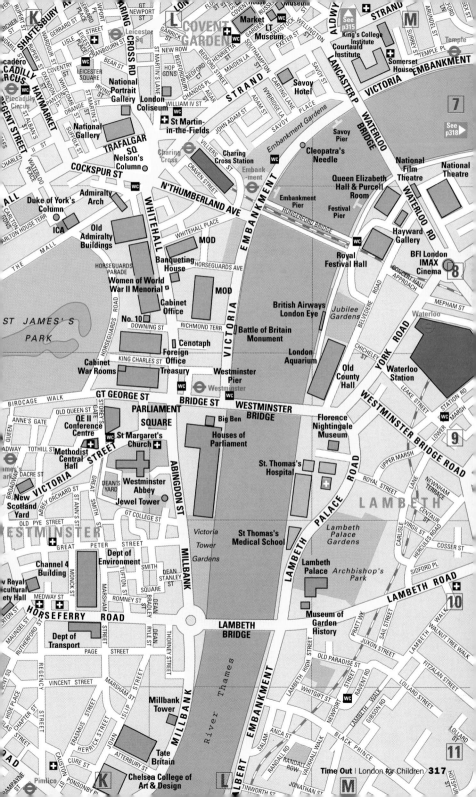

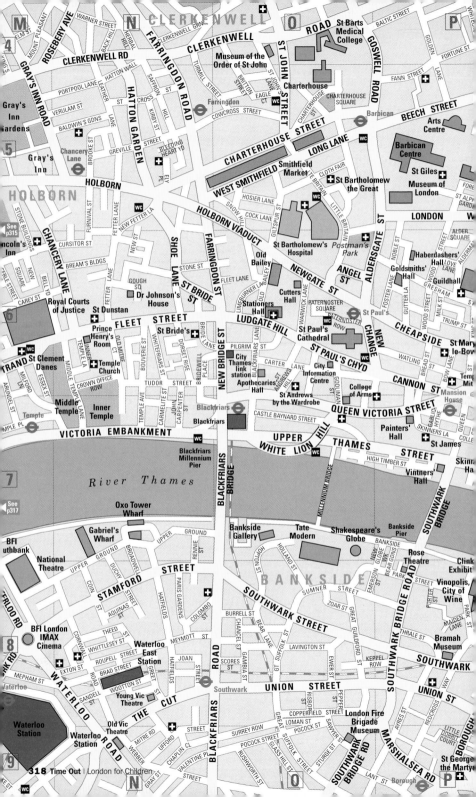

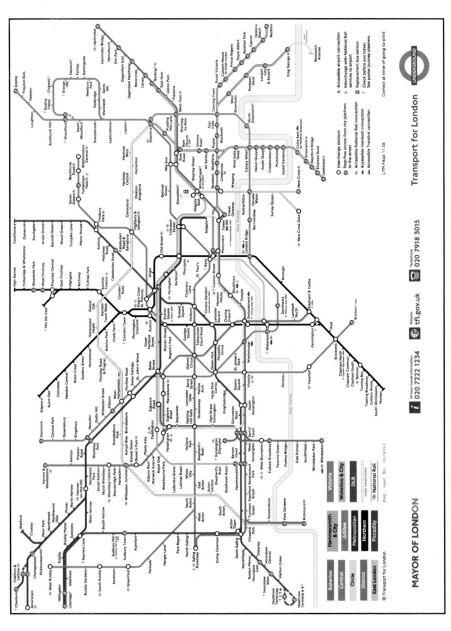

Tube Map